USAAF FIGHTERS
OF WORLD WAR TWO
IN ACTION

A factory-fresh P–51D breaks away from the camera plane, illustrating how the laminar flow wing had been filled and painted to maintain the desired airflow. At this point, Mustangs were being delivered without camouflage but the wings were always painted (although many times just the first third of the wing was filled and painted) as can be seen from the contrast between the silver paint and the bare metal of the gear doors and stress panels. Note the ejection chutes for spent shells and drop tank/bomb shackles. (NAA)

USAAF FIGHTERS
OF WORLD WAR TWO
IN ACTION

Michael O'Leary

BLANDFORD PRESS
POOLE · NEW YORK · SYDNEY

First published in the UK 1986 by Blandford Press
Link House, West Street, Poole, Dorset BH15 1LL

Copyright © 1986 Michael D O'Leary

Distributed in the United States by
Sterling Publishing Co, Inc,
2 Park Avenue, New York, NY 10016

Distributed in Australia by
Capricorn Link (Australia) Pty Ltd
PO Box 665, Lane Cove, NSW 2066

British Library Cataloguing in Publication Date

O'Leary. Michael D.
USAAF fighters of World War 2 in action.
1. United States. *Army Air Force*—History
2. World War, 1939–1945—Aerial operations,
American   3. Fighter planes—History
I. Title
940.54'4973   D790

ISBN 0 7137 1839 0

Typeset by Keyspools Ltd, Golborne, Lancs.
Printed in Great Britain by
R.J. Acford, Chichester

Contents

Introduction

United States Army Air Forces Fighters of World War Two shows not only the amazing growth of the American aeronautical industry but also outlines the development of the nation. In 1939, the aviation industry was a rather sleepy, backwater activity – only just beginning to respond to the frantic visits of the British and French Aircraft Commissioning Committees who were desperate to purchase combat aircraft. Fully aware of the growing German menace, both countries realized the American aeronautical effort was behind the times when compared to the very rapid developments on the Continent and in Europe.

Quantity, rather than quality, became the order of the day as massive orders were placed for a variety of combat aircraft – most of which were really obsolete when compared to what was coming from the German factories. This is not to say these were bad aircraft – some machines like the Lockheed Hudson and Curtiss Hawk 75 were rugged, dependable machines but they did not offer enough in the way of performance or armament. Some aircraft, like the Brewster Buffalo, were unmitigated disasters (see *United States Naval Fighters of World War Two*).

Huge orders from abroad, coupled with increased American government fear that the war which was obviously brewing in Europe would lead to American involvement, caused a rapid expansion in the country's aeronautical plants as unprecedented orders demanded construction of new plant space and the hiring of thousands of new workers. This increase in military development did not proceed smoothly since much of the American population (and government) favored the curious policy of isolationism. Protected by vast stretches of ocean to the east and west and with friendly neighbors to the north and south, Europe was perceived by Americans as a vague and distant place – best left to carry out its own affairs with a minimum of American aid or interference.

With the start of World War Two, vicious aerial fighting took place which quickly pointed out how unwise it had been for industry to ignore German developments. Soon, just Britain remained and that island nation began churning out thousands of Hurricanes and Spitfires to help stem the projected Nazi invasion. Drawing upon combat experience, an order was placed by the British with an upstart American company for a new fighter – and the North American Mustang was born. Other companies employed visionary designers, such as Lockheed's Kelly Johnson, who saw the shapes of future fighters and were fully capable of translating their ideas into fighting machines. Once started, the flow of new American designs was truly staggering: Lightning, Thunderbolt, and Mustang – aircraft with high performance and capable of seeking and destroying the enemy in any location. Adopting the mass production techniques developed by Henry Ford in his automobile factories, tens of thousands of new warplanes were on the way to the fighting fronts – aircraft not only superior to what the enemy could put in the air but also available in overwhelming numbers. As the aircraft industry developed, so did the American populace. The Great Depression was now at an end, high-technology aeronautical industries forecast the way of the future as huge numbers of Americans left farms to be employed in industry for the first time, and, most importantly, the average American citizen began to perceive the size and importance of the world around him.

As with any volume of this size, the number of individuals who offered assistance and information would fill up several pages of closely-packed type. However, I would like to make mention of a few individuals who went out of their way to provide assistance: USAF Major William Austin of the USAF's Magazine and Book branch; Mr Gene Boswell, now retired from Rockwell; Mr Robert Ferguson of Lockheed-California; Mr Larry Gann of McDonnell Douglas; and Ms Lois Lovisolo of the Grumman Corporation. Special thanks is also due to Barry Gregory and Michael Burns who got the project on its feet and offered guidance towards completion. Also, I would like to thank my parents for their continued interest and support.

Michael O'Leary
Los Angeles, January 1986

Seversky P-35
The Army's First Modern Fighter

Seversky's stubby fighter introduced modern features to the Army but was a disaster in combat.

Modern is a relative term. When the Seversky P–35 entered service with the Army Air Corps in 1937, the popular press made a great deal of the 'aerial superiority' of the new fighter. However, to pilots of the 34th Pursuit Squadron stationed in the Philippines on 10 December 1941, the burning hulks of their shattered P–35s did not live up to their press.

During the 1930s, a one-legged former Czarist Russian aristocrat had a very profound effect on American military aircraft design. Alexander P. de Seversky had been born in Tiflis, Russia, to a wealthy family. During the start of World War One, he entered the Imperial Russian Naval Air Service but on his first combat mission he had the misfortune to have his aircraft hit by anti-aircraft fire during an attack on German naval units in the Gulf of Riga. Seversky managed to bring his burning aircraft down for a rough crash-landing in the open sea but a bomb had hung up on its rack and detonated upon impact with the water. The explosion instantly killed Seversky's observer and blew his own right leg off. Rescued by friendly forces, Seversky was rushed to a hospital and his life was saved. While recuperating from his wounds Seversky demanded an artificial limb so that he could get back into the air! His superiors figured that the mad

A beautiful view of Army Air Corps peacetime flying. This Seversky P–35, assigned to the 27th Pursuit Squadron of the 1st Pursuit Group, is seen in flight near its home base of Selfridge Field. The P–35 was the Army's first 'modern' fighter which meant that it was all-metal, had an enclosed cockpit, and featured retractable landing gear. These innovations did little for the fighter since it had poor performance and limited armament. Note the unit's diving eagle insignia on the side of the fuselage. (USAF)

Seversky's P–35, in an incredibly complex aeronautical evolutionary process, had its beginnings in this aircraft – the SEV–3. Painted a gaudy metallic gold, the design of the SEV–3 seemed ultra-modern when it appeared during the Depression year of 1933. Seversky was an advocate of the streamline school of design that was flourishing during this period and the SEV–3 embodied the theory perfectly. (Seversky)

Russian's flying days were over but they had yet to come under the full influence of the persuasive Seversky. Once he had mastered the use of his new leg, Seversky took a training aircraft aloft to renew his piloting skills and then assaulted his superiors with requests to be returned to combat status. They finally gave in, and Seversky found orders to report to a combat unit.

Entering combat with an enthusiasm that bordered on mania, Seversky attacked every German aircraft that he spotted with a wild abandon. His score of enemy aircraft confirmed destroyed mounted, and he soon had thirteen to his credit and was ranked as Russia's third highest ace. During 1917, Seversky was ordered to travel to the United States on a fact-finding mission to check on that country's supply of raw and finished war materials. Seversky crossed the country, visiting war plants and talking to high-placed officials. While Seversky was in the United States, the depressing news of the Russian Revolution reached him. Deciding not to return to a country dominated by the hated Communists, a type that he detested even more than the Germans, Seversky made the choice to stay in the United States and work to become a citizen of the country that he had quickly learned to admire.

During the early 1920s, Seversky met General Billy Mitchell and the friendship that developed between the two airmen was to have a profound effect on Seversky's views of airpower. Mitchell was the outspoken advocate of the superiority of airpower but he was fighting against the old school of Naval and Army officers who viewed aircraft as little more than wasteful playtoys. Mitchell's views eventually led to his court martial but Seversky passionately agreed with the General's view that a nation, to be strong and independent, had to have an air arm that could disable enemy forces at will.

Along with his new citizenship, Seversky had acquired a fanatical patriotism that many found cloying but his fervor was honest and it drove Seversky on in an attempt to produce the world's most modern combat aircraft. Seversky was also a prolific writer and began a series of magazine articles and books that served as his forum for the development of airpower.

Seversky began to design features that he considered essential for modern aircraft and, during the 1920s, patented various devices that included an anti-spin parachute, advanced wing flaps, gyroscopic bombsight and a method for mid-air refueling. Seversky also assisted Elmer Sperry with the development of the autopilot. Seversky had developed friends in many high places in the military and one of his proudest moments came during 1926 when he was commissioned as a major in the Army Air Corps Reserve, a rank that he proudly used for the rest of his life.

Seversky felt that, in order adequately to develop his aeronautical ideas, he should try to raise capital to open his own aircraft factory. In 1931, during the height of the American Depression, Seversky, with his enthusiastic personality, managed to bring together enough funds from investors to rent a hangar at the Edo Aircraft Company's College Point, Long Island, New York, factory, and there he set to work on developing his ideas into the design of an actual aircraft. Two years later, Seversky found that he was growing out of his small space and moved to Farmingdale nearby in Long Island.

After his move, Seversky added another fellow Russian to his small working staff. Alexander Kartveli became chief designer and his brilliance was to lead to the P–47 Thunderbolt of World War Two fame. Kartveli had the ability to take Seversky's ideas and form them into working blueprints from which construction of the company's first aircraft could begin.

The first effort from the Seversky factory embodied all the elements of the streamlining craze that permeated the 1930s. The SEV–3 (also the first of Seversky's rather complex designation system) was a bulky yet sleek twin-float amphibian that carried three and flew for the first time in 1933. Made entirely of metal, the monoplane design appeared to the public to be the most modern thing in the air. Beside the gold-painted aircraft with the bold Seversky insignia emblazoned on the fuselage, the contemporary biplanes looked absolutely primitive.

The SEV–3 featured an unusual float system that pivoted about the end of a built-up cantilever strut and was able to travel up and down in the vertical plane. The wheels were recessed directly into the floats and attached, via the main strut, to the wing structure – thus making them completely independent of the floats. When the wheels were retracted for aquatic operation, the floats were automatically locked at the correct angle while small wheels mounted in the water rudders at the rear of the floats could once again adjust the floats for ground operations when the regular tail wheel, enclosed in a large fairing, would be

employed. The SEV–3 had a very low streamlined canopy which hampered vision but added to top speed. A window was added on each side of the fuselage by the pilot's feet so that he had some form of downward vision – essential during landing and take off.

Seversky was anxious to establish the company's name in the aeronautical world so he took the metallic gold aircraft on a number of record runs, the first being on 9 October 1933 when he piloted the aircraft from Roosevelt Field for an amphibian speed record of almost 180 mph. After this record flight and a number of promotional visits to East Coast military and civil airfields, the SEV–3 was taken back to the Farmingdale factory where the amphibious landing gear was removed and a conventional gear was installed, the two main legs being wrapped in huge streamlined fairings. In the landplane configuration, the SEV–3 demonstrated a top speed of 210 mph which quickly brought attention from the military.

Probably due to Seversky's close association with the military over the years and his many high-ranking friends, it was not a great surprise when the Army Air Corps issued a requirement for a basic trainer that had a great deal of resemblance to what the SEV–3 had to offer. Once again, the SEV–3 was returned to the factory and a number of modifications were undertaken so that the aircraft could compete in the Air Corps' evaluation program for a new trainer. Visibility is one of the prime requirements for a training aircraft and that was not a feature which the SEV–3 could claim, so the rear fuselage decking was cut down while a larger canopy with a much better view was added. The dual control system and dual instrument panels were installed

The SEV–3 on the ground, illustrating its unique adjustable amphibious gear. Registered X–2106, the aircraft carried a crew of three. The canopy was built especially low to reduce drag and considerable glazing was added to the sides of the fuselage to help improve the very limited visibility. The Seversky logo, which could also be read 'Sever the Sky', was emblazoned on the side of the fuselage. (Collect-Air Photos)

and the third crew position was deleted, while the engine mount was lengthened to compensate for the changes in the center of gravity.

The modified aircraft was redesignated SEV–3XAR (the added letters standing for Experimental Army). Flown by Army pilots, the SEV–3XAR was quickly accepted (could there have been any doubt as to the outcome?), and a production order was given for 30 aircraft to be designated BT–8. Seversky had achieved his first production contract and now he felt that he could conquer new fields in aviation. The ability of the basic SEV–3 design to be molded and adapted to new mission requirements was just beginning and such a history of modification to a basic design was not to be equaled.

The BT–8 trainers were not world beaters in looks but apparently they performed their role competently although there is little remaining history surviving as to their operation, and it is interesting to note that there were no follow-on orders.

Kartveli took the SEV–3XAR back into the shop soon after the Army testing trials and the aircraft once again emerged as an amphibian but with a new designation and powerplant. Now the SEV–3M (for military), the aircraft carried a 715 hp Wright R–1820–F3 in the nose. Seversky was soon stumping the country with the aircraft and set an impressive speed record of just over 230 mph on 15 September

Here, the SEV–3 is seen fitted with its ground only landing gear which was enclosed in huge hand-formed aluminum spats. In this form, the SEV–3 was capable of speeds up to 210 mph and performed better than virtually all aircraft of the period, and the aircraft attracted considerable interest from the Army Air Corps. Note the folding hatch on the side of the pilot's cockpit.

At this stage, the Army demanded a number of changes in the Seversky design and X–2106 emerged from the Farmingdale factory with a greatly enlarged canopy and a new designation. SEV–3XAR. The third seat was eliminated as was most of the fuselage glazing. This became the basis for the AAC's BT–8 contract. Within three months the SEV–3XAR was back on its amphibious gear, giving an idea of the changes that the aircraft could handle. The aircraft wound up its life when it was sold illegally to Spain for use in that country's Civil War. The machine arrived in Spain during 1938 in float plane configuration but the floats were soon removed and land gear was fitted. It was assigned to the Republicans' Group 71 in company with

French Dewoitines where it served as a communications aircraft and did not receive any armament. It was generally flown by a veteran of the Lacalle Squadron, Augusto Lecha. On the morning of 6 February 1939, the squadron received orders to regroup on a field at Banolas (province of Genoa). The SEV–3 took more than half an hour to get off and when it arrived at Benolas, Group 71 did not exist – it had been destroyed by a surprise bombing attack. Lecha tried to land, but without wind indication, and he turned the aircraft over on the bombed airfield. The Seversky was abandoned on the spot. It is not known if it still retained the metallic gold paint scheme.

1935. The South American country of Colombia was impressed with the aircraft and ordered six (which were built as SEV–3MWW) for the Colombian Naval Air Service which used them as reconnaissance amphibians.

During 1934, work had begun on a second prototype in the Farmingdale factory that was completed as an SEV–3M. However, before the second aircraft could be completed, Kartveli decided to modify the prototype to yet another new configuration . . . this time as a single-seat pursuit.

In the meantime, while work was progressing on the conversion of the first aircraft, the second prototype was finished as the SEV–2XP (which, in Seversky terminology, equated to two-seat experimental pursuit). This aircraft featured the huge spatted landing gear of the SEV–3XAR and the engine of the SEV–3M. The two crew-members sat under a sliding canopy and the rear occupant had a .30 caliber machine gun on a swivel at his disposal. Making its first flight in the spring of 1935, the SEV–2XP once again impressed Army officials who felt that a specification should be drafted which would call for production of a fighter in the prototype's category.

Seversky felt that the aircraft would make a good fighter for the Army and an excellent replacement for the outmoded Boeing P–26 but little did he know that Curtiss had been very busy designing and building a new fighter, the Model 75. The new Curtiss design was

submitted to the Army at Wright Field during May and proved to have impressive performance along with the added benefit of retractable landing gear.

Doubts ran high at the Seversky factory as to whether their new design could best the aircraft from Curtiss. The SEV–2XP was to arrive at Wright Field for testing during June but it had to be withdrawn due to an accident during the journey. History has revealed that the accident was a fabrication on Seversky's part in order to gain more time to modify the two-place fighter. Working around the clock, Kartveli redesigned the SEV–2XP into a single-seat aircraft that had rather crude retractable landing gear which folded straight back into the wing, leaving large fairings covering the strut and wheel. A quick redesignation of SEV–1XP, and the aircraft was off to Wright Field for evaluation during August.

The SEV–1XP followed the lines of the previous Seversky machines and was not a bad looking aircraft. The engine of the SEV–2XP had been replaced with a 950 hp Wright R–1820–G5 Cyclone with a new three-blade propeller. This combination gave a top speed of 289 mph, which was below the performance specifications issued by Seversky. Examination of the engine revealed that it was not developing full power. However, this drop in speed was not a serious problem since the Curtiss Model 75 was suffering similar engine troubles. Army officials were about to issue a contract to Seversky when Curtiss lodged an official com-

The SEV–3XAR resulted in the rather grotesque BT–8 basic trainer. Seversky's contacts in the military resulted in his first production order for an aircraft that the Army did not really need. Seen here in its blue and yellow training colors, this BT–8 carries the Wright Field badge on the side of the fuselage.

plaint relating to the fact that the Seversky entry had more time since the 'accident' to undergo modifications.

The Material Division, afraid to enter into a contract that might end in a law suit, decided to delay the selection until April 1936, at which time another fly-off would take place between the competitors. By that time, two other aircraft had entered the arena. These machines were the Consolidated Special and the Vought V–141, but neither aircraft was really in the running as they failed to meet a number of Air Corps specifications.

In the time leading up to the April fly-off, Kartveli had been busy reworking the SEV–1XP. The aircraft was fitted with a new engine, the 950 hp Pratt & Whitney R–1830–9 Twin Wasp. A smaller cowling was installed while the tail area was redesigned and the Air Corps armament of one .30 and one .50 caliber machine gun was installed in the upper fuselage decking. The aircraft received yet another designation change to SEV–7 by the time it reached Wright Field for the fly-off. Curtiss had also been busy improving the Model 75.

Once again, both the Model 75 and the SEV–7 were plagued by a number of minor but

*S*ticking to the same basic theme, Seversky came up with the SEV–X–BT, a retractable gear version of the BT–8 trainer. The project did not progress past the prototype X189M. (Seversky)

*S*een as the SEV–1XP, the form of the future P–35 is virtually jelled in X18Y (which started out life as the two-place fixed gear SEV–2XP). In competition with the Curtiss Hawk 75, it became very clear that the Army favored Seversky's design even though the aircraft was having troubles with its engine. The SEV–1XP won out over the Model 75 although the Model 75 was the winner in the long run. (USAF)

performance-degrading problems. The SEV–7 came out on top in the Army's point system, and a contract was awarded on 16 June 1936 for the construction of 77 fighters with the new Army designation of P–35.

Seversky began work on a company-funded prototype for the series that was designated AP–1 (for Army prototype). Given the civil registration of NR1390, the aircraft served as a test bed for a number of Kartveli modifications. Problems plagued the P–35 and by the time the first prototype reached the Army during July 1937, top speed had fallen to a very disappointing 281 mph.

In order to promote the P–35, Seversky came up with the very clever idea of sending some of his 'near' P–35 products to the Cleveland National Air Races, an event that was immensely popular with the 1930s public. Millionaire Frank Fuller flew an SEV–S2 (later, just S–2) in the 1937 Cleveland event and came in first while Frank Sinclair took fourth place in the Bendix Trophy Race with the S–1, which was the rebuilt SEV–1XP! Seversky also intended to enter the AP–2 NR1250, which was similar to the P–35 but had a new canopy and a new wing center section that incorporated inward, flush-retracting landing gear. While en route to Cleveland, and being flown by Seversky, the AP–2 had a landing gear failure and had to be withdrawn from competition.

Seversky found that the publicity gained at the air races was extremely useful so a number

of other aircraft built on the same basic design as the P–35 were put together. During this time period, American oil companies were very interested in promoting aviation and most usually had a stable of high-performance aircraft and famous aviators. Shell Oil Company contracted with Seversky to build a racing aircraft designated DS (Doolittle Special) for Jimmy Doolittle. The DS followed basic P–35 lines and was powered by an 850 hp Wright R–1820–G5 Cyclone. Doolittle was quite pleased with the speedy aircraft and flew it as his own personal mount for the next three years.

The AP–7 was built from the wreckage of the AP–2 and was powered by a Pratt & Whitney R–1830 Twin Wasp of 1,200 hp. Given the registration of NX1384, the AP–7 was flown by Jacqueline Cochran. While delivering the AP–7 to Miss Cochran at Burbank, California, Seversky set a new speed record by covering the continent in ten hours, three minutes and seven seconds. After racing in the Bendix Trophy Race of 1938, the aircraft was returned to the factory and modified with a new wing leading edge, inward retracting landing gear and a number of other small modifications in preparation for the 1939 Bendix but the aircraft was completely destroyed in a hangar fire at Miami before the race.

Seversky also kept a close eye on the export market and sold his aircraft whenever a likely customer appeared. One example each of the

After winning the Army contract, the amazing career of 18Y continued. Redesignated S–1, the aircraft was flown by Seversky test pilot Frank Sinclair to fourth place in the 1937 Bendix Trophy Race. These races served as a billboard for the flamboyant Seversky to display his wares.

two-seat SEV–2XP and the SEV–2PA–A and the SEV–2PA–1 amphibians were sold to the Soviet Union which, after a brief testing period, re-shipped them to the Spanish Republican forces for use in that country's Civil War. Two SEV–3XARs, fixed gear land aircraft, were sold to the Mexican government. Seversky also made a very controversial sale to the Japanese government when he supplied that nation with 20 SEV–2PA–B3 two-seat fighters in 1939. The Imperial Japanese Navy intended to employ the SEV–2PA–B3 as a long-range fighter to escort their bombers deep into China. The Japanese designated the type as A8–V1, but quickly found that the aircraft did not live up to its performance claims and was inferior to Japanese types currently in service. The SEV–2PA–B3 was relegated to reconnaissance duties over central China.

The contract with the Japanese had a disastrous effect on future business for Seversky. The secret nature of the Seversky negotiations with the Japanese angered the American government who, in turn, apparently exerted considerable pressure on the Air Corps not to order any more P–35s and, instead, to concentrate on the loser of the contest, the Curtiss Model 75!

Using much of the wrecked airframe of the AP–2, the AP–7 (registered NX1384) was built. The aircraft was an attempt to get as much performance out of the basic P–35 design without radical modifications. Fitted with a Pratt & Whitney R–1830 Twin Wasp of 1,200 hp, the aircraft was flown to victory in the 1938 Bendix Race by Jacqueline Cochran. Before this event the plane had been flown by Seversky on a cross-country speed dash for a record ten hour, three minute and seven second crossing. After the Bendix the AP–7 was returned to the factory for drastic modification.

While no actual evidence was uncovered that Seversky acted illegally, his sale of aircraft to Japan was extremely unpopular with the public and the company quickly began to experience severe financial difficulties. While Seversky was in England trying to convince the British that the P–35 was just what they wanted (fortunately, they knew better), the Board of Directors ousted Seversky and re-organized the company in order to avoid bankruptcy. The new organization became known as the Republic Aircraft Corporation.

During the transition between the two companies, negotiations had started with Sweden for the purchase of a modified version of the P–35. During February 1939, Sweden placed an order with Republic for 100 EP–106s (the company designation of EP–1 was also used), and 50 SEV–2PA–204A two-place fighters that were to be equipped as dive bombers. The first batch of EP–1s was completed during January and was shipped to Sweden where they arrived the following month, and were delivered to *Flygflottilj* 8 where they replaced Gloster Gladiator biplanes. The Swedes, in dire need of new aircraft, signed another order for a further 60 EP–1s.

Events soon turned sour for Sweden when the United States placed an embargo on all military goods to that country and, on 24 October 1940, claimed all the completed and uncompleted Swedish aircraft in the United

States. At this time 40 EP-1s had been delivered. The embargoed aircraft were given the designation P-35A and 17 were immediately crated and shipped to the Philippines to bolster that area's defenses. The Swedish version of the P-35 was equipped with a 1,050 hp Pratt & Whitney R-1830-45 radial and had a greater armament of two .30 caliber machine guns in the upper cowling and two .50 caliber machine guns in the wings. Only two of the SEV-2PA-204A dive bombers had been delivered and the remaining machines were taken over by the Army Air Force (redesignated the previous June) and assigned to training units as AT-12 Guardsmen advanced trainers.

When initial deliveries of the P-35 to Air Corps units began with the first aircraft going to Wright Field during May 1937. It was found that the aircraft had dangerous spinning and stalling characteristics while performing aerobatics and a modification was undertaken that added several degrees of dihedral to the outer wing panels which helped the situation but the P-35 remained placarded against certain aerobatics during its military life. The P-35 (the fighter was never given a popular name) took up active service with the famous 1st Pursuit Group at Selfridge Field, Michigan, with final aircraft delivery taking place during August 1938, months behind time. Before the last P-35 had been delivered to the 17th, 27th and 94th Pursuit Squadrons that made up the Group, an order was received instructing that the unit would receive the Curtiss P-36 as replacement. This meant that the 1st would have P-35s and P-36s serving at the same time while one new fighter was phased out and the other new fighter was phased into service. Pilots found the P-35 a pleasant aircraft to fly but quickly realized that it was no combat machine. Sluggish in performance and undergunned, the P-35 was woefully outdated by the new aircraft coming into service in Europe and Japan.

The bulky fuselage of the Seversky had enough room for the crew chief to go along for a ride during check flights, locking himself in the spacious baggage compartment – access to which was gained by a large door in the side of the fuselage. During the P-35's brief combat career, the large fuselage held several people as P-35s were evacuated in the face of advancing enemy forces.

The P-35As that were sent to the Philippines were assigned to the 21st and 34th

Reappearing from the Farmingdale plant, NX1384 had a new look. A new, more modern wing had been fitted with landing gear that retracted flush towards the center line. The modified AP-7 was to participate in the 1939 Bendix with Jacqueline Cochran at the controls once again. However, the plane was destroyed in a hangar fire before the event. Note that the Seversky logo has been replaced with that of the new Republic Aviation Corporation. (Republic)

The aircraft that cost Seversky his future in military aviation. Completely unmarked except for the letter R on the fin and under the left wing, the SEV–2PA–I was built for Russia, who ordered one example along with two other Seversky aircraft. These planes also found their way to Spain after a brief testing period by the Russians. The next export order was from Japan who purchased 20 SEV–2PA–B3 two-place fighters (almost identical to the SEV–2PA–A) during 1939. This contract was carried out with a great deal of secrecy on Seversky's part and was so unpopular with the military and the public alike that Seversky was booted from the controlling position of his company which reorganized as the Republic Aviation Corporation. Used by the Japanese Navy in China, the Seversky's were not particularly well liked but the fact remains that they were the only American-built aircraft to serve in squadron strength with Japan during World War Two.

Pursuit Squadrons. The first 17 aircraft were reinforced by a further 31 machines shipped from Farmingdale. When the aircraft arrived in the Philippines it was found that all instructions and manuals were in Swedish as were all the instruments and cockpit notes. Mechanics struggled with primitive facilities to erect the fighters and make them airworthy. Long-range plans called for the P–35As to be transferred to the Philippine Air Corps where they would replace the antiquated Boeing P–26 while the Army Air Force units in the area would be equipped with new Curtiss P–40s. However, the Japanese were to have other plans.

For being such a strategic area, the Philippines had been greatly neglected as the United States tried to build up its strength in other

parts of the Pacific. The admittedly obsolete P–35As and P–26s were absolutely no deterrent to Japanese aggression as the Army soon discovered.

Throughout 1941, a number of frantic changes were made in the organization of the defense of the Philippines. The Philippine Department Air Force was comprised of a single group, the 4th Composite Group, that included the 28th Medium Bombardment Group, the 2nd Observation Squadron (both based at Clark Field, 60 miles North of Manila), and the 3rd, 17th, and 20th Pursuit Squadrons based at Nichols Field which was located just south of the city. Lt Boyd D. 'Buzz' Wagner was given the command of the 17th PS and this young and innovative fighter pilot whipped the poorly-equipped P–35A unit into fighting shape as they received new P–40s. Along with the diverted Swedish P–35As, the Philippine Department Air Force gained another bit of international flavor when they received 11 A–27s that had originally been intended for delivery to Siam before that country was overrun by the Japanese. The pursuit squadrons received these aircraft for training and the pilots had to puzzle once again over instructions and instruments in Siamese.

Staffing the pursuit squadrons was a problem; most of the ground staff was on hand but pilots were in short supply and, for a time, the squadrons could only muster half strength. On 4 December, the squadrons began to receive

new-in-the-crate Curtiss P–40Es. The new fighters were eagerly assembled just as fast as the ground crews could work. At this time, the 34th, commanded by Lt Samuel W. Marrett, was moved to a newly prepared field with the rather romantic name of Del Carmen. However, Del Carmen was no tropical paradise – rather it was a stinking hell hole that the pilots and ground crew instantly began to detest. The raw dirt strip was located near the small town of Floridablanca which, in itself, had little to offer except for impoverished Filippinos. The dirt and dust that was kicked up as each Seversky took off from Del Carmen caused a hazard by greatly reducing visibility and taking two or three minutes to settle. The dirt also played havoc with the worn-out systems and engines of the P–35As; overhauls were needed but the facilities were so primitive and the lack of parts so critical that the pilots had to keep flying machines that probably would have been grounded at Stateside bases. Radio communication between Del Carmen with Nichols and Clark was poor at best and the one radio set was prone to breakage.

The moment of truth for the American air arm in the Philippines came at 12:00 pm on 8 December 1941 (7 December Hawaiian time) when the Japanese, in coordinated attacks, quickly swept across the main bases. At 4:00 am that morning, messages had arrived at Clark signalling Pearl Harbor had been attacked by the Japanese. The airmen were

During February 1939, the Swedish government placed an order for 100 improved P–35s, designated EP–I, (known as the J9 in Swedish service) and 50 SEV–2PA–204A two-place fighters to be equipped as dive bombers. One of the two-seaters is seen here after undergoing flight tests and before being shipped to Sweden.

The EP–106s were delivered to the Swedish Air Force in natural metal finish with national crown insignia in six positions. The aircraft was powered by the Pratt & Whitney R–1830–45 of 1,050 hp which gave a top speed of just over 300 mph. The Swedish aircraft were more heavily armed than their American counterparts, two .30 caliber machine guns in the nose and two .50 caliber weapons in the wing. Sixty of the fighters had been delivered to Sweden by May 1939 when the American government put a complete embargo on military sales to that country. The remaining aircraft plus a further order for 20 went to the Army as P–35As.

assembled and told of the news; they were surprised that Pearl had been hit but not surprised that the Japanese were finally on the move against America. Bombs were taken out to the operational aircraft to be loaded for a strike against Formosa, the most likely enemy target. However, it was decided that the bombs would not be loaded in case a special strike was called and a different bomb load would be needed. It was also thought that having the bombed-up aircraft sitting on the field would not be safe in case of an enemy air raid. The bombs were left by the aircraft where they could be quickly loaded. Communications were extremely poor and many pilots did not know of the attack on Pearl until several hours later. The pilots at Del Carmen were totally unaware as nobody bothered to radio the field.

A morning patrol of P–40s was launched as soon as there was enough light while a Douglas B–18 Bolo rattled aloft for patrol duty with a load of bombs. At Nielson Field the staff of the Far East Air Force (FEAF) gathered to discuss the critical situation. A number of divergent opinions were voiced but there was a consensus that the limited supply of Boeing B–17 Flying Fortresses should be immediately

launched on a reprisal raid against Japanese-held Formosa. The assembled group of officers was shocked to a man when General Brereton announced 'No, We can't attack till we're fired on'. Major General Lewis H. Brereton had recently been appointed commander of the American air arm in the Philippines and his decision to avoid a direct attack on the enemy was not popular.

On 8 December 1941, the inventory of the 24th Pursuit Group was not particularly impressive: the 3rd PS, 18 P–40s in tactical commission at Iba; the 17th PS, 18 P–40s in tactical commission at Nichols Field; the 21st PS, 18 P–40s in tactical commission at Nichols Field; the 20th PS, 18 P–40Bs in tactical commission at Clark Field; and the 34th PS, 18 P–35As in tactical commission (22 in actual commission) at Del Carmen. This gave the 24th Pursuit Group a total of 90 first-line combat aircraft with which to oppose an enemy of unknown, but probably considerable, strength. Also, to be included with the inventory of combat aircraft, were a number of Boeing B–17C Flying Fortresses and obsolete Bolo bombers and various communication and light transport aircraft.

P-35 of the 17th Pursuit Squadron of the 1st PG with the unit's famous black and white eagle proudly displayed on the side of the fuselage. Squadron color was white and the cowl ring was thus painted. This view of the P-35 gives a good idea of the aircraft's large canopy and the pilot's positioning on the highest point of the fuselage for the best visibility. Note the polished face of the propeller while the rear portion of the blades were Flat Black. While in military service the P-35s suffered from a number of maintenance problems, including leaking fuel tanks. The fuel tank system in the P-35 was rather interesting since the entire wing center section formed a gas tank, there were no bladders or metal tanks as the wing structure formed the basis for the fuel container. When the aircraft were delivered to the 1st PG, tiny leaks of fuel from the center section were apparent. However, after some time in the air and a number of hard landings, the rivets began to loosen up and fuel began to cascade in quantity. This situation had to be rectified and the fix fell to unfortunate airmen who had to remove the small center section access plates and paint the entire inside of the unit with a sealer. This unpleasant job had to be repeated three or four times before the unit was sealed but then, with time, the sealer began to crack and shrink and the fuel once again began leaking. Another maintenance problem concerned itself with the engines which threw off excessive amounts of oil when running. It was not uncommon for a 1st PG crew chief to be standing at his aircraft's parking spot with a bucket full of gasoline, waiting for 'his' P-35 to return from a flight. Sometimes, if the aircraft had been on a high-altitude mission, the entire accessory section of the engine was awash with oil. The crew chief would remove the cowling of the P-35 and begin sloshing in the gasoline in an effort to remove the oil and return the fighter to the pristine shape of the pre-War Army aircraft. (E. Strasser)

Although the P-35As were listed as operational, they were, in fact, only marginally so. The aircraft had been poorly maintained and many were in need of engine and airframe overhaul while spare barrels for the machine guns were in such short supply that many of the aircraft were forced to fly with worn out guns. The fact that many of the manuals for maintaining the P-35s were written in Swedish did not help. Many of the P-40s were also marginally combat ready because they had just been uncrated and some had not even been air tested. The P-40s of the 18th did not have an average of over three flight hours each. The pilots were unfamiliar with their aircraft and had little chance to practise aerial maneuvers or test the guns of the P-40s.

Between the hours of two and three pm, the primitive American radar set located at Iba picked up a large formation of aircraft coming in towards the main Philippine island of Luzon (on which the important American bases were located). The aircraft were presumed to be Japanese and their intentions hostile. In the early sunlight of the morning of 8 December, P-40s of the 3rd Pursuit Squadron roared aloft with the orders to attack the incoming forma-

tion if it came within 20 miles of the coast. However, the poorly equipped P-40s had not been fitted with any form of oxygen equipment which limited operations to around 15,000 ft and, in any event, the Allison engines performed very poorly above that altitude. The radar operators saw the tracks of the two groups of aircraft converge. The pilots of the P-40s never saw the Japanese who were at much greater height. Oddly, the Japanese formation turned back and the P-40s returned to land.

The Americans had mistakenly presumed that the Philippines would be the first objective of the Japanese and confusion among the military units in the Philippines was rampant as word spread of the attack on Pearl Harbor. How had the enemy ventured over 5,000 miles from the Philippines without being spotted? When would an actual strike on Luzon come and where would it come from?

Confusion was in the extreme that morning as the 17th PS climbed into the humid air to fly a covering patrol over Clark. Fearing a surprise Japanese attack, the B-17 Flying Fortresses, which were sitting targets, were ordered into the air and the crews began taking the four-engine bombers aloft at 8:30 am. A number of mechanical problems kept some of the bombers on the field and the launching of the fleet took some time. The Fortresses had arrived in the Philippines, for the most part, in the shiney natural metal finish that typified the aircraft of the peacetime Army. An attempt was made to camouflage the B–17s as the chances of open conflict grew. There was only one paint spray gun available at Clark (another interesting oversight in the supply of the American forces in the Philippines) and it took a considerable time to camouflage each of the large bombers.

Initial Japanese bombing attacks took place at Baguio and Tuguegaro while the 20th tried to engage the marauding enemy formation that was flying at 22,000 ft. Most of the P–40s had an impossible time struggling to this altitude but a few of the pilots (presumably with huge lung capacity) managed to get their fighters to the bombers' height but the few shots fired were inconclusive. The first act of overt Japanese aggression had been committed against the Philippines and the FEAF was now officially at war.

Through confusion and extremely poor military planning which had the high-ranking Army ground officers and high-ranking Army air officers almost quarreling in their differing opinions, the B–17s began to return to Clark at around 10:30 after aimlessly circling the immediate area. As the Fortresses landed, ground crews frantically began the lengthy refueling process with Clark's limited equipment. Many of the bombers needed minor repairs and adjustments and all of the servicing procedures took time. Some officers wanted the B–17s to get into the air as soon as possible to avoid being on the ground in case of attack. To this day a controversy still exists as to why the bombers remained on the ground during this critical time period. General Hap Arnold stated after the war that he had never been able to get 'the real story of what happened but, as common with American thinking of the period, the Far East Air Force had woefully underestimated the strength and ability of the Japanese armed forces'.

At about noon Iba was hit by Japanese bombers just as aircraft of the 3rd PS were coming in to land for refueling after a patrol. Some of the P–40s managed to struggle back into the air as enemy bombs were demolishing the field. The few P–40s that became airborne spotted what they thought to be a formation of P–35As, but, upon investigation, the 'P–35As' turned out to be a pack of Zeke fighters. The Zekes began a textbook strafing attack on Iba. The airfield, through the effects of the highly accurate bombing and strafing, was completely destroyed and the flyable aircraft headed for the small strip at Rosales. Casualities at Iba were as high as 50 per cent.

At 12:40 it was Clark's turn for the attentions of the Japanese. It was a disaster for the FEAF. Over 50 enemy aircraft hit Clark with little warning. The first indication of an air raid for many of the airmen was the sight of bombs exploding on the field. There were no American fighters in the air as most were on the ground refueling (again another glaring example of military incompetence). The enemy bombers came over in perfect formation at high altitude and only four P–40s of the 20th PS managed to get into the air among the explosions. Clark was devastated by the severity and accuracy of the attack. Many of the major buildings were demolished and communication with other bases was cut. Zeke strafers came in after the bombers and increased the toll of American men and aircraft. Most of the B–17s had escaped destruction in the initial bombing attack but the Zekes quickly took care of that and soon many of the Fortresses were in flames. Anti-aircraft protection at Clark was inadequate with old-fashioned weapons that were so slow on their mounts that they could not track the fast, low-flying fighters. Crewmen ran to their Fortresses and tried to put up a defensive fire from the bombers' machine guns and many of the gunners died at their positions. Only a few enemy aircraft were destroyed or damaged but the Zekes that fell to the P–40s were among the first confirmed and credited American kills of the war.

Back at Del Carmen, the men of the 34th PS were ignorant of the rapid happenings at Iba and Clark but at the sight of the huge smoke clouds billowing from Clark, the pilots ran to the P–35As and the crew chiefs had the engines running in short order. As soon as the P–35As were airborne and gaining altitude, they tangled with a pack of Zekes that had been strafing Clark. Several of the Zekes were hit as were the P–35As but no aircraft were lost in the P–35A's first taste of action. The out of the way location of Del Carmen made it an ideal target for local fifth columnists, called Sakdalistas, who lit fires in the bush and cane fields around the airstrip in an attempt to attract Japanese aircraft. Patrols sent out to stop the fire-setting never found any traces of the Sakdalistas, who always managed to slip away after starting their fires. After the brief skirmish, the P–35As returned to Del Carmen to regroup and try to figure out what was happening. Del Carmen's thick, choking dust did the tired P–35A engines no good and the strain of the mass launching caused several of the engines to break down.

Mechanics worked frantically on the tired P–35As as the depressing news from Clark and Iba – as well as other Luzon locations – began to filter in to Del Carmen. Through heroic efforts, almost all of the P–35As were made airworthy and stood ready for missions on 9 December against the very powerful enemy but the Japanese did not show up because of storms over their bases on Formosa. On 10 December, the Japanese began to make landings at Vigan and the FEAF made a maximum effort to get every available aircraft into the air. The B–17s that escaped destruction at Del

Although the P–35 was basically a rugged machine problems arose because of a great deal of hand fitting of parts on individual machines, resulting in non-interchangeable parts. This caused many maintenance problems but the P–35 was unique in Army history as being declared obsolete while aircraft were still being delivered to the Army. (Collect-Air Photos)

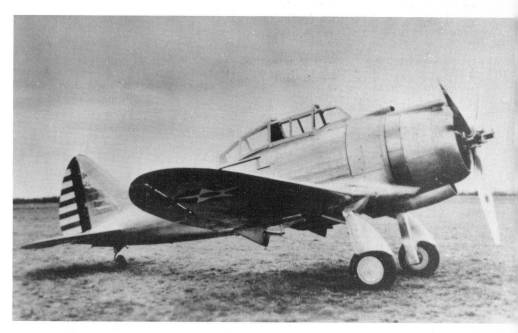

Only two Swedish machines had been delivered before the embargo, and the remaining two-seat aircraft were impressed into the US Army as AT-12 Guardsmen. This particular example is seen at Wright Field where it is being tested with a fin of greatly increased area.

Monte and a couple that had been patched up at Clark were bombed up while the remaining P-40s were armed as escorts. The patched and damaged aerial armada set out to Vigan but the P-35As, which were to escort the bombers, could not make the rendevous point because of their slow speed. The tired engines of the Severskys began to malfunction and, one after another, the stubby fighters began to turn back to Del Carmen. However, Lt Sam Marrett stubbornly continued on with the remaining fighters and attacked the landing enemy with extreme vigor and determination. The Japanese had not expected any aerial opposition and the casualties on the ships and ground were heavy. If more aircraft had been available there would have been a good chance that the enemy landings could have been completely routed. Unfortunately, Lt Marrett was killed by anti-aircraft fire as he pressed his attacks home at ship mast height.

The surviving P-35As headed back to Del Carmen but luck was just not with the Severskys. While landing at Del Carmen, the P-35As were hit by 12 strafing Zekes and a dozen of the fighters were destroyed and six more were damaged. The Squadron, now commanded by Lt Brown, was almost instantly reduced to a ground unit. The Japanese began to make many more landings in the face of dwindling American airpower and the P-35A squadron did not get aircraft airborne again until the 25 of December when they acquired a few P-40s.

The confusion and rapidly changing events that followed the Japanese landings on Luzon saw the squadrons break apart from their rigid pre-war order into loose-knit units that began operating from any airstrip they could find. The part played by the Severskys (individual aircraft were scattered at several fields) in the last days before Japanese victory in the Philippines was small, their performance made contact with raiding bombers difficult and they were at the mercy of the Zekes. However, the P-35As did participate in strafing attacks on enemy shipping and troop concentrations. The number of serviceable P-35As varied from day to day as the ground crews made heroic efforts to patch together flyable aircraft out of wrecks. The engines of the P-35As gave considerable trouble because of the effects of the clouds of thick choking dust thrown up at the primitive airstrips from which they were operating. Fighting in conjunction with the rapidly decreasing numbers of P-40s and B-17s, the remains of American air power in the Philippines managed to make life for the Japanese difficult.

As the Americans were forced to move from one temporary airstrip to the next, the spacious aft fuselage of the P-35A allowed several men or extra parts to be accommodated with ease. The P-35As were usually flown at tree-top heights during these reshuffling flights to avoid the attentions of prowling enemy fighters. Many of the P-35As had been given crude camouflage paint schemes to help avoid detection. As the situation in the Philippines became more and more desperate and evacuations were beginning, the active role of the P-35A in combat had basically come to an end. However, two patched-up P-35As managed to make it to Bataan on 5 March. It is thought that these aircraft were used for supply and reconnaissance work as the island made a last-ditch stand against hordes of Japanese. Captain Hank Thorne made the last P-35A flight out of Cabcaben airstrip with two pilots in the rear fuselage and a small load of bombs to drop on the Japanese after takeoff as he headed for safer territory. Thus the brief and not very heroic saga of the Philippine Severskys came to an end as all American resistance in the Philippines collapsed in surrender on 6 May with the fall of Corregidor.

The P-35s that were left in the United States were dispersed to training units or used as base hacks. Since the type was not a particularly loved aircraft, the P-35 soon became a rare sight at an operational base and most were scrapped or sent to mechanic training schools. The Severskys in Sweden did not see action but were used by that air force until the early 1950s when the last of the type was retired. Today, the United States Air Force Museum has on display an EP-1 (donated by Sweden) and an authentic P-35 that was discovered in a trade school. Thus Seversky's portly and much modified basic design can now stand beside the more famous fighters of World War Two, showing how it pointed the way towards the high-performance propeller-driven combat aircraft of that conflict.

SAM MARRETT – FORGOTTEN HERO

The heroic actions of many American fighter pilots during the early days of the fighting in the Philippines have gone largely unrecorded.

Lieutenant Sam Marrett viewed his new command and their airstrip with a great deal of distaste. Firstly, Del Carmen was not his idea of a well-maintained fighter base. Situated in Philippine agricultural land not far from Clark Field, Del Carmen consisted of a rough dirt strip with dust so thick that the slightest movement stirred up clouds of choking intensity. The facilities at Del Carmen were almost non-existent. Electricity was minimally provided by one small generator and quarters for the officers and men consisted of rows of tents. There were no eating, sanitary, or operational facilities and the supplies of fuel and ammunition were miniscule. Secondly, the aircraft that had been assigned to Marrett's 34th Pursuit

Squadron were a cruel joke – worn-out Seversky P–35As, much like the aircraft that they had been trained on back in the States. They had been promised brand-new Curtiss P–40Es.

Marrett, a lanky native of New Braunfels, Texas, was as green as the other pilots of his squadron. They had arrived in Manila aboard the ss *Coolidge* on 20 November 1941 with great hopes of setting up a modern pursuit unit, yet the young pilots only had training time entered in their log books. Marrett and his men were ordered to Nichols Field where they were greeted by the sight of 25 P–35As, their 'new' fighters. Some of the aircraft had been given a coat of drab camouflage paint but most were still finished in their natural metal skin and bright Army Air Corps markings. Everyone in the Philippines seemed to believe that war was coming and coming soon but Marrett and his men assembled their ground crews and began working on the almost impossible task of forming a combat unit within what most military officials figured would be a very short period of time.

Rather than center all aircraft at the few main bases on the island of Luzon, it was decided to transfer fighter and bomber units to more primitive 'hidden' airstrips that would not be well-known to the Japanese. Del Carmen certainly filled the primitive aspect but Marrett busied himself in setting up his unit in the best possible manner. Little could be done to make Del Carmen more palatable to the men, but a few temporary sheds were erected along with a crude control tower that gave the field a bit more presence as an operational military organization. The P–35As, however, proved to be a more difficult matter. The clouds of dust that were thrown up each time an engine started did little good for the engines or the airframes and systems. The dust penet-

Through poor communications and bad military leadership, American forces in the Philippines were caught with their proverbial pants down. These destroyed P–35A fighters were gleefully photographed by the victorious Japanese after the capture of American airfields. Note that aircraft 25 has been camouflaged, which was a difficult operation since only a couple of spray guns were available on the island of Luzon.

Another demolished P–35A seen after being caught in a Japanese strafing attack. Note what appears to be hastily applied light bomb racks over the word Army. The military operation of the P–35A in the Philippines was extremely limited.

rated everything and played havoc with the radial engines which were long overdue for overhaul to begin with. The mechanics had to labor under additional difficulties since the aircraft were originally built for Sweden and many of the servicing instructions and manuals were in Swedish.

A limited amount of practice flying was carried out along with gunnery practice but the pilots soon discovered that the gun barrels were almost worn out and firing results were wildly inaccurate. Cut-off from activity at Clark Field and having to rely on a primitive radio for communications the young pilots of the 34th felt completely disconnected from the outside world. Water had to be dragged by bucket from a nearby polluted stream and boiled before it could be consumed and the various ills of living in the open in a tropical environment began to play unpleasant tunes with the men's physical well-being.

When the war started on 8 December, it was almost as if Del Carmen had been forgotten, the base did not receive word of the Pearl Harbor attack until five hours after Clark Field had been notified. Marrett immediately mustered his men and explained the situation as crew chiefs topped off the fuel tanks and loaded ammunition. The Severskys did not have self-sealing fuel tanks or armor protection and the pilots were not pleased with what they considered to be flying coffins.

The confusion that resulted from the news of the Pearl Harbor attack left many of the young pilots puzzled. Almost everyone was sure that the Philippines would be attacked first if the Japanese declared war on the United States and, after several hours and no action, some of the fliers began to feel that the news of the

Pearl Harbor attack was false and broadcasted by the Japanese as part of some elaborate plot. Still, the pilots sat in the sweltering cockpits of the P–35As, parachutes strapped on and everything ready. As the day wore on, the heat became too intense and the pilots abandoned the cockpits for the shade offered by the wing. Shortly before one in the afternoon, Marrett and the men of the 34th spotted huge clouds of black smoke pouring into the sky from nearby Clark Field. Without warning, the attack had come.

Without waiting for orders, Marrett jumped into the cockpit of his Seversky, whose engine was already ticking over courtesy of the crew chief, and led his squadron out onto the crude runway. Amazingly, all the P–35As managed to get airborne through the clouds of dust, even though the last aircraft were probably flying on instruments. With throttles to the firewall, the 34th headed towards Clark. The enemy bomber formation had passed overhead in parade-ground drill at great height, but they were followed up by low-flying Zeke fighters which were strafing everything in sight. Sam Marrett and his fighter pilots ran right into this hornet's nest but, in the ensuing dogfight, not one P–35A was lost although several suffered battle damage and a number of Zekes felt the sting of the P–35A's two .30 and two .50 caliber machine guns. The Zekes broke off contact and headed back to their bases in the Philippines, and Marrett patrolled the skies over Clark, noting with a sick feeling the many burning B–17s and P–40s on the ground. When fuel began to run low, Marrett took the 34th back to Del Carmen where the aircraft were refueled and rearmed. If the pilots had suffered low morale before the attack, then it

was even worse now for they had been completely powerless to stop the destruction of Clark Field.

Although Marrett had the P–35As prepared for instant scramble, most of the day was spent sitting by the aircraft and waiting for the enemy to return, but they did not. Communications with Clark were limited and the next day saw the 34th constantly in the air on patrol for Japanese, but a series of storm systems were keeping the Japanese on the ground in Formosa although the men of the 34th had no way of knowing this. However, fifth columnists were busy on the ground, sneaking close to Del Carmen and setting fires in the bush in hopes of directing Japanese bombers to the airfield. Ground personnel were kept busy trying to put out the fires and taking the odd pot-shot at what they thought were the fifth columnists. By the end of the day the pilots were exhausted and defects had cropped up on some of the aircraft, meaning that the mechanics would have a very long night. However, Marrett received orders late in the day that the 34th was to retreat to an equally primitive field, San Marcelino, for the night because of the threat of bombing attack.

On the morning of the 10th, the 34th was back at Del Carmen and Marrett found urgent orders awaiting him. Every Seversky was to get into the air and head for Vigan on the northern coast of Luzon where the Japanese were making their first landing. A P–40, airborne just before dawn, had spotted the enemy fleet and brought back the message to Clark. Patched-up B–17s and P–40s from Clark, joined by some of the B–17s that had escaped destruction at Del Monte, were airborne and headed for Vigan with the objective of doing as much damage to the enemy as possible.

The ground crews swarmed around the P–35As in an attempt to put fuel in the aircraft for the flight to Vigan. Time was critical and Marrett stood in the cockpit of his Seversky, surveying the sky for any sight of the enemy. Once again, the P–35As struggled through the dust cloud and became airborne. However, the time spent on the ground meant that they could not rendezvous with the aircraft from Clark which were already heading towards Vigan, and the slow speed of the P–35s prevented them from catching up.

Departing Del Carmen in two flights of eight aircraft, one flight led by Marrett and one by Lt Ben S. Brown, the Severskys soon began encountering problems. One by one, the fighters began turning back with engine problems. The high-time powerplants and the effects of the dust were taking their toll and a nervous Marrett watched as his formation steadily decreased. When the 34th approached Vigan only seven P–35As were still in the air, two in Brown's flight and five with Marrett.

The depressing sight of a huge Japanese naval force greeted the small group of pilots. Close to shore were the transports and landing craft while farther out stood the warships, destroyers and cruisers. The B–17s and P–40s had finished their attacks and smoke was rising from where bombs and bullets had found their mark. This also meant that the Japanese were now fully alerted to the fact that American airpower in the Philippines still had some sting and anti-aircraft guns were being erected as the P–35s appeared on the horizon.

What good the lightly-armed P–35s could do against the formidable Japanese force was debatable but Marrett knew that the 34th would have to attack. The pilots knew that the Filipino troops would not be able to hold the enemy off for more than a brief period so, just like in training school, the P–35s broke formation in a perfect peel off and, with engines screaming, dived on the enemy. The little fighters roared among the shipping, sending volleys of machine gun fire into the surprised Japanese who had not expected the small force to commit themselves to battle.

Marrett, flying right above the surface of the ocean, selected a transport and held the trigger down as he watched his bullets slam into the lightly armored superstructure. Racking the Seversky around in a dangerous tight turn just a few feet above the water, Marrett went back for another firing pass as the Japanese gunners were blazing away with everything they had. Shells were kicking up water spouts around Marrett's aircraft as he centered his sights on the transport. Again he flew straight and level and poured gunfire into the middle of the ship. One of the 34th's pilots yelled to Marrett over the radio to abandon his attack because it was becoming too dangerous. Marrett persisted on his run and pulled over the ship's mast at the last possible instant. However, Marrett had waited too long. The 10,000 ton transport had apparently been carrying shells and ammunition and, just as Marrett cleared the superstructure, a violent explosion blasted the enemy vessel in two and, at the same time, blew the right wing off Marrett's P–35A which instantly flipped over and plunged into the ocean. It was all over in a second. The Japanese ship literally disappeared in the massive explosion. The surviving 34th pilots decided that

they had done all that was possible and began a hasty retreat to Del Carmen.

By the time the fighters had got back into Del Carmen, the ground crews had managed to patch together most of the fighters that had aborted but one of the P–35As returning from the strafing attack crashed into the jungle when the engine stopped, the pilot parachuting to safety. As the fighters were being rearmed, a dozen Zekes hit the strip in a surprise raid and their shooting, as had been discovered at Clark Field, was very accurate. With little in the way of anti-aircraft, the Americans were helpless and dived for cover into trenches or foxholes. After the Zekes left and after the fires and explosions had quieted down, the 34th discovered that 12 of the P–35As were smoking ruins and another six were very badly damaged. It looked like the 34th was out of the fighting business. Lt Ben S. Brown took over the unit after Marrett's death and had the men move their living quarters deeper into the jungle while they patched the wrecks together to look like operational aircraft. This deceived the Japanese who paid much time and attention to destroying the already destroyed P–35s.

To be expected, morale – already reaching bottom – really took a dive with the death of Marrett and the virtual destruction of all the Severskys. The pilots and ground crews were almost completely cut-off from any news of the war, even though Del Carmen was fairly close to Clark Field, and the young pilots felt as if they had been deserted. Even the patching up of the ruined Severskys after each bombing raid could not take up all their time and the situation was beginning to get very critical when Captain Harold Munton decided to do something about it. Munton had come to Del Carmen to set up the new Air Depot at the field and, as the men of the 34th were beginning to rebel and getting ready to take to the hills, Munton took it upon himself to take charge.

Captain Munton forced the squadron to take a hold of itself as a unit and initiated a move to Orani on the morning of the 26th; all members were able to receive a Christmas meal the night before from the operators of a nearby sugar mill. The command of the 34th was taken over by Lt Robert S. Wray and was soon flying reconnaissance missions with the P–40s that had been assigned to that base. Munton then went on to transport all Depot supplies to Bataan Field and was later in charge of supplies at that base. The few remaining P–35s left on Luzon flew reconnaissance missions until the last two flyable examples were taken to Bataan on 2 January.

Those hectic first days of America's entry into World War Two meant that records were slim and that many heroes went without the recognition that they deserved. On the day that Marrett was killed, Captain Colin Kelly in a B–17 Flying Fortress made an attack on a Japanese vessel and was awarded a posthumous Medal of Honor when he was killed trying to bring the damaged aircraft back to base. The American propaganda mill, desperate for some good news, amplified Kelly's attack on the ship to make it appear that the vessel was a carrier or a battleship and that it was sunk. The craft Kelly and his crew attacked was actually a cruiser and damage to the vessel was probably light. This event completely overshadowed Marrett's courageous attack in an obsolete aircraft but he was eventually awarded a posthumous Distinguished Flying Cross.

SEVERSKY P–35 SERIAL NUMBERS AND SPECIFICATIONS

Serial Numbers

P–35	36–354 through 36–429
P–35A	41–17434 through 41–17493

Specifications

P–35

Span	36 ft
Length	25 ft 2 in
Height	9 ft 1 in
Wing area	220 sq ft
Empty weight	4,315 lb
Loaded weight	6,295 lb
Max. speed	282 mph
Cruise speed	258 mph
Ceiling	31,000 ft
Rate of climb	2,400 fpm
Range	450 to 1,100 miles
Powerplant	Pratt & Whitney R–1830–9 of 950 hp

P35A

Span	36 ft
Length	26 ft 10 in
Height	9 ft 9 in
Wing area	220 sq ft
Empty weight	4,575 lb
Loaded weight	6,723 lb
Max. speed	290 mph
Cruise speed	260 mph
Ceiling	31,400 ft
Rate of climb	1,920 fpm
Range	600 to 950 miles
Powerplant	Pratt & Whitney R–1830–45 of 1,050 hp

Curtiss P-36
It Fought For Both Sides

The P–36 was the eventual winner in the Seversky/Curtiss fighter contest but its main claim to fame was that it would evolve into the P–40.

Lt G. H. Sterling, sweating in the cockpit of his Curtiss P–36A, was wishing that he had an aircraft with more horsepower, more guns, more maneuverability ... more everything. It was 0855 hrs on the morning of 7 December 1941, and, over Wheeler Field, Lt Sterling was having very little time to think about much else except surviving. Sterling had managed to get off the ground at Wheeler Field with two

other 46th Pursuit Squadron P–36As. With huge columns of smoke billowing up from Pearl Harbor and the airfields in the vicinity, it was not hard for the P–36 pilots to find action. Anti-aircraft fire, now that the initial surprise of the devastating Japanese attack had somewhat passed, was pouring into the sky and any aircraft was considered a target – even if they were friendly. Just before 0800 hrs, aerial units of the Imperial Japanese Navy had staged a perfectly executed attack on American bases located on the Hawaiian island of Oahu. Dive and horizontal bombers, torpedo aircraft and a variety of fighters smashed the American

Perhaps the grandest hour for the P–36 in American skies was at the Cleveland, Ohio, National Air Races during September 1939. The P–36s of the 27th Pursuit Squadron were given individual and wildly imaginative 'camouflage' schemes on the excuse of an upcoming 'war game' but the war game was never held and it is more likely that the pilots and crews of the 27th just wanted to make a grand entrance to the Air Races, which were the most important aviation gathering in America. At the same time, the 1st PG has left a puzzle for historians that probably will never be solved – namely in defining the colors used on the P–36s. Aircraft No 59 carries the insignia of the 27th Pursuit Squadron and was probably painted in washable colors of dark green, brown, white, and orange. Many of the colors used on the P–36s were non-standard so it is impossible to match them to official color designations.

facilities with precision in the initial assault. At 0840 hrs, a second wave of enemy aircraft continued the attack. The Navy had suffered the worst losses in its long history. *Arizona, California, West Virginia* were sunk, *Oklahoma* had rolled over, and the *Nevada* was blazing from numerous hits. Smoke and explosions were filling the air over Pearl as the P–36s clawed for altitude.

About 25 bombers had hit Wheeler Field shortly after 0800, causing heavy damage to the aircraft that were parked closely together and to the facilities and hangars at the Army base. During a brief lull in the aerial attack, the three P–36As managed to get into the air with orders to proceed to Bellows Field to patrol the area and attack bombers at will. With throttles all the way to the stop, the P–36As dodged bursts of anti-aircraft fire as they headed towards Bellows. Bellows had not been hit as hard as Hickam or Wheeler but nine Zekes had strafed the field without opposition or any positive results from the limited anti-aircraft fire that the Army was able to put up. The Curtiss fighters arrived over Bellows shortly after the strafing attack and spotted the forms of nine Val dive bombers heading towards Bellows. The pilots immediately waded into the surprised enemy formation. Sterling kicked his rudder pedal over hard as he selected the fat fuselage of a Val that had broken formation. Closing rapidly against the fixed-gear bomber, Sterling quickly settled the aircraft in his sights and hit the trigger, sending off several bursts of .30 and .50 caliber machine gun fire from the two guns located in the upper forward fuselage. Although the firepower of the P–36A was anything but adequate, the well-aimed bursts from Sterling's guns were devastating against the unarmored Val. With its fuel tanks unprotected, the steel-jacketed slugs from the P–36A instantly turned the Val into an inferno and the blazing aircraft plunged to the ground – the two Japanese airmen going to meet their ancestors much sooner than they probably wished. Enemy aircraft were everywhere over Oahu so targets were not a problem but the ill-equipped hunters soon became the hunted. Superlative Mitsubishi Zeke fighters – a type unleashed with complete surprise against the Americans – were soon after the P–36As. One of the other Curtiss pilots managed to flame another bomber before being pounced upon by the fighters. Two of the three P–36As managed to get back to Wheeler but Lt Sterling – the first American pilot to score a victory over Pearl – had fallen to the guns of the avenging Zekes.

The Curtiss P–36A had had its moment of combat glory – at least in Army hands – on 7 December 1941. From that point, the woefully inadequate fighters were retired to second-line

duties or to training units. However, history books would have to record the significant fact that the first Japanese aircraft to be claimed as destroyed by the USAAF was a victim of the Curtiss P–36A and a brave pilot.

The Curtiss P–36, along with the Seversky P–35, was the bridge between biplanes and modern fighter aircraft for the USAAF. As stated in the chapter on the P–35, both aircraft were entered in a particularly hard–fought contest that was to have curious final results. Both machines were less than adequate in all categories of performance but they did manage to change the rather staid thinking of the American military and to help aircraft factories tool up for the coming conflict.

If the P–36 had served with just the US Army, then its story would have been short indeed. The build-up of war tensions meant that European nations – as well as many other smaller countries – were frantic to obtain as many combat-ready aircraft as they could as soon as possible. The Curtiss design happened to be at the right place at the right time. The P–36 design was available to be quickly mass-produced and supplied to foreign nations and it was with some of these countries that the design achieved its greatest success.

Curtiss began prototype construction of its 'Hawk 75' design as a private undertaking.

The Curtiss Model 75 (carrying the civil registration of 17Y) in flight near the Curtiss factory in Buffalo, New York. This was the aircraft with which Curtiss entered the Army pursuit aircraft competition during May 1935 but lost out to the Seversky P–35. Yet, in a curious reversal of circumstances, the Model 75 was the eventual winner. Principal designer of the Model 75 was the talented Donovan A. Berlin who had left Northrop to join Curtiss. Carrying s/n 11923, the Model 75 was originally powered by the Wright R–1670 900 hp radial, an unfortunate choice. Engine problems dogged 17Y and the first replacement engine was the Pratt & Whitney R–1535 of 700 hp but, since this was basically an obsolete powerplant, it was quickly replaced with a Wright R–1820 Cyclone. These engine problems were a major factor in the contest with the P–35 and 17Y (now designated Model 75B since the engine change) lost out in the fly-off of April 1936. This aircraft eventually gained new life when it was converted to the XP–37. Color scheme for 17Y consisted of blue fuselage and yellow flying surfaces – an evident attempt to impress the Army with an aircraft painted up in their standard color scheme.

The Army was interested in obtaining an aircraft to replace the little Boeing P–26 Peashooter and the new contract would be extremely lucrative and one that would bring prestige and fortune to the winning company. Like the P–35, the prototype Hawk 75 did not offer anything completely new in aviation terms but it did combine a number of factors, such as retractable landing gear, all-metal construction and enclosed cockpit, into a fighter that could be classified as 'modern' in appearance but not in performance – especially when one considers that the Hurri-

Curtiss did not completely lose out in the fly-off contest with the Seversky P-35, for the Army, not all that pleased with the Seversky, decided to issue Curtiss with a contract for three developmental YIP-36 aircraft to be powered by the same Pratt & Whitney R-1830 that lugged the Seversky through the air. The combination of airframe and new engine changed the downward slide of the Model 75's career. This YIP-36 is seen in natural metal finish with the yellow and blue Wright Field arrow on the side of the fuselage.

One of the three YIP-36s seen at the Buffalo, New York, airfield. These aircraft were extensively flown with the new engine installation and proved quite popular with factory and Army test pilots. Given the Curtiss factory designation of Model H75E, the three YIP-36s were delivered during March 1937 and carried the standard inadequate Army armament of the time period: one .30 and one .50 caliber machine gun firing through the propeller and located in the upper fuselage decking. The YIP-36s could be distinguished from production machines by the lack of cowl flaps on the smooth NACA cowling. It is interesting to note that the three aircraft had different prices: $48,432, $43,477 and $73,477. These prices are a bit deceptive since the Army supplied such essential items as engine and guns. Note the cumbersome retractable landing gear which, while being retracted, swiveled 90 degrees before entering the wells in the wing.

cane, Spitfire and Bf 109 were all under development at the same time.

Since the Model 75 was a privately-funded venture, the prototype had to be given a civil registration – X17Y. Curtiss rather optimistically committed the aircraft to an Army-style paint scheme of blue fuselage and yellow flying surfaces. The new aircraft was powered by the experimental XR–1670–5 radial built by Wright (a division of Curtiss). The radial was composed of 14 cylinders arranged into two rows and was theoretically capable of pumping out 900 hp.

Curtiss factory test pilot Lloyd Child took the new aircraft up for its first test flight on 13 May 1935 but reported that the aircraft did not handle all that well and power from the engine was disappointing. The XR–1670–5 was totally unsatisfactory and it was temporarily replaced with an obsolete 700 hp P&W R–1535.

Seven hundred horsepower was not enough for a plane like the Model 75 so the engine mount was redesigned and the airframe was fitted with a Wright XR–1820–39 single-row radial of 950 hp. Child felt that the extra real horsepower improved the handling and performance of the machine so, on 27 May, the aircraft was submitted to the Army's Material Division for testing.

The Army was looking for a cleanly designed fighter (incorporating the 'modern' innovations previously listed) but they were limiting the usefulness of the design by specifying the carriage of two guns and a speed up to only 300 mph. Curtiss was in for a surprise – figuring that the fighter contest was in their pocket – for none of the other designs were ready and the Seversky entry had been mysteriously pulled out from the competition due to a questionable 'accident'. Actually, the so-called accident gave Seversky time to install crude retractable landing gear on his design and make it more competitive with the Model 75. The Army went along with the idea – feeling that the 'accident' should not deprive Seversky of his chance at the brass ring! Designer Donovan Berlin and the management of Curtiss protested at the decision but the Army felt that their action was warranted and stuck to the time extension. However, the modified Seversky entry and the Model 75 both suffered technical and engine troubles at the next gathering date and the Army once again extended the contest, this time until April 1936.

Both manufacturers took the extra time to develop and refine their fighters. The Model 75 had a new engine installed, this time an 850 hp Wright Cyclone, and the fuselage around the engine installation of X17Y was slightly redesigned while rear vision panels were placed in the fuselage behind the canopy. These modifications resulted in a designation change to H–75B. Thus modified, the aircraft entered the contest but the extra work had not completely cured the Curtiss fighter of its problems. During a short period of testing time, four engines had to be changed on the Curtiss because of failures, but all the fault was not on the side of the Curtiss entry as the Seversky was enjoying less than qualified successes. Curtiss had promised a top speed of 294 mph at 10,000 ft but the fighter was only able to produce 285 mph. The P–35, when the Army announced the results of the testing, proved to be a winner with a total of 812 points gained in the various categories (this was for the aircraft equipped with the Pratt & Whitney radial). Worse still, Seversky also took second place (792 points) with the aircraft powered by a Wright Cyclone. The H–75B dragged in at third with a not too exciting showing of 720 points.

This rather bleak picture was not all that bad for – although Seversky had many friends in the military – the Army was not satisfied with the company's ability to mass-produce a combat aircraft. To get around putting all their eggs in one basket, the Army issued a Service Test Order (AC 9045) to Curtiss for three service evaluation aircraft based on the H–75B but to be powered by the more reliable and powerful Pratt & Whitney R–1830 Twin Wasp. Since service test aircraft were assigned the Y1 designation, there never was a prototype (X) for the P–36, the designation the Army had given the new fighter. Curtiss was pleased with the contract, especially in the light of the fact that the 75 series was picking up increased export interest.

The Y1P–36 aircraft benefitted from additional detail design and clean-up work and the type was given the factory number of 75E. A new cowling housed the much more reliable P&W radial and the three aircraft, delivered in gleaming polished metal finish with Army markings, were sent to Wright Field for intensive testing. The R–1830–13 engine swung a three blade Hamilton Standard constant speed propeller and could deliver 950 hp. Since these were service test aircraft, the three machines were handed over to regular squadron pilots from the 1st Pursuit Group who put in about 60 hours of flying time, doing everything from slow flight testing to full power dives. The comments of these pilots were noted and recorded for a final summary. After the period of testing, a three-page report was carefully prepared by Colonel Frank Kennedy who summed up the test results. On the negative side, the pilots had felt that the cockpit was very hot; the heat came from defects in the firewall which, while it let in large amounts of engine heat, also allowed deadly gases to seep into the cockpit. Controls were also reported to be heavy when flying at high speeds, or at the beginning of a spin or snap roll. The combat pilots felt that the handles for the flaps and landing gear were too close together which could result in an embarrassing and expensive mistake. Engineers had noticed a structural weakness in the wing and a lack of strength in the gear attachment point. Lesser complaints included the fact that the baggage compartment was too small. On the positive side, the testing revealed that the re-engined P–36 performed aerobatic maneuvers with considerable *élan* and that vision from the cockpit was good. The Y1P–36s displayed very stable flight attitudes while ground handling and take-off characteristics were also good.

Curtiss went to work on the complaints. They reinforced the wing structure and landing gear attachment points, and modified the cowling to included cooling gills so that improved air circulation could take place while the engine was running on the ground. The controls were also modified and this was perhaps one of the most significant changes undertaken by Curtiss for the control system modification turned the P–36 into a beautifully flying aircraft with superb control harmonization. The P–36 was now able to roll at a faster rate than even the vaunted Spitfire.

Less than pleased with the delivery and performance of the Seversky P–35, the Army issued a contract, huge at the time, to Curtiss for the production of 210 P–36A fighters, costing $4,113,550 – the largest contract price for American aircraft. Curtiss was very pleased with the obvious victory over Seversky. The prestige of the Army contract would also bring foreign orders from governments who felt more confident in buying an aircraft already ordered in large quantity by the US Army.

The Curtiss P–36A was to be built entirely out of metal with a cantilever multi-spar wing that was skinned with 24ST Alclad. The fuselage was an aluminium monocoque. The retractable landing gear was of a patented Boeing design and Curtiss had to pay royalties to Boeing for each set of landing gear constructed.

The P–36A wing was built in two pieces and the wing tips were easily detachable. The airfoil was a NACA 2215 section at the root, tapering to a NACA 2209 section at the tip. The wings were joined at the centerline by a heavy ribbing and a large number of strong bolts that linked the two halves in a tight bond. The outer panels of the wing were sealed to help the aircraft to float in case it had to be ditched in the sea. Not quite sure of the merits of retractable landing gear, Curtiss built a strong skid into the forward centerline portion of the lower fuselage to reduce airframe damage in a wheels-up landing.

The hydraulically operated split flaps enabled a low landing speed of 74 mph to be achieved while also shortening the take-off run to 750 ft with a bit of wind coming over the nose. The wing area was to prove to be a weak point in the P–36. Structural wrinkles appeared around the landing gear/wing area due to hard landings or from being subjected to particularly hard g forces. Reinforcement was attempted in the form of thicker wing skinning and extra rib webs but this never entirely solved the problem.

The fuel situation was taken care of with three tanks that held a total of 162 gallons, giving a range of about 820 miles at economy cruise. Although different powerplant combinations were experimented with, the standard P–36A engine remained the Pratt & Whitney radial turning a Curtiss Electric three-blade propeller that was capable of full feathering as well as constant speed.

The tail section was also cantilever and used the NACA 0009 section and was entirely covered in Alclad except for the rudder and elevator which were finished in the traditional fabric covering as were the ailerons.

Designated P–36A, the production model of the new Curtiss fighter was not much different

from the service test machines. The propeller was changed to a Curtiss Electric fully-feathering three-blade unit while the engine was produced to the latest modification standards, with the addition of flaps on the rear of the annular cowling to aid cooling. Brand new, the P–36A could nudge over 300 mph but it had a ridiculously inadequate armament of one .30 and one .50 caliber gun. The smaller weapon was equipped with 500 rounds while the .50 had only 200 rounds. This curious throw-back to World War One standards went in the face of effective European and Japanese cannon armament which had been developed, tested and put into service. Even the British standard .303 caliber aerial machine guns was tempered by the fact that these guns were usually installed in some number – eight guns in the early Hurricanes and Spitfires.

The first production P–36A (Curtiss Model 75L) was delivered to the Army during April 1938 but deliveries of further machines did not proceed all that smoothly. Apparent lack of design foresight and production line quality control led to a weakness in the fuselage and wing that followed the P–36A through its short career with the Army. Testing of the first P–36A (s/n 38–001) during aerobatics brought back the problem of skin wrinkling and buckling in the area of the landing gear wells and on certain sections of fuselage skinning. Curtiss tried to correct the problem with thicker skin but apparently the problem went deeper – to a poorly designed structure – and it was not resolved.

Service P–36As went to the 20th Pursuit Group and its three squadrons – the 55th, 77th and 79th – at Barksdale Field in Louisiana, but serviceability was extremely poor and groundings were frequent. Controls on the Curtiss production line apparently did little good, for the Army would usually ground a newly delivered aircraft until they had made their own modifications. The three squadrons had a hard time coming up to operational strength – they had given up their Boeing

*L*ine-up of P–36As from the 79th Pursuit Squadron of the 20th Pursuit Group. The aircraft in the lead was the mount of the squadron commander and can be identified by the two bands around the rear fuselage which were painted in yellow as was the large band around the engine cowling. Yellow was the color assigned to the 79th PS. Lightly armed and less than overpowered, the P–36 would have been a poor opponent for the Bf 109 that was flying with the Luftwaffe. (Barksdale AFB)

P–26s in anticipation of getting the P–36As. Flying hours were low as aircraft had to be grounded each time a skin wrinkle was found so that its entire airframe could be carefully inspected by Army mechanics for any signs of structural failure.

Factory changes were common for the P–36A at Buffalo and, by June 1939, Curtiss had instigated no fewer than 81 changes. These caused an increase in airframe weight and an obvious decay in performance and most factory-fresh P–36As with the new modifications would have had a hard time topping 300 mph. Pilots of the 20th PG were also having difficulties getting enough flying hours to keep current and had to borrow training aircraft to fly. The Boeing P–26s that had equipped the 20th PG were transferred to overseas units where a few later saw action in the Philippines and a number were destroyed on the ground in the initial attack on Pearl Harbor.

The Seversky P–35 and the P–36A gave the Army inadequate new fighters that were not only poorly armed to fight but were also limited in the types of combat maneuvers which they could perform. The Army, in concern for its pilots' safety, limited the top speed to 250 mph and strictly limited rough, combat-style maneuvers. One Army document lists, on 30 April 1939, the fact that 47 of the 61 P–36As based in America were grounded due to problems.

The 1st Pursuit Group, based at Selfridge Field in Michigan (and mentioned in the chapter on the P–35), was to give up its Seversky fighters for P–36As during 1938 but the problems with the Curtiss aircraft severely hampered the 1st's plans. The 17th, 27th and 94th Pursuit Squadrons made up the 1st PG but only the 94th was able to equip with the P–36A by the time the year closed. Even then, the 94th was not up to strength and had to fill in with P–35s. The 27th began taking on P–36As during 1939 but also could not come up to strength. The 17th stayed with the P–35. While operating both types, the 1st PG was able to experience the frustrations caused by the many troubles that the P–35 and P–36 generated.

Developmental work continued at the Curtiss factory on the P–36 and several other versions were produced to test armament configurations. P–36A 38–020 was modified to carry a Twin Wasp of 1,100 hp and was given the designation P–36B in November 1938. Another P–36A was fitted with a turbosupercharger and had the airframe lightened a bit in an attempt to increase performance, but the increase was negligible and the aircraft was put back into stock configuration after testing.

The P–36D saw the conversion of P–36A 38–174 to mount a Twin Wasp R–1830–17 of 1,200 hp. The nose armament was modified to carry two .50 caliber weapons while modified outer wing panels carried two .30 calibers with 500 rpg on each side. The 147th P–36A, 38–147, became the XP–36E when the wings were modified to carry a total of eight .30 caliber guns with 500 rpg; the nose armament was eliminated. S/n 38–172 became the XP–36F when Curtiss installed one 23 mm Danish Madsen cannon with 100 rpg in a fairing under each wing panel; the XP–36F kept the standard nose armament. The increased weight and drag from the cannon pods reduced the top speed to an unimpressive 265 mph and development was discontinued.

The Army was not pleased with the performance of the P–36As that were beginning to arrive at squadron level, so the last 30 aircraft of the contract were uprated to become the P–36C. The P–36C was powered by the 1,200 hp Twin Wasp R–1830–17 radial while the outer wing panels were modified to take an additional .30 caliber gun with 500 rpg. A distinctive identifying feature of the P–36C was the cartridge container case that was mounted below the wing gun. Even with the increased drag of these units, the P–36C's speed rose a bit because of the extra horsepower. Modification of other P–36 airframes to XP–37, XP–42 and XP–40 prototypes is dealt with in the chapters concerning those aircraft.

As more P–36As became available, more units were equipped with the fighter, but it was rapidly becoming very obsolete as a result of the military developments in Europe. Curtiss fighters went to the 35th and 36th Pursuit Groups at Moffett Field, California, and Langley Field, Virginia, where, instead of arriving as operational fighters they were utilized as combat training aircraft.

America's far-flung outposts often received hand-me-down aircraft and Alaska was certainly no exception. In any upcoming threat of global conflict, Alaska was considered to be relatively safe from any enemy incursion – little did Washington know that the Japanese had mapped out a most effective invasion plan of Alaska via the long string of bleak and dismal islands known as the Aleutians.

Alaska was a vast uncharted frontier in the late 1930s and airfields capable of accepting modern military aircraft were virtually nil. Construction workers were sent to Anchorage to build a modern facility, Elmendorf Field, in 1940 but, by July 1940, when the first Army Air Force representatives arrived in Alaska, only a portion of the construction had been undertaken and completed. Since Anchorage is located at the end of a long inlet, the yearly temperatures, moderated by the influence of ocean currents, are considerably milder than in the interior of Alaska. The first temporary

hangar at Elmendorf was erected during the first months of 1941 and the officers in charge of the project decided that it was time for tactical aircraft to be transferred from the continental United States to the northern outpost. During February, the first combat aircraft arrived – 20 carefully crated P–36A fighters belonging to the 18th Pursuit Squadron. These were soon joined by 12 equally obsolete Douglas B–18A Bolo bombers of the 73rd Bombardment Squadron (Medium) and the 36th Bombardment Squadron (Heavy).

The Army Air Force effort in Alaska was consolidated under the title of Air Field Forces, Alaska Defense Command, on 29 May. The organization assumed the responsibility of training personnel, repairing and maintaining aircraft and preparing aerial defense methods for Alaska. Since the weather conditions in this part of the world were completely different to those in the United States, it was essential that pilots be fully trained to fly within the confines of Alaskan weather. Navigation aids were primitive, so it was also necessary that each

pilot become acquainted with every airfield and its surrounding points of identity. There was initially some conflict between the Navy and the Army concerning the roles of defense that each service should undertake but these differences were smoothed out by close co-operation.

As the war in Europe escalated, the importance of Alaska to America rapidly became clear. The Aleutian chain of islands provided many natural harbors for enemy landing forces who could set up temporary harbors and airfields that would be very difficult to dislodge. Ground forces in Alaska were fairly immobile because of the difficult nature of the terrain

Side-view of a P–36A assigned to the 36th Pursuit Squadron of the 8th Pursuit Group. The 36th PS could trace its history back to the 36th Aero Squadron of World War One and its P–36As carried the squadron's insignia on the sides of the fuselage, which consisted of a golden orange bordered in blue, 'a flying fiend' proper with a gutte de sang dropping from tongue, blue helmet and white goggles with black rims on an irregular cloudlike background. The 36th PS operated the P–36 from 1939 to 1940, during which time it also had on charge YP–37s and A–17s.

A P–36A from the 1st Pursuit Group shows off the aircraft's clean and simple lines to advantage. The plexiglass panels behind the sliding canopy offered a limited degree of visibility to the rear. Pre-war aircraft serving with the Army were maintained in pristine condition by individual crew chiefs and their helpers. This P–36A, carrying the group's insignia on the fuselage sides, was photographed on 22 October 1939. (E. Strasser)

and the weather, so they were basically tied to their stations and the Army felt that an intergrated system of airfields would be the only way to ensure the mobility needed in case of enemy invasion.

New airfields were rapidly put under construction during the summer of 1941 and by that fall, Elmendorf, Ladd, Kodiak, Yakutat and Nome airfields were all capable of supporting at least one fully equipped combat squadron while a dozen auxiliary landing fields were being constructed which would increase safety and the mobility of the air forces. Once the Curtiss P–36As had been uncrated and assembled, the difficult Alaskan weather did not

provide many operating problems, although preheating of the engine and oil was standard procedure during the cold months. The P–36As flew a variety of patrols, airfield scouting missions and survey flights but they were quickly phased out when newer P–40s became available. However, on 7 December 1941, the only operational combat aircraft in Alaska was the motley force of 20 P–36As and 12 Bolo bombers. The Alaska Defense Command thus became the only Army overseas air force which did not have one up-to-date combat aircraft immediately prior to the outbreak of the American entry into World War Two.

Another vital American defense location was the Panama Canal, that small but vital waterway which bisects Central America. Air defense in the Canal Zone had existed since 1917 but it was only during 1939 that the Army realized that the most likely form of attack against the Canal would come from the air. The bases in the Canal Zone had been

around for a while but were not completely finished or equipped. Personnel were also poorly trained and were usually engaged in constructing facilities rather than perfecting the tasks for which they were trained. The Canal certainly had more aircraft available than in Alaska but, once again, these machines were mostly obsolete and ineffective. New bases were being established in areas such as Puerto Rico, and the Caribbean area aerial defenses were consolidated under the command of the new Caribbean Air Force during May 1941 with the focus point of operations being the Panama Canal. Three main air bases formed the aerial defense basis of the Canal: France Field was located on the Atlantic side, Albrook Field was on the Pacific side and Howard Field was three miles from Albrook. These three bases were backed up by seven auxiliary fields and a number of emergency landing strips that had been cut out of the surrounding jungle and bush. By 7 December 1941, only 183 aircraft, out of the allotted total of 396 planes, had been assigned to Canal Zone bases. Many of these aircraft were obsolete by any standards and included the Boeing P–26 and Northrop A–17. The start of World War Two saw P–36As operating with the 16th Pursuit Group and its 24th, 29th and 43rd Pursuit Squadrons. Located at Albrook Field, the 16th was saddled with a mixture of P–36As and P–26s. Also at Albrook was the 32nd Pursuit Group which had a mixture of P–36s, P–26s and a few P–40s for its 51st, 52nd and 53rd Pursuit Squadrons. The P–26s and P–36s were replaced with P–40s as soon as the new aircraft became available, most of the P–36s being sent back to the States. The P–36 apparently did not see any action while in the Canal Zone against the German U-Boats that occasionally slipped in close for a look, although one of the U-Boats met its end by coming to the surface at the wrong place and wrong time – just when a patrolling B–18 Bolo happened to be passing overhead (the B–18 was a contemporary of the P–36 and just as obsolete but, like the P–36, it managed to capture a brief moment of glory).

The air defense of Hawaii had reached a much more advanced level than in either Alaska or the Canal Zone, probably due to the lengthy and heavy American military presence in the Hawaiian Islands. The roster for 7 December 1941 was impressive: 754 officers and 6,706 enlisted men formed the human component of the Hawaiian Air Force, which was concentrated on the island of Oahu. This force was broken down into the 18th Bombardment Wing at Hickham Field and the 14th Pursuit Wing with the headquarters at Wheeler Field. The 18th was made up of the 5th and 11th Bombardment Groups (Heavy), the 58th Bombardment Squadron (Light) and the 86th Observation Squadron based at Bellows Field, about 28 miles from the headquarters at Hickham. The 14th consisted of the 15th and 18th Pursuit Groups at Wheeler (one squadron was undergoing training at a small field called Haleiwa in the northern part of the island). The Hawaiian Air Force was in better physical shape than any other overseas Army Air Force command, for about half of their 231 combat aircraft could be considered modern. The modern portion consisted of 12 Boeing B–17D Flying Fortresses, 12 Douglas A–20A Havocs, 12 Curtiss P–40Cs and 87 P–40Bs. On the debit side were 33 B–18A Bolos, 14 Boeing P–26 Peashooters ... and 39 P–36As along with the usual assortment of observation, training and transport aircraft.

This force had been rapidly built up since the beginning of 1941 when the total aircraft count stood at only 117 machines and all of them were considered obsolete. During February 1941, Hawaii was reinforced with 31 P–36s which, along with pilots and ground crews, arrived aboard the carrier *Enterprise*. The P–36As were rapidly supplemented with the arrival of P–40s, also transported by carrier from California.

Army pilots flew intensive practice missions from the various fields on Oahu during 1941, but a number of curious deficiencies in the air defenses persisted. Anti-aircraft defenses were primitive. The new radar that had been placed on the island's mountains was not given the full attention and respect that it deserved. The Army continued to park its highly polished aircraft in close rank formation – making perfect targets for bombing or strafing aircraft. Facilities and hangars remained uncamouflaged but some of the newly arriving aircraft such as the P–40s and some of the B–17s were wearing the new Olive Drab and Neutral Gray camouflage paints. The atmosphere at the Army and Navy bases on Oahu was almost one of an exclusive club – for good

Immediately prior to World War Two, the P–36 was a common sight on most American military airfields. This highly polished example belonged to the 79th Pursuit Squadron of the 20th Pursuit Group and the yellow diagonal stripe meant that the aircraft was assigned to B Flight Leader. The 79th PS operated the P–36 from 1938 to 1940. Insignia on the side of the fuselage was that of the 79th PS. P–36 equipped units often carried either the squadron's or unit's insignia on the sides of the fuselage. (W. T. Larkins)

reason. The pilots that made up the pre-war Army Air Corps and later the Army Air Force were just about the best to be had; add to this the lush tropical atmosphere of Hawaii and the fact that the wars in China and Europe seemed very, very far away, and one can understand this curiously detached view.

However, on 26 November, a large Japanese task force sailed from Hitakappu Bay in the Kurils; it included six aircraft carriers, two battleships, two cruisers, nine destroyers, three submarines and a train of support vessels. Plans for the attack on the American fleet and Army airfields at Oahu had been undertaken during the summer of 1940 and completed by November of that year. The Japanese picked highly qualified crews for the surface

With everything down, a P–36A comes in for a landing. This view shows off the aircraft's split flaps to advantage. Note that the pilot has the canopy slightly opened and that the air vents, located directly below the windshield, are fully open. Aircraft is in the markings of the 79th Pursuit Squadron and the band around the cowling is painted yellow. (W. T. Larkins)

vessels and aircraft and these crews trained at a breakneck pace for an attack which, the Japanese hoped, would completely eliminate American influence in the Pacific. The Japanese did not have really up-to-date information on the number of ships in the main naval base at Pearl Harbor but they hoped to sink or heavily damage at least four American carriers and four battleships. These victories would be accomplished by a fleet of Val and Kate bombers acting in the roles of horizontal, dive and torpedo bombers. The new Zeke fighters would provide protection and would attack targets of opportunity. At 0600 on the morning of 7 December from a location 200 miles away, the Japanese fleet launched the first strike force of 50 Zekes, 50 horizontal bombers, 40 torpedo planes and 50 dive bombers. Just 45 minutes later, the second wave of aircraft – 50 horizontal bombers, 80 dive bombers and 40 fighters – launched towards Oahu.

One of the six Oahu radar stations remained operational on that sleepy Sunday morning

and reported a large force of aircraft at 0702 about 130 miles away. Apparently, after some consideration as to what was the correct procedure to follow, the radar station operator telephoned the news to the main information gathering center. Since Navy aircraft were expected to be participating in maneuvers and Army B–17s would be arriving over Oahu that morning, the information was shuttled aside, especially since the Army officer on duty that morning was there for training and observation and did not feel that it was his duty to pass the information to operational units. The radar unit continued to track the enemy force towards Oahu where it lost them. At 0755, a force of aircraft heading toward the huge base at Pearl was seen near the Hickham Field hangar line. A minute late both bases came under devastating attack.

The attack on Pearl Harbor was savage and decimating. The pre-war American military was particularly sleepy on Sunday mornings, and 7 December was no exception. The Japanese could not have wished for a better

scenario. There were about 169 naval vessels in the Oahu area that morning and 87 of them were destroyed. The Navy and Marine Corps suffered 2,086 officers and men killed and 749 wounded. The one bright point in the attack was the fact that the carriers – a particularly valuable target that the Japanese wanted to destroy – were not at Pearl Harbor. The American carrier force had departed Pearl a few days previously on other missions and their escape from certain destruction at Pearl meant that the Japanese had to pay very heavily in the days to come for their sneak attack on Pearl.

The heavy clouds of smoke from the burning battleships and installations covered the sun and obscured the fact that a few American fighters were managing to get off the ground to engage the Japanese. Along with the pre-war habit of lining aircraft in close rank formation, the fear of sabotage (Oahu had a large Japanese population, thought to be sympathetic with the homeland) had caused the Army to issue an order on 27 November that all aircraft

would be grouped in tight units rather than being widely dispersed and ready for immediate action. The Japanese could not believe their eyes as they saw the tightly packed concentrations of fighters and bombers and the Zekes raked the aircraft with machine gun fire and cannon shells. Sometimes the aircraft were so close together that if one exploded, it stood a good chance of taking the remaining aircraft with it. However, at about 0830, four P–40s and two P–36s managed to get into the air from Wheeler. Three P–36As of the 46th Pursuit Squadron were in the air at 0850 while six pilots of the 47th PS, in training at Haleiwa, managed to get to their aircraft by automobile and roar aloft. Haleiwa was probably not known to the enemy or not considered a strategic target since it did not come under attack. These pilots managed to carry out a number of sorties between 0815 and 1000, with some enemy aircraft claimed as destroyed or damaged. Lt George Welch (later to become a test pilot for North American Aircraft and die in the crash of a prototype F–100 Super Sabre)

claimed four enemy aircraft destroyed while flying a P–40. Lt John L. Dains alternately flew three sorties in P–40s and P–36s but was shot down on the third sortie by American anti-aircraft fire.

After the enemy attacks were concluded, some form of order was attempted – which was difficult since virtually every military base appeared either to be destroyed or burning. Every available aircraft was put into the air – there were not many left airworthy – to avoid further Japanese attacks and to search with vengeance for the enemy carriers. The P–36As, along with P–40s, O–47s, A–20s, B–17s and B–18s patrolled to the limits of their

Dressed in their 1930s 'Bowery Boys' overalls and floppy hats, a trio of mechanics wait for the pilot of this 77th Pursuit Squadron, 20th Pursuit Group, P–36A. Note how the designator 'PT99' has been applied under the left wing. Location of the designator was rather capricious – the amount of space under the wing usually specifying location. Squadron color was bright red. The straight up and down red band around the rear fuselage signified that this aircraft was the 'A' Flight Leader.

Banking for the benefit of the camera plane, this P–36C of the 27th Pursuit Squadron displays its highly individual water-based camouflage acquired for the 1939 National Air Races. This aircraft, thought to be PA 44, shows off the cowl flaps to advantage. The YIP–36s did not have the flaps which were used to cool the engine. Also note that part of the rear fuselage plexiglass panels have been painted over.

endurance for the enemy fleet, but with no success. The Japanese fleet had arrived and left completely unseen by the Americans. The Roberts Commission, set up to investigate the raid, stated on 26 December: 'A total of ninety-six Army planes were lost as a result of enemy actions, this figure including aircraft destroyed in depots and those damaged planes which were subsequently stripped for parts.' A total of 600 Army personnel were killed or wounded.

The Pearl Harbor attack spelled the end for a strange decade of American isolationism. The blackened hulks of the great ships and the flattened hangars testified to the fact that the American awakening to what was happening in the rest of the world was sudden and painful. The elite Army Air Force and its proud polished aircraft were a thing of the past. The Curtiss

P–36, after 7 December, was relegated to second-line and training duties – they even disappeared quickly from these roles – and American began to tool up for a new air force equipped with aircraft that would smash back at the enemy.

The Curtiss P–36 and its brief moment of glory were forgotten in the following four years of war but, during the 1950s, a civilian example of a P–36 turned up at a small airfield in Florida. Seldom flown by its owners, the little fighter was eagerly acquired by the United States Air Force Museum who restored the craft with a colorful war game camouflage. Proudly on display at Wright Patterson AFB, the Curtiss P–36 stands as a reminder of the dark days of 1941 and the price that was paid for the lack of vigilance.

The Curtiss 75 series achieved its greatest success while in the service of other nations. Although it is outside the scope of this volume to give full histories of each, these are important episodes in the P–36 story and the following summary outlines the service of the aircraft with a number of different nations.

ARGENTINA Occupying the 'boot' of South America, Argentina maintained a strategic position during World War Two for shipping or submarines attempting to cross into the Pacific by the long and arduous route around South America. The Argentinian government, during the late 1930s, was being courted by both German and American interests who realized the importance of the nation. Accordingly, the air arm of Argentina began to acquire a distinctly cosmopolitan look with Focke Wulf Fw 44J *Stieglitz* trainers being license-built, beginning in 1937, as negotiations were going on with Curtiss to license-build Hawk fighters. The government had acquired the second demonstrator Hawk – with the US civil registration NR1277 – and, after having some of the country's top pilots test the aircraft, placed an order for 30 H–75O fighters. At the same time as the order was placed, a request for license manufacture of the type was also lodged.

The H–75O had the fixed landing gear deemed more suitable for less sophisticated nations, and was similar to the Thai Hawk but had a redesigned exhaust system, 875 hp Cyclone powerplant and four .30 caliber machine guns – two in the nose and two in the wing. License manufacture was undertaken by the government factory *Fabrica Militar de Aviones* at Cordoba and a total of 20 Hawks were completed with the first being delivered on 16 September 1940. The Hawks were supplied to the *I, II* and *III Regimientos de Caza* where they became the nation's first modern fighter. The accident rate was fairly low and 45 of the total of 50 Hawks remained in service by 1945. Serving well into the 1950s, the H–75O was well-liked by pilots, the more senior of whom were known for putting on flashing aerobatic displays over local towns and bases. Several continued to fly into the 1960s as well-maintained pets of high-ranking officers. It is thought at least one H–75O still survives in Argentina. Construction numbers of the Curtiss-built H–75Os were c/n 12769 through 12797.

BRAZIL It was decided to supply Brazil, another large South American country of strategic importance, with ex-Army P–36As as part of an attempt to bolster that country's defenses. Beginning in 1942, ten P–36As were supplied to the *Fôrça Aérea Brasileria* by whom

they were used as first-line fighters along with a small number of Curtiss P–40Es. As more P–40s became available, the P–36As were assigned to the advanced trainer role. The following list gives an account of the P–36As supplied to Brazil:

FAB Serial	Army Serial	Curtiss C/N
FAB 1	38–054	12468
FAB 2	38–039	12453
FAB 3	38–043	12457
FAB 4	38–159	12573
FAB 5	38–051	12465
FAB 6	38–158	12572
FAB 7	38–175	12589
FAB 8	38–106	12520
FAB 9	38–060	12474
FAB 10	38–053	12467

These two views of the 27th PS's No 50 P-36C illustrate that the water-based camouflage was applied with completely different patterns on both sides of the fuselage – thus confounding current aero historians even further. This aircraft was flown by John C. Kilborn during the races but normally was the mount of the squadron's executive officer, Capt Israel. Note that the 'B' Flight Leader stripe is still visible. This particular aircraft was painted in shades of black, medium grey, tan, white, and dark green. (E. Strasser)

BRITAIN The Royal Air Force became the depository of a considerable number of Hawks, many arriving as a result of the fall of France. However, in RAF service, the Hawk (or Mohawk as it was named by the British) did not, in common with several other American aircraft ordered in quantity, see any action in the North-West European theatre of war, being rated as a second-line aircraft and not really suitable for combat over Europe; it did, however, see action in less-known combat zones.

During June 1941, as the fortunes of France went from bad to worse, some French pilots decided to set course on their own – seeing the fall of France as an imminent fact – and headed for Britain with their *Armée de l'Air* Hawks. The British were certainly not puzzled by their arrival for that country had become a landing ground for aircraft of many nations since Hitler's *Blitzkreig* had begun to move upon Europe. With the collapse of France and the setting up of the pro-Nazi Vichy government, the remainder of the Hawk contracts placed with Curtiss were transferred to the Royal Air Force.

Britain received about 225 Hawk fighters, both escaping aircraft from France and aircraft supplied new from the Buffalo factory. The Hawk became the first American fighter in service with the RAF with the arrival of the first French H–75A1s, which were given the

P–36C No 67 was known by the 27th PS as 'Old Barber Pole' because of its striped appearance. This P–36C was flown by Lt William J. Feallock. Colors, from cowl to tail, ran black, grey, dark green, white, brown, chrome yellow and then began to repeat with the last color being white. The supposedly easily removable paint proved to be a surprise for the ground crews when they found that repeated scrubbings were necessary to remove the 'temporary' camouflage.

Interesting because of its excellent detail of a pre-war Army Air Corps pilot's flight gear, this photograph shows the commander of the 27th PS, Major Willis R. Taylor, in a rather dramatic pose as he issues orders to the squadron prior to a mass take off at Cleveland. (Selfridge Field)

During the many pre-war tests involving the correct use and application of camouflage, this P–36C was drawn from the 23rd Composite Group to test an Olive Drab and Neutral Gray scheme. Serial number 38–202 was one of 30 P–36Cs, being the last group of aircraft on the P–36A contract, modified to the C version after P–36A 38–85 was fitted with a single .30 caliber gun in each wing. Production P–36Cs were powered by R–1830–17 radials of 1,200 hp.

British designation Mohawk Mk 1 while the H–75A2s and 3s became Mohawk Mks II and III. The first three marks of Mohawks came directly from France, but the Mohawk Mk IV was the Cyclone version designated A4 which was delivered new from Buffalo after the transfer of the contract to Britain from France. These aircraft had been modified at the factory to fit British specifications, including the fitting of six .303 caliber machine guns, two in the nose and four in the wing, British throttles, instruments, and other miscellaneous equipment. The first five Mohawk Mk IVs to arrive from Curtiss were uncrated in July 1941 and two of them, allotted RAF serials AR644 and AR645, were sent to the Aeroplane and Armament Experimental Establishment at Boscombe Down for intensive testing. A French Hawk 75A–2, No 188 had been borrowed by the British for testing before the fall of that country, so the type was not entirely new. The

Hawks were found to be very maneuverable aircraft but in no way were they comparable to the Messerschmitt Bf 109Es and Fs that were roaming the skies of Europe at will. The borrowed French Hawk was test flown against a Supermarine Spitfire Mk I, K9944. At slower speeds, the Hawk could outmaneuver the Spitfire because of its excellent aileron response and, at higher speeds in a dive, the Hawk could break away from the Spitfire by executing a rapid aileron turn that the Spitfire could not follow due to its much heavier aileron pressures. However, the Spitfire's superior speed allowed it to run away from the Hawk. Take-offs and climbs for the Hawk were found quite good compared to the early model of Spitfire with its two-pitch propeller, and torque from the Hawk's engine was much less pronounced on take-off. The Spitfire's speed was much better and the aircraft had a great development potential compared to the Hawk.

When Mohawk Mk IVs began to arrive in considerable numbers in Britain they were assembled and flown to Maintenance Units away from possible German bombing attack and held in reserve against the German invasion which was thought to be coming soon. However, with the possibility of invasion rapidly diminishing as the months passed,

Mohawk Mk IVs were disassembled and transferred to other countries.

The Mohawk Mk IV did see some combat with the RAF, but in a rather unlikely location. No 5 Squadron, RAF, was based at Dum Dum, Calcutta, India, and, in late 1941, began receiving some Mohawk Mk IVs to replace their totally antiquated biplanes. Another RAF squadron stationed in India, No 146, also began converting from biplanes to Mohawk Mk IVs but these aircraft were soon transferred to No 5 Squadron, leaving No 146 to re-equip with the notorious Brewster Buffalo and wonder what they had done wrong. No 5 Squadron took its Mohawks into combat for the first time on 17 June 1942 as bomber escorts. After their debut, the Curtiss fighters were used for just about every combat role possible and it was not until June 1943 that the antiquated Curtiss fighters were replaced with Hurricanes. Another squadron, No 155, was also equipped with Mohawks during July 1942 at Peshawar. This squadron saw considerable action with their Hawks – from interception of Japanese aircraft to dive bombing in Burma. The Mohawks were grounded several times due to oil distribution trouble with the Cyclone engines. No 155 Squadron saw heavy action at Imphal during February and March 1943 as it worked in conjunction with the British Army and the squadron soldiered on with its tired and obsolete Mohawks until January 1944 when they were replaced with Spitfire Mk VIIIs. Mohawks in service with No 155 included AR649, AR677, AX889, BJ451, BS731, BS798, and BT470.

CHINA During the first part of 1938, the Chinese government placed an order with Curtiss for 112 H–75M fighters, the production version of the 75H. Armed with four .30 caliber machine gunes, the Chinese felt that the H–75M would be a match for the fixed-gear Mitsubishi Type 96 Claude which, at that time, was the most advanced Japanese fighter in China. The Chinese order for 112 aircraft was to be supplied to that country in major component form for assembly by the Central Aircraft Manufacturing Company at Loi-Wing. Chinese pilots were notoriously poor

and Hawks were wrecked almost faster than CAMCO could assemble them. In order to save oriental face, the Chinese accused Curtiss field representatives of incorrectly aiding in the assembly of the machines but Curtiss countered with an explanation that the faults were directly the result of Chinese incompetence. A typical incident occurred during one formation flight when six out of the 13 Hawk fighters crashed and were destroyed while attempting to land. Japanese bombing attacks also managed to take their toll of H–75Ms. Madame Chiang Kai-shek once bemoaned her pilots' ability by saying: 'What can we do, what can we do? We buy them the best planes money can buy, spend so much time and money training them, and they are killing themselves before my eyes. What can we do?' Claire Lee Chennault had been hired to shape up the Chinese air arm but it was a hard job and eventually had to be done with mercenaries.

Chennault, as a gift, had been presented with H–75H demonstrator NR1276 and found the aircraft a delight.

'I fell in love with the Hawk Special the first time I flew it and asked Madame Chiang to buy it for my personal plane. She paid Curtiss Wright $55,000 for the plane. It was in the Hawk Special that I got my first taste of Jap flak and fighter tactics, and that I learned some of the lessons that later saved many an American pilot's life over China.

'The difference between Japanese and American equipment was crystal clear in the air over the Yangtze Valley. Japanese had featherweight monoplanes and twin-float

View of a P–36C that illustrates to advantage the fairing mounted under each wing to accommodate the installation of the .30 caliber guns. Note the retractable air scoop immediately behind the lower cowl ring. Photographed on 8 June 1940. (E. Strasser)

The beautiful and highly polished Model 75H demonstrator NR1276 complete with the light blue and white Chinese national insignia. Two examples of this simplified, non-retractable gear version of the Model 75 were built and promoted as Hawk 75s as can be seen from the logo under the canopy. NR1276 was sold to China where it became the personal mount of Claire Chennault, leader of the American Volunteer Group in China, who commented: 'I fell in love with the Hawk Special the first time I flew it and asked Madame Chiang to buy it for my personal plane.' The second Model 75H demonstrator was sold to Argentina (while in Curtiss ownership it carried the civil registration NR1277).

seaplane fighters that sacrificed everything else for incredible maneuverability. In a turning, tail-chasing dogfight they were poisonous. Even then it was evident that Japan was thoroughly committed to building planes as expendable items, counting on a short combat life and depending on production for replacement rather than on field repair and maintenance to put damaged planes back into action.

'My Hawk was built ruggedly with maeuverability sacrificed for heavy firepower (this is Chennault's own statement – from a man used to pre-war Army biplanes with two guns – and not quite accurate since the soon to be encountered Zeke carried a cannon), dura-

bility, and diving speed. To get the last mile of straightaway speed we stripped the Hawk of every bit of the non-essential "hardware" so dear to American manufacturers. Since there were no air-to-ground communications in China, the radio was removed, and I generally carried my thick, heavy bedroll in the radio compartment directly behind the pilot's seat. On more than one occasion when I unrolled this pack for the night, Japanese bullets fell from the blanket folds.

'Surviving ten months of combat and operational flying under the roughest field conditions, the Hawk Special finally met an ignominious end in a ground loop caused by a ham-handed American test pilot. The cowling had been bent by Japanese bullets and the test pilot was taxiing out for a trial hop with the repaired cowling when he wrapped up the Hawk on the ground.'

The completion of the H–75M order led to interest in the more advanced retractable gear Hawks and the H–75A5 Cyclone-engined fighter was built under license in China by CAMCO after the delivery of one complete aircraft and sets of parts from Curtiss. Powered

by the GR–1820–G205A, the fighter was armed with six .30 caliber guns. Plans for mass production collapsed when, on 26 October 1940, a heavy Japanese bombing attack destroyed the CAMCO plant at Loi-Wing. Surviving jigs and material were later transferred to India.

FINLAND The Finnish people suffered greatly in the war with the Russians which began with a massive Soviet invasion on 30 November 1939. After 104 days of costly fighting, a peace treaty was signed on 12 March 1940 and the Finns soon began to rebuild their badly depleted armed forces. Peace was to be a short-lived commodity and, in June 1941, what became known as the 'Continuation War' broke out with Russia. Previous to this the Finns had purchased 21 ex-*Armée de l'Air* H–75A3s from the Nazis. These aircraft had been overhauled by the Germans and fitted with German equipment, instruments and radios by *Espenlaub Flugzeugbau*. This marked an era of cooperation between the Finns and the Germans in an effort to expel the Soviet invaders and regain captured Finnish soil. The Finns also obtained eight ex-Norwegian

75A6s and seven 75A4s. Small numbers of ex-French Hawks were also acquired during the coming years. The Finnish Hawks enjoyed considerable success and several aces came from the ranks of Hawk pilots.

FRANCE France was the best customer for the export 75s but it was also with this country that the Hawk would see action against Allied forces in one of the most regrettable incidents of World War Two. During the late 1930s the French were frantically rearming but their industry seemed incapable of logical production – airframes would be ready but engines would be incomplete, complete aircraft would be parked at the manufacturer's airfields ready to go except for some vital missing part which a subcontractor could not supply on time. The French were also building some of the most grotesque aircraft ever to take wing during this period, especially bombers. However, lessons were being learned but time was at an absolute premium and there was not enough of it.

A French pilot familiar to American aviators for his winning 1936 Thompson Trophy performance in a Caudron racer, Michel Detroyat, flew the Hawk 75B demonstrator at the Cleve-land National Air Races and reported back to French military officials that the aircraft had superior handling qualities, creating official interest in the purchase of the aircraft to supplement the fighter forces of the *Armée de l'Air.*

The French Purchasing Commission filed an order for 100 H–75A1 fighters during May 1938, to supplement the Morane Saulnier 406 in French service. Powered by a Twin Wasp radial capable of producing up to 1,050 hp and armed with four 7.7 mm machine guns and French instruments, throttle and radio, the French Hawk was also equipped with rudimentary armor protection, a feature lacking in the American P–36As. The four guns gave the 75A1 a heavier armament than the P–36A but a lighter gun load than any other operational French fighter of the time. The French Hawks would be built with airframe jigs and tools purchased by the French.

Assembly of the first French Hawks proceeded rapidly, as did all the Hawk 75s, (especially since the French were demanding early delivery as a contractual obligation) and the first two aircraft were test flown at Buffalo during December before being disassembled for sea shipment via the SS *Paris* to Le Havre. A further 14 Hawks were shipped to France as testing aircraft while the first two were retained to become pattern aircraft for license manufacture. The remainder of the Hawk order was sent in broken-down sub-assemblies and these were put together by the French. All aircraft of the initial contract for 100 machines had been assembled and flown by 12 May 1939.

The French had been particularly alarmed by the victories achieved by the Junkers Ju 87 *Stuka* during the Spanish Civil War. The *Armée de l'Air* wanted a fighter that could catch and destroy the dread *Stuka*, even when the bomber was in its infamous dive. If facts and results had been studied more closely the French would have found out that the *Stuka*, courtesy of excellent dive brakes, was extremely slow in its bombing dive, allowing the pilot considerably more time to aim his bomb accu-

A *French Hawk H75–A2. One hundred of these aircraft were delivered, beginning during May 1939. These aircraft were powered by the R–1830–S1C3G radial of 1,050 hp and were armed with six 7.5 machine guns, two in the nose and four mounted in the wing.*

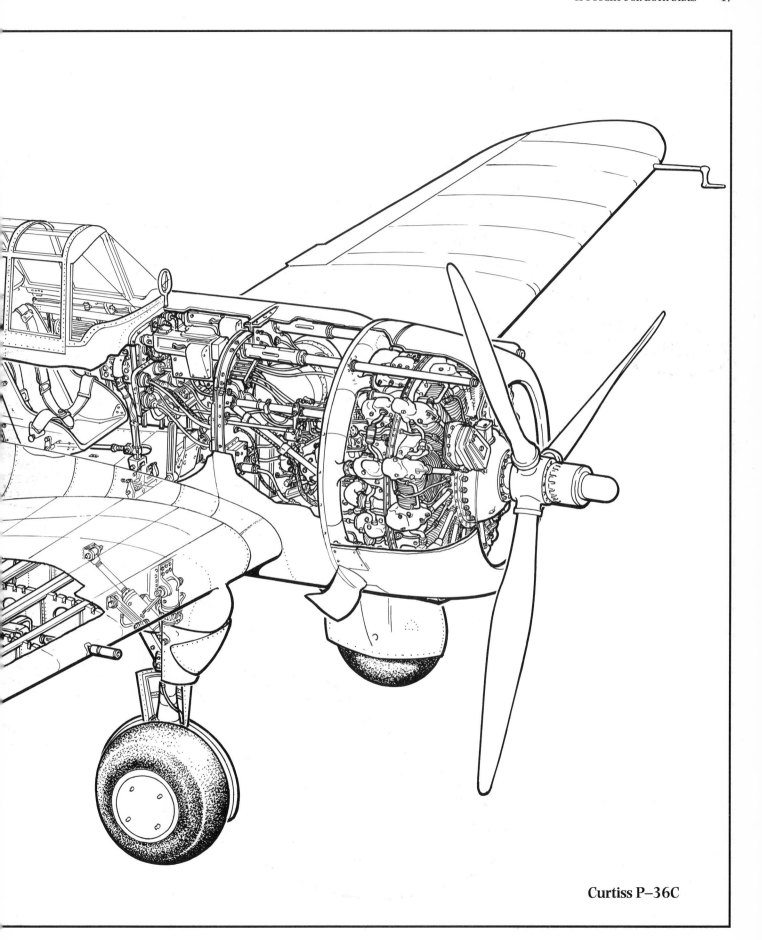

Curtiss P–36C

rately. In all truth, the *Stuka* was only a useful weapon for bombing roads clogged with fleeing civilians or for attacking targets that lacked fighter or anti-aircraft protection.

Proof was wanted of the Hawk's diving capabilities so factory test pilot Lloyd Child was assigned to fly the first French Hawk for diving tests on 9 December 1938. Child proceeded to take the Hawk up to 22,000 ft and in a power dive he brought the aircraft to within 1,500 ft of the ground. The French were quite pleased with the results and released a news bulletin stating that the Hawk had set a world diving speed record of 575 mph. Viewed in cold and analytical light, the figure was probably erroneous because of the lack of precision of the aircraft's instruments. During World War Two it became rather common for test pilot's to

The Curtiss designation of Model 75A was given to one of the research and development aircraft which was registered NX22028. This aircraft was flown in a number of different configurations as it tested a variety of equipment, including the ungainly supercharger on the side of the fuselage as seen in this photograph. The aircraft crash-landed following an engine failure and was scrapped.

claim that they had broken the sound barrier during power dives. Yet this was far from the truth as the recording instruments were sometimes as much as 200 mph off the mark. It would have been impossible for the airframe of a propeller-driven World War Two fighter to penetrate, much less break, the sound barrier. The Curtiss performance had impressed the French to such a degree that another batch of Hawks was ordered.

In the meantime, testing of the aircraft assembled in France revealed a number of weaknesses. Along with the inadequate armament, the guns tended to freeze when at high altitude and the fuel transfer system was considered too complex, but the lack of self-sealing fuel tanks drew the loudest complaints from pilots. Even with these negative testing results, Hawks were rapidly beginning to enter service with the *Armée de l'Air*, with the *4éme* and *5e Escadre de Chasse* converting during March 1939.

The second batch of Hawks, designated H-75A2, had a further machine gun in each wing panel and some of the fuselage structural modifications that had been adopted for the

Army P-36As. The first 75A2s began arriving in France during May 1939 and 100 aircraft of this type were ordered. September 1939 found the *Armée de l'Air* equipped with the 200 Hawks it had originally ordered. The Hawks were in service alongside the MS 406 which was similar in many ways to the British Hurricane. The closing possibility of war led the French to order more Hawks – 135 75A3 and 285 75A4 fighters. The A3 was equipped with a more powerful Twin Wasp while the A4 had the Wright GR-1820-G205A Cyclone 9 radial of 1,200 hp. When France surrendered, 110 A3s had been taken on strength but a smaller number was actually ready for combat because of late delivery of French systems. Only a few A4s arrived in France before the surrender. After the fall of France, 17 A4s that were en route by ship were disembarked in Martinique and six were dropped off at Guadeloupe. These aircraft had been on the French carrier *Bearn*. The fighters sat in crates for over two years before being shipped to Morocco and assembled, their unreliable Cyclones being discarded in favor of Twin Wasps.

The combat career of the Hawk in French

service was violent and brief. On 8 September 1939, French Hawks intercepted a force of *Luftwaffe* Bf 109s and claimed two destroyed. This initial victory for the Hawk elated the French pilots but, unfortunately for the *Armée de l'Air* aviators, the victories were not to be a sign of future fortunes. The French army began to make small attacks in the Saar River area in an effort to prevent the Germans from applying total military strength against Poland and to test out French equipment. The Germans took great umbrage at these military forays and launched their Messerschmitt fighters against the French aircraft supporting the army with telling effect.

At the start of the war, the Hawk fighter equipped four *Groupes de Chasse*: I/4, II/4, I/5 and II/5. Curtiss fighters were assigned to protect bomber and reconnaissance aircraft flights during the early days of the war and losses began to mount as the formations were attacked by Bf 109Es, but the French pilots did manage to score a number of victories so the aerial fights were not completely lopsided, especially since the Bf 109E was superior to the Hawk in all aspects of combat.

The winter of 1939/40 was extremely cold and, during the period that became known as the Phoney War, aerial combats were restricted. Hawks would occasionally attempt to intercept and destroy high-altitude German reconnaissance flights, usually undertaken by the unattractive Ju 86P, but the fighter's lack of performance virtually guaranteed that the photo missions would be a success for the Germans. During the Phoney War, the French made efforts to increase their military strength but the government acted a bit like a chicken with its head cut off and considerable military advantage was lost by the time the Germans launched their massive all-out *Blitzkreig* against France on 10 May 1940.

The German *Panzers* poured into the Benelux countries and France like a sharp knife slicing through the weakest of substances. The French and the British Expeditionary Force went into action but communications soon collapsed and, for all intents, both armies were soon involved in a rout. The Germans had smashed through the front-line defenses and, in a bold stroke, made a rush to the Channel coast, avoiding combat with the best Allied divisions and being able to advance on them from their weak rear positions.

The Hawks were soon engaged in heavy action, taking off from their bases to intercept enemy bomber formations and to defend their own runways. *GC* I/5 ran into a large force of vaunted *Luftwaffe Stukas* that was in the process of attacking French ground forces and the fighters fell on the dive bombers with vengeance. The *Stukas* were slaughtered, 16

being claimed as destroyed. Strangely, this decisive encounter did little to stem the fear of the *Stuka* and its myth of incredible power continued well into the Battle of Britain. The Hawks were also given additional duties of supporting land forces: *GC* I/4 was assigned to the 2nd Army in the Ardennes, and II/4 and II/5 patrolled the eastern section of France and covered the 2nd and 3rd Armies.

The French and British forces were pushed with great speed toward the coast where Hitler figured they could be annihilated, but he did not figure on the amazing rescue from the beaches of Dunkirk. Hawks hurriedly flew off to protect Paris but Paris was soon occupied and the Hawk pilots attempted to fight a rear-guard action as they retreated from one base to another. Parts were in short supply and the supply system itself had been completely destroyed as the Germans cut the country to pieces. By June the military situation was virtually hopeless, the RAF had all but ceased to exist over France and the Italian *Regia Aeronautica*, convinced that France had just a short time left, gallantly joined the battle with their Nazi allies. Hawks began to break down as their unreliable Cyclone 9 engines failed under the pressure of combat and many Curtiss fighters were withdrawn from combat because of the lack of engine parts. On 10 June, the fifth and final Hawk equipped group, *GC* III/2, joined the war after suffering heavy losses with their MS 406 fighters.

The surviving Curtiss fighters were ordered to withdraw to North Africa during June but some pilots did not like the idea and headed for England instead, giving the RAF their first Mohawks. When the surrender, or armistice depending on viewpoint, took effect on 25 June, the five Curtiss-equipped fighter groups were in North Africa, having made the journey between 18 and 20 June. As per the armistice, these fighters were ordered to be disarmed – especially when some of the French pilots indicated that they wanted to head to the RAF base at Gibraltar and continue the fight.

One of the strangest periods in the history of World War Two began after the fall of France. This was the establishment of the French Vichy Government, an administration of Frenchmen who were to 'rule' the country while obeying their new German masters. The French quickly settled into this arrangement with a speed which astonished the Germans. Paris became a must tourist spot for German soldiers and *Luftwaffe* aviators and the French citizenry responded with extraordinary zeal in the turning in of Jews and other 'undesirables' to the Germans.

The British were now standing with their backs to the wall. Their European allies had been efficiently demolished one by one by the

German war machine which seemed to be unstoppable. The British made a direct appeal – or threat – to the French to attack the Germans with their fleet of warships at Mers el Kebir, or scuttle them. The French did not seem in a mood to sink their ships nor to attack the Germans with them (the French fleet could have posed a major problem for the rapidly expanding German forces). The Royal Navy launched a carrier-borne attack against the French warships on 3 July 1940, causing considerable damage and casualties – enraging the French into action to attack the primitive Royal Navy aircraft, which included Fairey Swordfish biplanes and Blackburn Skuas. The Hawks were able to repel some of the attacks and were credited with the destruction of two Skuas. The Germans were impressed, from a propaganda viewpoint, in the fact that ancient hatreds had been stirred in the clash with the aerial forces of Britain and France. The Germans also quickly moved in large numbers of fighters to protect their newly acquired French 'friends' against future attacks. French pilots were rewarded for their exploits by being given a greater degree of freedom and having their monthly flying hours allotment raised.

The Hawks added the colorful yellow and red tail stripes to their regular earth tone camouflage schemes to display the fact that they now obeyed orders from the Vichy government. Hawk units were moved to different bases as the need arose or as new threats were felt in French North Africa. When Charles De Gaulle's soldiers – supported by the Royal Navy – attempted to invade Senegal, Hawks of *GC* I/4 added a distasteful chapter to French history when they attacked and strafed their own countrymen. The Hawks were instrumental in repulsing six different landing attempts. In order to punish the British and the Free French for their transgressions, the Vichy government sent a heavy bombing attack against the British garrison on Gibraltar.

Perhaps the oddest episode in the already strange career of the French Hawks was the pitched battle with the US Navy that took place during Operation Torch – the invasion of North Africa – on 8 November 1942. Operation Torch was one of the first large-scale American military moves and one that was vitally important to the war in Europe. A rather motley invasion force had been assembled by the Americans for the attack but the invasion (including the carrier *Ranger*) went to schedule, going in favor of the Americans from the start. However, Hawks of *GC* I/5 and II/5 were scrambled to intercept incoming American aircraft and they did just that. The Grumman F4F Wildcats that were protecting the American dive bombers met the enemy

with considerable strength and élan. The French were also bent on extracting a high price from the invaders but the outcome was never really in doubt although the costs were high. Fifteen Hawks and eight French pilots were lost while at least seven Wildcats were destroyed in a fight that saw pilots machine-gunned while hanging from their parachutes. American pilots were full of zeal to retaliate against the Axis for Pearl Harbor and the 'turn-coat' French were treated with little respect. The end of the day's fighting had virtually finished off the Hawk in French service while opening a new front in the war against Italy and German.

HOLLAND The Netherlands originally placed an order for the Cyclone-powered H–75A7 fighter during 1939. The original order was for 35 aircraft but this number was cut down to 20 fighters after political haggling. Armed with four machine guns (two in the nose, two in the wing) these fighters had yet to arrive in Holland when the Germans poured across the border on 10 May 1940. The fighters were sent instead to the extensive Dutch holdings in the Netherlands East Indies which were in danger of imminent invasion from the Japanese who had their eyes trained on the islands' excellent natural resources. The fighters were assembled and local modifications were undertaken, including an attempt to improve the reliability of the Cyclone 9. When the war in the Pacific began, the Dutch were quickly equipping their Hawks to carry small underwing bombs for the ground attack role and the aircraft began missions against the rapidly advancing Japanese. The Dutch fighters were quickly eliminated either through accidents or by enemy fighters and Dutch Hawks had ceased to exist by the middle of February.

INDIA Since India had received a great deal of the residue from the damaged Chinese Hawk production line, including many jigs and partially completed airframe components, it was natural that India would attempt to build Hawks for its air force. Accordingly, an order was issued to Hindustan Aircraft Ltd that called for the construction of 48 H–75A fighters to be powered by Cyclone 9 radials. India had obtained a licensing agreement with Curtiss and the first Royal Indian Air Force Hawk

Hawk H75–A7s put up an heroic fight when the Japanese invaded the Netherlands East Indies. The Japanese invaded Java on 2 March 1942 and landed 85,000 troops while another large invasion fleet was just offshore. Some of the Hawks had been destroyed on the ground while others managed to oppose the overwhelming enemy forces, but it was just a short few days until most were destroyed and Java surrendered on 5 March. This patrol of Hawks was photographed from a Lockheed 212 bomber.

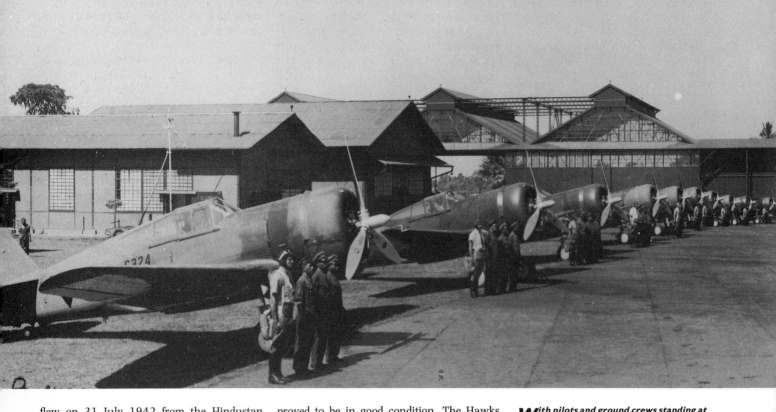

flew on 31 July 1942 from the Hindustan factory. Hindustan had acquired an enviable reputation for high-quality aircraft workmanship and it was not surprising that USAAF activity, which was increasing at a break-neck pace in India, would require additional maintenance, repair and rework facilities for the fleets of transport aircraft that would begin the regular shuttle service over the 'Hump'. Contracts were placed with Hindustan for such work and due to the pressure from Army work, production of the Hawk was dropped after only a further four examples had been completed.

IRAN (PERSIA) The vital oil-producing country of Iran had definite pro-Nazi ties before the start of World War Two. To prevent possible German occupation, Allied forces occupied the country on 25 August 1941. The Iranian military was primitive in the extreme but they had ordered ten H–75A9 Cyclone 9 fighters (apparently Seversky was not the only American aeronautical company who would eagerly sell warplanes to countries with questionable political leanings). The British expeditionary forces discovered the ten Hawks still in Curtiss factory packing crates – the reason for the lack of Iranian interest in assembling and flying the aircraft has been lost to time – and the aircraft on close inspection,

proved to be in good condition. The Hawks were brought up to more or less RAF standards and transferred to No 5 Squadron, which is mentioned in the notes on RAF Mohawk operation.

NORWAY When the Germans moved against Norway on 9 April 1940, the small air arm of Norway was able to field only a few fighters to attempt to stem the might of the *Luftwaffe*. Re-equipment of the air force had just begun as Norway had ordered 12 H–75A6 fighters with Twin Wasp engines and four .30 caliber machine guns. At the same time the initial order was placed, a licensing agreement was reached which called for the production of 24 more Hawks in Norway. The order was placed in the autumn of 1939 and, realizing that they had waited too long, Norway placed another frantic order for a further 12 A6s but, due to the lack of time and the speed of the Germans, the Norwegian Hawks were never to see service in that country.

While assembly of the first Hawks had begun at the factory at Kjeller, another order was placed for 36 Hawk H–75A8s that had the Cyclone 9 engine and two .50 caliber guns in the nose and four .30 caliber weapons in the wing. The Germans attacked Norway and Denmark with Operation *Weserubung* on 9

With pilots and ground crews standing at attention, these Curtiss H75–A7s are seen on display at Bandoeng, Java, Netherlands East Indies. Twenty A7s were ordered, equipped with Cyclone engines, by the Netherlands but the aircraft were all diverted to the East Indies after the German invasion of Holland. (Curtiss Wright)

Opposite top and bottom
H75–A8s being flown by Free Norwegian pilots training in Canada. Norway had ordered 36 A8s with R–1820–G205A Cyclone engines of 1,200 hp but the Germans invaded the country before deliveries could be made. Six of the aircraft were allocated to the training program in Canada while the remainder were taken on by the US Army and designated as P–36Gs.

April 1940 and an initial bombing attack on the air force factory at Kjeller demolished the first four 75A6 fighters. German forces found eight other A6s in their factory crates at Oslo harbor and these were the aircraft that were later sold to Finland.

PERU The 36 Hawk H–75A8 fighters that had been ordered by Norway were undelivered when that country fell. The aircraft were transferred to Canada where they served as trainers for the Free Norwegians who were learning to fly at Canadian bases. The aircraft were eventually purchased by the American government, overhauled, and sent to Peru as P–36Gs to reinforce that country's small air arm. Thirty aircraft were supplied (USAAF serials 42–36305 through 36322, and 42–108995 through 109006) and their civil designated Wright Cyclone engines were re-designated with the military terminology of R–1820–95. At least one of these aircraft is currently preserved in Peru.

PORTUGAL The rather impoverished country of Portugal was extremely anxious to maintain some form of neutrality to keep out the Germans during the early days of World War Two. Its military forces were basically just a token and the aerial defenses were sadly lacking. Having had fairly close relations with the British, who had supplied Gloster Gladiator biplanes during 1938, the Portuguese sought further aid via the ancient Alliance Treaty of 1373 and the British responded with a dozen Mohawk Mk IVs which they were more than happy to get rid of. The *Arma da Portugal* was probably hoping for something with a bit more performance than the Mohawk but the fighters were gladly accepted (RAF serials were AR642, AR643, AR652, AR664, AR666, AR668, AR671, AR673, AR679, AR680, AX882 and AX886). Unfortunately one of the Mohawks was destroyed immediately upon arrival and the surviving fighters were coded 480 to 490. The Mohawks served at various bases in Portugal and were transferred to the Azores in 1944 to protect those vital islands. The Mohawks proved to be faithful mounts in Portuguese service and actively participated in the defense of the Azores until 1945 when the aircraft were withdrawn and scrapped.

SOUTH AFRICA After the threat of invasion by the Germans had passed, the British were eager to get rid of the Mohawks that they had held in reserve. A willing customer was South Africa which needed more modern aircraft for its air force. An eventual total of 72 Mohawk

Mk IVs was received in South Africa. The first unit to operate the type was No 4 Squadron which equipped with Mohawks during May 1941. The Mohawks were used as operational trainers. Only one unit, No 6 Squadron, was operational with the Mohawk, for home defense duties, but they were phased out when the threat of aerial invasion passed.

THAILAND (SIAM) Twenty-five H–75N fixed gear Hawks were ordered by Thailand with deliveries starting during November 1938. Originally only fitted with the standard twin nose guns, provision was made to carry a podded .30 caliber gun under each wing panel. Some aircraft were later modified to carry the Danish 23 mm Madsen cannon under the wing. Curtiss records show only 12 construction numbers – c/n 12756 through 12767 – assigned to the Thai order. The Thai Hawks saw action, initially in the Thai invasion of French Indochina during early 1941 and some victories over French aircraft were claimed but the French denied these claims. When Japan invaded Thailand on 7 December 1941, the Hawks were again in action but, being no match for the Japanese, one-third were soon lost before the cease-fire. The Japanese tested some of the captured Thai Hawks. One H–75N is currently preserved in Bangkok.

CURTISS P–36 VARIANTS, SERIAL NUMBERS AND SPECIFICATIONS

Curtiss Variants

Model 75 Prototype for series. First flew during May 1935 carrying civil license NX17Y. Modified several times, including 75A with 900 hp XR–1670–5 and 75B with 850 hp XR–1820–39. One .50 and one .30 caliber machine gun in nose. Painted yellow and blue.

Y1P–36 Three test examples ordered during July 1936 and delivered in February 1937. Differed from Model 75 by having modified cockpit and canopy, and retractable tail wheel. Powered by 950 hp R–1830–13. Designated Model 75E. Designated P–36 after completion of testing. Delivered in natural metal finish.

P–36A Curtiss Model 75L. Similar to the Y1P–36 but with 1,050 hp R–1830–13 and three-blade constant speed propeller, and cowl flaps. Armed with one .50 and one .30 caliber machine gun in upper engine and accessory compartment. Order for 210 aircraft at $4,113,550 was largest fighter order since World War One. Delivery of P–36As started during April 1938 and, after 177 were completed, the remainder were finished as P–36Cs. USAAF s/n 38–1 and 38–85 were converted to prototype P–36Cs while 38–20 temporarily became the sole P–36B. S/n 38–10 was converted to the prototype XP–40 while 38–4 became the XP–42. P–36As were delivered in natural metal finish.

P–36B During November 1938, 38–20 was converted to P–36B standard by the installation of an 1,100 hp R–1830–25. Aircraft reverted back to to P–36A standard after testing completed. Natural metal finish.

P–36C Similar to P–36A. Equipped with 1,200 hp R–1830–17 with additional armament of two .30 caliber machine guns mounted in the wing. Other small improvements. Delivered in natural metal finish.

XP–36D P–36A 38–174 converted to carry four .30 caliber wing guns and two .50 caliber nose guns.

XP–36E P–36A 38–147 modified with eight .30 caliber wing guns and one .50 caliber nose gun.

XP–36F P–36A 38–172 equipped with two Masden 23 mm cannon mounted under the wing, but retained standard P–36A nose armament.

P–36G–CU Aircraft originally ordered for Norway but sent to Canada to train free Norwegian pilots after Norway had fallen to the Germans. Later designated RP–36G–CU and entered USAAF service. A number were later supplied to Peru.

Model 75A–1 Similar to P–36A but with four 7.5 mm guns (two in nose, two in wing). Powered by 1,050 hp R–1830–SC3–G engine. One hundred to France. Some escaped after French surrender to UK and were designated Mohawk Mk I in RAF service.

Model 75A–2 Similar to A–1 but with four wing guns and two nose guns. One hundred to France. Escaping aircraft to UK became Mohawk Mk II.

Model 75A–3 Similar to A–2 but with 1,200 hp R–1830–S1C3–G engine. France ordered 135 but only about 60 were delivered. Others diverted to French Morocco; 20 to UK as Mohawk Mk III.

Model 75A–4 Similar to 75A–2 but with a 1,200 hp GR–1820–G205A. Only 284 built out of French order for 795. Majority of order taken over by RAF as Mohawk MK IV.

Model 75A–5 Export version for China. Prototype and several sets of components supplied to China for license manufacture. Powered by Wright GR–1820–G205A and armed with six .30 caliber machine guns. Only a few were built in China before the factory was badly damaged by a Japanese bombing attack. Surviving jigs and tooling went to the Hindustan Aircraft Factory at Bangalore, India. Production began in late 1941 but only five aircraft were built before new projects were undertaken. These aircraft were taken over by RAF as Mohawk Mk IV.

Model 75A–6 Similar to Hawk 75A–2. Armament consisted of four .303 machine guns. Norway ordered 12. License-manufacturing was requested from Curtiss for building a further 24 A–6s by the Army Aircraft Factory. It quickly became apparent that these aircraft could not be manufactured in a short period of time, so a further 12 were purchased from Curtiss. However, due to the war, these 12 aircraft were not delivered to Norway but sent to France and then, after the fall of France, to England. Original group captured by Germans and eight sold to Finland.

Model 75A–7 Twenty aircraft ordered by the Dutch for the Royal Netherlands Army's Air Division, after political squabbling had reduced the original order for 36 aircraft. Powered by the GR–1820–G205A and was armed with one .50 and one .30 caliber weapon in the nose and one .30 caliber gun in each wing panel. When the German invasion began, the aircraft were sent to the Netherlands East Indies. While in the East Indies the .50 caliber gun was replaced with a .30 caliber weapon because of the shortage of ammunition.

Model 75A–8 Order placed by Norway during January 1940 for 36 A–8s powered by GR–1820–G205A Cyclones, and armed with two .50 caliber guns in the nose and four .30 caliber weapons in the wing. After the fall of Norway, the newly completed aircraft were delivered to the Norwegian training center in Canada. On 5 May 1942, the USAAF purchased 18 of the A–8s, refurbished them as P–36G–CUs and supplied them to Peru. On 29 May 1942, the USAAF purchased 12 more A–8s and supplied ten to Peru, the remaining two aircraft apparently being converted to parts.

Model 75A–9 Ten purchased by the Imperial Iranian Air Force, and delivered during the summer of 1941 but never uncrated. Taken over by the British as Mohawk Mk IVs. Powered by R–1820–G205A, and armed with six .30 caliber guns.

Model 75H Model 75B rebuilt and fitted with an 875 hp GR–1820–G3 and a fixed and spatted landing gear to simplify maintenance in primitive countries. Registered NR1276, aircraft went to China. Second prototype 75H (similarly equipped to the Y1P–36) had underwing racks. Registered NR1277, the aircraft was sold to Argentina.

Model 75M Production version of the 75H with modified landing gear fairings and four .30 caliber guns. China ordered 112.

Model 75N Similar to the 75M but purchased by Thailand, which ordered 25. They differed from the 75M by having the landing gear fairings redesigned. Two .30 caliber guns in the nose with two 23 mm Masden cannon in fairings under the wing.

Model 75O Thirty aircraft purchased. Similar to the 75N but with electric cooling gills at the rear of the cowling and a redesigned exhaust system and armed with four .30 caliber Masden machine guns. License construction begun by *Fabrica Militar* and 20 Hawks were built in Argentina.

Serial Numbers

Model 75	NX17Y
YP–36	37–68 through 37–70
P–36A	38–1 through 38–180
P–36B	38–20
P–36C	38–1, 38–85; 38–181 through 38–210
XP–36D	38–174
XP–36E	38–147
XP–37F	38–172
P–36G–CU	42–38305 through 42–38322; 42–108995 through 42–109006

Specifications

Model 75B

Span	37 ft 4 in
Length	28 ft 1 in
Height	9 ft
Wing area	236 sq ft
Empty weight	4,049 lb
Loaded weight	5,075 lb
Max. speed	285 mph
Cruise speed	260 mph
Ceiling	32,500 ft
Rate of climb	2,500 fpm (initial)
Range	730 miles
Powerplant	Wright XR–1820–39 of 850 hp

Y1P–36

Span	37 ft 4 in
Length	28 ft 2 in
Height	9 ft
Wing area	236 sq ft
Empty weight	4,389 lb
Loaded weight	5,437 lb
Max. speed	294.5 mph
Cruise speed	256 mph
Ceiling	35,100 ft
Rate of climb	3,145 fpm
Range	752 miles
Powerplant	Pratt & Whitney R–1830–13 of 1,050 hp

P–36A

Span	37 ft 4 in
Length	28 ft 6 in
Height	12 ft 2 in
Wing area	236 sq ft
Empty weight	4,567 lb
Loaded weight	5,650 lb
Max. speed	300 mph
Cruise speed	270 mph
Ceiling	34,000 ft
Rate of climb	3,400 fpm
Range	825 miles
Powerplant	Pratt & Whitney R–1830–13 of 1,050 hp

P–36C

Span	37 ft 4 in
Length	28 ft 6 in
Height	12 ft 2 in
Wing area	236 sq ft
Empty weight	4,620 lb
Loaded weight	6,150 lb
Max. speed	311 mph
Cruise speed	270 mph
Ceiling	33,700 ft
Rate of climb	3,100 fpm
Range	820 miles
Powerplant	Pratt & Whitney R–1830–17 of 1,200 hp

P–36G

Span	37 ft 4 in
Length	28 ft 10 in
Height	9 ft 6 in
Wing area	236 sq ft
Empty weight	4,541 lb
Loaded weight	5,750 lb
Max. speed	323 mph
Cruise speed	262 mph
Ceiling	33,600 ft
Rate of climb	n/a
Range	1,003 miles
Powerplant	Wright R–1829–95 of 1,200 hp

Model 75R

Span	37 ft 4 in
Length	28 ft 6 in
Height	12 ft 2 in
Wing area	236 sq ft
Empty weight	5,074 lb
Loaded weight	6,163 lb
Max. speed	330 mph
Cruise speed	302 mph
Ceiling	n/a
Rate of climb	3,000 fpm
Range	600 miles
Powerplant	Pratt & Whitney R–1830–SC2–G

Model 75

Span	37 ft 4 in
Length	28 ft 7 in
Height	9 ft 4 in
Wing area	236 sq ft
Empty weight	3,975 lb
Loaded weight	6,418 lb
Max. speed	280 mph
Cruise speed	240 mph
Ceiling	31,800 ft
Rate of climb	2,340 fpm
Range	547 miles
Powerplant	Wright GR–1820–G3 of 840 hp

Model 75A–1

Span	37 ft 4 in
Length	28 ft 7 in
Height	9 ft 4 in
Wing area	236 sq ft
Empty weight	4,483 lb
Loaded weight	5,692 lb
Max. speed	303 mph
Cruise speed	260 mph
Ceiling	32,800 ft
Rate of climb	2,340 fpm
Range	677 miles
Powerplant	Wright R–1820–G105 of 900 hp

Curtiss XP-37
Variation On A Theme

This design represented a search for a practical formula for high-speed fighters

During the 1930s the odd pastime of air racing was at a fever pitch in America. While air racing was also popular in Europe, it seemed that the American designs were creations of brute horsepower while the British and Continental racers tended towards highly developed small powerplants and extremely refined airframes. In the States the 'barnyard' designers were slapping together machines that were showing their heels to the best pursuits owned by the Army. Such actions were, of course,

embarrassing to the Service who prided itself on the performance of its elite pursuit squadrons. Aircraft such as Wedell-Williams, Lairds, Gee Bees, and a whole crop of other unusual racers were making history by constantly raising the top speed of aircraft. Records did not last more than a couple of months in this mad quest for the goddess of speed. The path towards this goal was paved by broken aircraft and broken pilots but they usually died as heroes, adulated by a public that the popular press claimed was 'air-minded'. Whether this simplistic phrase was true or whether the masses enjoyed the sport of aircraft rushing

The Curtiss XP–37 certainly looked different when it was rolled out of the Curtiss plant during April 1937. The cockpit was placed to the rear of the fuselage because of the space taken up by the Allison engine, three radiators, turbosupercharger, and fuel cell. Visibility was extremely poor and the engine and turbo unit gave many problems. No armament was ever fitted to the prototype and it appears that the YP–37s were to be fitted with two .30 caliber guns in the nose but were never so equipped. Two lessons were learned from the P–37: not to put the cockpit in the rear fuselage, and to position the turbosupercharger in the bottom of the fuselage where it would not interfere with the location of the pilot and other equipment. The XP–37 was retired from flying after only 150 hours. (USAF)

around a pylon course at unheard of speeds with the chance of a gruesome accident always in the cards is a topic that is open to considerable speculation. The point is that these civilian pilots were taking the glory away from the military and the Army did not like that one bit.

Most of the crop of really fast racers were small machines powered by very large radial engines: Placement of engine and fuel were important and the pilot wound up where there was room. The best example of this spacing problem was the barrel-like Gee Bee racer which had an immense radial tied on to the smallest airframe possible. The only room for the pilot was in the extreme rear fuselage where his head was literally touching the vertical fin. The rest of the aircraft was occupied by fuel and engine. Now this was fine (perhaps fine is not the right word since only one pilot that raced a Gee Bee survived and that pilot was none other than Jimmy Doolittle whose skills can safely be classified as above

average) for a racer whose only goal was to break and make records but the Army cast a glance at these glamorous machines and was able to see the future; no longer would the biplane fighter dominate the air, for the monoplanes had too much to offer. The sleek racers were also having their effect on established airframe manufacturers who were quickly, and usually without any credit or compensation, adopting the best features of the racers to aircraft which they were trying to pedal to the military.

Curtiss had lost an important contract to Seversky for building the first modern fighter for the Army. However, all was not lost for the Hawk 75 series as the Army eventually bought the aircraft as the P–36 and Curtiss would go on to reap the benefits of a number of foreign contracts. Curtiss designers decided that something could be done to the basic Hawk 75 airframe to jazz up the design and give the appeal of the civilian racers. Curtiss submitted a quickly prepared outline for the new aircraft to the Army who immediately snapped at the proposal and assigned the designation XP–37 to the new aircraft. On paper the plane looked most impressive and certainly would have looked right painted up in gaudy civilian colors and parked on the ramp at the world-famous Cleveland National Air Races.

Assigned the company designation Hawk 75–I (the I standing for inline engine) the aircraft was to be basically a P–36 airframe with drastic modifications. Power was to come from a turbocharged Allison V–1710–11 that was capable of 1,150 hp. The contract was signed on 1 April 1937 (researching aviation history leads to many fascinating gems of information – one being the number of aircraft that either flew for the first time or had contracts signed on April Fools Day) and the Army was most anxious to test the new plane with its projected top speed of at least 340 mph.

Room for the inline engine, GE turbocharger and fuel cells meant that the pilot would have to be assigned to the rear confines of the fuselage. As mentioned, this was probably all right for a racer with just one function but for a military combat aircraft the choice was less than ideal.

The exhaust was tunnelled back into the fuselage and through the turbocharger while three radiators were supplied with air from scoops in the cowling. The Army, hoping great things from the prototype, also placed an order for 13 YP–37 service test aircraft which would be equipped with V–1710–21 engines and

improved GE B–2 turbochargers, a number of minor airframe changes, and a 25-in extension to the rear fuselage behind the cockpit. The YP–37 was quickly put together, using the airframe of the Model 75 prototype, and was in the air by the end of April.

Problems immediately cropped up and the prototype was plagued with engine and turbo problems while the test pilot complained of the non-existent visibility from the cockpit. The aircraft was transferred to the Army in June and the same problems kept appearing while the top speed was well below the quoted figure. The aircraft was eventually sent to a mechanic's training school after only 150 hours flying time.

The YP–37s did not perform any better and most were rarely flown, the highest time example had only just over 200 flying hours. The aircraft were quickly scrapped or sent to mechanic's training schools where they were taken apart and put back together countless times by students who were having the fine art of taking care of aircraft beaten into their heads. One YP–37 was transferred to the National Advisory Committee for Aeronautics (reason unknown) and it survived until 1946 when it was scrapped.

The idea presented by the P–37 series was certainly not unworkable for Curtiss had another aircraft under development that would perform much better and would create aeronautical history and that aircraft was the P–40.

CURTISS YP–37 SERIAL NUMBERS AND SPECIFICATIONS

Serial Numbers

XP–37	37–375
YP–37	38–472 through 38–484

Specifications

YP–37

Span	35 ft 3.5 in
Length	32 ft 11.5 in
Height	11 ft 1 in
Wing area	236 sq ft
Empty weight	5,592 lb
Loaded weight	6,700 lb
Max. speed	325 mph
Cruise speed	293 mph
Ceiling	34,000 ft
Rate of climb	3,000 fpm
Range	n/a
Powerplant	One Allison V–1710–21 of 1,150 hp

Lockheed P-38 Lightning — The Fork-Tailed Devil

Although its development took longer than originally planned, the Lightning became one of the greatest fighters of World War Two.

As Lt Benjamin Kelsey surveyed the crumpled wreckage of the Lockheed XP–38 interceptor, he probably reflected on the radical new aircraft's future with the Army Air Corps as well as his own career. The circumstance of a lieutenant wrecking a brand new fighter was not a happy one – even though Kelsey had held that lowly rank for nearly ten years! This was not because of any incompetence on Kelsey's

part, but rather the opposite, since he was one of the best test pilots in the Army. Kelsey's lack of promotion was due entirely to the slow pace with which the Army Air Corps of the 1930s progressed. There were few aircraft and few positions to fly them, so promotions were more than agonizingly slow – they were almost non-existent, even if individual pilots were rated more than outstanding. That fact did not help Kelsey on 11 February 1939, for the new and glistening aircraft that would have pushed the Army Air Corps into the forefront of military aviation was nothing more than scrap.

During the 1930s, the Army Air Corps was stocked with a curious collection of 'combat' aircraft. A majority were 'O-birds', lightly armed observation craft that performed little in the way of function besides providing a platform for pilots to fly. The pursuits of the day were little more than glorified sport planes, built for a war that would never happen, while strategic bombing rested on the broad fabric wings of aircraft whose design would not have been out of place during the Great War.

The Army was not completely deaf to the appeals by far-sighted officers for new, dy-

namic aircraft which would inject needed life into the Air Corps and provide America with a realistic defense capability, but the government, still struggling with the disasterous effects of the Great Depression, was almost completely reluctant to supply the Army with money for anything as frivolous as aircraft.

From 1935 to 1937, the growing menace of a Hitler-dominated Germany began to register on even the most isolationist of American politicians and some money began to flow from the depleted government coffers to the military for limited research and development on advanced aircraft projects.

The fact that money was now available meant that the few Army officers who were concerned with aircraft development could now start voicing ideas as to the direction of fighter design. Observations in Europe had led to the idea that American aircraft development was much too conservative and that funds should be allocated to companies which had

designers who could creatively form new concepts and put them into production. One of the developmental projects envisioned was a twin engine interceptor that would be capable of carrying a heavy armament to high altitudes which would be achieved via new turbosuperchargers that were also being developed. The new design would have long range and be able to climb quickly in order to intercept high-flying bombers. Also, a tricycle undercarriage was specified so that ground handling could be simplified. The requirement was given the title of 'Specification X–608' and was circulated among interested aircraft manufacturers, which meant virtually all aircraft builders, since the industry was in a depressed economic condition and military contracts were something to fight over.

One of the companies that was deeply interested in the 1937 specification was Lockheed Aircraft Corporation. The company, located in Burbank, California, had gone through many ups and downs over the past decade as the poor world-wide economy decimated the aviation manufacturing community. Lockheed had developed a reputation for designing and building high-performance aircraft that offered advanced aerodynamics and an ability to grab records and headlines. Pilots of the caliber of Amelia Erhart, Wiley Post and Howard Hughes had flown Lockheed aircraft such as the Vega and Lodestar to garner new speed and distance records. Nevertheless, profits were small and, during a few years, the company quite often went into the red. The Models 10, 12 and 18 airliners were gaining acceptance among the growing air transport system, but lucrative government contracts were needed to assure stability and growth.

Lockheed responded promptly to Specification X–608, which required an aircraft that could climb to 20,000 ft in six minutes and offer a top speed of 360 mph at altitude by assigning its best engineers to come up with a 'paper aircraft' that would satisfy the specification. One of Lockheed's brightest lights in the engineering department was an unassuming young man named Clarence Johnson. Nicknamed 'Kelly', Johnson had been hired as a graduate from the University of Michigan in 1933, after a senior designer had been impressed by a report (a critical one) that Kelly

had written on a Lockheed transport. Johnson would go on to have what reasonably could be described as one of the most impressive careers in American aviation, designing such diverse aircraft as the U–2, F–104 and the always amazing SR–71 'Blackbird'. However, in 1937 Kelly was still proving his stuff and looking forward to bringing some of his radical aeronautical concepts to fruition.

Johnson looked at X–608 with a critical eye and realized that the biggest handicap would come from the lack of a suitable powerplant. Working with experienced Lockheed engineer Hal Hibbard, Kelly immediately began making sketches of proposed aircraft. The interesting common denominator of the drawings was that all the designs had two engines. One engine would simply not provide the performance for the top speed or the rate of climb required by the Army. Kelly was always one to keep aircraft designs as sleek as possible and for a powerplant he chose the V–12 Allison V–1710 since it could develop at least 1,000 horsepower and its low frontal area offered better streamlining. It was also the only high horsepower American inline engine in series production.

Initial sketches showed a wide variety of possible configurations – combined pusher and puller engines, all pushers or all pullers with engines on the wing or buried in the fuselage. Lockheed had been considering a high-performance military aircraft for the past year to be produced as a private venture in hopes of capturing Army orders so useful contacts had already been made with influential Army officers and they were given advanced 'previews' of the new Lockheed designs in order that the company could benefit from their criticism.

The new interceptor was assigned the designation Model 22 by the factory. Attention rapidly settled on one of the paper aircraft that had elegant twin booms with a fuselage pod mounted on the wing between the booms. Power was to come from twin Allison engines (V–1710–C series) that could produce a maximum of 1,150 hp each, and high-altitude performance would come from twin General Electric turbochargers located in the booms and connected to the engines through a complex system of tubing. Tricycle landing gear, the nose gear in the fuselage pod and the main gear in the spacious booms, was provided to help ground handling. Another radical design feature was the armament system. Concentrated in the nose, it comprised a large cannon with a battery of machine guns, giving the interceptor unprecedented fire power. The armament was not immediately finalized since a variety of cannon was under consideration, but, by putting all the armament in the nose, a

The highly polished XP–38 epitomized the Art Deco elegance of the late 1930s – an era when streamlining was applied to even the most mundane of household items. March Field, whose barren terrain can be seen in the background, was selected as the test base for the XP–38 mainly because the Army Air Corps field was fairly close to Burbank and away from prying eyes. Although the entire production run of P–38s looked similar, the XP–38 was almost completely different than the production aircraft. By comparing with other Lightnings illustrated in this chapter, several important differences are evident including the hand-made extremely tight cowlings around the Allisons and the small radiator openings. A small retractable airscoop can be seen immediately below the left cowling. The photograph was taken shortly before the start of Ben Kelsey's ill-fated cross-country speed dash. (Lockheed)

concentrated stream of lead and high explosive could be accurately aimed at an enemy with devastating results.

The Army officer in charge of overseeing the development of the new interceptor was none other than Lt Benjamin Kelsey who, from his Wright Field office, carefully went over proposals entered by Lockheed and other manufacturing concerns. Kelsey was impressed by the sheer power represented by the Model 22 and he recommended, after Lockheed president Robert Gross delivered the Model 22 drawings to Kelsey during February 1937, that the Army issue a prototype contract to the Burbank firm.

After consideration by other Army officials, the government issued Air Corps Contract Number 9974 to Lockheed on 23 June 1937 for the construction of one XP–38 that was to carry the Army serial 37–457. Lockheed was extremely pleased with this bit of work

although they realized that the new XP–38 was radical and one aircraft might not lead to production if the aircraft did not perform correctly. Johnson, ever the optimist, predicted that the XP–38 would fly at 400 mph, some 40 mph faster than the speed that the Army had calculated. The magic figure of 400 mph really appealed to the Army since a very high top speed would help impress Congress when it came to ordering more aircraft.

Lockheed began construction of the XP–38 in a partitioned portion of one of their Burbank hangars. Model 22 was classified as a secret project so access to the area was limited but most employees certainly knew what was going on, a far cry from the company's now famous 'Skunk Works' (started by none other than Kelly Johnson), a branch of Lockheed created to develop extremely classified projects. As with most aircraft of the period, even for those as advanced as the XP–38, construction

progressed rapidly. Actual metal cutting and work began in July 1938 and the fighter was physically complete by the end of the year.

For a fighter, the XP–38 was certainly like nothing else that had flown in America. First of all, it was just plain *huge*. Weighing in at a bit over 15,000 lb and with a wing span of 52 ft, the XP–38 looked more like a stylized bomber than an interceptor. Lockheed had come up with a beautifully sleek installation for the twin Allisons and the cowlings were so snug that they would have looked more at home on the front of a custom-built European racing machine. Every bit of the latest aeronautical technology had been employed in the airframe. The flush riveting was first-rate, the polished metal barely marred by any sort of bump or protrusion that could harm streamlining. Lockheed workers took special care and pride in what they built and, with the XP–38, this dedication really showed.

Large Fowler flaps, employed by Lockheed with great success on their transport aircraft (business for which had picked up considerably – especially since the British were placing large orders for a modified transport that was to gain fame as the Hudson bomber) were added to both of the XP–38's wing sections in order to improve low-speed handling characteristics, while the installation of the large Allison gave the engineers some headaches since a failure of one engine while the aircraft was at low speed could cause lots of trouble. The right engine was modified to turn opposite from the left unit, thus the propeller of the right engine would turn in a clockwise direction to counter the torque forces of the left propeller. The pilot, on takeoff and landing, would not have to put up with the tremendous pulling force created by the torque of two engines turning in the same direction.

The long slim booms that took the place of a

Magnificent aerial photograph of a YP–38 cruising over Pasadena, California. The YPs were basically test machines and in no way represented combat ready aircraft. Armament for the YP was to include a 37 mm cannon, two .50 caliber machine guns and two .30 caliber weapons but these were never fitted. The good visibility from the P–38 cockpit is evident as is the large 'steering wheel' which was unusual since most fighters employed a stick-type control column. The windshield was a curved piece of plexiglass and no armor protection was fitted. Test pilot Milo Burcham is in the cockpit. (Lockheed/X2081)

Tension from the rapidly approaching war was clearly evident when this camouflaged P–38D arrived at the Naval Air Station at Oakland, California, on 16 November 1941. The aircraft had been carrying the pre-war identifier 99–51P on the vertical fins but this had been quickly sanded off in the favor of security. The identifier meant that the aircraft was assigned to the 51st Pursuit Group, 16th Pursuit Squadron, out of March Field. This P–38D was a long way from combat fighting since its guns had not been installed, some form of gun port covering being attached in their place. (W. T. Larkins)

normal fuselage, housed General Electric Type F turbosuperchargers and the main landing gear, and supported the graceful twin tail unit. The pod for the pilot was mounted on the very substantial wing center section between the two engines. The nose landing gear was housed in the forward portion of the pod below the armament. The design crew liked the idea of centering the heavy armament for several reasons: ease of maintenance; a more concentrated cone of firepower could be achieved by a gathered battery of weapons compared to guns spread out over a wing; and the center of gravity could be more accurately maintained. The XP–38's armament had been standardized on one 23 mm Madsen cannon (although a 22.8 mm T1 cannon was considered as a replacement in case the Madsen was not available in sufficient quantity) and four Browning .50 caliber M2 air-cooled machine guns with 200 rounds per gun. However, the XP–38 prototype was never fitted with the proposed armament.

Unlike other fighters either in production or under development, the XP–38 was designed from the outset to have metal-covered control surfaces rather than the more traditional fabric-covered units. Since the new aircraft would be operating at high altitudes and at high speeds, the metal covered surfaces would be more efficient when recovering from high speed dives as well as not being easily prone to damage. The controls were manually operated and were dynamically balanced, but this would be changed much later in the P–38 production line.

Lockheed, Allison and General Electric worked closely together as the prototype was built to insure that the operation of the engines

at high altitude would be as efficient as possible. A complex network of tubing connected each engine to its individual turbosupercharger in the tail boom. The turbine wheel was located in a semi-flush housing atop each boom over the trailing edge of the wing. As the aircraft gained altitude, the turbosupercharger would begin to function, taking exhaust gases from the engine to the turbine by means of the tubing system. The turbine would be spinning at tens of thousands of rpm, compressing the exhaust gases and passing them through an intercooler in the leading edge of the wing and then channeling the compressed and cooled gas back down the throat of the engine to maintain manifold pressure and offer greatly improved performance at altitude. Such a complex system has to have problems and the P–38 series would be bothered with developmental bugs in the turbosupercharger system but a more pressing problem was that of adequately cooling the tightly-cowled Allisons.

Hibbard and Johnson knew that the engines would have to be cowled as sleekly as possible to obtain maximum streamlining but the best location for the radiators and oil coolers posed a problem. Openings would have to be as large as possible so that cooling air could do its jobs but, at the same time, the openings would have to be as small as possible so that performance would not be degraded by the additional drag. The XP–38 presented particular difficulties since it had two of everything. The radiators were located in the middle of the boom and were housed in large blisters that had their opening in the front and a controlled shutter at the rear. The oil coolers were immediately behind the spinners. Once again, the cooling fluid (Prestone) had to be pumped from the radiator to the engine via tubing and a series of pumps but this function did not provide completely adequate cooling for the Allisons and overheating was a major problem during much of the P–38's operational career.

When basically completed, the XP–38 was trucked from Burbank to the Army's March Field in Riverside. The lengthy journey was accomplished with a great deal of secrecy and the XP–38 was carefully wrapped in canvas to prevent prying eyes from getting a close view of the new aircraft. March, an Army bomber base, offered long runways and, in those days, it was remote from major population centers. After the aircraft arrived, several days were spent reassembling the fighter and then several more were required to service it and make sure that the engines and systems were functioning correctly. Lt Kelsey carefully supervised the assembly of the fighter and made sure that he learned how the aircraft functioned so that, hopefully, nothing would

come as a surprise during the first flight.

The first step in finding out whether a new aircraft is ready for flight is a taxi test. During these tests, the aircraft is trundled down the runway at various speeds and the pilot and crew hope that any possible flaw will be discovered at this time. Kelsey quickly found that the XP–38 had a number of disturbing problems, one of which almost resulted in the loss of the prototype even before it had flown. As the speed of the taxi tests increased it became apparent that the XP–38 did not have sufficient braking power. One high speed taxi test resulted in the brakes becoming extremely hot and losing all function. Kelsey was sitting atop an out of control 15,000 lb monster that was rapidly eating up the remaining portion of March's runway. The XP–38 shot off the end of the paved area and bounced through the grass and dirt, hit a ditch and stopped. By the time that Kelsey had unstrapped and clambered from the cockpit, Lockheed engineers had already arrived in speeding cars. The frightened team inspected their creation, running hands over the sleek skin to feel for any deformation of structure. After a quick walk around they were surprised and delighted to find no damage. Now, something had to be done about those brakes.

March Field was home to a number of different types of Army bombers so, after the XP–38 was moved to one of the hangars, Lockheed engineers did some quick scavenging through the Army's spares bin and found some items that they could put to use. Using a cylinder from a Northrop dive bomber and an extra small tank to contain additional hydraulic fluid, the engineers and mechanics attached the pump and tank inside the XP–38 so that the pilot, when the brakes began to fail, could pump additional fluid into the brake reservoir thus providing increased braking pressure and cooling. This was an emergency lash-up, Kelsey and Lockheed both realizing that the brakes would be good for only one or two landings. Kelsey decided that the best way of getting the XP–38 safely back to its parking spot would be to bring the big fighter in over the fence at the slowest possible speed – right on the edge of the stall – so that the fighter could use the long runway to stop with absolutely minimal braking. Kelsey and the Army, both entering a new phase of high performance aerodynamics, learned that dragging an aircraft in over the runway threshold at a very low speed was both unwise and unsafe.

Work and maintenance was finally completed on 27 January 1939 and on a clear California morning, the XP–38 was pulled from its hangar and a series of final checks began. The fighter looked truly beautiful in its polished natural aluminium finish, the only markings being the colorful pre-war Army red, white and blue rudder stripes and the blue cocarde, white star and red center painted on the outer wing panels. Even the three-bladed Curtiss propellers had been carefully polished. The attention to detail on the XP–38 was very evident, the hand-made cowlings were wrapped as tightly as possible around the Allisons while every item that stuck into the slipstream had been made as small as possible and this included the air scoops for the radiators.

Kelsey, dressed in the standard Army garb of the period, boarded the fighter, went through a brief engine check to keep temperatures in the green and began to taxi towards the runway, using the rudders for directional control and staying off the brakes as much as possible. Slowly but positively advancing the large throttles with his left hand while feeling the speed build up through the big control column, Kelsey made the decision to go after rolling a couple of hundred feet. Speed quickly built up. A tug on the control column lifted the nose wheel into the air and the XP–38 lifted from the runway, the roar of its twin Allisons turned

An interesting comparison that illustrates the relative size of the Lightning next to a Supermarine Spitfire Mk V W3119. The Lightning could usually be spotted at some distance by enemy pilots who often took the opportunity to give the fighter a wide berth. The Spitfire was probably in Burbank to do comparison testing with the American fighters that were being produced in the Southern California area. (Lockheed/Y6787)

into a muted rumble as the exhaust gases passed through the turbosuperchargers. However, it was not to be a smooth flight and only Kelsey's skill would save the new fighter from destruction. Just after the main wheels lifted from the March Field concrete a dreadful flutter set in, causing the instrument panel to disappear in a violent blur. Fighting to maintain control with the vibrating wheel that was trying to shake itself out of his hands, a quick glance out of the cockpit nearly caused Kelsey's heart to stop – the wingtips were shaking so violently that they were travelling three feet up and down!

Kelsey grabbed the flap handle and pulled the flaps up – the Fowler flaps had been half down, a procedure for take-off that had been recommended by Lockheed engineers. As the flaps came up into the wing, the intense flutter stopped – only Kelsey was still shaking.

Reducing speed and keeping the nose high, Kelsey flew the XP–38 near March Field for 34 minutes – making the gentlest of maneuvers and trying to figure out what caused the fighter to nearly shake itself to pieces. During the intense flutter, Kelsey had noticed a portion of flap shaking particularly violently. The fact that the flutter had disappeared when the flaps were retracted led the Army pilot to attempt a landing with the flaps in the full up position. Since the flaps had to stay up, Kelsey was forced to keep the fighter's nose at about an eighteen degree up angle during the approach, and the fins of the twin rudders contacted the runway before the main wheels.

Once back on the ground, the XP–38 was closely examined and the cause of the flutter was immediately discovered. Three of four soft aluminium control rods for the flaps had broken due to the intense flutter which in turn had come about from lack of gap sealing and poor flap installation. This matter was quickly rectified by adding steel control rods, cutting away some parts of the wing skin and providing adequate gap sealing for the flaps. Damage to the fins was also repaired. Still, the flap arrangement was far from ideal, but Kelly Johnson modified the flaps sufficiently on the YP–38 to rid the aircraft of the problem.

It was urgent that the testing program continued as quickly as possible, so by 10 February the XP–38 had completed five additional flights, accruing nearly five hours of flying time. With the flutter gone, Kelsey found that the XP–38 was a dynamic aircraft which handled really well for all its size. Developmental problems occurred with the engines and turbosuperchargers but this was expected and both Lockheed and the Army felt like they had a winner on their hands.

Official Army testing of new aircraft was carried out at historic Wright Field near Dayton, Ohio, so the XP–38 would have to be transported to that location. Lockheed felt that too much time would be involved by taking the prototype apart and shipping it by rail. Kelsey then decided the easiest way to get it to Dayton would be by air. To gain some publicity at the same time, the Army decided that Kelsey should attempt to set a speed record between

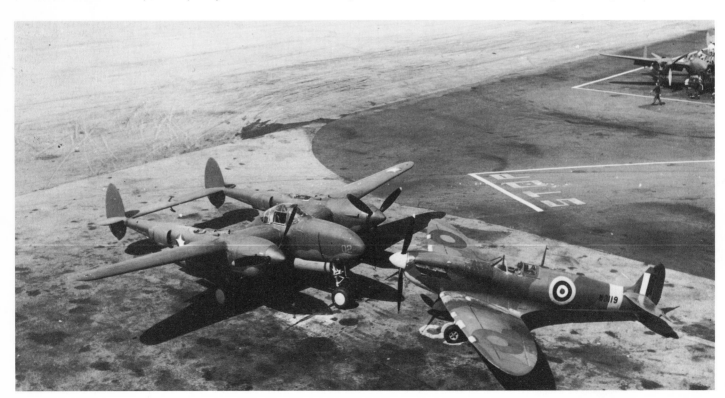

Los Angeles and Dayton. A stop at Amarillo, Texas, was planned.

Fully fueled, the XP–38 departed March Field on 11 February and Kelsey was going to rely on its cruise performance and not push the engines or the airframe in order to set a record. Quickly into the flight profile, Kelsey realized that the XP–38 was really moving. He was at Amarillo in just two hours and 48 minutes. Rapidly refueling, it was on to Dayton in two hours and 45 minutes. Chief of the Army Air Corps, General Hap Arnold, was on hand to greet Lt Kelsey and discuss the flight. General Arnold had been under pressure to get the Army Air Corps in the news with positive items. The European air forces were setting records constantly and the Army needed a morale boost that would also help in obtaining contracts for new aircraft. The cross-country speed record was, at that time, held by Howard Hughes. Since a cross-country speed dash was not considered from the start of the XP–38 flight, the time spent on the ground at Amarillo meant that Hughes' overall record could not be beaten but his total hours in the air record could be taken if the Army acted rapidly. After a brief discussion, Arnold said 'Take it' and the sleek silver fighter was on its way to Mitchel Field Long Island, New York, as soon as fuel and oil supplies could be replenished. The wisdom of sending such a new and basically untested prototype would probably be questioned by today's strict aeronautical testing standards but procedures were much more lax in 1939.

Averaging 360 mph, a tired Kelsey began his descent into Mitchel Field when the carburetors began, apparently, to pick up ice. Carb ice comes about in certain weather conditions when, with the engines at reduced idle, ice begins to form in the throat of the carburetor and, if the ice builds up enough, the fuel supply to the engine can be choked off. Most aircraft are equipped with carburetor heaters, a system that supplies heat to the carbs when the engines are at low power, virtually eliminating the chance of ice forming. The P–38 had such a system. Kelsey had the carb heat turned on during his descent but, unknown to him, the deadly ice had started to form in the carb throats. Kelsey carefully brought the flaps down, reduced power even further and raised the nose in order to bring the XP–38 in as slow as possible since the braking system was still less than adequate.

As he approached the runway's threshold, Kelsey saw that he was a bit low so he eased the throttles forward and was faced with the shocking realization that there was no power. The forward movement of the throttles produced absolutely no response from the engines and the XP–38 slammed into the ground short of the runway's threshold, destroying the gleaming prototype. Kelsey escaped with minor scrapes.

Lockheed and the Army were now faced with the problem of having an interesting concept but no hardware to back up the program. The Army reconsidered the Lockheed aircraft and, on 27 April 1939, instigated a contract with Lockheed for thirteen service test YP–38 aircraft. Hap Arnold had been one of the supporters of the program and he campaigned with the government for the new aircraft. The fact that the contract was issued so quickly really was due to how persuasive Arnold's argument was. The XP–38 had never really established any performance or combat specifications that the Army could study and consider, and they were basically taking the word of one man, relying on his uncanny judgement that Lockheed could produce what the Army needed.

Contract 12523 spelled out the terms for the production of the YPs but the YP was to be a much different aircraft than the XP and problems were to develop. Lockheed gave the YP a new company designation, Model 122, and the engineering team went to work on refining and developing the basic design which would need extended development to make into a combat ready fighter.

Improved Allisons were used in the YPs.

Pre-war long-distance pilot Jimmie Mattern shows how the Lightning handles with one engine out to a young Army pilot uncomfortably crammed behind Mattern in the space previously occupied by the bulky radios. The Lightning could be quite a handful on one engine, especially if the engine was lost during landing or takeoff. Many fatal accidents resulted when the stricken P–38 began a roll that could not be corrected before slamming into the ground. Mattern attempted to illustrate that the Lightning was not a killer on one engine but he advised that a critical engine loss during landing or takeoff was best handled by immediately pulling power off the remaining engine and crash-landing straight ahead. Serial number 42–67079 is a P–38H–5–LO. (Lockheed)

These were the new F series powerplants, – V–1710–27 (F2R) and V–1710–29 (F2L) engines, which had both propellers turning outboard in an effort to reduce airflow turbulence over the tail surfaces. The fact that both propellers were turning outboard meant that the effect of torque, if both engines were operating correctly, was counteracted as in the earlier XP configuration. British contracts for Hudsons had brought new prosperity to Lockheed and the company management had enough sense to see that aviation's dark age was at an end and massive orders for military aircraft were in the very near future. The company made plans to expand rapidly its Burbank facilities and work force.

As design work continued on the YPs, a decision was made to change the cannon armament to the Colt Browning 37 mm weapon with fifteen rounds. The machine guns were changed to two .50 calibers with 200 rpg and two .30 caliber weapons with 500 rpg. Since the XP–38 had been virtually handbuilt from engineering drawings, the YPs had to be designed with large scale production in mind. Other detail changes included modifications to the turbosupercharging system,

radiators and cockpit, and the addition of mass balances on the horizontal stabilizer. Fillets between the fuselage pod and the wing center section were also eventually added. The cowlings were gradually expanded to allow for better cooling and the radiator wells were also enlarged. The Army was concerned about overall weight and specified that the YPs weigh 1,500 lb less than the XP, imposing further design problems since weight tends to rise as aircraft become closer to being produced to military standards.

The new aircraft did not go without notice in Europe. French and British Purchasing Commissions were soon at Burbank to be briefed on the P–38 and to visit the new production line and view the technical staff at work. Both commissions liked what they saw and orders, huge for the time, were placed. The French wanted 417 to be designated Model 322–F, while the British opted for 250 Model 322–B during May 1940. The Army was not far behind the two Europeans, and an order for 66 Model 222 fighters, to be designated P–38, was entered in July.

As engineers struggled to make an aircraft that could be mass-produced, the production

Sergeant pilots relax on the desert sand of Muroc Air Base (now the site of Edwards AFB) as they watch four of their peers return from a training flight on 12 March 1942. Aircraft are P–38Fs of the 95th Fighter Squadron. (Lockheed)

P–38Fs of the 95th Fighter Squadron are seen on a patrol along the Southern California coast. Stationed at Mines Field, the 95th would go on to compile a distinguished combat record. It is interesting to note that the 95th was originally composed of enlisted pilots although many of the pilots would rise to high rank as the war progressed. This formation photo was taken from a Lockheed Hudson bomber. (Lockheed)

For all its size and bulk, the P–38 was an exceptionally clean aircraft – especially when viewed from head-on. Carrying twin drop tanks this factory-fresh P–38 is seen on a test flight from Burbank but the meaning of the rather unusual nose marking, an 'M' and an arrow, is unknown. Of interest are the polished alumimum 'mirrors' attached to the inside of each nacelle, one of which can be seen on the right nacelle. These were added to enable the pilot to watch the main gear, letting him make sure they were either up or down since the gear was not visible from the cockpit. (Lockheed)

line for the thirteen YPs got underway as frantic building at the Burbank airport rapidly began to expand Lockheed's facilities. Though XP–38 construction had proceeded at very fast speed, the YPs were dragging their feet as change after change had to be done to the technical drawings as well as to the partially completed airframes. During this critical period in history, time was something that was just not available in surplus quantities. France fell to the German *Blitzkreig* shortly after negotiations for the Model 322–F had been completed and suddenly Britain was left alone, looking across a small channel of water at a hostile Europe and licking its wounds from the pounding that the British Expeditionary Force

had taken at Dunkirk. Aircraft were being built by the hundreds and pilots were being trained as fast as possible, but the Royal Air Force was not in an ideal position to meet the *Luftwaffe* in aerial combat.

The Army Air Corps watched the unfolding events in Europe with horror and attempted to spur Lockheed and the production of the new fighter. The first YP did not fly until 16 September 1940 when test pilot Marshall Handle took the fighter up from Burbank for a short proving flight. Although the YP looked a great deal like the XP, the YP was basically a new aircraft and the Army knew that testing would have to be intensive to prove the new design ready for military service. However, the flow of YPs from the factory was not especially fast but the Army wanted more and increased its order to 673 machines. The thirteenth YP was not delivered until May 1941 but flying hours were being built up as quickly as possible by Lockheed's test pilots and new problems soon developed.

The weight of the YP–38 came in at 11,171 lb empty and 13,500 with a normal load so the design team had been able to knock

the weight down a bit but not as much as the Army desired. Weight was not to be the main problem once the flight test program for the YPs had started, rather a new and frightening aerodynamic force called compressibility came into focus. Defined, compressibility means that, as an aircraft travels faster through the atmosphere, air molecules begin to compress around certain points of the airframe. If the compression occurs around vital control surfaces, then the flying quality of the aircraft can drastically be affected and this is exactly what happened to the YPs.

Lockheed test pilots such as Jimmy Mattern (holder of the impressive 1930's long-distance flight records in a Lockheed Vega) had been test hopping the YPs and then turning them over to the Army for extensive test flying. One of the Army's favorite test maneuvers of the period was called, by a popular name, the power dive. The test pilot would take the aircraft up to altitude and then push the nose down and get going as fast as possible to see how it would handle and how it would recover. It was not uncommon for prototype aircraft *not* to recover or to break up from the

great pressures exerted in pulling up from a power dive, so the test pilots were more than earning their modest salaries.

During one of these testing flights, Major Signa Gilkie had taken a YP up to altitude and then nosed the aircraft into a screaming power dive with the throttles of the Allisons pushed all the way forward. The sleek YP picked up speed like a rocket and the altimeter unwound like an elevator with its cables cut. The pilot felt the control column becoming nose heavy as the air speed passed 500 mph and Gilkie began to pull back on the column to ease out of the dive. He quickly discovered that the column would not move, no matter what strength he exerted, and that the nose was tucking under even further causing the YP to head straight down at an ever increasing speed. Jumping out and relying on a parachute was a distinct option but the pilot realized that the chance of surviving such a high speed jump was not good and the fact that the large tail surfaces were just waiting to squash the unwary pilot who did not carefully exit the cockpit.

Trying to move the control column back and forth did no good since the column reacted like

it had been set in cement. Desperate to do something which would stop the dive, Gilkie grabbed the elevator trim mechanism and added nose-up trim. The trim tab, located on the horizontal stabilizer, is usually utilized for making small adjustments during flight to trim the aircraft and reduce pressure on the control column. It was a combination of using the trim and the fact that the YP was rapidly entering the thicker air of the lower atmosphere that caused the nose to begin to rise. The test pilot was able to regain control and easily pulled the fighter back into level flight, at which time he headed back to Burbank to have a very close talk with the design team and to examine the airframe for signs of overstress.

A close examination of the YP did not reveal any signs of airframe fatigue but reports from other pilots began to tell a strange story of the tail surfaces buffeting and vibrating at certain power settings and speed ranges. Lockheed test pilots began experimenting with a couple of the YPs and found that the vibration was indeed present – looking over their shoulder they could see the tail moving in a blur. As mentioned previously, this type of flutter or

White spinners contrasting brilliantly with dull camouflage, this P–38H–5–LO was assigned to a training unit in Orlando, Florida. The large numbers in the oval on the side of the engine nacelle denote the training role. Barely seen in the deep shadows under the wing center section are two 1,000 lb bombs. Orlando was the site of the Army Air Force's Tactical Training Center where pilots were given training in the fighter-bomber role. (USAAF)

vibration was regarded as extremely serious since it could possibly separate the tail from the booms. Hibbard and Johnson quickly went to work on this problem and found that fitting pod/wing fillets cured the problem which turned out not to be flutter but rather a vibration in the tail caused by an airflow disturbance at the pod/wing juncture. Testing at the Cal Tech wind tunnel helped cure the problem and fillets were soon fitted to all the YPs and became a standard item for production aircraft.

Testing of the compressibility problem continued and one YP was fitted with boosted trim tabs which would give the pilot an easier way of pulling the aircraft out of the dive. However, the new tabs did not cause the problem to go away and Lockheed test pilot Ralph Virden

The real failure of the Lightning production run was the Royal Air Force's Model 322, or Lightning Mk I. Originally, 243 Mark Is were ordered but the type proved to be so dismal that the British refused to accept the aircraft. Delivered without turbosuperchargers and with propellers that rotated the same way (causing extreme torque), the Mark I could not even come close to its projected performance specifications. Most were taken on charge by the Army who assigned the planes to unfortunate training units where they were universally hated by instructor and student alike, both realizing the aircraft's deadly characteristics. Still carrying its RAF serial of AE992, the Mark I also still has its RAF day-fighter camouflage with USAAF insignia painted over the British roundels.

Lightning Mk I AE979 seen on a test flight from the Burbank factory. This high-angle view illustrates the lack of turbosuperchargers, normally located in the top portion of the tail boom, which made the Mk I a slug that could not fight its own shadow. (Lockheed)

was killed when the tail of the number one YP came off on 4 November 1941 during the recovery from a power dive. The compressibility problem would not easily be solved and would affect production aircraft, as we shall see later in this chapter.

As testing of the YPs continued, the first of the 66 P-38s began to take form. These aircraft were identical to the YPs except for some minor changes. Lessons in Europe saw the addition of armor plate protection for the pilot and the elimination of the small .30 caliber weapons in favor of more .50 caliber

machine guns. The XP and YPs had all been left in their beautiful polished natural aluminium finish but there could be no doubt that the new P-38s were machines of war for they left the production line in a coat of Olive Drab and Neutral Gray, giving them a singularly purposeful look. The production run of P-38s did not proceed smoothly; one aircraft was pulled out for modifications and designated XP-38A for testing with a pressurized cockpit, while 36 were completed as P-38Ds. The P-38D saw the deletion of some items that the Army figured were not necessary, such as the

high pressure oxygen system (a safer low-pressure system was added), while more armor and self-sealing fuel tanks were fitted in an attempt to make the design combat worthy. Armor glass was installed over the instrument panel along with fluorescent instrument lights for night flying. A retractable landing light was put in the wing. The maximum internal fuel capacity was reduced to 300 US gallons from 410 US gallons in an effort to keep weight down. Some of the P-38s and P-38Ds were set aside for research and development use and some of the modifications were strange, such

received their fighters in the spring of 1941, the nose cannons had not been fitted and the aircraft were really not combat ready. However, the 1st was ready to test their new fighters in a realistic combat environment and the twin-tailed P–38s went to Louisiana and the Carolinas for the extensive war games which were carried on through September to November. The pilots of the 1st were able to test their aircraft against other Army fighters such as the P–35, P–36 and P–40, finding the P–38 generally superior in all categories.

While the 1st PG was trying out its new aircraft, Lockheed decided that the P–38 needed a name and came up with the appellation of 'Atlanta'. Such a name conjures up a nightmare of an entire generation of American fighting aircraft named after second-line cities. The mind boggles at such fearsome aircraft as the Cincinnati, the Detroit or even the Milwaukee. Fortunately, the British were also in the market for the P–38 and they had much more experience naming aircraft (even though, British names ran the gamut from the ridiculous – the Tomtit – to the sublime – the Fury), whereas the Army and American manufacturers simply settled for numbers. The British liked the name Lightning and, after consideration, so did Lockheed. The new fighter received a name that would prove to be most appropriate.

When France fell during June 1940, the French order for Model 322s was added to the British order. The French and British aircraft had several major differences when compared to their American counterparts, differences which negated the Lightning's main virtues. First, the Model 322s had V–1710–C15 engines *without* turbosuperchargers which had less horsepower (1,090 hp at 14,000 ft) than the American variants and were geared to have the propellers rotate in the *same* direction. Apparently, the thought behind this disastrous combination was that the engine and propeller combination would be the same as the Allisons used in the Royal Air Force's Curtiss Kittyhawks, and therefore interchangeable. However, the deletion of General Electric turbosuperchargers was not solely due to a requirement of the British specification; rather, it was the fact that production at GE could not even keep up with the US Army's demands. The British were faced with accept-

as those to P–38 s/n 40–744 which had a cockpit installed in the left boom to test the effects of an asymmetrical layout on the pilot whose sense of balance could have been disturbed by the placing of his seat away from the aircraft's centerline. [This aircraft, along with other Lightning modifications, can be found in the sub-chapter titled 'Lightning Oddities'.]

Lockheed was having a bit of a problem getting P–38 production on a schedule which would make the Army happy; the rapid expansion and the hiring of thousands of new workers was causing expected confusion, but management felt the situation would soon be sorted out and the production rate for the new fighter would rapidly rise. With P–38s and P–38Ds being added to the inventory, the Army made the decision to send the fighters to the 1st Pursuit Group, Selfridge Field, Michigan. Many of the 1st's pilots had test flown YP–38s and the Army felt that the experience gained in the type would help to introduce the P–38 more quickly to operational service.

The fact that P–38s were now in unit service did not mean all that much. When the 1st PG

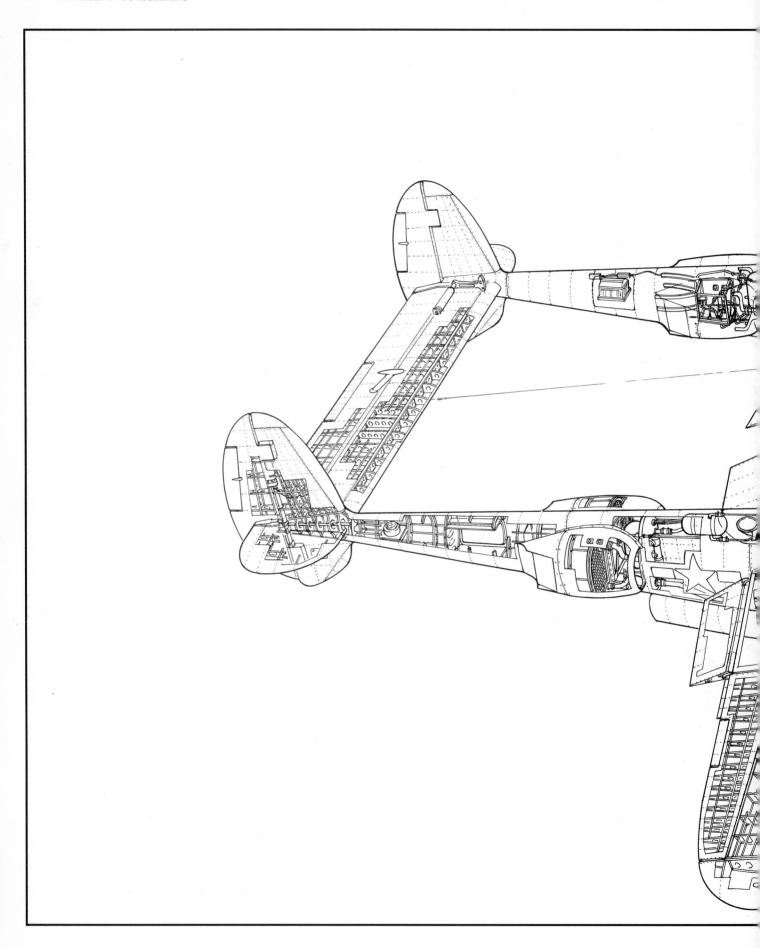

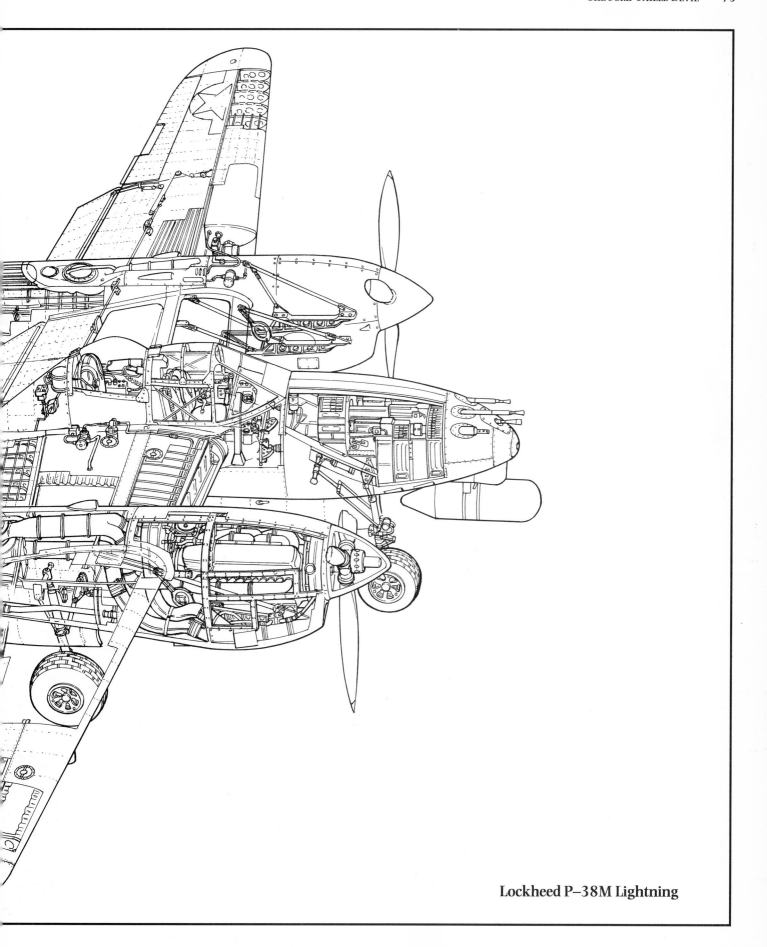

Lockheed P–38M Lightning

ing the aircraft without the units or having the fighters stored in the open until the turbosupercharger became available.

Given the designation of Lightning Mk I, the first aircraft flew from Burbank in Royal Air Force colors during August 1941 but the second did not get airborne until October. British pilots stationed in America went to Burbank to fly the new fighter and they were unanimous in their dislike of the British variant. Performance was considerably below specifications and above 12,000 ft the Lightning Mk I was virtually useless.

So rapid was the British condemnation of

the Model 322 that only one example, with RAF serial AF106, was even shipped to Britain. There it was tested, again with negative results. It was reported to have good handling characteristics but the restrictions on performance made the fighter of little use for combat over Europe. The British were quick to cancel their large orders with Lockheed but the Army was equally quick to pick them up. A Lightning Mk II had also been planned but only one example was finished in British markings before that order was also dropped. The Mk II had more powerful Allisons, turbo-superchargers and other uprated equipment. These aircraft were also taken over by the Army. Comprising 524 machines the Army divided the batch into P–38Fs (150 Mk IIs), the P–38G (374 Mk IIs) and the P–322 (140 Mk Is). Most of the P–322s, a very unusual designation for an Army aircraft, were sent through a re-engineering depot to receive

more powerful Allison F series engines and then scattered around the country to various training bases. Few student pilots remember the P–322 with any fondness since, even with the new engines, it was still underpowered with vicious engine cut-out characteristics. Quite a few P–322s were operated by the USAAF in RAF camouflage and serials.

As the end of 1941 loomed closer, more variants of the Lightning came from the Burbank production line but it was not until the P–38E and the P–38G that the Lightning became combat ready. The P–38E (Model 222–62–09) was the first major production version of the Lightning and it was considered as an interim step to the combat-ready P–38G. On the P–38E, the 37 mm cannon was replaced by a license-built Hispano 20 mm weapon with 150 rounds of ammunition. Once again, most of the P–38Es were scattered to training units, but the Army and Lockheed

These four pilots have a reason to be happy: they have just completed a successful ferry flight from America to Britain. From the left to the right are Colonels Ben S. Kelsey, Cass S. Hough, James E. Briggs and John K. Kerheart. These long-range ferry flights proved that the Lightning could avoid the U-boat menace and fly directly to the battlefronts. (Lockheed)

A P–38H–5–LO displays the short-lived red border around the national insignia (used only from July to August of 1943). The P–38H was equipped with Allison V–1710–89/–91 engines that gave improved altitude performance. The H model also introduced automatic engine controls, larger oil coolers and improved turbosuperchargers. Maximum take-off weight increased to over 20,000 lb. (Lockheed/V7823)

With production increasing, Lightnings found themselves on every warfront. This well-worn P–38, named Golden Eagle, is receiving another bomb mission marker on the side of the nacelle. Pilot Captain Billy Beardsly and crew chief TSgt V. DeVito are seen adding to the tally. Operating in the China-Burma Theatre, the P–38 has its own Chinese guard. When the photograph was taken in 1945, Golden Eagle was billed as one of the oldest fighter planes in the inventory of the 14th Air Force. (USAF/54130)

ferried long distances overwater. Fortunately, this plan never got beyond the tail modification stage. Others were used to tow gliders while 41–2048 was converted to dual controls and used to test various airfoil sections.

Along with 377 Army ordered machines, the P–38F series incorporated 150 Lightning Mk IIs originally intended for the RAF. Retaining the same armament as the P–38E, the Fs were powered with 1,325 hp Allison V–1710–49/–53 engines. These machines were produced in five different batches, each with its own set of updates and modifications. The F series included the first Lightnings to carry drop tanks (P–38F–5–LO): two 155/165 US gallon tanks could be carried on pylons located between the engines and the fuselage pod; two 1,000 lb bombs could also be fitted to the pylons in place of the drop tanks.

Built with 1,325 hp Allison V–1710–51/–55 engines, 708 P–38Gs (Model 222–68–12) were ordered in six blocks by the Army. The P–38G was generally similar to the F but with some detail refinements including an updated radio package, a new oxygen system, strengthened pylons that could carry 1,600 lb bombs, and winterization equipment. The P–38G–13–LO and P–38G–15–LO (a total of 374 aircraft designated Model 322–68–19) came from the British order for Lightning Mk IIs.

While Lightning production was rapidly building up, the Japanese struck American military installations at Pearl Harbor, Hawaii, on 7 December 1941 with a devastating blow. A panic immediately swept America concerning a possible invasion of the West Coast. Intelligence was limited and rumors were rife, reports of Japanese submarines off Los Angeles and of paratroopers landing in the desert caused a wave of anti-Japanese sentiment resulting in the interning of all West Coast Japanese – even if they were American citizens.

It must be remembered that the threat of a Japanese invasion was a very real possibility and to counter the threat the 1st Pursuit Group with its testing and training P–38s and P–38Ds was rushed to California to provide a modicum of air defense capability. The 1st was one of America's most historic air units and it is fitting that the unit was quickly moved to counter a possible threat. The 1st PG had been formed in France on 5 May 1918 and immedi-

did retain some of the aircraft for modification and testing purposes. Those assigned to training units carried the 'R' prefix, indicating that the aircraft was for a non-combat role. Thus, the Army operated RP–38s, RP–38Ds, and RP–322s as of 1942 when the designation change came into effect.

As detailed in our 'Lightning Oddities' section, many RP–38Es were put to extremely strange uses. Several had a cramped second seat installed directly behind the pilot where an unwilling student could be crammed for a demonstration of the Lightning's handling. Another was fitted with a massive, upswept tail in the anticipation of adding floats to the airframe, creating an aircraft that could be

A determined looking Major Herbert E. Johnson is seen with his P-38 after a mission to Brunswich, Germany, escorting Flying Fortresses. During this raid he shot down a pair of Focke Wulf Fw 190s. (USAF/50179)

ately went into action using a variety of foreign-built equipment that included the Nieuport 28, SPAD and Sopwith Camel. Two of the 1st's most distinguished pilots would go down in the history books: Captain Edward V. Rickenbacker became America's leading ace, while 2nd Lt Frank Luke, Jr, became known as the unit's maverick. In 1939, the 1st was reconstituted and consolidated into the 1st PG (Interceptor) in December 1939 and the 1st PG (Fighter) in March 1941.

The P-38s of the 1st arrived at the Naval Air Station in San Diego amid a flurry of activity and military preparations. Although the ground crews, spare parts and supplies did not arrive until a few days later, by train, and some of the early P-38s were completely unarmed, the Lightnings were immediately ordered into the air on combat patrols, and the pilots headed aloft – not really knowing what to look for since they could be opposing anything from high flying recon aircraft to an entire Japanese battlegroup.

The 1st soon moved to sprawling March Field near Riverside, California, to join the 14th Pursuit Group (the term fighter would replace pursuit early in 1942) which was in the process of equipping with Lightnings to form the only really modern high altitude defense available on the entire West Coast. Launching from March, the P-38s patrolled up and down the coast, usually heading up to Santa Barbara and then turning back towards San Diego before returning to March. Since Los Angeles was the main center for aircraft production, it was a prime target for a possible Japanese attack. However, as the weeks slid by it became obvious that the Japanese were not coming and it was time to send the Lightnings to confront the enemy directly.

Early in 1942, the United States Army Air Forces felt that combat ready Lightnings should be sent to Britain to reinforce America's growing presence in that island nation. Getting the P-38s to Britain was another problem. U-boats were taking a heavy toll of supply ships but flights across the Atlantic were still in the pioneering stage and considered very hazardous. With the P-38F and the development of reliable drop tanks, an island-hopping route would get the Lightnings to Britain safely and in record time. With drop tanks the P-38F had a maximum ferry range of 3,100 miles, demonstrated by Lockheed test pilot Milo Burcham; this was an exceptional range but probably could not be achieved by the average service fighter or average service pilot.

The Army notified the 1st and 14th Fighter Groups that they would be the first Lightning units to deploy to Britain, so both units pulled up stakes in California and headed for the East Coast for final training and modification of the P-38s for the long overwater flight. Starting in June 1942, groups of P-38s headed for Britain by flying via Goose Bay in Labrador, Bluie West One in Greenland, and Reykjavik on Iceland, landing at Prestwick, Scotland. Usually using a B-17 'mother ship', these flights were quite successful and the time gain over surface transportation was obvious.

By August, the Army Air Force had eight-one P-38Fs in Britain and preparation was underway to deploy the fighters in combat.

Half a world away, other P-38s were being readied for combat to fight in one of earth's most inhospitable climates: the Aleutians. Japan had been quick to realize the significance of the chain of islands that led directly into the American possession of Alaska. They knew that, by occupying the islands, a dagger could be aimed directly at Alaska – drawing America's limited military might away from the war in the Pacific. Accordingly, the Japanese landed in battalion strength on the Aleutian's Attu and Kiska islands. The occupation of these two islands became a thorn in America's side and a major effort was undertaken to dislodge the Japanese.

American military presence in Alaska had always been a rather token effort, but with the

P–38J–25–LO 44–23654 drops a 1,000 lb bomb during a training flight. Part of the P–38's great versatility was the fact that it could easily be converted to a 'B–38', a long range bomber carrying more bomb load than a B–25 Mitchell. During these bomber raids, the 'B–38s' were led by 'Droop Snoot' Lightnings with a lead bombardier who would give the entire B–38 formation the signal when to release their bombs. The bomber Lightnings would usually be protected by an equal number of P–38s although, once their bombs were released, the bombers would immediately revert to their fighter status. (Lockheed/E. Miller)

Dramatically illustrating the change-over from Olive Drab and Neutral Gray camouflage to natural metal finish, is Lockheed P–38J–10–LO 42–68040 seen taxiing down a row of camouflaged fighters at Burbank. The Army dropped camouflage to speed production, gain a couple of miles per hour, and reduce overall costs. The small opening in the extreme forward portion of the nose cone is for a gun camera although this installation was less than ideal since the guns made the camera vibrate, quite often making the film illegible for intelligence officers. The gun camera was moved to the wing with the P–38L. (Lockheed/T1262)

Japanese invasion a force of P–38s was gathered and sent on the long flight north. The 11th and 18th Fighter Squadrons of the 28th Composite Group were equipped with tired P–40s and P–39s so the new squadron of P–38s was most welcome. The islands of the Aleutians are spread over a 1,200-mile strip of ocean so incredibly hostile that a pilot would die after just a few minutes of exposure to the frigid water. The Kittyhawks and Airacobras were limited in range and their single power-plants offered no margin of safety. The Japanese were expanding efforts in digging in and fortifying the two islands against American attack. A few limited air clashes had taken place before the arrival of the P–38s and several Japanese aircraft had been destroyed by the P–40s.

The P–38s were soon put into action, their range stretched to the maximum, and an attack was launched on the enemy base at Kiska. Some ships in the harbor were bombed and shot up while the ground installations and airfield were given a good working over, much to the surprise of the enemy who probably thought that such an attack was impossible. American engineers began to construct airships on the islands nearer the enemy and some of the problems associated with the long-

range missions began to disappear, but it is a sobering fact that only ten of the original 31 Lightning pilots survived their Aleutian tour. Most were victims of the foul weather and freezing sea. Parts for the fighters were non-existent and wrecks had to be scavenged by the mechanics for every useable piece. Some of the damaged aircraft which were still flyable were flown all the way back to Texas for repairs but this was not an easy flight and several pilots were lost.

Engineers had established bases on Adak and Amchitka, putting strike forces much closer to the enemy and attacks were launched whenever weather permitted. Pilots of the 54th FS were regularly hitting the Japanese in company with the P–40s and P–39s, and the B–24 Liberator heavy bombers and during September 1942, the 54th, 11th and 18th Fighter Squadrons were amalgamated into the 343rd Fighter Group, 11th Air Force. The enemy was always ready to oppose the attacking Americans but the fight slowly began to tilt in favor of the Americans. P–38s went up for mission after mission, usually carrying a 500 lb or 1000 lb bomb under one wing and a fuel tank under the other. The Japanese always put up a fairly stiff resistance and the Zeros were tough opponents. Aerial slaughters that

*A*llison V–1710 is lowered into position on a P–38J as it moves down the Burbank production line. Known as QEC (Quick Engine Change) unit, the engine and auxiliary systems were contained in a power 'egg' that could quickly be removed and replaced with a new unit, thus greatly reducing the number of manhours needed for an engine change. (Lockheed)

soon became common over the South Pacific were not unknown in the Aleutians. On 24 May 1943, a group of 25 Betty bombers was intercepted and all but three were destroyed.

On 11 May 1943, the Navy landed an invasion force on Attu and, after three weeks of fighting, the Japanese force of 2,300 was overwhelmed. In July, Kiska was invaded but the Americans were suprised to find that the Japanese had left in their ships during a heavy fog, leaving piles of abandoned military equip-

ment. P–38s were to be stationed in the area for the rest of the war, but the heavy fighting at the top of the world was over.

Back over the North Atlantic, the ferry flights to supply the USAAF effort in Britain were continuing and Lightnings were regularly crossing but losses were incurred. Six P–38s and their two B–17 mother ships went down in Greenland on 27 June 1942 after bad weather prevented them from landing at their assigned base. The aircraft all safely crash-landed on the ice cap and none of the pilots were injured but it was a few days before they could be removed. The aircraft were left where they went down. In 1983, with a growing interest in the history of World War Two and its artifacts, an expedition was launched from

America to find and recover the fighters and bombers. The featureless terrain of the ice cap proved to be a major problem but, by using sophisticated sonar gear, large metal targets were found buried under *seventy-five* feet of solid ice! The expedition had to abandon its base camp with the onset of winter and there has been some discussion of going back and melting the ice with a jet engine but such an undertaking would entail a vast expenditure.

Other Lightnings went down on the ferry route but their pilots were not so lucky – they simply disappeared. The Germans did not like the idea of the aerial supply line but there was little they could do about disrupting the flow, not like the U-boat's slaughter of Allied transports. However, the Germans did develop several clever means of damaging the supply line. Powerful radio beams were used to misdirect Allied aircraft and Germans speaking perfect English were employed to give incorrect orders over the air. Far ranging Focke Wulf Fw 200 Condors went out over the Atlantic to observe the flights and attack any possible stragglers. The hunter became victim on 15 August when a Condor was jumped by a P–38 from the 27th FS and a P–40 from the 33rd FS, both out of Greenland. The Condor was sent down on fire into the ocean for the honor of being the first German aircraft destroyed by the USAAF during World War Two in the European Theatre of Operations. The 27th FS had been on its way to England when orders directed them to remain in Greenland to bolster the island's P–40 defense. The long-range Lightning proved to be a great threat to the prowling Focke Wulfs and the Germans were much more careful about sending out the lumbering four engine aircraft. The 27th only stayed in Greenland for two months before departing to Britain but they had helped dilute the German threat.

The Olive Drab and Neutral Gray Lightnings of the 14th Fighter Group arrived in Britain at the end of August, their unique configuration capturing the fancy of every British schoolboy. The Lightnings were not immediately ready for combat and practice flying, tactics and local familiarization flights had to be undertaken, but the deployment of the P–38 in a combat situation was not to have as much to do with the Lightning's battle readiness as with international politics.

President Roosevelt and Prime Minister Churchill felt that the opening of a front on enemy territory was a political and military necessity. Several influential generals were pushing for a major landing in France but the politicians were against the projected invasion, feeling that the situation was not right for such a major military move. Stalin was also against a direct invasion of France, but he did favor heavy intervention on some other front to take the immense German pressure off Russia. A major attack, Operation TORCH, was planned against North Africa but there was considerable military opposition to this move and it took almost ten days of heavy arguing before Roosevelt won out and the invasion was planned. Currently, some historians feel that this major delay of landing forces in France gave the Soviets a distinct advantage in later claiming all of Eastern Europe.

Operation TORCH needed a vast amount of planning and material to ensure its success – failure at that point in the war would have spelled disaster. Due to the pressing needs for effective airpower in the invasion, a new air force was created – the USAAF 12th Air Force. Aircraft were urgently needed to fill the new air force, but were not yet coming from America's increased production lines to fill the needs of the Allies' far-flung military operations. Accordingly, the USAAF looked to the 8th AF in Britain to see what could be taken without decreasing the effective strength of the 8th. The P–38s of the 14th FG were an obvious

answer since the unit had not been fully committed to combat; in fact, the unit had only flown a few combat bomber escort missions during October 1942.

In October, orders were received to move the 14th, its pilots, aircraft and other ranks to a new secret location. Spare parts and ground personnel were loaded aboard cargo ships – the men having absolutely no idea of where they were going – while the P–38s launched to Gibraltar, timed to arrive on 8 November, the day planned for the invasion. Once again, the pilots had little idea of what was going on but some of the more politically astute must have figured that a strike at Vichy-occupied North Africa was in hand.

The strike at North Africa was indeed an attempt to open a new 'front' on basically what would be the easiest military target. The invasion would give the Allies a needed emotional boost while attempting, for the moment, to pacify the Russian demand for the opening of a major offensive on the German military machine in the west. Trouble would be encountered because the Allies were attacking

not only the enemy but also the French who inhabited the area. Many French had escaped during the initial German invasion but many more had stayed, more or less leading the everyday existence that they had before the start of the war. The French government and military forces in the area had been quickly reorganized by the Germans with Vichy figureheads who obeyed the orders given by their masters.

Overall military commander for TORCH was General Dwight Eisenhower. Air Marshal Tedder's command included the newly formed Desert Air Force which, in itself, included the equally new USAAF 9th AF. Jimmy Doolittle commanded the 12th AF. Field Marshal Erwin Rommel commanded the elite *Afrika Korps*. Historians would later write that such a gathering of capable leaders had the makings

Inverted 'Christmas tree' rocket launchers, standard installation on P–38Ls, could also be attached to other variants of Lightnings by simple modifications at forward bases. An improvement over the earlier bazooka style launchers, the rocket trees carried a total of ten 5-in high velocity rockets. (Lockheed/P9906)

of one of the war's most epic fights. In Egypt, General Bernard Montgomery's British 8th Army was taking advantage of the victory at El Alamein in Egypt in October 1942, and was applying considerable harassing pressure on Rommel that would be very useful for TORCH.

The logistics for such an invasion, while not approaching the scope of the later Normandy landings, were immense. The Allies poured ashore on 8 November 1942 at Casablanca, Safi, Fedhala, Port Lyautey and Oran, catching the enemy, if not entirely by surprise, at least in a state of confusion. The French *Armée de l'Air* put up its Curtiss Hawk 75s and a few brief but bloody air battles ensued with US Navy Wildcats and Dauntlesses and British Seafires, during which both sides suffered losses.

The French did not really have much of fight in them and a surrender was worked out on 11 November, the day which the Gibraltar-based Lightnings flew their first missions. The Lightnings had departed Gibraltar on the day of the invasion and landed on the airfield at Tafaraoui on the 11th. The 14th FG pilots were basically on hostile soil by themselves since the supply train with their ground crews and spare parts had not yet arrived. As the days passed, more P-38s arrived along with the missing ground crews and operations were undertaken on a limited basis.

The Germans were by no means hiding and when the 48th FS moved to the famous Maison Blanche airfield during the middle of the month, the *Luftwaffe* caught them by surprise in a strafing and bombing attack that knocked out airfield facilities and crippled seven of the Lightnings. This was just the first of several visits that the Germans paid to the field – a raid on 20 November destroyed over 20 Allied aircraft.

Besides the use of fast-moving bombers and Stukas during the *Blitzkrieg*, the Germans never took full advantage of developing an efficient ground attack force that could directly and repeatedly hit Allied airfields, destroying aircraft and equipment on the ground. The slim Allied airpower force in North Africa is an ideal example of the *Luftwaffe*'s blundering since the few ground attack missions against the Allies did a tremendous amount of damage to already limited resources, but they were never pressed to full advantage.

The Lightning pilots, besides putting up with the German hit-and-run raids, had to cope with the harsh realities of living 'in the field'. Living conditions were, at best, primitive and pilots found themselves living in tents, in structures made of discarded fuel barrels or, quite often, just in the open where they had to put up with dust when it was hot and an incredibly tenacious mud when it rained. The ground crews maintained the Lightnings as best they could in these harsh conditions, but mechanical and engine failures were not uncommon. Along with the growing score of *Luftwaffe* and Italian aircraft destroyed, the P-38 pilots were also beginning to take heavy losses; when the 14th Fighter Group was withdrawn from combat at the end of January 1943, 32 of the original 54 pilots had been lost in combat or in accidents while the Group claimed 62 enemy aircraft destroyed.

As Operation TORCH progressed, the P-38 forces consolidated and gradually began to increase their firepower as new aircraft and pilots arrived. Rommel began moving his famed *Panzer* units against the Allies in a series of daring attacks that usually resulted in heavy losses on both sides, but the sharp conflicts mainly resulted in German defeats or stalemates. The Germans were receiving a great deal of their supplies by air and Allied intelligence felt that if the aerial supply train could be broken, then there was a good chance of the entire German military machine in North Africa grinding to a halt. The P-38s of the 1st and 82nd FGs became part of Operation FLAX, a massive Allied effort aimed at attacking and destroying German supply lines.

The German transport fleet consisted mainly of slow, ungainly Junkers Ju 52 trimotors that were efficient cargo haulers but easy aerial targets for fighters. The other main *Luftwaffe*

Carrying two 500 lb bombs, Lightnings taxi for takeoff on a dive bombing mission against von Runstedt's forces during December 1944 which, at this time, was within fifteen miles of this P-38 base in Belgium. These Lightnings were from the 485th Fighter Squadron, 370th Fighter Group, and carry the identifying code 7F. It is interesting to note the colorful checkered nose on the P-38J in the right background. Some P-38s, such as the one in the foreground, had the extreme tip of their nose cone highly polished with a white band added behind the polished area. This was done with the hope of confusing the German pilots into thinking that the fighter was an unarmed 'Droop Snoot' Lightning. (USAF/58856)

*B*riefly at rest, a 9th AF P–38 is seen parked among the ruins of a forward air base in Belgium shortly after the D-Day invasion. (USAF/55542)

This was just the beginning of the slaughter of the *Luftwaffe* transports.

For the next several days, Lightnings, P–40s and Spitfires attacked huge formations of German aircraft and, although Allied aircraft were always lost in these swirling battles, the Germans really came out on the losing end, hundreds of transports falling to the Allied fighters. The *Luftwaffe* became unable to protect the transport flights and supply missions became virtual suicide trips. By destroying the German transports, the Allies took a major step in gaining control of the airspace over North Africa. The German/Italian armies began to crumble, with a massive surrender of men coming in mid-May. Field Marshal Rommel and most of his staff managed to escape the final defeat. Rommel continued to fight the Allies on different portions of the battlefront until after the Normandy Invasion when he was forced by Hitler to commit suicide.

The Lightning had proven itself in a wide variety of missions: the high-altitude fighter sweeps, bomber escort, medium altitude dogfights, ground attack missions and recon flights. The harsh conditions of North Africa had taken a heavy toll of Lightnings and USAAF pilots but the aircraft had established itself as a valuable military tool and new combat areas were rapidly opening.

Back in Burbank, Lockheed was paying attention to reports from their field representatives and the USAAF. Hundreds of modifications were incorporated into the Lightning production line while the design department came up with new variants. Reports from the combat areas had told of power falling off above 25,000 ft. Automatic oil radiator flaps were fitted to the new P–38H (226 P–38H–1–LO variants constructed) that not only enabled the Allison V–1710–89/91 powerplants, with a take-off rating of 1,425 hp, to run cooler but let the pilot keep military power on the engines above 25,000 ft where 1,240 hp per engine could be achieved. The P–38H–5–LO (375 built) had the more powerful B-33 turbosuperchargers installed in the booms.

Major improvements were introduced with the P–38J. One of the key identifying features of the earlier Lightnings was the elegant swept-back 'shark' air intake behind and below the spinner which gave the Allison engine installation an extremely streamlined appearance. Although the installation was streamlined, cooling became a problem as demands on the Lightning increased. A P–38E (s/n 41–1983) had been modified at the factory to

transport was the even more ungainly Messerschmitt Me 323, a variant of Germany's massive glider transport powered by six engines. Slow, unmaneuverable and not very well armed, these transports were usually protected by hordes of fighters that would slowly weave back and forth over the transport flights. However, the transports were so slow that the fighters would have to reduce speed drastically and then gently maneuver in S turns to keep their own speed even further down. High-performance engines were often victims of fouled plugs as the fighters flew for extended periods at the reduced power settings.

Operation FLAX proposed to blast through the enemy fighter defense and decimate the aerial supply line. The first major encounter happened on 5 April 1943 when Lightnings of the 1st and 82nd FG flew their usual bomber escort mission and ran into 65 Ju 52s which they bounced from high altitude, roaring directly through the defending fighter formation and hitting the transports. Eleven of the Junkers fell into the ocean near Cape Bone along with several of the escorting fighters.

These Lightnings serve as a symbol of the overwhelming American airpower that blasted the Axis into rubble. Beautiful formation of D-Day striped Lightnings practice in England before a mission over the Continent. This formation was developed for the 'B–38' bombing raids. A 'Droop Snoot' Lightning would lead the formation on a bombing attack at altitudes over 20,000 ft. (USAF/51937)

incorporate larger radiators and much larger scoops under the engine. This did detract from streamlining but, at the same time, offered an impressive increase in power. With the larger radiator area and new Prestone coolant scoops mounted on the booms, the Allisons could operate more efficiently. Testing with the P–38E had proven the installation more than satisfactory and the modification was incorporated into the new P–38H production run. The P–38J (Model 422–81–14) kept the same engine installation as the P–38H but the

increased cooling meant that power at 27,000 ft would go from 1,240 to 1,425 hp. War emergency power selection at that altitude would take engine power to 1,600 hp for a few minutes. The Model 422–81–14 was built in large numbers: ten P–38J–1–LOs, 210 P–38J–5s and 790 P–38J–20s. Each block variant had improvements that included the addition of two 55 US gallon fuel cells in the space previously occupied by the intercoolers (J–5) which increased internal fuel to 410 US gallons. Flat armored windshields were added to the J–10 along with other minor improvements.

The Model 422–81–22 production was divided into two main batches; the P–38J–15–LO (1,400 built) had an updated electrical system while the J–20 (350 built) had new turbosupercharger regulators. The Model 422–81–23 block consisted of 210 P–38J–25s that had

dive flaps located under the wing that were electrically powered and they were also fitted with ailerons that had power boost systems. These new variants would soon be on their way to all corners of the globe, replacing earlier Lightnings and giving the USAAF a fighter that was greatly feared by the enemy, *Luftwaffe* pilots calling the P–38 'the Forktailed Devil'.

After the Allied victory in North Africa, USAAF units re-equipped and built up strength before entering combat over the Mediterranean in preparation for the invasions of Sicily and Italy. One of the first targets was the fortress island of Pantelleria, the site of heavy enemy concentrations and location for one of the Allies' more ambitious experiments: to destroy completely, an enemy target from the air. Every aircraft that could carry a bomb was thrown into the attack on Pantelleria and for days on end the island was repeatedly blasted until final victory was achieved. Lightnings of the 1st and 82nd FGs carried out hundreds of strafing and dive bombing missions against the stronghold. USAAF pilots had to be particularly careful when taking the '38 out for a dive bombing run since the problem of compressibility was still plaguing the design. Pilots had to monitor carefully their speed since it built up so quickly and to allow for loss of control which could quite often be followed by airframe disintegration.

Lightnings had joined other Allied air units in hitting targets in Sicily during July 1943 in preparation for Operation HUSKY – the invasion of Sicily and the first probe into the 'soft underbelly' of the Axis. Battling in the Mediterranean proved to be anything but soft and the enemy was not only well-equipped but also tenacious. Sicily was invaded on 10 July 1943 but did not fall until 17 August.

After the capture of Sicily, the three Lightning groups (the 1st, 14th and 82nd) began concentrated attacks against the Italian mainland – bombing, escorting and intercepting. On 1 November, a change in paperwork assigned the three P–38 groups to the Fifteenth Air Force, giving the Lightning pilots the main assignment of escorting heavy bombers to enemy targets in Austria and other Axis locations such as Greece, the Balkans, France and Italy. These missions were hazardous since they were over enemy territory for a good portion of the flight time and opposition from the *Luftwaffe* and flak batteries was intense.

Proponents of the Lightning maintained that the P–38 would make a good pin-point bomber since it had twin-engine reliability and could easily carry a 1,000 lb bomb for a long distance. Usually, another aircraft or a modified Lightning provided the role of pathfinder for the Lightning force and, after some practice, the first of these pioneering missions was flown on 10 June 1944. Nearly 50 82nd FG P–38s dropped their 1,000 lb high explosive bombs on an oil refinery in Rumania. These refineries had been subject to constant American attention and, while never being able to knock them out completely, enough damage was done to hinder the German's war effort. The targets were very heavily defended and the Lightnings paid dearly on this first mission. The 'bombers' were escorted by an equal number of P–38s that kept a look-out for enemy fighters. Near the target area, a massive dogfight developed and 22 Lightnings fell in the fight, devastating losses that were not really equal to the results obtained.

The Fifteenth Air Force kept hammering German and Axis targets thus drawing valuable supplies, men and material away from the Western and Eastern fronts and sending them south to fight the American advances. For aviators of the Fifteenth, their zone of combat was extremely dangerous if they were shot down and it was not uncommon for pilots and crews to be badly beaten or killed by hostile civilians – rescue, oddly enough, coming only

when the Germans intervened to haul the downed fliers to a prison camp.

Raids on German and Italian airfields proved to be an effective but dangerous way of reducing the enemy's air force. The P–38's heavy, concentrated armament was particularly useful in this role although liquid-cooled engines could easily be damaged by small arms fire. One epic raid on 25 August 1943 sent 65 Lightnings from the 1st FG and a near equal number from the 82nd FG out to demolish the enemy airfields that surrounded Foggia, Italy. In order to achieve total surprise, the Lightning pilots flew on the deck and the raid hit the enemy so quickly and so hard that very little anti-aircraft fire was received. The raid was a total success and about 200 German and Italian aircraft were destroyed or damaged in exchange for two P–38s being lost. Such massive losses did not stem the enemy's will to fight and huge dogfights were still the rule of the day, neither side giving quarter.

General Montgomery made his landing in southern Italy on 3 September 1943 to be followed by General Mark Clark and the American 5th Army on 9 September near Salerno.

The 'soft underbelly' was not living up to its name and the Germans fought back so fiercely that the Allied high command suddenly became fearful of the final result of the invasion.

Once again, every available P–38 was thrown into the battle but the heavy aerial fighting had reduced the number of Lightnings available for combat. Prime targets were German troop and supply concentrations along with the enemy airfields. The three weary Lightning groups could muster a bit less than 250 of the twin-tailed fighters and quite a few of these machines would be destroyed or damaged during the September fighting. Airfields felt the bite of the Lightning and on 18 September, nearly 300 more hostile aircraft were destroyed or damaged when the airfields around Foggia were once again raided. Foggia was denied to the enemy on 27 September when it was overrun by units of the American

Ninth Air Force Lightning pilots, their briefing for the day's mission completed, pile into trucks for a ride to the hardstands where their fighters were parked 'somewhere in England'. Note the diversity of uniform dress. (USAF/A55543)

A fully modified 'Droop Snoot' Lightning seen in Britain. The forward section of the P-38J's fuselage pod containing the guns and ammunition was removed and a new nose section was built housing a bombardier, bomb sight and associated navigation equipment. (Lockheed/P8486)

8th Army. Lightnings began to use the airfields and the pilots were amazed to see the stacks of destroyed Axis aircraft – the fields looked like massive scrap yards. The devastating attacks and the slowly advancing infantry were finally taking an irreparable toll on the Germans. With Italy's surrender, many of the former enemy airfields were occupied by Lightnings and the bomber force, each step closer to the heart of Germany, but the Germans in Italy fought on, hard.

By February 1944, the newer P-38Js were arriving in Italy and the Lightning groups began to venture further into enemy territory. Plans for co-ordinated raids into Germany and

Austria were undertaken by the Eighth and Fifteenth, putting the enemy in a pincher and reducing his forces even more. Using their increased range, the Lightnings participated in some of the epic air battles over Austria and Germany. At this stage of the war, the *Luftwaffe*, although reeling could be counted on when bomber raids hit strategic targets. The Germans would throw everything into these aerial battles but aircraft such as the Bf 110 and Me 210 were easy prey for the Lightnings. Experienced *Luftwaffe* pilots in Bf 109s and Fw 190s were more than a handful and the pilots of such caliber had to be respected. Still, it was a war of attrition and, bit by bit, the Germans were able to put fewer aircraft into the air while the Allies were able to get more and more over the target areas.

As the war progressed into mid-1944, ground attacks had virtually stopped all rail traffic in the portion of Italy still held by the

Germans. Lightnings and Thunderbolts attacked anything that moved and it was not safe for the enemy to use roads or rails in the daylight. With the Normandy invasion, Lightnings of the 1st and 14th FGs staged through Corsica to support the Allied landings. These missions were less than easy and in a few days 23 P-38s were knocked down. German air opposition began to fall off drastically over Italy during August and September and the bombers were able to pound targets more effectively. Photo recce Lightnings ranged far into enemy territory, bringing back damage reports and finding new targets. The war, for the Fifteenth, from late 1944 on was to be one hard and long advance. The enemy remained dangerous and Lightning losses, although decreasing in number, continued until the final victory. As aerial targets became harder to find, the Lightnings intensified their ground attack efforts even though these missions were very dangerous. For example, on 14 April 1944, 15 Lightnings were shot down during strafing and bombing attacks on enemy positions. When, on 2 May, more than one million Germans surrendered, the war in Italy was finally over.

Since the Fifteenth Air Force had absorbed virtually all of the Lightnings in Britain, it is interesting to note that the Eighth Air Force did not begin to re–equip with the P–38 until September 1943 when the 55th FG and its P–38Hs arrived at Nuthampstead. By mid-October, the unit was ready for combat and began to fly missions over France and other occupied countries. Re-equipping with P–38Js during December 1943, the 55th now had the range to escort bombers all the way to Berlin and back – a distance of 1,300 miles, thus becoming the first Lightning unit capable of

protecting the hard-pressed bombers through an entire mission; the first mission of this type taking place on 3 March 1944.

The 55th FG was to be joined by other Lightning units: the 20th FG in December 1943, the 364th FG in March 1944, and the 479th FG in May 1944. The 55th was originally equipped with P–38Hs which were not really suited for high altitude operations. Pilots complained of bitter cold at altitude and cases of frostbite were recorded. Even though the aviators were encased in leather and lamb's wool, the cold of the high European skies was like a prolonged torture and pilot efficiency rapidly dropped. The P–38Hs were also prone to windshield icing and fogging of the cockpit plexiglass – certainly not a safe situation in a fighter aircraft where visibility often meant the difference between life and death. At altitude, there was also a problem with overboosting

the Allison engines, much the same problem as suffered by P–47 pilots with their turbosupercharged P&W R–2800s. Blown engines were not uncommon among the more inexperienced pilots and the Allison, in the ETO, began to get a reputation as a 'boat anchor'.

Since the Army and manufacturers had so many field modification kits to update or modify their combat aircraft, it does not seem unreasonable that some form of efficient heater and windshield de-icer could have been devised and quickly added to the P–38Hs. As it

Kicking up a trail of dust, a P–38J lands on a newly made airstrip near the Omaha beachhead, Vierville sur Mer, France. Photographed on 10 June 1944, the Lightning was the first aircraft (besides light observation types such as the L–4 Cub) to land on the strip. These airfields made safe havens for damaged Allied aircraft that were unable to get back across the Channel. (US Army/190118–S)

was, many Lightnings that went out on the early ETO missions simply never came back – whether from enemy action, engine failure or other reasons – and pilot morale began to take a distinct downward turn which was unusual for American fighter groups.

Increased instruction on the correct operating of the Allisons at altitude began to cure some of the overboosting problems but it was obvious that high altitude brought out many problems with the P–38H and there was relief when the more advanced P–38Js began arriving in the United Kingdom, although the supply of the J was not as fast as the fighter

groups wished. The J, along with its increased range, featured improved cockpit heating and windshield de-icing systems while the new radiator system helped a bit with the overboosting problem and engine failures decreased. The more reliable cooling and improved superchargers meant that more power could be obtained from the Allisons at higher altitude but it was not uncommon to have mixed formations of Hs and Js until the supply of Js greatly increased towards the middle of 1944.

The 55th FG was basically fully equipped with pilots and aircraft but the other groups were only partially operational at first and took a while to build up to combat readiness. Beacause of this, FGs would usually send their limited number of aircraft out with the 55th on bomber escort missions. By combining forces, two FGs could usually get around 90 Lightnings airborne for the bomber escort missions. Since the Lightnings were larger than their

fellow escorting Thunderbolts, German pilots could usually spot the P–38 sooner and they would stay away from the twin-boomed fighter. The trips deep into Germany were no piece of cake, even in the improved P–38Js, and losses were common due to mechanical failure, flak and fighters. Many P–38s did make it back to base with one engine out, thus proving the feasibility of the twin-engine concept.

The Lightning did not serve solely in its role as high-altitude escort. A major modification was undertaken on some of the fighters that led to the new name of 'Droop Snoot' along with a rather ungainly profile. The nose section and armament of the Lightning were removed and a new nose was installed that included a plexiglass dome in the extreme forward nose with a seat and associated equipment for a bombardier. Although the new position certainly could not have been too comfortable for the unfortunate in the nose, the modification did give the Lightning new

On 11 March 1943, these four 9th Fighter Squadron P–38 pilots accounted for five Japanese aircraft during a raid on Dobodura airstrip. From left to right: Lt T. R. Fowler (1 victory); Capt Sidney Woods (1); Lt J. C. Mankin (1); and Lt Dick Bong (2). Bong would go on to become America's ace of aces with forty victories. The heat and humidity of New Guinea meant that the pilots wore only the lightest of khaki uniforms. (US Army/168528)

versatility and the 'Droop Snoots', modified at Lockheed's major overhaul center at Langford Lodge, Ireland, were spread around the combat units.

The idea behind the 'Droop Snoot' was simple and effective: the bombardier-equipped Lightning would lead the fighter P–38s that had been fitted with a 1,000 lb bomb on one of the underwing pylons (a fuel tank would be on the other) and the 'Droop Snoot' would do all the navigating to the target. When approaching the target, the bombardier would take over the formation and all the bombs would be dropped on his order. This method of delivering high explosives to the enemy was effective and bombing altitudes were usually 20,000 ft and above. After bomb release the P–38s could defend themselves against fighter opposition. While in the bomber configuration, other 'regular' P–38s would circle the 'B–38' formation for protection on the run-in to the target area.

As Mustangs and Thunderbolts took the bombers to Germany, the Eighth decided to employ the P–38s in ground attack as well as escort missions. From 6 June 1944, the P–38s were in the air all day, escorting and attacking targets of opportunity although, from this point on, German fighter forces rapidly began to decrease in number and quality so ground attack missions became more and more common for the USAAF fighters.

When General James H. Doolittle took command of the Eighth AF in the middle of 1944, he made a sweeping decision that would drastically affect the role of the P–38 in the ETO. His decision was that the P–38 and P–47 groups should be equipped with the P–51 Mustang. Doolittle felt that the Mustang was a more efficient and more cost effective aircraft than either the Thunderbolt or the Lightning and that it could perform the high-altitude escort and ground attack role more effectively. The decision was not overly popular with the P–47 commanders since they had grown to love their big fighters and had learned to take advantage of the Thunderbolt's great diving speed, massive firepower and strong airframe. P–38 group commanders seemed to take the decision a little bit more philosophically since they realized that the P–38J was only just becoming a fully combat effective aircraft and, besides, many of them had the chance to fly Mustangs and realized the potential of North America's sleek fighter.

The Ninth Air Force, whose mission was primarily tactical, sent its first combat Lightning patrol out on 25 April 1944 with its 474th FG but the Ninth was to be also effected by Doolittle's orders. Although the Ninth had gotten two other Lightning groups (the 367th and 370th) operational, the units found themselves quickly converting to the Mustang and the Thunderbolt.

The Lightning's role in the ETO was not particularly long nor particularly covered in glory but every British schoolboy that saw the Lightning's distinctive shape was fascinated by the 'Yank' warplane and probably carries the memory with him today. Although the Lightning had given distinguished service in North Africa and Italy, had taken the bombers to Berlin from Britain and had performed invaluable recon work, its true fame was yet to come: the Lightning would achieve immortality over the vast Pacific, fighting the Japanese.

The Lightning met the Japanese for the first time in an unlikely location which was also one of the most hostile places on the face of the earth: the Aleutians. The Japanese, wishing to secure as many fronts against the weakened Americans after Pearl Harbor, invaded the island of Kiska in the Aleutian chain off the northwest tip of Alaska during June 1942. The enemy quickly set up fortifications, an airfield and a crude port that could receive both warships and floatplanes. As mentioned earlier in this chapter, the Aleutians proved to be such a hostile environment that more aircraft were lost to the terrible weather than to the enemy. However, the early P–38s used in the fighting gave good service and scored the first Lightning victories over the powerful Japanese.

The enemy moved quickly after Pearl Harbor, capturing one Allied stronghold after another until it seemed the Japanese tidal wave could not be stopped. Australia was a particular plum which the Japanese had been eyeing for quite some time, as the huge island continent would serve as an ideal base for future conquests. The rag-tag US Fifth Air Force which was headquartered in Australia had a motley collection of fighting machines, some of them survivors of earlier, disastrous battles with the Japanese.

The first Lightnings in Australia were not desperately needed fighters but four F–4 photo recon birds that arrived on 7 April 1942 under the command of Major Karl Polifka and designated as the 8th Photographic Squadron. They were needed just as badly as combat aircraft since Allied commanders had little idea what the Japanese were doing. Reports from the coast watchers were often out of date because of the time that it took them to reach headquarters, but a fast-moving aircraft equipped

By all accounts, Thomas B. McGuire was an unpleasant man with a large ego but he was also a top-notch fighter pilot. Caught up in the ace 'race' with Dick Bong, McGuire was always a step or two behind Bong. McGuire had started out his military career flying Airacobras in the Aleutians and he took the 'race' very seriously. When Bong was sent back to the States after breaking Rickenbacker's WWI record, McGuire thought that he had the field to himself and was not pleased when Bong returned for a second tour. Bong raised his score to forty and was sent home for good so McGuire tried frantically to break the forty mark. When McGuire got his score up to thirty-eight, General George Kenney (who favored the easy-going Bong) grounded McGuire until Bong could be fully honored upon his return home. Airborne again after a few days on the ground, McGuire went after a Japanese fighter at very low altitude and, in the rush for a victory, committed one of the most basic errors: stalling the P–38. The fighter slammed into the ocean and he was killed.

with reliable cameras could carry out recon missions over vast stretches of territory, relying on speed advantage to stay out of the reach of enemy fighters. Quickly moving to the famous Port Moresby airstrip, the 8th began operating from New Guinea searching out enemy airfields, shipping and troop concentrations, and bringing back hundreds of high quality photographs that could be interpreted carefully to gain valuable knowledge upon which future raids could be based. These four F–4s provided virtually the entire intelligence on which the early battle strategy against the Japanese empire would be based.

The first fighter Lightnings to arrive in

Australia consisted of 25 P–38Fs that were assigned to the 35th Fighter Group as the 39th Fighter Squadron, which converted from very tired Bell Airacobras. The Lightnings' first combat base was Jackson Field, Port Moresby. The P–38Fs had been plagued with mechanical problems during training in Australia and some of these problems continued in New Guinea when the squadron was taken into combat under the command of Captain George Prentice. Entering combat in October, it was not until 27 December 1942 that the 39th scored its first success when eleven Japanese aircraft were knocked down in exchange for the loss of one F model. One of the pilots achieving two victories was Lt Richard Bong who would go on to become America's ace of aces.

Major General George Kenney was in charge of the Fifth and he was a proponent of the P–38 from the start. Lobbying hard and long, Kenney was not successful in getting the numbers of Lightnings that he required. P–38s dribbled into the Fifth's inventory and many of the missions had to be flown with a mixed gaggle of very tired P–40s and P–39s. The Lightning was very fast, heavily armed and, while not as maneuverable as the Japanese fighters, could still tackle the enemy if they did not attempt to engage in a dogfight at low or medium altitudes. An extra bonus was the two engines which gave pilots an extra chance of survival when operating over the unchartered Pacific. Kenney's demands did produce a limited flow of Lightnings and the second unit to form with the new fighter was the 8th FG with the 49th FG following shortly. However, the fighters were in such short supply that each Fighter Group could only form one Lightning squadron apiece. The Thirteenth Air Force, operating out of the Solomons, also wanted P–38s because of their range and twin engines and the 339th FS, 347th FG was equipped with Lightnings and began operating out of Henderson Field, Guadalcanal, with its first combat occurring on 18 November 1942 when the Lightnings flew a bomber escort mission.

Late 1942 and early 1943 saw the small numbers of Lightnings combined with Bell P–39s, P–400s and Curtiss P–40s and sent out on endless missions to combat the Japanese. Even though the Bells and Curtisses were outmoded they did an excellent job attacking Japanese ground and shipping targets while performing creditably in aerial combat. The P–38s also participated in the ground attack missions and quite often they were called upon for long range escort missions with the Mitchells, Fortresses and Liberators. With the American high command deciding that new fighters must first be supplied to USAAF units

in Britain, the pilots and commanders in the Pacific knew that they had a long, hard war in front of them with only the barest minimum of warplanes to put up against the enemy.

Adversity often breeds success, and the pilots and mechanics of the Fifth and Thirteenth Air Forces literally performed miracles by keeping the Lightnings operational and by beating, over and over, the Japanese – an enemy that probably thought their secure island bases would never be challenged, much less defeated. One of the greatest of all Lightning missions was flown on 18 April 1943 when pilots from the Thirteenth's 18th and 347th FGs literally assassinated one of Japan's greatest commanders.

American cryptographers had scored a major coup when they broke the Japanese secret code which was used to transmit important messages across the Pacific. The code breakers discovered that Admiral Isoroku Yamamoto (one of the main planners of the Pearl Harbor attack) would be flying to Ballale airfield on Shortland Island in a Betty bomber. Several other Bettys would be in the flight, also carrying high-ranking Japanese. The flight would be protected by Zeroes but the Japanese thought that the vast stretches of Pacific airspace would make an American interception of the flight unlikely, which was probably true if the code had not been broken.

With only a short time to prepare, P–38Fs and Gs were equipped for the long range flight and a mix of 165 and 310 US gallon drop tanks were added to the underwing pylons. The pilots were briefed on the mission and its importance – both in propaganda and in the denying to the Japanese one of their greatest military minds. Timing was absolutely essential since range was a prime consideration and a mistake in timing could cause the P–38 flight to miss the enemy formation completely. Sixteen P–38s launched from Henderson Field, Guadalcanal, on the 18 April and headed out

Major Richard Bong, America's ace of aces with forty confirmed victories, stands by P–38J—20–LO 44–233461, one of several Lightnings that he flew in combat. Bong, regarded by the military as a 'boy next door' type (and heavily promoted as such), survived his combat tours without a scratch only to die after returning to Burbank to fly a new P–80 jet fighter. The engine quit shortly after takeoff and crashed into a parking lot on 6 August 1945.

on the 500-mile flight to Shortland Island. The enemy was intercepted on schedule and the P–38s immediately attacked the Betty bombers. The Betty carrying Yamamoto was hit repeatedly by shells from Captain Thomas Lanphier Jr's guns and it rolled over and plummeted into the jungle, killing all aboard. [The wreckage of the Betty was recently discovered, covered by jungle growth, and the special seat in which Yamamoto sat was recovered.] Another Betty and five fighters were dispatched before the Lightnings turned and headed home, leaving the Japanese naval command stunned over their loss.

General Kenney's requests for more Lightnings kept falling on deaf ears. Although the 475th FG was able to equip completely with Lightnings during August 1943, this was not a signal of improved conditions. The 475th was able to keep operational with hard work and creative repair of damaged aircraft since replacement parts and engines were in very short supply. On the debit side, the 35th and 49th FG had to *drop* their only P-38 squadrons because of insufficient numbers and convert to Thunderbolts. The long and costly fight towards the end of 1943 saw heavy casualties for both sides as fierce air battles raged over contested islands. Giant dogfights regularly took place, but, when the final results were analyzed, the Japanese kept coming out on the losing end. The vast loss of aircraft and experienced pilots, many whose service dated back to the Manchurian campaign, was to be an irreplaceable blow to the Empire. The Japanese scheme for training new pilots was not sufficient to supply needs and, rather than

revise and form a more sensible training program, a new training program was instigated that produced hurriedly trained aviators that were not really fit for combat. The Japanese were also having the same problem with their aircraft. The Zero was a superb dogfighter, perhaps the best ever built, but once the Americans learned the rules of the game, the Zero was an easy mark with its fragile construction, lack of armor protection and non-sealing fuel tanks. American pilots, particularly P-38 pilots, began building rapid scores over the enemy.

The American P-38 aces were a mixed bunch, ranging from rather unpleasant career builders to quiet introverts. One of the quieter ones was Daniel T. 'Preacher' Roberts. Roberts had intended to become a minister, hence the nickname, but the coming war convinced him to join the Army and take up flying – winning his wings just a few weeks before Pearl Harbor. Roberts did not drink, did not use profanity and was not a hell-raiser – making him a bit

P-38s were often very colorfully marked as is the case with Pappy's Birr-die, the P-38 flown by Major Pappy Kline shortly after he took over the 431st Fighter Squadron following the death of Tom McGuire. (N. Krane)

different from his fellow fighter pilots. Sent to combat with the 80th FS, 8th FG, Fifth Air Force, Roberts was shipped to Darwin, Australia, to fly P-39s and P-400s and it was in these obsolescent fighters that he gained his first two victories. After the unit had been operating in New Guinea and seeing heavy action, it was pulled back to Australia for re-equipping. Roberts, now a captain, was pleased to see the new fighters were P-38s, and the squadron returned to Port Moresby in March 1943, beginning combat missions soon after.

Roberts found the P-38 to his liking. On one of the first combat patrols, the squadron ran into a huge formation of enemy aircraft, estimated at 20 Val dive bombers and an equal number of escorting Zeros, that was on its way to attack Allied shipping in Oro Bay. The P–38s screamed into the enemy, catching the Japanese by surprise. Roberts sent a burst into a Val and saw pieces of it fly off but he was then attacked by three fighters. Yanking the '38 around, Roberts got beneath one of the Zeros and blew off a wing with a burst of machine gun and cannon fire. The rest of the squadron was doing equally as well and, when the combat ended, eleven Zeros and three Vals had been knocked down – Roberts being credited with two.

When the 475th FG became an all-Lightning unit in May 1943, experienced officers were sought out to join the group. Accordingly, Roberts was transferred to the 475th's 433rd FS in order to instruct younger pilots on the virtues of the P–38. Roberts' talent was sufficiently appreciated that he was made squadron commander on 4 October 1943. His main tactic was to have the squadron stick together and hunt like a wolf pack rather than to rely on individual action.

Roberts' score continued to grow when he destroyed three Zeros over Rabaul on 23 October. The Zeros were attempting to intercept a flight of Liberators that the 433rd was protecting and the resulting battle decimated the determined enemy. The last two months of 1943 merged into a blur of constant missions as the P–38s flew several times a day. The least liked target was Rabaul, very heavily defended by anti-aircraft guns, but it was frequently visited by American bombers that were attempting to knock out the airfields in the area. The P–38s had to fly at reduced speed when protecting the bombers and were quite often subjected to intense flak. One memorable mission on 9 November saw 20 enemy fighters attack Roberts' 433rd Squadron and the group of B–25 Mitchells that they were defending. His P–38s had to stay near the bombers and were subjected to repeated attacks but the P–38s of the 431st and 432nd Squadrons were providing high cover and their diving passes eventually broke the enemy's will, but not before three Lightnings fell in flames. The bombers got through and blasted their targets.

Flying fighter aircraft in the heat of combat calls for immense skill and judgement and the slightest error can be fatal. On 9 November, Roberts' squadron was once again on a bomber escort mission to Rabaul and, once again, were met by a determined enemy. Roberts got a long burst into a Hamp which smashed into the ocean and exploded. By this time the dogfight had descended to virtually sea level and wingtips were almost hitting the water as the fighters maneuvered into firing positions. A single Zero was spotted racing low, heading for its home airfield. Roberts, his wingman and

another Lightning pilot spotted the Zero and took off in pursuit. The Zero pilot saw his pursuers, kicked in right rudder in an attempt to make a very tight turn which the P–38s would not be able to follow. Roberts rolled his Lightning hard right but his wingman, acting a split-second too slowly, smashed into the tail booms of his leader's aircraft. Both fighters exploded and fell into the ocean. Preacher Danny Roberts was dead. He had shot down 15 aircraft and the 433rd, during his 37 days of command, had destroyed 55 Japanese aircraft with a loss of only three Lightnings. His story was not atypical.

The American war machine in the Pacific began to pick up speed and compile victory after victory over what was thought to be an invincible enemy. The American public, most only dimly aware of the exotic battle locales mentioned on the radio news reports, began to idolize the young pilots and their distinctive twin-boomed fighters that would not give way to the enemy. War correspondents did their part, sending long stories back home on how the Lightning pilots were enduring hardship on the ground as well as in the air to defeat the enemy. It was a deadly battleground over the vast jungles or over the brilliant blue Pacific where no quarter was given. Back home, a popular song was written about the P–38 while women wore P–38 silhouettes as jewelry – made out of the new 'miracle' material lucite.

General Kenney's long argument to get more Lightnings to the battlefront was finally paying off and aircraft directly off the production line were shipped to the Pacific. The newer variants of the Lightning were much better suited to Pacific operations and, with their improved range and increased horsepower, began to take an even bigger toll on the Japanese. By the middle of 1944, the Fifth and Thirteenth Air Forces were consolidated into the Far East Air Forces (FEAF) under Kenney's capable command. Kenney was now able to field five P–38 groups (8th, 18th, 49th, 347th and 475th) and among these groups were many aces whose scores were rapidly on the rise. Over 40 pilots were to become aces in the Pacific by flying Lightnings exclusively. In the summer of 1944, the enemy was in retreat – giving up each island in a bloody and costly battle which usually left most of the Japanese defenders dead – and the Lightnings were ranging far and wide on a variety of missions including dive bombing, fighter sweep, escort and recon.

The press had developed a contest between two P–38 pilots, Dick Bong and Tom McGuire, whose scores were rising. In actuality, it *was* a contest since McGuire was determined to become the top scoring American pilot. McGuire, by reports from the people who

served with him, was an unpleasant individual with an immense ego but, at the same time, he was also a very good fighter pilot. Bong, on the other hand, projected an image of the 'All-American Boy'. By late 1943, it was clearly apparent that the race was on. However, when Neel E. Kearby and his 348th FG equipped with Thunderbolts entered the area, it became a three-way race. Kearby, an aggressive commander and pilot, rapidly pushed up his score with the powerful P–47D. On one mission, on 11 October 1943, he blasted seven enemy fighters but was only credited with six because his gun camera ran out of film! Kearby's race was ended on 9 March 1944 when he was shot down and killed. His official score stood at 22.

Using Captain Edward Rickenbacker's WWI score of 28 German aircraft destroyed as a watershed mark, the press gleefully reported on the exploits of the two pilots. Bong, 49th FG, was the first to reach the 'magic' score, but he was soon sent home on leave to give War Bond lectures. Thomas McGuire, 475th FG, took advantage of Bong's leave to raise his score to 28 and was irritated to discover that Bong was to be sent back to the Pacific for a second combat tour. Bong tackled the enemy with his usual skill and daring, running up his score to 40 destroyed by 17 December. Having been awarded the Medal of Honor earlier, Bong returned to the United States a hero and was sent on an extensive press and patriotic tour around the country. McGuire, once again taking advantage of Bong's absence, made a determined effort to raise his score as high as possible but, on 7 January 1945, he committed a basic error that ended the race. McGuire and three other P–38s were dogfighting with a single Japanese fighter when he racked his P–38 in a tight turn, entered a high speed stall and spun into the ocean. McGuire's final score was 38 destroyed and he was awarded a posthumous Medal of Honor. Bong did not enjoy his title for long. During August, he was killed when the new P–80 jet fighter he was flying crashed shortly after take-off from Burbank.

One reason that so many pilots were successful with the P–38 in the Pacific is the fact that the later versions of the fighter were superb fighting machines. The factory had been working constantly on improving the aircraft, and one of the major improvements was the addition of dive brakes which would fight the compressibility problem in a steep dive. The flaps were attached to the main spar outside each engine nacelle. The flaps could be activated instantly via a button on the control wheel, enabling the pilot to recover from a dive bombing run or after building up speed to escape an enemy fighter. A Lightning was fitted with the brakes during February 1943

*The colorful nose art on **Windy City Ruthie** illustrates ten kills along with various crew names. Since the P–38 had so much room for names and personal markings, it was not uncommon for the crew chiefs to decorate the engine nacelles with their own art, leaving the fuselage pod for the pilot.*

and was flown by none other than Colonel Ben Kelsey who felt that the device should immediately be incorporated into the P–38 production line. However, due to politics and other bureaucratic considerations, the dive brake was not incorporated until 14 months later! This damning bit of negligence certainly cost many P–38 pilots their lives while restricting the fighter from becoming a very efficient warplane. The modification was not incorporated until the P–38J–25–LO.

As the island-hopping war drew near to the Home Islands, P–38s were regularly overflying areas such as Formosa and Korea. Bases in the Philippines and Ie Shima provided the staging points needed for the long-legged Lightnings. Saved from a costly final combat by the

dropping of two nuclear bombs on Japan, the Lightning had the honor of being the first Allied fighter to land in Japan after the unconditional surrender of that country on 15 August 1945.

Unfortunately, there was no career for the Lightning after the end of World War Two. Many aircraft were not even brought back to the United States for disposal. Instead, a demolition man would throw a grenade into the cockpit and the mangled fighter would be pushed into a pit by a bulldozer – an inglorious end for the Army fighter that had defeated the Japanese. The military decided to standardize on the P–51 as the main propeller-driven fighter back in the States. Besides, all those new jets were coming into service and the Army did not want 'obsolescent' propeller-driven fighters. The final indignity was that the Army did not even bother to save a Lightning for Hap Arnold's proposed air museum.

Some mention should be made of the brief foreign use of the P–38. During World War

Two, the Lightning was operated by the Free French in some numbers in the *Forces Aeriennes Françaises Libres.* Operating photo recon variants, the French performed useful work in North Africa. One of the most famous French Lightning pilots was the author Commandant Antoine de Saint-Exupery who simply disappeared off southern France on 31 July 1944. The Australians received three F–4s whose entire service life amounted to less than three months. China received an unspecified number of fighter and photo recon Lightnings. Some Lightnings that had force-landed in Portugal during 1942 were retained and operated by the Portuguese Air Force. After the war, Italy received 50 Lightnings to help re-equip its new air force while a handful went to Honduras in Central America. Today, the Lightning is an extremely rare type with only a few in museums. However, about six are still flown by civilian collectors and serve as a reminder of the greatest twin-engine propeller-driven fighter.

BLACK BIRDS

The war ended before the P–38M night-fighter had a chance to prove itself in combat.

The young pilots who reported for duty as night-fighting trainees were more than a bit disappointed when they saw the sort of aircraft that lined the hot ramp at Williams Field in Arizona. It was early 1943 and the hopes of a rapid entry into service by the advanced Northrop P–61 Black Widow were becoming dim because of developmental problems with the big twin-engine fighters. The aircraft which awaited the trainee pilots were a mixed and motley bag of RP–322 Lightnings and Douglass P–70s.

The RP–322 had come about through a strange gestation. The British, during their massive aircraft orders of 1939 and 1940, contracted with Lockheed for 667 P–38 figh-

ters. However, the British apparently wanted to keep the big fighters as simple as possible so they specified in the contract that the counter-rotating propellers and turbosuperchargers (this particular item being in short supply) be removed in the Lightning Mk I. Without this equipment, the twin-tailed fighter was limited to low altitudes and engine-out flight became a real difficulty. After testing the first few of these machines, the British decided to cancel their order and around 138 completed aircraft were transferred to the Army with the designation RP–322.

The Army did not quite know what to do with their new mount so they were assigned as restricted twin-engine trainers and sent to various training fields in the American Southwest. These were the aircraft with which the new pilots were burdened. (The Douglas P–70s are another story and their lack of success is described in a separate chapter.)

In the Army's quest to build an effective night fighter force, most hopes were pinned on the massive Black Widow but, with delayed deliveries, some sort of make-shift night fighter force had to be concocted. These trainee pilots who were gathered at Williams were to become the central core for the 418th and 419th Night Fighter Squadrons but there was a long way to go before they became an effective unit. Training in the RP–322 and P–70 gave valuable twin-engine experience but both aircraft were so slow that they stood little chance of catching the more advanced enemy aircraft. Various tactics were experi-

Posing for the Lockheed photographer during a test flight from the company's Burbank, California, facility is P–38M 44-27234. During test operations in warm Southern California the radar operator must have baked in his tight fitting bubble. All Ms were conversions of P–38L aircraft. Note the unpainted stainless steel panels that surround the turbosuperchargers on top of the twin booms. (Lockheed)

*F*uture P–38 night fighter pilots were horrified to find that part of their training would be undertaken with obsolete and dangerous RP–322 fighters abandoned by the British. Originally designated Lightning Mk Is by the RAF, the British fighters were a far cry from the American operated P–38s. The British wanted nothing to do with contra-rotating propellers and turbosuperchargers – against Lockheed's strenuous advice – and the resulting aircraft was a poor performer with dangerous engine-out flying characteristics. The USAAF assumed the bulk of the order and made the aircraft restricted pursuit trainers with the designation RP–322. The fledgling night fighter trainees flew these machines and equally obsolete P–70s. A well-worn RP–322, still retaining its RAF serial AF101, is seen undergoing engine tests at Newark, New Jersey, on 16 April 1946.

*T*he night fighting P–38Ms certainly had a distinctive look in the air. With their sinister all-black paint scheme, radar nose and antenna for the radar sprouting under the outer wing panels, the P–38M looked every inch the fighter that it was. (Lockheed)

P-38M has the chocks pulled away in preparation for a test flight from the Lockheed plant. Note how the radar operator was able to see over the pilot's head. (Lockheed/AD-6546)

mented with in the clear night skies over Arizona but an effective method of dealing with enemy aircraft at night did not evolve. They key to the whole operation lay with an effective radar system and the speed to intercept and destroy the night intruders.

By the end of their training period as night fighter pilots, the group of students realized that the Black Widow would not be forthcoming and resigned themselves to the fact that they would be going overseas with P-70s. At least the Douglas twin-engine fighters were superior to the RP-322s – but then, just about anything was superior to the RP-322!

The night fighter pilots were sent by ship to Guadalcanal where they arrived near the end of 1943. The 418th Night Fighter Squadron had been activated on 17 March 1943 and its first overseas base was Milne Bay, New Guinea, which was occupied on 2 November 1943. The 418th NFS pilots had high hopes of taking

care of any Japanese night intruders and devised a colorful emblem to be carried by their aircraft. Official records describe the insignia as:

Over and through a blue-green disc, a king bee black and golden orange, wearing a red crown, holding aloft a lighted lantern proper with the right foreleg, and grasping a gray machine gun in the left foreleg, tip-toeing across a white cloud formation in base, and peering over the edge with a look of ferocity on his face; a crescent moon and two stars of yellow in the background.

In operation, the P-70 proved to be a failure in most respects and some of the enemy bombers could actually outrun the modified Douglas light bomber. The 419th NFS arrived at Guadalcanal on 15 November 1943 and immediately began experiencing the same problems as the 418th. Supplies of P-70s were not sufficient to bring the units up to full strength so each squadron was assigned a

small number of P-38H Lightnings which was a great improvement over the RP-322.

With mixed bags of Lightnings and P-70s prowling the skies, pilots began working on tactics to intercept enemy bombers. The P-38s were stock day fighters with absolutely no radar or any other equipment for finding the enemy at night. The Lightning pilots would wait until the enemy aircraft were over target and, hopefully, illuminated by the defender's searchlights. They would then try to pick out the outline of the enemy aircraft and intercept. This was a dangerous method of operation because the P-38 was subjecting itself to anti-aircraft fire from the defenders as well as to being spotted by the bomber's gunners.

419th pilot Lt Donald Dessert checked out in the first P–38H assigned to the unit and flew the first of the searchlight patrols between 1945 and 2145 hrs on 10 December 1943. This patrol did not have any result and other pilots were equally baffled in trying to find the enemy by searchlight. The method had been used in Britain during the early days of World War Two with some success but it was a still far from ideal method. Ground Control Intercept (GCI) radar was installed later to help vector the P–38H pilots towards the enemy but this did little good. A fast, powerfully armed fighter with its own radar was needed and the Black Widow was still months away.

With almost 400 night missions being flown by the end of 1944, the 419th pilots only claimed three enemy aircraft. One pilot, Henry Meigs, nailed two Mitsubishi G4M Betty bombers over Guadalcanal and was awarded the Distinguished Flying Cross by Admiral 'Bull' Halsey who was probably happy to see something finally happening with the night fighter unit.

The American talent for improvising in the face of adversity came to the fore during the quest for an efficient night fighter. Pilots and mechanics of the 6th Fighter Squadron (whose ancestry goes directly back to the 6th Aero Squadron of World War One) fitted out at least two P–38G Lightnings with a second seat and a radar unit mounted in a drop tank. The SCR–540 gave the two man crew the 'night eyes' they needed but the New Guinea detachment of the 6th was disbanded before the ingenious 'Rube Goldberg' invention could be put to combat use. Other modifications by other units were also apparently carried out and the 547th NFS in the Philippines modified at least two single-seat P–38J fighters with APS–4 radar but the results of most of these field modifications are lost to time.

As with most ideas, it seems that the thought of converting the Lightning into a real night fighter came to a number of men at roughly the same time. The Lightning was a good choice for the mission: it had excellent visibility, long range, heavy armament and the added reliability of a second engine. Stateside, at least one P–38J had been reworked to carry AN/APS–4 radar in a large fiber pod. During initial tests, the pod was carried under the rear

The pilot's position in the P–38M was basically the same as on the P–38L. (Lockheed)

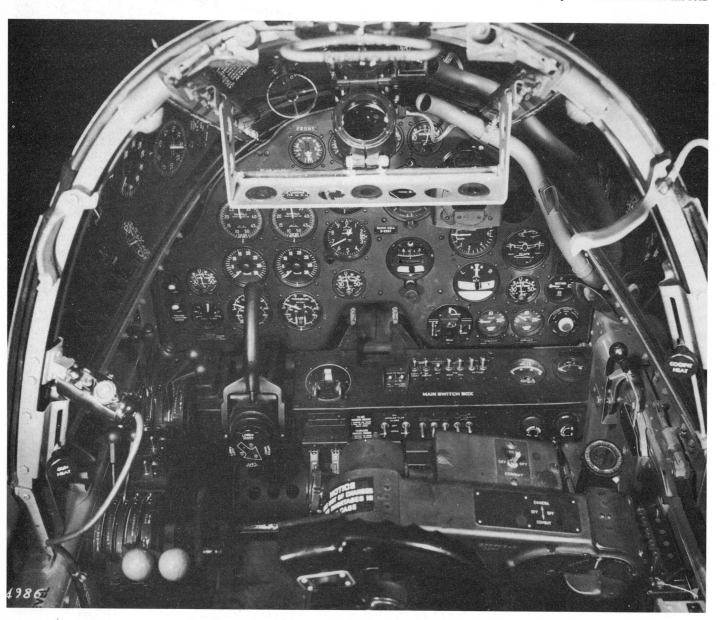

On the P–38M, the scope for the radar unit
projected directly into the R/O's face. If the
war had continued there was some discussion of
using the basic two-seat P–38M concept as a dual
control trainer. Note how the black paint quickly
scuffed and chipped away. (Lockheed/AD–6541)

Working accommodations for the P–38M crew
were far from ideal. R/Os were probably
ideally of small stature for, with a back pack
parachute, the R/O's head was firmly jammed
against the top of the bubble canopy.
(Lockheed/AD–6540)

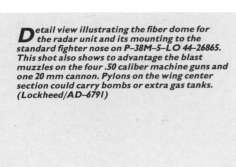

Detail view illustrating the fiber dome for the radar unit and its mounting to the standard fighter nose on P–38M–5–LO 44–26865. This shot also shows to advantage the blast muzzles on the four .50 caliber machine guns and one 20 mm cannon. Pylons on the wing center section could carry bombs or extra gas tanks. (Lockheed/AD–6791)

fuselage but it was quickly damaged by the rain of expended cartridges when the machine guns and cannon were fired. The pod was later moved to an outboard wing panel and the installation worked fairly well. A number of Lightnings had been converted in the field to two-seat configuration. These aircraft were often used as squadron hacks and to give the ground-bound mechanics a taste of what flying was like (or to carry the mechanic after an engine overhaul – a method which was sure to result in excellent workmanship during the engine rebuild). Other two-seat modifications were used to carry high-ranking officers on fast – and heavily escorted – trips over battlefields to see what the situation looked like from the air. The P–38 was fully capable of carrying a second seat but the installation – usually in the space directly behind the pilot – gave little room.

All these factors were eventually combined and, during the last months of 1944, the Army contracted with Lockheed for the conversion of a P–38L into the new role of night fighter. While all this was happening, deliveries of P–61 fighters to combat units had started and the Black Widow, while it had a number of problems, was infinitely better than any other Army attempt at a night fighter. The 418th NFS quickly dumped all but two of their P–38s, but these two aircraft continued night operations and, on 22 February 1944, Lt Dorval Brown made the first nocturnal bombing drop on Rabaul in company with Captain Emerson Baker in the other Lightning. These non-radar P–38s still had no success in tracking enemy fighters but they did participate in night-time harassment missions against the Japanese.

Serial number 44–26865 became the first P–38M (there were no XP or YP M models, the series just assuming immediate production). Modifications included the installation of the radar in a large fiber pod under the foward nose, blast muzzles on the weapons to prevent the pilot's night vision from being ruined and a

After the war, the P–38Ms were quickly disposed of, most having only a few flying hours. P–38M–1–LO 44–53085A, still with factory stencilling applied, is seen 'out to pasture' in company with at least two other Ms. At least one M was supplied to the air force of Honduras but it was probably operated as a day fighter.

second seat for the radar operator behind the pilot. The radar operator (r/o) sat perched higher than the pilot with the viewing port for the radar set projecting directly into his face. To give the r/o some headroom, his position was fitted with a blown bubble canopy but, even so, it was a very tight fit and the r/os would have to be chosen with a regard to their height or lack of it. The first flight for the night fighting Lightning took place on 5 February 1945, by which time the P–61 was firmly established in service and setting an impressive record against rapidly dwindling enemy air forces. The USAAF ordered 75 M models but this seemed almost a token gesture since the war was obviously winding to a conclusion.

Flight testing of the P–38M started in July 1945 at Hammer Field, the large night fighter base just east of Fresno, California. Testing revealed that the M had a better performance envelope than the P–61 but that the P–61 was better suited as a night fighter. Records on the deployment of the P–38M are not entirely clear but it does appear that only four made it to the Philippines before the war ended. However, P–38Ms were stationed in Japan with occupation forces, but the majority of completed aircraft were either scrapped or put for sales as surplus. A couple of P–38Ms appeared at the post-war Cleveland Air Races and at least one was sold to the air force of Honduras as a day fighter. This aircraft survived a long period of service, although gathering only a few hours of flying time, before being returned to America. Today, this P–38M is beautifully restored and displayed at the Champlin Fighter Museum, Mesa, Arizona, as the sole surviving example of the Lightning night fighter.

LIGHTNING ODDITIES

Like any other World War Two production
fighter, the P–38 was subjected to a wide
variety of modifications – some successful,
some not . . .

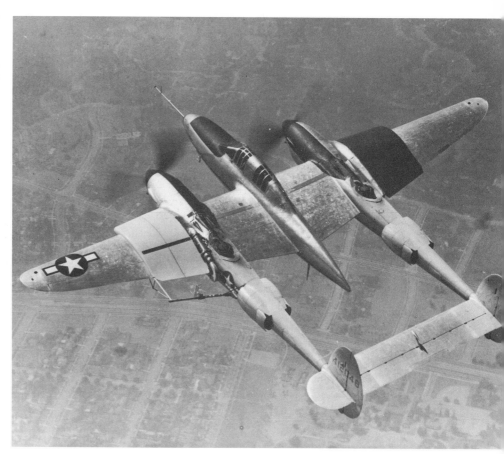

*Certainly one of the worst looking
modifications ever performed on a P–38, this
one-off Lightning was a drastic conversion of P–38E
41–2048 and was used for a wide variety of tests. In
this photograph the aircraft, dubbed 'Swordfish', is
testing airfoils. Note what appears to be a spray
boom behind the airfoil addition on the left and the
extra and complex ducting near the wing root.
Thirty inches were added to the front portion of
the center fuselage pod and forty-eight inches to
the rear, and two cockpits were installed. This
creation first took to the air on 2 June 1943 and
Tony Le Vier found that the aircraft dived at a
faster speed than any other Lightning. The
Swordfish survived the war and was used by
Lockheed to test concepts for other aircraft (as it is
doing in the photograph), but was eventually
surplused and turned up as a civilian aircraft with
at least four seats! The Swordfish finally met its
doom in the early 1960s when it was destroyed in a
crash. (Lockheed)*

*A*ttractively decked out in bare metal finish, a red fuselage stripe, red, white and blue tail stripes, and the name **Piggie Back** on the boom intake, P–38F–1–LO 41–7485 was retained by Lockheed for use as a development airframe. In this role the P–38 was modified to have a second seat directly behind the pilot. From this extremely uncomfortable position, pilot trainees were to be introduced to the wonder of Lightning operations. The use of such a trainer was limited but it would be of value to illustrate some of the P–38's more dangerous flight characteristics such as engine out operation. Flown by famed 1930's record flight pilot Jimmy Mattern, the P–38 was used briefly in this role before the idea was dropped. Note the ADF 'bullet' under the nose. This aircraft did not carry any armament. (Lockheed)

*A*nother bizarre P–38E conversion was this aircraft which featured drastically upswept tail booms in an attempt to cure the early Lightnings' problems of compressibility in a dive. The idea behind the upswept tail was to raise the unit above the disturbed airflow from the wing and thus aid in control during high speed dives. Serial number 41–1986 was flown by Lockheed test pilot Ralph Virden but he was killed when the aircraft failed to pull out of a high speed dive. Engineers eventually found the answer by installing new wing fillets, a modification that would not slow down the production line because of drastic airframe modifications. (Lockheed)

Opposite
One of the many weapon configuration experiments carried out by Lockheed with the Lightning was this modification of a P–38F to carry two torpedoes. Fitted with sway braces, the torpedoes were dropped without any problem but the concept was not put into operation. This aircraft also has its nose armament removed. (Lockheed/Z3561)

Right
Yet another P–38 weapon configuration experiment, the P–38F in the photograph is equipped with four bazooka-style rocket launchers that each carried three 4.5 in rockets. (Lockheed/Z5600)

Opposite below
Well-worn RP–38 40–744 Jollie was subject of an interesting modification. Army scientists were studying the effects on the human body of flying in a different position other than the center line of the aircraft. The Germans were also experimenting with this concept and the Army found that the easiest test bed for conversion was, of course, the P–38 with its twin booms. 744 was accordingly modified to carry an extra cockpit in the left boom in place of the turbosupercharger and testing was carried out at Wright AAFB in Ohio. (Lockheed/F1361)

Certainly the most colorful Lightning ever built, P–38J–20–LO 44–23296 was painted a glorious bright red overall with the name Yippee painted on the nose and under the wing in white with a black outline. The unusual paint scheme was applied to celebrate the 5,000th Lightning built. The aircraft was used for publicity and war bond drives before going into regular military service. (Lockheed/T9813)

Among the armament experiments with the Lightning was this P–38L–1–LO with 14 rockets mounted on zero length launchers under the wing. Rocket mounting was eventually standardized on the 'Christmas Tree' arrangement that had the rockets mounted in clusters of five. (Lockheed/S5858)

One of the more interesting modifications to be forced on the P–38 airframe was the addition of tow harnesses to the rear of the tail booms that enabled the Lightning to test its capabilities in hauling Waco CG–4A combat gliders. Seen during an initial test, the P–38 is still on the ground as the CG–4 begins to rise in the air. Plans were under way to enable the P–38 to carry as many as three CG–4s into combat but the idea was dropped when the decision was made to delegate the transport of gliders to cargo aircraft such as the C–46 and C–47. (Lockheed)

S- 5858

'*Droop Snoot*' *Lightnings (about 25 had been so modified) were replaced by the more sophisticated P–38L Pathfinder aircraft. The Pathfinder had a greatly extended nose that carried AN/APS–15 radar (Bomb Through Overcast) which was called 'Mickey'. The operator sat behind the radar and had two windows from which he could contemplate the outside world. This prototype aircraft was photographed at Lockheed on 6 June 1944 and the XP–58 can be seen parked in the background. (Lockheed/S527)*

PHOTO FIGHTERS

Although totally unarmed, these Lightnings made an invaluable contribution to the war effort by being able to photograph enemy territory in considerable detail.

An F–5B–1–LO 42–67332, is seen in company with P–38J–5–LO 42–67183 during a photo flight over the San Gabriel Mountains near the Lockheed plant in Burbank, California. The F–5B–1–LO was the reconnaissance version of the P–38J–10–LO and 200 were built, four being transferred to the Navy as FO–1s. Most of the early photographic Lightnings were painted in a strange color scheme with what was known as Haze Paint. The original Haze Paint was found to actually make the aircraft more visible at altitude so there was a fairly rapid shuffle to find a replacement. Sherwin-Williams Paint Company and Army officials came up with what was known as 'Synthetic Haze Paint'. This color scheme consisted of Sky Base Blue and a synthetic haze enamel called Flight Blue. The Lightning test aircraft was painted overall Sky Base Blue and then Flight Blue was sprayed over the shadow areas of the aircraft and in light coats on the side of the fuselage pod and booms. The new combination seemed to work fairly well and was adopted by March 1943 as the official paint scheme for the F–5s coming off the Lockheed line. However, the interpretation of this scheme was open to question and, depending if the aircraft was painted at the factory or in the field or modification depot, there was a wide difference of application style. The F–5B in the photograph also carries the short-lived red surround to the national insignia. (Lockheed)

From D–Day minus seven until D–Day plus fourteen, F–5s took 3,000,000 aerial photographs of the Normandy coast and General Eisenhower credited the F–5s with furnishing him with the most valuable information on invasion progress during the period. General Hap Arnold once commented: 'Our photo-reconnaissance pilots are instructed to fly on the theory that fighter planes win battles while camera planes win wars.' The warmly dressed pilot of this Lockheed F–5A watches while camera gear is installed in the spacious nose compartment that held guns and ammunition for the P–38s. This particular Lightning is painted with Haze Paint. The original application of Haze Paint was a bit complex: the Lightning was supposed to be painted overall black, a thin coat of haze being applied over the top of the aircraft and down the sides which resulted in a very dark blue color. Heavy haze was then sprayed on the undersurfaces and the remainder of the aircraft, producing a very light blue color. The point between the heavy and light coats of haze was sprayed with a medium coat of the paint and the resulting color was a sort of a medium blue. Needless to say, this process was time consuming and it took a full working day just to let the paint dry and extreme quality control and good lighting were necessary to have the paint applied according to specification. The finish itself quickly changed color and weathered in the sun and, as previously mentioned, the Haze Paint became very visible above 20,000 ft when, due to changes in lighting, the colors intensified. During October 1942, Lockheed was told to drop the Haze Paint and replace the color scheme with the ordinary Olive Drab/ Neutral Gray scheme. However, the Army was still not convinced that Haze Paint was all that bad – anything that gave the unarmed photo planes an extra chance of survival was seriously considered – and development proceeded to Synthetic Haze Paint. (H. W. Kulick)

Opposite
Since many of the photo Lightnings were painted at British depots where they were prepared for service with combat units, it was not uncommon that some of the aircraft were finished with the paints that were at hand. This F–5B appears to be finished in an overall single color, the most likely shade being British Photo Reconnaissance (PRU) Blue. (Lockheed)

Right
F–5A–10–LO 42–13291 during a test flight from the Burbank factory. The color scheme on this aircraft is extremely dark, indicating that the aircraft was finished in an overall dark blue color or, perhaps, the black base coat prior to the application of Haze Paint. The F–5A was the reconnaissance version of the P–38G and 181 aircraft were built. (Lockheed)

Very well-worn F–4A (based on the P–38F) shows off its Haze Paint to good avantage. The theory behind the haze scheme was that the application of colors would 'break up' the lines of the Lightning and cause the reconnaissance aircraft to blend with the sky. Lockheed records indicated that all twenty F–4As built were painted in the haze scheme before they left the factory. Primitive field conditions and extreme weather quickly took a toll on the carefully applied paint. This aircraft carries the yellow surround to the national insignia and the wheel covers have been given an individual touch by being painted white with a red star. The use of the yellow surround on the insignia was a common practice in the 12th Air Force during 1942 as an identification feature.

An F–5B beats up its British base prior to landing. A large nude has been added to the side of the fuselage pod. This aircraft appears to be painted RAF Photo Reconnaissance (PRU) Blue rather than in a Synthetic Haze camouflage. The high altitude capabilities of the Lightning helped the unarmed aircraft evade enemy fighters. (USAF/52750)

Opposite above

F–5E–2–LO 44–23226A seen on 7 November 1944 at the large aircraft ferrying depot in Newark, New Jersey. A total of 705 P–38J and P–38L fighters were converted to F–5E configuration. Note the patches over the gun ports and the bulged camera window located in the access hatch. One hundred P–38J–15–LO fighters were built into F–5E–2–LOs. As the war progressed, F–5s were delivered from the factory in bare metal finish and they were painted, if at all, at the base air depots prior to being delivered to combat units. The '172' stencilled on the nose and tail is the last three digits of the construction number.

Opposite below

A dramatic view showing off the graceful lines of the photo Lightning to excellent advantage. The Lockheed F–5 featured an extended and rounded nose that could house a variety of cameras. Ports for the cameras can be seen in the most forward portion of the nose cone and under the nose, directly in front of the nose gear door. The ADF loop can be seen to the rear of the underside of the fuselage pod, in front of the three standard identification lights. The two stub pylons under the wing center section could carry droppable fuel tanks and the extension on the left stub housed a gun camera (presumably eliminated on the reconnaissance versions). (Lockheed)

The F–5G's extended nose gave the aircraft a rather awkward look while on the ground. F–5G–6–LO 44–26592A was converted from a P–38L–5–LO and the long nose carried several cameras in a variety of locations. 6592A is seen at Newark, New Jersey, on 10 July 1945.

LOCKHEED P–38 LIGHTNING VARIANTS, SERIAL NUMBERS AND SPECIFICATIONS

P–38 Variants

XP–38 A highly advanced long-range fighter with two Allison V–12 engines, propellers rotating towards fuselage pod and with provision for four .50 caliber guns and one 23 mm weapon in the nose, but these were not installed. The aircraft quickly set records when first flown during January 1939 but the single prototype was destroyed in a crash on 11 February. Highly-polished metal finish. Lockheed Model number 022–64–01.

YP–38–LO Thirteen pre-production service test examples (Lockheed Model 122–62–02). Most were delivered in natural metal and sprayed aluminum finish. The Allison engines were equipped with outward rotating propellers. Armament consisted of two .50 caliber, two .30 caliber and one 37 mm weapons.

P–38–LO The first production version (222–62–02), with 30 built. Limited armor protection and four .50 caliber guns and one 37 mm cannon. Most, if not all were delivered in Olive Drab and Neutral Gray camouflage. Most were used for training.

XP–38A–LO Experimental conversion of P–38–LO 40–762 to test a pressurized cockpit (622–62–10).

P–38D–LO Model 222–62–08. Basically the same as P–38–LO but with more military equipment added including self-sealing tanks and extra armor. Flares were also added along with a low-pressure oxygen system. Thirty-six were built, all delivered in Olive Drab and Neutral Gray finish.

P–38E–LO Basically the same as the P–38D but the hydraulic system had been reworked. The 37 mm cannon was replaced with a more reliable 20 mm Hispano weapon. Some aircraft had Curtiss Electric propellers and most had the SCR274N radio. A total of 210 was built, some converted as F–4–1–LO.

P–38F–LO Lockheed Model 222–60–09. Variants of the F received new model numbers: the F–1 became Model 222–60–15, F–5 Model 222–60–12; other models became 322–60–19. It had pylons inboard of the engines for the carriage of 2,000 lb of bombs or external fuel tanks. The F–15 saw the introduction of a modified Fowler flap.

P–38G–LO Basically the same as the F except for new engines (V–1710–51/55) and revised internal radio gear. The G received Lockheed Model number 222–68–12. (G–13 and G–15 were Model 322–68–19; these machines were RAF Lightning Mk IIs that were not delivered).

P–38H–LO Lockheed Model 422–81–20. Powered by two Allison V–1710–89/91 engines equipped with automatic oil radiator gills for improved cooling. The underwing carriage of weapons or fuel was increased to 3,200 lb. 601 built and 128 were finished or converted as photo recon F–5C–LO.

P–38J–LO Model 422–81–14 covered the J–1 and J–5; 422–81–22, the J–10; 522–81–22, the J–15 and 20; and 522–87–23, the J–25. The J introduced the most distinctive physical change in the Lightning series, the large chin radiators for improved cooling. All J variants, except the J–1, had more fuel capacity. With the J–10, a flat, optically perfect bullet-proof windshield was finally introduced. The J–25 had the new dive brakes and power assisted ailerons. The majority of these aircraft were delivered in natural metal finish. A total of 2,970 was built, including F–5E/F–5F photo recon variants.

F–38K–LO One aircraft only, Model 422–85–22. Basically the same as the P–38J, but the Allison V–1710–75/77 engines were equipped with paddle-blade propellers. The earlier XP–38K–LO was a P–38E conversion.

P–38L–LO/VN Model 422–87–23. Basically the same as the P–38J but with V–1710–111/113 engines, and the landing light now in port wing. 3,810 J–LOs were built, and 113 L–VNs were constructed at the Vultee plant. Connections for ten 5 in rockets under the wing.

P–38M–LO The Model 522–87–23 was a conversion of the basic P–38L airframe into a two-seat night fighter (75 built), with radar mounted under nose in pod. Solid black finish.

Other Variants

XFO–1 Five F–5B–LOs assigned to the US Navy in North Africa and given Bureau Numbers 01209 through 01212.

F–4–1–LO An unarmed photo recon version of the P–38E, equipped with K17 cameras and autopilot. F–4–1–LO, Model 222–62–13, numbered ninety-nine aircraft with serials 41–2098/2099. 2121–2156, 2158/2171, 2173/2218, 2220. The F–4A–1–LO used the P–38F as the basic airframe and twenty were built (41–2362/2381). Most were delivered in special blue/gray 'haze' camouflage.

F–5–A F–5A–LO was a version of the P–38G modified for photo recon (Model 222–68–16, s/n 42–12667/12686. F–5A was Model 222–62–16 (s/n 41–2157); F–5A–3 Model 222–68–16 (s/n 42–12767/12789); F–5A–10 was Model 222–68–16 (s/n 42–12967/12986, 42–13067/13126, 42–13267/13326). Most were delivered in 'haze' camouflage schemes.

F–5B Adaptation of P–38J–10–LO airframe to photo recon standards. Designated Model 422–81–21, 200 were built (s/n 42–76312/67401, 42–68192/68301).

F–5C Model 222–68–16, a modification of the P–38H to a photo recon aircraft with 123 built.

XF–5D Model 222–68–16. A rebuild of the F–5A–10–LO, modified with a plexiglass nose cone and prone observer's position. Two .50 caliber guns and a vertical camera were fitted.

F5E A photo recon modification of the P–38J. F–5E–2–LO was Model 422–81–22 (P–38J–15–LO) with 100 built; F–5E–3–LO Model 522–87–23 was a conversion of 105 J–25–LO airframes; F–5E–4–LO Model 422–87–23 was a conversion of 500 L–1–LO fighters.

F–5F–3–LO Model 422–87–23 recon modification of the P–38L–5–LO.

F–5G–6–LO Model 422–87–23. Basically the same as the F–5F–3–LO but different cameras.

Model 322 Lightning for the RAF. 243 Mk Is were ordered (AE978/999, AF100/220), but just one was delivered, the rest being taken over by the USAAF as P–322 and flown in a training role. An order for 524 Mk IIs was cancelled. The Mk IIs had serials AF221/744 assigned.

Serial Numbers

XP–38–LO	37–457
YP–38–LO	39–689 through 39–701
P–38–LO	40–744 through 40–773
XP–38A–LO	40–762
P–38D–LO	40–774 through 40–809
P–38E–LO	41–1983 through 41–2097, 41–2100 through 41–2120; 41–2172; 41–2219; 41–2221 through 41–2292
P–38F–LO	41–2293 through 41–2321
P–38F–1–LO	41–2322
P–38F–LO	41–2323 through 41–2358
P–38F–1–LO	41–2359 through 41–2361
P–38F–LO	41–2382 through 41–2386
P–38F–1–LO	41–2387
P–38F–LO	41–2388 through 41–2392
P–38F–1–LO	41–7484 through 41–7485
P–38F–LO	41–7486 through 41–7496
P–38F–1–LO	41–7497
P–38F–LO	41–7498 through 41–7513
P–38F–1–LO	41–7514 through 41–7515
P–38F–LO	41–7516 through 41–7524
P–38F–1–LO	41–7525
P–38F–LO	41–7526 through 41–7530
P–38F–1–LO	41–7531
P–38F–LO	41–7532 through 41–7534
P–38F–1–LO	41–7535
P–38F–LO	41–7536 through 41–7538
P–38F–1–LO	41–7539 through 7541
P–38F–LO	41–7542 through 41–7543
P–38F–1–LO	41–7544
P–38F–LO	41–7545 through 41–7547
P–38F–1–LO	41–7548 through 41–7550
P–38F–LO	41–7551
P–38F–1–LO	41–7552 through 41–7680
P–38F–5–LO	42–12567 through 42–12666
P–38F–13–LO	43–2035 through 43–2063
P–38F–15–LO	43–2064 through 43–2184
P–38G–1–LO	42–12687 through 42–12766
P–38G–3–LO	42–12787 through 42–12798
P–38G–5–LO	42–12799 through 42–12866
P–38G–10–LO	42–12870 through 42–12966; 42–12987 through 42–13066; 42–13127 through 42–13266; 42–13327 through 42–13557
P–38G–13–LO	43–2185 through 43–2358
P–38G–15–LO	43–2359 through 43–2558
P–38H–1–LO	42–13559; 42–66502 through 42–66726
P–38H–5–LO	42–66727 through 42–67101
P–38J–1–LO	42–12867 through 42–12869; 42–13560 through 42–13566
P–38J–5–LO	42–67102 through 42–67311
P–38J–10–LO	42–67402 through 42–68191

P–38J–15–LO	42–103979 through 42–104428; 43–28248 through 44–29047; 44–23059 through 44–23208
P–38J–20–LO	44–23209 through 44–23558
P–38J–25–LO	44–23559 through 44–23768
XP–38K–LO	41–1983
P–38K–1–LO	42–13558
P–38L–1–LO	44–23769 through 44–25058
P–38L–5–LO	44–25059 through 44–27258; 44–53008 through 44–53327
P–38L–5–VN	43–50226 through 43–30338
P–38M–LO	44–25237 (converted from P–38L–5–LO for prototype; other serials random)

Specifications

XP–38

Span	52 ft
Length	37 ft 10 in
Height	12 ft 10 in
Wing area	327.5 sq ft
Empty weight	11,507 lb
Loaded weight	15,416 lb
Max. speed	413 mph
Cruise speed	n/a
Ceiling	38,000 ft
Rate of climb	20,000 ft in 6.5 min
Range	n/a
Powerplant	Two Allison V–1710–11 of 1,150 hp each

YP–38

Span	52 ft
Length	37 ft 10 in
Height	9 ft 10 in
Wing area	327.5 sq ft
Empty weight	11,171 lb
Loaded weight	14,348 lb
Max. speed	405 mph
Cruise speed	330 mph
Ceiling	38,000 ft
Rate of climb	3,330 fpm
Range	650 miles
Powerplant	Two Allison V–1710–27/29 of 1,150 hp each

P–38

Overall dimensions	as YP–38
Empty weight	11,670 lb
Loaded weight	15,340 lb
Max. speed	390 mph
Cruise speed	310 mph
Ceiling	n/a
Rate of climb	3,200 fpm
Range	825 to 1,500 miles
Powerplant	Two Allison V–1710–27/29 of 1,150 hp each

P–38D

Overall dimensions	as YP–38
Empty weight	11,780 lb
Loaded weight	15,500 lb
Max. speed	390 mph
Cruise speed	300 mph
Ceiling	39,000 ft
Rate of Climb	20,000 ft in 8 min
Range	400 to 975 miles
Powerplant	Two Allison V–1710–27/29 of 1,150 hp each

P–38E

Overall dimensions	as YP–38
Empty weight	11,880 lb
Loaded weight	15,482 lb
Max. speed	395 mph
Cruise speed	n/a
Rate of climb	n/a
Range	500 miles
Powerplant	Two Allison V–1710–27/29 of 1,150 hp each

P–38F

Overall dimensions	as YP–38
Empty weight	12,265 lb
Loaded weight	18,000 lb
Max. speed	395 mph
Cruise speed	305 mph
Rate of climb	20,000 ft in 8.8 min
Range	350 to 1,900 miles
Powerplant	Two Allison V–1710–49/53 of 1,325 hp each

P–38G

Overall dimensions	as YP–38
Empty weight	12,200 lb
Loaded weight	19,800 lb
Max. speed	400 mph
Cruise speed	340 mph
Rate of climb	20,000 ft in 8.5 min
Range	275 to 2,400 miles
Powerplant	Two Allison V–1710–51/55 of 1,325 hp each

P–38H

Overall dimensions	as YP–38
Empty weight	12,380 lb
Loaded weight	20,300 lb
Max. speed	402 mph
Cruise speed	300 mph
Rate of climb	2,600 fpm
Range	300 to 2,400 miles
Powerplant	Two Allison V–1710–89/91 of 1,425 hp each

P–38J

Overall dimensions	as YP–38
Empty weight	12,780 lb
Loaded weight	21,600 lb
Max. speed	414 mph
Cruise speed	290 mph
Rate of climb	20,000 ft in 7 min
Range	450 to 2,600 miles
Powerplant	Two Allison V–1710–89/91 of 1,425 hp each

P–38L

Overall dimensions	as YP–38
Empty weight	12,800 lb
Loaded weight	21,600 lb
Max. speed	414 mph
Cruise speed	n/a
Rate of Climb	20,000 ft in 7 min
Range	450 to 2,625 miles
Powerplant	Two Allison V–1710–111/173 of 1,425 hp each

Bell P-39 Airacobra — The Art Deco Failure

The Bell Airacobra did not live up to its initial concept as a fast-climbing interceptor, but distinguished itself in the low-level ground support role.

If life were more simple and only one word could be used to describe the design trend of an entire decade, then the word *streamline* could be used to cover the ten years of the 1930s. The 1920s are fondly remembered as the 'Roaring Twenties'; a term that came about by the rebelling of the younger generation away from the horrors of the First World War and towards a new openness and frankness that was working its way on what had been a staid and upright society. The 1920s were a period of wild pranks, stunts, and fun. The bubbling gaiety of the period collapsed with the spectre of world-wide Depression which covered the globe during the last two years of the decade. A gray drabness encircled America and the European nations while food and steady employment became the paramount objective in nearly every mind.

The 1930s began with the Depression but slowly began to work their way towards a different view on the world. The non-stop quest of entertainment and thrills of the Roaring Twenties was gone and, in its place, was a concerted effort toward goals. Many of these goals were involved with the new technologies that had sprung up with the century: the automobile, the high-speed train and, perhaps most importantly, the aircraft.

National pride began to manifest itself in record setting events; the longest distance covered, the fastest speed, the most people carried. Perhaps it was the concept of speed that most captured the mind of the general public during the 1930s. Speed, once a limited commodity reserved just for the very rich, had become a national stimulant which made the middle-class realize that perhaps, just perhaps, the magic carpet of world travel was unfolding each time the daily newspaper was opened and the news of yet another daring speed or distance record leapt off the pages.

The clumsy wire-braced cloth and wood biplanes that had characterized the early days of aviation quickly fell by the side of the runway as manufacturers began to build aircraft which could cash in on the sudden mania for high speed. The concept and execution of aeronautical design was still suffering birth pangs as engineers sat down at their drafting boards and began to puzzle over the many ingredients needed in the elusive search for speed. The engineers realized that the most essential item would be a slick, smooth airframe that could pass through the air with the least amount of resistance or drag. The design of such a clean airframe presented problems with structural strength. Before speed became a paramount consideration aircraft had been built a bit like sea-going sailing ships. Strength was built in with judicious use of plenty of wood, metal fittings, nails, and miles of bracing wire. This combination of materials was just not conducive to the slim shape that was needed to smoothly penetrate the ocean of air.

One of the first service test YP–39s seen during a test flight from the Bell factory. The highly-polished natural metal aircraft shows the streamlined concept so popular with designers of the 1930s. This particular aircraft has no armament. (Bell)

While being drag inducing, the wire braced structures were also strong and aeronautical companies had a devil of a time combining the needed strength with the required streamlining. Many early attempts ended in disaster, often with fatal results, as new designs suddenly converted themselves to junk when a wing or tail surface failed under pressure of the high speed that was being sought.

In the aeronautical industry lessons were quickly learned since mistakes, as well as being fatal, could put fledgling companies out of business overnight. The lust for speed began to work, and as the miles per hour edged up the scale, the public's imagination was hooked. Records began to tumble. Wiley Post, a black patch over one eye, flew the beautiful Lockheed Vega *Winnie Mae* around the world in seven days, 18 hours and 49 minutes during July 1933. The sleek Vega and its colorful pilot were overnight heroes and the tempo of the worship of speed increased at a fever pitch. Pilots transversed the globe in new creations, each hoping to cut hours off the previous record. Flashing propellers carved the skies as a variety of innovative aircraft and daring pilots, many of them female, quested for fame and money. The names of the aircraft and pilots became household words even though most people did not understand the technical workings behind these feats; they could, however, feel the heady rush of speed as the skies were split asunder by the roar of aero engines.

The feeling of speed and the allure of streamlining began to make itself felt in the everyday, non-technical, world. Designs for the home began to take on a sleek, smooth look. The lines of automobiles began to look less boxy and more "aeronautical", a term that the auto

Bell's first and only aircraft before the Airacobra was the FM–I Airacuda. Certainly one of the most radical American aircraft of the time, the XFM–I first flew on I September 1937 and was intended as a bomber destroyer. The five-man crew had a heavy armament at their disposal including the unique installation of a gunner and a 37 mm cannon in the front of each nacelle which housed a pusher Allison engine. Problems with weight and performance eventually killed the Airacuda concept but it did establish Bell as a manufacturer with different ideas. (Bell)

manufacturers were only too quick to promote. The streamline look touched virtually every facet of 1930s life: passenger trains became streamliners, ocean-going vessels stressed their elegant and fast service; the young air transport industry began to cater for passengers by building aircraft that could reach their destinations almost as quickly as the record setting aircraft. The quest for the ideal form of the fleet-footed god Mercury even took on its own names, 'Art Deco' and 'Modernism' were the terms most heard. They referred to the sleek, modern art forms that were being experimented with in everything from building design to everyday furniture. It was truly a period of daring experimentation with line and shape.

This almost fun-filled quest for speed was not lost on the military minds of the major powers. They viewed the search for speed and great

load carrying ability with something less than the joy of a headline seeker. Germany had taken the genius of their aeronautical designers to heart and given them free rein with the development of their 'airliners' and 'mail planes'. The Germans were prevented from designing and building military aircraft and the modern designs from Junkers, Heinkel, and Dornier captured speed and load records as they zipped between European capitals in the service of the national airline, *Lufthansa*. It seems as if the aeronautical press of the period, perhaps caught up in the euphoria of record-setting, failed to notice that the German designs, while beautifully efficient, really did not seem to be ideally suited to carrying passengers. Did the available room inside the rounded fuselages not seem more likely as a home for high-explosive bombs rather than fare-paying passengers? The questions were on the minds of a few, but their warning voices were lost in the rush of progress and Adolph Hitler quietly went about building his secret *Luftwaffe* while his *Lufthansa* 'airliners' mapped out Europe and proved that certain loads, not necessarily passengers, could be quickly transported over major European airfields, harbors, and cities.

In America and Britain, bomber design had lagged far behind the creative efforts of the Germans. Many of the bombing aircraft still bore a great deal of resemblance to their World War One ancestors. During the early and

middle 1930s, the bi-winged, wire-braced bomber with limited range, limited bomb load, and limited defensive abilities was the order of the day. The role of the bomber was an offensive tool that was to be used to hammer an enemy's strategic targets into rubble. The idea of wanton bombing of civilians and cities had not really been voiced. Some American and British designers saw the streamlined shapes of the German aircraft as the way of the future and realized that the biplane bomber was just as outmoded as the sailing ship. Unfortunately, money for defense orders was in short supply but firms such as Boeing, Martin, and Douglas were able to carry on creative aeronautical design work with a limited amount of money allotted by the government. Aircraft orders of the day were considered good if the requested aircraft numbered in the dozens.

America also maintained a rather outdated concept with their fighter (then called 'pursuit') aircraft forces. Once again, military thinking had proven to be stuck in the mud as the accepted doctrine of the day was the 'ascendancy' of the bombardment forces over the pursuit forces. The reason for this doctrine was perhaps explained by the curious American policy of isolationism. Americans realized that their country was large and new and that potential enemies were far removed; certainly Mexico and Canada were not threats in the twentieth century although this had not proven true during the early days of the nation. Coupled with this realization of being separated from potential enemies by vast areas of ocean was the feeling that the activities of Europe and Asia were so foreign as not to be related in any way to the American style of life. The vast number of European immigrants that had flooded into the country were viewed with a hostile suspicion by 'native' Americans; a feeling which was not alleviated by the fact that the immigrants usually grouped together by ethnic or religious ties in ghetto communities, allowing for little outside contact. The Depression put so many pressures upon the average working man and his family that very little thought was given to the outside world while the system of news communication to the general public left a lot to be desired. Only the movies and the daring exploits of aviation's record seekers seemed to offer any escape from the harsh realities of daily life.

The pioneer of the American concept of strategic bombing, General Billy Mitchell, had been discredited and court marshalled for his radical views during the 1920s. He must have been a bit rueful as he saw the growing importance with which the American military held the bombing aircraft. It was true that the American bombing aircraft of the early 1930s were primitive but the policy of placing importance on strategic bombing aircraft would eventually lead to such great combat aircraft as the Boeing Flying Fortress and the Consolidated B–24 Liberator. However, it was the fighter aircraft that was to really suffer from this policy. The most modern pursuit aircraft that the United States Army Air Corps could field during the early 1930s was the Boeing P–26 Peashooter. This curious looking little design was the first monoplane pursuit to enter service with the American military. Although being modern in having one wing instead of two, the aircraft was primitive in the fact that it had an open cockpit, large spatted drag-producing fixed landing gear, wire-braced wings, and an armament of two rifle caliber machine guns which dated back to World War One. The Peashooter would probably have made a fine sport plane for the wealthy pilot but it was not a true fighter or even a pursuit because many of the foreign bombers that it would have to fight if a war broke out during the mid-1930s had a higher top speed!

During the middle of the decade it was becoming increasingly obvious to those concerned with foreign affairs that trouble was rapidly developing in Europe and the areas of Asia which could be affected by the aggressive new policies of Japan. Military planners were suddenly aware that American defensive and offensive aircraft were woefully outdated and something had to be done to strengthen the Air Corps' striking power. As the decade drew to a close plans were underway which would develop the specifications for a whole new generation of American fighters but these aircraft were still far from the production lines. American aeronautical companies were seeking new designs which would combine the speed and power that had represented many American record flights. New innovations were needed, and needed quickly, and few companies realized the fact more than the Bell Aircraft Corporation and its president, Lawrence D. Bell.

Larry Bell was the model of an American

A turbosupercharged Allison V–1710–17 that developed 1,150 hp powered the XP–39. Weighing in at only 5,500 lb loaded, the XP–39's performance was sparkling. However, Army muddling caused the performance to rapidly drop off when it was decided to order the P–39 without the turbosupercharger and to change the role of the fighter from fast-climbing interceptor to ground support. Note the higher canopy and small fin which were dropped on other versions. Intakes on the fuselage were neatly faired. The aircraft was photographed at Wright Field, Ohio, during February 1939. (USAF)

Opposite
X P–39 after modification to X P–39B configuration. The aircraft was fitted with the lower canopy line, carburetor intake behind the canopy, and intakes in the wing root. Aircraft was highly polished natural metal when it was photographed on 20 November 1939. (USAF/19661)

The YP–39s were not equipped with the turbosupercharged Allisons and performance fell off. However, the aircraft were highly polished and did not carry full military equipment so the performance was still better than the actual combat equipped versions that followed. (Bell)

capitalist who employed his industrious mind to establishing his own corporation and making a profit, hopefully in the shortest time possible. Bell had served as a vice-president with Consolidated Aircraft before that company had decided to pull up roots at its Buffalo, New York, factory and move to sunnier climes in San Diego, California. Bell, apparently liking what New York had to offer, decided to resign and set up his own company in Buffalo. The parting was friendly and the first contract obtained by the new Bell plant was from Consolidated for the manufacture of the retractable wing tip floats for that company's famous PBY Catalina. Bell knew that expansion and large profits could not be realized from sub-contract work and his small staff of 50 employees. Accordingly, Bell decided to under-

take a radical aeronautical project to develop a heavily-armed fighter which would be a completely new concept for Air Corps planners.

Larry Bell and his chief designer, Robert J. Woods, came up with an aircraft that was so startlingly different that even today's aeronautical buffs are puzzled how a new company could have manufactured such an unusual creature. The aircraft was the XFM–1 Airacuda and it embodied a twin-engine pusher configuration with a gunner operating the heavy armament of a single 37 mm cannon in each nacelle! The Airacuda first got into the air on 1 September 1937, and its gleaming polished aluminum airframe appeared to have jumped directly out of one of the countless pulp adventure magazines of the period. It was powered by two turbosupercharged Allison V–1710–13 engines. Their lengthened nacelles overlapped the leading edge of the wing and were equipped with a streamlined canopy and cabin in which a single gunner was installed. These unfortunate individuals were left on their own with the massive 37 mm cannon. The rest of the crew was ensconced under a large green house in the nose of the fuselage while a rear gunner operated a .50 caliber machine gun that was mounted in a large blister, one on each side of the fuselage.

The unusual creation probably had Air Corps officials more boggled than anything

else but the military decided to order, a preproduction batch that would be designated YFM–1. With the turbosuperchargers Bell figured that the YFM–1 could top 300 mph at 20,000 ft. However, in a burst of stupidity that seemed rampant at the time, the Air Corps substituted the turbosupercharged engines with altitude-rated Allisons that limited top speed to 270 mph and dropped the effective ceiling to 12,600 ft. One of the reasons given for the dumping of the turbosupercharger concept was the fact that a turbo had exploded on the YFM–1's first test flight on 28 September 1939. The YFM–1 featured a number of modifications including the placement of the radiator openings in the wings rather than on the top of the nacelle as on the XFM–1. The offensive armament was improved with a .30 caliber Browning being added to each nacelle while the rear defensive position was strengthened with the addition of two .30 caliber guns. The rather bulbous blisters were replaced with a retractable top turret that housed a single .50 caliber while a sliding hatch on the belly revealed another .50. The two .30s were fired

B ell's XFL–1 was an attempt to sell the P–39 design to the Navy as a carrier fighter. Flying for the first time on 13 May 1940, the XFL–1 was powered by an Allison V–1710–6 and was fitted with conventional landing gear. However, only one example was built. (Bell)

Airacobra Mk I AH621 is seen during flight test trials in North America. Aircraft has various non-standard modifications including 12 exhaust ports with a bulged fairing and modified fin and rudder. RAF pilots and groundcrews both loathed the aircraft. (Bell)

from side windows. Underwing racks could even accommodate a load of small bombs that could have been dropped on enemy bomber formations or on ground installations. The FM–1 was a very interesting concept and one of the most heavily armed fighters ever built but the engine substitution had doomed the project to slower speeds at lower altitudes where many bombers could have outrun the fighter or simply flown above it. Nine of the YFM–1s were built with conventional landing gear but the three YFM–1As that came along in October 1940 incorporated tricycle landing gear, which was to become a Bell landmark in fighter design. The performance of the Air-acuda just did not match up to its exciting looks and most contemporary fighters could have been more than a match for the FM–1.

Even though production orders were not forthcoming, Bell was able to prove that his company could develop startling concepts featuring innovative aeronautical creations. Mr Bell and his design staff were now more than ready for their next project, a project that would garner exactly 9,572 more orders than their first unusual creation!

As previously mentioned, Air Corps think-ing during the 1930s meant that the pursuit aircraft would have to include such interesting and diverse duties as close support for the ground pounders and coastal defense in its repertoire. The item of coastal defense was highly stressed by the military and many concrete forts were built on the east and west coasts which enclosed massive 'disappearing' rifles that could lob shells 20 miles at an approaching enemy fleet and hit them with virtual pin-point accuracy. Of course, the builders of these magnificent weapons did not take into account the fact that the defenses would be immediately obsolete if the invading enemy fleet came in aircraft rather than ships.

A similar lack of reasoning extended to aircraft for there were no real interceptors in the Air Corps inventory nor was there any sort of pursuit that could effectively deal with night attacks by enemy bombers.

Outmoded Curtiss P–36s and Seversky P–35s would have been hard pressed to inter-cept the new Japanese and German bombers of the late 1930s. These fighters were slow, had poor rates of climb, and featured light arma-ment. A new fast climbing machine with a high top speed and heavy armament to blast the bombers were needed and Larry Bell was convinced that his company was going to build the interceptor.

Bell engineers felt that the new interceptor should have a very heavy armament which would spell doom for the bombers that the aircraft was to attack. Most fighter aircraft had stayed with the traditional World War One armament of two rifle caliber machine guns that would be almost ineffective against the new generation of all-metal bombers, many of which carried considerable amounts of armor

*C*amouflage scheme for the RAF's Airacobra Mk I was an American interpretation of the British orders and was changed to conform with British specifications when the aircraft arrived in England. (Bell)

*T*his technical manual illustration gives some idea of the length of the drive shaft and reduction gear for the Allison installed in the Airacobra Mk I. (Allison)

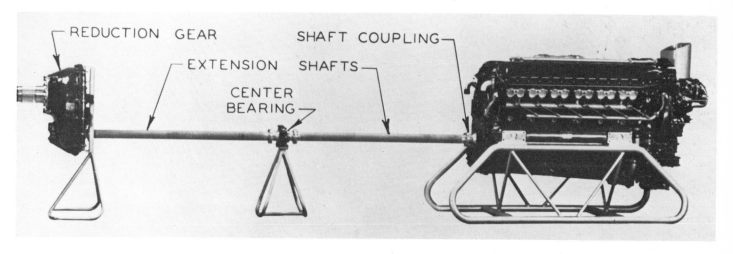

plating. Bell's chief engineers, Bob Woods and Harland Poyer, were in favor of combining a very heavy cannon along with several machine guns. The choice of the cannon was a foregone conclusion, The Oldsmobile T4 37 mm gun. This accurate but slow-firing weapon had been installed in the Airacuda and considerable experience had been obtained with the gun by Bell.

The next problem facing Bell was where to put the heavy gun. A single-engine fighter was extremely limited for placement of such a large weapon and it did not have the convenient nacelles of the FM–1 which easily housed the weapon. Thus the shape of the Bell interceptor was to be dictated by the gun and the aircraft that was to be built would be virtually unique.

The designers felt that an interceptor should have as much weight gathered around its center of gravity as possible. This would make the aircraft less prone to weight changes as ammunition and fuel were expended. It was also felt that the aircraft would be more maneouverable. The initial sketches prepared by Bell placed the engine directly in the middle of the airframe. A long drive shaft would pass through the forward fuselage and attach to the propeller assembly. This drive shaft would also serve as the ideal location for the cannon which would then fire directly down the center line of the fighter, making aiming of the weapon extremely easy. Since the engine was amidships, a great deal of room was left in the

Opposite above
Since the RAF rated the Airacobra as a failure and cancelled their order, the USAAF had to take over 179 examples. These machines were all equipped with 20 mm cannon and many carried their RAF camouflage along with RAF serials while in USAAF service. AP375 has been partially repainted in USAAF Olive Drab. Note the long length of the 20 mm cannon barrel. The name **One for the Road** has been painted on the nose in white.

When the RAF rated the Airacobra a total failure in operational service, the USAAF took back 179 of the machines – a fact that made the American pilots assigned to the aircraft distinctly unhappy. Many of the machines were sent to Burtonwood Airdrome where they were fixed up and outfitted for the long trip to Africa where the USAAF felt that the aircraft's ground attack capabilities could be put to good use. The aircraft were left with their original camouflage and RAF serials. BX187 is seen ready for the ferry flight. The camouflage paint has had various comments chalked on by the crew chief relating to the aircraft's mechanical condition. Note the US insignia with a yellow outer ring, and the large ferry tank installed under the fuselage. In the background can be seen the base's 'boneyard' – a collection of wrecked and damaged aircraft that have been gathered for scrapping or salvage of parts. These wrecks include B–17s and B–24s and one solitary Airacobra Mk I. Examining the original print with a high-power magnifier, one can see the wingless Bell fuselage being eagerly stripped of parts by two crew chiefs who apparently intent on getting a few extra spares for their own aircraft! (USAF/78997AC)

Everything ready, the pilots warm up their Airacobra Mk Is for the long flight to Africa. This photograph was taken at the 91st Bomb Group base in Bassingbourne, England, on 10 March 1943. One of the ferry flights to Africa had an inadvertent and unusual side effect. During the flight a number of Airacobras lost their way and were forced to land in neutral Portugal. Eighteen Airacobras were welcomed by the Portuguese when they landed at Portela de Sacavem Airport at Lisbon. The aircraft were quickly grabbed by the Portuguese and on 23 June 1943 they equipped a new fighter unit, Esquadrilha OK. The aircraft were given serials ranging from 301 to 318 and were flown fairly regularly by the Portuguese pilots who seemed to enjoy the machines. The Airacobras were withdrawn from front-line service during 1946 and scrapped. In this photograph, the second Airacobra from the left is BX249. (USAF/69358AC)

nose, even after installation of the cannon, so Bell was able to apply their famous nose gear which had been developed on the Airacuda. The nose was also able to accommodate two .50 caliber machine guns. Needless to say, the Army was most impressed with the sleek, streamlined plans and, on 7 October 1937, a contract was issued for a single prototype that would carry the designation of XP–39.

The choice of engine was limited to a variant of the Allison since there were no other inline American liquid-cooled powerplants of enough horsepower. Bell decided to go with the V–1710–17 which could develop just over 1,100 hp and was fitted with a turbosupercharger that would be on the port side of the fuselage. In order to keep the design as sleek as possible, Bell located the intakes for cooling air in slim pods on each side of the fuselage. Other intakes were molded into the wing root where they blended with the clean lines of the design. Development of the XP–39 was kept very secret and the public was not aware of the aircraft until it was announced on 9 February 1939 – a comfortable amount of time since the prototype had been placed on flatbeds and sent

by rail to Wright Field where it was flown for the first time on 6 April 1938.

The new fighter appeared to be what the Army had been hoping for – a clean, fast climbing aircraft that could pack a considerable wallop. However, the situation was soon to change. The XP–39 had been flown in a very light condition, armament and a number of other military items not being installed. The National Advisory Committee for Aeronautics (NACA) had studied the XP–39 and recommended changes which would affect the final production aircraft. Even though the prototype was extremely light at well under 6,000 lbs it was felt that a military equipped XP–39 would not weigh in at much more than 6,500 lbs and that the performance the aircraft had demonstrated, including a climb to 20,000 ft in five minutes, would be relatively intact. NACA and Army decisions were to forever adversely affect Bell's slim fighter.

Some of the Army brass, being of the 'old school' which insisted that aircraft should operate subordinate to ground forces, managed to force through a view, aided by NACA data, that the P–39 should be built for a close-

Many P-400s were sent to the South Pacific where they participated in the early heavy fighting against the Japanese invaders. A number were retained in the States for the training role, illustrated by this well-worn example with large training codes on the nose and still retaining its RAF camouflage. The aircraft was from the USAAF Training Command's Central Instructor's School and was photographed during early December 1943 at Matagorda, Texas, which was an auxiliary field of Foster Field. (USAF/22504)

Mechanic checking over the Curtiss Electric propeller of a service test YP-39. Service test aircraft were built in batches of 13 and distributed to various fields for intensive testing. Note the small fairings over the nose machine guns. (USAF)

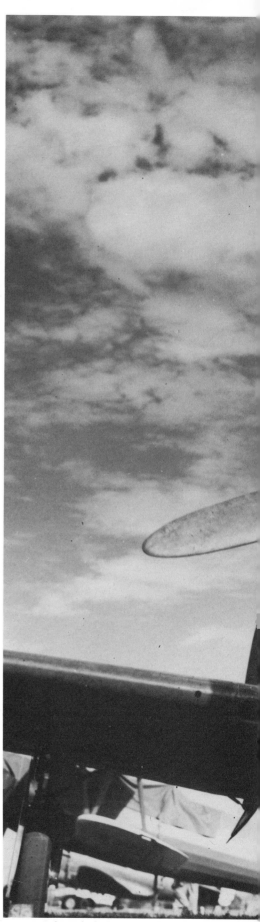

support role which, of course, takes place at low altitude. Bell was dismayed when the Army and NACA requested that a number of changes be made to the P-39, especially since 13 YP-39 service test examples, which had been ordered on 23 April 1939, were already on the production line.

The most damaging change insisted on by the Army was the deletion of the turbosupercharger which would not be needed since the aircraft would be operating at lower altitudes. Little thought was apparently given to the fact that new German and Japanese fighters were capable of flying and fighting at altitudes higher than which the non-turbo equipped P-39 could attain. NACA felt that the high canopy line should be reduced, making the aircraft a bit cleaner. The coolant radiator was moved to the wing center section causing the carburetor air intake to be moved to a position atop the fuselage, directly behind the canopy. Several other small changes such as the addition of landing gear fairings were also incorporated. Power was to be supplied by the low-altitude rated V-1710-37 Allison which effectively put the end to the P-39 as an interceptor, once again leaving the Army

without an effective high-performance fighter.

As these changes were ordered, Bell modified the prototype to conform with the modifications and the aircraft was redesignated XP-39B. The 13 service test YP-39s began to enter Army test groups on 13 September 1940 and, one year earlier, Bell had secured an almost $3 million order for the development and production of the Airacobra, as the type had been named.

The YP-39s were fitted with armament but immediately had two extra .30 caliber guns mounted in the nose between the two .50 caliber weapons. Testing with the XP-39B revealed that climb and top speed had decayed considerably but maneuverability at lower levels was quite good and the Army was pleased with the changes that they had ordered. Maneuverability had also been enhanced by the addition of a larger vertical tail on the YP and XP-39B.

The YP-39s were extensively flown by service pilots while Bell geared up for the job of mass-producing fighting aircraft. Up to this point the only aircraft Bell had produced had been a few of the unsuccessful Airacudas so the massive orders for the P-39 which, follow-

Head-on view of a YP-39 illustrates the streamlined shape of the Airacobra. The thick short wing was not suited for dog fighting. The 37 mm cannon was the heaviest weapon to be carried by an American World War Two production fighter. (Bell)

ing a newly established Bell tradition, had taken up the name Airacobra. The Army felt that the many changes which had been applied to the original P-39 concept should result in a change of designation with the new fighter being the P-45. However, it was finally decided to let the P-39 designation stay and the original order for 80 aircraft under the P-45 title was changed to read P-39C. The first production Airacobras were very similar to the service test aircraft but, after 20 P-39Cs had been constructed it was decided to change the remaining 60 aircraft on the contract to P-39Ds that would have four .30 machine guns in the wing in place of the two .30 caliber weapons in the nose. With these various modifications, the Airacobra's weight began to creep upwards and, with the low power avail-

able from the non-turbosupercharged Allison, it was obvious that the design was going to be in for trouble.

The Airacobra, for all its radical looks, was a conventionally constructed all-metal aircraft. The airframe was very sturdily built, a construction technique that was to become a Bell trademark, and this toughness stood the fighter in good stead when it entered the deadly arena of aerial combat. The fuselage of the Airacobra comprised two sections, a forward and an aft unit. The forward section carried the main portion of the entire fuselage – the wing center section, nose wheel bay, nose armament, engine bed, extension shaft and propeller gear reduction assembly mounts, and mountings for all the engine accessories.

The cabin for the pilot, oil and engine cooling systems, and ammunition boxes for the nose guns were all fastened to the forward unit. Needless to say, since all this important equipment was concentrated in one unit then that unit had to be of exceptional strength. To achieve that strength, the unit was built up

from two longitudinal beams which were cradle-shaped in profile. Each beam was manufactured of extruded aluminum angle sections that were tied together with almost solid reinforced aluminum webbing. To this cradle a series of aluminum bulkheads was added to give the fuselage the desired shape. Two of the bulkheads were steel castings and attached to the wing section to create a very substantial unit. A thick aluminum deck plate was riveted to the tops of the bulkheads and went the entire length of the longitudinal beams. Forged angle members were mounted to the rear of the beam to form the bed for the Allison engine.

The forward unit of the fuselage was covered with aluminum sheet skin that was riveted to the bulkheads. The skin on the forward section of this unit and under the pilot's cockpit was .051 sheet while the remainder of the unit was covered in .032 sheet.

The cockpit was an integral unit of the forward section and fume-tight bulkheads were provided between the engine compartment and the cockpit and between the armament in the nose and the cockpit. This unit was very sturdy and saved many an Airacobra pilot's life during a crash landing when, quite often, the only intact portion remaining would be the cockpit area. The fume-tight bulkhead's success was a matter open to speculation for Royal Air Force tests conducted on their Airacobra Mk Is found a lethal concentration of gases in the cockpit after the nose weapons had been fired. The RAF ordered its pilots to wear oxygen masks from the time of engine start until engine shutdown when flying the Airacobra. Many American pilots also wore oxygen masks full time when flying the Airacobra although this was quite often extremely uncomfortable when flying the aircraft on low-level missions in the sweltering South Pacific.

The aft section of the fuselage carried the entire tail section and was of ordinary semi-monocoque construction. The unit was covered with .032 sheet aluminum.

The cockpit had been arranged for maximum visibility and the canopy was the closest thing to a full bubble unit when the Airacobra entered service, being built up from six plexiglass panels while the windshield was formed of $\frac{1}{4}$ in laminated bullet-proof glass. An unusual feature of the Airacobra was the entry method for the pilot. Most fighter aircraft are extremely awkward to enter but the Airacobra offered all the comfort of a family sedan with two full-size doors which afforded easy access (and escape) to the aircraft. The doors even had $\frac{21}{64}$ in laminated glass windows that could be rolled up and down via automobile-like handles. Both doors could be jettisoned in case

of an emergency and the pilot could then either roll out of his seat or, if speed was low enough, get out on the wing before jumping. Indicating how people have grown in the past forty years, the Airacobra cockpit was designed for a 5 ft 8 in pilot that would weigh in at 200 lbs with parachute and survival gear attached. The pilot was protected by a sturdy roll-over structure directly behind his seat that was capable of supporting a weight greater than the aircraft. This unit was built out of two main beams of very heavy gauge aluminum that were joined together by bulkhead sections and heavy-gauge skin that was riveted to the beams and bulkheads. This unit was further strengthened by the use of wire bracing that was tightened by turnbuckles.

The Airacobra's wing had a NACA airfoil that started with an 00015 section at the root of the wing and traveled to a 230099 section at the tip. The wing was of all-metal construction with stamped and pressed ribs and flush riveted aluminum skin which gave a very smooth surface. The wing was equipped with Frise-type ailerons, which were fabric covered (as were the moveable surfaces on the tail). Split trailing edge flaps were also installed.

The armament of the Airacobra was, at that time, the heaviest ever carried by an American production fighter. Replacing the concept of pursuit aircraft having just two rifle-caliber machine guns, the sting of the P–39 made a lasting impression on the Army Air Force whose fighter aircraft would, from that point, be substantially armed. When the armament of the P–39C was revised producing the P–39D, the Army had a fighter that could

carry a 37 mm cannon, two .50 caliber and four .30 caliber guns. The 37 mm cannon was mounted on the fuselage center line just above the extension drive shaft from the Allison. The barrel of the cannon passed through the reduction gearbox and the propeller hub. The two nose mounted Browning M2 machine guns were installed just in front of the pilot's position and synchronized to fire through the arc of the propeller while the four .30 caliber weapons were installed in pairs in each outer wing panel.

All weapons were manually charged and electrically fired by solenoid units that were activated by the two firing switches located on the pilot's control column. One button was for the operation of the cannon while the other button operated the machine guns. In the P–39D the .50 caliber weapons were equipped with blast tubes to minimize flash. Each nose machine gun had its own ammunition holder that accommodated 200 rounds. Spent cases and their connecting links were disposed of via ejection chutes. The .30 caliber weapons were divided with two guns in each outer wing panel and each pair shared a 1,000 round ammunition box.

The real punch from the Airacobra was, of course, the 37 mm cannon. Although slow

The two fighters that typified the Army's airpower during the late 1930s. The P–40 and P–39 were photographed at Indianapolis, Indiana. Maj James H. Doolittle, who became famous during the war for his daring bombing attack on Japan, was flying the P–40 and was visiting Allison in Indianapolis in his position as inspector of engines for the Air Corps. The P–39C was flown by First World War Ace Lt Col H. Weir Cook, a resident of Indianapolis, on duty with the procurement director at Wright Field.

firing, a hit from the cannon would usually destroy an aircraft or a ground vehicle. The cannon was fed by a circular endless-belt holder that was wrapped around the nose machine guns. This holder carried 30 rounds for the cannon and the spent shells were also ejected from under the nose.

The Airacobra was well armored in vital areas with homogenous steel plate, face-hardened steel plate, and, as mentioned, armor glass. Armor was installed around the propeller reduction gear box, the bulkhead between the gun bay and the pilot, and in front of the windshield. Armor was also installed on the turnover structure while more armor protected the oil tank.

Second Lieutenant James C. Robertson of the 39th Pursuit Squadron, 39th Pursuit Group, waves at the cameraman during a night mission from Nachitoches Airport, Louisiana, during 1941 war games exercises. Airacobra is a P–39D. Aircraft is camouflaged in Olive Drab and Neutral Gray with Black designators. Red cross behind the engine exhausts was a marking for the war game. (USAF/22844)

The P–39C and P–39D were pressed into service as quickly as they came off the Bell production line. The Army was desperate for new fighters and the Airacobras were looked upon as being deliverance from the primitive aircraft with which they had been operating. This was a fighter, the Army hoped, that could compete with the best European fighting machines. Unfortunately, the officials did not know just how wrong they were.

The first outfit to receive the Airacobra was the 31st Pursuit Group who immediately put their new machines to work by taking them to the huge First Army war game that took place in the Carolinas during September 1941. (It should be noted that the rather curious designation of Pursuit was dropped during May 1942 for the more descriptive term of Fighter.) The 31st Pursuit Group was activated on 1 February 1940 and its first aircraft was the Airacobra. Commanded by Col John R. Hawkins, the 31st contained three squadrons initially; the 39th, 40th and 41st Pursuit Squadrons. The pilots were pleased with their new

mounts and, since they only had more obsolete Army aircraft to compare the P–39 with, initially thought that the Airacobra was quite a machine, although they were soon to learn the hard way that it was not.

The giant war games that took place during September through November were to prove that America was not ready for the war engulfing the rest of the globe. However, the games did bring to light the fact that a considerable amount of the Army's textbook tactics – both in the ground and in the air – were completely out of date and revisions were undertaken to correct the problems and to lay down a solid foundation of tactics which would prove to be of use once America entered the war.

During the war games the Airacobras of the 31st Pursuit Group, flying with the 'Blue Forces', roared into the air on countless missions to support Army troops, intercept 'enemy' bomber formations, and tangle with opposing fighters. During these three months certain unsettling facts concerning the P–39

Undersurface view of an early production P-39D shows details such as the retractable landing lights and shell ejection chutes. Legend 'U.S. Army' was painted in Insignia Blue. (Bell)

began to appear. Firstly, it became quickly obvious that the P-39 would not be capable of fighting above 12,000 ft due to the lack of a turbosupercharger on the Allison. Secondly, the Airacobra was prone to a number of maintenance problems including a weak nose gear that would quite often give way when operating off unprepared fields. Thirdly, it became obvious that the performance of Bell's fighter – even under 12,000 ft – was not all that sterling and the P-39 would be badly pressed by a quality fighter such as the Messerschmitt Bf 109. The armament of the P-39 was substantial and the aircraft was pleasant to fly, being described by one pilot as 'a good high-performance sport plane for a wealthy civilian pilot'. However, at this point the Army was stuck with the Airacobra since they had nothing else besides the P-40 to fall back on.

The British and French, during their frenzied aircraft buying missions prior to the start of World War Two, investigated the new product from Bell with considerable interest. On 13 April 1940, the British Aircraft Purchasing Commission decided that – based on figures issued by Bell – the Airacobra would make an ideal fighter for the Royal Air Force and a

contract was placed that called for the delivery of 675 Airacobra Mk Is, as the type would be designated in RAF service. However, the British soon found out that several 'mistakes' had been made when ordering the aircraft. All performance data had been based – and not very conservatively based – on the highly polished, low-weight prototype rather than the P-39D to which the Airacobra Mk I was basically identical. Originally having the name Caribou, the Airacobra Mk I differed from the P-39D in having British radios, gunsight, and detail differences. Also, the hard-hitting 37 mm cannon was replaced by a 20 mm Hispano M1 with 60 rounds. The RAF had experience with this weapon and selected it instead of the 'unknown quality' Oldsmobile weapon.

Bell made a great deal of publicity over the RAF order and posed camouflaged examples for press cameras to show how America was supplying its ally with the latest in aeronautical technology. After the Airacobra Mk Is were test flown, they were disassembled, carefully crated and shipped to Britain where the first example was erected and flown on 6 July 1941. Arrivals of crated Airacobras began to

increase and the first RAF unit to equip with the type was No 601 (County of London) Squadron, an auxiliary unit that had been activated with the start of the war. The Airacobra, used to the US Army's beautifully prepared long concrete runways, was not going to react well to the standard RAF field which was grass and short and would have been classified by American pilots as 'unprepared'. The Airacobra Mk I was a bit of a ground lover and RAF pilots transitioning to the type must have had their share of thrills as they saw the hedges at the end of the runway rapidly approaching while the Airacobra seemed to have other ideas on its mind beside flying. The Air Fighting Development Unit at Boscombe Down, responsible for testing and setting up tactics for new fighting aircraft, found the Airacobra Mk I to be woefully inadequate but the aircraft was duly issued to No 601 Squadron who, with considerable misgivings, gave up their trusty Hawker Hurricanes.

By September 1941, No 601 Squadron was ready for a 'press day', an event which meant that the Airacobra Mk Is would be lined up in impressive rows with the pilots and ground crews standing around looking 'smart' for the propaganda photographs and probably hoping Jerry would not send a bombed-up intruder over to disrupt the event.

The Squadron immediately had maintenance problems with the Bell fighters, including landing gear problems while operating from muddy grass fields. If mud got inside the wheel wells of the Airacobra during takeoff then,

USAAF armorers load up a P–39D with .50 caliber bullets. However, the people in this staged photograph were going to run into some problems since they were trying to load the .30 caliber wing guns with .50 caliber shells! This view also shows good detail of the Curtiss Electric propeller which was finished in a silver anodized color. (USAF/21744)

quite often, the gear would not want to come down for landing. This would result in belly landings if all gear legs were jammed in the up position or, if one or two gear legs came down and the others did not, the pilot would simply jettison the car doors and take to his parachute. No 601 Squadron established itself at the historic Duxford aerodrome near Cambridge (today the site of the huge collection of vintage aircraft belonging to the Imperial War Museum) and, on 9 October, began flying reconnaissance missions over Dunkirk and other areas of the French coast, and attacking targets of opportunity. However, the pilots hated the aircraft and the Airacobras began breaking down with such frequency that squadron serviceability rates began dropping to the zero mark, an embarrassing situation for the hard-pressed mechanics. The Airacobra was withdrawn from RAF operational use

during December, examples in England being shuttled off to the Russians whom the British felt would take anything, while a few examples were retained for mundane test work. The remainder of the contract was rejected, leaving the US Army with the type.

A bit over 200 Airacobra Mk Is were eventually shipped to Russia while 179 were taken over by the Army as P–400s. These aircraft usually retained standard RAF day fighter camouflage and serials but had American national insignia. Some P–400s were retained in the training role while the majority were shipped off to Australia where the need for fighting aircraft was desperate after 7 December 1941. One pilot commented that 'the P–400, like the rest of the Airacobra series, was pleasant to fly, but we felt more comfortable with that big 37 mm up front rather than the puny 20 mm that the Brits had installed.

B*ell P–39D–1–BE equipped with the 20 mm nose gun. With the P–39D series a small dorsal fin fillet was added.*

E*ngine run-up for a well-worn P–39D–1–BE. The long barrel of the 20 mm cannon is evident. The belly fuel tank has been modified with the rear portion sectioned off, perhaps as a non-standard napalm bomb. (Bell)*

A *training school group of P–39D–1–BEs. Stateside training aircraft could be identified by the large numbers painted on the fuselage. (USAF/22521)*

C *ockpit of a P–39D. The Airacobra's cockpit was designed for a 5 ft 8 in pilot who weighed 200 lb with parachute and full flight gear. For larger pilots the cockpit was definitely on the cramped side but the roll down windows helped a bit when the aircraft was on the ground. (USAF)*

We knew that if we hit something with the 37 mm that it was going to be heavily damaged if not destroyed.'

The Airacobra was deployed to the vital Canal Zone in Panama before the outbreak of the war to bolster the weak defenses. The fact that defenses for the Canal were weak came upon the Army like a bolt of lightning when they realized that a co-ordinated attack by Japanese and German submarines could spell doom for the Free World's important transportation route. The Army decided to double the number of pursuit aircraft at the Canal in August 1939, and Curtiss P–36s and Douglas B–18s were sent to Albrook Field which was in the throes of rapid expansion. By the end of 1939 and the start of 1940, it was evident to the American government that the Germans, who had strong connections in Latin America, were stirring up trouble and anti-American feelings. On 17 June 1940, the Canal Zone and the Hawaiian Territories were alerted against the possibility of immediate attack by German forces in the Canal and by the Japanese in Hawaii. This alert, although proven inaccurate but prophetic in many ways, served as another order for more aircraft for the Canal's dozen airfields. Twenty-four P–39Ds were dispatched to the Canal Zone along with a larger

number of P–40s. These aircraft helped modernize the area's defenses which were also bolstered by the addition of an early radar unit.

Operating out of the more primitive Canal airfields, the Airacobra ran into the same enemy that the RAF had encountered: landing gear failure. Between 1941 and 1942, eight P–39Ds suffered accidents during landing, another 20 were victims of gear failure, while 16 crashed into the sea or jungle. The original batch of Airacobras was supplemented by further aircraft sent from the States to constantly replenish the diminishing number of fighters. Units of the 6th Air Force which operated the P–39 in the Canal Zone included the 43rd, 24th, 31st, 52nd, 53rd, and 51st Fighter Squadrons. The P–39s are not recorded as having seen any action during their assignment in the Canal Zone although some of the antiquated B–18 Bolo bombers slugged it out with the U-boats which they found on the surface and, in a couple of instances, the B–18 crews found themselves floating in life rafts on the surface of the Atlantic watching the U-boat sail away and wondering where they went wrong. Pilots of the Airacobras that went down at sea were faced with the possibility of becoming a meal for the sharks which abounded in unpleasant profusion while those that went down in the jungle had the possibility of becoming the main course for the equally unpleasant native population. Several times it was suspected that natives had done away with pilots who had been forced to bail out of malfunctioning Airacobras. One pilot commented: 'When one of our boys went missing with the possibility of having been killed by the natives, our squadron would mount an "unofficial" mission against native encampments where the firepower from the guns and the effects of 500 lb bombs leveled several villages whose inhabitants were taken by surprise from our low-flying Airacobras.' Although probably satisfying for the pilots participating in these revenge missions, they certainly did nothing to improve the natives' disposition the next time they saw a white devil

The Airacobra had to prove itself during an extensive series of war games held in the Southern States during the later part of 1941. These aircraft are from the 31st Pursuit Group which, with its 39th, 40th and 41st Pursuit Squadrons, flew in support of Army units that were maneuvering in the field. These factory-fresh aircraft did not carry nose guns. (USAF)

floating to the jungle in his parachute. Since chances for combat were slim, pilots blew off steam by 'rat racing' down the many rivers in the area while trying to pick off alligators with the 37 mm cannon.

As 1941 continued, P–39s were rapidly reaching USAAF squadrons and, after the 31st Pursuit Group, the 58th Pursuit Group received its Airacobras. The 58th, consisting of the 67th, 68th, and 69th Pursuit Squadrons was activated on 15 January 1941, and served as a replacement training unit for pilots until 1943. The Group operated a mixed bag of aircraft that included P–35s, P–36s, P–40s, and P–39s.

By the time of 7th December 1941, some P–39s had been transferred to Hawaii but most were destroyed or damaged on the ground during the Japanese raid. The mass confusion following the Japanese attack had every fighter unit in the Pacific clamoring for more aircraft. Frantic shipments began from American West Coast ports as crated parts and aircraft were shipped around the clock. With

such frenzy and poor intelligence reports coming from areas under attack, it was not uncommon for aircraft to arrive at their destinations lacking vital parts to make them airworthy. The first unit to have the distinction of taking the Airacobra into combat was the 8th Pursuit Group. This historic unit was, in December 1941, part of the aerial defense force for New York City but was quickly moved to the Pacific in the early part of 1942 with headquarters at Brisbane, Australia. Once arriving in Australia, the Group immediately began assembling their aircraft and deploying them to forward operating bases in New Guinea. The 8th PG was joined by the 35th Fighter Group (carrying the new Fighter designation) during July of that year with more Airacobras and the 39th, 40th, and 41st Fighter Squadrons which had originally been attached to the 31st FG, the first USAAF unit to operate the P–39.

The Airacobra pilots detached to the airstrips in the steaming jungles of New Guinea were to face problems that were totally alien to the average American airman. First, they were

in an area where America had never been and the few available maps were so riddled with inaccuracies that they were virtually useless. Secondly, intelligence reports were so wildly inaccurate that the pilots really did not know what they would be facing; rumors ran rife. Thirdly, the USAAF pilots had come to realize that the Airacobra was a dog and that they would be opposing Japanese warplanes whose reputation had made them seem invincible.

The P–39s operating in this area were a mixed bag that included P–39Ds and Airacobra Mk Is from the cancelled British order. Parts and maintenance manuals were in short supply as the ground crews labored to prepare as many P–39s for combat as possible. Not only were the pilots faced with the possibility of flying fighters that could not be adequately maintained, they were also faced with the harsh reality of flying over stretches of water where, if forced down, chances of rescue were remote. Such was the fighting spirit of the American pilots and the desire to strike back at the enemy that the dangers were forgotten as

Airacobras bravely ventured across the ocean to new forward bases and onto sweeps, attacking Japanese shipping or targets of opportunity.

The 347th Fighter Group was activated at New Caledonia on 3 October 1942, with a mixed bag of P–400s and P–39D–1–BE Airacobras which were also equipped with the 20 mm cannon. Detachments of this Group, which was attached to the 13th Air Force in January 1943, were sent to Guadalcanal where they flew protective patrols, supported ground forces, and attacked shipping. The 67th Fighter Squadron, attached to the 347th FG, shot down a Zero on 22 August – one of the earliest victories to be scored by an Airacobra during those dark days. Heat, humidity, poor maintenance, and disease all took their toll on the American pilots who operated from crude airstrips under the most primitive of conditions.

Back at the Bell factory in New York, work was carried out on further versions of the Airacobra even as reports came in challenging the usefulness of the design. The designations P–39F and P–39G were assigned to aircraft essentially similar to the P–39D–1 and P–39D–2 but equipped with the Aeroproducts constant-speed hydraulic three-blade propeller rather than the Curtiss Electric propeller. Most of the different versions of the Airacobra, as seen from the specifications tables, were created by engine, propeller or minor equipment changes. The final versions, the P–39N and P–39Q, were built in the most numbers of any Airacobra. These aircraft were mostly supplied to Russia via the Lend-Lease program.

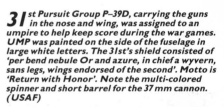

31st Pursuit Group P–39D, carrying the guns in the nose and wing, was assigned to an umpire to help keep score during the war games. UMP was painted on the side of the fuselage in large white letters. The 31st's shield consisted of 'per bend nebule Or and azure, in chief a wyvern, sans legs, wings endorsed of the second'. Motto is 'Return with Honor'. Note the multi-colored spinner and short barrel for the 37 mm cannon. (USAF)

Russia had a huge appetite for aircraft and seemed to take anything they could get. A wartime press release from Bell gives an idea of the manner in which 1940s America regarded their ally:

'Buffalo-built Bell Airacobras are proving the ideal plane for Russian winter fighting. This was explained in a report received by the British Information Services from official London sources. The Russians call the P–39 the "Flying Cross."

'It was mid-winter of last year when the Airacobra first flew in Russia, but the first authentic reports are just filtering through. Indications are that the approaching Soviet Winter will find the P–39s operating in the same fashion as last year. Explaining how the Airacobras had to be assembled in sub-zero temperatures, the British report continues:

'"The aerodrome runways were of snow, rolled hard enough to support the weight of an aircraft, the surface anything up to three feet above the level of the ground underneath. The Airacobra is the right aircraft for these conditions as it cannot ground-loop nor turn over on its nose. [Note: like the performance specifications for the RAF's Airacobra I, these statements are not exactly true!] Judgment of

landings is also rather harder on snow and once again the nosewheel undercarriage scores. Also it was found almost unnecessary to use brakes after landing on snow while the take-off was only slightly lengthened.

'"The squadron re-equipping with the Airacobras collected the aircraft and began a few weeks of intensive training. The Airacobra was christened 'The Flying Cross' and the two things which the Russians chiefly praised were the armament – for obvious reasons – and the metal propeller which they said was preferable to wood when ramming."

'Explaining how the planes are assembled, the report adds:

'"The mechanics were divided into erection gangs, each of which was responsible for the complete erection of an aircraft. As soon as the aircraft is allotted to a gang, it sets to work on it with eagerness, their one aim being to send it on its way to the front as soon as possible. First, all the loose items of equipment are carried into the hangar where they are guarded as personal property. Next a tractor is attached to the fuselage cradle and it is dragged into its erection bay. Finally a labor gang is called and the wings are lifted and carried into the hangar. It must be admitted that the labor gangs are unskilled and the wings get rather roughly handled but the Airacobra is tough and damage was rarely serious.

'"The erection mechanics work with a will. They have been trained the hard way with too few tools and too little equipment; their skill with the tools to which they are accustomed is striking. They have very great ability at impro-

visation. They quickly appreciate the object of the special purpose tools but unfortunately the efficient use and handling of such equipment is outside their experience.

'"Sooner than expected, a new Airacobra with red stars stands out in the snow, its sleek lines emphasized by the stubby I–16 fighter which stands beside it."'

Production of the P–39N and P–39Q totalled 7,000 units and virtually all of this group was transferred to the Soviet Union where the fighters were put to good use attacking tanks and ground targets. The Russians particularly liked the damage that the 37 mm cannon could do to German armor. In the air, the P–39 was no match for experienced *Luftwaffe* fighter pilots who blasted them out of the air with alarming regularity. Germany's greatest ace, Erich Hartmann, recalls attacking Russian Airacobras: 'I got behind the Airacobra, closed

right in, and after a short burst the enemy fighter went down and crashed with a tremendous explosion ... I was happy to get this Airacobra down.' Hartmann destroyed at least 33 Airacobras but admits that the type could be dangerous when in the hands of a very experienced pilot. The Soviets had a unit of Airacobras flown by their top aces, called the 'Red Guards', and the Germans realized that this was a very dangerous group.

The ultimate version of the P–39, the Q Model, had all wing guns deleted and replaced with a pod under each wing that held one .50 caliber machine gun. On many Qs, even this reduced armament was eliminated – relying strictly upon the nose guns. Many pilots felt that the weight loss aided performance a bit and, at that stage, the overweight Airacobra needed every bit of help it could find. Only 75 P–39Qs were retained by the USAAF and passed on to the 332nd Fighter Group in Italy

during February 1944. The pilots of this unlucky unit probably could not believe that they would receive such an outmoded fighter so late in the war but, fortunately, the Airacobras were replaced in a couple of months with P–47 Thunderbolts.

Probably the strangest model of the Airacobra was the XP–39E. Only three models of this aircraft were manufactured and it was intended as a test vehicle for the new Continental V–1430–1 engine. The XP–39E featured a laminar flow wing and various other modifications. Each aircraft had its own modified stabilizer of different shape and configuration. The XP–39E never flew with the Continental since that engine was not ready so Allison V–1710–47s were installed. Intended to be put into production as the P–76 with an order for 4,000 aircraft, the 'new' fighter was wisely cancelled during May 1942.

The use of the Airacobra in the Pacific

40th Pursuit Squadron Airacobras deployed during 1941 war games. Note the white crosses painted on the fuselages to designate that the aircraft were assigned to the games. When operating from unimproved strips during war time, a fault in the landing gear system quickly became evident. The nose gear was particularly weak and would collapse under difficult circumstances. Mud getting into the wheel wells would prevent the landing gear from locking when they were extended. (USAF)

spread during 1942 and 1943 and the USAAF and USN fought a desperate battle against superior forces with excellent equipment. The pilots of the outmoded and outperformed Airacobra were pressed into inventing tactics by which they could lure the Zekes down to low altitude where the P–39 stood a better chance of survival. Wishing not to dogfight with the enemy, a decision that would have been fatal, the P–39 pilots would try to make one high speed pass at the enemy and then escape at full throttle. If they could hit anything during this

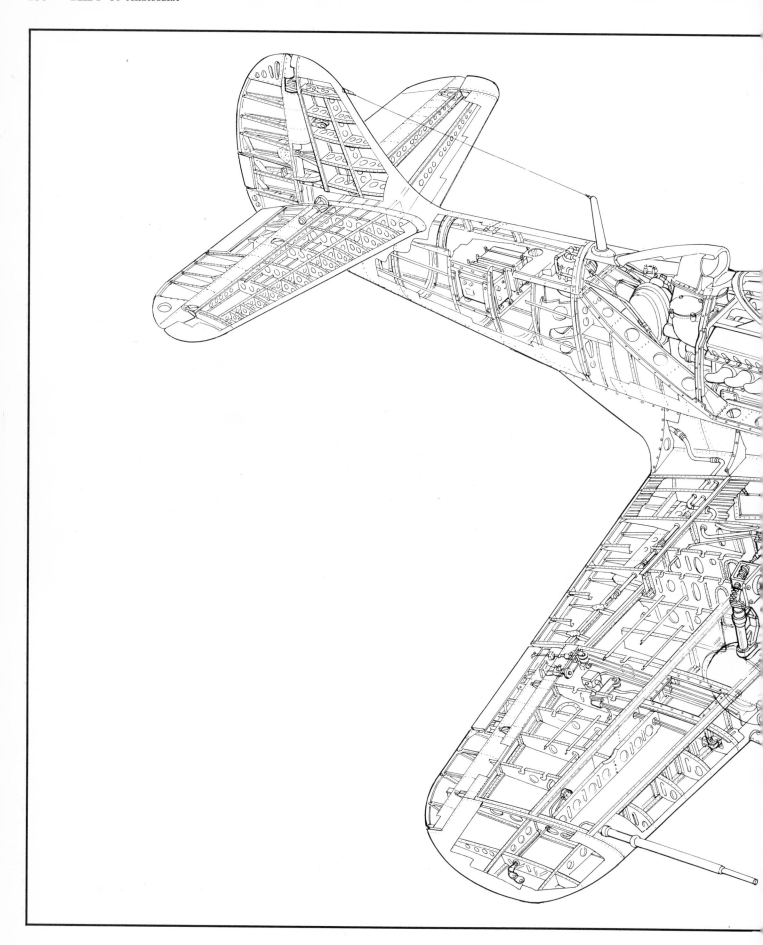

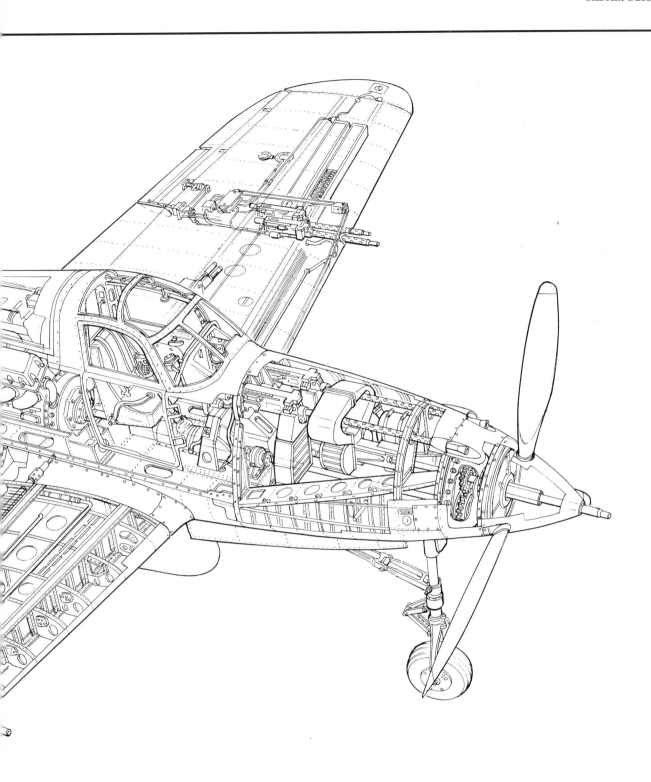

Bell P–39D–2 Airacobra

pass, destruction of the lightly built Japanese aircraft was almost assured. One pilot recounted that, during a head-on pass with a Zeke, a shell from the 37 mm cannon slammed into the Japanese fighter which instantly disintegrated. During combat more flaws with the Airacobra began to reveal themselves. One of the most discussed was the mysterious 'tumbling'.

A virtual mythos has been built out of the question of whether the Airacobra went through a peculiar aerodynamic maneuver which was given the name tumbling. The tumble was taken to be an inadvertent maneuver which was so unconventional that

Airacobras everywhere: elements of the 31st Pursuit Group undergoing maintenance during war games. Most of the systems in the Airacobra were easily accessible via large panels that could be taken off the airframe. (USAF)

there was no known recovery method. During this maneuver the Airacobra was reported to tumble tail over nose. The only recommended procedure was to get out of the aircraft as fast as possible since it would be dropping like the proverbial iron brick. Interviewing surviving Airacobra pilots leaves the tumble with part of its mystery still intact. Many pilots have flatly denied that this strange maneuver could take place while others recall that they 'heard about it' from other pilots but even fewer state that they have actually done it. Usually the tumble would come about during aerial combat when the Airacobra pilot would be entering a very tight maneuver and high-speed stall the P–39. It was thought because of the unique mid-engine installation of the P–39, which had much of the weight centered around the middle of the airframe, that the high-speed stall would throw the aircraft into the end-

over-end tumble. The problem, or the rumor of the problem, became so severe that Bell sent a field representative to the South Pacific to help iron out the trouble. Lt Col Richard Kent recalls the problems of tumbling: 'Another deadly factor in the P–39 was also due to the short wings and resultant airflow. When performing aerobatics at altitude or in ship-to-ship combat that resulted in an unco-ordinated turn or too tight a turn, the plane was said to stall without warning and tumble end over end. Several pilots have told me this happened to them and it took 15,000 ft to recover. This tumbling characteristic was debatable – it never happened to me and, intentionally and unintentionally, I stalled the plane in almost every conceivable situation but at high enough altitude to recover. Perhaps I was just lucky to stall it in such a way to avoid the tumble. These stalling factors, however,

caused many pilots to avoid flying the P–39 whenever possible and contributed to its reputation as a dangerous plane to fly.'

Edwards Park recalls tumbling in his *Nanette*, one of the finest and most evocative books written on World War Two aerial warfare: 'When you flipped on all three gun switches and fired your entire arsenal, there was a great roaring noise – *braaaaap* – and the cockpit filled with smoke so your eyes ran, and your airspeed dropped off a little. All this weight of armament tended to compensate for the engine being mounted amidships. But after you'd spent some ammunition the center of gravity would slide back, and the plane could do some strange things. It could tumble, for example. That means somersault, nose and tail swapping places as it drops out of the sky. No plane ought to do that.

'I did it once, practising acrobatics in Florida. I was on my back ("... and there I was on my back with nothing on but the radio ..." – fliers' joke back then) and managed to stall out, and she tumbled once, the sun swinging down past the nose, and then the earth, while we fell 12,000 ft. Absolutely terrifying.'

Lack of range, poor maintenance reliability, and the mentioned poor performance gave Airacobra pilots nightmares in the South Pacific. Fighting alongside equally outmoded P–40s, USAAF pilots had to face formations of Japanese bombers well protected by Zekes and Oscars. Japanese bombers, especially the Betty, were well-armed and quite fast but they suffered the fatal flaw of all Japanese combat aircraft – lack of armor and self-sealing fuel tanks. Ben Brown recalls interception missions against the Bettys: 'If the bombers had the slightest lead on us the pilots would firewall the throttle and run away which was a bit embarrassing for fighter pilots. Once the old P–39 got up around 300 mph, it would shake and make a terrible racket like an old dowager protesting a ride in a fast car. The Jap gunners with their 20 mm cannons in the tail were good and we would have to be careful approaching the Bettys if and when we could catch them.'

Pilots of 35th Fighter Group valiantly went out on several missions each day to intercept Japanese raiders. Results of these air battles were usually rather inconclusive, with both sides taking losses. The aerial defense of Australia and New Guinea took place from primi-

Conditions in the Aleutian chain were often less than ideal. These unfortunate pilots are being driven out to their P–39Fs as the squadron dog faithfully tags along on the rain-soaked ramp. This photograph was taken on 3 November 1942 at Adak. (USAF)

*P*ilot and crew chief strike a casual pose amidst the squalid living conditions at Kodiak, Alaska, on 7 August 1942. The P–39F is parked on a dirt revetment with belly drop tank and bombs stored nearby. (USAF)

*T*he distinctive wolf's head insignia marked this P–39F as belonging to the 57th Fighter Squadron at Kodiak, Alaska. Photographed on 7 August 1942. Note belly tank installation. The P–39F was equipped with the Aeroproducts propeller built by General Motors. (USAF)

tive air strips that took a toll on both aircraft and pilots. The Airacobras were constantly suffering from mechanical problems, their Allison engines overheating almost as soon as they started. It became common practice to tow the Airacobras to the end of the runway rather than taxi them. This way the coolant would not overheat in the high jungle temperatures. The pilot would then start the Allison, perform the briefest of engine run-ups, and then get the aircraft into the air as quickly as possible. This lack of run-up quite often meant that engine problems would not surface until the P–39 was in the air – often with

disastrous results. The toll of physical problems with the pilots was also high – jungle fever, malaria and dysentery running wild in the unimproved jungle camps. Still, daily missions were flown against the enemy. Pilots began to realize that having the engine behind them was not all that valuable. The Japanese pilots had been trained to shoot at the wing roots of American aircraft – quite often the location of fuel tanks – but would usually miss and the bullets would thud into the engine and accessories compartment. The lack of an engine up front meant that the pilot would have little to protect him in case of a crash landing in a rocky or wooded area. A plus factor was the fact that the Airacobra's rounded belly seemed to be ideally suited to water crash landings. The aircraft would gently skip like a rock and then settle down on the surface of the ocean, giving the pilot a chance to crawl out and take to his life raft, not like the later P–51 which would violently dig into the water because of its belly scoop and be on its way to the bottom within a few seconds.

The dogged responsibility felt by American pilots in defending Australia meant that their attacks on the Japanese bomber formations were savage and determined. The Japanese were startled by this showing and had to regroup and lick their wounds. The P–39s, P–400s, and P–40s of the 49th, 35th and 8th Fighter Groups began attacking Japanese ground targets as well and it was discovered that the Airacobra made a stable dive bomber. Field modifications were undertaken and the P–39s were able to handle a 500 lb bomb on a center section rack under the fuselage. The usual tactic was to dive quite low and release the bomb with a sharp pullout to escape the blast effects and to get away from anti-aircraft fire. Two squadrons led by the redoubtable Buzz Wagner arrived in New Guinea during April of 1942 and immediately put their Airacobras to work attacking anything that looked even vaguely Japanese. Air bases were attacked, ships were strafed and fuel dumps were blown up. The enemy soon begun to develop a healthy respect for the punch of the Airacobra.

Airacobras flew daily air patrols over Port Moresby, hoping to catch Japanese raiders before they could drop their bombs. It was hard, gruelling work with little in the way of thanks. The military realized the plight of the Airacobra pilots and began to take measures to replace the P–39 as soon as possible. Lockheed P–38s were shipped to the Pacific as fast as they could come off the production line to replace Airacobra equipped units but the unlucky 347th Fighter Group did not give up their Airacobras until August of 1944, by which time they were doing mainly ground

This P–39F was assigned to the Training Command's Central Instructor's School. Note the red bordered national insignia. (USAF/28072)

P–39L 42–4558 belonging to the 93rd Fighter Squadron, 81st Fighter Group, in Tunisia during 1943. Aircraft had a very patched-up Olive Drab paint scheme and carried the name The Pantie Bandit *on the nose along with the painting of a cartoon animal.*

P–39N–1–BE undergoing an in-the-field engine change somewhere in North Africa during 1943. The P–39N was fitted with an Allison V–1710–85 driving an Aeroproducts propeller.

P–39N with the characteristic heavy grey exhaust stain of the Allison engine on the side of the fuselage. 42–8896 carried the name III Winds on the nose section. Photograph taken 28 June 1943

at Gray Field, Washington. Aircraft was assigned to the 353rd Fighter Squadron. (USAF/25404)

*T*he Russians received the majority of the 4,905 P–39Q Airacobras built. This example is seen at Praha during May 1945. The P–39Q had fittings for carrying an optional two .50 caliber machine guns under the wings but this example

does not have them fitted. The Russians were fond of painting patriotic slogans on their aircraft, as can be seen from the inscription above the exhaust stacks.

P–39Qs of the 333rd Fighter Squadron, 318th Fighter Group, at Bellows Field, Hawaii, in 1943. The 333rd FS operated the Airacobra from 1942 to 1944. (J. Maita)

Line-up of P–39N–I–BE Airacobras at a Stateside training base. A large number of the 2,095 N Model Airacobras was sent to the Russians. (USAF)

support work and letting the aerial fighting go to the newer aircraft.

Many Airacobras were shipped off to the Aleutians Island in Alaska to help fend off the threat of Japanese invasion. Some of the Aleutians were actually invaded and occupied by Japanese who immediately began building bases for aircraft and ships. The conditions in the Aleutians were as bad as the South Pacific except instead of the terrible heat everything was cold – very cold. Airacobra pilots quickly discovered that the heaters in their aircraft were totally unsuited for the cold weather at the top of the world and they attempted to do everything possible to keep warm. Every panel line was taped over, newspapers were stuffed inside the nose to plug air leaks, and pilots dressed in as many layers of clothing as possible. Weather conditions contributed to the destruction of many P–39s, strong crosswinds caused the P–39s to go out of control, heavy fogs and low cloud banks would hide airfields, ocean landings would result in almost instant death because of the freezing water and, on top of all this, the Japanese were busy attacking the Americans whenever possible.

The enemy felt that a foothold in the Aleutians could be the basis for future incursions into Canada and eventually the United States. Submarines could be replenished and sent south to attack the important Pacific shipping lines.

USN aerial units and the 54th Fighter Group attacked the enemy on Kiska Island whenever possible. Airacobras strafed and bombed enemy supply dumps and airfields, also shooting up Japanese float planes that would be tied up in the harbor. The P–39s destroyed 20 enemy aircraft during their time in the Aleutians – losing one pilot in aerial combat, the commanding officer of 42nd Squadron. Many Airacobras, however, were written off in accidents – usually caused by the poor weather conditions or by mechanical problems. Once again, the Airacobra – although outclassed – helped stem the threat of a Japanese victory.

In Europe, the USAAF's Airacobra-equipped units suffered the same fate that had befallen the other squadrons in the Pacific and Aleutians. The 31st Fighter Group had been reorganized with the 307th, 308th, and 309th Fighter Squadrons and sent to England in July of 1942. The squadrons were quickly pushed into action but one sweep into Europe with 12 Airacobras – and the loss of six – quickly convinced the American military to pull the Airacobra out of the arena of combat in Western Europe. The 31st Fighter Group re-

equipped with Spitfires and enjoyed much more combat success. The only other P–39s to operate with the USAAF in Europe saw action in Italy. Other units went to North Africa where the 81st and 350th Fighter Groups operated in the Operation Torch landing. In these theaters the Airacobra was used as a ground support aircraft and was usually protected by medium- and high-cover fighters. The 81st and 350th Fighter Groups saw heavy action as they followed the Allied advances in Italy, attacking German armor, supply depots, and troop concentrations.

Foreign air forces also used the Airacobra. Beside Russian and British use, the P–39 saw service in Portugal where examples that had been forced to land while on ferry flights were impressed and used as interceptors. The Portuguese eventually got their hands on 18 Airacobras, which they purchased from America after the end of the war. The American pilots that had been flying these aircraft were interned but usually managed to 'escape' back to England or to North Africa via merchant ships. The Portuguese *Arma da Aeronautica* were more than pleased to have what they considered modern aircraft.

The Airacobra also saw service in the markings of the Royal Australian Air Force. The RAAF operated a mixed bag of P–39Ds and Fs, amounting to an original batch of 22 aircraft serialled A53–1 through A53–22. Several others were given to the RAAF by local USAAF units and the aircraft were pressed into service when the threat of invasion from Japan was at its strongest. When the prospect of invasion decreased following several Allied victories, the surviving Airacobras were returned to the USAAF.

The French had been first to order the Airacobra but the fall of that country prevented any machines from being delivered. However, France eventually did receive about 200 Airacobras when the USAAF began to supply Free French units in North Africa. The French were pleased to get the aircraft, many of which were distinctly tired, but were less than thrilled with their American instructors. The French, apparently still smarting from American attacks on French naval and air units and along with the typical French intransigence toward foreigners, made life miserable for the American fighter pilots that had been assigned to teach the French the finer points of flying the Airacobra. The French would only acknowledge the presence of the Americans during flying instruction and then retire to their tents or bars to pretend that the Americans did not exist. The French were eager for any aircraft that could attack the Germans and they put their machines to good use attacking German armored units and providing ground support for troops. The French were probably the last to keep the Airacobra in service, retiring the type in 1947.

After the capitulation of Italy, America quickly began building up that country's air force to help battle with the stubbornly retreating Germans. After training, a number of Italian P–39Q equipped squadrons began operations against the Germans on 18 September 1944. These aircraft made some sorties but contributed little to the Allied victory in Italy.

Thus the Bell Airacobra, originally intended as America's premier fast climbing interceptor, found itself as an overweight and underpowered aircraft that could not fight above 12,000 ft. The Airacobra's greatest achievement was the fact that it was there and ready to use when an ill-prepared America found itself thrust into a strange and foreign war. Today, two flying examples of the Airacobra are operated by the Confederate Air Force and Kalamazoo Air Zoo where they are admired as rare examples of America's fighting aircraft from the darkest days of World War Two.

P–39Q 'Tarawa Boom De-Ay' with underwing gun packs at Oahu Field in Hawaii during the Spring of 1944. Note the three Japanese kill marks under the windshield. (USAF/65220)

A P–39Q on its way to Russia. Airacobras being sent to Russia were ferried from the United States over Canada to Alaska where they were picked up by Russian pilots. The Russians liked the 37 mm cannon for attacking armor. (E. Deigan)

P–39Q in the lead with two P–39Ns in the
background. These aircraft were assigned to a
training school. Note the underwing gun pods on
the P–39Q. (USAF)

*P*ossibly the ugliest fighter aircraft
modification during World War Two was the
TP–39. Converted from small batches of Fs and Qs,
the TP was a dual control trainer that put the
second seat in the nose section where the
armament would have gone. The TPs were not
armed and had additional dorsal and ventral fins
added for stability.

*Q*uite often it is what is in the background
of a photograph that is more interesting than
the main subject. Behind this P–47 Thunderbolt are
part of the Navy's collection of F2L–1K Airacobras.
These machines, still in Army paint but with Navy
painted on the nose, were to have been used as
targets but it is not known if they were radio
controlled as Navy records are sketchy.

INTRODUCTION TO THE AIRACOBRA
By Ben L. Brown

Spoiled by the sparkling performance of the P–51C, Ben Brown found the Airacobra a disappointment.

My introduction to the Bell Airacobra came about in a rather pedestrian manner. I had gone through flying school in Texas with the Royal Air Force rather than the USAAF. The RAF method of teaching was considerably different and quite rigorous. The top ten students in my class were treated with a few hours in a factory fresh P–51C from the North American plant in Dallas. That was some machine compared to the trainers we had been flying and it was an experience I will never forget. Since I was number two in class standings I was able to get in a few more minutes flight time in the Mustang.

At the RAF school we flew 80 hours in Stearmans and then went directly to the AT–6 for 140 hours of flight time. The basic stage with the BT–13 trainer was completely eliminated. Our top ten students comprised four Americans and six Britons. The location was at Terrill, and it was the first such school in the United States that the British had talked the Americans into creating. Other schools were established in Lancaster, California, two in Oklahoma City and one in Florida. We had a terrific navigation program that was as comprehensive as the USAAF's navigator school. We also got to fly long cross-country missions along with plenty of low-level training and night flights.

After graduation we were sent to Las Vegas, Nevada, for fighter indoctrination training. The base had a number of mixed variants of P–39s for us to learn on and we were given three or four days of ground instruction before being allowed to fly the aircraft. The situation was much more casual than it is today because the aircraft that we flew were not multi-million investments but rather worn out obsolete fighters. The P–39 was an easy aircraft to fly and we quickly piled up the required number of hours. Some of our aircraft had 37 mm cannons while others were equipped with the 20 mm unit. The 37 mm cannon was fun to fire but a problem arose because the slow firing cannon had a completely different missile trajectory to the machine guns so it was very hard to get all the guns hitting the same target.

When we completed training we went to San Francisco and were put upon one of the deluxe pre-war cruise ships that had been converted to a troop carrier and steamed away to Honolulu. From Hawaii we went to Townsland, Australia, and that is where the USAAF had a forward strip. The base was equipped with P–40s and P–39s and we were not too pleased to be back with the Airacobra because even at that early date in the war the pilots realized that the Airacobra was a dog but we just did not have anything else at the time. We quickly began flying missions against the Japanese – going after their shipping, supply

Ben Brown flew P–39s for two and a half months in action against the Japanese from Townsville, Australia. He commented: 'The P–39 was a lot of fun to fly if you did not have to worry about somebody shooting at you or, conversely, if you had to try to shoot at somebody. It was a nice looking airplane but, on final summation, it was a bad aircraft – a dog that could not do the job for which it was designed.'

depots and bombers. The Airacobra's lack of range would mean that on many occasions we would have to deploy to primitive forward bases. The Airacobra had some trouble at these bases if mud got inside the wheel wells during takeoff. This would quite often cause the landing gear to not lock when lowered, resulting in a crash landing.

I always flew the Airacobra down low since it was really worthless above 12,000 ft. The South Pacific climate meant that you wore the least amount of clothes under that plexiglass hot-house. I just wore shorts, parachute, Mae West and a baseball cap. I never wore an oxygen mask because it was just too uncomfortable at low altitude. I also wore just the standard headset without any other form of ear protection which I now regret since the Airacobra was extremely noisy inside – it produced a noise unlike any other aircraft and the effect on the ear-drums was permanent. One nice feature was that we could roll the windows down in flight to get some extra air. This had to be done at lower speeds because at higher speeds a suction would be created inside the cockpit that would swirl everything around.

A typical mission in the Airacobra would involve getting up in the morning, going to the briefing, going to the airplane, getting in it and taking off. I never even once looked over the aircraft, never even kicked the tires, just got in and flew the thing if the crew chief said it was ready to go. Of course I was only 20 years old and stupid. After the war when I continued flying I would very carefully check out the aircraft before taking it up. Survival makes one more cautious.

Starting the Airacobra was always a thrill. The thing would buck, gasp and snort and feel like it was tearing itself into a million pieces. All those gears and long drive shaft contributed to a feeling that the P–39 was going to tear itself apart until you got the revs up to about 1,200 rpm and then the damn thing would smooth out. For starting we had to be towed out to the runway because, with the high jungle temperatures, the Airacobra would overheat very quickly on the ground. Once we started the engine we were on our way after a very brief run-up. This, of course, would lead to problems and several times during takeoff pilots found themselves in gliders when the engines quit. I remember watching several P–39 'gliders' go crashing through the jungle at the end of the strip, tearing off both wings, ripped off the tail section and finally sliding to a stop as a complete ruin. The pilots would open the car door and casually stroll away as if nothing had happened.

Once airborne we would stay low and head out for our assigned target. Quite often we would run into enemy aircraft and if they did not want to tangle with us they would simply open the throttle and outrun the Airacobras. We had a bad time with the Betty bombers that we would try to catch for they were fast and if they had a head start we would be hard-pressed to catch them. Once the P–39 got a bit over 300 mph it felt it was going to fall apart – shaking, vibrating and making the most god awful noise. Actually, we were probably lucky that we did not engage the enemy more often. If we had some height and were intercepted by Zekes we would dive away for the Airacobra went down like a rock and no Zeke could keep up with it and those that did usually did not live to tell the story for the Zeke's most vulnerable position with the P–39 was in a dive – especially if there were several of us and one of the Airacobras could get behind the Zeke while in the dive and blow him out of the air with a squirt from the cannon.

Our missions were usually short because of the range of the P–39 and we would return to base, execute a fighter break over the airfield and come in to land, switching off the Allisons as soon as possible to prevent overheating. The mechanics would then take the aircraft, go over them, reload the guns and prepare them for the day's next mission. In the meantime we would go to our tents and attempt to relax and play cards.

Our missions took us to such delightful places as Biak, Finchaven, Port Moresby and other tropical paradises. The coastwatchers would tell us about Jap ship movements and off we would go. Without our belly tank we only had a two hour range so we would use the tank on the way out and then drop it before attacking the enemy. We liked going after the shipping as the cannon would make a nice hole in the Jap ships. The cannon was slow firing and there was a built-in delay switch so that the gun could not be fired too quickly and burn up the barrel.

I did just about every maneuver that I could think of in the P–39 except for spinning the aircraft. Even at that young stage of my life I was smart enough not to attempt spinning a fighter aircraft. I had heard about 'tumbling' but it never happened to me. The P–39 was a lot of fun to fly if you did not have to worry about somebody shooting at you or, inversely, if you had to try to shoot at somebody. My crew chief had painted a shark's mouth on the nose of my Airacobra along with the inscription *Mabel's Boy*, my mother's name. It was a nice looking airplane but, on final summation, it was a bad aircraft – a dog that could not do the job for which it was designed. After two and a half months of flying the Airacobra we were very relieved to receive brand-new P–38s. Now we could do some damage to the Japs.

COBRAS TO ALASKA
By Ben L. Brown

To keep the Russians supplied with combat aircraft, an aerial highway was created between the United States and Alaska.

The *Wehrmacht* was knocking on the door at Stalingrad during 1942. US aircraft deliveries to Russia had bogged down. To remedy the problem, F. D. R. Roosevelt gave top priority to the shipment of aircraft to the Russians, and the 7th Ferrying Group of the Alaskan Division of the Air Transport Command was given the task of getting the planes to the Russians.

In all, 6,000 aircraft were delivered to the Russians via Great Falls, Montana, north to Fairbanks, Alaska, and on to Russia. I was one of the 7th Ferrying Group pilots who delivered these aircraft. As I review and recall these incidents that happened over 30 years ago, I realize what a great chapter in my life took place. Few pilots in our armed forces ever had such a great opportunity to fly all types of aircraft to so many places in the world. As all former ATC pilots will agree, this was one great time and it will never happen again. It was fantastic in so many respects that I, and many of the oldtimers like myself, wish that we could do it all over again for just a few days.

The ATC was a giant operation. Beside the ferrying division, it operated aircraft transporting VIPs, parts and supplies, medical evacuees, and all types of military personnel, and, at the time, was probably the largest airline in the world. It trained and retrained personnel constantly. Ground crews went to school to learn their jobs and later returned to school to learn about new aircraft. All pilots coming into the ATC were sent to various schools for retraining. Even airline pilots and former civilian instructors were sent to training schools. Former combat pilots and new pilots right out of flying schools were checked out in various aircraft or sent to instrument schools. The ATC made the best effort of any branch of service to train everyone to do his best at his particular job. I was happy to have been a part of this organization.

Ferry pilots were a colorful group of characters; many were former instructors, airline pilots, combat pilot and crop dusters. These men had a lot of experience and know-how in flying the unusual in all types of weather and situations. A pilot had to be versatile because he never knew what type of aircraft he would be ferrying next. Some pilots were single-engine fliers, others were strictly twin-engine, and those that loved to fly them all were called Class 5P pilots and they flew in any type of weather. Many of us had 'green' instrument cards that put us up in some of the roughest weather that one can imagine . . . this was long before ILS and GCA.

A typical trip from Great Falls, Montana, would take us away from our base for 35 to 45 days. It would run something like this: Go to Seattle, pick up a B–17G and take it to Elgin Field, Florida. From there, hop a commercial airline (ATC pilots had a top priority rating which guaranteed them a seat even if a paying passenger had to be removed) and head for Farmingdale, Long Island. There, pick up a P–47D and ferry it to Oakland, or perhaps head for Nashville and pick up a B–24 for Sacramento. Then, pick up a P–51D and head for Newark, go to Buffalo and take a P–39 or a P–63 to a training base in the South. Eventually you were re-routed back to your home base to pick up your pay and *per diem* and get your mail, have a few days rest and then head for the north country. They might keep you on the Alaskan run for a month and then back again on the road in the States or South America. In three years of this type of flying I managed to check out and fly over 55 various types of military aircraft.

My first assignment north was greatly anticipated and I looked forward to it because it sounded so different according to all the stories I had heard from other pilots. My home base was Gore Field, Montana, an enlarged commercial field taken over by the Army. It was situated on top of a plateau overlooking Great Falls, about 800 ft above the city. Located ten miles east of Great Falls was another field called East Base where all aircraft going north were processed and winterized.

Here we encountered the Russians – not many, but a chance to see a few. The Russian purchasing commission had a delegation of civilian and military personnel stationed there to observe and count the aircraft they were going to get. They were unusual in that they never socialized with us and never ventured out alone but always in groups with one acting as interpreter. Several admitted they spoke English and all carried a small translation book. Later on I managed to get friendly with some of them but they maintained a very reserved atmosphere at all times. In the mess halls they sat by themselves and when they would go into Great Falls for a movie or a visit to a bar they would stick together like glue.

On one occasion I was invited over to their big table at the Silver Dollar Saloon to help them order some food and drink. After they chatted in Russian they finally began asking a few guarded questions about America. My answers were what any American would give about our customs, cars, people, homes, living conditions, etc. They were shocked to see the number of cars in the streets, especially in wartime, and when I began asking similar questions about their country they became very quiet and suddenly forgot their English. One man usually carried the money to pay for everything and what a roll of greenbacks he carried! It seemed they were always loaded with money.

Later on I did some of the checkout work and gave cockpit checks to some of their pilots when a new or updated aircraft came through. My personal thoughts were that these pilots were rough and showed no flying *finesse* at all. Overall, I would judge them to be poor and men I would have washed out.

The closest I came in contact with the Russians was having two Russians assigned to fly along with us from Great Falls to Fairbanks in a new B–25J. They were to observe and also to get some time and experience in the Mitchell. They spoke English quite well and had been in combat on the Eastern Front flying various Russian fighters and using our P–39s to knock out German tanks. They were going to be used as navigator pilots flying their group in B–25s from Fairbanks back to bases in Russia. It seemed that they did loosen up a great deal once they were away from Great Falls and were on their own. They talked more freely than ever and did a great deal of drinking when on the ground.

In Fairbanks we had no contact at all with the Russian crews that flew in to pick up their aircraft except for a cockpit check and some ground school sessions with interpreters. The Russians would fly in on C–47s and in a few days perhaps 35 to 50 pilots would be ready to take back all the aircraft that had accumulated over the past few weeks. Then there would be a great assembly of pilots and aircraft with a mass departure. The B–25 was used as the navigator ship and all aircraft would end up flying a loose formation and just follow him back to Russia. Later in the war we saw a number of women pilots who were sent along to do the flying and they flew anything that was on the ground and ready to go.

I began flying P–39Qs late in 1943 and after the usual ground school for flight review, routes, radio frequencies, emergency procedures, we were issued our flight equipment for the Alaska flight. It consisted of a backpack parachute, a .45 caliber automatic and a special pillow-type cushion we sat on that contained all our emergency food rations, extra ammo, and flares. Not much to take with you if you had to jump. In winter, we had big flying boots, parkas, hats, and gloves – all furlined and it was a hell of a job getting into and out of a 39 or 63 while enclosed in all this bulk.

Radio equipment was primitive with LF ranges but later on, VHF came into use. Most aircraft had ADF or loop-type ADFs which were fairly accurate but the further north you flew the worse the radios operated. The major air bases along the route were at Whitehorse and Edmonton. The other refuelling stops at first were dirt strips with tents. Later they were updated with hangars and black top and the usual tarpaper shacks and pot-bellied stoves. At first, maps were inaccurate with many major landmarks often shown 15 to 20 miles from their actual positions and many of the peaks were higher than shown. The Canadian Rockies were always to our left and we followed the Alaskan Highway, or had it in view for about 900 miles out of the 1,935 mile route from Great Falls to Fairbanks.

When ferrying fighters we flew in better weather since we had no wing de-icers and we would always fly 500 ft on top if the weather was poor and would make a flight plan only if our destination was open. But with the other type aircraft we flew in any kind of weather. With luck we made 800 miles the first day, other times we would fly only as far as good weather would allow. A typical trip in Kingcobras would be to leave Great Falls in the morning, land at Edmonton for fuel and lunch and then take off for Fort St John. We would stay overnight there and in the morning we would clear for Whitehorse, refuel and go on into Fairbanks. Sometimes we made the trip in two days but that was rare. After making our delivery to Fairbanks we would catch a C–47 flight back to Great Falls, flown by Western Airlines pilots under contract to the Army.

Weather was our greatest enemy and one problem which we could not control. Summer was the best time from May through October when most days were clear and only the usual summer rain and thunderstorms were seen and avoided. But the winter months were horrible. At times temperatures went to 55 below and many air bases would sock in zero-zero within three minutes and aircraft would not start until the bush pilots taught us about diluting the gas with oil. When the temperatures were low, aircraft were put into hangars and started inside. Then the doors would be opened quickly and you taxied out and called the tower as you rolled along for takeoff instructions. Many of our ferry flights took two weeks because of bad weather and sometimes you would be weathered in for a week at one base.

Getting down to the business of flying, P–39s and P–63s were where the action was. The similarity of the two aircraft was apparent when you got into the cockpit. Both aircraft were mainly electrical in operation; the gear, flaps and the props were General Motors Aeroproducts units that were linked with the throttle. Some P–39s came through with Curtiss Electric props. The 63 was a bigger aircraft

The Russians received the majority of the P-63 Kingcobras produced yet they never paid for them, ignoring the terms of the American Lend-Lease contract.

in all departments and a great improvement over the 39. The fuel arrangement was similar and both carried about the same quantity of fuel. The 63 had 68 gallon tanks in each wing and 75 gallon auxiliary tanks under each wing. The 39s had 60 gallon tanks in each wing and early models carried a big 175 gallon belly tank between the main landing gear and it was a handicap in flying, affecting airspeed and flight characteristics.

The major improvements that Bell made with the P-63 were the laminar-flow wing, four blade propeller and two larger coolant radiators to overcome the ground heating problem that the 39 had. As a rule, the 63 encountered no ground heating problems at all unless it was extremely hot and there was some traffic delay in getting off the ground.

The early model P-63s had a 1,325 hp Allison and later on they installed the new 1,510 hp Allison in the C model. The 63 could climb to 10,000 feet in a shade over two minutes while the 39 took about three minutes to do the same. The 63 was about 25 to 30 mph faster than a 39 in both cruise and top speeds. On ferry flights we cruised the 63 at about 250 mph IAS versus 230 mph for the 39. The 63 grossed 8,800 lbs on takeoff and the 39 grossed out at 7,700 lbs, which made a great deal of difference in takeoff, climb and general flight operations. On our ferrying

flights no oxygen was carried so we limited our flights to 10,000 ft or below. A few times, in order to get above weather we encountered en route, we had to get up to 15,000 ft or higher for short periods and then come back on down again. But usually we stayed down around 5,000 ft above the terrain and on many trips we cruised at 500 ft or below and flew low the entire leg of that part of the trip just to sightsee. As we approached our landing destination we would pull up to around 1,000 ft and make the usual traffic pattern.

Of course, the tricycle landing gear was the best part of flying 39s, 38s, and 63s. You could taxi faster, had greater ground visibility and the landings and takeoffs were simple compared with the conventional type of landing gear. Ferrying the aircraft with auxiliary tanks under each wing was not too pleasant for many reasons. If you had engine failure on takeoff you could not or did not hardly have time to release the tanks and in flight they slowed you down about seven to ten mph and you were not supposed to exceed about 275 IAS with the tanks attached. However, we exceeded this airspeed on many occasions and few tanks ever popped off. But they could be released electrically if necessary by hitting the wing tank switches and pressing the top button on the stick. The P-63 had delightful flight characteristics. Using 54 inches manifold pressure for takeoff, accelerating rapidly, and with proper trim, the Kingcobra would fly itself off the ground. Torque was no problem, or at least not as bad as in the P-51, but right

rudder had to be used in most takeoffs to ensure a good straight pattern.

Back to the Alaska ferry flights. Fairbanks is where the fun began and the excitement really made the adrenalin flow. Crews were assigned from Gore Field on the day before the flight. Anywhere from three to 15 pilots were sent over to East Base for briefing and aircraft assignments. The size of the flight depended on how many aircraft were ready to go and how many qualified pilots were available. Usually the flight was made up of five to seven aircraft. The flight leader ran the show. He was a pilot who had five or more trips to Fairbanks and he was given a secret flight number for the trip as aircraft numbers were never used en route. So the flight leader designated who was to fly number two, three, four, etc. As an example, the flight number might be 150 and each pilot was designated 150A (Able), 150B (Baker) and so forth. The takeoffs and landings were a set procedure throughout the trip. Formation flying was a must and any pilot who later turned out to be poor in formation flying was usually relegated to some other type of flying. At this point none of us realized that our flight tactics would later be the same ones that the Blue Angels and other flight demonstration teams use in their operations.

The pilots were driven out to the planes took their usual pre-flight walk around their aircraft and got seated and ready to start engines. On a signal from the flight leader, all engines were started after the flight leader got his going. The flight leader handled all radio transmissions to the tower, range stations, etc. After permission to taxi was given, the flight leader began to taxi and each wing man followed out to the run-up area at the end of the active runway. After all run-ups were completed the flight leader got clearance for all members of the flight to taxi onto the runway. The leader was in the center with each wing man staggered to his right and his left. After all flight members were on the runway and holding, the flight leader began his takeoff roll. After he broke ground he continued a normal climb straight out for a longer than usual period and then began a shallow turn to the left. As he broke ground, the number two man started his roll, and as he broke ground number three began his roll and this took place until all flight members were airborne.

The last man usually had to make a quickie left turn shortly after takeoff to catch up with the rest of the flight. After all members joined up on the leader in an echelon formation, the leader made shallow turns to get us all lined up for a flight over the field on the heading we were to take toward our first ground reporting station. After we left the area the flight broke up into a loose formation and we followed the flight leader from station to station until we approached our first refueling stop. Now the important part of formation flying was that many times we took off in good weather and then had to climb up through a solid overcast from 100 ft to 500 ft thick to get 500 ft on top, and likewise we had to regroup to make it back down through an overcast before landing. So we held a tight formation going up and coming down through the stuff. Our takeoff and landing minimums for fighter aircraft were usually 1,000 ft overcast and three mile visibility. The C–47s could be flown with 300 ft and one-half mile for takeoff and 500 ft and one mile for landing.

About ten miles from touchdown, the flight leader would call us all in for a close-in right or left echelon formation depending on the field and runway we were going to use. He would call the tower and request a straight-in approach. ach. Our usual tactic was to barrel in across the field at 400 to 500 ft and make a tactical peel-off and pull up to about 1,000 ft, drop the gear, and each wing man would space himself accordingly. The flight leader would land on the left side of the runway, number two would land on the right, and so on until all members had landed, usually three aircraft were on the runway at one time completing their landing

and getting off onto a taxi strip. Now, where some of the crazy weather came into play up in this part of the country was that the temperature and dew point were close so much of the time that the fields would sock in within two minutes, and sometimes the last man to land could hardly see the field. On several occasions the last man did not make it and pulled up and climbed back up through the overcast and circled, staying up there until someone came up to guide him back down and make an instrument approach when the field opened up a bit. We usually carried enough extra fuel to go on or return to the first emergency strip nearby which was open or had better landing minimums. You could get back up easily but it was getting down that was tough, and many times the older pilots had to help out a new man.

After a few trips north, we began to get to know most of the personnel at the various air bases en route and knew just about what we

could get away with regarding aerobatics, buzzing, and low altitude antics. Edmonton, Whitehorse and Fairbanks were big and you did not fool around at these fields, but the others were usually more relaxed and most anything was acceptable. Places like Watson Lake, Northway, Fort St John, Grand Prairie and Snag were small enough where you could get away with a lot of clowning around. A number of times we would be weathered in at one of these primitive strips and if we could not continue for a day or two, many of us would just takeoff and fly around the area and scout the countryside, put on little airshows, buzz the hell out of everything in the area, lakes, animals, and just have fun.

Many pilots would not do any of this and just stayed on the ground and would not break any rules. Some fields, in spite of the location and facilities, offered good food and had lots of recreation material. If a number of flights were all going north at once we would all agree to

Lt Ben Brown outfitted for a spot of cold weather flying in a Russian P–63. The area over which the P–63s were ferried was, in many parts, uncharted and being forced down could spell doom for the pilot. (B. L. Brown)

Above
Bell P–63 Kingcobras are given a final check at the factory before being allocated to ferry pilots who would begin the long flight to Alaska. The ramp at the Bell factory is literally covered with the red-starred machines. (Bell)

Above right
Another Kingcobra work of art was produced with Little Marge, a P–63C–5–BE. It is interesting to speculate exactly what the rather conservative-minded Russians had to think about all the scribbling on their new fighters. (B. L. Brown)

Above centre

This P–63C carries some more of Lt Brown's artwork. The car door entry and exit system on the P–63 was almost identical to the early Airacobra. (B. L. Brown)

Right

To help relieve the boredom of the long ferry flights, the pilots would chalk markings and messages on the Kingcobras. Lt Brown added his mother's name and a shark's mouth on 42–70763. On the original print the designation block under the pilot's door can be seen to read: 'US Army Air Forces USSR', giving an indication of the aircraft's Lend-Lease identity. (B. L. Brown)

stop at a certain base for a big party. Everyone carried liquor and did some bootlegging on the side and one of the big sports we enjoyed was playing poker. Everyone usually had plenty of money and the stakes were plenty high. Thousands of dollars were on the table during a day and each pot was easily worth a hundred or more. Crap shooting was also a favorite. Most of the pilots were on good terms with the base personnel but I did witness a few disputes that came to blows.

USO shows came through at times. No top entertainment but they made a good effort. Of course, many of the men were interested in the ladies who were in the show but they were nothing to get excited about as a rule and most of the base personnel had not been away from their girl friends or wives for too long a time so they were not too excited over the whole thing. I remember landing at Snag on one trip and the men on the field had no liquor or beer at all and were anxious to buy most anything. I auctioned off several fifths of average liquor I had for $60 a fifth (that's the most I ever received) with the usual price being $25 to $30.

The route to Ladd Field, Fairbanks, was designed to be about as safe as possible under wartime conditions. Radio facilities improved each month and by the end of the war the trip was very pleasant. We flew over vast areas of flat terrain and the huge Canadian Rockies on our left were beautiful to see and one never tired of looking at them. Many times the ground below was obscured by an overcast but the Rockies were always sticking above everything, and snow-covered. We used to fly over to them as they were quite close at certain places along our route and we liked to fly around the peaks and down into the valleys where we would see many types of deer, moose, antelope, bear, horned sheep, and even see eagles cruising around at various altitudes. At times geese by the hundreds would be spotted flying at 3,000 ft.

One of the most amusing and exciting incidents took place at Watson Lake. Several flights were weathered in for over a week and life was pretty boring. You can do just so much drinking, gambling, eating and sleeping. It was spring and the lake was still frozen. Several of the pilots with lots of energy decided to get some rifles and scout around, maybe shoot a rabbit or something. They started walking out across the field toward the trees and paralleling the lake when they literally ran into an Alaskan brown bear with a cub. In their excitement to get away, one of the pilots fell down and his gun accidentally discharged. The big mother bear became enraged and charged, chasing one of the pilots across the field. She nearly caught up with one pilot and

when another pilot fired off a shot slightly wounding the bear that only made matters worse. They headed for a small shack at the edge of the field and went inside, only to have the bear continue on right into the shack. They went out the back door in a great rush, the bear slowed down and tired out, let matters stand and limped back to her cub.

In the three years of operation of flying aircraft to Alaska, over 20 pilots were killed and many were forced down due to weather or mechanical difficulties, and I believe that only five never made it back. One pilot took about six weeks to walk out but he made it. Survival was questionable in winter and everyone who flew prayed his aircraft would not malfunction until he was close to a field or emergency strip. Some fields were so small and had so few RCAF personnel manning them that if you got caught in bad weather or at night, you had to buzz the field in order for them to turn on the lights.

Of the 40-plus trips I made north, I had only two close situations. One was lucky – we had just passed over Grand Prairie and had made our position report and were just about out of sight of the field when I noticed my oil pressure needle was slowly going down to zero. I immediately called the field for an emergency landing and peeled off to the left, my flight of five P-63s following me on in and by the time I hit the runway for a quickie cross-wind landing, the needle was on zero and I had to be towed in to the ramp. My flight continued on later in the day by tagging onto a flight that was passing by and I stayed a couple of days until the leak was repaired and then I took off and tagged along with another flight north.

The roughest situation was later on when I took off with a flight leaving Watson Lake. I sprung a coolant leak on takeoff and at 800 ft had no place to go. I could not make it back to the field at all, trees were everywhere and the engine froze and stopped. I soon found out that a fighter goes nowhere without that big prop turning. This is where the emergency procedures came into use. I merely pulled the emergency door handle, the door fell off and I rolled out the right side and away I went into the blue. When faced with a no-choice situation, you soon learn what to do real quick. My small 24 ft chute opened up quickly and I came down without any problem, except with my winter equipment increasing my weight I hit pretty hard in the trees and fell right on through down to the ground. Luckily the Alaskan Highway was a few miles away and I hiked over to it and started back to the field. After an hour or so from the time I hit the silk, some of the base personnel came rumbling down the stone and dirt highway and picked me up. Rescue was unknown up in that

country and we were told that your chances of getting found in winter were practically nil. It would have been great if we had helicopters at that time for that is the only thing that would have been able to get any of us out.

Another sidelight was having some female ferry pilots go north with us on some trips. They were known to all as WASPS and were very good pilots. I had met many of them while flying throughout the country. They flew mostly fighters but some were checked out in twin-engine as well. Many of the WASPS were stationed at Dallas or Long Beach. On one trip, two WASPS flew P-63s north with us. One of these girls was a Chinese-American who was later killed while landing at a field in the States. The WASPS proved to be a real asset and made the trip more enjoyable.

By the early summer of 1945, deliveries of Russian Lend-Lease aircraft came to a virtual halt. The war had ended with Germany, the defeat of Japan was near, and no further aid was needed. It seemed odd to see the air bases kind of dry up. By late summer many pilots and ground personnel were now being discharged if they had enough 'points'. Everyone was leaving or being transferred. Those of us who stayed in continued to ferry aircraft within the States, picking up planes from various air bases that were closing down and ferrying them to storage centers. The big storage bases then were Kingman, Arizona; Walnut Ridge, Arkansas; and Muskogee, Oklahoma. All kinds of aircraft imaginable were being flown to these bases; many were being stored and thousands of others were busted up for scrap value. By the winter of 1945, the bases in Montana were almost entirely closed. Gore Field was closed and personnel were either discharged or transferred; the big East Base was kept for future use.

In early 1946, the big storage bases were bursting at the seams with aircraft. It is a sight I shall never forget. One cannot comprehend the sight of thousands of beautiful aircraft of all types just sitting there in the sun and going to waste. I flew aircraft that had only 50 hours on them to these bases where they were pushed out into the field to sit and die. I had half seriously thought of flying a P-51 or a P-63 to my home and hiding it somewhere. I do not think anyone would have ever noticed that it was gone. They never would have missed it. This was the end of an era, one that will never exist again. We who lived and participated in those years never knew how wonderful it was until we got home and found out as time went by that now again we wished we could make just one more trip north. No other generation will ever experience a situation exactly like ours. It was great while it lasted.

BELL P–39 AIRACOBRA VARIANTS, SERIAL NUMBERS AND SPECIFICATIONS

Variants

XP–39 Prototype. Allison V–1710–17. No armament. One built.

XP–39A Proposed YP–39 fitted with V–1719–31 high-altitude powerplant. Not built.

XP–39B Prototype reconfigured with NACA and Army modifications.

YP–39 Service test aircraft. Fitted with 37 mm cannon and two .30 and two .50 caliber machine guns in the nose. Allison V–1710–37. Thirteen aircraft built.

P–39C First production variant. Originally to be designated P–45 because of changes from prototype. Armed with 37 mm cannon and four nose guns. Twenty built and three shipped to Britain via Lend-Lease. Allison V–1710–35 engine.

P–39D Fitted with self-sealing tanks and extra armor plate. Provision for carriage of drop tank or 500 lb bomb. D–2 armed with 37 mm cannon, two .50 caliber nose guns and four .30 caliber guns in the wing. D–1 fitted with 20 mm cannon in place of 37 mm weapon. The D–3 and D–4 were ground attack versions with extra armor plating. Total of 923 constructed. Allison V–1710–35.

Airacobra Mk 1 RAF variant. Same as the P–39D except for substitution of 37 mm cannon with a 20 mm cannon. Allison V–1710–E4 (export version of –35). Eventually rejected by RAF; 675 ordered with 212 diverted to USSR (54 lost during U-boat attacks on convoys), and 179 aircraft taken over by USAAF after 7 December 1941 as P–400.

XP–39E Three early production P–39Ds modified to flight test the new Continental V–1430–1. Modified with laminar flow wing and different tail configurations on each aircraft. Never flown with the Continental and instead powered with Allison V–1710–47. Eventual production as P–76 planned but cancelled. Three aircraft were used for test work with the new P–63.

P–39F Same as P–39D–1 with Aeroproducts propeller instead of the Curtiss Electric unit. Some modified as P–39F–2 with ground attack and recon. duties. Total of 229 built.

P–39G Same as P–39D–2 but with Aeroproducts propeller. However, aircraft not built under this designation (*see* P–39K–1, P–39L).

P–39K–1 First 210 aircraft of the P–39G order. V–1710–63 engine and Aeroproducts propeller.

P–39L Total of 250 built from P–39G order with Curtiss Electric propeller.

P–39M Total of 240 built. Allison V–1710–83 with Curtiss Electric propeller.

P–39N Allison V–1710–85 and Aeroproducts propeller with 11 ft 7 in diameter. Later production Ns had reduced internal fuel capacity. Total of 2,095 built.

P–39Q Two .50 caliber machine guns carried under wings in pods but these were deleted on many aircraft. Retained 37 mm cannon and two .50 caliber machine guns in nose. Some fitted with four-blade Aeroproducts propeller. Most sent to Russia under Lend-Lease. P–39Q–10 and above had propeller setting linked to the throttle for automatic adjustment. P–39Q–21 and 25 fitted with four-blade propeller. Allison V–1710–85. Total of 4,905 built.

TP–39Q Dual control indoctrination trainer modification of P–39Q.

A–7 Radio controlled target drone conversion of Airacobra. Apparently not built.

Serial Numbers

XP–39	38–326
YP–39	40–027 through 40–039
XP–39B	38–326
P–39C	40–2971 through 40–2990.
P–39D	40–2991 through 40–3050, 41–6722 through 41–6841, 41–6842 through 41–7052, 41–7057 through 41–7058, 41–7080 through 41–7115
P–39D–1	41–28257 through 41–28406, 41–38220 through 41–38404, 41–38563
P–39D–2	41–38405 through 41–38562
XP–39E	41–19501 through 41–19502 and 42–71464
P–39F	41–7116 through 41–7344
P–39J	41–7053 through 41–7056, 41–7059 through 41–7079
P–39K	42–4244 through 42–4453
P–39L	42–4454 through 42–4703
P–39M	42–4704 through 42–4943
P–39N	42–4944 through 42–5043, 42–8727 through 42–9126
P–39N–1	42–9127 through 42–9726, 42–18246 through 42–18545
P–39N–5	42–18546 through 42–19240
P–39O–1	42–19446 through 42–19595
P–39Q–5	42–19596 through 42–20545
P–39Q–10	42–20546 through 42–21250
P–39Q–15	44–2001 through 44–3000
P–39Q–20	44–3001 through 44–3850, 44–3859 through 44–3860, 44–3865 through 44–3870, 44–3875 through 44–3880, 44–3885 through 44–3890, 44–3895 through 44–3900, 44–3905 through 44–3910, 44–3915 through 44–3919, 44–3937 through 44–3940
P39Q–21	44–3851 through 44–3858, 44–3861 through 44–3864, 44–3871 through 44–3874, 44–3881 through 44–3884, 44–3891 through 44–3894, 44–3901 through 44–3904, 44–3911 through 44–3814, 44–3920 through 44–3936, 44–3941 through 44–4000
P–39Q–25	44–70905 through 44–71104
P–39Q–30	44–71105 through 44–71504
Airacobra Mk I	AH570 through AH739, AP264 through AP384, BW100 through BW183, BX135 through BX434

The following serial numbers are of interest to the Airacobra chronicle:

XFL–1	Highly modified Naval version of the Airacobra. One aircraft built, BuNo 1588.
F2L–K	Airacobras obtained by the Navy for use as drones. It is not known if the aircraft were radio controlled. Seven aircraft obtained, including BuNo 91102 and 91103 (102 was P–39Q–10–BE/ 42–20807, 103 was P–39Q–5–BE/42–19976). The other five aircraft carried BuNos 122447 through 122451.

Specifications

XP–39

Span	35 ft 10 in
Length	28 ft 8 in
Height	11 ft
Wing area	200 sq ft
Empty weight	3,995 lb
Loaded weight	5,550 lb
Max. speed	390 mph
Cruise speed	n/a
Ceiling	32,000 ft
Rate of climb	3,800 fpm
Range	n/a
Powerplant	Allison V–1710–17 of 1,150 hp

XP–39B

Span	34 ft
Length	29 ft 9 in
Height	11 ft 10 in
Wing area	213 sq ft
Empty weight	4,530 lb
Loaded weight	6,450 lb
Max. speed	375 mph
Cruise speed	310 mph
Ceiling	36,000 ft
Rate of Climb	2,800 fpm
Range	600 miles
Powerplant	Allison V–1710–37 of 1,090 hp

YP–39

Span	34 ft
Length	30 ft 2 in
Height	11 ft 10 in
Wing area	213 sq ft
Empty weight	5,042 lb
Loaded weight	7,235 lb
Max. speed	368 mph
Cruise speed	257 mph
Ceiling	34,500 ft
Rate of Climb	2,700 fpm
Range	600 miles
Powerplant	Allison V–1710–37 of 1,090 hp

P–39C

Span	34 ft
Length	30 ft 2 in
Height	11 ft 2 in
Wing area	213 sq ft
Empty weight	5,070 lb
Loaded weight	7,275 lb
Max. speed	379 mph
Cruise speed	274 mph
Ceiling	33,200 ft
Rate of climb	n/a
Range	500 miles
Powerplant	Allison V–1710–35 of 1,150 hp

P–39D

Span	34 ft
Length	30 ft 2 in
Height	11 ft 10 in
Wing area	213 sq ft
Empty weight	5,462 lb
Loaded weight	8,200 lb
Max. speed	368 mph
Cruise speed	213 mph
Ceiling	32,100 ft
Rate of Climb	2,720 fpm
Range	800 miles
Powerplant	Allison V–1710–35 of 1,150 hp

XP–39E

Span	35 ft 10 in
Length	31 ft 11 in
Height	11 ft 10 in
Wing area	236 sq ft
Empty weight	6,936 lb
Loaded weight	8,918 lb
Max. speed	386 mph
Cruise speed	205 mph
Ceiling	35,200 ft
Rate of climb	2,800 fpm
Range	500 miles
Powerplant	Allison V–1710–47 of 1,325 hp

P–39K

Span	34 ft
Length	30 ft 2 in
Height	11 ft 10 in
Wing area	213 sq ft
Empty weight	5,658 lb
Loaded weight	8,400 lb
Max. speed	368 mph
Cruise speed	213 mph
Ceiling	32,000 ft
Rate of climb	2,800 fpm
Range	750 miles
Powerplant	Allison V–1710–63 of 1,325 hp

P–39N

Span	34 ft
Length	30 ft 2 in
Height	12 ft 5 in
Wing Area	213 sq ft
Empty weight	5,657 lb
Loaded weight	8,200 lb
Max. speed	376 mph
Cruise speed	n/a
Ceiling	32,000 ft
Rate of climb	2,600 fpm
Range	750 miles
Powerplant	Allison V–1710–85 of 1,200 hp

P–39Q

Span	34 ft
Length	30 ft 2 in
Height	12 ft 5 in
Wing area	213 sq ft
Empty Weight	5,645 lb
Loaded weight	8,300 lb
Max. speed	385 mph
Cruise speed	n/a
Ceiling	35,000 ft
Rate of Climb	2,700 fpm
Range	650 miles
Powerplant	Allison V–1710–85 of 1,200 hp

Weight vs Horsepower

Many of Bell's problems with the Airacobra can be related to rapidly escalating weight which was not backed up by more engine power. This list gives a quick idea of the performance problems that beset the series.

	Max. Weight	Max. Horsepower
XP–39	5,550 lb	1,150 hp
XP–39B	6,450 lb	1,090 hp
YP–39	7,235 lb	1,090 hp
P–39C	7,275 lb	1,150 hp
P–39D	8,200 lb	1,150 hp
XP–39E	8,918 lb	1,325 hp
P–39K	8,400 lb	1,325 hp
P–39N	8,200 lb	1,200 hp
P–39Q	8,300 lb	1,200 hp

Armament

XP–39	None
XP–39B	None
YP–39	37 mm cannon/two .50 caliber MGs/two .30 caliber MGs
P–39C	37 mm cannon/two .50 caliber MGs/two .30 caliber MGs
P–39D	37 mm cannon/two .50 caliber MGs/four .30 caliber MGs
Airacobra Mk I	20 mm cannon/two .50 caliber MGs/four .30 caliber MGs
P–39D–1/D–2	20 mm cannon/two .50 caliber MGs/four .30 caliber MGs
P–39Q	37 mm cannon/two .50 caliber MGs/optional two .50 caliber MGs in wing

PART TWO

Curtiss P-40
A Fighter For All Seasons

Although basically obsolete at its time of entry into military service, the P–40 fought throughout World War Two and give outstanding service to the Army and America's Allies.

The morning sun rose to greet a bright and clear day over Wheeler Field, the United States Air Corps base just south of Ford Island, Honolulu, Oahu, Hawaiian Islands. The early rays glinted dully off the flat Olive Drab camouflage of the Curtiss P–40s of the 15th and 18th Pursuit Squadrons, 14th Pursuit Group, which were lined in neat and orderly rows, much as if the aircraft were waiting for an inspection or for the admiring glances from thousands of spectators at an air display. However, this was not to be just another typical day in paradise – it was the morning of 7 December 1941 and disaster was just moments away.

About six miles south from the large Wheeler base was Bellows Field, temporary home of the 47th Pursuit Squadron, 14th Pursuit Group, with 12 P–40Cs. Eight P–40Bs from the unit had been dispersed to a small dirt strip at Haleiwa, for training.

There was a distinct tension at the many

Racing back and forth across the Atlantic at full speed, dodging U-boats and long-range Fw 200s, the USS Ranger supplied American forces in the North African campaign with vitally needed Curtiss P–40F fighters. Powered by a Merlin, s/n 41–13352 is seen as it begins the take-off run as the carrier nears the coast. Carrying a large American flag on the fuselage for additional recognition, the P–40 pilots found little problem in taking off from the short carrier deck. This particular machine carries basic Royal Air Force camouflage of Middle Stone and Dark Earth upper surfaces with Azure Blue under surfaces. (USN)

X *P–40 in flight near the Buffalo factory in its original configuration with the radiator and airscoop located behind the trailing edge of the wing. Flying for the first time on 14 October 1938, the XP–40 was to undergo many modifications and the radiator installation was to eventually be moved under the nose. Original armament proposals were to have one .30 and one .50 caliber Browning machine gun mounted under the top cowling. Armament was not fitted and small metal blisters can be seen fitted on the two streamlined fairings for the weapons. Finish was overall highly polished natural metal. (Curtiss-Wright)*

A *s P–40 production increased, Curtiss-Wright proudly released this photograph with the caption 'One day's output of Curtiss P–40 fighters for national defense'. Little did the company realize how the production line would soon expand. Photographed on 13 September 1940, the day the War Department authorized an additional order for 540 aircraft, the P–40s are having their Allisons run in prior to test flying. (Curtiss-Wright)*

military bases in the Hawaiian Islands and the past months had seen countless rumors sweep through the bases. The rumors usually concerned the Japanese and the hostile movements of the Empire in the Far East and Pacific. Alerts had passed through the island's bases – aircraft rumbled aloft for patrols, ships headed out from the congestion of Pearl Harbor into the clean, open seas while Army personnel manned sand-bag reinforced machine gun pits. Yet the alerts had a feeling of unreality. No effective defensive action was taken.

The pre-war Army Air Corps was almost a country club. There were few aircraft and few pilots but most of those pilots had been hand-picked and there was a distinct clanishness in the organization. The aircraft, most considered obsolete by European war standards, were well-maintained, but, in reality, they had been built for a type of war that would never come. The colorful Army Air Corps colors were rapidly giving way to the dull camouflage so

effectively displayed on the newly arrived Curtiss fighters, rushed to the island in a vague attempt to reinforce the pitiful air defenses that surrounded the Navy's massive port.

On a peak near the coast, the Army had erected one of the new radar detection units. The radar's signal swept out to sea, searching for 'blips' that could well mean the start of a Japanese invasion. However, radar was new fangled and to Army officers, many of whom had been trained in cavalry charges with drawn sabres – and still took that type of tactic seriously – the radar unit was more of an extravagant toy from Washington to be tolerated but not taken seriously.

It was Sunday morning, a notorious time on American pre-war military bases since it was a period to 'stand down', to relax, to engage in sports or to socialize at the officers' club. Even with the many alerts that had passed through the island, this Sunday was really no different to any of the others that had passed before. At the airfields, the pristine fighters stood quietly, their neat rows in contrast to the way they had been scattered about in previous weeks when it was decided to disperse them to make them less vulnerable to a possible air attack. The military had a great distrust of many of the islanders (lots of whom were of Japanese ancestry) and this fear of the 'Yellow Peril' and possible sabotage to the aircraft, which could not be properly guarded in their dispersed positions, led to the unwise order to move all the aircraft to central parking areas where they could be put virtually wingtip to wingtip. This made guarding them against some sort of sabotage much easier, but it also made for one hell of a target.

Unknown to the Americans (only due to faulty intelligence and failure of high ranking officers to draw obvious conclusions from assembled facts), Vice Admiral Chuichi Nagumo had already launched a large force of attack aircraft from his carriers, which were about 200 miles north of Oahu. Led by the daring and experienced Commander Mitsuo Fushida, the aerial warriors consisted of the new and deadly Zero fighters, Val dive bombers and Kate torpedo bombers.

Tension among the Japanese was very high since they knew that at some point the Americans would have to detect such a large fleet of aircraft and ships, but their main defense was the incredible discipline common to Japanese military aviators combined with complete radio silence.

Fushida must have felt a sense of accomplishment as he watched the formation of 183 aircraft fly through the still air, the early morning light beginning to turn dark shadows into hauntingly beautiful pastel shades – the

rising sun throwing its rays through a cloud to form a sunburst effect not unlike the Empire's flag. Fushida became very excited by this natural phenomenon, viewing it as a mystical sign portending the success of the sneak attack.

The lone radar operator sitting in his hut atop the Oahu hill began picking up blips of targets that were over 130 miles away. Frantically he called the lieutenant who was his commanding officer and reported the unprecedented sighting. The lieutenant thought very little of the importance the enlisted operator was putting on the huge number of blips. The report was passed to a central information center where it was filed for later inspection.

The Japanese force flew over the beautiful beaches of Oahu totally unopposed, the only spot of trouble coming when a light civilian aircraft blundered near the formation of warplanes. It was briefly attacked but managed to escape.

Without any warning, the Japanese aerial armada swept over the American Fleet – Fushida, stunned by the enemy's lack of response, radioed the coded message *Tora, Tora, Tora* (Tiger, Tiger, Tiger) that would let Nagumo know the targets had been reached with total surprise. The Japanese force split apart, some going to attack the anchored fleet while others struck at the airfields to neutralize the aerial defenses which could ruin their mission.

Zeros and Vals blasted the ranks of P–40s at Wheeler. That they were neatly arranged was bad enough, but there was no way that they could respond to the attack since they were neither fueled nor armed! This was another of

the anti-sabotage plans to prevent one burning or exploding aircraft from igniting the entire row. The P–40s were instantly riddled by cannon shells and bullets from the Zeros or blown apart by bombs from the Vals that descended on the field in screaming dives. The results of the attack on Wheeler were devastating; 62 P–40Bs were destroyed and not even one of them had the chance to fire a shot in anger.

Meanwhile, at Bellows just one enemy aircraft attacked the airfield but the P–40s were in the same condition as those at Wheeler – unarmed and unfueled. Pilots and ground crews frantically began getting their fighters ready for flight at about 0840 hrs, knowing full well that one enemy aircraft would merely signal the arrival of more. Just as some of the P–40s took off, a flight of Zeros hit the field. The P–40s stood no chance as they began to burn on the runway or crashed shortly after take-off. Of the 12 P–40Cs on the field, only two survived the attack.

In the crazy panic that gripped the island during the attack, some pilots of the 47th Pursuit Group somehow managed to stay cool and drive to Haleiwa where their P–36As and P–40Bs were stationed. The ground crews had quickly realized the seriousness of the situation as they saw long columns of black smoke come from the bases and heard the terrific din of combat – the Curtiss fighters were ready for combat, engines ticking over as the crew chiefs sat in the cockpits hoping that their pilots would be alive after the initial attacks.

Due to the success of the initial wave of Japanese aircraft, the fleet had launched a follow-up second wave of 183 aircraft that proceeded to blast targets left over from the

Two P–40s formate for the camera plane, the closest aircraft being s/n 40–309. Except for three early production aircraft, the P–40 was the first fighter to be delivered in camouflage to the Army. Standard paint for the P–40 was Olive Drab and Neutral Gray with red, white and blue tail stripes, no national insignia on the fuselage, and standard insignia on the wings. As can be seen, these aircraft were unarmed. Also note the lack of armor glass in the windshield. (Curtiss-Wright)

first attack. The air was full of enemy aircraft and increasing bursts of anti-aircraft fire as the P–40Bs clawed skyward. A quick plan had been devised while they were on the ground to patrol the coast, then land at Wheeler for more fuel and information if available. From the air they could view the devastation of Pearl Harbor and surrounding areas. Coastal patrol proved fruitless so the fighters recovered at Wheeler, having to taxi between rows of burning aircraft to get fuel, the burning wreckage of dozens of Curtiss fighters proving the folly of becoming a sitting duck. Information was fragmented at best. All the Army knew was that they were under attack.

The P–40 pilots spent the least amount of time on the ground as possible. Airborne once again, Lts Ken Taylor and George Welch quickly ran into the enemy and engaged two aircraft, sending them down in flames. Unknown to the P–40 pilots, the P–36As had engaged the enemy shortly before – thus having the honor of drawing the first blood over Pearl. The pilots headed back to Wheeler for more fuel and, while landing, were shot at by panicked anti-aircraft gunners, a P–36A falling in flames.

Airborne, the small fighter force engaged a group of attacking aircraft heading for Ewa and managed to destroy two of the aircraft and break up the attack. Orbiting over the sprawling base, the pilots slowly began to realize that the enemy had departed, leaving behind a vast pall of smoke and fire. Returning to refuel and rearm at Wheeler, the aircraft were soon back in the air for no one knew if another wave would soon be on its way. Rumors rapidly flashed from one end of the island to the other

concerning sightings of enemy paratroopers or landing parties. Fortunately, all proved to be false but the one inescapable fact was that the American fleet and the Army Air Corps had taken a mauling from which it appeared doubtful that they could recover.

For the Curtiss P–40, the attack had been its first chance to do combat in US Army service. The very few fighters that got off the ground acquitted themselves well but Army fields were packed with the wreckage of a fighter force: only two of the 12 P–40Cs were usable while 62 of the 87 P–40Bs had been knocked out of action. It was indeed a surprise attack and a masterpiece of enemy planning but the specter of the P–40 would rise from the ashes at Hickam, Wheeler and Bellows to dog the Japanese Empire until the end of the war.

During 1936 and 1937, rapid advances were being made in the design of pursuit/fighter aircraft by the major powers. Curtiss, with the P–36 contract firmly established, sought to

increase its contract base by offering new fighter designs to the Army. The design team at Curtiss had always been a bit conservative and, when they could, would retain as much of a previous design as possible in order to save the company money and to reduce overall design time. Donovan Berlin felt that by taking the basic P–36 airframe and adding a new powerplant and a few updates, a new fighter could be developed which would offer enough of an increase in perforrance to interest the Army.

The problem would be the engine. The only inline military powerplant in American production was the Allison V–1710. Donovan liked the lower frontal area of the V–12 but was a bit disheartened by the rather low horsepower figures. Assured by Allison that the V–1710 had a great deal of growth potential, Donovan began with two designs. One, the Model 75I, evolved into the P–37 and was a failure, as recounted in an earlier chapter. The other, the Model 75P, took

advantage of Allison's development of a gear-driven supercharger to boost performance at altitude. With this engine, Curtiss felt that a converted P–36 could give a top speed of 350 mph. The Army began to take interest.

By March 1938, a proposal was approved that would see the tenth production P–36 pulled from service and modified to carry the new engine and supercharger. Donovan designed a new cowling that wrapped closely around the V–12 while the radiator was placed in a scoop under the rear fuselage, slightly behind the pilot. Armament remained the same inadequate mix as on the P–36.

Typical of the period, construction of the new fighter was very rapid and, designated XP–40, the fighter made its first flight on 14 October 1938. Right from the beginning, the XP–40 displayed many problems. The Allison V–1710–19 (maximum 1,160 horsepower) and airframe combination could only attain 299 mph. Also, the radiator was not providing adequate cooling. Some quick re-engineering

P–40 belonging to the 20th Pursuit Group, 55th Pursuit Squadron, assigned to March Field, California, photographed at Oakland, California. Although an operational group, the 55th was also responsible for testing the new aircraft. As can be seen, this is a fully armed fighter with two nose guns and two wing guns. The legend U.S. Army was painted under the wing in Insignia Blue. (W. T. Larkins)

took place and the radiator was shifted to a new position under the nose. Not only did this increase the top speed to 342 mph because of a drastic decrease in drag, but the new position also provided better cooling.

The modified XP–40 was ready in time for the big Air Corps fighter fly-off at Wright Field. The eclectic gathering at Wright included two other Curtiss products, the P–37 and Hawk 75R, while other designs represented included the Bell Airacobra, Lockheed Lightning and Seversky AP–4. The Army inspected designs, went over plans, checked performance figures and let the aircraft represented by flying prototypes be taken aloft by Army and company test pilots. Taking place during January 1939, the XP–40 achieved what Curtiss had been hoping for: an immense contract for 524 production aircraft worth $12,872,898, the largest contract issued since World War One. Two of the other competitors went on to achieve their own success but, for Curtiss, this victory led to lucrative future contracts.

The Curtiss plant at Buffalo immediately began to gear up for large-scale production and, fortunately, the fact that most of the tooling employed on the P–36 could be immediately transferred to the new P–40 line saved much time.

Test pilot Lloyd Child took the first production P–40 aloft on 4 April 1940. Of the 524 aircraft order, the first 199 were P–40s, with

White-nosed P–40 of the 8th Pursuit Group. The first P–40 was lightly armed by European standards with two .50 calibers in the nose and two .30 calibers in the wing. The extremely clean cowling around the Allison V–1710–33 was the work of designer Don Berlin. Deliveries of the P–40 began in June 1940. (USAF)

the new model number of Hawk 81A, and this group was delivered in the amazingly short period between 1 June and 15 October 1940! The P–40 was armed with only two .50 caliber machine guns with 200 rpg, and they were delivered without armor protection, armor glass or sealing fuel tanks, stupid omissions considering the period and the fact that designers knew better since they regularly received reports on aerial battles over Europe. Interestingly the P–40 was the first fighter delivered to the Army in the new overall camouflage of Olive Drab and Neutral Gray, only the first three aircraft being left in natural metal finish.

The Army's base at Langley Field, Virginia, was selected as the first operational P–40 base. Many early P–40s were diverted to Wright Field for intensive testing but the honor of being first to operate the type went to the 8th Pursuit Group which consisted of the 33rd, 35th and 36th Pursuit Squadrons. The 8th was to test out the basic combat usefulness of the design, define the airframe's limits and

develop basic combat tactics. P–40 expansion continued with the equipping of the 20th Pursuit Group at March Field, California, and of the 31st Pursuit Group at Selfridge Field in Michigan.

The new P–40s really looked warlike but Army pilots were disturbed by the lack of the equipment previously mentioned. A main complaint was the totally inadequate armament system. This was cured in a rather unusual manner. During the initial stages of P–40 design and construction, many foreign countries were scrambling for the few combat designs produced in America. On 25 March 1940, President Roosevelt deflated the bubble of isolationism a bit when he allowed friendly foreign countries to purchase American combat machines on a 'cash and carry' basis. Curtiss salesmen opened their doors to the British and French who placed large orders for the new fighter. However, this meant that the aircraft would probably have to be taken out of the Army order so that the vitally needed

warplanes could get to their new destinations. This decision did not displease the Army since that organization was not all that happy with the P–40 and the extra time the delay would give them could be employed to their benefit, adding the requested combat items and increasing the armament.

The British requested that their aircraft be fitted with more guns, so the wing was redesigned to mount four .30 machine guns along with the two .50 caliber units in the nose. The first P–40s (or Tomahawk Is) to be received by Britain were actually from the French order since the country fell to the German onslaught before the fighters could be delivered. Unsuitable for aerial combat with the Germans, the Tomahawks were assigned to the Army Cooperation role and it was felt that they could give valuable low-level service in the event of a German invasion.

The US Army liked the four gun wing and 44 wings were grabbed from the British order and added to P–40 fuselages, the new variants

becoming P–40Gs. Some of these aircraft were supplied to the Soviet Union but the remainder were sent to March Field, Hamilton Field and Pope Field.

The Tomahawk Mk Is divested from the French order to the British following the fall of France were unarmored and did not have self-sealing fuel tanks, but the 90 French aircraft remaining on the Curtiss production line were modified at British insistence to have an armor glass windshield, some armor protection and self-sealing tanks. Other modifications included adding standard British instruments and equipment such as throttles that the pilot pushed forward to add power and pulled back to decrease power. For some reason, the French insisted on using throttles which operated in the opposite manner. As can be imagined, forgetful British pilots probably soundly cursed the French after moving the throttle incorrectly. These modified aircraft were given the designation of Tomahawk Mk IIA, as were a further 20 aircraft built es-

pecially for British contracts. Another 930 fighters were constructed as Tomahawk Mk IIBs which had .303-in wing guns, British equipment, a revised fuel system and provision for the carriage of a belly tank. Although they were given the name Tomahawk, Americans usually referred to the fighters as P–40s – no matter what model.

Of the British order, 100 Mk IIs supplied to the Chinese government for the newly organized American Volunteer Group (AVG), formed by General Claire Chennault with the understanding and assistance of the American government. Popularly known as the Flying Tigers, Chennault and his assistants recruited

This unarmed P–40 carries the tail code '20 MD' which signified that the fighter was assigned to the Wright Field Material Division, where it was probably used for testing. The tail wheel appears to be permanently fixed in a down position although the P–40 did have a retractable unit that was completely covered by small clam shell doors. (USN/80G–15488)

American pilots from the USAAC, USN and USMC, although a few civilian pilots also joined the organization. The chance to fly in combat, exotic travel, good pay (along with a cash bonus for every enemy aircraft shot down) and the complete cooperation of the government made the job a fighter pilot's dream and applicants were pushing each other aside to sign the papers.

Making their way to China in a variety of ships, the rather diverse AVG pilots found the reality less attractive. Most were appalled by the condition of Chinese airfields, overall poor quality of the aircraft being operated by the Chinese and overall poor quality of the Chinese pilots themselves. Chennault's agents in the United States were gleefully spending Chinese gold on a wide variety of aircraft, everything from transports to second-rate fighters such as the Curtiss Demon – an underpowered, under-armed disaster that met a quick end with the enemy over China.

The P-40s' arrival was met with anticipation since the pilots knew it would give a much more even footing with the Japanese than any warplane operated by the Chinese. Fearsome shark's mouths were added to the P-40's sleek cowling, a by no means new idea. Chennault had seen a color illustration in the *India Illustrated Weekly* depicting No 112 Sqn, RAF, operating from the Libyan desert with shark's mouths on their P-40s. Impressed by the looks, Chennault had the insignia copied for his P-40s. Chennault was always a bit puzzled by the fact the AVG had been dubbed the 'Flying Tigers' by the media and it was not until just before the AVG disbanded that some form of appropriate insignia to go along with the name was created. At the request of the Chinese Defense Supplies organization in Washington, Roy Williams, an artist with Walt Disney Studios in Hollywood, created the AVG insignia. The attractive emblem consisted of a winged tiger flying through a large stylized V which stood, of course, for victory. By June 1941, the Flying Tigers had set up base at Toungoo, Burma, and were test flying their P-40s which had arrived in crates aboard transport ships. The AVG had several primary objectives, one being the disruption of Japanese bombing raids, another the protection of the area between Lashio and Chungking where the vital Burma Road kept war supplies flowing to the fighting front.

General Chennault was planning a battle strategy by which he could attack and destroy Japanese aircraft and airfields. Chennault re-alized that the average Japanese aviator was very disciplined and rarely disobeyed orders or used individual initiative. By using his P-40s in daring strikes that the enemy could not anticipate, Chennault hoped to create an element of fear in the Japanese mind to such an extent that they would believe that the fanged aircraft were invincible!

Chennault planned to have the AVG constituted with three squadrons, creatively designated Nos 1, 2 and 3, each fielding 18 P-40s, but as the AVG worked up to combat strength, Pearl Harbor was attacked and the United States was formerly at war. To get the three squadrons closer to the enemy, Chennault moved the AVG to Kunming, a name that would go down in the annals of aerial combat.

Maintenance of the P-40s was a problem, and spare parts were almost nonexistent, although some P-40s were cannibalized for spares. When the AVG flew its first mission on 20 December, all the squadrons were not up to the planned strength. Flying from Kunming, the 1st and 2nd Squadrons surprised ten Ki-21 bombers and blasted six from the sky in a stunning defeat for the Japanese. The Japanese had grown so sure of aerial superiority over the Chinese that the bombers did not even have a fighter escort ... a conceit which was soon to change.

Chennault and the Chinese had developed a 'bamboo telegraph' by which forward posts would pass back reports of advancing Japanese aircraft until the message reached the AVG. With this form of communication, Chennault managed to avoid one of his real nightmares – being caught on the ground like the Americans at Pearl Harbor. The General was very excited about the first combat mission, as he recalled after World War Two:

This was the decisive moment I had been awaiting for more than four years – American pilots in American fighter planes aided by a Chinese ground warning net about to tackle a formation of the Imperial Japanese Air Force, which was then sweeping the Pacific skies victorious everywhere. I felt that the fate of China was riding in the P–40 cockpits through the wintery sky over Yunnan. I yearned heartily to be ten years younger and crouched in a cockpit instead of a dugout, tasting the stale rubber of an oxygen mask and peering ahead into limitless space through the cherry-red rings of a gunsight.

The 3rd Squadron, AVG, was sent to Mingaladon airfield near Rangoon, Burma, on 12 December to assist the Royal Air Force Brewster Buffalo and Hurricane squadrons in the defense of that important city. While over Rangoon, the AVG saw heavy action during a ten-week period. That, according to Chennault, 'saw the AVG with between twenty and five serviceable P–40s', but they acquitted themselves with distinction, as Chennault recalled:

This tiny force met a total of a thousand-odd Japanese aircraft over southern Burma and Thailand. In thirty-one encounters, they destroyed 217 enemy planes and probably destroyed forty-three. Our losses in combat were four pilots killed in the air, one killed while strafing, and one taken prisoner. Sixteen P–40s were destroyed. During the same period the RAF, fighting side-by-side with the AVG, destroyed seventy-four enemy planes, probably destroyed thirty-three, with a loss of twenty-two Buffaloes and Hurricanes.

Chennault could be proud of his men and their P–40s along with the fact that the tactics he used against the Japanese were paying off. The General advocated hitting Japanese aircraft once, preferably diving from an altitude advantage, and then zooming away – definitely not staying around to dogfight. This was the same tactic employed by the more successful fighter commanders in the Pacific once the war began to move against the Japanese. Even though the P–40 was not heavily armed, a well-directed burst could usually tear an unarmored Japanese plane to pieces.

Suddenly, the AVG and its commander were world-wide news and reporters kept showing up with regularity at the AVG airfields. Not many were well-liked and some were physically ejected from the bases. However, there was no denying the AVG's fame and Winston

Churchill paid the AVG the following compliment, 'The victories of these Americans', he wrote to the Governor of Burma, 'over the rice paddies of Burma are comparable in character if not in scope with those won by the RAF over the hop fields of Kent in the Battle of Britain.'

The AVG fought hard and well for six months, eventually claiming a total of 286 enemy aircraft destroyed. As so many P–40s had been lost in accidents as well as combat, the original 100 aircraft were considerably depleted, and 30 P–40Es were supplied to the unit. Since America was fully involved in the war, the AVG became a bit of an embarrassment because American pilots were virtually running wild against the Japanese and collecting 'bounty' money for each enemy aircraft that they destroyed. The AVG was incorporated into the United States Army Air Forces on 5 July 1942 with the designation of the 23rd Pursuit Squadron, China Air Task Force. The unit was commanded by Chennault, who did not like the idea of disbanding the AVG, as crusty and demanding of his pilots as ever. Of the original AVG pilots, just a few decided to stay with the new unit, others returning back to their original branches of service (a young pilot named Pappy Boyington decided to return to the Marines and make a name for himself in the South Pacific), while others simply retired. It is worth noting that the new unit would not slacken its high goals and they continued to fight the enemy with unabated ferocity.

Back at Curtiss, new variants of the P–40 were being created in an effort to update the fighter's capabilities. As mentioned, the AVG had received 30 of the new P–40Es and this model was a significant advance in the evolution of the fighter.

Curtiss constructed 23 P–40Ds (Curtiss Model Hawk 81A–1) with a 1,150 hp Allison V–1710–39 located in a redesigned nose section. The engine had a spur reduction gear which meant that the entire engine installation was shorter while having a higher thrust line. The increased horsepower offered hope of a better performance. The –39 was capable of operating at a war emergency power rating of 1,470 hp for five minutes, while the 1,150 hp rating could be maintained up to 11,500 ft if the throttle was pushed into the military power setting.

With the slightly shorter redesigned nose, which destroyed the shark-like contours of the earlier P–40D, the P–40D's nose guns were eliminated, but the wing was modified to hold four .50 caliber Browning machine guns. Detail modifications that had come about through the earlier models' combat experience were also made. Additional armor plate was

added to the cockpit and to vital areas in the airframe, and improved radios were located behind the pilot, while other detail refinements made the P–40D a more combat-worthy aircraft.

Concerned about the P–40D carrying only four guns, the Army Air Forces specified that future deliveries should have six .50 caliber wing guns. This change quickly came about and the new model, the P–40E, also picked up a new name: the Warhawk. To show how quickly aircraft design was changing, the P–40E had even more improvements including a centerline shackle that could carry an external fuel tank or a 500 lb bomb, giving the P–40E a new ground attack role. The remainder of the airframe behind the firewall was basically the same as on earlier P–40s and this caused some trouble.

The increased horsepower, weight and shorter nose combined to make the P–40E a much more sensitive fighter to fly when compared to the earlier variants. Stability became much more of a problem and P–40E pilots had to be particularly aware of the fact, under certain conditions and loadings, the controls could become very difficult to move and became almost frozen in high speed dives. Also, the short fuselage/higher horsepower combination caused torque to become more noticeable as the throttle was advanced for take-off. Many P–40Es were demolished in ground loops by inexperienced pilots who did not compensate for the increased torque by adding more rudder and trim. This problem became serious enough for the Army to issue special instructions for operating the P–40E.

The anticipated improvement in performance with the P–40E did not really materialize since the aircraft was heavier. However, the P–40E was marginally faster at all altitudes than earlier models. The Army contracted for 820 P–40Es. Deliveries had commenced before Pearl Harbor, and 74 P–40Es were operational in the Philippines with the Army on 7 December 1941. These aircraft had been assigned to the 24th Pursuit Group, tasked to defend the Philippines, not an easy task when one considers that the Philippines comprise over 7,000 islands! The 24th Pursuit Group was made up of the 3rd, 17th, 20th and 21st Pursuit Squadrons but not all were completely equipped with P–40Es since P–40Bs were still on the inventory.

America had a long and complex relationship with the Philippines, many American officers regarding the Philippines as a strategic base for American surveillance of the Pacific. Forces on the Philippines were attacked almost ten hours after the initial raid on Pearl Harbor but those ten hours were not used for obtaining maximum readiness – instead it was a

period of confusion with one rumor after another causing a virtual panic among some sectors.

Aerial defense of the Philippines depended on a rather motley bag of flying machines totaling 162 aircraft. Many were obsolete – the Philippine 6th PS was flying seven Boeing P–26 fighters with open cockpits and fixed landing gear – but there was a mixed force of 107 P–40Es and Bs. Some of the P–40s were still in their packing crates – newly arrived, there had not been time to unpack and assemble the fighters for test flying. Other pursuits that rounded out the collection included P–35As. American strength was concentrated at Clark Field (20th PS with 18 P–40Bs), Nichols Field (17th PS and 21st PS each with 18 P–40Es) and Iba Field (3rd PS with 18 P–40Es and six P–35As).

As with other American Pacific bases, much was lacking in the Philippines. Communications were very poor and quite often did not function at all while commanding officers had a limited overall view of the entire military situation. Oddly enough, other more basic problems were to plague the Americans. The pilots were not well versed in aerial gunnery, maintenance on the aircraft was marginal and many of the subsystems gave trouble or simply would not work in the vile tropical climate. Particularly vexing was the fact that considerable portions of ammunition for the P–40 guns were faulty so, in an overall view, the Americans had virtually everything going against them except for one element: courage.

After word reached the Philippines of the Pearl Harbor attack, there was discussion of launching immediately an air strike against Japanese bases in Formosa. This would almost certainly have been a suicide mission because it would have been flown by a handful of Douglas B–18 Bolos and early model Boeing B–17 Flying Fortresses, but such a raid could have caused the enemy some damage and delayed his military plans. However, the American military command was in such confusion that it was just not possible to plan the raid.

Iba Field scrambled some P–40s on a search mission but there was no interception. They were probably chasing an elusive Japanese recon aircraft since Iba's primitive radar, the

Tigers on the prowl. These Tomahawks of the American Volunteer Group came from a batch of 100 H81–A2s that had diverted from the Royal Air Force order. The American government 'allowed' Chennault to recruit aviators directly from military service and many pilots were lured by the chance to get into combat. Pay was around $750 per month with 30 days leave per year, free quarters and servants, money for food and, perhaps more importantly, a $500 cash bonus for each Japanese aircraft destroyed. Chennault did not go wanting for volunteers.

Although the AVG quickly established itself as a deadly force that the enemy had to reckon with, the AVG's airfields were often exposed to air raids if the 'bamboo telegraph' early warning system did not work. This Tomahawk has been blown apart by a bomb hit. The upturned wing shows the Chinese national insignia to advantage (light blue and white) along with the landing light position and the twin barrels for the wing mounted .30 caliber machine guns.

only unit in the Philippines, was recording *something* on its scope. Throughout the day (it was 8 December in the Philippines), the P–40s patrolled the sky and chased misinformation. Through inept tactical command in not keeping a standing air patrol of as many fighters as possible, only two P–40s were airborne when the Japanese finally came at noon.

Once again, ineptness had the P–40s lined in neat rows at Clark and the Japanese struck with fury at the B models and other aircraft on the field. The results were predictable. Some of the P–40 pilots attempted to get into the air. Four were shot to pieces by Zeros during the P–40s' take-off rolls. Three fighters did get airborne and two of the pilots managed to

destroy three of the enemy fighters, so at least some blood was drawn.

Errors compounded errors and, as the 3rd PS attempted to land at Iba when they were low on fuel, they managed to run directly into the initial Japanese attack on that field. Five P–40s were immediately destroyed in the air, three crashed when they ran out of fuel but one pilot got two Zeroes before his engine coughed into silence, starved of fuel. The 3rd was decimated: only two P–40Es remained in combat-worthy condition.

The attack was a classic of Japanese planning. The bombers approached in parade ground formation (the total number of bombers was reported as being between 54 and 72 aircraft). Zeros came in low to strafe and attack any airborne fighters while the bomber crews concentrated on the bomb run, probably not realizing that the P–40s, even if airborne and fully fueled, could not have reached their 28,000 ft altitude in time to interfere with the bomb run – if, in fact, they could have reached it at all with their altitude-limited Allisons.

The 3rd's two remaining P–40Es were flown

to the rough and crude airstrip at Florida Blanca where they joined the 17th and 21st PS. This small airstrip was apparently, at that time, unknown to the Japanese, so the pilots had a chance to regroup and consider their position which, no matter how it was viewed, was poor.

The Japanese attack had decimated American forces in the Philippines and the sad fact was that the Americans had known that the attack was coming but had not been able to muster any sort of logical defense. Of the P–40s, 26 had been destroyed, leaving eight operational P–40Bs and 38 P–40Es to face a further onslaught by an enemy which would not give any quarter.

Operating out of well-established bases in Formosa, the Japanese had plenty of time to consider their next move against the Americans; they also had the resources in men and equipment unavailable to the US Army. For each Zero lost in combat, the Japanese could rely on their supply line for a replacement. The US Army, already with a very limited number of P–40s, knew that no spare parts would be forthcoming and the only way damaged aircraft could be put back into the air was with ingenuity and makeshift parts.

Surviving P–40s were constantly scrambled to intercept Japanese aircraft but the missions were usually futile since there was no method of early warning and the Japanese bombers were either too high to intercept or the warnings turned out to be false. The Zeros were another matter since they came actively looking for the American fighters. Meetings with the formidable Japanese fighter were not all one-sided and the Americans began to build a meager collection of victories. Lt Boyd 'Buzz' Wagner, Commanding Officer of the 17th Pursuit Squadron, became America's first ace on 13 December. On that day he destroyed four Mitsubishi K–27 Nates to add to the two that he had flamed the day before. Wagner was a natural fighter pilot and he aggressively fought the enemy wherever they appeared. Wagner was in action constantly from the initial raid. On 16 December, he flew, along with Lt Russell Church, what was to be described by Army historians as the first planned American attack of the war. Wagner and Church attacked Vigan Field, which the Japanese had occupied on 10 December. Several enemy aircraft were strafed and destroyed and airfield buildings were attacked. Church was shot down and killed but Wagner returned safely.

After the attacks of 8 December, the Japanese had kept up constant pressure on the Americans with air raids and naval bombardments. On the 10th the enemy began landing in force in Luzon and the situation really was hopeless since there was little that the small group of fighters could do. The Philippines had been written off by the American government, who virtually ignored the many messages requesting aid. On the 21st a huge force landed at Lingayen Gulf and headed for Manila.

Surviving Flying Fortresses, a valuable warplane that could not be caught on the ground by fighters nor fall into the hands of the Japanese, were evacuated to Australia but they would return, via Del Monte, for continuing attacks on the invading force. Even the most optimistic knew that the Philippines would fall. Buzz Wagner, wounded on the 22 December, had, on the 23rd been evacuated to Australia with seventeen other pilots who formed the core of Army pilots there to continue the fight against Japan.

As the enemy moved on Manila, about 20 P–40s were still operational and flying attack missions. When it was decided to pull out from Manila and regroup at Bataan, everything useful that could be hauled from Nichols Field was moved and then the Army blew the gasoline stores and planted explosive charges in the runway to deny it to the Japanese.

From Bataan, the fight continued and a few meager victories were obtained by the P–40 pilots. The decimated squadrons were regrouped into a single unit as the Bataan Air Force. Surplus personnel were issued with rifles and formed into an infantry unit. When Manila fell on 2 January 1942, P–40s were operational, but nine of these were sent to Mindanao. Only six made it – the other three crashed on the way. The six P–40s, along with two P–35s, flew recon missions from Mindanao. Eight P–40s were left for the defense of Bataan but these were reinforced when joined by three of the Mindanao P–40s that had been sent back north one week later.

Captain Ed Dyess became commander of the Bataan Field Flying Detachment. He had at his disposal the rag-tag collection of P–40s, a couple of light planes and two Stearman biplane trainers. Dyess and his pilots hit the enemy every day, sometimes flying fighter patrols, sometimes attack missions or recon flights. There is little doubt that the P–40s became a major problem for the enemy who thought that Bataan would be an easy victory.

Robert W. Prescott stands by his highly decorated Tomahawk which he flew with the 'Hell's Angels' squadron of the American Volunteer Group. Commissioned as an ensign in the US Navy during 1940, Prescott served as a flight instructor until September 1941 when he was approached by one of Chennault's people to join the AVG. After AVG service, he returned to the United States and, following the war, established the famous Flying Tiger Line.

It was not until 3 April 1942 that the Japanese finally broke through the defensive lines of Bataan's 47,000 defenders. To do this, the initial enemy invasion force had to be heavily reinforced. For five days the Americans and Filipinos fought but it became clear that the battle for Bataan was over and General Jonathan Wainwright and 11,500 men retreated to Corregidor Island to continue the battle. Wainwright ordered the remaining troops to surrender to the enemy. By this time only one P–40 was still flyable and it was flown to Del Monte by Captain Moore and eventually joined four other P–40s in northern Mindanao. Corregidor finally fell on 6 May and General Wainwright ordered all American resistance in the Philippines to cease.

Colonel Robert L. Scott in the cockpit of his P–40K before takeoff from Kunming, China, for a mission. When this photograph was taken on 4 January 1943, the AVG had been incorporated into the 14th Air Force. This close-up view gives a good look at details such as the rear view mirror and gun sight. (USAF/23481–B)

Although the battle for the Philippines had taken a heavy toll of the enemy, it extracted an even heavier toll from the Americans and Filipinos, many of whom were murdered outright after the surrender. The battles for Manila, Corregidor and Bataan had been burned into the collective American memory along with a resolve to destroy the Japanese Empire. MacArthur's 'I shall return' would not be a hollow promise.

The surviving pilots from the Philippines who made it to safety in Australia were almost shell-shocked. They had seen grueling combat in the harshest of conditions but rest came only momentarily to these aviators. An attempt to rebuild the 24th Pursuit Group was undertaken but aircraft were in short supply. A consignment of P–40Es was shipped to Australia and the 3rd, 17th and 20th Provisional Pursuit Squadrons were activated at

Amberly Field, Brisbane, but the units were drastically understrength. At this stage in the war, the oil producing Dutch East Indies were a prime target for the Japanese, and British and Dutch air units were attempting to defend the resource-rich islands. The Army decided to send the Provisional Squadrons to Java even if they were not ready for combat and, in February 1942, the 17th Provisional Pursuit Squadron arrived in Java with 13 pilots and 12 P–40Es at Blimbing, combining with an obsolete RAF and Dutch force that was already being sorely pressed by the Japanese. Java was to be a disaster for the American squadrons and the 20th PS, which followed the 17th with 18 P–40Es, arrived with only ten aircraft. On the flight to Java, the 20th kept running into the enemy and Zeros accounted for eight of the Americans lost on the island-hopping ferry flight to Java. On the plus side, the P–40s got three Zeros during the fighting. Fairing even worse, the 3rd lost nine out of 18 P–40s that crashed in a fog bank during the flight to Java.

The situation in Java was much like a repeat of the Philippines, and the Allied aerial units were once again decimated by an aggressive enemy. The invasion of Java took place on 1

March and the pilots of the provisional squadrons, (or, at least, the survivors, for nine had been killed and four were missing), were pulled off the island and returned to Australia aboard ships that managed to avoid Japanese raiders. During their very brief time in Java, the provisional squadrons destroyed at least 50 enemy aircraft but the story of these heroic pilots has never been fully recorded. In one last attempt to bolster Allied forces, a transport brought 27 crated P–40s into Java at night but the defense had virtually collapsed and the crated fighters had to be pushed into the ocean so they would not fall into Japanese hands. However, the Japanese did manage to get a couple of complete P–40s and these were taken back to Japan where they were evaluated and then used in various propaganda movies, constantly being 'shot down'.

Half a world away in the Aleutians, P–40s were beginning to face the Japanese in that cold and hostile environment. Before the Japanese surprised the Americans by establishing their foothold in the Aleutians, the Army had reinforced its far North airfields with P–40Es to be operated by the 11th and 18th Pursuit

P–40Es of the 16th Fighter Squadron, 51st Fighter Group, lined-up for takeoff in China on 24 October 1942. The lead aircraft was flown by Lt Dallas Clinger. Retaining the markings of the AVG, American national insignias replaced the Chinese roundel on surviving AVG planes. It is interesting to note that only five AVG pilots and 17 mechanics accepted the USAAF's offer to join with the new 23rd Fighter Group of the China Air Task Force commanded by Chennault. These aircraft arrived in standard desert camouflage. (USAF/74265)

Lt R. E. Smith on the wing of his P–40E Katydid at Peishihwa, China, 20 October 1942. Assigned to the 16th FS, 51st FG, Smith and fellow pilots reinforced the 23rd when General Chennault noticed that the squadron's pilots (at that time based in India) were exceptionally skilled. A deal was worked, and the 16th was on its way to China where it compiled a valiant record. (USAF/74268)

Squadrons, 28th Composite Group, during April 1942. The P–40E was a tough aircraft, suited to operating in the vile weather of the Aleutians. From their bases on Attu and Kiska, captured on 7 June, the Japanese struck at the Navy's Dutch Harbor base on Unalaska, causing considerable damage. Poor weather kept the P–40s from participating in the initial defense of Dutch Harbor, fog having enshrouded their strips at Cold Bay and Otter Point on Umnak.

The Japanese were launching air strikes from the carriers *Ryujo* and *Junyo* while some of the floatplanes were staging from the enemy's new bases. The situation had improved by the time of the second attack on Dutch Harbor and P–40Es intercepted the carrier's formations, knocking down only two of the enemy while losing three P–40s.

Large aerial battles never took place. The P–40 aerial battles were sporadic but, whenever the weather permitted, attacks against the enemy's ground bases were carried out with savage effect. The weather was the major enemy, for both sides, and the Japanese suffered as much as the Americans and the Canadians. The RCAF had two Kittyhawk squadrons, Nos 14 and 111, aiding the American defensive position. The Japanese were operating a squadron of Zeros off their land bases along with several dozen Zero floatplanes. Equipped with a large central float and two outriggers, the sea-going Zero was a formidable opponent despite the fact that the

floats caused drag and lowered overall performance. The floatplanes were good targets when they could be caught at anchorage and riddled by .50 caliber bullets. The Japanese realized that the war at the top of the world was going nowhere and that the Americans were determined to regain the lost territory, so, under the cover of darkness and fog, the Japanese forces quietly slipped away – leaving little but wrecked Zeros for the surprised Americans to discover.

Along with every other variety of aircraft based in that hostile area, the Aleutians ate up many P–40s, but, overall, the P–40 gave a good account of itself, proving that its robust structure could stand punishment and that it made a good platform for ground attack missions.

As with the Bell Airacobra, the P–40 design suffered from poor performance over 12,000 ft due, mainly, to the rapidly decreasing power available from the Allison as it passed this altitude. In the Philippines, where early warning was not available, the P–40 pilots were constantly frustrated by not being able to catch Japanese bombers before they hit their targets. The enemy, often flying above 20,000 ft, simply could not be reached by the hard-pressed fighters. The lack of effective engine boost rendered the design effective only at low to medium altitudes. The airframe, using mid-1930s technology, did not offer the refinements needed to achieve higher speeds.

*R**oyal Australian Air Force Curtiss Kittyhawk IAs (similar to the P–40E) display a wide variety of markings and camouflage finish as they are prepared for a strike against Rommel's forces. The CV codes mean that the aircraft was assigned to No 3 Squadron. Each aircraft appears to have a different camouflage pattern or different colors. Undersurfaces were painted a deep Azure Blue that photographed almost black. The photograph was taken shortly after the squadron, commanded by Squadron Leader Bobby Gibbes, had downed his 200th enemy aircraft on 28 October 1942. Gibbes accounted for a Bf 109 over Fuqa to bring the total to 200 and his own score at the time to 9¼.*

Even with so much against it, the P–40 could be flown to victory by aggressive and dedicated aviators such as the AVG pilots who became aces by regularly blasting experienced Japanese out of the sky. Unlike Bell, Curtiss hoped the P–40's altitude performance could be improved by mating the airframe with the legendary Rolls-Royce/Merlin.

The Merlin, with its efficient supercharging, offered superb high altitude performance and, early during 1941, the Army obtained a Merlin Model 28 from the British and sent it to Curtiss for installation in the second P–40D airframe, s/n 40–360. The two primary identifying characteristics of a Merlin-powered P–40 were the lack of an airscoop atop the engine nacelle and different exhaust stacks. Several locations were tried for the radiator, but the final installation was basically similar to that of the Allison-powered aircraft. Production began with the P–40F, 699 being purchased as the Model H87-B3. The engine was

a Packard V–1650–1 (licence-built Merlin 28) that could pump out 1,120 hp at 18,500 ft via its single-stage two-speed supercharger. A maximum top speed, using war emergency power, of 364 mph could be obtained at 20,000 ft – a considerable improvement over the Allison aircraft. Armament was the same as the P–40E's. Many modifications were undertaken during the P–40F production run, which totalled 1,311 fighters, so dash numbers were used to tell the difference between models.

From the P–40F–5 on, all fuselages were increased in length by 20 inches to improve directional stability and counter torque from the Merlin – even the Allison models could ground loop quickly if the pilot let his attention slip during landing or takeoff. The fuselage stretch also helped smooth out the P–40's lines. A minor change, replacing the electric cowl flaps with a manual system, resulted in the P–40F–10, while the F–15 was optimized to operate in cold weather and the P–40F–20 had a new oxygen system.

At a later date, a rather curious change took place when some P–40F airframes, assigned to the training role, had the Merlin engines replaced with Allisons! This turn-around was called the P–40R but government records are unclear as to how many airframes were actually converted. An Army document states that 600 fighters were converted at random but another source states that only 123 machines received Allisons. However, it is thought that around 300 fighters were re-engined when demand for the Merlin rapidly increased among other more combat effective aircraft.

The designation Hawk Model H87–B3 also covered the P–40L which was, basically, very similar to the P–40F–5. However, the main difference between the two Merlin-powered aircraft was that the L was a lightweight variant. The Curtiss fighter had always been on the heavy side and the weight reduction program was another attempt to extend the basic design's useful life. Weight was pared by eliminating two of the .50 caliber wing guns and associated fittings and ammunition. A 37 US gallon forward wing fuel tank was also dropped while the remaining four .50 caliber Brownings had their ammunition reduced by 70 rounds per gun (281 to 201). The first 50 P–40L–Is had the short fuselage of earlier models but the P–40L–5 (220 built) had the longer fuselage and fittings under the wing for rocket stubs, making the design even more effective in the ground attack mission. More changes resulted in the P–40L–10 (148 built) which had armor eliminated from the coolant tank, a relocated fuel pump, deletion of some warning lights and the addition of sway braces to stabilize the belly drop tank. The P–40L–15 had such minor changes as a new carburetor air filter and signal lights; 112 were built. The final L variant was the L–20, 170 being built, which had an SCR–695 radio and an installation for an incendiary grenade. The pilot could activate the grenade after a crash landing to make sure that the aircraft would not fall into enemy hands. However, a well-placed hit could also set off the grenade and demolish the P–40 in the air so it is probable that the grenades were rarely installed. With the P–40F and L came the new name Warhawk.

The weight savings program dumped around 450 lb from the P–40L airframe but, in the field, some of this weight was added back when the deleted armor and missing guns were replaced – the weight savings slipping to about 250 lb for an overall speed gain of only 4 or 5 mph.

The RAAF made very good use of their P–40s in the ground attack role, called 'Kittybombers'. The pilot of this aircraft is seen being guided out by a crewman on the wing prior to a strike against enemy targets. Poor visibility over the nose and clouds of sand kicked up by turning propellers made the wingman a real necessity. Loaded with three bombs, the Kittybomber was heading for the frontline of the 8th Army to support the British push against Rommel.

*I*nteresting high angle view of a Royal Air
Force Tomahawk Mk IA when this particular
aircraft was under test at Duxford. Camouflaged in
Dark Green and Dark Earth with Duck Egg Green
undersurfaces with Sky spinner and Sky 18 in rear
fuselage band the Tomahawk, even though new,
shows how quickly this paint would chip and
weather. Extensive retouching is evident. The
British found that the Tomahawk was no match for
the Luftwaffe, handling characteristics were
generally satisfactory but that the fighter was
prone to ground looping. (Air Ministry 10559A)

*C*lassic view of a short fuselage P–40F over
an extensive cloud layer. Finished in standard
factory markings, the photograph shows the main
identifying feature, the lack of an air scoop atop the
cowling along with new exhaust stacks, to
advantage. Many of the Merlin-powered P–40Fs
were sent to North Africa for combat against the
Luftwaffe.

Kittyhawks and Warhawks were fighting on almost every combat front during 1943. The redesignated American Volunteer Group, the 23rd FG, was carrying the war to the Japanese – reinforced by shipments of new P–40Es and Ks. However, the Ks were already veterans of fighting in the Western Desert with the British and they were distinctly war weary. The fact that the 23rd FG was cut off by thousands of miles of hostile territory from Allied bases, including one of the world's most hostile mountain chains, the Himalayas, led to the instigation of one of the most famous supply lines of World War Two. The Air Transport Command was established to supply the 23rd FG. Brave transport crews flew obsolescent aircraft over the 'Hump' to keep the 23rd going ... virtually everything the unit needed came by air including fuel, parts, engines, food and medical supplies. The route was extremely hostile and the weather could change radically within the matter of a few hours. It is not surprising that many of the transports just simply disappeared during the long flights.

The 23rd FG destroyed 150 Japanese aircraft during nine months while losing only 16 P–40s to the enemy, a fine kill to loss ratio. In order to bring the 23rd FG more into the structure of the rapidly expanding USAAF, the unit's parent organization – the China Air Task Force – was disbanded and immediately incorporated during March 1943 as the 14th Air Force with Chennault as a major general and commander.

Thousands of miles away, P–40s were fighting a deadly battle against the Axis in North Africa. In the Western Desert, the Allies were up against the genius of Erwin Rommel and his *Afrika Korps* who, in a brilliant campaign initiated on 26 May 1942, began a rapid move against various British military installations that had been regarded as fairly secure. Capturing the huge fort at Tobruk on 13 June, Rommel mauled Britain's Eighth Army in a series of battles that, for a time, appeared to completely defeat the Allied forces in the area.

The British kept retreating until they were able to form a defensive line near El Alamein. All around this tiny village the British dug in, planted land mines and prepared to meet the full might of the *Afrika Corps* and its Italian allies. Rommel realized that the British had a sound defensive position – protected by the ocean on one side and by impassable marshes on another – but he also felt that if he could successfully breach British defenses then the Germans could be completely victorious in North Africa. However, Rommel did not count on the tenacity of Allied airpower and the damage that aircraft, especially the hard-pressed P–40s, could cause to his armor and infantry.

From July to September, Rommel threw his forces against the British, causing heavy losses among his own forces and doing little to dislodge the British forces who were being supplied by sea. General Bernard Montgomery arrived in Egypt during August to mastermind a plan that called for the defeat of Rommel. On 23 October, the British, in a daring frontal attack, blasted through Rommel's vaunted *Afrika Korps* in what would become known as the Battle of El Alamein and, combined with the Allied Operation TORCH, Rommel was suddenly very much on the defensive and in retreat to more friendly territory.

Prior to the major battles, the Desert Air Force had been operating a variety of very tired Tomahawks but, when Montgomery gave complete control of the aerial war to Air Marshal Tedder, the situation began to change. Tomahawks had been hitting the Germans and Italians whenever possible. RAF mechanics had improvised crude but effective bomb racks under the Tomahawk's wings which could carry a variety of nasty weapons that caused much grief among the enemy. The Tomahawk was also enjoying success in aerial combat and several British and Commonwealth pilots became aces while flying the aircraft. Although outclassed by the more advanced German machines such as the Bf–109, the Tomahawk was capable of blasting the Italian's lightly armed biplanes and bombers. German and Italian transports also fell victim to aggressive P–40 attacks. Royal Australian Air Force Wing Commander Clive 'Killer' Caldwell would go on to record over 20 victories against the enemy while flying the P–40.

Rumbling through the thick dust of an Alaskan summer, this fiercesome P–40E belonged to Major John Chennault, Claire Chennault's number one son. Using a Bengal tiger as a model, the P–40E was a distinct change in art from the fanged AVG aircraft.

Caldwell also pioneered the P-40 as a low-level attack bomber and his squadron, No 112, soon adapted to the role – paving the way for hard-hitting attacks against the Germans. The P-40s operated from a variety of desert airstrips, ranging the gamut from terrible to awful. The P-40's rugged construction helped overcome many of the obstacles such as rutted landing areas and incredibly contrasting temperatures. Desert sand and dirt played havoc with the Allisons and even the fitting of temporary, crude air filters that helped keep some of the debris out of the engine did not alter the fact that the engine had to be changed at alarming rates. Due to the nature of the terrain, combat damaged aircraft or P-40s that had engine trouble and had nowhere to go

but down, usually could pull off successful belly landings. Most airfields kept a fleet of salvage vehicles at the ready to head out into the desert, dismantle the damaged P-40, and return to base where the fighter could either be repaired or broken down for parts. Pilots who were not immediately found by Allied troops had interesting experiences dealing with locals in their search for food, shelter and transportation.

Tomahawks and Kittyhawks of the Desert Air Force aggressively took the war to Rommel, hitting vital fuel and supply depots, infantry and even attacking the fearsome German armor. Rommel fully realized the damage that the air attacks were doing to his forces but his ability to cope with the air war seems to have been limited. Had Rommel coordinated with the *Luftwaffe* to form an effective defense against the Allied air forces, which were small, the entire shape of the desert war could have been altered drastically.

Through the disastrous months of May and June, P-40s had covered the British retreat and caused damage to the advancing enemy. Pilots took full advantage of the P-40's good low-level handling and literally flew on the surface of the desert to avoid anti-aircraft fire. The P-40s and pilots of the Desert Air Force flew countless missions but, even though men and machines became very tired, they kept on fighting. In August, the Army Air Force came into the fight with P-40K and F models of the 57th Fighter Group when the unit arrived in Palestine to bolster Allied air strength.

The squadrons of the 57th FG (64th, 65th and 66th) went into combat with a mixed bag of Merlin- and Allison-powered P-40s. The P-40K, initially ordered on 28 October 1941 with deliveries starting just in time for aircraft to be sent to the 57th, was basically a P-40E airframe fitted with an Allison V-1710-73 powerplant and a center-line shackle for a 500 lb bomb. P-40K-1 through -5 had the

P-40K assigned to the 333rd Fighter Squadron, 318th Fighter Group, at Bellows Field, Hawaii, during 1943. Markings of interest include the giant national insignia under the wing and the short-lived red outline to the insignia.

Shot-up former enemy staff car served as crew transport for the pilots of the 64th Fighter Squadron, 57th Fighter Group, 9th Air Force, during their operations in North Africa. Flying constant ground attack missions, the 'Sky Scorpions' had a large dark grey scorpion painted on the nose with red details and trim. One of their P–40Fs is seen in the background.

standard short fuselage but, with the P–40K–10, the extended fuselage was incorporated into the production line. Short fuselage Ks were fitted with a small dorsal fin that helped directional stability. The Allison had a higher blower gear ratio linked to an automatic pressure regulator which improved engine life through a smoother operation of the powerplant. The Ks, which became the heaviest aircraft of the P–40 series, were fitted with six .50 caliber Brownings in the wing.

The 57th FG was attached initially to the hard-pressed British units and almost immediately went into action with the first American victory over the desert being scored on 9 August when two Messerschmitt Bf–109s were knocked down. The pilot, Lt Bill O'Neill, was not in the best of shape after the dogfight since his P–40 had taken cannon and machine gun hits. Finding that he could not make it back to base, O'Neill selected a flat spot of desert and made a belly landing.

Learning ground attack tactics from their British Allies, the Americans went to work on the German positions with the individual squadrons attached to British wings. By the time of the Battle of El Alamein, the 57th finally fought as a group and soon became the cornerstone of the new 9th Air Force which was organized by General Lewis Brereton and operated under the direction of the British-run Mediterranean Air Command. With ground attack being the primary mission, aerial victories were not that easy to come by but the 57th began to build up a respectable score. On 13 October, P–40Fs of the 65th FS tackled two dozen Bf–109Es in a swirling dogfight and two of the enemy were destroyed for the loss of one Merlin-powered Warhawk.

As the El Alamein battle began in earnest, enemy aerial activities took an upswing and it was not unusual for the P–40s to run into formations of Junkers Ju 87 Stukas and Italian Fiats. These slow aircraft were easy prey, especially when the 109s were not escorting them, and the 57th chalked up 27 victories by the end of October. The first American P–40 ace in the Desert War was Lt Lyman Middleditch who shot down three Bf–109Es on the 27 October to become an ace.

Alarmed by the Allied push, German high command replaced some of the desert fighter pilots with aggressive aviators fresh from the Eastern Front. The effect was immediate and the P–40s began to suffer increased losses. It was obvious that the hard-pressed 57th would need support so the 79th Fighter Group boarded the USS Ranger for a dash across the Atlantic (the 57th had travelled the same way, the carrier launching the P–40s as the coast was neared). The 79th FG operated P–40Fs and was a boost to American combat operations in the area but received an early blow when commanding officer Lt Colonel P. McGoldrick's P–40F was hit by anti-aircraft fire during a ground attack mission. McGoldrick guided the stricken Warhawk into a successful belly landing but the fighter hit a land mine and the commander was killed.

American operations in the area greatly increased with Operation TORCH on 8 November 1942. A P–40 unit, the 33rd FG, was carried aboard the USS Chenango and launched on the 10th and 12th of the month. The short-lived fighting was already over but the P–40 ran into disaster that had nothing to do with the enemy. As the US Navy had found to their cost, most landing areas in the combat zone

were treacherous and in poor condition, the soil content being porous and very soft. During the two days, 77 P–40s of the 33rd launched from the Chenango and ran into a thick bank of fog with one P–40 being immediately lost. No less than 17 more were either destroyed or damaged in ground loops or turn overs during landing. The decimated group was reinforced by 35 P–40s flown off HMS Archer.

After their initial bitter opposition to the Allies, the French forces in North Africa capitulated to the military strength of the invasion force. Not wanting to take French citizens as prisoners of war, a deal was struck whereby French pilots could be absorbed into new anti-Nazi squadrons and take up the fight against their former commanders. Accordingly, orders were cut to supply the Armeé de l'Air with 30 P–40Fs to form new combat units in Morocco. These aircraft were drawn from the ill-fated 33rd FG. Hurriedly painted in French national markings, the pilots were given quick instruction in the operation of the Warhawk and then left on their own. Presumably one of the main points of instruction was to point out the fact that the American throttle operated in completely the reverse way to standard French units! This probably caused some humor among the British pilots present who had earlier had to cope with eccentricities of the throttles on Tomahawks

that the RAF obtained from French orders after the fall of France!

The 33rd FG finally made it into action when it arrived at Thelepte on 6 December, relieving the P–38s of the 94th FS, 1st FG. It is not clear why the Merlin-powered P–40Fs were selected to operate in North Africa but the high command must have been pleased with the aircraft for two more groups were sent to the area. The 324th FG (314th, 315th and 316th FS) and the 325th FG (317th, 318th and 319th FS) became available for combat in February 1943, the 325th flying off the *Ranger* – whose crew had now become very adept at handling and launching Army fighters. The new P–40Fs arrived at an appropriate time since the *Afrika Korps*, retreating into Tunisia, had met up with fresh German and Italian combat forces and had managed to blunt the forward thrust of the British Army.

Rommel, by now much more aware of the effectiveness of Allied airpower, came up with a daring new plan: he would launch an attack that would overrun Allied airfields and accomplish the dual objectives of destroying aircraft while capturing fuel supplies needed for his mechanized units. The key to this quick thrust was an area known as the Kasserine Pass, through which the panzers could make their run directly at the Allies.

Massing his forces, Rommel stormed through the pass but was met by heavy Allied resistance. His armored units mauled, Rommel had no choice but to retreat once again. Bottled in against the sea and surrounded by victorious Allied units, the Germans were not about to give up and the bloody fight continued.

Operational losses among the Warhawk units had been high and the 33rd FG was especially mauled with only a dozen P–40Fs remaining operational. The French, flying as the *Group Lafayette*, had also lost ten of their limited numbers of aircraft so both units were ordered back to Casablanca to rebuild their strength. The French received three dozen P–40Ls and formed three squadrons that picked up the insignia and traditions of famous World War One units: *Sioux*, *Cigognes*, and *Diables Rouges*. Returning to combat in March, the French compiled a brave record against *Luftwaffe* Fw 190s and Bf 109s.

On 18 May 1943, the last fighting Axis units in North Africa surrendered to the Allies and,

A ceremony honoring Curtiss aircraft production is seen in this photograph of C–46 Commando transports and P–40N–1 and N–5 fighters illustrating both types of canopies used on the planes. Some of the planes are in standard Olive Drab and Neutral Gray camouflage with Army markings while others are in desert finish with no national insignia, these aircraft intended for Britain and other Commonwealth nations. (Curtiss-Wright)

Improvised bomb mount on a 14th Air Force P–40E. The 'homemade' mount, created by ground crews, carried three 70 lb incendiary bombs. Field modifications such as this were common and typical of American ingenuity under combat. Note the wooden sway braces.

One of the worst possible areas for a serviceman to be assigned during World War Two: the Aleutians. This airfield was set up by US forces on Amchitka, about seventy miles from the Japanese held island of Kiska. These P–40s are almost frozen in place, heavy canvas covers on the flying surfaces and canopy attempting to keep ice off the airframe. (USN)

P–40N Warhawk operated with No 120 Squadron of the Royal Netherlands Indies Army Air Force. Operating out of Biak, New Guinea, the aircraft flew ground attack missions against the Japanese. Wham Bam! *carries the serial C3–503, the last three digits being repeated on the drop tank.*

by this time, there were five Warhawk groups in action in North Africa (33rd, 57th, 79th, 324th and 325th). There is no doubt that the Curtiss fighters played an important role in defeating what was once a nearly invincible enemy.

Individual acts of heroism by the North Africa P–40 pilots caught the public's attention and one such event was when Major Philip Cochran, 33rd FG, skipped a 500 lb bomb directly into the Hotel Splendida, Kairouan, which just happened to be the location of German headquarters. Artist Milton Caniff was quite taken by the pilot's many daring actions and he was soon immortalized in the cartoon strip *Terry and the Pirates* as the rough and tumble 'Colonel Flip Corkin'.

P–40s also participated in the 'Palm Sunday Massacre' which took place on 18 April 1943. The Germans, desperate to supply their troops, were launching huge flights of transports that soon became prime targets for fighters. Even though the transports usually had a cover of *Luftwaffe* fighters, the Americans always broke through the protective umbrella and got at the slow and lumbering aircraft. On 18 April, 47 Warhawks from the 57th and 324th, launched from El Djem on a combat patrol with 12 Spitfires flying high cover. The transports were spotted flying very low in an attempt to avoid detection – there were over 90 of the vulnerable aircraft when they were spotted by the Warhawks.

The results of the aerial melee were amazing. In a dozen minutes the Warhawks and Spitfire had shot down 58 lumbering Junkers Ju 52 tri-motor transports, 14 Italian Macchi 202 fighters and four Bf 109s for the loss of six P–40Fs and a Spitfire. This was a stunning blow to the Germans but they continued their supply flights, each time losing more aircraft, until the losses made the operations impossible.

With the surrender of North Africa, it was time for the Allies to move on to other German strongholds in Sicily and Italy. One of the more interesting targets was the island of Pantelleria which became a target for Allied airpower in an experiment to see if an enemy stronghold could be forced to surrender as a result of aerial attack alone. For a month, Allied aircraft pounded Pantelleria day and night – reducing most of the island to rubble and the final result was just what the Allies wanted – the Germans surrendered on 11 June. The battle for Pantelleria thus went into the history books as the first enemy position to be overcome by airpower alone.

From Pantelleria, the Allies looked across the Mediterranean at Sicily – a prime target since it pointed straight up Italy into Occupied Europe. The Germans, of course, knew the strategic importance of Sicily and had heavily fortified the island while providing some of its top bomber and fighter units to operate off the island's airfields. Sardinia, another island 175 miles northwest of Sicily, was also a prime target for the Allies and the Mediterranean was about to see incredibly fierce aerial fighting. The P–40s were to be in the thick of it.

The battle for Sicily began on 10 July 1943, while strikes were also carried out against Sardinia during the same period. Major Robert Baseler, a pre-war Army Air Corps pursuit pilot and one of the war's outstanding individual pilots, had taken command of the 325th FG. A large and colorful man, Baseler, decided to extend his personality to the unit's aircraft by having their tails emblazoned with yellow and black checks, giving the unit the nickname 'Checkertails'. With the *Luftwaffe* contesting every inch of airspace above the islands, it was not long before the 325th entered action and an epic dogfight took place on 30 July when 20 P–40Fs engaged a large force of enemy fighters at low level over Sardinia. The experienced P–40 pilots immediately tackled the swarm of 109s, many being flown by brand-new fighter pilots. The result was a slaughter. At low level, the P–40 had a slight edge on the Messerschmitt and the American pilots were all experienced aviators with superior training so when the battle ended, 21 Messerschmitts had been knocked down for the loss of just one P–40F.

The 33rd FG had established an air base on Pantelleria where it was joined by a unique P–40 unit, the all-Negro 99th FS. With segregation being a common American practice

*C*arrying the insignia of 28 air forces with which Curtiss fighters of all types flew during World War Two, this 15,000th Curtiss fighter was rolled off the assembly line at Buffalo, New York, on 22 November 1944. The Curtiss P–40N–40–CU carried the Japanese victory tally amassed by Tex Hill while the German kills were the 20¼ victories gained by Group Captain Clive Caldwell. (Curtiss-Wright)

Opposite above
*T*he RAAF supplied 95 Kittyhawk Mk IVs (P–40N) to the Royal Netherlands Indies Army Air Force. Used by No 120 Squadron (whose Dutch pilots had been trained at Jackson, Missouri), the aircraft were supplemented by P–40Ns from USAAF stocks. Initially fighting with Australian units, the squadron began operations out of Java after that island was captured. Note the rather crude application of the national insignia on Snafu.

*K*ittyhawk Mk IV (P–40N–5–CU) FX594 seen after arriving in Britain for testing. The RAF contracted for 536 Mark IVs, the majority going to North Africa and no squadrons were ever formed with the type in Britain. The N–5 had a revised pilot seat, the increased rear window area and modified canopy, wing bomb racks and additional fuel tankage. Twenty-seven inch magnesium wheels were added to help save weight. (Ministry of Aircraft Production/13246C)

at the time, it was decided that an all-black fighter squadron with black crewmen would be a good way to employ blacks in the war while not breaking the Army's strict color line. The 99th arrived at Casablanca during April 1943 with 27 new P–40Ns, the first of its type to reach North Africa. The P–40N (Curtiss Models H87V and H87W) was the final production version of the fighter and it was also produced in the largest numbers (5,220 aircraft). Originally to have been powered by the Merlin and designated P–40P, all attempts possible were made to reduce weight on the N and the results were successful since the P–40N became the fastest production P–40 with a top speed of 378 mph. Power was provided by the Allison V–1710–81 which could pump out 1,200 hp. The P–40N–1 had the four-gun wing with reduced ammunition, reduced fuel load, no wing racks and new radios. However, pilot and systems protection was increased with the use of additional armor. The N model went through many changes, finally working up to a P–40N–40 variant. Significant changes were introduced with the N–5 which had wing bomb racks; the N–15 brought the six-gun wing back into use; the N–20 had the modified, squared-off canopy for better visibility; and the N–40 had the Allison V–1710–115 engine.

Command of the 99th went to Lt Colonel Benjamin O. Davis, Jr, and he and his unit were carefully instructed in the art of P–40 combat by none other than Phil Cochran, commander of the 33rd FG. By the time that the 99th was based on the defeated island fortress, it had already flown strike missions against Pantelleria. Cochran had been particularly careful instructing the young blacks on tangling with the Germans at low altitude. His suggestion that the pilots turn into the attacking fighter was a good one and several pilots quickly scored victories even though their mission was ground support. Ranging over Sicily and Sardinia, the 99th saw plenty of action and quickly gained respect for their Warhawks and the ability to take punishment and get them back home over long stretches of water.

With the eventual capture of Sicily after very heavy losses inflicted by determined Germans, the P–40s began the long slog up through Italy meeting an enemy that would not give ground – even though the Allied high command felt that Italy would be a push-over. It was anything but and the P–40s flew countless ground support missions and gave good account of themselves when they were bounced by enemy fighters. The P–40s attacked anything that moved and, on 4 August, even took on a submarine that had been caught above water. Three P–40s from the 325th repeatedly strafed the sub and claimed the U-boat as damaged, but it was later credited to the unit as sunk. Since ground support was so important in the Italian campaign, two P–40 groups (the 57th and 79th) were withdrawn from the Desert Air Force and sent to Italy. During October 1943, the 57th and 324th began turning in their

well-used P–40s for new P–47s but since supplies of the Thunderbolt were slow to arrive, it was not uncommon for mixed formations of Warhawks and Thunderbolts to attack targets together.

During January 1944, the 33rd, 79th and 324th FGs and their P–40s and some P–47s moved to Naples to support new Allied landings that were to be made on 22 January. The P–40s flew constantly during the invasion, attacking the various German counter-thrusts and cutting avenues of supply. The *Luftwaffe* came over the invasion beaches in force and P–40s were able to claim victories, including the 99th FS.

A decision to redistribute American airpower resulted in the 33rd FG being withdrawn from combat and sent to India after compiling an outstanding combat record which included 131 enemy aircraft destroyed in the air. On the debit side, the 33rd FG lost 48 pilots to enemy action and accidents. The 33rd's P–40s were assigned to the 27th and 86th Fighter Bomber Groups, both these units had previously been operating A–36s.

After the slaughter of American forces at Pearl Harbor, P–40s were in demand for other threatened bases in the South Pacific. With the capture of Guadalcanal, the Americans had vital airbases which the Japanese did their best to dislodge. Navy and Marine Wildcats fought alongside Army P–40s and P–39s in conditions that were so bad that they are difficult to describe. Through superior tactics and personal courage, the American pilots overcame every possible difficulty to emerge victorious.

America's Allies in the Pacific received large numbers of various P–40 models. The Royal New Zealand and Royal Australian Air Forces used the fighter to advantage, first to defend their islands from the aggressive enemy and then to carry the war to Japan. Originally starting the war with just one P–40 squadron, the RNZAF P–40 component eventually grew to seven squadrons. Small but highly trained and motivated, the RNZAF fought the enemy over New Guinea and in the Solomons, their distinctive white-trimmed P–40s blazing a trail of glory.

The RAAF would have a total of eight P–40

The last Curtiss P–40, an N–40–CU, was delivered to the Army by Curtiss during the early part of December 1944. With the production line for fighters closed down, Curtiss switched production to the twin engine Curtiss C–46 Commando transport. Late model P–40Ns were delivered in an overall silver lacquer finish. (Curtiss-Wright)

P–40Ns assigned to the AAF Tactical Center at Orlando, Florida, where actual combat situations were replayed and carefully examined in an effort to improve American tactics. The lead P–40N, aside from its giant shark mouth, carries a four color fuselage band.

A few P–40Ns were converted to TP–40N dual control trainers. The top of the fuselage was cut away fairly extensively, new plexiglass added along with a full set of dual controls. To keep an eye on what the student in front was doing, the instructor had an elaborate reflective system of mirrors.

squadrons and many of these aircraft were thrown into the defense of the huge island when it appeared that the Japanese invasion was a certainty. Going aloft from Milne Bay and Port Moresby, RAAF P–40s tackled incoming enemy air raids with such effectiveness that the plans for invasion were stilled. RAAF Kittyhawks carried the island-hopping war to New Guinea and other tropical hell holes. The Army Air Force went to the air defense of Australia when a detachment of the 49th FG arrived at Horn Island, Queensland, during March 1943 and immediately went into combat with Zeros. After the enemy threat was stopped, the unit transferred to New Guinea.

Using New Guinea as a staging area, the P–40 forces rapidly built up and the 8th, 49th, and 347th Fighter Groups were operating from the island with a variety of P–40 models.

In Hawaii, the 15th and 318th Fighter Groups equipped with P–40s to defend the islands against another attack. As the war progressed and more island bases were gained, as the P–40's influence began to spread and the effectiveness of the aircraft as a fighter bomber was not doubted. The Germans had found out that the P–40 could be a handful at low altitudes and the Japanese had to learn the same tough lesson. P–40 units were constantly updated with new aircraft as they became available, especially after the American mass supply line was established.

Even though the P–40 was not a top-line fighter, many pilots in the Pacific became aces. One of the outstanding young pilots who flew the Curtiss fighter was Robert B. Westbrook. Arriving with the 44th FS at Guadalcanal, Westbrook displaying uncanny marks-

manship and excellent flying skills which would stand him well in future meetings with the Japanese. Lt Westbrook's P–40s joined the P–39s and few P–38s that were daily flying and fighting from the island's airfields. Henderson Field had grown considerably since its capture from the Japanese a few short months before Westbrook's January 1943 arrival but conditions were still far from ideal.

The 44th immediately went into combat and Westbrook and his Warhawk became engaged in a major air battle on 27 January when a mixed group of AAF P–40s, P–39s and P–38s and Marine Wildcats scrambled aloft in the face of an enemy bombing raid. The American formation was struck by Zeros as they were still climbing toward the bombers and the sky was suddenly full of battling fighters. The situation was not going well for

P-*40N P-11265 of the Chinese Air Force shortly after the end of the war. The Chinese Air Force used many Curtiss fighters and virtually every model was employed in combat at one time or another.*

the Americans as two P-38s were almost immediately shot down, quickly followed by two P-40s. Westbrook found a Zero on his tail so he pushed the stick forward and advanced the throttle, using the P-40's diving speed to get away from the enemy fighter. On his way down, a formation of three Zeros passed in front of his gunsight and, with lightning reactions, Westbrook sighted one aircraft and gave it a healthy burst – blowing off a wing. The Americans claimed the destruction of nine Zeros in exchange for the two P-38s.

After the Guadalcanal campaign came to an end during February, the 44th was assigned the role of bomber escort and they accompanied a variety of Allied bombing aircraft of the Thirteenth Air Force to attack targets on other occupied islands. Having closely to watch their charges, the P-40s were not able to pursue the enemy fighters after fending off their initial passes. Such tactics did not allow the fighter pilots to build up their scores but it

did allow the bombers to complete their missions with minimal losses.

The Japanese took the loss of Guadalcanal and its vital bases and ports as a major blow and kept sending over bomber and fighter raids on a regular basis. Crude radar units installed near the airfield were able to pick up some of these raids and allowed American fighters the time needed to gain altitude and get into position. During one such interception on 7 June, Westbrook was in the air for over two hours as he tangled with 50 Zeros, claiming two of the enemy as destroyed.

On 1 July, Westbrook was assigned to fly one of eight P-40s providing cover for Allied shipping in Rendova Harbor. A formation of 30 Japanese fighters and bombers attacked the ships and a swirling dogfight developed, also involving Marine Wildcats and New Zealand Kittyhawks. Westbrook's marksmanship paid off and he was credited with a Val and a Zero. Promoted to captain and sent to Australia for rest and relaxation, Westbrook was given training in the new P-38 and he traded in his old P-40 for the twin-engine fighter. At the time, Westbrook had seven victories and was the second ranking ace in the Thirteenth AF.

The RAF, RAAF and RNZAF flew substantial numbers of P-40 variants but their heroic operations with these aircraft are outside the scope of this book. Other Allied nations also flew P-40s and included the Free Netherlands Air Force, China, Canada, Brazil, France, Russia and South Africa. Operations in Russia are not available in this country but one can be sure that the P-40s sporting the red star did as good a job as they did for the other nations.

Although the P-40 series never achieved the publicity or glamor of the later fighters, the type fought all the way through World War Two and was a faithful, rugged fighter that could be counted on when there simply was nothing else available. A grand total of 13,738 P-40 aircraft was built, the last (a P-40N-40) leaving the factory on 30 November 1944. Except for a few aircraft types that were produced in very limited numbers, the end of P-40 production spelled the end for Curtiss as a major fighter manufacturer since the company was never able to come up with an acceptable advanced aircraft. Today, around a dozen P-40s of various models remain flyable, examples of a heroic time when America and its Allies had their backs to the wall.

HAWKS FOR TRAINING

Modified Curtiss P–40s were used as combat trainers.

The main problem with introducing any single-seat high-performance fighter aircraft to a freshly graduated student pilot is that of correct training. World War Two fledgling pilots were turned loose from their Texans (no easy aircraft to fly) and expected to perform with alacrity in a wide variety of combat aircraft. However, the transition did not always go smoothly – the new pilots were quite often intimidated by the fighters which usually had at least twice as much horsepower as their more familiar advanced trainers.

Sometimes second-line or retired fighter aircraft such as the P–36 were used to smooth the transition into the new aircraft but training accidents rose at a rapid rate as more and more new pilots were hurriedly stamped out from training schools. The USAAF could ill-afford to lose aircraft at such a rate so several schemes were considered. One plan was to extend the training schedule but pilots were badly needed at the combat units so a second, more novel, plan was tried out. Fighter aircraft were modified to carry a second cockpit and set of controls so that instructors could brief the students on the operation of the fighter. Virtually every fighter type in the USAAF inventory was modified to have a second seat (the work usually being done at base or depot level) but the P–40 series had perhaps the largest number of conversions.

One of the earliest P–40 two-seat conversions took place with P–40K–10–CU 42–10181 and this particular Hawk was not even planned to fly! Aircraft mechanics had developed an unfortunate trend of damaging their aircraft as they taxied them for engine runs or maintenance checks, so, utilizing damaged and surplus airframe parts, some Curtiss employees at the Company's Camp Curtissair in Buffalo, New York, used their ingenuity to develop a two-seat tricycle gear training version of the Hawk. All military systems including guns and armor plate were removed and the canopy was completely cut away to allow for a second cockpit which had, it appears, the windshield from a P–36. Used at the USAAF's Technical Command School, the ground-bound Hawk was used to teach mechanics the correct use of engine and propeller controls and how to apply the brakes without turning the fighter onto its nose. The contraption, although odd looking, functioned in its role and soon gathered a collection of dents and bumps. In its new role, it was re-designated TP–40K–CU.

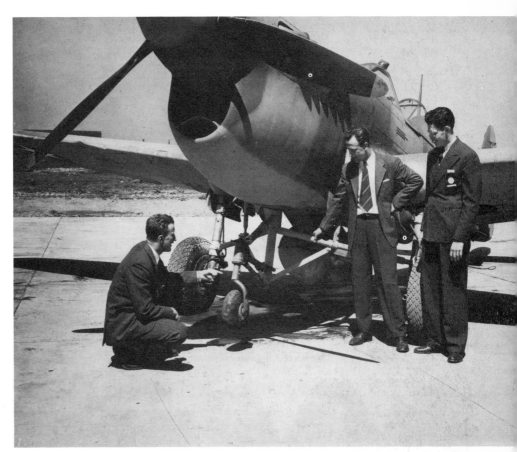

Curtiss engineers from Camp Curtissair examine their handywork on the modified P–40K. A P–40 tailwheel was pressed into service as a nosewheel to insure that the mechanics did not put the P–40 up on its nose as they practiced with the engine controls and the brakes. Named Susie Q, *the aircraft was assigned to the USAAF's Technical Training School. Needless to say, the P–40 did not fly in this configuration. (Curtiss-Wright)*

**W**ith the war over, the Hawk trainers were quickly dumped from USAAF inventories. TP–40N–5–CU 42–105927 is seen awaiting scrapping. Note placement of serial under the wing.

The first Hawks to be modified into two-seat trainers were a pair of P–40Es. The fuel tank behind the pilot's seat was removed along with the armor plate, rear vision panels and upper fuselage decking. Adding a second set of controls is not an overnight modification and it took some good design and engineering work to get the controls and a second instrument panel installed. A plexiglass 'tunnel' connected the two cockpits and the second seat was provided with a standard P–40E sliding canopy that moved on rails to the rear. A communications system between the two crew members was also installed. Full armament was retained. All in all, the modified P–40 was not a bad looking aircraft – it was reasonably proportioned and did not have the ungainly lines of the Bell TP–39. These two P–40s, which were repainted in the standard Olive Drab/Neutral Gray camouflage scheme after the modification work had been completed, were, according to some sources, redesignated as P–40ES but this designation does not show up in any USAAF/USAF serial and designation listing. Many other P–40Es were modified in the field as two-seat aircraft although these machines rarely featured dual controls and were used mainly as hacks or as high speed transports.

The next step in the evolution of the P–40 as a trainer was also, numerically, the most important. Around 30 P–40Ns were exten-

sively modified to the trainer role with modifications similar to those carried out on the two P–40Es. Once again, the fuselage fuel tank was removed and the area where the second seat was to be installed was extensively reworked with dual controls and an instrument panel installed along with a gun sight and intercom system. A plexiglass tunnel connected the two cockpits but the instructor in the rear position was given further visibility of his charge's actions and reactions via a large mirror mounted on the tunnel. These modified Ns were redesignated TP–40N and assigned to various training units around the country where they gave many graduating student flyers their first real experience in flying a combat machine. Production of trainer P–40s, along with other contemporary fighter conversions, never really got underway because improved training began turning out pilots who had a better understanding of the high performance machines that they would be flying.

With the end of the war, the training Hawks were quickly shuttled off to scrapyards but one has survived. Purchased by legendary movie stunt pilot Paul Mantz for his fleet of movie aircraft, TP–40N–40–CU 44–47923 (registered N923) has appeared in many movies and TV series and still operates from the Kermit Weeks Air Museum in Florida.

LAST OF THE HAWKS

The Curtiss P–40Q was an attempt to extend the P–40's life past a practical point.

In order to improve future prospects for Curtiss, company engineers began a program to revise the basic P–40 design into a fighter that could be viable when compared to the more advanced Mustangs and Thunderbolts pouring off the production lines. However, the P–40 design was steeped in mid 1930s techniques, making modernization extremely difficult. Design modifications such as a cleaner airframe, bubble canopy, revised cowling, improved cooling system and uprated powerplant were considered by Curtiss and the result was designated the Model 87X.

As with many of the Curtiss modifications, lineage of changes and conversion are a bit complex. During 1943, a P–40N, unofficially designated XP–40N, had been modified to carry a bubble canopy. The rear fuselage decking was cut away and the new unit was

Emblazoned with a set of tiger's teeth, the second XP–40Q is seen on a test flight. By the time that this photograph was taken, the XP–40Q had 'clipped' wing tips to gain a bit more speed. Note the sleeker nose cowling which tightly fitted around the radiator for the Allison V–1710–121 of 1,425 hp, and the streamlined air intake in the right wing. Painted in the standard Olive Drab and Neutral Gray scheme, the aircraft also carried the briefly used red surround to the national insignia. (Curtiss)

Another view of the second XP–40Q shows the new bubble canopy to good advantage. Even though the airframe was streamlined and lightened, the XP–40Q could not compete with the newer Mustang and Thunderbolt. The XP–40Qs were armed with only four .50 caliber Browning machine guns in order to save weight. (Curtiss)

Parked on the ramp for the 1947 Cleveland Air Races, the XP-40Q-1 (42-45722) proved to be a bit of a dark horse. The pilot did not qualify for the Thompson Trophy Race, but took off anyway and joined in the pylon bending melee. The engine caught fire, and the pilot baled out safely. (H. G. Martin)

Not an unattractive aircraft, the XP-40Q was limited by its mid 1930s design philosophy. 42-45722 was a converted P-40K-1-CU airframe. Note how visibility was improved by the bubble canopy. A slab of bullet-proof glass was mounted inside the curved windshield to offer the pilot frontal protection. This aircraft survived to be sold surplus. (USAAF)

added, improving visibility considerably, but the work required to change the production line was considered excessive and the bubble canopy project was shelved until it was dusted off for the Model 87X. Designated XP-40Q, the Model 87X comprised several airframes. For conversion work, two P-40Ks (42-9987 and 42-45722) and one P-40N (43-24571) were used. One of the P-40Ks was fitted with an Allison V-1710-121 of 1,425 hp. The cooling intakes were relocated in the wings while the cowling was very closely fitted to improve streamlining as much as possible, but the resulting cowling was still mated to the rather dumpy P-40 airframe and this first P-40K conversion retained the standard framed canopy. The second XP-40Q had the bubble canopy, but the wing mounted cooling system,

which proved to be a bit troublesome, was discarded, and the more conventional forward chin scoop system was used, although the new scoop was considerably reduced in frontal area. This second aircraft was designated XP-40Q-1. Fitted with four blade propellers and an engine equipped with water injection, the Q's were the fastest of all Hawks at 422 mph – still considerably slower than the P-51 and P-47.

The third modification, XP-40Q-2, featured clipped wing tips (the wing on the Q-1 was also later clipped) and other small improvements but no orders were given for the P-40Q and the design was phased out in favor of more modern and efficient warplanes.

P-40Q-1 s/n 42-45722 survived the scrapping drives at the end of World War II

and, with very low airframe hours, was purchased for a few hundred dollars by Joe Zeigler who wanted to race it in the post-war Cleveland Air Races. Given the civil registration NX300B and race number 82, the XP-40Q was entered in the 1947 Thompson Trophy Race but did not make the final race of 12 aircraft. Somehow, in the confusion of the start, Zeigler managed to get airborne and joined in the race where he quickly advanced to fourth place but the engine then failed and caught fire. The pilot jettisoned the canopy, which hit a woman spectator and injured her, and managed to parachute to safety from a low altitude. The burning XP-40Q plunged into a rail yard and exploded, a rather ignoble end for the last of the Curtiss Hawks.

CURTISS P-40 HAWK VARIANTS, SERIAL NUMBERS AND SPECIFICATIONS

Variants

XP-40-CU Curtiss Model 75P. Conversion of P-36A airframe s/n 38-10 with Allison engine. Many modifications were carried out during testing, including moving the radiator from under the rear fuselage to under nose. Accepted by Army on 16 October 1938. Polished metal finish.

P-40 Curtiss Model 81A-1. The initial production model (no service test examples under YP designation). Two .50 caliber Brownings in nose, two .30 caliber guns in wings. Twenty were eventually sent to Russia.

P-40A One P-40 (s/n 40-326) fitted with a camera and mount in rear fuselage with photo/recon window.

P-40B Model 81A-2. Updated combat version of P-40, fitted with bulletproof windshield panel, self-sealing tanks and armor protection, and increased armament, with two extra .30 caliber weapons in wing.

P-40C Curtiss Model 81A-3. Similar to P-40B but with extra military equipment and newer self-sealing fuel tanks. Total of 193 constructed.

P-40D Model 87A-2. It had an enlarged radiator for better cooling. The nose guns were dropped, but four .50 caliber weapons were fitted in wing. The canopy was improved and modified while the rear fuselage was slimmed and slightly shortened. It had modified landing gear legs. Under fuselage rack for 500 lb bomb; wing contained rack for four 50 lb bombs. Total of 23 built.

P-40E Model 87A-3. Similar to P-40D but with six .50 caliber guns in the wing. P-40E did not have underwing racks; 820 built. P-40E-1 had strengthened wings and external stores racks; 1,500 were delivered. Many of these aircraft were Lend-Lease machines.

XP-40F Model 87D. Modified P-40D (s/n 40-369) re-engined with a 1,300 hp Rolls-Royce/Packard V-1650 Merlin 28.

YP-40F Model 87D. P-40F 41-13602 used for engine testing.

P-40F Similar to XP-40F but powerplant was standardized on the V-1650-1 without the air intake on top for cooling. Six .50 caliber guns in wing. Provision for 170 gallon external fuel tank under fuselage. Name Warhawk introduced. From P-40F-5 onwards, all aircraft were delivered with the fuselage lengthened 19.5 inches, and the fin and rudder moved rearward of the horizontal stabilizer. P-40F-10 had manual cowl flaps. P-40F-15 was modified for cold weather service. P-40F-20 had a demand-type oxygen system.

XP-40G P-40 s/n 39-221 with updated combat equipment, self-sealing fuel tanks, armor protection and export H-81-A2 wings.

P-40G 44 produced by mating updated P-40 fuselages to H81-A2 wings. The aircraft were based with the 95th AB Group, Hamilton Field; 1st AF Base Group, Pope Field; and 32nd AB Group, March Field.

P-40K Similar to P-40E but with a V-1710-73 engine and large fillet around vertical fin. The P-40K-5 was similar but had a rotary valve cooler. The P-40K-10 had the long fuselage of the P-40F-5; some were winterized for cold weather operations. The P-40K-15 also had a long fuselage, and was winterized, and the emergency hydraulic system was eliminated and the battery moved forward. 1,500 lb of bombs could be carried under wing and on the fuselage center line rack.

P-40L Similar to P-40F but the aircraft was subjected to an intensive lightening program, with two .50 caliber guns eliminated, some armor dropped and fuel capacity reduced. It was powered by a V-1650-1 Merlin. P-40L-5 was the same as the -1 but had the long fuselage and rocket fittings under wing. The P-40L-10 had some internal equipment relocation, armor removed from coolant tank, and sway braces added from fuselage drop tank. The P-40L-15 had a new air filter for engine carburetor and aircraft signal light added. The P-40L-20 had an SCR-695 radio and provision for installation of an incendiary grenade for, presumably, setting the aircraft alight if forced down in hostile territory. A total of 700 of the series was built.

P-40M Similar to P-40K but with an Allison V-1710-81 engine and modified cowling with cooling grill ahead of exhaust; it had the long fuselage, and six .50 caliber guns in wing. The P-40M-5 had strengthened ailerons and a new carburetor air filter. The P-40M-10 had a fuel pressure warning light, air vapor eliminator and visual landing gear indicator. A total of 600 of the series were built.

P-40N Model 87W. Similar to P-40M. Four .50 caliber wing guns, pilot armor. The lightweight program included removal of front wing tanks, lighter wheels and improved radiators. The P-40N-5 had an SCR-696 radio, recognition lights, improved pilot's seat and the addition of external bomb racks. The P-40N-10 had cold weather gear, oil dilution and rate of climb indicator. The P-40N-15 had 137 gallon wing tank restored and six .50 caliber guns in wing.

P-40N The P-40N-20 introduced a new look for the Warhawk with a new canopy that gave improved visibility with less frames and a cut-back rear fuselage. Six wing guns and provisions for carrying three 500 lb bombs. The P-40N-25 had some small internal modifications and non-metal self-sealing tanks. The P-40N-30 also had minor updates. The P-40N-35 had new ADF and radio with other small changes. The P-40N-40 had V-1710-115 with automatic boost and propeller control along with revised armor, new exhaust and new oxygen system. Total of 5,210 P-40Ns constructed.

XP-40Q The XP-40Q-1 was modified a P-40K (s/n 42-9987) with an 1,425 hp Allison V-1710-121 and a four-blade propeller, four .50 caliber wing guns and wing leading edge radiators which were later repositioned under the nose. Two XP-40Q-2 aircraft were built (P-40K s/n 42-45722 and P-40N s/n 43-24571) with cutdown fuselage, bubble canopy and squared off wing tips.

P-40R Around 300 P-40Fs and Ls were fitted with Allison V-1710-81 powerplants when Merlin supplies became scarce. P-40Fs that were re-engined were designated P-40R-1 and the P-40Ls became P-40R-2s.

Export Variants

H81A-1 Similar to the P-40, with two .50 caliber guns in upper portion of cowling and two .303 guns, one in each wing, these were not Lend-Lease machines but were purchased by the British directly from Curtiss. The 142 aircraft delivered, with RAF serials in the BK852 through BK853 and AH741 through AH880 groups, were operated with the RAF's Nos 13, 94, 171, 286 and 400 Squadrons.

H81A-2 This variant was similar to the P-40B. 100 built for the RAF but the order went to the American Volunteer Group and the billing to China. The aircraft arrived in Rangoon from May through October 1941. Serials AM370 through AM519, although not all these used.

H81-A2 Similar to the P-40, this variant was called the Tomahawk Mk II by British. It had the same armament as the Tomahawk Mk 1. They had British radios and other equipment. 110 were delivered to Britain, but many were transferred to Russia. Again, they were not Lend-Lease aircraft.

H81-A2 & -A3 Lend-Lease aircraft operated under designation Tomahawk Mk IIB by the RAF and similar to P-40C with three .303 Brownings in each wing and two .50 caliber guns in the fuselage, many were transferred to Egypt, South Africa, Russia and Canada.

H87-A2 Similar to the P-40D, with four .50 caliber guns in the wing, they were designated Kittyhawk Mk I in RAF service. 560 were delivered and 17 were sent to Turkey, 24 to Canada and six to Russia.

H87-A3 & A4 Similar to the P-40E and provided under Lend-Lease, the models were designated Kittyhawk Mk IA in RAF service. 1,500 were delivered, many of which were sent to the RAAF, RNZAF and RCAF.

H87-B3 P-40F and P-40L under Lend-Lease, designated Kittyhawk Mk II in RAF service. 230 aircraft were delivered.

Kittyhawk Mk III P-40Ks and Ms that were apparently not allocated a foreign model number by Curtiss. 364 aircraft were delivered.

H87-V & -W Lend-Lease P-40N-1 through P-40N-35. For RAF service, 458 were delivered, many of which were transferred to the RAAF and RNZAF.

Serial Numbers

XP–40–CU	38–10 (conversion of P–36A)
P–40–CU	39–156 through 39–220; 39–222 through 39–289; 40–292 through 40–357; 39–290 through 39–679 were cancelled
P–40A–CU	40–326
P–40B–CU	41–5205 through 41–5304; 41–13297 through 41–13327
P–40C–CU	41–13328 through 41–13520
P–40D–CU	40–359 through 40–360; 40–361 through 40–381; 41–13696 cancelled
P–40E–CU	40–358; 40–382 through 40–681; 41–5305 through 41–5744; 41–13521 through 41–13599; 41–24776 through 41–25195 (Lend-Lease aircraft for RAF, serialled ET100 through ET519); 41–35874 through 41–36953 (Lend-Lease aircraft for RAF, ET520 through EV699)
XP–40F–CU	40–360 (conversion of P–40D)
YP–40F–CU	41–13602
P–40F–CU	41–13600 through 41–13695
P–40F–1–CU	41–13697 through 41–14299
P–40F–5–CU	41–14300 through 41–14422
P–40F–10–CU	41–14423 through 41–14599
P–40F–15–CU	41–19733 through 41–19932
P–40F–20–CU	41–19933 through 41–20044
XP–40G–CU	39–221 (conversion of P–40)
P–40G–CU	42–14261 through 42–14274; 42–14277 through 42–14278; 42–14281
P–40K–1–CU	42–9727 through 42–9729 (cancelled)
P–40K–5–CU	42–9730 through 42–9929
P–40K–10–CU	42–9930 through 42–10264
P–40K–15–CU	42–10265 through 42–10429
P–40K–1–CU	42–45722 through 42–46321
TP–40K–CU	42–10181 (conversion of P–40K)
XP–40K–CU	42–10219 (conversion of P–40K)
P–40L–1–CU	42–10430 through 42–10479
P–40L–5–CU	42–10480 through 42–10699
P–40L–10–CU	42–10700 through 42–10847
P–40L–15–CU	42–10848 through 42–10959
P–40L–20–CU	42–10960 through 42–11129
P–40L–25–CU	42–11130 through 42–11253 (cancelled)
P–40M–1–CU	43–5403 through 43–5462
P–40M–5–CU	43–5463 through 43–5722
P–40M–10–CU	43–5723 through 43–6002
P–40N–1–CU	42–104429 through 42–104828
P–40N–5–CU	42–104829 through 42–105928
P–40N–10–CU	42–105929 through 42–106028
P–40N–15–CU	42–106029 through 42–106405
P–40N–20–CU	42–106406 through 42–106428; 43–22752 through 43–24251
P–40N–25–CU	43–24252 through 43–24751
P–40N–30–CU	44–7001 through 44–7500
P–40N–35–CU	44–7501 through 44–8000
P–40N–40–CU	44–47749 through 44–47968
XP–40Q–1–CU	42–9987 (conversion of P–40K)
XP–40Q–2–CU	42–45722, 43–24571 (conversion of P–40K and P–40N)

Royal Air Force Serial Numbers

Tomahawk Mk I	AH741 through AH880 (all RAF serials selected from designated blocks
Tomahawk Mk IIA	AH881 through AH990
Tomahawk Mk IIB	AH991 through AH999; AK100 through AK570; AM370 through AM519; AN218 through AN517
P–40B–CU	BK852, BK853
Kittyhawk Mk I	AK571 through AK590; AK591 through AK999; AL100 through AL230
Kittyhawk Mk 1A	ET100 through ET519; ET520 through ET999; EV100 through EV699
Kittyhawk Mk II	FL219 through FL448; FS400 through FS499
Kittyhawk Mk III	FL710 through FL730; FL875 through FL905; FR111 through FR140; FS100 through FS269
Kittyhawk Mk IV	FR884 through FR885; FS270 through FS399; FT849 through FT954; FX498 through FX847

Specifications

XP–40

Span	37 ft 4 in
Length	31 ft 1 in
Height	12 ft 4 in
Wing area	236 sq ft
Empty weight	5,417 lb
Loaded weight	6,870 lb
Max. speed	342 mph
Cruise speed	299 mph
Ceiling	n/a
Rate of climb	n/a
Range	460 to 1,180 miles
Powerplant	Allison V–1710–19 of 1,160 hp

P–40

Span	37 ft 4 in
Length	31 ft 9 in
Height	12 ft 4 in
Wing area	236 sq ft
Empty weight	5,376 lb
Loaded weight	7,215 lb
Max. speed	357 mph
Cruise speed	277 mph
Ceiling	32,750 ft
Rate of climb	3,000 fpm
Range	650 to 1,400 miles
Powerplant	Allison V–1710–33 of 1,040 hp

P–40B

Overall dimensions as P–40	
Empty weight	5,590 lb
Loaded weight	7,600 lb
Max. speed	352 mph
Cruise speed	280 mph
Ceiling	32,400 ft
Rate of climb	3,000 fpm
Range	730 to 1,230 miles
Powerplant	Allison V–1710–33 of 1,040 hp

P–40C

Overall dimensions as P–40	
Empty weight	5,812 lb
Loaded weight	8,058 lb
Max. speed	345 mph
Cruise speed	270 mph
Ceiling	29,500 ft
Rate of climb	2,690 fpm
Range	n/a
Powerplant	Allison V–1710–33 of 1,040 hp

P–40D

Span	37 ft 4 in
Length	31 ft 2 in
Height	12 ft 4 in
Wing area	236 sq ft
Empty weight	5,970 lb
Loaded weight	8,810 lb
Max. speed	359 mph
Cruise speed	260 mph
Ceiling	30,500 ft
Rate of climb	2,590 fpm
Range	800 to 1,200 miles
Powerplant	Allison V–1710–39 of 1,150 hp

P–40E

Overall dimensions as P–40D	
Empty weight	6,300 lb
Loaded weight	9,250 lb
Max. speed	354 mph
Cruise speed	300 mph
Ceiling	29,000 ft
Rate of climb	2,050 fpm
Range	700 miles
Powerplant	Allison V–1710–39 of 1,150 hp

P–40F

Span	37 ft 4 in
Length	33 ft 4 in
Height	12 ft 4 in
Wing area	236 sq ft
Empty weight	6,590 lb
Loaded weight	9,350 lb
Max. speed	364 mph
Cruise speed	290 mph
Ceiling	33,500 ft
Rate of climb	3,250 fpm
Range	575 miles
Powerplant	Packard V–1650–1 of 1,300 hp

P–40K

Overall dimensions as P–40F	
Empty weight	6,400 lb
Loaded weight	10,050 lb
Max. speed	363 mph
Cruise speed	295 mph
Ceiling	28,000 ft
Rate of climb	2,000 fpm
Range	350 to 1,600 miles
Powerplant	Allison V–1710–73 of 1,325 hp

P–40L

Span	37 ft 4 in
Length	31 ft 8.5 in (33 ft 4 in for P–40L–5 through L–20)
Height	n/a
Wing area	236 sq ft
Empty weight	6,340 lb
Loaded weight	9,200 lb
Max. speed	370 mph
Cruise speed	295 mph
Ceiling	36,000 ft
Rate of climb	3,300 fpm
Range	750 miles
Powerplant	Packard V–1650–1 of 1,300 hp

P–40M

Overall specifications as P–40F	
Empty weight	6,470 lb
Loaded weight	9,100 lb
Max. speed	360 mph
Cruise speed	275 mph
Ceiling	30,000 ft
Rate of climb	2,200 fpm
Range	350 to 1,600 miles
Powerplant	Allison V–1710–81 of 1,200 hp

P–40N–20

Overall specifications as P–40F	
Empty weight	6,155 lb
Loaded weight	11,500 lb
Max. speed	350 mph
Cruise speed	290 mph
Ceiling	31,000 ft
Rate of climb	2,100 fpm
Range	350 to 1,800 miles
Powerplant	Allison V–1710–99 of 1,200 hp

XP–40Q

Span	35 ft 3 in
Length	35 ft 4 in
Loaded weight	9,000 lb
Max. speed	422 mph
Ceiling	39,000 ft
Powerplant	Allison V–1710–121 of 1,425 hp

Seversky XP-41
On The Road To Success

This was an attempt to advance American fighter design to the high level achieved by European contemporaries.

Admittedly Alexander de Seversky did jump on his own bandwagon to a great degree and the title 'prophet of aviation' was probably invented by some public relations type within the Seversky works but, ego thumping aside, Seversky was very interested in fighter development and the improvement of what he considered to be a weak US defense position.

The P–35 had been the first American 'modern' fighter but that certainly did not mean that the type could not use a good deal of upgrading. Modern in the sense that it was all metal with an enclosed cockpit and retractable landing gear, the P–35 was still rather primitive in concept and no match for its European contemporaries. Not adequately armed, underpowered and not very maneuverable, Seversky realized that the goal of a high-performance American fighter was still a long way off. Seversky and the Air Corps set aside the last production P–35, USAAC s/n 36–430, for modification and improvement towards the goal of a heavily armed fighter that could take on all comers – a goal that Seversky saw as the answer to American mastery of the air.

One of the most noticeable modifications to

The Seversky XP–41 at Wright Field where it underwent testing. The lines of the forthcoming P–43 and P–47 are clearly evident in this experimental fighter, the last aircraft to bear the Seversky name. The wide track landing gear retracted flush with the bottom of the wing, greatly improving streamlining and ground handling when compared with the P–35. Equipped with an improved Pratt & Whitney R–1830–19 of 1,200 hp, the XP–41 had an intake for a turbosupercharger fitted in the root of the left wing. The supercharger was installed in the fuselage directly behind the rear wing root. The XP–41 was never fitted with armament. (USAF)

the XP–41 was the elimination of the crude and bulky landing gear that left half its structure hanging in the P–35's slip stream. A rugged wide track gear was installed with folding gear door flaps that, when retracted, fitted completely flush against the bottom of the XP–41's wing. Fitted with an uprated Pratt & Whitney R–1830–19 engine of 1,200 hp, the XP–41 also had a very neat air scoop installed in the front portion of the left wing root to draw air for a two-stage supercharger that was positioned in the bottom of the fuselage just behind the wing root. The fuselage had been extended by about two feet, helping to get rid of the bulky and top heavy look of the P–35.

Flown for the first time during March 1939, the XP–41 was the last fighter to bear the Seversky name before the company changed directors and became Republic Aviation Corporation. During flight testing the XP–41 showed itself to be a reasonably performing aircraft with a top speed of 325 mph at 15,000 ft and extremely good ground handling qualities courtesy of the new landing gear. The Army liked the idea of the XP–41 but preferred other ideas that were already on the drawing board and which would develop into the P–43.

Seversky had the satisfaction of seeing a rapid evolution in his designs that would lead to the air superiority fighter for which he had been hoping. The P–43 would not be the answer for the heavily armed juggernaut of the air but the P–47 would, and, if one looks at the XP–41 from certain angles, the emerging Thunderbolt can clearly be distinguished.

Seversky went on to somewhat of a literary career after his ouster from the new Republic Aviation Corporation and his *Victory Through Airpower* would prove that he was indeed a prophet of the coming war in the air and he certainly could take some satisfaction that his actions were to lead directly to one of America's most successful fighting aircraft during that conflict.

SEVERSKY XP–41 SERIAL NUMBER AND SPECIFICATIONS

Serial Numbers

XP–41	36–430

Specifications

XP–41

Span	36 ft
Length	27 ft
Height	12 ft 6 in
Wing area	220 sq ft
Empty weight	5,395 lb
Loaded weight	6,600 lb
Max. speed	325 mph
Cruise speed	292 mph
Ceiling	n/a
Rate of climb	n/a
Range	720 miles
Powerplant	Pratt & Whitney R–1830–19 of 1,200 hp

Curtiss XP-42
Another Attempt At Streamlining

Trying to find a winning answer in the battle between radial and inline engines, Curtiss came up with this modification of the P–36.

During the late 1930s the debate raged hot and heavy as to what was the best powerplant for a pursuit aircraft. Proponents of streamlining, their aircraft design's flowing lines highlighting the Art Deco movement of that period, demanded closely cowled liquid-cooled inline engines that could make the front end of their aircraft as pointed as a bullet. Followers of the radial engine felt that their powerplants could produce more raw horsepower than the available inlines, especially with the rapid development that was taking place in the radial engine field. However, they were also concerned that the radials were bulky looking engines that did detract from the overall smooth airflow needed for a fighter aircraft. Curtiss walked both sides of the fence as their graceful P-6E biplane pursuit featured a tightly cowled Curtiss Conqueror liquid-cooled inline while their new monoplane Hawk 75 had a radial. Concerned over the problem of gaining extra miles per hour from streamlining and not knowing what the Army really wanted, Curtiss decided to modify the fourth production P–36 (s/n 38–4)

to test an experiment in attempting to closely cowl a radial engine. The idea was also being developed by several other manufacturers (see the chapter on the Vultee P–66).

The modified P–36 was designated XP–42 by the Army and was soon ready for flight testing. Pratt & Whitney had rightly claimed that the saving of weight in a pursuit aircraft was just as important, if not actually more so, as streamlining. Accordingly they subjected several of their engines to ground tests whereby long drive shafts and tight cowlings were added. Cooling proved to be a big problem but a series of tests with large controllable exit gills seemed to hold the cooling problem to a reasonable level. The XP–42 was fitted with a special Pratt & Whitney R–1830–31 of 1,050 hp and flight testing began in March 1939. The original nose was a bullet-shaped affair that really did give the appearance of an inline powerplant. Cooling was controlled by a very narrow high-velocity intake that wrapped around the cowling directly behind the spinner. This installation was soon found to be unsatisfactory especially during taxiing when the engine temperature would go into the red in a matter of seconds. That cowl was scrapped and other answers were sought

A close-up view of one of the cowling arrangements applied to the XP–42 during its testing period. This cowling features fixed air scoops above and below the massive spinner. The cooling gills can be seen at the rear of the cowling in the closed position. This arrangement was a bit better than the original long cowling that had a very narrow air duct wrapped around the entire cowling directly behind the spinner. However, cooling problems cropped up with this installation and the XP–42 finally settled on a cowling that made it look more or less like the P–36 that it really was. The high quality of workmanship is evident in the polished cowling which was made entirely by hand. (H. W. Kulick)

The fact that the XP–42 was the fourth P–36 (38–4) may give a hint on why the numeral four appeared on the vertical fin. Extensively tested by Curtiss, the Army, and NACA during its life-time, the XP–42 never contributed greatly to the advancement of aeronautics. The yellow and blue Wright Field 'arrow' was carried on the sides of the XP–42's fuselage.

which led to a variety of noses being stuck on to the XP–42 in a search to overcome the problem of cooling. One installation had an air scoop installed below the spinner with a smaller one above the spinner. Variations of scoop size followed. Another cowling was almost the size of the one on the original P–36 but featured a small front opening and a large spinner wrapped around the three blade Hamilton Standard propeller. All the experiments carried out with the XP–42 were interesting and varied as to the degree of success but Pratt & Whitney's final assumption that weight was more important than streamlining was correct.

Pratt & Whitney's main competitor was Allison and the design of their liquid-cooled inline was rather dated while the engine was quite heavy with its systems of radiators and cooling pipes. P&W felt that the horsepower of their engines could be developed to such a point that the advantage of streamlining and liquid-cooled powerplants would be negated and they were right, especially in the instance of the superb R–2800 that was to power the majority of America's naval fighters during World War Two.

And what of the XP–42? Its handling qualities were quite nice and, after testing, the aircraft was shuttled around to a number of different units and appeared in a wide variety of markings including a very unusual wash-off water color camouflage for a 1940 war game. The XP–42 flew at different Stateside bases during the War as a hack and was eventually scrapped during the early part of 1947 but it had proven the value of the theory behind high-power radial engines.

CURTISS XP–42 SERIAL NUMBER AND SPECIFICATIONS	
Serial Numbers	
XP–42	38–4
Specifications	
Span	37 ft 3.5 in
Length	28 ft 6 in
Height	11 ft 1 in
Wing area	236 sq ft
Empty weight	4,818 lb
Loaded weight	6,260 lb
Max. speed	315 mph
Cruise speed	286 mph
Ceiling	n/a
Rate of climb	n/a
Range	730 miles
Powerplant	Pratt & Whitney R–1830–31 of 1,050 hp

Republic P-43 Lancer — The Inbetween Fighter

Not really a success, the P–43 was certainly pointing the way towards that elusive goal.

Alexander Seversky was forced out of his company in September of 1939 when the board of directors did a complete reorganization of the company's structure and assets. The new company was to be known as Republic Aviation Corporation but a number of Seversky's concepts were to linger on with the new entity. The XP–41 had pointed in the direction in which Seversky wanted to head

with his fighter development and, with the shift of power, the development continued but in a bit different direction. On 12 May 1939, a contract had been signed by Seversky and the USAAC to develop a modified version of the XP–41 and the AP–4. The AP–4 was a company project (given the civil registration NX2597) that was an attempt to develop advanced features for fighters. Powered by a Pratt & Whitney turbosupercharged R–1830–19, as was the XP–41, chief designer Alexander Kartveli attempted streamlining the

With tufts of yarn taped to the wings to observe air flow, the first YP–43 Lancer, 39–704, seen undergoing flight testing. The YP–43 was a rather neat design with many features that would be seen in the later P–47 Thunderbolt. Having been developed from the XP–4I and the AP–4, the YP–43 never had an X designation, progressing directly to the Y – or service test status – designation since so much prototype work had already been done with the two previous aircraft. The intake for the turbosupercharger was moved from the XP–4I's wing root location to inside the cowling and under the engine on the YP–43. (Republic)

radial powerplant in a manner somewhat similar to the Vultee P–66 prototype.

The engine was extremely closely cowled and a huge spinner was fitted to the propeller hub, giving a rather bullet-like shape. Cooling was to be provided by retractable airscoops but, like the Vultee experiment, the idea was a failure and high engine temperatures could not be reduced so a more standard cowling was fitted to the AP–4. Flight testing with the AP–4 and XP–41 gave the newly formed Republic some valuable experience with turbo-superchargers – an item that was to prove essential in later fighters. Accordingly the contract for a new fighter would incorporate all the worthwhile features of these two aircraft. Given the designation YP–43, 13 aircraft were ordered for testing by the Army.

Kartveli decided to clean up his new design and give it some of the features of the combat aircraft which were making their appearance in the skies over Europe. The crash of the AP–4 when the turbosupercharger exploded in flight did not slow down the program but it did direct attention to that unit, which was a complex bit of machinery and would give trouble during the war years. It should be noted that there

was no X version of the P–43. Apparently the Army felt that enough experience had been gained with the earlier P–35, XP–41, and AP–4 to proceed directly to the order for the 13 aircraft under the Y designation which was assigned to indicate service test aircraft.

Power for the YP–43 was to be supplied by the Pratt & Whitney R–1830–35 that gave 1,200 takeoff horsepower. The boxy center section of the P–35's wing was eliminated, being replaced by a straight-through graceful elliptical wing that was almost identical in shape to the wing on the P–47 series that followed. A more powerful-looking cowl surrounded the engine and the air intake for the turbosupercharger had been moved from the wing root on the XP–41 and AP–4 to a position inside the cowl and just beneath the engine on the P–43. Armament was also revised and the new fighter would carry two .50 caliber machine guns in the upper cowling along with a .30 caliber gun in each wing panel, not a quantum jump in armament but at least it was a step in the right direction and heading towards the heavy armament being carried by European and Japanese fighting aircraft.

The YP–43 eliminated most of the stubby looks which had been a trademark of the Seversky P–35. The YP–43 had provision for carrying two .50 caliber air cooled Browning machine guns in the upper cowl and two .30 caliber guns in the wing. The first YP–43 was lost in a ground looping accident that led to the modification and extension of the tail strut by ten inches. The longer unit could not fully retract so a hinge was provided on a strut allowing the tail wheel to fold back against the tail cone so that the force of drag on the exposed unit would not be as great. (Republic)

The first YP–43, USAAC s/n 39–704, was handed over to the Army in September of 1940 and the remaining dozen aircraft had been delivered by April of 1941. Given the name Lancer, the YP–43s were dispersed to various Army fields for a period of extensive testing. A rather humorous story has been recounted involving the first YP–43 and the future Gen Mark Bradley concerning the problem of ground looping. As stated in the chapter on the P–35, that aircraft had a nasty habit of very violent ground looping and usually wound up on its back inflicting heavy damage to the airframe and, occasionally, the pilot. Bradley felt that the ground looping tendency (common to almost all aircraft with a tail wheel) could be dampened if not entirely eliminated

by installing a strong tail wheel lock which he felt would improve directional control on the ground. Testing this theory proved to be a bit of a problem as the YP–43 immediately did a very violent ground loop, flipped over, and broke into several pieces! An answer to ground looping was eventually found by increasing the height of the tail wheel strut, thus giving the fuselage a better angle which helped reduce the chance of the ground loop. However, the ten inch extension to the tail wheel strut meant that the unit could not completely retract inside the fuselage so a rather neat little hinge was added to the strut which let the wheel fold back against the tail cone, helping eliminate some of the drag from the unit.

Testing proved out the fact that the YP–43, while a considerable improvement over the P–35, was still not what the Army wanted. Also the increasing tempo of aerial warfare in Europe had quickly made the aircraft obsolete. Republic was going to stake its future on a new aircraft that would have carried the designation P–44 and the name Rocket. To be powered by an R–2180 the Rocket was to offer high performance but, before metal could be cut, events had outstripped this design so Republic and the Army progressed to the P–44–2 which was to be powered by the Pratt & Whitney R–2800; history was to be made when the aircraft's designation was changed to P–47.

There was to be a bit of trouble, however, between the demise of the YP–43 and the rise of the P–47 and that problem was mainly time. It was going to take a considerable amount of

Well-worn P–43 after the end of the war in the big aircraft graveyard at Chino, California, where thousands of aircraft were scrapped. This aircraft did not escape the scrapper's torch and was melted down in 1946. Serial number 40–2894 was the fourth P–43A constructed. (W. T. Larkins)

time for the Republic production line to spool up for building the new fighter and, rather than lay off many skilled workers that would be hard to replace at a later date, it was decided to build more Lancers to keep the production line open until the introduction of the new fighter. The P–43 was not *that* bad a plane and perhaps, the Army and Republic reasoned, it could be used for an advanced fighter trainer.

Contracts were drawn between Republic and the Army which called for the construction of 54 P–43s that would be virtually identical to the YP–43. It was soon apparent that more orders would be needed to keep the production line moving up until the introduction of the Thunderbolt so it was decided to convert the lapsed order for 80 P–44–1 Rockets into P–43As. The A model of the Lancer was equipped with the P&W R–1830–49 that, courtesy of the turbosupercharger, could keep pumping out 1,200 hp right up to 25,000 ft – otherwise it was identical to the earlier Lancers. Deliveries of the P–43A started during September 1941 and were complete by March of next year. Once again it was decided that some more Lancers had to be built to keep the line going and, in a manner which probably would be highly suspicious in today's world, funds were taken from the Lend-Lease program and 125 P–43A–1 Lancers were built ostensibly for China which had always been a dumping ground for unwanted aircraft. Thus the continuation of the Republic's Farmingdale, New York, production line had been assured by the production of a small group of 'inbetween'

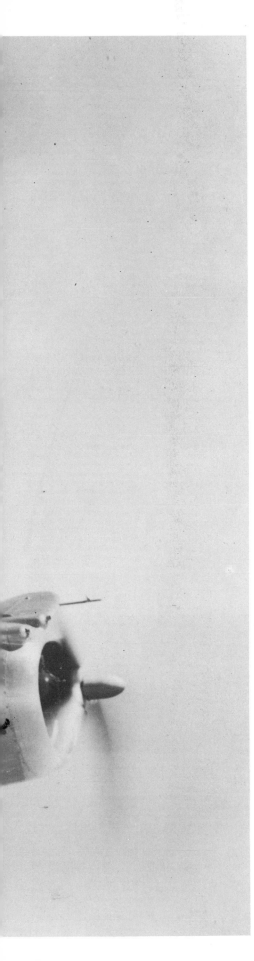

A classic view of the Army's pre-war fighting aircraft. A YP–43, in which the armament has been installed, leads a formation consisting of a P–40, P–39, and P–38. The Army's preference for liquid cooled engines is quite evident in this view. (USAF)

The Republic P–43 was remembered by a Flying Tiger pilot, who had a chance to observe closely the aircraft being operated by the Chinese Air Force, as 'a fine looking aircraft but underpowered and underarmed when it had to face the Japanese fighters and, like the RAF Buffaloes, was doomed to lose the fight.'

fighters that bridged the gap between 1930s thinking and one of the most successful fighter aircraft to be produced during the course of World War Two.

Little is known about the operation of the Air Corps Lancers although several pursuit squadrons were formed and the aircraft were apparently reliable if not the greatest of performers, although they were a big leap over the P–35. Many of these fighters eventually found their way to secondary units where they served as advanced trainers as the Army felt that Lancers could not be committed to a combat role. During 1942 the Army decided to convert all surviving YP–43s, P–43s, P–43As, and P–43A–1s (17 of which were retained by the Army from the Chinese order) to have a photo reconnaissance capability. Modified with a variety of camera installations the Lancers, depending on photographic equipment, adopted the designations of P–43B (150 conversions) and P–43C (two conversions) while P–43D and E models were apparently never taken up.

The Chinese P–43A–1s were equipped with R–1830–57 engines and had four .50 caliber Brownings (two in the nose, one in each wing) and featured vitally important self-sealing fuel tanks along with the ability to carry a small load of bombs. The fighters, at least 108 of the order, were shipped to China where they did see action against the Japanese but since the Lancer was a bit sluggish in the performance and maneuverability departments they probably did not fare well against the nimble Japanese fighters.

Eight Lancers found their way to Australia to take up service with the Royal Australian Air Force although it is not clear if these aircraft were already in Australia under Army service or whether they were specially shipped to Australia. Painted overall dark green the aircraft were assigned to No 1 Photographic Reconnaissance Unit where they were given RAAF serials A56–1 through A56–8, with

A56–5 being written off in a landing accident at Coomalie Creek during December 1942. It is thought that these Lancers were probably used for very high altitude reconnaissance of Japanese bases and fleet units.

The nearly forgotten Lancer formed the technological bridge to new aircraft while fighting in some of the more forgotten theaters of the war. Its service record is almost unknown and the type is virtually disregarded today. Not one example survived the scrapping of the Army Air Force after the end of World War Two which is too bad as the Lancer would have made a fine museum exhibit as an aircraft which soldiered on until something better was available.

REPUBLIC P–43 LANCER SERIAL NUMBERS AND SPECIFICATIONS

Serial Numbers

YP–43	39–704 through 39–716
P–43	41–6668 through 41–6721
P–43A	40–2891 through 40–2970
P–43A–1	41–31448 through 41–21572

Specifications

P–43A–1 Lancer

Span	36 ft
Length	28 ft 6 in
Height	14 ft
Wing area	223 sq ft
Empty weight	5,995 lb
Loaded weight	8,485 lb
Max. speed	356 mph
Cruise speed	275 mph
Ceiling	36,000 ft
Rate of climb	2,800 fpm
Range	1,450 miles max.
Powerplant	Pratt & Whitney R–1830–57 of 1,200 hp

P–43 Lancer

Span	36 ft
Length	28 ft 6 in
Height	14 ft
Wing area	223 sq ft
Empty weight	5,650 lb
Loaded weight	7,940 lb
Max. speed	345 mph
Cruise speed	270 mph
Ceiling	38,000 ft
Rate of climb	2,850 fpm
Range	1,300 miles max.
Powerplant	Pratt & Whitney R–1830–47 of 1,200 hp

Curtiss XP-46
The Ugly Duckling

Attempting to benefit from the lessons of combat in Europe, Curtiss produced an aircraft which was grotesque in the extreme.

There can be no doubt that the Curtiss P–40 series of fighters deserve the title of classic. Heavily influenced by 1930s thinking and showing little brilliance, the P–40s were available in considerable numbers when they were most needed. However, during and after the P–40, virtually every aircraft in the fighter category produced by Curtiss was a failure. Not only were they failures but they were also some of the ugliest aircraft ever made. A perfect example of the rapid drop in the fortunes of Curtiss was the XP–46.

Observers from Curtiss who had been sent to England and Europe before the outbreak of World War Two returned to the parent company with a number of suggestions as to future directions for proposed fighters. Heavily influenced by the early Spitfires and Messerschmitt Bf 109s, a smaller fighter than the P–40 with a battery of at least eight .30 caliber machine guns and a slotted wing to improve control during combat was suggested. Preliminary work on the aircraft, which was hoped to be a successor to the P–40, was handed over to the Army Air Corps who approved of what they saw and issued a production contract for two prototypes on 29 September 1939.

Production for the P–40 was rapidly building up when the order for the new fighter prototypes was received and Curtiss planned to use an uprated Allison, a V–1710–39 of 1,150 hp, to power the new aircraft, thus

The first XP–46 to fly was actually the second aircraft, 40–3054, which had been designated XP–46A. Curtiss attempted to profit from the rapid development in fighter aircraft design in Europe. Intended as a possible replacement for the P–40 series, the XP–46 was to be smaller with more power, better combat maneuverability, and a heavy armament. However, the aircraft had sluggish handling qualities, and all-round unsatisfactory performance, worse than that of the P–40s already in production. Never fitted with the proposed armament of eight wing mounted .30 caliber machine guns and two .50 caliber guns in the nose, the XP–46 was quickly cancelled by the Army. (USAF)

assuring a common engine design for the two types. With the liquid-cooled Allison and a smaller airframe than the P–40, Curtiss designers predicted a top speed over 400 mph – how they came up with this unrealistic figure is open to conjecture. The quality of work coming from the Curtiss design department also leads to interesting speculation on the creation of the North American NA–73X – the aircraft that led directly to the Mustang. North American, having little experience in the military combat aircraft field, was forced by the Army to purchase vast amounts of Curtiss wind-tunnel data for what, the Army hoped, would be a good education from Curtiss. Unfortunately for Curtiss, North American had their own fighter ideas and did not let the rather dated concepts from Curtiss slow down work on the NA–73X – contrary to some ill-informed aircraft historians who have misguidedly suggested that the Mustang was really designed by pirating of Curtiss data.

The second XP–46 was the first to fly, on 15 February 1941, and was designated XP–46A. Designed to carry an armament of eight .30 caliber machine guns in the wings and two .50 caliber guns in the nose firing through the propeller arc, neither aircraft ever had the armament installed. The XP–46 was a rather portly, slab-sided affair with a low canopy situated over the wing. Bearing some resemblance to the P–40, both XP–46s were delivered without armament or radios to expedite flying schedules. Once in the air, the aircraft were found to be sluggish and slower than contemporary P–40s then in service. Work on both aircraft was quickly terminated and it is presumed that the machines were scrapped soon afterwards. The XP–46 proved that revamping a dated concept did not work and although the company was to go on and build thousands of P–40s, Curtiss, through lack of imagination and poor design, was out of the fighter business.

CURTISS XP–46 SERIAL NUMBERS AND SPECIFICATIONS

Serial Numbers

XP–46	40–3053
XP–46A	40–3054

Specifications

XP–46

Flight tests on the XP–46s were not completed because of the obvious inferiority of the design so performance specifications should be regarded as estimates.

Span	34 ft 4 in
Length	30 ft 2 in
Height	13 ft
Wing area	208 sq ft
Empty weight	5,625 lb
Loaded weight	7,665 lb
Max. speed	355 mph
Cruise speed	327 mph
Ceiling	28,000 ft
Rate of climb	2,000 fpm
Range	325 miles
Powerplant	Allison V–1710–39 of 1,150 hp

Republic P-47 Thunderbolt — Heavyweight From Farmingdale

The biggest single-seat combat aircraft of World War Two, and one of the best, the P–47 could tackle several different missions and perform all of them well.

Seversky's (and later Republic's) experience with the P–35 and P–43 series of fighters had led to the conjecture that an improved version of the P–43 could supply the Army with a heavyweight fighter that would be capable of performing ground attack as well as interception duties. Alexander Kartveli, Seversky's chief designer, felt that there could be several avenues down which the new design could proceed. First, a basic redesign and moderniza-

tion of the P–43 was an easy possibility. Secondly, since the Army was so drawn to the Allison inline, Kartveli felt that a major redesign of his basic fighter concept could be undertaken so that the Allison could be accommodated. However, there was the possibility of sweeping the design board clean and coming up with an entirely new prototype.

The Army had shown some interest in the idea of using an Allison but Kartveli, studying the results of the early aerial fighting over Europe, decided that it would be wise to mate a new, slimmed-down airframe to the Allison. However, during 1939 Kartveli came up with drawings and projected performance figures

A pilot and his aircraft: Captain E. A. Sprietsma stands by his P–47D during an apparent display of American military might for visiting British citizens. This view illustrates the P–47's rugged landing gear and the unpainted barrels of the four .50 caliber machine guns. The first Thunderbolts to enter combat were C models and a shipment of these aircraft arrived in Britain a few days before the end of 1942, startling British pilots with their size. The fuel tank upon which the Captain is resting is one of the paper/plastic composition 108 gallon droppable auxiliary tanks that extended the Thunderbolt's range for bomber escort missions.

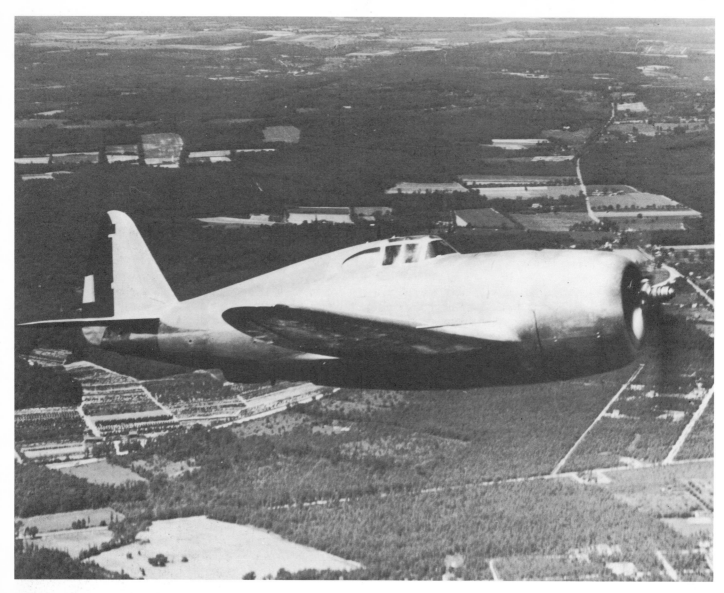

The XP–47B seen in flight during May 1942. On the aircraft's first flight, the cockpit filled with smoke and test pilot Lowery Brabham made a precautionary landing at Mitchel Field. The prototype did not last long, although it did last long enough to acquire an Olive Drab and Neutral Gray camouflage scheme, for it crashed on 8 August 1942. The rear fuselage had become enveloped in fire (probably from an exploding turbosupercharger) and test pilot Fillmore Gilmer wisely decided to take to his parachute – the experimental fighter crashing in Long Island Sound. (Republic)

for the new Allison-engined project, which was given the company designation of AP–10, but, when it was time during August 1939 to submit the design, now envisioned as strictly an interceptor, to the Army, some problems arose. The Army did not feel that the new aircraft was suited to mass production techniques. However, they felt that the projected performance estimates were very encouraging so the data was submitted to the Army's experimental flying section at Wright Field in Ohio where the design was given a complete going over.

Army engineers had several helpful suggestions that increased the AP–10's chances for production. Kartveli's initial design work had attached the Allison to the smallest airframe he could design. His reasoning was that superior performance could be achieved by keeping the frontal area as low as possible, the overall weight low and the armament fairly restricted to decrease space and save weight. Wright

Field had a few other ideas to make the aircraft more suitable to the Army. They enlarged the design slightly, increasing weight and wing area. Oddly, since current battlefield reports were flowing in from Europe, Wright kept Kartveli's restricted armament of one .30 and one .50 caliber machine gun housed in the upper section of the cowling. However, they did add two pylons under the wing that could carry small bombs.

At this point, one of those strange twists that makes aviation history such a fascinating subject took place. With a projected top speed of 415 mph, the Army wanted to get the revised AP–10 into production as soon as possible. Accordingly, the Army issued the project with two designations: XP–47 for a fully combat furnished prototype and XP–47A (to be delivered before the XP–47) which would be an experimental prototype that would not be fitted with military equipment and would be used strictly to prove that the design was airworthy and suitable for production.

The company was thus faced with a very ambitious project: build a relatively lightweight (something Seversky could not have been accused of previously doing) new fighter with a liquid-cooled engine and have it flying in the very short space of nine months. Problems quickly arose when the Army tried to obtain final permission for contract funding. An investigation into the type quickly showed some major deficiencies that were of serious concern to the contract makers. The rather primitive armament was immediately rejected in the light of European experience, while wing loading (the wing was a tiny 115 sq ft in area) was felt to be much too high and the top speed, based on the projections from other manufacturer's new designs, was felt to be too low. These considerations led the design team back to the drawing board where the new design was hacked about, the wing area increased, the armament uprated with the addition of one .30 and one .50 caliber machine gun and the weight increased to accommodate the various modifications. Kartveli felt that he could hold the top speed figure but he knew that the climb rate, a prime consideration for an interceptor, would decay with the additional size and weight.

By the start of 1940, the combat situation was changing so rapidly in Europe that American manufacturers were almost overwhelmed with design changes to keep up with what the foreign air forces wanted. Seversky had become Republic by the end of 1939, and the new company was continuing to modify the basic AP–10 design to satisfy Army requests. More weapons were to be added along with armor protection and self-sealing fuel tanks. More work was, of course, needed to complete design drawings and the final completion date of the XP–47A kept slipping. Republic could probably see that the idea of producing the new fighter was rapidly fading. The old Seversky company always favored big radial engines and, despite the change in name and the reshuffling of top management, the idea that a big radial was better than the Allison was still very popular.

Once again Kartveli and his team went back to a blank sheet of paper in order to save the company from losing what would certainly be a large and very lucrative contract. Pratt & Whitney had introduced their R–2800 Double Wasp which promised, with fairly minimal development, to produce over 2,000 hp. Not only was the horsepower impressive, but the R–2800 had a surprisingly low frontal area for an engine of its cubic inch capacity. Taking the criticisms of the Army and of the European air forces to heart, the team incorporated the engine into an entirely new airframe because the AP–10 was much too small to handle the R–2800. The new airframe was not unlike earlier Seversky efforts. Throwing American caution to the wind, a battery of six .50 caliber machine guns was mounted in the wing which also had two underwing pylons. Considerable armor, self-sealing fuel tanks and other combat updates were added. When the paper design was completed, even the engineers were surprised. They had created a monster – a fighter aircraft that, at almost 12,000 lb, was over twice the weight of the XP–47!

Even though the new aircraft was completely different from the XP–47/XP–47A, it retained the same designation and was just given a new model number, XP–47B. The new design was a heavyweight in more ways than one, but its large size did not mean that performance had completely decreased. It had, in fact, remained fairly high – especially at top speed (projected at 400 mph at altitude) and its firepower was tremendous, more than any

Showing the distinctive white bands added to the Thunderbolts as an identification aid are P–47D–1–RE Thunderbolts of the 62nd Fighter Squadron, 56th Fighter Group. The national insignia has had a thin yellow surround added for the same purpose. These special identity markings were applied because of the P–47's similarity in appearance, when viewed from a distance, to the Luftwaffe's Focke Wulf Fw 190. (USAF/24914)

In the company of a lone Mustang, P–47D–11–RE Thunderbolts are seen at the 2nd Base Air Depot in Lancashire, England, on 10 March 1944. The Base Air Depots, or BADs, were responsible for readying recently arrived aircraft for delivery to combat units. At this time, new updates or specified field modifications were added and the aircraft were thoroughly test flown to make sure that they were in good mechanical condition. (USAF/76512)

other operational American fighter by a wide margin.

After evaluating the new paper design, the Army placed an order for the P–47B on 6 September 1940 and it was a most impressive order: 773 aircraft were to be built and the prototype had not even been constructed! All data, parts and tooling for the earlier Allison version of the P–47 was either scrapped or dispersed to the National Advisory Committee for Aeronautics (NACA) where it was tested and studied. In the meantime, Republic was busy expanding its facilities and preparing the thousands of detailed drawings which are required to build a fighter.

The R–2800 would be equipped with a large turbosupercharger and the placing of this sophisticated piece of equipment was of prime importance. It was decided, after examining the initial sketches for the large fuselage, to place it to the rear of the fuselage. An elaborate system of ducting would enable the unit and the engine to perform with utmost efficiency, providing the necessary boost to the engine to provide high-altitude performance of the highest quality. This system of ducting was complex and would cause some problems during

the early production run of P–47s – but more about that later.

With its big, heavy fuselage, large cowling and massive turbosupercharger, the P–47B was mounted, rather surprisingly, on a very attractive wing with elegant elliptical outer panels not unlike those on the Seversky P–35. To absorb all the power possible from the R–2800, the P–47B was fitted with a four-blade controllable pitch propeller that had a huge 12 ft 2 in diameter, immediately giving the designers fits over how to install the propeller without making landing gear that would look like stilts and take up all the room for guns in the wing. Vought had been faced with the same problem with their R–2800–powered Corsair (although this machine had a three-blade propeller) and they had opted for an inverted gull center section that would provide plenty of propeller clearance along with a landing gear leg of regular proportion. Republic decided to use a telescoping gear leg that would be about nine inches longer when extended than when retracted. This gave more than adequate room in the wing for the six .50 caliber Brownings; in fact, there was so much room that the armament was soon expanded to a devastating eight .50s.

In today's terms, the large fuselage could certainly be classified as 'widebody' and the Republic engineers took advantage of the space to install a large (300 US gallons) fuel tank to feed the hungry R–2800 – one of the radial's bad points was that its fuel consumption was almost double that of the Allison. The cockpit was extremely spacious and the instru-

ments were fairly well laid out and convenient to the pilot's reach. The canopy was a rather slipshod affair, hinging over to the side and making entrance and exit rather difficult, especially in the event of an emergency. Production P–47Bs favored a sliding canopy – like on the Curtiss P–40 – which was much easier to jettison in case the pilot had to parachute from his striken fighter.

There was only one XP–47B model and no service test YP–47s, a rather unusual departure from Army practice, but an indication of how desperate the service was for advanced fighters. The XP–47B was virtually hand-built by Republic workmen. This aircraft, after testing by the factory and by the Army, was retained by Republic for further test and modification. The second P–47B, although classified as the first production machine, was actually another handbuilt prototype to be used by the Army for proving the concept.

Republic's chief test pilot, Lowrey L. Brabham took the XP–47B up for the first time on 6 May 1941, flying from Farmingdale, Long Island. Republic's airfield, at this time, was unpaved and recent rains had left the surface of the runway questionable for operations. It was decided to fly the XP–47B over to Mitchel Field, a nearby Army base, for landing.

Even with the muddy field, the prototype took off smoothly – being lightly loaded for the first flight. Brabham grabbed some altitude and began circling over the two airfields, jotting down performance notes and waiting for company officials to drive to Mitchel to witness the landing. Suddenly the cockpit be-

*D*ramatic view of a Thunderbolt attacking an
enemy flak tower and giving it a good hosing
down from the eight .50 caliber machine guns.
There were few targets that could stand such
punishment. The photograph was taken from a
frame off the gun camera of the Thunderbolt flying
directly behind its attacking companion. Note how
the identity bands stand out from the Dark Olive
Drab finish. (USAF/51036)

*W*ith a wave from the starter, two bombed-up
Thunderbolts begin to trundle down an
English runway on their way to France. Both
aircraft carry 108 gallon drop tanks made out of
compressed paper impregnated with plastic on
their center-line racks. These tanks were made in
England and were much less costly than the metal
units. (USAF)

gan to fill with smoke and Brabham, attempting to clear the noxious fumes, opened a small sliding panel on the canopy to get outside air but all this accomplished was to suck in additional smoke (some oil had spilled onto the ducting of the turbosupercharger and caused the thick smoke. It was not serious but Brabham, of course, did not know this). Breathing as little as possible, Brabham waited until he saw the company cars on the Mitchel ramp and then landed the XP–47B smoothly.

The company knew that they had a winner from this first test flight but the cautious test pilot recommended certain changes – some of which were easy, some of which took time. One of the most important findings was that the pilot had felt a slight amount of flutter in the controls. Flutter was a serious problem. If it reached an advanced state, it could rip the wings or tail off the most sturdily constructed warplane. It was decided to leave the XP–47B at Mitchel and Republic engineers cured the

problem by fitting stiffeners to the wing. Brabham was also not pleased with control response, which he felt was rather sloppy, but the engineers had a solution for this problem too.

Further flight tests revealed more problems, especially as the big fighter headed for the high altitude from which it was to operate. The 40,000 ft ceiling of the XP–47B was unexplored territory for a heavy fighter and among the problems encountered was the failure of the R–2800's ignition harness above 30,000 ft, causing the big engine to backfire, run poorly and lose power. Solving this problem took quite a bit of time and experimentation with many different types of ignition harnesses but it was eventually conquered by the pressurization of the harness. High altitude also had a drastic effect on engine oil, the oil boiling and foaming and not forcing its way through the engine which would quickly self-destruct without the lubricating fluid. By using a different type of oil and a different method of cooling and distribution, this problem was also beaten.

During early flight tests, Brabham began to explore the XP–47B's performance envelope. During a power dive he found that the new fighter accelerated like nothing else flying. The

A *P–47C–2–RE, 41–6209, receives an engine run-up before take-off. At altitudes below 15,000 ft the new Fw 190 proved to be more than a handful for the big American fighter but at heights over that figure it was another story as the turbosupercharger started playing its magic for the R–2800. Above 15,000 ft the P–47 could outrun and even out turn the Fw 190. (USAF)*

big fighter gathered speed very quickly, reaching its critical Mach number of about .8, or around 550 mph. This high speed also had a heavy price since the controls became very heavy and considerable force had to be exerted by the pilot to pull out of the dive. Upon landing, Brabham was surprised to find that the majority of the fabric on the tail surface controls was ripped. The immense pressure of the air had literally caused the fabric covering to explode – a situation that could have caused Brabham to lose control. The control surfaces on the Thunderbolt eventually had aluminum covering but the first production units retained the fabric controls.

The Army had not been naming its fighters, just giving them designations. The British had started the practice of giving names to their aircraft and these names were easily recognized by the public after the start of World War Two. American manufacturers soon began to take up the trend, especially since they were selling the majority of their product to the British. A Republic official came up with the name Thunderbolt and the new prototype was

so designated. It turned out to be a very good name and summarized many of the aircraft's performance attributes.

The program was moving into high gear and the first four 'production' Thunderbolts were quickly assimilated into the rigorous testing regime. Each one of these machines had minor differences such as changed canopies – the original system of a car-type door and hinged canopy was dropped as being too dangerous in case of an emergency – slight modifications to the airframes, and changes to the controls.

The four prototype/production machines were flying by March 1942 but disaster struck soon after. One of the Republic test pilots had taken a Thunderbolt up to investigate diving characteristics but pilot and fighter were soon a smoking crater on a local golf course. Even though Brabham and the engineers had recommended metal-covered controls, some of the very early P–47Bs still had the fabric-covered units and it was the destruction of the fabric that caused this particular crash. Even though the modifications were being carried

out on the production line, the pressure of flight testing was such that another P–47B was lost in May due to the same problem. In this case, the pilot managed to bail out of the stricken fighter and descend by parachute into Long Island Sound where he was rescued by a passing boat.

The Army was pressuring for early delivery of the fighter since America was now involved in the war and every aircraft was desperately needed somewhere on the Army's global conflict map. The first operational P–47B was handed over to the Army on 26 May 1942 but the new fighter would be deployed in an interesting manner that would involve combining training with operational experience for the new Thunderbolt pilots.

During 1942, the threat of some sort of German attack or mini-invasion along the East Coast of America was a very real problem. Some high-ranking officers felt that a German attack on one of the many vulnerable war plants would give the Germans a psychological

victory while causing damage to the war effort. One of the most vulnerable areas was the then-remote Long Island, home of Republic. The Army decided to take the first production Thunderbolts and form a protective squadron at Farmingdale. The Thunderbolts would provide an umbrella against possible German air attacks while giving the pilots excellent training in the new aircraft.

The recently formed 56th Fighter Group was given the task and its three squadrons were dispersed to Farmingdale; Bridgeport, Connecticut (home of Vought); and Bendix, New Jersey. Arriving with Airacobras, the unit began to transition to the big fighter. As with most transitions, problems were encountered. The young pilots were not used to the lumbering take-off of a loaded Thunderbolt. The aircraft ate up an amazing amount of runway and a slight burp or malfunction in the engine would mean that the fighter would not achieve flight and end up plowing at high speed through the trees at the end of the runway.

Fortunately, the Thunderbolt was so rugged that the pilot would usually survive with minimal injuries. The development was costly and a check of Republic's records reveals that over half of the 56th Fighter Group's Thunderbolts had been wrecked by the end of June 1942. Still, valuable lessons had been learned and these were passed back to the engineers and incorporated into the production line, making the P–47 an even better fighter.

By August, the Thunderbolt had been red-lined at 300 mph following several accidents (some fatal) that came about as a result of high altitude flight and power dives. A remedy was found in strengthening the tail area which

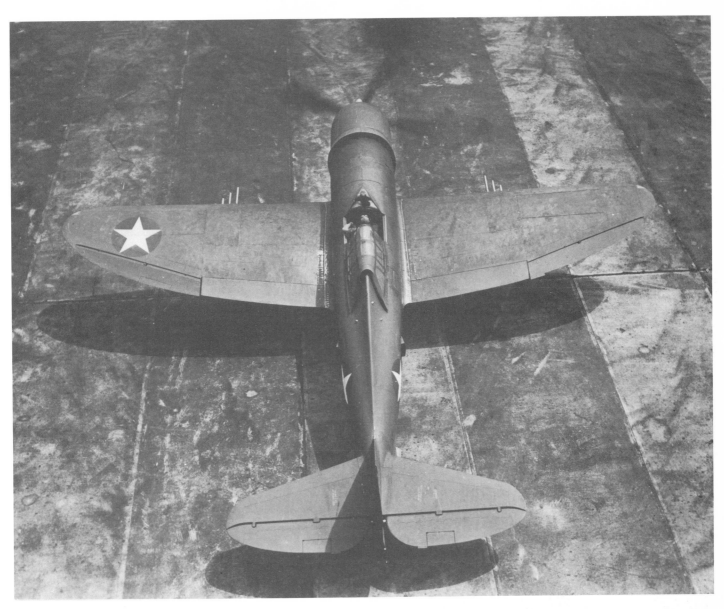

*H*igh-angle view gives an idea why the early
Thunderbolts were called 'razorbacks'. This
view also emphasizes the Kartveli wing shape and
the huge nose that made forward visibility difficult
while the Thunderbolt was on the ground.
(Republic)

Opposite above
*D*own and out: a P–47D blazes after crash
landing with battle damage in Belgium. The
pilot managed to get away before the aircraft was
completely consumed by the flames from the
fuselage tank. Pilots disliked the large fuselage
tank for it was prone to catching fire or blowing up
in accidents such as this. (USAF/56625)

*B*adly-bent P–47D–22–RE 42–25710 of the
351st Fighter Squadron, 353rd Fighter Group
did not quite make it back to base on 3 May 1944
and crash landed in a field. USAAF personnel
prepare to remove the guns and ammunition that
made such good souvenirs for young lads in the
area. (USAF/69591)

eliminated a high-speed flutter that had torn
the rudders from some aircraft. During the
high altitude flights, Republic and the Army
were both delighted to find that the Thunderbolt was indicating performance figures higher
than those the designers had originally calculated. It was almost 30 mph faster at altitude
than expected. The Army realized that the
Thunderbolt would be a most potent
warplane.

The Thunderbolt could, from its high-
altitude perch, dive like the proverbial brick
which gave rise to the myth that the P–47 had
broken the sound barrier during a power dive.
At this point, the sound barrier was not
particularly well understood. The barrier
varies with altitude, density of the air and
temperature – anywhere in the low- to mid-
700 mph region. Two Thunderbolt pilots were
amazed to find their airspeed indicators re-
gistering well over 700 mph after power dives.

Figuring out the variables previously mentioned, the Army proclaimed that the sound
barrier had been broken. Both Thunderbolts
had received physical damage after the Friday
the 13th dives during November 1942, an
indication of the tremendous stresses that had
been placed on the airframes. The aviators
related that the aircraft were almost uncontrollable and that recovery from the dives
was more a matter of luck than anything else.
However, as understanding of the physical
characteristics of the sound barrier and aerodynamic compressibility grew, the Army realized that there was no way in which the
Thunderbolt or any other propeller-driven
fighter could break the sound barrier no matter
what distance they dived. The bulky airframe
of the Thunderbolt reached compressibility
well before the barrier and the actual speed of
the dive was probably somewhere in the region
of the high 500s. Engineers would come to

realize that a sleekly-styled airframe propelled by a jet or rocket was needed to slip past the barrier, but that does not in any way take away from the bravery of the young Army pilots who ventured to the threshold of a new dimension in aerodynamics.

The Army had contracted for 171 P–47Bs and these machines were completed in just six months at Farmingdale as the company prepared for the much larger contracts that were following. The P–47 would hold the record for the largest number of an American fighter to be built, 15,683 units. The next variant was the P–47C, similar to the P–47B except that the forward fuselage was eight inches longer in order to move the engine farther forward in an effort to improve the center of gravity. A center-line pylon was added to carry a bomb or fuel tank. The vertical and horizontal tail control surfaces were modified and strengthened and the space made available by the fuselage stretch was used to house a 30 US gallon water tank that supplied liquid for the R–2800–59's injection system. The selected new variant of powerplant was not available for the first 112 P–47C–1s so they were fitted with the same engine that powered the B, the R–2800–21, which did not have water injection. With the water injection, the P–47C–5's horsepower rating jumped from 2,000 to 2,300 hp at 27,000 ft.

The small number of P–47Bs remained basically trainers, allowing pilots their first introduction to the huge new fighter. The 56th Fighter Group kept up its rigorous flying schedule although, as previously mentioned, accidents took a large toll of the P–47Bs but the Thunderbolt was being brought up to combat readiness. It would soon be time to unleash Republic's new warplane on the Axis.

The Army extensively tested several P–47Cs at Wright Field finding, perhaps rather surprisingly considering its size, that the Thunderbolt had the fastest roll rate of any Army fighter. General flying characteristics were found to be more than satisfactory and the main criticisms seem to have centered around vision over the nose while the aircraft was on the ground and during landing and take-off. Vision in the air was also a problem since the canopy frame was heavily braced, the metal strips serving as blinders for the pilot. All in all, the Army judged the P–47C to be a satisfactory warplane and approved the variant for combat.

American mass production techniques have already been mentioned. The combat demand

The terrain of Northern Burma was some of the worst in the world so the pilots of these bare metal P–47Ds were probably very glad about the reliability record of their R–2800 powerplants. The China-Burma-India Theater had several Thunderbolt units including the 33rd, 80th and 81st Fighter Groups.

Harsh climatic conditions and primitive operating conditions at air fields in the CBI were extremely harsh on aircraft but the tough Thunderbolt proved to be a perfect weapon in this theater.

for the Thunderbolt was such that two new factories had to be put into production in the least possible time. Evansville, Indiana, was a new site, while Thunderbolts were built under license at the Curtiss-Wright plant at Buffalo, New York. The Evansville plant was started in early 1942 and the factory's first Thunderbolt was flown in September – while the factory was still being finished around the production line! The license production of the Thunderbolt by Curtiss did not go as smoothly as Evansville, which became an excellent example of mass production, and the P–47Gs (basically similar to the P–47C) suffered from poor quality control and very slow delivery – only delivering 354 aircraft before closure.

The Army began making plans for the deployment of the P–47C to Britain and paperwork began to create new squadrons that

would take the Thunderbolt into combat. The P–47's immense hunger for fuel (up to 130 gallons per hour at high cruise power – compared to about 60 for the P–51B) would limit the type's radius of action to about 200 miles but the fighter would be able to provide vital escort for Liberators and Flying Fortresses as they battled their way to targets over *Luftwaffe* infested France.

Republic and the Army decided that, after initial factory and Army test flights, the P–47s would be crated and shipped to Britain for assembly, test flights and delivery to combat squadrons. The first deck cargo Thunderbolt arrived in Britain on 20 December 1942 and was assigned to the 4th Fighter Group. The 4th was the follow-on to the RAF's Eagle Squadrons – combat units of American volunteers flying Spitfires for the British. At the time of the Thunderbolt's arrival, the 4th was the only fighter group under the command of the 8th Air Force whose bombers were being mauled daily due to the lack of appropriate fighter protection.

The 4th's base at Debden became the Thunderbolt's first United Kingdom home. Deliveries of aircraft began to build rapidly during January 1943 and pilots began flying the new fighters but trouble quickly arose as pilots familiar with the sleek petite Spitfire tried to master the powerful and portly P–47C, delaying the vitally needed fighter's entry into combat. The first combat sweep took place on 10 March 1943 when 14 P–47Cs ventured over enemy-held territory. However, technical problems gave so much trouble that the next combat mission did not take place for another month while crew chiefs and mechanics made the P–47C more combat worthy, modifying and repairing equipment that would only malfunction when sent into the rigors of high-altitude combat.

As the 4th struggled with its new aircraft, the officers and men of the 56th Fighter Group began arriving by ship in Britain for stationing at their new base, Kings Cliffe in Northamptonshire. A third fighter group, the 78th, was also formed to fly Thunderbolts and was based at

A view that emphasizes the brute power of the P-47. For such a heavyweight, the Thunderbolt had a very clean head-on profile, the R-2800 merging smoothly into the barrel-like fuselage. S/n 42-75568 is a D-11-RE of which 400 were built powered by a 2,300 hp R-2800-63 with water injection. Note the eight unpainted gun barrels and extremely wide track of the landing gear that gave the P-47 good ground handling characteristics (besides the poor visibility over the nose). (Republic)

Line-up of killers. This photograph reveals the difference in markings on several ETO Thunderbolts, the first two being painted in Dark Olive Drab and Neutral Gray followed by a bare metal P-51D and a bare metal P-47D with a gaily checked cowling. Mr Ted, the second P-47 in the line carries the white and black checkered cowling of the 78th Fighter Group.

In an attempt to increase the P–47's already large capacity for ground attack, these bazooka-like tubes carrying 4.5 in rockets proved to be effective for destroying a variety of ground and shipping targets. (Republic)

Goxhill in Lincolnshire. The fact that three new combat groups were being pushed into the field caused trouble enough but, to add to this, only the 4th had combat experience, only the 56th had flown the P–47, but the 78th had done neither! The problems that the 4th was having as their Thunderbolts dropped out with mechanical woes were tripled with the addition of the new groups. USAAF and Republic field service teams frantically shuffled between the bases, quite often learning new techniques for the care and feeding of the Thunderbolts as they worked side by side with squadron crew chiefs.

Training accidents began to take their toll although pilots that had to make belly landings after engine failure were often amazed by

the strength of Republic's fighter as it plowed through stone walls, trees and hedgerows with aplomb. As the three groups flew more and more hours, there were fatal accidents – it must be remembered that, according to one source, the 56th, while flying P–47Bs Stateside, lost 14 aircraft and 13 pilots. Mysterious engine failures at high altitude were eventually traced down to fuel flow problems and Pratt & Whitney field service representatives made the necessary modifications. Ignition harnesses were prone to succumb to the damp British weather and the failure of the harness would also lead to the engine stopping. A liberal coating of a special grease to the harness prevented moisture from affecting the electrical flow to the problem that plagued early Thunderbolt combat missions, pronounced static and electrical interference over the radio making communications all but impossible, was traced to the immense amount of static electricity generated by the harness and

escaping from small gaps in the engine's magneto seals. The problem was partially corrected by sealing the gaps but it took pressurized magnetos to cure the problem of unwanted static completely.

The USAAF was anxious to mount a large scale P–47 mission to show the Allies that the new fighter could do what was advertised. To gather a fairly large number of airworthy Thunderbolts, it was necessary to draw upon all three fighter groups to produce 24 P–47Cs for a mission on 8 April. The Thunderbolts, which had by now acquired white recognition stripes on the forward cowling and vertical tail to aid other pilots and gunners in identifying the new type, ventured out over Pas de Calais but, like the previous few missions, no contact was established with the *Luftwaffe*. Drawing aircraft from the three groups became a standard practice for the next few missions but results were still zero, except for the Thunderbolts – a couple of aircraft were lost due to

The fuel situation was difficult to cure in its own right. A rather crude compressed paper jettisonable tank was fitted to the belly pylon of some Thunderbolts in the field to give some extra range. This tank, which had a capacity of 200 US gallons, giving about 1.5 hours of flying time at low cruise settings, was not pressurized and fuel had to be drawn before the aircraft got over 20,000 ft. Since it would be of only limited use, the tank was only partially filled, used during the long climb and jettisoned as the pilot switched over to internal fuel. With typical Yankee ingenuity, field engineers took some of the small drop tanks left over from P–39 operations, pressurized the units, and installed the tanks, with appropriate feed lines, to the center line shackle. The new tanks worked very well but were capable of holding only 75 US gallons of additional fuel. New tanks meant that the P–47s could guard the bombers deeper into enemy territory and many *Luftwaffe* pilots were totally surprised to have a pack of Thunderbolts on their tail as the Germans attempted to attack the bombers. Larger fuel tanks were modified for use on the P–47 and British-built paper tanks could carry 108 US gallons.

The struggle to extend the P–47's range was reduced by the arrival of the first P–47Ds in Britain during April 1943. The first Ds were very similar to the C but many internal modifications had been made by the factory to improve the ducts for the turbosupercharger, simplify the engine controls, add more armor for the pilot and vital systems and many other small detail modifications that would make the Thunderbolt a better fighter. A major step forward came with the P–47D–15 which introduced two underwing pylons that could carry either 1,000 lb bombs or additional fuel. However, when this heavily loaded, the ammunition per gun had to be reduced from 425 to 267 rpg and on some aircraft the number of Brownings was reduced to six. The bombing capability was totally opposite to the P–47's original role of stratosphere fighter but, as events would prove, it was to be a capability that would cause considerable damage to the Axis.

With the aircraft now arriving in a steady stream from the two factories (some were lost in U-Boat strikes on the supply ships), new fighter groups were created to handle the

engine failures but the pilots were rescued as they bobbed around the English Channel in their life jackets.

It was just a matter of time until the Thunderbolts ran into action and on 15 April 1943, P–47Cs from the 335th Fighter Squadron, 4th Fighter Group, met and defeated two Focke–Wulf Fw 190s over France – the very beginning of a long run of Thunderbolt victories. Since the P–47 was the only Allied fighter with a radial engine and, from a distance, looked a bit like an Fw 190, gunners quite often fired first and asked questions later – many times apparently ignoring the white identification stripes. During the first few months in service, Thunderbolts were regularly fired on as they returned from missions over occupied Europe.

The USAAF felt that the P–47s and pilots were ready for their first high altitude escort mission and, on 4 May, a mixed group of Thunderbolts joined the bomber stream for

Antwerp as the Flying Fortresses battled their way to the heavily defended target. Streaming contrails, the Thunderbolts lazily S-turned over the bomber formation – providing an umbrella for the lumbering Boeings.

Once again, problems were encountered as the P–47s escorted the bombers. Some of the aircraft had very rough running engines, not an ideal situation for the pilot of a single-engine fighter over Nazi territory, while fuel consumption ran higher than had been estimated – even at the reduced power settings which were employed to stay in formation with the bombers. The R–2800's sophisticated fuel control system was the cause of some of the problems, especially since the engine was coupled to the huge turbosupercharger. If the system was operated slightly out of kilter, cylinder heads could be damaged and this would be the first step to engine failure. Educating the pilots helped to eliminate the problem.

An essential pre-start procedure was pulling the Thunderbolt's propeller through several revolutions to free any oil that may have gathered in the bottom cylinders which could cause engine damage when started. This white and black checkered cowling 78th FG P-47D-22-RE was flown by Captain Q. L. Brown who had 13 kills at the time the photograph was taken. (USAF 51369)

Thunderbolt – the 352nd, 353rd, 355th, 356th, 358th, 359th and 361st. Since the Curtiss factory was not producing aircraft as quickly as Republic and since the Curtiss line was beset with a number of serious problems, it appears that most of the Curtiss-built P-47Gs were reserved for Stateside training units and that none was sent to combat zones.

The Thunderbolt quickly began to gain fame as it operated with the fighter groups in Britain. The 56th Fighter Group, in particular, which was led by Colonel Hubert 'Hub' Zemke quickly headed to the top of the scoreboard. Zemke had built up a good background of Thunderbolt experience with the P-47B when the 56th was Stateside and he was a prime advocate of the big fighter's destructive power. Zemke had compared the P-47C against the captured flyable *Luftwaffe* fighters which were

operated by the British as training aids for combat pilots. Zemke found out that the early Fw 190A was quite a handful but it could be met and defeated on its own ground by the Thunderbolt, if the big fighter was precisely flown to take advantage of the German machine's weaknesses. The much smaller Fw 190 could accelerate faster than the P-47C in all phases of flight, but given some time, the P-47 could usually overhaul the German in a long run. The Fw 190 could outclimb the P-47 and initially outdive it, but the P-47C, with its tremendous diving capabilities, could quickly catch the German. The Focke-Wulf was at an advantage in a close-in dogfight, especially if the P-47's speed could be reduced to below 250 mph – giving the agile German fighter a chance to maneuver inside the P-47's turning radius. The cannon-armed German could do great damage to the Thunderbolt's rugged airframe but the Fw 190 was virtually doomed if it took a direct burst of fire from all eight of the .50 caliber Brownings.

Zemke concluded that the P-47 would be most effective against the German fighters if the 56th operated above 15,000 ft where the

big turbosupercharger would really start pumping extra power to the R-2800 while the German's power scale would begin slightly to drop off. Dogfights were not recommended, so Zemke devised a dive and zoom tactic which was most effective when employed against the *Luftwaffe*. P-47 pilots were instructed to take advantage of height when engaging the enemy and then dive on the target for a firing pass, zoom climbing for altitude after the pass and then setting up for another firing run. This way the Thunderbolt pilot could avoid being drawn into a dogfight where he would be at a disadvantage.

Pilots of the 56th and other P-47 fighter groups found that the fighter's huge, fat fuselage was an ideal canvas for personal insignia and the Thunderbolt units became some of the most colorful of the war. All the early Thunderbolts were delivered in the standard Olive Drab and Neutral Gray camouflage colors. Early P-47s arriving in Britain had USAAF cocardes on the fuselage sides as well as on the upper left and lower right wings. Since AA gunners were having a hard time with the P-47, the white bands previously mentioned were applied and the cocardes were outlined with a ring of yellow paint to make them stand out. Still, this was not enough and further identification measures were carried out by applying very large cocardes under both wings and they were changed to the more familiar 'star and bar' insignia at a later date, usually by just painting bars onto the cocardes. Unit identification was by painting the unit's two code letters on the side of the fuselage flanking the national insignia along with the individual aircraft's identification letter. Thus, the 56th FG had code HV applied to their aircraft and these code letters were usually in white on the Olive Drab planes. High ranking aces usually had their own aircraft and the pilots could quite often choose their own individual code letters, an example being the code letter A used by Francis Gabreski of the 56th FG.

Later model Thunderbolts, with their underwing pylons, were well-suited to the ground attack role yet the USAAF wanted to continue using the P–47 as a high altitude escort fighter for the bomber streams. Fighter pilots being what they are, unofficial strafing and bombing missions were carried out over France and the Low Countries by P–47 pilots looking for something exciting. There is no doubt that these missions were exciting for there were few things more well defended than a *Luftwaffe* aerodrome. *Luftwaffe* flak groups had a well-deserved reputation but certainly they must have been surprised as a Thunderbolt came roaring across the airfield at full power, its eight .50s chewing up everything in front.

Tales of the exploits of these daring pilots soon got around to the various Thunderbolt bases and gun camera film confirmed the damage that an individual aviator could do to parked aircraft or to supply trains which criss-crossed Europe, carrying Nazi supplies. The Thunderbolt was about to be born into a new and deadly role.

The first formal P–47 ground attack mission took place on 25 November 1943. The 351st Fighter Squadron of the 353rd FG was launched on an attack against the *Luftwaffe* airfield at St Omer. Rather than coming in on the deck, the bombed-up Thunderbolts attacked from 10,000 ft – dropping down in an extreme 60 degree dive before releasing their 500 lb bombs. Strafing attacks were then carried out. The mission was a success. Although the *Luftwaffe* flak was very accurate, it was soon discovered that heavily damaged Thunderbolts could often limp back to Britain with the fuselage and wings riddled by shell bursts. The rugged R–2800 was also capable of absorbing considerable damage – something that the inline engines with their sensitive cooling systems could not do. Losses did begin to mount rapidly, however, with these ground attack missions because the role was much more hazardous than the aerial combat mission. Along with the flak, flying low and fast very close to the ground had its own hazards and it was not uncommon for the young pilots to fly into the ground as they concentrated on strafing a target. Low flying Thunderbolts would sometimes be enveloped in the explo-

sion of the target they were attacking – sometimes they would come flying out of the other side of the fireball, sometimes not. For those pilots who were coming back to Britain in a damaged P–47 and could not make it, the Channel offered a watery landing spot but at least it would not be in Occupied Europe. Pilots forced down in the water could have the comfort that the RAF's efficient search and rescue service would be out looking for them. Also, in a unique role, Thunderbolts of the 5th Emergency Rescue Squadron prowled the Channel with flares and dinghies strapped under their wings.

Early experience with the Thunderbolt in the ground attack role convinced the Army that they were on to a good idea. The new P–51B Mustang that was coming into service promised to be the ideal long-range escort fighter for it offered the fuel economy and performance needed for the mission. This would mean that P–47 units could gradually be freed from their escort flights and assigned the mission of destroying the Germans on the ground.

Along with the new assignment, Thunderbolts were also sporting a new look for, as of the P–47D–21, the aircraft were being delivered to combat units in natural metal finish and it soon was common to see flights with Thunderbolts in both finishes.

With the paper 108 gallon tank mounted under the fuselage, this yellow-nosed P–47D–11–RE 42–75549 of the 376th FS, 361st FG taxis out for a mission.

Rather opposite from the cartoon cutie on the nose, Princess Pat carries a very lethal load under the fuselage. The fragmentation bombs would explode on contact and cover an area with thousands of razor-sharp bits of shrapnel that would shred virtually anything. These weapons were particularly effective on convoys of German rolling stock. Marauding P–47s would knock-out the lead vehicle and then destroy the vehicles at the end of the convoy. The rest of the now-trapped Germans could be destroyed almost at leisure. (USAF)

Squadron commanders were busily studying the results of the earlier ground attack missions. It was apparent that the most effective method of attacking the Germans, particularly the aerodromes, on the ground was by coming in as low and fast as possible. Although the P–47 made a good dive bombing platform, attacking from heights of 10,000 ft and above would give the Germans too much warning and the effective flak units could cut the attackers to pieces. The German early warning system, especially in forward areas, was not very effective and coordinated attacks by the P–47s could chop an airfield to pieces – especially the very vulnerable armed and

fueled combat aircraft that were parked in the open. Pilots were warned to make only one pass and then high tail for safety since the flak, once alerted, would be very dangerous. Of course, the last pilots in this type of attack would be subject to intense return fire.

In order to accommodate the growing number of P–47 units in England, a new air force was created – the 9th Air Force. Originally operating out of the Middle East on a much smaller scale, the 9th was restructured to control the USAAF's tactical air forces. The first assigned combat units for the 9th began arriving in late 1943 with Thunderbolts. The first unit was the 358th Fighter Group but with the decision to use the P–51B and C Mustang as the primary fighter escort type the 358th was assigned Thunderbolts and transferred to the 9th AF from the 8th who, in turn, was given a new Mustang unit.

It was planned to use Thunderbolts from the 9th on missions when the 8th AF needed additional escort strength. The first of these actions that took place in strength happened

during March 1944 when Thunderbolts of the 365th, 366th and 368th FGs joined with the 8th's Mustangs for sweeps over Europe. As the dedicated role of the 9th was tactical air support, Thunderbolts, also in March, began taking on increasing numbers of ground support missions. The P–47s also went after the new V–1 launching sites in an attempt to stop the flow of the deadly robot bombs. Other missions went after anti-aircraft units that were causing heavy losses among USAAF medium and light bomber units. These were hazardous targets to attack but by coming in at very low altitude the necessary element of surprise could usually be achieved.

Modifications were being introduced at a very rapid rate on the Thunderbolt production lines as lessons learned from combat experience were translated into engineering data. The Curtiss production was still below target, and the slow deliveries and shoddy workmanship resulted in the line being closed down prematurely. Since the P–47 was one of the first aircraft to use the Army's new system

of dash numbers (D–6, D–11, etc) to identify successive airframe or engine modifications or changes, the Thunderbolt was distinguished by a vast collection of dash number designations (these are explained in some detail at the end of this chapter). Early modifications included strengthening the wing pylon to carry heavier bombs (D–15), while the Hamilton Standard paddle-blade propeller replaced the standard Curtiss Electric unit, beginning with the D–22–RE, although the Curtiss Electric propeller was reintroduced on later models. This new propeller allowed the engine's power to be transferred more efficiently, especially at low altitude. The new propeller also greatly increased the aircraft's climb performance – going from 2,700 fpm (sea level) to 3,100 fpm. There were also attempts to reduce the P–47's weight to make room for further performance increases and the D–23 had its weight dropped by 200 lb to 10,500 lb. There were also various attempts by Republic to increase the P–47's performance through some drastic modifications; these sometimes very unusual

attempts are illustrated in the section 'Experimental Thunderbolts'.

As with the Mustang and other early war Allied fighters, the P–47 had a blind spot to the rear due to canopy and high-back fuselage design – the 'razor backs'. It became obvious that the P–47 would, at some point, have to be modified to give a better fighting view. Republic decided that a bubble-style canopy would give the best view, and obtained a unit from a British Hawker Typhoon. This was installed on a P–47D which received the experimental designation XP–47K. With the cut-down rear fuselage and new canopy, the P–47's rather bulky looks were streamlined a bit and the reports from the test pilots were uniformly enthusiastic about the greatly increased view. Farmingdale and Evansville both tooled up for the new variant, which was to also be produced with a larger fuselage fuel tank. The Farmingdale aircraft was the P–47D–25–RE and was fitted with the Hamilton Standard propeller while the Evansville production aircraft was the P–47D–26–RA

A typical scene during the hard winter of 1944–45. Photographed on Christmas Eve 1944 in Belgium, Doogan, a P–47D–22–RE 42–26041 of the 22nd FS, 36th FG, heads out for a mission over a snow-covered taxiway. Marked with a red nose and rudder, the aircraft is carrying two 500 lb bombs under the wing and fragmentation bombs on the fuselage shackle.

with the larger-diameter Curtiss Electric propeller. With such drastic modifications, it would have greatly simplified the designations by introducing a new model number but this was not to be.

As P–47 deliveries had settled down to a steady flow to American units, the P–47 could be supplied to the Allies who had been requesting the big fighter. The largest foreign user of the fighter was the Royal Air Force which eventually received a total of 830 P–47s. The RAF's first Thunderbolts were tested in Britain but it was decided to use the type in the Pacific where the RAF needed a modern heavyweight fighter. Designated Thunderbolt Mk I, the RAF received two batches of these aircraft (D–20s),

A delivery pilot prepares to mount a factory fresh P–47D–25–RE at Farmingdale. Another presentation aircraft, this machine carries the inscription of the donor, town and State on the side of the fuselage. The large piece of armor plate that was incorporated into the seat headrest can be seen clearly. (Republic)

Opposite above
Royal Air Force number FL844 was one of the first group of Thunderbolt Mk Is delivered. Finished at the factory in standard RAF day fighter camouflage, the Thunderbolt was regarded initially by the RAF with a bit of scepticism because of its large size, especially by pilots who had been flying the petite Spitfire. (MoD)

A Royal Air Force P–47D–30–RE, KJ346. Designated Thunderbolt Mk II, the aircraft carried the Lend-Lease legend 'United Kingdom Government' above the small standard data block on the left side of the fuselage below the canopy. It is seen before delivery at the major aircraft depot in Newark, New Jersey.

allocated the serials FL731–850 and HB962–HD181, a total of 240 machines. The Thunderbolt Mk II was identical to the D–25. These were serialed HD182–301, KJ128–367, KL168–347 and KL838–887.

A good majority of these aircraft were shipped directly to British depots in India where they were assembled and test flown before being assigned to combat units. No 146 Squadron, under the command of Squadron Leader L. M. O'Leary, was the first RAF unit to receive the fighter and the Republic beast was a welcome replacement for such obsolete aircraft as the Curtiss Mohawk and Hawker Hurricane. As with any new fighter coming into service in a rough and tumble combat area, the P–47 had more than its share of maintenance and supply problems. The unit started its conversion to the Mark I in May 1944 but it was not until September that operations really got underway with any regularity. As in Europe, the RAF put their Thunderbolts to work attacking ground targets, airfields and the Japanese in the air. Compared to the earlier under-armed fighters that the Thunderbolt replaced, the P–47's firepower was absolutely devastating against the lightly constructed Japanese combat air-

craft. The Japanese philosophy of building light, unarmored aircraft that sacrificed protection and structural strength for performance was proven to be an incorrect procedure as the P–47's eight .50s demolished aircraft after aircraft.

The British found, as had the Americans, that it was unwise to dogfight with a Japanese fighter so they employed the American tactic of diving and zooming on the enemy wherever possible. The Mark Is were also equipped to carry three 500 lb bombs and were used in the dive bombing role against anything that moved. The Thunderbolts were a great boost to the RAF's offensive against the Japanese and, as more became available, the Japanese began to fall back against the devastating aerial assaults in Burma.

Operating in the hot and humid weather of India and Burma caused the aircraft to suffer from various engine, accessory and instrument ailments, while the heat and heavy combat loads meant that the ground-loving Thunderbolt's take-off roll could be even longer than usual. Runs over one mile were not uncommon and many British pilots must have had their fingers crossed as the jungle at the end of the runway loomed closer. One comforting fact was that if the P–47 failed to become airborne then its amazing structural strength would usually enable the aviator to survive after the fighter scythed down a large portion of the jungle foliage.

Eventually, in South East Asia Command (SEAC), Mark Is served with Nos 5, 34, 113, 123, 135 and 146 Squadrons, and Mark IIs with Nos 5, 30, 34, 42, 60, 79, 81, 113, 123, 131, 134, 135, 258, 261 and 615 Squadrons, the policy being to use the Thunderbolt MK II as the major RAF fighter type in the area. At the end of hostilities, with the run-down of SEAC, the RAF had little use for the Republic fighter that had served them so well, while the

Thunderbolts on patrol: returning from a mission, these Royal Air Force Thunderbolt Mk Is belonging to No 134 Squadron roar over FL884 as mechanics look on. (RAF)

terms of the Lend-Lease agreement specified that American aircraft at the end of the fighting had to be either purchased, returned or scrapped, so the majority of P–47s were simply destroyed at their combat bases by either being bulldozed into a pile or having a hand grenade thrown into their cockpits. The Spitfire became the major RAF fighter in the area.

As the American air offensive against Nazi Germany began to push deeper into enemy territory and the P–47 pilots began racking up huge numbers of air and ground victories, the Army decided that it was time to send the big fighter to the Pacific. Thunderbolts were being produced at such a high rate by the two factories that supply would not be a problem.

Australia was a prime target for Japanese

raiders during the early portion of the war and the Allies were fearful that an invasion of the huge island continent was an all too real prospect. The capture of even a portion of Australia would give the enemy an excellent foothold as well as many new ship and aircraft bases from which they could continue their conquests. Embattled New Guinea was a Japanese staging base for Australian attacks and even though the Allies held a good chunk of New Guinea, the situation on the island was not clear cut and the fighting was daily and fierce. In June 1943, 59 P–47s arrived by ship in Australia where they were assembled, flight tested and then flown to Port Moresby, New Guinea, for the 348th Fighter Group which had recently arrived from the United States.

Assigned to the small but effective 5th Air Force, the 348th set up home at Port Moresby

and soon joined the 5th in the lengthy and dangerous attacks against the many Japanese bases along the hostile northern coast of the island. Most of the bases were extremely close to the coast since the jungle foliage of New Guinea was so heavy that considerable time and manpower would have had to be spent to hack airfields out of the jungle.

The 348th was scheduled for bomber escort duties but the fuel consumption of the R–2800 meant that some field modifications had to be made to make the flight safe for the P–47 pilots. Crew chiefs constructed a bulky, rather ugly 200 US gallon tank that could be fitted to the center line shackle and, with fuel system modifications, this unit bumped up the range a bit so that the P–47s could take the bombers back and forth. This modification was typical of the hard working Army ground crews who would labor day and night to find solutions for the problems that came up in this new theater of war. Each tank was virtually hand made and it meant that when one was dropped in combat or for another reason, a replacement

would have to be fashioned. Pilots attempted to keep the tank attached but the unit did have to be jettisoned if the enemy was encountered since the fuel tank handicapped maneuverability as well as reducing top speed.

The Americans, like the British, discovered that the firepower of the P–47 would vaporize any Japanese fighter but the P–47 pilots also quickly learned to respect the highly trained Japanese aviator and to avoid deadly dogfights at all cost. With operational missions beginning in July/August, the 348th's presence was a great help for the American bombers whose raids on the Japanese bases caused the enemy to go after the bombers with fanatical determination. Besides the massive fuel consumption – a problem which was never really fully overcome with the earlier Thunderbolts since there was a physical limit on how much extra fuel they could safely carry – the P–47s proved reliable work horses as they operated out of New Guinea and fighters returning from escort missions often attacked Japanese shipping when they could find them and combined

Throttle back, canopy open, a P–47D–28–RA 42–29064 comes in for a landing at Okinawa. Photographed during September 1945 at the big Naha base, this Thunderbolt displays the large black Pacific identification stripes. Note the colorful pre-war style rudder stripes. (R. Hegge)

attacks from massed .50 calibers often sent smaller enemy ships to the bottom.

As more of the fighters became available by the end of 1943, it was finally possible to convert some of the Bell P–39 Airacobra and Curtiss P–40 groups to the P–47. These inadequate fighters had served long and well against the aggressive enemy but it was with much relief that the pilots were finally able to get their hands on a more modern fighting machine.

As aircraft supplies to England became more of a certainty, the flow of combat aircraft to the Pacific began to increase and by the end of 1943 several hundred P–47s were available for combat assignment. By the early part of 1944, three P–47 groups (the 35th, 58th and 348th FGs) were flying combat and using the

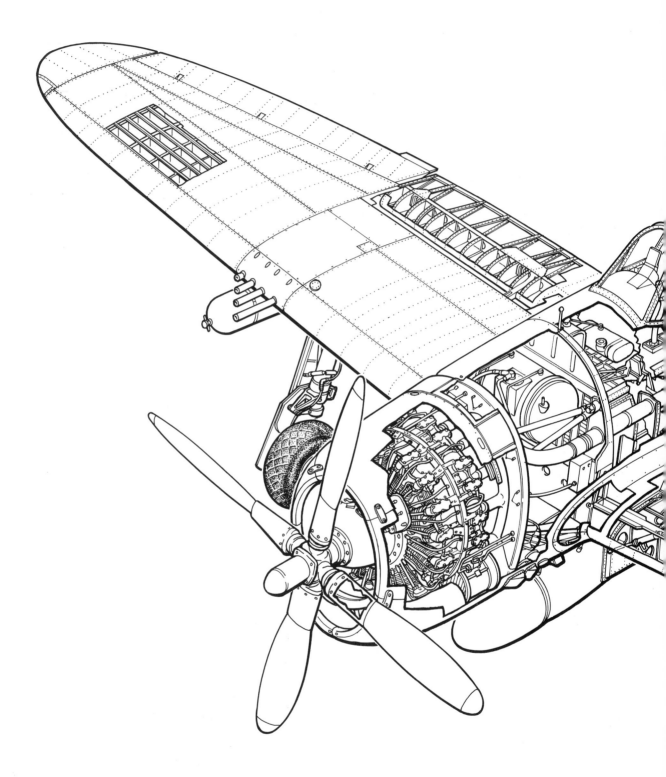

Republic P–47D–25–RE Thunderbolt

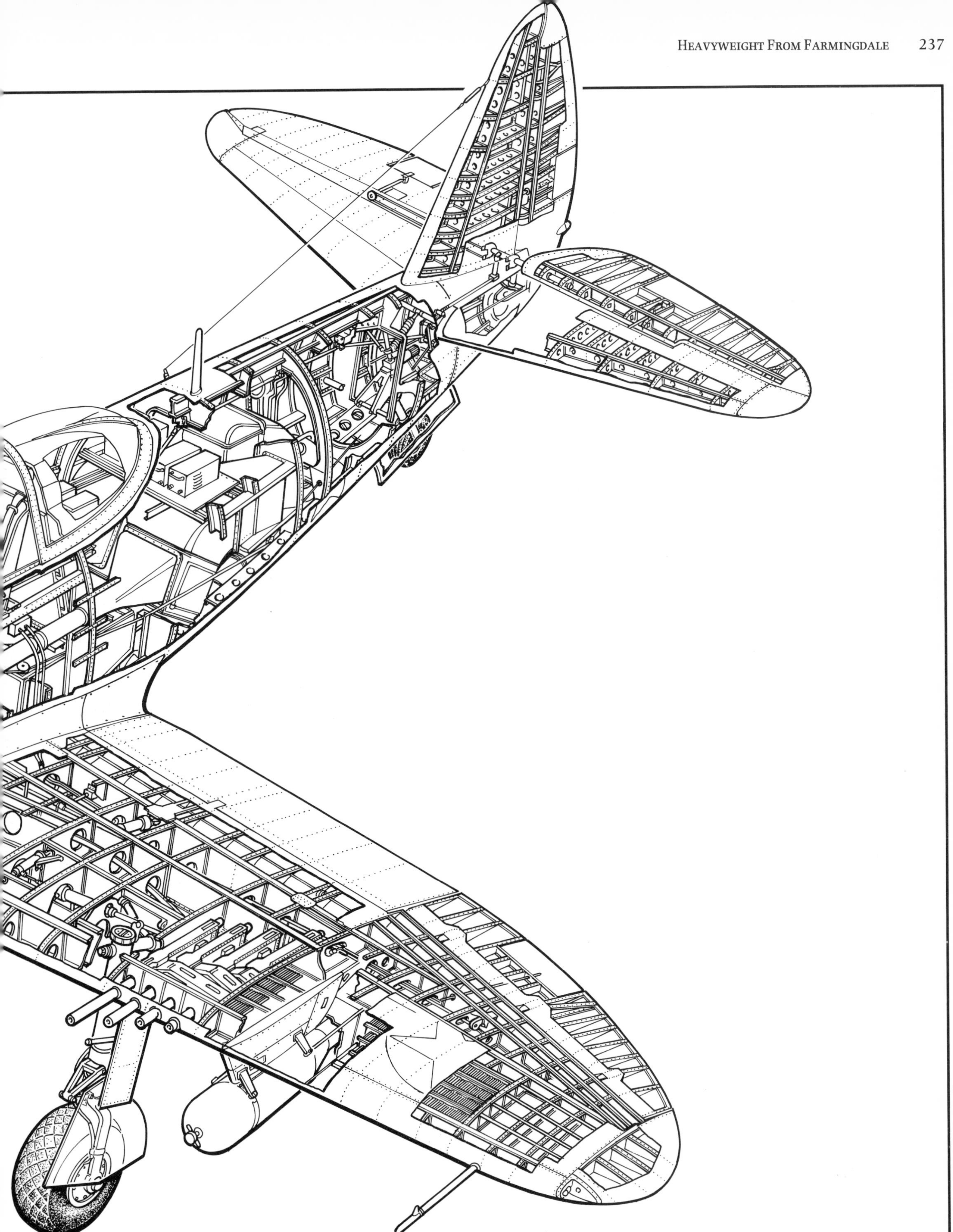

*R*eady for a civil owner or the scrap heap: Curtiss-built TP–47G–I0–CU (the T prefix did not indicate a dual-control aircraft but, rather, its assignment to a training unit) is seen at Chino, California, immediately after World War Two. Chino was one of several bases in the United States that quickly set to work scrapping America's vast aerial armada. Out of the hundreds of combat aircraft sent to Chino, none were left within two years. This well-worn P–47G had been attached to a State-side training unit. (W. T. Larkins)

Thunderbolt to good effect against enemy aircraft and heavily-fortified ground targets. One of the real heroes to fly the P–47 during this period was Colonel Neel Kearby, commander of the 348th FG. Kearby loved the big fighter and played upon its many strengths to achieve victories over the enemy.

Neel Kearby was a natural leader and his fellow officers held him in high esteem. His training and tactics not only developed the Thunderbolt's talents but also those of the pilots that served with him. After the arrival of the 348th FG late in 1943, Kearby quickly began rolling up a very impressive string of victories with the P–47 and was soon one of the top three aces, ranking with Richard Bong and Thomas Lynch. On one mission alone, on 11 October 1943, Kearby attacked and destroyed seven Japanese aircraft but his gun camera recorded only six of the victories before running out of film! Without doubt, Kearby

stood an excellent chance of becoming the top ranking American aerial ace but he was killed in action on 9 March 1944 when his score stood at 22 enemy aircraft confirmed. Colonel Kearby's death was a big blow to the men of the 348th FG but the war was moving very rapidly and the tide of victory was definitely flowing in the favor of the Allies. Kearby's successor, Major Bill Dunham, continued the Thunderbolt's success with the 348th, scoring 16 victories and sinking two Japanese ships in the process.

The Thunderbolts prowled far and wide over the Pacific, their only limitation being the fuel hungry R–2800s. Even with large drop tanks, running out of fuel was always uppermost in the P–47 pilot's mind – more so than running into a flock of Zeros. Even with fuel restrictions, the P–47s met and defeated the best the Japanese could offer. Quite often the victories were spectacular, such as the time when P–47s from the 342nd FS intercepted 15 Betty bombers, escorted by three Tony fighters, near Cape Gloucester on 26 December 1943. Most of the P–47s had a height advantage over the Bettys so they utilized their tremendous diving speed to ram into the middle of the bomber formation. The combined effect of the 19 P–47s' Browning machine guns chopped up the enemy formation and the lightly-armored

Bettys were torn to pieces, 14 falling in flames along with two of the escort. The Bettys did not even drop their bombs. One P–47 pilot, Lt Lawrence O'Neill, accounted for four of the bombers. None of the Thunderbolts was lost in the action. Such incidents were not isolated exceptions and aerial massacres such as this foretold the complete destruction of the Japanese military machine.

The skies over New Britain were hotly contested and just the next day, 27 December, the Japanese once again made concentrated attacks against Allied positions and once again lost heavily. The 340th FS knocked down eight Val dive bombers and seven Zeros in just a few minutes of fighting while the 341st FS shot down 13 Zeros – all with no losses to the P–47 units.

As 1944 progressed, the Thunderbolt units moved towards Japan as America's war policy of island-hopping captured more and more enemy-held islands. The fighter preferred for these lengthy Pacific overwater missions was the Lockheed P–38 Lightning, whose twin engines offered a considerable margin of safety, but it was not available in as large numbers as the P–47 and P–38 units did not really begin to proliferate until later in the Pacific war. Thunderbolt range was still a problem but some unique modifications were

An RAF armorer makes last minute checks on his Thunderbolt Mk I before a mission. This photograph illustrates the small style of roundel that was used by the RAF in Burma and it also shows the large 165 gallon drop tanks to advantage. (RAF)

undertaken, such as the installation of a huge 300 US gallon tank under one wing with a 165 US gallon tank under the other letting the P–47s fly from Morotai to Balikpapan – a distance of nearly 1,000 miles – so that 5th AF bombers could be protected while they hit the enemy's important oil production plants in Borneo. The Japanese guarded the plant with some of their best fighter pilots and the bombers were taking losses so fighter protection was essential. Aircraft of the 40th and 41st FS of the 35th FG flew this first very long distance mission on 10 October 1944 and the results were immediate. Enemy fighters were met and defeated while the losses to the bomber force were dramatically reduced. These missions were not easy to plan and each step had to be carefully drawn out so that the pilots would have a chance to return with enough fuel to make it back to Balikpapan. With the outsize fuel load, the P–47s were hard to fly and the effect of flying long hours at high altitude was physically very trying for the pilots. Only a few missions of this type were undertaken but they greatly helped the 5th's fleet of Consolidated Liberators pound the enemy refineries to ruin.

As the American military effort moved closer to Japan, the enemy's aerial forces were literally blown out of the air as P–47s, P–51s and P–38s scrambled for the few remaining targets. Unknown at that time was the fact that the Japanese had pulled back many of their combat aircraft to Japan to prepare them for the suicide attacks that would take the Americans completely by surprise. Back in the United States, Republic was rapidly moving ahead with new variants of the basic design that would make the P–47 an even more potent weapon.

In Europe, many of the P–47 groups were having their aircraft replaced with the Mustang and by the start of 1945, only the 56th FG still had the P–47 and they were getting a brand-new version, the P–47M, that promised much superior performance to the earlier Ds that they had been flying. The P–47M was powered with a P&W R–2800–57 that could churn out a maximum of 2,800 hp with a Curtiss Electric propeller giving a top speed of 473 mph at 32,000 ft. The airframe was basically that of the P–47D–30 but the more powerful engine also incorporated other refinements that included an improved turbo-supercharger, modified ignition, and more efficient fuel flow controls that would improve the engine's fuel specifics. The increased horsepower rating meant that the P–47M pilots would be able to pass the fastest Mustangs at altitude but it would be at a price since the big radial running at full power would consume an astonishing 330 plus gallons per hour. The new engine controls, however, would aid the P–47M pilot in reducing the aircraft's fuel consumption at cruise to about 100 gallons/hour which was an improvement over earlier models.

Only 130 P–47Ms were produced and the 56th FG received virtually the entire production run but trouble soon followed. With the constant rush of wartime production, complete testing was sometimes not undertaken. What worked under hasty factory testing would not function under operational conditions. This, unfortunately, was true with the P–47M. M model pilots were horrified to find their engines stopping completely or cutting in and out once they reached cruising altitude. Missions were hastily aborted and maintenance men were puzzled. Other engine problems began to manifest themselves, including corrosion and low cylinder head temperatures which affected the correct operation of the engine. The problem soon grew to nightmare proportions when it became obvious that

The first production P–47N, 44–87784, was retained by the factory for testing. Special markings include a yellow cowl and tail section along with the designation 'NI' on the cowl and fuselage. Virtually all of the N production came from the Farmingdale factory. (Republic)

every P–47M operated by the 56th was stricken with the same problem.

Since this was a major difficulty, the Army threw in its best maintenance men while representatives from Pratt & Whitney and Republic also began working around the clock to cure the ills of the M. Once again, the ignition leads were suspect and they were replaced with a different type but the engine problems continued and it seemed that the –57 was an engine which would not run. Airflow to the cylinders was modified so that the heads could heat to the most efficient temperatures. It was discovered that the sensitive engine/turbosupercharger controls were not being correctly operated, so additional training for the pilots was required along with some modifications. A great deal of minor modifications and tuning meant that the engine gradually gained a degree of reliability but, eventually plagued by just too many problems, the engines of every operational M were changed in an attempt to gain combat readiness.

As the war in Europe fought to a close, the P–47M was finally operationally deployed during April 1945 and its high top speed meant that the Luftwaffe's more advanced adversaries such as the Me 262 jet could, if conditions were right, be caught and destroyed. The rocket-powered Me 163 was another matter and these aircraft, which were fortunately deployed in a limited number, were extremely difficult to destroy and could usually only be attacked after they had exhausted their fuel supply and were heading back to home field. For all its speed and power, the P–47M remained a 'limited production' version.

Republic planned to keep the growth of the Thunderbolt advancing after the M ceased production and the next variant on the line was the P–47N, considered by many pilots to be the ultimate Thunderbolt. Designed with the Pacific and extra range in mind, the P–47 had its fuel capacity increased by 200 more gallons of fuel held in the wing. In addition to the eight .50 caliber Brownings it had stubs and wiring for eight or ten 5 in HVAR rockets under the wings. To add further lifting capability, the wing span was increased by 18 inches and its square wing tips became a P–47N recognition factor. In order to distribute the aircraft's increased weight more efficiently, the landing gear was redesigned and the tread was increased by 24 inches. Power came from the same R–2800–57 that had given the 56th so much trouble but refinements in production and a complete revision of power and turbosupercharger controls had made the –57 reliable. To reduce the

Thunderbolts of the 345th Fighter Squadron, 350th Fighter Group on patrol. Tail band was dark blue with a yellow lightning bolt.

After the end of the war, the Thunderbolt soldiered on with various Air National Guard units. Before rules were drawn up for individual State insignia and markings, most P–47s merely had any reference to the USAF removed and the designation 'NG' applied. Lead aircraft is a P–47D–30–RA 44–21080N.

Opposite above
Classic shot of P–47N–1–RE 44–88104 framed by the .50 caliber gun of a White halftrack at Ryukyu Retto, 1945. The N had the so-called long range wing that added 18 inches in span and 22 square feet in area. A fully-loaded N could tip the scales at an amazing 20,700 lb. This example is carrying 165 gallon P–38 drop tanks. (USAF/65093)

As can be seen from the different colored lines on P–47N–5–RA 44–88613A, photographed at Fort Dix, New Jersey, on 18 December 1945, was fitted with a replacement cowling. Also note the rocket stubs under the wing along with the deployed landing light. Only 149 Evansville Ns were completed before the contract was cancelled due to the end of the war.

strain of long overwater flights, a General Electric C–1 autopilot was installed in the cockpit and proved to be very useful. The extra weight became very noticeable in the take-off run and almost 1,000 more feet was required to become airborne when fully loaded.

Combat-ready P–47Ns were coming off the Farmingdale factory by the end of 1944, while Evansville kept building Ds and did not convert to the N until almost the end of the war. The first unit to receive the P–47N was the 318th Fighter Group on the small island of Ie Shima where the American pilots immediately began encountering hostile aircraft. As the mighty American task forces approached Japan, the enemy began to unleash some of the aircraft that were held in reserve and the powerful P–47N proved to be particularly valuable since it could hit the enemy in the air and on the ground. With its load of weapons, two 300 US gallon drop tanks under the wings and a 110 US gallon center line drop tank, it became the heaviest single-engine fighter of World War Two – exceeding 21,000 lb.

Ie Shima, the place where famed journalist Ernie Pyle was killed by a sniper, is located off the coast of Okinawa only 325 miles from the Home Islands, enabling the P–47Ns to roam freely over mainland Japan where enemy fighters rose with regularity to oppose the invaders. The quality of the individual Japanese aviator had fallen greatly by 1944 but the surviving older aviators were still very dangerous. The new P–47Ns had so much power at hand that individual American pilots were often able to inflict disproportionate damage on the enemy, such as during May when two P–47N pilots from the 318th FG became instant aces when they each destroyed five enemy aircraft during one mission. This type of event was not uncommon and many P–47N pilots, who probably thought they would not encounter enemy planes from the 'defeated' Japanese, were delighted to be knocking down the enemy in numbers.

Ie Shima began to receive some more Thunderbolts as the war against the mainland intensified and two new groups, the 413th and the 507th, were formed. Since Okinawa was becoming a main American staging base, the Japanese had something special in mind for the contested island: The Divine Wind. Japanese *kamikazes* attacked Okinawa and the fleet in during May 1945 and the P–47Ns of the 318th were constantly airborne, attempting to destroy the enemy aircraft before they could

*S*een during 1948 is P–47D–40–RA 45–49283N of the New Jersey Air National Guard. Even though overshadowed by the Mustang in the ANG role, the Thunderbolt remained in service until 1952.

*P*ilot of a Connecticut ANG P–47N–25–RE prepares to start the aircraft's engine. The P–47 did not get to see service in Korea like the Mustang but 150 were in storage and 350 in Stateside service during 1950.

hit the ships. Even though the P–47s and their pilots did a magnificient job, the suicide air-craft accomplished their mission with deadly precision. On 25 May, the enemy came in force and the 318th accounted for 34 *kamikazes* in the space of just four hours as virtually every type of Japanese combat aircraft went on a one-way trip against the American fleet. The extra power from the R–2800–57 was par-ticularly useful as the P–47s dove on the low-flying targets that were going full throttle at the nearest American ships. The fighting became heavy and desperate even though the eventual outcome was not really in doubt. One P–47N pilot managed to blow a *kamikaze* out of the air with an underwing rocket after he had run out of ammunition for the .50s which was the first time this type of victory had been accredited to a pilot in the Pacific.

The Japanese did not have a sufficient supply of aircraft or pilots to keep up the suicide attacks and by June it was fairly rare to see an enemy aircraft heading for the fleet. The Thunderbolts, at this point, began to rove on ever increasing search and destroy missions during which an epic 1,800-mile flight took the P–47Ns of the 507th FG all the way to Korea. Eighteen enemy aircraft were destroyed on this flight for the loss of one P–47N. Since aerial targets were rapidly disappearing, the P–47s concentrated on anything that moved on the ground and, as in Occupied Europe, Japanese rail and road traffic was slaughtered. The atomic bomb settled the question of inva-sion and the last P–47 victory of the war was scored by a 318th FG pilot who clobbered a Frank fighter near Osaka on 14 August 1945.

The end of the war in the Pacific saw P–47s as part of the occupying air force but, as with many other aircraft companies, orders for new Thunderbolts were rapidly axed at Farming-dale and Evansville. Over 6,000 P–47s on order were dropped while work on the remain-ing machines was completed rapidly. Like many other warhorses, the P–47 did not really have much of a role in the post-war Army. Thunderbolts were rapidly sent to storage bases where they were scrapped but a few units of the rapidly developing Air National Guard soldiered on with Republic's rugged fighter until the early 1950s. A few foreign air forces also received Thunderbolts and put them to good use. Both Mexico and Brazil had combat squadrons formed under the USAAF during the war and these countries continued to fly it after the fighting had stopped. China, France and Russia also flew them while the Mutual Aid Program supplied the portly figh-ters to some Central and South American countries. Today, the Thunderbolt remains mainly a memory but there are a few flying examples that still grace American airshows to remind the public of World War Two's largest single-engine fighter that accomplished its mission with honor and efficiency in every theater of World War Two.

EXPERIMENTAL THUNDERBOLTS

The basic Thunderbolt airframe served as the basis for a number of interesting modifications and experiments.

The first experimental Thunderbolt was, of course, the prototype XP–47B. A logical outgrowth of the unsuccessful P–35 and P–43, the XP–47B was a massive aircraft that dwarfed its test pilot. American observers in Britain during the early part of World War Two were impressed by the eight machine guns carried aloft in the wings of Spitfires and Hurricanes but they were not impressed by the caliber, figuring that the

Browning-built .50 caliber weapon in similar numbers would have a punch that few bombers or fighters could withstand, so heavy armament became one of the prime design considerations for the Thunderbolt. First flown on 6 May 1941 by Lowery L. Brabham (seen standing next to the bare metal prototype), the Thunderbolt was regarded by sceptics as being too big and too heavy to make an efficient fighting aircraft. (Republic)

During the early days of World War Two it was thought that pressurized fighters would enjoy a considerable advantage in combat. However, the problems of pressurizing a small fighter were considerable. Since the Thunderbolt had very good high-altitude performance, Republic figured that the aircraft was big and strong enough to handle the pressurization system and the last P–47B airframe on the Republic line was modified into the XP–47E. The system was difficult to install and perfect, cockpit sealing being a big problem. The canopy was reworked into a smaller hinged unit but delays in perfecting the system meant that the XP–47E did not fly until September 1942 and then its performance was judged not to be all that much better than standard production line Thunderbolts. The unarmed XP–47E was reportedly finished in an overall blue/gray color scheme. (Republic)

Undoubtedly the most radical-looking Thunderbolt, the XP–47H was built to test the 2,500 hp Chrysler 16-cylinder, inverted-vee, liquid-cooled XI–2220. Two P–47D–15–RA airframes were removed from the Evansville factory to be modified into the XP–47H. Envisioned as only a flying test-bed, all armament was removed along with other military systems. Once again, conversion was more difficult than anticipated with delays in the Chrysler engine production causing many headaches. The XI–2220 was an enormously complicated bit of machinery and the installation in the basic Thunderbolt airframe meant that many structural modifications had to be designed. (Republic)

Most obvious modification to the XP–47H was the addition of a huge snout and intake for the cooling radiator. Problems with the engine and its installation dragged on for so long that the XP–47H did not fly until July 1945. The original Chrysler design called for the installation of an axial-flow supercharger but the unit could not be developed so a General Electric CH–5 turbosupercharger was installed as a replacement unit. Hoping for a top speed of 490 mph, the best that the XP–47H could do was 414 mph and the project was dropped after consuming considerable funding. (Republic)

The XP–47J resulted from an attempt to reduce airframe weight and increase engine power. The initial plans for the XP–47J called for a fan-cooled R–2800–61, contra-rotating propeller, and improved General Electric turbosuperchargers. Despite intensive efforts by Curtiss and Aeroproducts, a suitable propeller could not be produced. A Curtiss paddle-blade unit was installed and the cooling fan was intended to produce a long, slim nacelle which would cut down on the large, flat drag-producing surface of the R–2800 engine. Armament was reduced to a planned six .50 caliber guns with 1,602 rounds and smaller fuel tanks carrying only 287 gallons. First flying on 26 November 1943, the XP–47J was soon back on the ground after the engine self-destructed with only ten flight hours recorded. A new engine was installed but the XP–47J was not back in the air until March 1944. The XP–47J soon showed itself to be a very hot performer with straight and level speeds of 500 mph being recorded. A new turbosupercharger was installed and Republic claimed 504 mph on 5 August 1944 at 34,450 ft. Later USAAF testing only managed to get 493 mph and it is thought that the Republic claim could have been inaccurate because of faulty instruments. Development on the XP–47J was dropped when it was realized that the project would require 70 per cent new tooling for production. The XP–72 project was also showing considerable promise and this led to the final cancellation of the XP–47J. The XP–47J is seen on display after the war at the Wright Field victory air show. Note the Superman cartoon figure with a lightning bolt painted on the cowling. (W. T. Larkins)

P–47B 41–5938 was modified into the XP–47F to test a laminar-flow wing. Spanning 42 feet, the laminar flow wing had straight edges that gradually tapered to rounded tips. The XP–47F was sent to Wright Field during the fall of 1942 for testing before being returned to Republic for further work and flying. It was hoped that the drag-reducing laminar airfoil would considerably increase the Thunderbolt's top speed. The laminar flow wing required a great deal of work to achieve a smooth surface and testing revealed that the results were not much better than the standard wing. The XP–47F was transferred to NACA (National Advisory Committee for Aeronautics) for more testing but it was destroyed in a fatal crash near Hot Springs, Virginia, on 14 October 1943. (Republic)

The P–47K was modified from the last
D–5–RE. The top fuselage of the Thunderbolt
was cut down and a bubble canopy was installed,
much against the wishes of designer Kartveli. The
first bubble canopy became the definitive
production unit and intensive production of the
P–47K was planned but the addition of XP–47L
internal fuel tankage changed the designation back
into the D series contracts. The P–47K was
completed on 3 July 1943 and was eventually
modified to test the long-range wing that became
standard with the P–47N. (Republic)

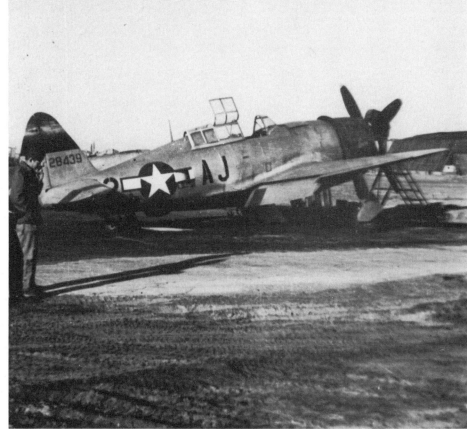

In the USAAF – at squadron level – there was
a great deal of freedom involved in the use and
modification of aircraft. Americans, naturally
rebellious and inventive, soon had fighter aircraft
struck off charge as 'war weary', a designation that
indicated they were unfit for further military
flying. Of course, some of these aircraft were
actually worn out but others were appropriated
for a variety of tasks. The pilots usually liked
taking their crew chiefs and other maintenance
personnel for rides but, in the Thunderbolt, there
was no room for an extra 'body'. Accordingly,
some of the 'war weary' aircraft were field
modified to have two seats for joy riding or flights
to other fields where liquor, women, cigarettes, or
food stuffs could be appropriated. 42–8439, a
P–47D–5–RE, has had a couple of canopies joined
together as one sliding unit with the portion of the
canopy for the passenger hinged to provide easy
entry and exit while a certain amount of the
fuselage decking has been cut away.

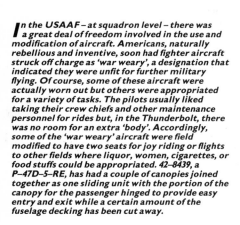

*N*o two field modifications for two-seaters were the same. This conversion has had the second seat installed under the standard canopy. Seen at a 9th AAF base in Belgium, Colonel Ray Stecker is buckling in his crew chief, SSgt Bailey Ingram. These two-seat conversions were also used to fly combat photographers or war correspondents to cover fighter sweeps. *(USAF/55090)*

*E*xperimental armament installation. The Thunderbolt flown by Colonel Fred Gray of the 78th Fighter Group had two 20 mm cannon manufactured by Oldsmobile mounted under the wing of this aircraft. It was thought that the added punch of the two cannon would be a real plus in strafing missions but the installation did not prove to be successful. The cannon added considerable drag and knocked top speed down by 50 mph. Streamlined fairings had been designed but were not installed when this photograph was taken on 24 October 1944. It was hard to beat the destructive power of the standard eight .50 caliber guns and the aircraft was converted back to standard configuration. The aircraft was at Duxford, England, when the photograph was taken. *(USAF/72320)*

PRODUCTION LINE

**These views illustrate the American capacity
for mass production of its weapons of war.**

With three facilities at their disposal, Republic managed to churn out over 13,000 fighters in 45 months. The plants at Farmingdale and Evansville were responsible for the main Thunderbolt production since the poorly managed Curtiss facility in Buffalo built only 354 P–47Gs in a year and a half, certainly equaling Brewster's disgraceful Corsair production record. This photograph illustrates how the Thunderbolt fuselages were mounted on moveable dollys that could be easily wheeled by construction personnel. The fuselages have been given a fresh coat of Olive Drab and Neutral Gray (the masking paper is still on the canopies) and rows of wings can be seen in the background, some bearing British camouflage and markings. Production was just changing over to uncamouflaged aircraft and a stack of bare metal fuselages can be seen sitting on their firewalls in the background. (Republic)

*A*pparently used as a training and assembly
aid, this complete – but unskinned –
Thunderbolt was mounted in flight attitude on a
dolly and could be positioned in various parts of
the factory for lectures on equipment installation.
This unique display was probably scrapped with
the end of the Thunderbolt production line in 1945.
(Republic)

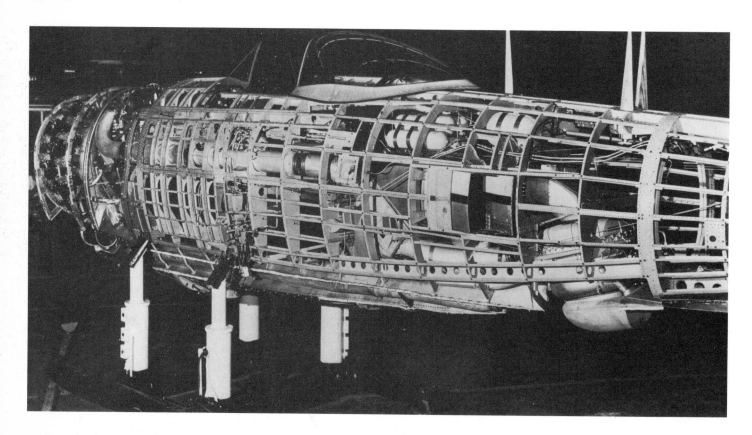

*C*lose-up view of the unskinned Thunderbolt
illustrates such equipment installation as
oxygen tanks and turbosupercharger. As can be
seen, there was little room left inside the P–47's
massive fuselage. The sliding bubble canopy offered
excellent visibility from its position on the
fuselage's high point. (Republic)

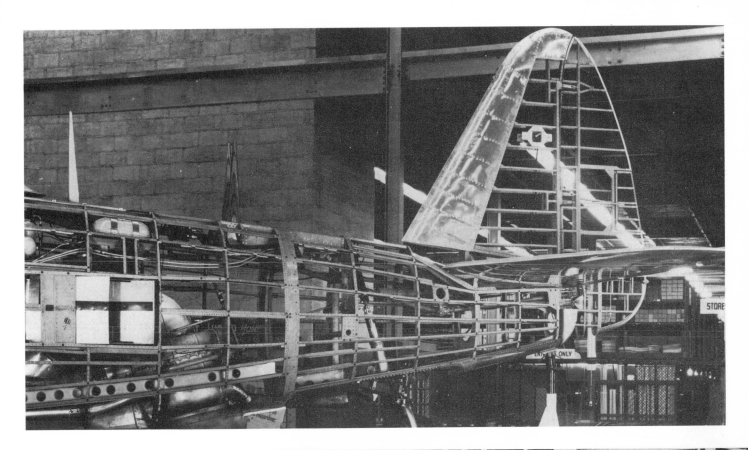

The tail section of the Thunderbolt was of equally strong construction as the rest of the aircraft. The door on the side of the fuselage was for turbosupercharger cooling, the ducting for which can be seen running to the forward fuselage. Note the positioning of the three antennas. (Republic)

As a row of nearly complete D–25s for the USAAF move forward, fuselages of RAF-camouflaged Thunderbolts are prepared for wing mating in the background. As each P–47 airframe came down the line, it had small carts of parts assigned to it so workers would not lose time by having to leave the main airframe to go to a central parts depot. As can be seen in this photograph of nearly completed aircraft, carts with all the cowling panels are parked in precise, marked-off locations. Note the large American flags hung from the rafters of the assembly building; these were usually supplemented by patriotic slogans or messages. (Republic)

*S*ome of the amazing American mass-production capability that stopped the Axis. This scene photographed on the Republic ramp at Farmingdale shows a variety of P–47D–30–RE and RAF Mk II Thunderbolts undergoing final checks and test flights before being handed over to the military. No less than 73 USAAF and RAF aircraft are present in the photograph which also gives a good idea of the differing Allied thoughts on camouflage, the USAAF by this time having gone to bare metal finish because of the turn in fortunes of war and because of the increase in speed due to the lack of the paint's weight and its drag-producing finish, while the RAF favored full camouflage. (Republic)

REPUBLIC P–47 MARKINGS AND INSIGNIA

The Thunderbolt's huge fuselage served as a canvas for pilots and ground crews.

*L*ouis the waiter stands beside a P–47D–21–RE for a bit of wartime propaganda. It was not uncommon for individuals or groups to raise bonds or funds that would buy 'presentation' aircraft for the USAAF or Navy. These aircraft would usually be marked with a plaque or insignia to honor their donor. These markings would quite often remain on the aircraft during its operational career. This view illustrates to good advantage the soft edge of the camouflage colors as they met around the wing leading edge and cowling. Also note how the colors continue onto the inside of the cowling while the landing gear wells were finished in yellowish-green zinc chromate. The Curtiss Electric propeller was finished in Black Shade 44 camouflage lacquer while the propeller hub and spinner were aluminum. The tips (four inches) of the propeller were finished in Yellow Shade 48 as was the data block on the hard rubber cuffs of the prop. (Republic)

*T*hunderbolts that marked a high-water point in production were usually conspicuously painted at the factory and the 10,000th Thunderbolt certainly was no exception. 44–20441 was a P–47D–28–RE and, after delivery, went on to serve with the 87th Fighter Squadron, 79th Fighter Group, in France. Seen in the cockpit as the aircraft prepares for its delivery flight is WASP pilot Teresa James. Female WASP pilots delivered all types of aircraft during the war, relieving men for combat duties. (Republic)

Thunderbolt number 15,000 was used for a victory rally before being shipped to an operational unit. Conspicuously marked, the Thunderbolt is seen in flight attitude with small practice bombs mounted under the wing. The stub rocket launchers are shown to advantage. (Republic)

Republic employees were not immune to the patriotic fervor that swept the country during World War Two. This P–47D–25–RE 42–26421A was the forty-fifth Thunderbolt to be purchased by workers for the USAAF. By the time that this photograph was taken, the Thunderbolt had seen some service and had taken on a distinctly 'used' look. Seen in Italy with 500 lb bombs under the wings, the P–47 was in service with the 66th Fighter Squadron whose insignia is prominently displayed on the nose. The 66th's insignia (approved on 2 January 1944) consisted of: on a background of white clouds in a fighting stance, a brown bird with white markings on head and arms and a white stomach, the body and head of a penguin with the yellow claws and beak of a falcon, holding a lighted cigar, wearing the clothes of a pug – a red cap with a visor pulled down and worn backwards, a yellow turtle-necked jersey with sleeves rolled up, and boxing gloves.

*A*ircraft were popular centerpieces for the huge war bond rallies that raised money for the government. This P–47D–27–RE 42–27206 illustrates its bare metal finish and insignia placement. Anti-glare panel was finished in flat green. The aircraft was on display in front of the US Sub-Treasury Building in New York for the Fifth War Loan Campaign. (Republic)

*A*n unusual and interesting post-war
Thunderbolt marking was carried on this
P–47D–30–RA 45–49329 assigned to Wright Field,
Dayton, Ohio. At that time (1947) Wright was still
used for considerable test flying (most test flying
would soon be transferred to Muroc Dry Lake)
and, since there were a number of commercial and
general aviation fields in the direct area around
Wright the Thunderbolt would go aloft to warn off
civil aircraft that may have been operating without
the benefit of a radio. Flying directly alongside a
small civil aircraft that was penetrating Wright
airspace, the lightplane pilot would quickly realize
that he was not wanted.

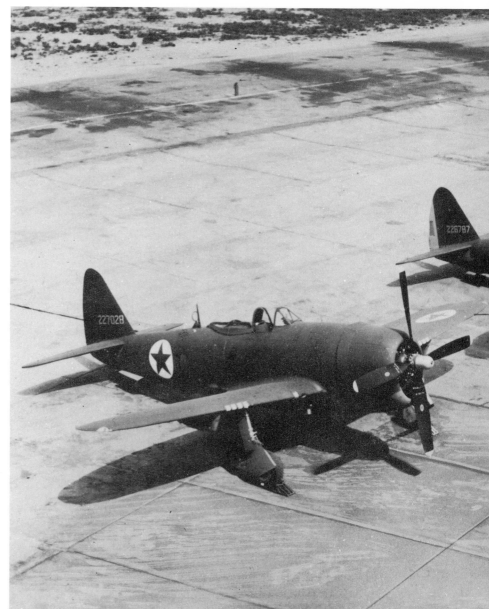

*B*eautiful factory photograph illustrating
Thunderbolts flown by four countries:
America, Russia, Brazil and Britain. It is
interesting to note that only the American aircraft
is left in natural metal finish while both the Russian
and Brazilian aircraft are painted Olive Drab and
Neutral Gray. The RAF Thunderbolt is finished in
Dark Green and Ocean Gray upper surfaces with
Medium Sea Gray lower surfaces. The Russian
national insignia consisted of a red star on a white
background but the white was usually painted out
with Olive Drab when the aircraft was sent to
frontline units. The Brazilian national insignia (in
this photograph it was painted on the top and
bottom of each wing and not on the sides of the
fuselage) consisted of a highly stylized five pointed
star in green and yellow with a blue and white
center and the fin flash was yellow and green. A
group of Fôrça Aérea Brasileira pilots was trained
in the US during the early part of 1944 as a P–47
combat unit under the command of Lt Col Nero
Moura. Upon reaching operational status the unit
was dispatched to Italy where it was placed under
the command of the 12th Air Force and it went into
action on 11 November 1944. The Brazilians
initially received 88 Thunderbolts but it is thought
that more were supplied to replace losses. After
the end of the war, the Thunderbolt was one of the
main components of the FAB and a further 25 were
obtained from US surplus stocks during 1955. One
P–47D was placed on a pylon for display in Brazil
after the type was withdrawn but it was blown up
during the student riots of 1969. (Republic)

Nine Japanese flags adorn the scoreboard on Captain J. E. Wolfe's P-47N-2-RE 44-87959. Captain Wolfe achieved a measure of distinction in the Pacific when he blasted a Japanese plane out of the air by using one of his wing mounted HVARs. Note the cover over the gunsight to protect the instrument from the harsh Pacific sun.

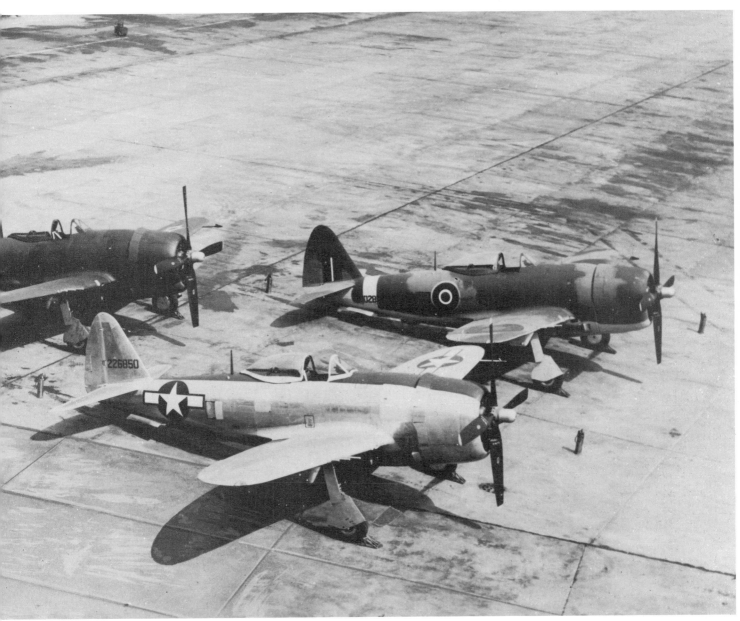

*T*he scoreboards on Thunderbolts quite often illustrated the variety of missions that the aircraft were capable of performing. Colonel J. L. Laughlin flew P–47D–30–RA 44–33287 coded B8–A with the 379th Fighter Squadron, 362nd Fighter Group and destroyed three German aircraft along with a German ship. Note how the swastikas are purposely painted in reverse.

*S*ometimes a slight over-application of the Thunderbolt's brakes could send the fighter up on its nose. That is what happened to P–47D–6–RE 42–74672 on 24 May 1944, sending one more propeller to the scrap heap. The P–47 belonged to the 350th Fighter Squadron, 353rd Fighter Group and carried the appropriate name El Shafto on the nose. Cowling was painted in yellow and black checks. Note the stencilling 'Hands off guns' applied to wing leading edge. (USAF/69592)

*A*nother Republic War Bond aircraft, this time number 62, carries the play-on-words name Maggie Zass and the 4K coding on the side meant that the P–47D–27–RE was assigned to the 506th Fighter Squadron, 404th Fighter Group. Pilots were often able to come up with very offensive names for their aircraft that, at first glance, appeared to be fairly innocent. The powers in command took a dim view of such fun and games and orders were regularly issued to cover up aircraft art work or to rephrase names. However, pilots usually found a way of getting around these orders.

*M*ajor Ernest D. Tibbets, operations officer for the 508th Fighter Squadron, and his Thunderbolt My Mozelle. At least 75 ground attack missions are recorded on the nose of the fighter in red. Coding 7J–F was painted in black. Nose band was red. Tibbets was killed in action on 8 December 1944 when he collided with (or rammed) a Heinkel He 111 after he complained twice over the radio that his guns would not fire. He was not flying his own aircraft at the time, rather he was in the air with the P–47 assigned to the squadron commander of the 508th which had a recent history of popping the gun circuit breakers when the firing button was pressed. Mozelle was the name of the Major's wife. (Col L. C. Moon)

*L*t Col Leo C. Moon's P–47D–27–RE
42–27221 coded 4K–L of the 506th Fighter
Squadron. Seen during December 1944 at St Trond,
Belgium, the Thunderbolt had been damaged by
flak numerous times during combat. On one
mission Moon (commander of the 404th Fighter

Group) lost the aircraft's pitot tube, hydraulic
system, left wing (which was later replaced),
supercharger and tailpipe to turbine and the
turbine itself along with 175 holes in the lower
fuselage. Moon commented 'I should have stayed at
home that day.' (Col L. C. Moon)

Left
*L*t Ben Kitchens in the cockpit of his P–47
with an impressive mission tally. Lt Kitchens
was killed in action on 24 June 1944 near Perriers,
France.

*M*oon's aircraft carried a small quarter moon
painted on the tail and, at a later stage in its
career, '7221 acquired a rather elaborate insignia
compared to the previous treatment. Name
translated to 'ill wind'. (Col L. C. Moon)

A patrol of P–47Cs of the 62nd Fighter
Squadron over Britain. These early
Thunderbolts were painted Olive Drab and
Neutral Gray and carry the white recognition
markings for ETO Thunderbolts on the tail and
cowling. The cowling band was 24 inches deep while
the vertical fin band was 12 inches wide and the
horizontal stabilizer bands 15 inches wide.

MEXICAN T-BOLT

In order to illustrate to the Axis the fact that Mexico had sided with the Allies, a token force of Mexican P–47s was deployed to the South Pacific.

Germany was anxious to commit as much subversion as possible in America's neighbor to the south, Mexico. America and the Mexicans signed an agreement on 1 April 1941 for the reciprocal use of military bases between the two countries. This would, of course, lead to American aid which the poorly equipped Mexican military desperately needed. On 29 May 1942, Mexico declared war on the Axis and thereby opened the channel for military equipment. The USAAF undertook the responsibility for training young Mexican aviators while the air force of Mexico was

to be expanded and modernized. By the start of 1945, the 201st Fighter Squadron of the Mexican Air Force had worked up to operational status with Republic Thunderbolts and the unit was sent to the Pacific as part of the Mexican Expeditionary Air Force, arriving in Manila on 1 May 1945. The Mexicans underwent quick tactical training from experienced American fighter pilots since the government was anxious to get the Mexicans operational against the Japanese for the political and propaganda – rather than military – value that such missions would accrue. (J. P. Gallagher)

The Mexicans began working in conjunction with the USAAF and flying ground support missions against the Japanese who were dug in on various sections of Luzon. Moving to Clark Field, the Mexicans were attached to the 58th Fighter Group which was also flying Thunderbolts. The Mexicans eagerly took to their assigned tasks but grumbled about the fact that the Americans had virtually destroyed all the enemy aircraft for they wanted to have a crack at the Japanese 'planes and pilots! P–47D–30–RA 44–33722 was photographed by James P. Gallagher during July 1945 when the 201st Fighter Squadron had been participating in a sweep over Formosa and the pilot of this aircraft noticed that his aircraft was using more fuel than it should have been. As the squadron returned to the Philippines, '722 diverted to Lingayen. (J. P. Gallagher)

Once on the ground, the USAAF mechanics at Lingayen gave the engine a quick going over, apparently correcting the problem for the Thunderbolt was fueled and the Mexican pilot was soon on his way back to Clark Field. Basically in standard USAAF markings and bare metal finish, the P–47D was identified as a Mexican aircraft by its vertical (reading from the inside of the rudder to the trailing edge) green, white and red stripes. (J. P. Gallagher)

The large black stripes on the wing and fuselage of the Mexican Air Force P–47 were identification bands used on Thunderbolts operating in the Pacific. Painted in glossy black, the stripes helped identify the Thunderbolts as friendly aircraft to trigger-happy gunners. Anti-glare panel was painted Olive Drab. (J. P. Gallagher)

T-BOLT PILOTS

These aviators made Republic's heavyweight one of the most deadly weapons of World War Two.

Colonel Francis S. Gabreski is the highest scoring surviving American fighter ace. Gabreski was at Pearl Harbor on 7 December 1941 but did not get airborne during the Japanese attack. Gabreski went with the 56th Fighter Group to Europe in 1943 and flew several missions with one of the Royal Air Force Polish squadrons but it was not until 26 November 1943 that he scored his first aerial victory. From that point on, victories began to build up and, by the time Gabreski was waiting for orders to go home during the summer of 1944, he had 27 victories, all in the Republic Thunderbolt. A mission on 5 July added another German victory to his scoreboard but, while strafing a German airfield on 20 July, he flew too low and bounced his P–47 off the ground, damaging the propeller. Crash-landing, Gabreski evaded capture for five days before being taken prisoner. Gabreski also scored 6.5 victories over enemy MiG-15s during the Korean War. He is a retired President of the Long Island Railroad. (USAF)

Robert S. Johnson entered the Army on 11 November 1941 with Class 42–F. Flying a total of 91 missions, Johnson scored 28 victories before finishing his tour and being sent home. During July and August, Dick Bong, flying a P–38, and Johnson, flying a P–47, toured the United States during a War Bond drive. Johnson commanded a P–47 operational training unit until the end of the war. (USAF/51225)

First Lieutenant Robert Johnson (left) shakes hands with Captain Walker M. Mahurin while the crew chief adds another victory to Mahurin's Spirit of Atlantic City, New Jersey. Mahurin left the USAF as a colonel after compiling an impressive record of 21 German aircraft, one Japanese aircraft, and 3.5 MiGs during the Korean War. Mahurin also had his share of luck, bailing out of Thunderbolts three times and crash landing once. Mahurin went down over Europe before D-Day but managed to get back to England via the French underground. During the Korean War, Mahurin's luck ran out when he was shot down and spent 16 months as a prisoner of the North Koreans. (USAF/73670)

Pilots of the 22nd Fighter Squadron, 36th Fighter Group, proudly stand by their chalk board with the latest tally of victories. This snap shot shows the squadron code of 3T and the red nose band. The diverse clothing of the pilots is also noteworthy.

Lt Martin Johnson sits on the horizontal stabilizer of his P–47, lifting three fingers to signify the destruction of a Fw 190, Bf 109 and Bf 110 during airfield strafing missions in France. On that mission, his P–47 suffered hits in the fuselage, elevator, tail wheel and turbosupercharger. Flak also severed a control cable and the tail wheel would not come down during landing – giving some idea just how accurate the German flak was and how hazardous it was to strafe the German airfields. (USAF/51417)

REPUBLIC P–47 THUNDERBOLT VARIANTS, SERIAL NUMBERS AND SPECIFICATIONS

Variants

XP–47–RE   Republic project that did not pass beyond initial design stage. It had a 1,150 hp Allison V–1710–39, and was armed with .50 caliber nose guns and four .30 caliber guns in the wing. Assigned serial 40–3051, the aircraft eventually turned into the XP–47B–RE.

XP–47A–RE   Same concept as above but with a lighter airframe and only nose guns retained. Serial 40–3052 was allotted but the project did not pass beyond initial design.

XP–47B–RE   First of the Thunderbolts with P&W XR–2800–2 of 2,000 hp. The turbosupercharger was mounted in rear fuselage. It first flew on 2 May 1941, but crashed and was destroyed on 8 August 1942. Bare metal finish. There were many design changes during the aircraft's life.

P–47B   Similar to the prototype but with many design detail changes including sliding canopy and metal covered control surfaces. GE A–13 turbosupercharger. Six or eight .50 caliber guns could be carried. The first example completed during December 1941. The first five aircraft became pre-production test and evaluation machines. Production aircraft were assigned to the 56th and 78th Fighter Groups. Delivered in Olive Drab and Neutral Gray standard camouflage.

P–47C   The C–1–RE had an R–2800–21 engine, and six or eight .50 caliber guns with 300 to 425 rpg, revised oxygen system and A–17 turbosupercharger regulator. First C–1–RE was completed on 14 September 1942. The C–2–RE had metal covered rudder and elevators; 128 were built. The C–5–RE just had radio and mast change; 362 were built.

P–47D   The D–1–RA, of which 114 were built, was the first Thunderbolt model built at the new Evansville (RA), Indiana, plant starting in December 1942. It was similar to the C–5–RE. The D–1–RE had additional cowling flaps, more pilot armor and a new radio and mast; 105 were built. The D–2–RA built at Evansville (200 aircraft), was similar to the D–1–RE. The D–2–RE (445 built) was similar to the D–1–RE with minor improvements to the fuel system. 100 D–3–RAs were built, and were similar to D–2–RE. The D–5–RE (300 built) was similar to the D–1–RE, but with modifications to the fuel and hydraulic systems. The D–4–RA (200 built) was similar to the D–5–RE. The D–6–RE (350 built) was similar to the D–1–RE but had two-point shackles for a bomb or drop tank under the fuselage. The D–10–RE (250 built) was as the D–1–RE, with minor changes in the hydraulic system and the addition of a GE C–23 turbosupercharger. The D–11–RE (400 built) was equipped with a 2,300 hp P&W R–2800–63 with water injection, while the D–11–RA was similar to the D–11–RE; 250 were built. The D–15–RE (496 built) had wing stations for a bomb or drop tank under each wing panel and the increased payload, giving the ability to carry up to two 1,000 lb bombs or three 500 lb bombs. The D–15–RA (157 built)

was similar to the D–15–RE. The D–16–RE (254 built) was similar to the D–11–RE but could use 100/150 octane fuel. Only 29 D–16–RA aircraft were built and they were similar to the D–16–RE. The D–20–RE (250 built) had a 2,300 hp P&W R–2800–59 along with a raised tail wheel strut, GE ignition harness and other slight modifications. 187 D–20–RAs were built and they were similar to the D–20–RE. The D–21–RE had manual water injection control but was similar to the D–11–RE, but aircraft were delivered in natural metal finish; 216 were built. The D–21–RA (224 built) was basically the same as the D–21–RE. 850 D–22–REs were built with a 13 ft Hamilton Standard paddle-blade propeller and A–23 turbosupercharger regulator. The D–23–RA (889 built) had a Curtiss Electric 13 ft paddle-blade propeller. The bubble canopy was introduced with the D–25–RE (385 built) which had increased oxygen supplies and repositioned integral equipment with increased fuel capacity (270 US gallons). The D–26–RA (250 built) was similar to the D–25–RE. 615 D–27–RE Thunderbolts were built and were similar to the D–25–RE except for minor fuel system changes. The D–28–RA (1,028 built) was similar to the D–26–RA. 750 D–28–RE aircraft were built, and were similar to the D–25–RE, but with a Curtiss paddle-blade propeller. 800 D–30–RE aircraft were built, similar to the D–25–RE, but with rocket stubs for five HVARs under each wing panel. The D–30–RA (1,800 built) was similar to the D–30–RE. The D–40–RA (665 built) introduced a dorsal fin for increased stability.

XP–47E   41–6065 converted to have a pressurized cabin. Modified a number of times during testing life, it carried an R–2800–21 and –59 with Curtiss Electric and Hamilton Standard propellers. Its performance was similar to that of the P–47B except for higher speeds with new engine and propeller so production was not warranted.

XP–47F   41–5938 was converted from a P–47B to test a new laminar flow wing. It was a test aircraft only, with no armament. It was lost in a fatal crash on 14 October 1943.

P–47G   Twenty G–CU Thunderbolts were built by Curtiss at Buffalo, with R–2800–21 engines and Curtiss Electric 12 ft 2 in propellers, but they were basically similar to the C–1–RE. The first aircraft was finished in December 1942. Forty G–1–CU, similar to the C–5–RE, sixty G–5–CU aircraft, similar to D–1–RE, and eighty G–10–CU aircraft, identical to the D–6–RE, and 154 G–15–CU, similar to the D–11–RE, were built. They were mainly assigned to the training role.

XP–47H   42–23297 and 42–23298 were converted from D–15–RA airframes and modified as test beds for the 2,300 hp Chrysler XIV–2220–1.

XP–47J   S/n 43–46952 fitted with a 2,800 hp R–2800–57 engine and cooling fan for the engine in a shortened nose and CH–5 turbosupercharger with many design detail changes. It was armed with six .50 caliber machine guns with 267 rpg. The project was dropped when the aircraft could not reach the top speed stated by manufacturer.

XP–47K   The last D–5–RE, 42–8702, modified to test bubble canopy. It later tested bigger wing for P–47N.

XP–47L   The last D–20–RE, 42–76614, modified into basically the XP–47K version, but with design detail changes. It later served as the test bed for R–2800–C engine.

P–47M   Three YP–47M–RE aircraft were built for testing with 2,800 hp P&W R–2800–14W and –57 engines with Curtiss Electric C642S–B40 13 ft diameter propellers, and the ability to carry six or eight .50 caliber guns with 267 rpg. The YPs tested the R–2800–C engines and related components. 130 M–1–RE Thunderbolts, higher-powered variants of the D–30–RE, were built, and all were sent to the 56th FG where dorsal fins were fitted as a field modification.

P–47N   One XP–47N, a converted D–27–RE, was built with an R–2800–57 and Curtiss Electric 13 ft diameter propeller, unilever power control, CH–5 turbosupercharger and a new long-range wing. They had a new engine mount and cowling with many design detail changes, 40 US gallon oil tank and the ability to carry six to eight .50 caliber machine guns. 550 N–1–RE models were built with the unilever power control dropped and replaced by automatic engine control unit and a new ignition harness. Extra fuel in the wing gave a total of 186 US gallons, and 300 US gallon drop tanks could be carried under each wing panel. 550 N–5–RE Thunderbolts were also built, basically similar to the N–1–RE but with minor detail differences including the addition of rocket launchers and AN/APS–13 tail warning radar and provision for GE C–1 autopilot. 200 N–15–RE aircraft were built, similar to N–1–RE except for the addition of an S–1 bomb rack and a new K–14A/B gun-sight, while the automatic engine control unit was dropped. 200 N–20–RE Thunderbolts were constructed, also similar to the N–1–RE except for new radio and other minor changes. 149 N–20–RAs, similar to the N–20–RE except for minor cockpit changes, were built. 167 N–25–REs were built, and were similar to the N–1–RE except for installation of automatic engine controls, auto-pilot, new cockpit floor and strengthened aileron to deflect blast from rocket firing. They were the final Thunderbolts built on the Farmingdale line, which closed during October 1945.

Serial Numbers

XP–47A–RE	40–3052 (cancelled)
XP–47B–RE	40–3051
P–47B–RE	41–5895 through 41–6064
P–47C–RE	41–6067 through 41–6123
P–47C–1–RE	41–6066, 41–6124 through 41–6177
P–47C–2–RE	41–6178 through 41–6305
P–47C–5–RE	41–6306 through 41–6667
P–47D–1–RE	42–7853 through 42–7957
P–47D–2–RE	42–7958 through 42–8402
P–47D–5–RE	42–8403 through 42–8702
P–47D–6–RE	42–74615 through 42–74964
P–47D–20–RE	42–25274 through 42–25322
P–47D–21–RE	42–25323 through 42–25538
P–47D–22–RE	42–25539 through 42–26388
P–47D–25–RE	42–26389 through 42–26773
P–47D–27–RE	42–26774 through 42–27384
P–47D–10–RE	42–74965 through 42–75214
P–47D–11–RE	42–75215 through 42–75614
P–47D–15–RE	42–75615 through 75864
P–47D–16–RE	42–75865 through 42–76118
P–47D–15–RE	42–76119 through 42–76364
P–47D–20–RE	42–76365 through 42–76613
P–47D–28–RE	44–19558 through 44–20307
P–47D–30–RE	44–20308 through 44–21107
P–47D–1–RA	42–22250 through 42–22363
P–47D–2–RA	42–22364 through 42–22563
P–47D–3–RA	42–22564 through 42–22663
P–47D–4–RA	42–22664 through 42–22863
P–47D–11–RA	42–22864 through 42–23113
P–47D–15–RA	42–23143 through 42–23299
P–47D–16–RA	42–23114 through 42–23142
P–47D–20–RA	43–25254 through 43–25440
P–47D–21–RA	43–25441 through 43–25664
P–47D–23–RA	43–25665 through 43–25753
P–47D–23–RA	42–27389 through 42–28188
P–47D–26–RA	42–28189 through 42–28438
P–47D–28–RA	42–28439 through 42–29466
P–47D–30–RA	44–32668 through 44–33867
P–47D–35–RA	44–89684 through 44–90283
P–47D–40–RA	44–90284 through 44–90483
P–47D–30–RA	45–49090 through 45–49554
XP–47F–RE	41–5938
XP–47E–RE	41–6065
P–47G–CU	42–24920 through 42–24939
P–47G–1–CU	42–24940 through 42–24979
P–47G–5–CU	42–24980 through 42–25039
P–47G–10–CU	42–25040 through 42–25119
P–47G–15–CU	42–25120 through 42–25273
XP–47H–RE	42–23297 and 42–23298
XP–47J–RE	43–46952
XP–47K–RE	42–8702
XP–47L–RE	42–76614
YP–47M–RE	42–27385 and 42–27386, 42–27388
P–47M–RE	44–21108 through 44–21237
XP–47N–RE	42–27387
P–47N–1–RE	44–87784 through 44–88333
P–47N–5–RE	44–88334 through 44–88883
P–47N–15–RE	44–88884 through 44–89083
P–47N–20–RE	44–89084 through 44–89283
P–47N–25–RE	44–89284 through 44–89450
P–47N–RE	44–89451 through 44–89683 (cancelled)
P–47N–20–RA	45–49975 through 45–50123
P–47N–RA	45–50124 through 45–55174 (cancelled)

Royal Air Force Serial Numbers

Mk I	FL731 through FL850, HB962 through HB999, HD100 through HD181
Mk II	HD182 through HD301, KJ128 through KJ367, KL168 through KL347, KL838 through KL887, and KL888 through KL976 which were cancelled

Brazilian Serial Numbers

P–47D–26–RE	42–26724 through 42–26773

USSR Serial Numbers

P–47D–10–RE	42–75201 through 42–75203
P–47D–22–RE	42–25539 through 42–25658
P–47D–27–RE	42–27015 through 42–27064, 42–27115 through 42–27164 (Seven aircraft were lost during delivery)

Specifications

XP–47B

Span	40 ft 9 in
Length	35 ft
Height	12 ft 8 in
Wing area	300 sq ft
Empty weight	9,189 lb
Loaded weight	12,700 lb
Max. speed	412 mph
Cruise speed	n/a
Ceiling	38,000 ft
Rate of climb	3,000 fpm
Range	575 miles
Powerplant	Pratt & Whitney XR–2800–21 of 2,000 hp

P–47B

Span	40 ft 9 in
Length	35 ft
Height	12 ft 8 in
Wing area	300 sq ft
Empty weight	9,346 lb
Loaded weight	13,360 lb
Max. speed	429 mph
Cruise speed	340 mph
Ceiling	42,000 ft
Rate of climb	2,560 fpm
Range	550 miles
Powerplant	Pratt & Whitney R–2800–21 of 2,000 hp

P–47C

Span	40 ft 9 in
Length	35 ft
Height	14 ft 2 in
Wing area	300 sq ft
Empty weight	9,900 lb
Loaded weight	14,925 lb
Max. speed	433 mph
Cruise speed	350 mph
Ceiling	42,000 ft
Rate of climb	2,400 fpm
Range	550 miles
Powerplant	Pratt & Whitney R–2800–21 of 2,000 hp

A factory-fresh Thunderbolt seen shortly after delivery to Curtiss-Wright where the aircraft was to be used in propeller testing. The aircraft is in basic Army markings with national insignia in four places, olive green anti-glare panel and black serial. The shiny finish was typical of Alclad aluminum in its finished state and the aircraft was not polished. Indeed, polishing would remove the ultra-thin protective covering over the aluminum, allowing the skin to corrode more quickly. This aircraft was later written off in a ground accident. (Curtiss-Wright)

P–47D–30		XP–47J		P–47N	
Span	40 ft 9 in	Span	40 ft 11 in	Span	42 ft 7 in
Length	36 ft 1 in	Length	33 ft 3 in	Length	36 ft 1 in
Height	14 ft 2 in	Height	17 ft 3 in	Height	14 ft 8 in
Wing area	300 sq ft	Wing area	300 sq ft	Wing area	322 sq ft
Empty weight	10,000 lb	Empty weight	9,663 lb	Empty weight	11,000 lb
Loaded weight	19,400 lb	Loaded weight	16,780 lb	Loaded weight	20,700 lb
Max. speed	428 mph	Max. speed	507 mph	Max. speed	467 mph
Cruise speed	350 mph	Cruise speed	400 mph	Cruise speed	300 mph
Ceiling	42,000 ft	Ceiling	45,000 ft	Ceiling	43,000 ft
Rate of climb	2,200 fpm	Rate of climb	3,100 fpm	Rate of climb	3,000 fpm
Range	475 miles	Range	765 miles	Range	800 miles
Powerplant	Pratt & Whitney R–2800–59 of 2,300 hp	Powerplant	Pratt & Whitney R–2800–57 of 2,800 hp	Powerplant	Pratt & Whitney R–2800–57, –73, or –77 of 2,800 hp
XP–47H		**P–47M**			
Span	40 ft 9 in	Span	40 ft 9 in		
Length	39 ft 2 in	Length	36 ft 4 in		
Height	14 ft 2 in	Height	14 ft 9 in		
Wing area	300 sq ft	Wing area	308 sq ft		
Empty weight	11,442 lb	Empty weight	10,423 lb		
Loaded weight	13,750 lb	Loaded weight	15,500 lb		
Max. speed	490 mph	Max. speed	473 mph		
Cruise speed	n/a	Cruise speed	n/a		
Ceiling	n/a	Ceiling	41,000 ft		
Rate of climb	n/a	Rate of climb	3,200 fpm		
Range	700 miles	Range	530 miles		
Powerplant	Chrysler XIV–2220–1 of 2,300 hp	Powerplant	Pratt & Whitney R–2800–57 of 2,800 hp		

Lockheed XP-49
The Lightning Replacement

This high-altitude fighter was built as a possible replacement for the P–38.

It is a curious truism in the world of military equipment that when a new weapon is built it is probably obsolete. This fatalistic attitude does hold a certain amount of fact for, in the field of aeronautics, today's development time for a new aircraft takes so long that, by the time it is in service, well over a decade has usually elapsed since the original thought crossed someone's mind. During the 1930s this time table was not so drastic but the amount of time between the creation of an idea and putting the idea into actual physical hardware was rapidly increasing. The increasing pace of aeronautical technology was causing the Army to worry, realizing that plans for new aircraft had to be made *before* the aircraft they would replace were in service!

Appearing at first glance to be a Lockheed P–38, the XP–49 was virtually a completely different aircraft although it did bear a great deal of resemblance to its older brother. Cancellation of the design's original powerplants, the Pratt & Whitney X–1800 of 2,300 hp, also meant a drop of over 75 mph in top speed when Continental's experimental XI–1430s were adopted. The prototype showed that it would not replace the P–38 as its performance was not really any better than the Lightning's. To get the aircraft into the air in the shortest possible time all military equipment, including the armament of two 20 mm cannon and four .50 caliber machine guns, was left out and never installed. (USAF)

One of the items that the Army had been worrying about was the high price of their new Lockheed P–38 Lightning. Even though the Lightning certainly looked like it was going to be a winner the Army was still having to labor under the hardship of a budget that was only just becoming free from the death grip of isolationism. Accordingly, the Army issued Circular Proposal 39–775 in hopes of finding an even better aircraft at perhaps an even lower price. But the Army was really grasping at straws in its search for the new long-range, twin-engine fighter because the winner was to be none other than Lockheed! The new aircraft was designated Model 522 by Lockheed after the original designation Model 222 had been assigned to the rapidly developing P–38. The new fighter, one of four proposals submitted by manufacturers, looked very similar to the P–38, Lockheed apparently deciding to capitalize on a winner, and was decidedly different from the Grumman XP–50 which garnered second place in the contest.

Power for the new aircraft was to come in the form of the equally new Pratt & Whitney X–1800 engine of 2,300 hp. The engine was a complex liquid-cooled sleeve valve affair that offered a high horsepower rating with slim frontal area. As mentioned previously, the Army and P&W decided that the company should wisely bow out of the liquid-cooled engine market and concentrate on its famous R–2800 and other radial projects. Thus Lockheed was left high and dry with a paper airplane and no engines to power the craft. A decision was made to switch to the Continental XI–1430 which was an inverted liquid-cooled V–12 engine that would develop only 1,600 hp, thereby dropping overall projected top speed from 475 mph to 400 mph.

The Army was left with a fighter that had just about the same performance as the P–38!

Stubbornly clinging to rapidly dwindling hopes, the Army proceeded with the Model 522, ordering the aircraft during October of 1939 and signing the formal contract on 8 January 1940. Construction went ahead and the XP–49 made its first flight on 11 November

Following a very brief period of testing, including a crash landing, by Lockheed, the XP–49 was transferred to Wright Field. A second seat had been installed in the cockpit to carry an observer. A series of flights to test the Continental engines was planned but only a few flights were made before the Army cancelled the engine program. The failure of one of the Continentals meant that the flying career of the XP–49 was over and it was shuffled off to one side of the airfield until the diabolical device in the photograph demanded a test specimen. The structure was a hydraulic drop test rig that was designed to test the strength of aircraft landing gear. The XP–49 was yanked up into the air and dropped onto the concrete to see how many G forces the airframe could withstand before incurring damage. Very few hard 'landings' were needed before structural damage began to appear in the tail and boom area. The XP–49 was scrapped soon after these tests were finished. (W. T. Larkins)

1942. All military equipment including the projected armament of two 20 mm cannon and four .50 caliber machine guns was left out in order that flight tests could be proceeded with in the greatest possible hurry. The experimental engines had to be changed after a few flights and, at this time, several minor modifications were also carried out.

During January 1943, the XP–49 was back in the air again but it suffered damage when a main gear leg failed to extend and the prototype slid in for a crash landing on the Burbank runway. The XP–49 was repaired but, by this time, the fact had dawned on the Army that the XP–49 was not going to outrun the P–38 which was already in service. Accordingly, the XP–49 program was shut down and plans were made to ferry the prototype to Wright Field where testing could be carried out on the Continental engines. A second seat was fitted in the cockpit for an observer, which must have been fairly cramped since it does not appear that the shape of the canopy was altered in the process. The aircraft made it to Ohio with no problem but various mechanical gremlins began to creep into the XP–49 after its arrival. Only a few flights were made and, by then, the Continental program was dead. XP–49 made only a few more flights before one of the experimental engines failed and the XP–49 sat out the rest of the war on the ramp. The aircraft's final contribution to the development of aviation was rather ignominious as the XP–49 was tied to a hydraulic lift which raised the fighter into the air and then, with considerable force, dropped the plane back onto the concrete ramp. This was to test how much force an aircraft's landing gear could take before the structure became damaged. As can be imagined it did not take very many drops before the XP–49 began exhibiting structural damage in the tail booms. The aircraft survived to be viewed at the massive Wright Field Victory Air Display after VJ Day but it was soon stripped of useful parts, which were few, and then chopped up for scrap.

LOCKHEED XP–49 SERIAL NUMBER AND SPECIFICATIONS

Serial Number

XP–49	40–3055

Specifications

XP–49

Since the aircraft completed only a few flights, performance specifications should be regarded as estimates.

Span	52 ft
Length	40 ft 1 in
Height	9 ft 9.5 in
Wing area	327.5 sq ft
Empty weight	15,400 lb
Loaded weight	18,825 lb
Max. speed	405 mph
Cruise speed	315 mph
Ceiling	30,000 ft
Rate of climb	3,500 fpm
Range	680 miles
Powerplant	Two Continental XI–1430–1 of 1,600 hp each

Grumman XP-50
A Twin For The Army

This interesting twin-engine aircraft only made one flight and it was not exactly successful.

One of the most radical American aircraft designs during the late 1930s was Leroy Grumman's XF5F–1 Skyrocket. This twin-engine, twin-tail, snub nose fighter was one of the most exciting looking aircraft when it appeared because all-metal monoplane fighters with *one* engine were just being accepted by the Navy. The Skyrocket was dubbed revolutionary for its configuration and its armament of two 23 mm Madsen cannon was considered quite extraordinary. However, as with so many of the mid to late 1930s projects, the Skyrocket just did not work out. The

aircraft went through a number of modifications including the addition of a more or less orthodox nose, conducted many flight tests and, eventually, gained enough data to pass on to the developing XF7F Tigercat which was put into quantity production for the Navy and Marines although it was too late to see action during World War Two.

Grumman quickly established itself, with large orders for the rugged little Wildcat fighter, as one of the main suppliers of aircraft to the Navy. This did not mean that Grumman was ignoring the possibility of lucrative Army contracts; on the contrary Leroy and his associates were giving much consideration to selling the Army a fighter.

Designated Grumman Project G–46A, this

new fighter had a marked resemblance to the developing XF5F–1 when Grumman offered a written proposal to the Army during the middle of 1939. Ordered by the Army on 25 November of that year, as the XP–50, the fighter was to have all the interesting features of its Navy stablemate. The XP–50 was a single place, all-metal, twin engine monoplane figh-

The Grumman XP–50 on its first flight. The fighter was to carry an armament of two 20 mm cannon and four .50 caliber machine guns but this was never fitted. Looking a great deal like the XF5F–I developed for the Navy, the XP–50 was to have a longer nose section which accommodated a nose landing gear. The crash of the experimental fighter was caused by an explosion and fire in one of the turbosuperchargers. The XP–50 had come in second to the Lockheed XP–38 on the initial Army design study. (USAF)

ter designed to meet the requirements of military forces for a high-performance pursuit and light bomber. Power came from two Wright GR–1820–G205 radials (military designation R–1820–67/–69) which had 1200 horsepower each at takeoff and 1000 hp at 13,500 ft, 900 hp at 14,000 ft. The engines were left and right hand rotation to nullify the effect of torque. The longer nose section helped stretch out the stubby lines that had made the XF5F–1 such a strange looking creature. Grumman also took a lesson from Bell Aircraft and added a nose gear to the lengthened nose. The pilot's cockpit was located mid-fuselage, between the two engines and afforded excellent visibility forward and upward. Downward visibility was hampered by the engines and wing.

Two armament packages were put forward for the XP–50. One package consisted of six .50 caliber Browning aircooled machine guns, four clustered in the nose and a single weapon in each outboard wing panel. Provision was made to supply approximately 500 rounds per gun. The second package consisted of four .50 calibers and two Hispano Suiza 20 mm cannon. Two machine guns would be in the nose with the two cannon, the remaining two weapons in the outer wing panels. Each cannon would be supplied with 60 rounds of ammunition. Provisions were made for installing a bomb rack under each wing which could mount a 165 pound bomb. A small window was installed in the bottom of the fuselage so the pilot could see directly below and readily acquire his target.

Construction of the fighter went quickly and the place was ready for its first flight on 18 February 1941. Grumman's chief test pilot Robert Hall did a thorough inspection of the fighter before taking the plane aloft for a 20-minute test flight. Few problems were encoun-

tered and Hall reported the XP–50 handled well in the air. Two further flights were made on 24 February but only added another 25 minutes of flight time. Lois Lovisolo, Corporate Historian for Grumman, generously supplied Robert Hall's log book so a historical summary of the XP–50's flight record could be prepared: The XP–50 flew again on 6 March (40 minutes), 7 March (12 minutes), 20 March (10 minutes), 21 March (15 minutes), 12 April (30 minutes), 14 April (25 minutes), 15 April (20 minutes), 18 April (50 minutes), 10 May (15 minutes), and 12 May (30 minutes).

The XP–50 was prepared for another test flight on 14 April and Hall departed the factory's Bethpage airfield for some air work over Long Island Sound. Fifty minutes into the flight, there was an explosion in one of the engines. Hall took immediate corrective action but a fire began to spread inside the nacelle and cowling. Hall jettisoned the canopy, undid his safety straps, rolled the XP–50 upside down, and let gravity do the rest. Descending in his parachute, Hall watched as the XP–50 pitched into a violent dive, impacting with the water below. The Army quickly lost interest in the XP–50, even though the fighter had rated second behind the Lockheed P–38 in desirableness and performance, and the idea of further development was quickly dropped.

Some of the money that had been allocated for the XP–50 was transferred to the study of a new design, the Model G–51. This aircraft was to incorporate many of the features of the XP–50 and its Navy stablemate, the XF5F–1. Both the Army and Navy were extremely interested and the design became the famous Tigercat. The Army reserved the designation XP–65 for the new fighter while the Navy took XF7F. Problems developed when the two services could not agree on a number of common items for the aircraft and the requirements for

the fighters began to become more divergent. Grumman decided that its future was with the Navy and the Army's XP–65 was quietly dropped. This was to be Grumman's last dealing with the Army for fighter aircraft and the company went on to become the supplier of some of the most famous naval fighters ever built (refer to *United States Naval Fighters of World War Two* from the same publisher as this volume). What Grumman did not learn was the extreme difficulty in producing a single fighter for both services; this eventually culminated in the disastrous General Dynamics/Grumman F–111B program of the early 1960s.

GRUMMAN XP–50 SERIAL NUMBER AND SPECIFICATIONS

Serial Number

XP–50	39–2517

Specifications

XP–50

Since the XP–50 did not complete its flight testing these performance specifications should be regarded as estimates.

Span	42 ft
Length	31 ft 11 in
Height	12 ft
Wing area	304 sq ft
Empty weight	8,300 lb
Loaded weight	10,600 lb
Max. speed	425 mph
Cruise speed	n/a
Ceiling	40,000 ft
Rate of climb	3,800 fpm
Range	1,250 miles
Powerplant	Two Wright R–1820–67/69s of 1,200 hp each

North American P-51 Mustang — The Long-Range Escort

Designed to a British requirement in just 117 days, the Mustang became the USAAF's most successful fighter of World War Two.

It was an early morning in October at Los Angeles' Mines Field. Typical for that time of the year was the fog, which had crept inland with the evening's darkness and had retreated with the morning sun – leaving only a thin mist from the nearby Pacific. North American Aviation Incorporated, which occupied the south-east end of the airfield, had row upon row of squat Texan and Harvard trainers parked on their large ramp area. These tough trainers, forming the basis of the Army Air Corps advanced pilot training program and serving as an advanced trainer for Commonwealth aviators, had placed North Amer-

ican on the aviation map and established the company's fortunes.

NAA had eventually emerged from a number of other corporate and conglomerate identities to join the rapidly developing aviation industry in Southern California. Mines Field was picked as the location for the manufacturing and testing of aircraft because it offered an established airfield, was close to the sources of supply, and – perhaps more importantly for a fledgling company – because it was cheap!

Founding of the factory took place in 1936 and the building covered 159,000 square feet and employed 150 persons in the manufacture and development of the NA–16 design that was eventually to turn into the Texan and Harvard, and of the Army Air Corps portly observation aircraft, the O–47.

By 1940, many of the events that plague a new company had been met and conquered and president James H. 'Dutch' Kindelberger had set NAA's collective sight on a bright and dangerous future.

That October morning in 1940 on the North American ramp began like most others. As the warming sun climbed in the sky and the Pacific mists evaporated, company test pilots were beginning their work. Mechanics were pulling covers off the engines and preparing the

The aircraft which started the Mustang line. Test pilot Vance Breeze is seen at the controls of the NA–73X as it orbits near Mines Field, Los Angeles. Of particular interest are the fine lines and finish of the aircraft, the pseudo Army Air Corps rudder stripes (the NA–73X was a civil registered prototype), the streamlined windshield and the short air scoop atop the intake. (NAA)

trainers for test and production flights. Parked among this gathering of work-a-day trainers was a flying machine so alien that it appeared as if it could have arrived from another planet. The rising sun glowed with an orange dullness off the aircraft's bright metal flanks and it seemed as if the machine would simply leap into its natural element. The aircraft was the NA–73X, the product of the collective genius that North American had been able to assemble and the first of a line of fighters that was destined to carve a respected name for themselves in the war-ravaged skies of Europe and over the watery vastness of the Pacific.

Perhaps only North American could have built the NA–73X for it was a young company, uncompromised by tradition and open to a rapidly developing aeronautical technology that was stemming from the war in Europe. The British Aircraft Purchasing Commission, which was transiting from one American

factory to another in a state of near panic, was purchasing aircraft in vast numbers; some of which could be best described as 'elderly' in aeronautical terms. Certainly some of these newly-purchased aircraft did sterling service for King and country but others, such as the Airacobra and Buffalo, were failures. The British realized that even though aircraft such as the Lockheed Hudson and Curtiss Tomahawk were performing adequately, they would soon be outstripped in fighting qualities by new German aircraft. However, the vast number of American aircraft that were being funneled to Britain and the Commonwealth nations did help and the British wanted to exploit the American techniques of mass production and advanced technology. Discussions opened between the British and North American with the idea of setting up a production line to build Curtiss Tomahawks under license. Kindelberger realized that there was little future in

For the NA–73X, disaster struck on 20 November 1940 when test pilot Paul Balfour ran a fuel tank dry with the result illustrated. Balfour landed gear down in a plowed field, the tires dug in and the NA–73X violently flipped onto its back. Balfour was virtually uninjured and wasted no time escaping from the crushed cockpit. Heavily damaged, most sources state the NA–73X was scrapped but it was rebuilt and continued a limited test career. Note the 'six-gun wing', the gun ports merely being all black paint: the NA–73X never carried armament. (NAA)

Unusual experiment to Mustang Mk II FR901, photographed during July 1943. In order to increase the type's range even further, these oversize fuel tanks were added under the wing. The Mustang Mk II was basically the same as the P–51A. (Air Ministry/12299C)

A familiar fighting compartment from an angle unfamiliar to pilots. A Mustang Mk I's fuselage center section on jacks with wing removed allows an interesting straight-in look. Photographed on 17 September 1941. (NAA/73–30–16)

building what he considered an obsolete aircraft under license from another company.

In a move that eventually changed aeronautical concepts, Kindelberger and his staff gave the British a counter-proposal that was revolutionary in both concept and undertaking. North American proposed to build, for the Royal Air Force, a brand-new fighter that would incorporate all the modern air fighting techniques that had been learned the hard way over Europe and Britain. At this stage of the European conflict, it was vital to get permission from the isolationist American government to proceed with such a project. Washington passed down its approval with the stipulation that North American and the British Aircraft Purchasing Commission hand over two of the early production aircraft to the Air Corps at no cost to the US government.

The British, enthusiastic to get approval, and North American, eager for a contract that would put them in the lucrative fighter business, saw no problem with this requirement.

Kindelberger and J. L. Atwood thrashed out a quick design sketch which the British looked over, approved, and then specified that they wanted an eight-gun fighter, that fit in with the armament then on the Spitfire and Hurricane, and that they wanted the new machine as quickly as possible.

Speed was to be the keyword in the production of the NA–73X as the fate of the contract would rest on how quickly the fighter could be designed and built. Learning hard lessons from the production of the Spitfire, which was a complicated aircraft to build, the North American design team was to be headed by Raymond Rice and ably assisted by Edgar Schmued as chief designer, Larry Waite and E. H. Horkey. The team quickly agreed to go with every revolutionary concept that they could develop provided that the concepts were efficient and easy to mass produce. Perhaps the most innovative feature was the employment of the then-new laminar flow wing. The airfoil for this wing had been partially developed by the National Advisory Committee for Aeronautics (NACA) and introduced several distinctive features. The greatest thickness in cross section of the wing had been moved well back and gradually tapered off to the trailing edge; this type of airfoil helped the air flow to remain smoothly flowing over the wing's surface beyond the points that it would have broken away into drag-creating eddies on a normal wing. This decrease in drag resulted, of course, in an increase in speed and lifting efficiency.

To make the NA–73X as aerodynamically clean as possible, the engineers incorporated

Flight of three P–51As with s/n 43–6237, a P–51A–10–Na, in the lead. These aircraft were equipped with four .50 caliber wing guns. Given the factory designation NA–99, 310 examples were built. These machines carry underwing canisters for the laying down of smoke screens.

the conical lofting method of streamlining which incorporated the smoothest airframe with all drag-producing areas reduced or completely enclosed within the structure of the airframe.

The powerplant for the NA–73X was another prime concern for the NAA group. The engineers wanted a powerful inline engine so that a highly streamlined nose could be employed in the design. The most powerful inline available in America at that time was the Allison V–1710 series of liquid-cooled V–12 powerplants. The Americans and British agreed to incorporate this powerplant into the new design.

The engineering team did a great deal of figuring over the exact spot at which to locate the radiator that was needed to cool the engine. Radiator location was a prime consideration in any fighter design that used a liquid-cooled engine for, in most instances, the radiator was just a large squarish lump of cooling core that greatly detracted from overall performance if much of its surface hung in the slipstream. They finally placed it below and behind the cockpit area where it could receive the maximum amount of air possible via an ingenious retractable air scoop while disturbing the airflow to the least possible extent. However, when some items are made more simple then other complex factors quite often appear. In the case of the NA–73X it was the amount of plumbing to connect the radiator with the engine and the fact that this method of cooling was very vulnerable to enemy gunfire.

NAA had been forced to purchase wind tunnel data on advanced fighters from Curtiss as part of the requirement for developing the NA–73X. This step was required since NAA had experience in neither wind tunnel work nor building high-performance fighters. However, many years later this was to give rise to the rumor that the NA–73X was merely a reworked Curtiss design. It appears that there is little to back up this statement and interviews with principals in the design of the NA–73X state that the rumor is simply not true; and, given the problems Curtiss designs were running in to, it is hardly likely that such an advanced design as the NA–73X came from Curtiss.

The British letter for go-ahead on the project had been given on 10 April 1940 (at this point the armament had been changed) while the formal contract had been signed by the various parties on 23 May. The NAA engineering team issued drawings to the fabrication shops in a never-ending stream that included 16-hour work days, seven days a week. The company was shooting for a delivery date of January 1941 but the aircraft was rolled out of the

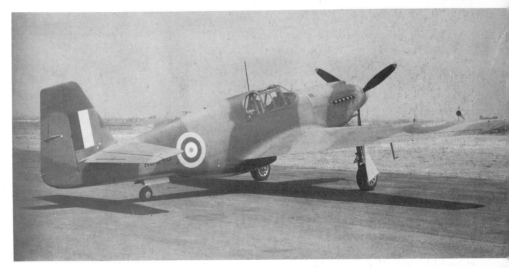

North American factory doors in 117 days although it was still incomplete in some details and rested on wheels and tires borrowed from the Texan production line! Another 20 days were to pass before the Allison engine was delivered and mated to the airframe; the mating took only one day.

The sleek, silver shape of the NA–73X looked like 'the right stuff' and the builders felt that they were going to have a winner. Under the bullet-shaped cowling, the Allison had been tested at over 1,100 hp. Allison engineers

Line-up of P–51s at Inglewood. AG459, the fifteenth Mustang Mk I, is in Army markings in the foreground. (NAA/73–80–112)

With the addition of dive brakes in the wing and bomb racks, the Mustang became the A–36A Invader attack bomber. Funds for 500 aircraft were issued on 16 April 1942. The first A–36 was flown by Bob Chilton on 21 September 1942 (s/n 42–83663). Illustrated is an MTO A–36A (normally known generically as Mustang).

One of the first Mustang Mk Is of the RAF order shortly after rollout from North American. Four .30 caliber guns were installed in the wing and two .50 caliber Brownings in the lower cowling. (NAA/73–0–11)

had fixed the critical altitude for the power-plant at 11,000 ft and here lay the inherent weakness in the design of the engine. This critical altitude figure meant that the performance of the fighter would start to fall off, even at maximum war emergency power setting, at any altitude over 11,000 ft. This meant that enemy fighters with a higher altitude performance could pick and choose combat.

Early in October, the flight test crew had commenced the running-in of the engine. For hours, the big Allison would be run up to maximum power, allowed to idle, and then run up again. The engineer in the cockpit found the bellowing from the exhaust stacks quite uncomfortable and soon procured a set of homemade ear covers to avoid the onset of premature deafness. This 'prototype' hearing shield, of course, developed into the ear coverings that are now so commonly seen at any international jet airport.

The ground run-in of the Allison proceeded in a smooth manner with few problems cropping up, which was a bit of a miracle considering the number of new features in the radiator systems. Small leaks were easily taken care of, the Allison engine being well-exposed when the simple cowling was removed.

As time for the first flight drew close, NAA realized that, while they did have test pilots, they did not have a *fighter* test pilot. At that time there were several very well-known aviators who operated on a freelance basis and let their reputations pull in first-flight assignments on new high-performance aircraft. One of these gifted individuals was the colorful and outspoken Vance Breese. North American contracted, for a reportedly very large sum, with Breese to fly the NA–73X. It was not unusual, in those heady days of rapid aircraft development, for Breese to test hop one aircraft and then fly to the opposite coast to test fly another manufacturer's creation.

The morning of 26 October found the NA–73X parked out on the NAA ramp, its elegant lines looking more like those of a European racing machine than a combat aircraft.

Breese settled into the cockpit, strapped on his parachute and safety harness, went over a mental checklist and then hit the starter for the Allison. The propeller jerked a couple of times and then, with a brief flurry of smoke from the exhausts, the Allison kicked into smooth-running life.

Breese let the engine warm up and then, accompanied by sharp cracklings from the exhausts, began taxiing the prototype down the taxi way. Breese had to S-turn the NA–73X so that he could see what was in front of the long cowling that seemed to stretch out forever in front of the streamlined windshield surface,

the NA–73X looked the part of a finely tuned machine – its sleek lines bespoke strength and a lack of any aerodynamic fat.

Standing on the brakes, Breese advanced the throttle until the airframe was vibrating with the pure passion of mechanical power, and then popped the brakes and pointed the nose down the center line of the runway. After rolling a few feet, he pushed the throttle to full military power – kicking in right rudder to compensate for the immense torque. The NA–73X leapt forward, sucked up its landing gear and pointed its sleek nose into the California sky. The first flight was a sedate affair as Breese had no intention of quickly pushing the machine into any possibly dangerous flight regimes.

Breese, being an extremely cautious test pilot, kept the runway at Mines Field always within sight as he tested the aircraft for about 20 minutes. The performance, Breese found, exceeded all previous estimates. Breese headed the aircraft back towards the airfield and made a perfect landing.

Three more test flights were made by Breese before going on to other projects to which he was committed. Paul Balfour was assigned to the post of chief test pilot for the NA–73X and, before his death in the early 1970s, Breese made the statement that he had bet a certain amount of money against NAA officials that Balfour would crash the NA–73X on his first flight. Unfortunately, Breese won the bet.

During the early morning hours of 20 November, the ground crew readied the NA–73X for its fifth flight. Balfour climbed into the cockpit with the Allison already running. In a few minutes he was making speed runs over the field. He made several passes over the timing crew stationed on the airfield in order to verify correct airspeeds. As he pulled up for another run, the engine coughed and began to run ragged. The Allison had run fine during an earlier ground test according to mechanic Olaf T. Anderson, 'At about 5:40 am I warmed the engine up as is the usual procedure before the flight. Oil and Prestone temperatures were normal (oil 65 degrees C, Prestone 95 degrees C). Oil pressure and fuel pressure were normal at 1,800 to 2,000 rpm. Oil was 80 lb and fuel 13 lb. The engine was run for five minutes and then shut down. When I started the engine for Mr Balfour before takeoff, it was a little hard to start (the Allison representative said their engines have a tendency to do such).'

After a few moments of rough running Balfour found himself in an aircraft that suddenly had no power at all from the Allison – it had come to a complete stop. Balfour glanced at the instruments but nothing appeared to be amiss. The loss of altitude incurred during the sweeping turn prevented the pilot from getting

back to the runway. Balfour dumped the flaps and landing gear during the last portion of the turn and directed the aircraft towards a ploughed field just west of Lincoln Boulevard.

Suddenly turned glider, the NA–73X whistled onto the field in the correct landing attitude but at almost the exact instant that it touched down, its tires dug into the soft earth furrows and the NA–73X catapulted through the air to crash onto its back. The built-up structure behind the cockpit saved Balfour from being crushed and he lost no time in unfastening his harness and crawling out of the side window to safety. The glistening NA–73X lay in the field, twisted and broken with gasoline dripping from ruptured tanks.

The prototype had gone from being a sleek aircraft to a pile of crumpled aluminum in just a few minutes. Investigation of the crash revealed that the Allison had run dry when the selected tank had been allowed to run out of fuel.

North American and the British both agreed that, in spite of the crash, they had a winning aircraft and the accident was in no way the fault of the design. Many aviation historians have stated that the badly damaged prototype was scrapped after this incident and that further testing was taken up with the early aircraft coming off the new production line.

Actually, the prototype was not scrapped. It was carefully lifted out of the field by a crane and transported back to the North American hangar where it was stripped apart and rebuilt in a very short time. R. C. 'Bob' Chilton was hired as chief test pilot to replace the unfortunate Balfour and a study of his log books indicates that he flew the rebuilt NA–73X on 3 April for a one-hour familiarization flight from Mines Field. Chilton also recalls that the NA–73X had made between five to six flights in the hands of another pilot immediately after the rebuild. Chilton's logs give details of the remainder of the flights in the NA–73X. They are summarized as follows:

12 April fuel flow test
  one hour
17 April landing speed and fuel flow test
  one hour 20 minutes
24 May test of new engine
  one hour 15 minutes
26 May carb metering test
  one hour 15 minutes
27 May carb and fuel system tests
  25 minutes
29 May carb and fuel system tests
  50 minutes
31 May carb and fuel system tests
  50 minutes
 1 June carb and fuel system tests
  45 minutes

3 June carb and stability tests
50 minutes
21 June Prestone thermostat test
35 minutes
12 July wake survey
one hour 20 minutes
15 July wake survey (last flight)
one hour

Thus it can be seen that the NA-73X accumulated very few flight hours but it did firmly establish the theories of the NAA design team. Bob Chilton remarked that 'the NA-73X was a clean flying aircraft with no bad vices. It was quite pleasant in the air and handled very similar to the production articles.' Chilton had quite a bit of fighter experience in the Army Air Corps before coming to North American, flying the Boeing P-12 and P-26, Curtiss P-36 and other fighter types. His expertise in the fighter field enabled the engineers to incorporate changes that would be beneficial to the combat pilot.

'I recall that the NA-73X was just pushed to the side after it had been retired from its last flight,' stated Chilton. 'It probably ended up on the company's junk pile but I do not recall seeing it there. It was a very attractive machine and its aluminum skin glowed with constant waxing by George Mountain Bear Lane, an American Indian whose duty was to keep the airframe as clean and highly waxed as possible to pick up those few vital miles per hour.'

With the first aircraft coming off the production line, North American and the British decided to use these aircraft for continued testing. 'The old NA-73X was no longer representative of the design,' said Chilton. 'We had orders on our hands for hundreds of new aircraft and the NA-73X had served its purpose. It had established the trend for what I believe was the finest propeller-driven fighter ever built by any country,'

The production aircraft had been named the Mustang by the British. The Royal Air Force designated the first model the Mustang Mk I. Flight testing was continued with AG345, the first production aircraft, which was flown for the first time on 23 April 1941 by Louis Wait. The fact that NAA had established an effective production line for the fighter was something of a miracle in itself and a fact that has been overlooked. Besides building a few O-47s, the main manufacturing thrust of the company was the Texan/Harvard trainer. Copying the same efficient style of production, a line was set up in new buildings at Mines Field which would easily accommodate a flow of sub-assemblies that eventually turned into a complete fighter. The Spitfire was a very complex aircraft and not really suited for mass produc-

tion techniques, and it is remarkable that 22,000 were built. However, the Mustang was the opposite as the airframe was extremely simple in execution – almost like a large metal model aircraft – and ideally suited to cranking out in huge numbers. Kindelberger kept pressuring for an advanced construction line, probably realizing that the coming war and the Army's growing interest in the type would lead to many more orders.

Mines Field was a busy place in 1941, Texans, a few new Mustangs and the new B-25 Mitchell bomber were all vieing for space on the NAA ramp. Aircraft workers were being hired by the hundreds as the company rapidly expanded. The initial order for the Mustang I amounted to 320 machines, later growing to 620 fighters, and, as typical of military aircraft, the price would exclude engine, armament, radios, etc. What the RAF was getting was the basic airframe and, although everything else would be added on at the NAA factory, the British government was responsible for purchasing and supplying the remaining items. The basic price for the aircraft was not to exceed $40,000 – a price that makes today's Mustang collectors wince.

AG346, the second production Mustang Mk I, was the first to be shipped to Britain. Disassembled and stored in a stout wooden crate, the fighter safely completed the hazardous ocean voyage, arriving at Liverpool on 24 October 1941. The aircraft was taken to Speke for assembling and initial flight testing which confirmed the results that had been noted in California with the NA-73X and AG345. Many British test and combat pilots tried their hand with the new warplane and found it satisfactory in its designed role.

Speed was, of course, of the absolute importance and new Mustangs were quickly flight tested at Mines Field, inhibited, disassembled, crated and shipped to Britain. U-Boats and Focke-Wulf Fw 200 Condors made the convoy voyage less than restful and some of the crated aircraft never arrived, going to the bottom with their torpedoed vessels.

Several small modifications were made on combat-ready Mustangs by the British including slight changes in the air duct system and radiator air scoop but a combat-ready Mustang Mk I was found to be 35 mph faster at 15,000 ft (375 mph) than the standard Spitfire Mk V but, above 15,000 ft, performance rapidly fell away due to the design defects of the Allison which, without a form of supercharging, was strictly a low to medium altitude engine. Most combat over Europe took place at medium to high altitude, rendering the Mustang unsafe, like the Tomahawk.

Some Mustang Mk Is went to RAF Duxford for air combat testing and compared favorably

with the Spitfire at lower altitudes. Few vices were unearthed – the British pilots particularly liked the logical American cockpit layout compared to some of the British fighters. At Duxford, the Mustang Mk I was tested against a captured Bf 109E and it again came away with a distinct edge in combat testing but the *Emil* was no longer in production at this point and newer and more deadly *Luftwaffe* fighters were coming off the production line.

In view of the Mustang Mk I's low altitude restriction, the British decided to continue to use the Spitfire as the standard fighter. The Mustang Mk I was rejected by the RAF Fighter Command and sent off to the new Army Cooperation Command – or to the Russians. Established during December 1940, the ACC was to coordinate air/ground activities with the Army – a vital task that was neglected with disastrous results by the British Expeditionary Force. The Mustang Mk I, planners felt, would be ideal for the ACC since it was fairly heavily armed and very maneuverable, had more than a decent range and could really get moving at low altitude where it would be most needed by the Army. Up until the advent of the Mustang Mk I, the ACC had been equipped with Westland Lysanders and Curtiss Tomahawks, neither ideal for operations over Occupied Europe. The squadrons with these aircraft began converting to the Mustang Mk I, probably with considerable relief, and it was planned to equip 18 squadrons but only 16 were eventually so constituted.

No 26 Sqn was the first unit to equip completely with the Mustang but there was a distinct problem at hand: there was really nothing to do with the Army. Kicked out of Europe at Dunkirk, the British Army had been remanning, re-equipping, training and generally licking its wounds back in Britain but there was nowhere to go with the British Army since an invasion of Europe was still only a remote possibility. The Mustangs had to have something to do so they were sent on armed recon missions over the enemy coast. The aircraft, usually in pairs – one aircraft equipped with an F24 aerial camera behind the pilot's seat – would intrude at high speed, photographing enemy fortifications and installations. The non-camera equipped Mustang Mk I would cover the photo plane, trying to fend off any attacking fighters. Coming in low and at high speed usually surprised the Germans but the *Luftwaffe*'s deadly anti-aircraft units were capable of extracting a heavy toll. The first operation, dubbed POPULAR, took place on 10 May 1942 when a single Mustang flew over the French coast, checking out enemy positions and actually strafing an airfield and a train.

From the first mission, use of the Mustang

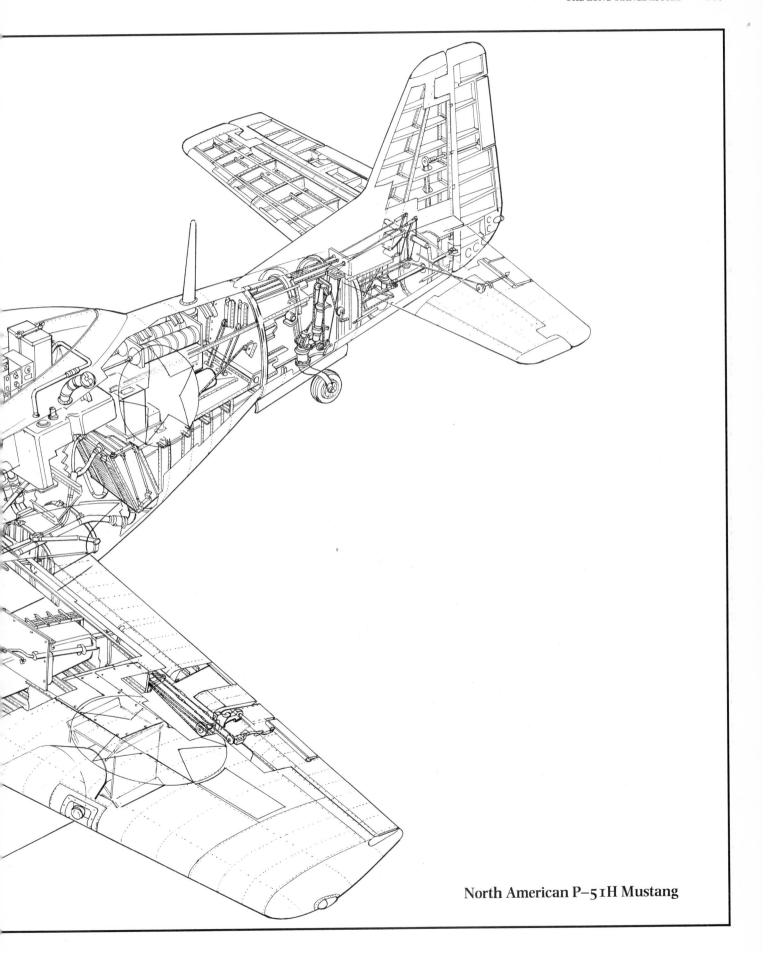

North American P–51H Mustang

Mk I began to intensify and the first aircraft was lost on 14 July when it flew into a target that it was strafing. This unpleasant incident was to be constantly repeated during the war. The combination of low-flying and high speed is extremely hazardous during war time and some pilots fell victim to 'target fixation' – a medical term that means the pilot becomes so intent on attacking his target that he literally flies into it, a victim of over-concentration. Heavy enemy flak was also an extreme hazard.

It appears that the honor of destroying the first enemy aircraft with a Mustang went to Flying Officer Hollis H. Hills of No 414 Sqn, a Canadian unit. Hills managed to bring down a low-flying Fw 190 that had attacked his wingman. Hills, oddly enough, was an American who had gone to Canada to fight and was a native of Los Angeles – birthplace of the fighter that he was flying.

The Mustang Mk Is actually did quite well when jumped by *Luftwaffe* fighters and, although they were primarily working in a recon/ground attack role, victories credited to the Mustang squadrons began to grow.

There were over 200 Mustangs in British service by October of 1942 and this number was in excess to ACC operations so Mustangs were sent on *Rhubarbs* – dangerous low-altitude search and destroy missions over enemy territory, 'down among the rhubarb', by pairs of aircraft. These aircraft fell under the orders of Fighter Command and were responsible for heavy destruction of enemy equipment and personnel.

The British eventually received 691 Mustangs from their original contracts. This number is arrived at because of losses at sea during shipping, the addition of a contract for 150 Mustang Mk IAs (equipped with four 20 mm cannon) and the addition of 50 USAAF P-51As to replace Mustangs 'borrowed' by the Americans from the production line.

The British Mustang Mk I squadrons fought through the war, serving long and hard and, with no further replacement Mustang Mk Is possible, steadily decreasing in numbers due to combat losses and accidents. The Mark I was unequalled for the low and fast recon and hit and run missions so vital to the war in Europe. The operation of these squadrons could alone fill a large volume. In June 1943, the remaining Mustang squadrons were assigned to the RAF's Fighter Command then to the 2nd Tactical Air Force in whose service they operated during the invasion of Europe. It is a sobering fact to note that, by the war's end, less than 100 Mustang Mks I or IA and P-51As were still operational. They had made an important contribution to the victory and became the first of the combat operational Mustangs, proving the type's worth.

THE MERLIN MUSTANG

It took an American airframe combined with a British engine to produce World War Two's greatest all-round fighter.

As mentioned previously, part of the American government's deal for the approval of production of the Mustang for the British was the handing over of two XP-51 aircraft from the British production run. These aircraft (the fourth and tenth) were free of charge but, instead of immediately subjecting the new type to extensive testing by qualified Army test pilots, they were shuttled about to different bases where they were flown by just about any pilot that wanted to take them up. However, the pre-War Army Air Corps was a small, elite bunch – not unlike the pre-War Royal Air Force – and word soon got around that this new fighter going to the British was a pretty interesting machine and certainly an improvement over the sluggish P-36 and P-35 fighters that most of the pilots were then flying.

Both XP-51s were at Wright Field, Dayton, Ohio, by the end of 1941. Wright Field, an historic location in the annals of aviation, was the Army's primary testing base for new aircraft and for aviation-related equipment. When the XP-51s arrived, it must be remembered that a vast new fleet of warplanes had been ordered by the Army and a wide range of these aircraft and their modified sub-types was being tested at Wright Field so it is not all that surprising that the two fighters were rather neglected.

Several detail changes were made to the two XP-51s including the modification and changing of the aileron brackets. Flying continued at off-and-on spurts. The pilots liked it but higher-ranking officers quite often seemed unaware of the type. Still, enough people kept pushing for the Army to develop and build the Mustang. However, on 7 July 1941, before the Army even started testing their aircraft, a curious event took place. The British were rapidly running out of ready money for their 'cash and carry' purchases of warplanes and equipment so, in a sweeping program that was to have profound effect, the American government created and instituted Lend-Lease. This concept would provide weapons to the British for minimal cash outlay, certain contractual concessions (America created virtually permanent bases in Britain) and the fact that the weapons would have to be either returned, paid for completely or destroyed at the conclusion of hostilities. Lend-Lease greatly increased Britain's 'purchasing power' and more orders poured into American factories – helping to wash away the last lingering traces of the Great Depression.

The Lend-Lease contract stipulated that the Army make the initial orders on Lend-Lease Mustangs for the British. On 7 July, a contract was placed for 150 of the new fighters. Intended for the British, the machines had the standard British armament deleted and four 20 mm cannons substituted. These fighters were known as Mustang Mk IAs by the RAF but the important fact is that fifty-five were kept by the Army, giving that service a solid Mustang base. Thus, Mustangs were actually being built for the Army even before the Army had evaluated the XP-51s to see whether they even wanted them!

The fact that the Army was not flooding North American with orders for the new warplane bothered Kindelberger considerably. He could see that rivals Lockheed and Curtiss were getting virtually everything that they wanted when it came to money for fighters so a new tactic was considered. Although it is not entirely within the scope of this book, the development of the A-36 is interesting because this aircraft helped to bring about the massive orders for the P-51 that the USAAF eventually placed. The effect of the *Luftwaffe*'s dive-bomber, or Stuka, forces had been horrifyingly portrayed across the country's newsreel screens. To the public, and perhaps the military, the dive-bomber was a terrifying threat that seemed unstoppable. Only experience would prove that the dive-bomber, although highly effective in its designed role, was at the mercy of a strong and forceful fighter force. America quickly realized that its armed forces were not equipped with this apparently so-effective weapon. Dutch and the design staff burned some of their famous midnight oil and, with a minimum number of modifications, converted the P-51 into a dive bomber. The Army loved the idea and ordered 500 of the machines on 16 April 1942. Equipped to take bombs, and with an effective dive brake in each wing, the new aircraft, designated A-36, was just what the Army wanted. Strangely enough, the modification worked and the A-36 became an extremely effective tool. It could deliver bombs right on target, was fast and had enough armament to defend itself. In fact, the A-36 became one of those aircraft that the Army wished they had ordered in considerably larger quantities for it fought until the end of the war when combat had depleted its numbers to almost nothing. The A-36 was named the Invader while the new P-51s for the Army were called Apaches but, fortunately to avoid confusion, these names were quickly dropped in 1942 and Mustang became the standard name.

America's precipitation into the war on 7 December 1941 had a very great impact upon the development of the Mustang. Virtually any sort of warplane was frantically being sought out and purchased. New versions of the Mustang were ordered and these included the P–51A which was basically similar to the P–51 but with cannons deleted and machine guns added. Many of these early Allison-powered aircraft were converted to photo-recon roles once they were in England, becoming F–6s. Other Allison aircraft were quickly shipped to India where they began compiling a heroic combat record with standard fighter units and with the Air Commando groups. It was quickly found that the Mustang could not dogfight with the Japanese aircraft but, below 10,000 ft, it had outstanding performance and could usually jump the enemy formations, shoot down some aircraft and then dive away

from pursuing fighters. However, above 10,000 ft performance began to fall off drastically because of the Allison's lack of horsepower at the higher altitudes. But the Mustang was performing excellent work and the combat bases wanted more. A critical supply situation developed.

The Army was to operate 819 Allison-powered Mustangs but this was nowhere near the number required and once these fighters were spread to training units, Britain, India and China the numbers of Mustangs operating in any one area became pitifully small. The Mustang was giving the Army what it wanted down low but at higher altitudes it was a victim of the Allison powerplant. Surely something could be done?

Looking back with the advantage of time and distance, it is surprising that the re-engining of the Mustang did not take place sooner. The fact that the P–51 *was* eventually re-engined came about from an almost one-man battle, a battle that was to radically change the course of World War Two.

Ronald W. Harker, who was in charge of test flying aircraft with Rolls-Royce engines for the famous company, had been invited to Duxford

Classic publicity photographs taken during March 1945 of pilots from the 353rd Fighter Group as they pose in front of Double Trouble Two, *a P–51D–20–NA 44–63684 flown by Lt Colonel William B Bailey. The Mustangs of the 350th Fighter Squadron were colorfully marked with yellow and black checkered noses and yellow rudders. (USAF/69528)*

The production of Merlin-powered Mustangs builds up at Inglewood. Testing of primered airframes is carried out under camouflage netting as more factory space is constructed. Note the four .50 caliber wing. (NAA)

to test fly one of the RAF's Mustang Mk I aircraft. Harker had heard about the fighter's good handling qualities so he quickly reported to the Air Fighting Development Unit where he tested AG422 on 30 April 1942. Even with the Allison, the Mustang was still an impressive machine and its handling qualities were better than the Spitfires which Harker was used to flying. More important, perhaps, was the fact that the Mustang had a huge capacity for fuel – three times that of the Spitfire Mk V. That the guns were close centered in the wing gave better accuracy which impressed Harker but the point that he remembered most strongly was that the Mustang, if perhaps combined with the fuel-thrifty Merlin, could strike from high altitude directly into the heart of Germany.

Full of enthusiasm, Harker returned to Rolls-Royce where he immediately began lobbying for a trial installation of a Merlin in a Mustang airframe. Rather surprisingly, his suggestion was not met with much interest, many of the British officials wishing to have little to do with an American-built aircraft. Harker persisted and managed to convince several high-ranking British and American officers of the feasibility of the project. Many of the senior officials at Rolls-Royce liked what Harker had to say for, if accepted, the engine change could result in a considerable increase in business. The director of R-R contacted several of his highly-placed friends and was able to convince Air Marshal Sir Wilfrid Freeman to send three Mustangs to the company's Hucknall facility for installation and modification.

Work progressed at a rapid pace with Rolls-Royce engineers performing much of the required detail work which included modified cowlings, motor mount and a revised cooling system. The first conversion flew on 13 October and housed a Merlin 65, the fighter having been designated Mustang Mk X. Serial AL975/G (the G indicated that the aircraft was a secret project and would have to be placed under constant guard) was piloted on the history-making flight by Captain R. T. Shepherd, Rolls-Royce's chief test pilot. AL975/G and the other two Mustangs chosen for the Merlin project were subject to constant modification and conversion as the company tried to meet the performance figures that the engineers had postulated. New propellers were tried, various modifications to superchargers undertaken, redesigns of the cowling and cooling system, and other detail modifications all led to an increasing performance and the realization that a truly long-range fighter was at hand.

Lt Colonel Thomas Hitchcock, American air attache in London, was a strong supporter of the Merlin modification and he wired officials in Washington and at North American of the success. Kindelberger, never particularly pleased with the Allison nor with the company's rather high-handed attitude toward North American, was more than pleased with the idea since the continued production of the Mustang was not an assured fact and a new engine offering greatly increased performance would certainly aid in obtaining further contracts from the Army. NAA design staff members were sent data from Rolls-Royce and

preliminary design work began on adapting the Merlin to a production line Mustang.

Rolls-Royce continued testing with their aircraft and a mock-up of a Griffon-powered Mustang was even undertaken. The Griffon, a larger, more powerful follow-on to the Merlin, was to be mounted in the middle of the fuselage, not unlike the Bell Airacobra, but the project never progressed past the mock-up and, unlike the Spitfire, the military Mustang was never to fly with the powerful Griffon V-12.

Negotiations were undertaken with Packard Motors for the license production of the Merlin in the United States and the lucrative contract was ideal for Packard who, as one of the nation's largest automobile makers, easily understood the basic principals of mass production of high-quality products. Continental Motors would also join the Merlin production plan as an additional source for the V-12 but the majority of American production would be handled by Packard.

North American's new Mustang would, because of the fairly radical design changes, get an equally new designation: XP-78. Two Mustang Mk IAs were drawn from the Ingle-

wood production line for conversion to carry the Packard V-1650-3 of 1,520 hp, the American system for designation of engines being entirely different from the British. While Merlin 65 would quickly identify the type of Merlin, the Americans preferred a longer designation: the V indicating the layout of the powerplant, the 1650 being the number of cubic inches, while the -3 stood for the type of modification to the basic engine. NAA produced a much more attractive installation for the Merlin than had Rolls-Royce modifications which were done more for quick testing than for production (although there were plans that, if the Americans did not care for the conversion, Rolls-Royce would set up a mini-assembly line to convert the RAF's serving Mustangs). Sleek stainless-steel covers wrapped around the exhaust stubs (a feature that was modified on production aircraft) while the air scoop blended gracefully with the lower portion of the cowling. An enlarged radiator air scoop held both the main radiator and the intercooler while the scoop itself was an excellent example of aerodynamic engineering. The airframe had been generally strengthened to accommodate the uprated

Lt Walter Goehausen (later Captain) in the cockpit of his P-51B-10-NA in which he scored a number of victories while with the 308th FS, 31st FG, 15th Air Force. Goehausen flew a total of 61 long-range Mustang missions during which he destroyed ten German aircraft including six Bf 109s, three Fw 190s and one Ju 88. Three of the Bf 109s were destroyed during one fighter mission over southern France. Goehausen was sent back to the United States where he became an instructor in Mustangs. He is currently a Boeing 747 captain with Pan American Airways. (National Archives/ 208-AA-113GG-2)

engine while new ailerons had been installed, although they were at this point still fabric covered. The prototype was also fitted with a four-blade Hamilton Standard Hydromatic propeller which was 11 ft 2 in in diameter. Armament would consist of four or six Browning .50 caliber guns in the wing although one of the XP-78s retained four 20 mm cannon.

Painted in standard Army Olive Drab and Neutral Grey, the first Inglewood Merlin Mustang flew on 30 November 1942 but, by this time, General Hap Arnold, convinced that the new fighter would be splendid, had placed orders on behalf of the Army for over 2,200 of the new warplanes, firmly setting North American on the path to becoming one of America's greatest fighter firms. The Army had had a

*E*xtremely well-worn F–6C (P–51B–1–NA) carries the name **Hun Flusher** and an impressive score board of reconnaissance missions. Flown by C. W. Kinyon, ZM*J was assigned to the 12th Reconnaissance Squadron, 67th Reconnaissance Group, 9th Air Force. White spinner and nose band served as a recognition aid.

*M*ixture of bare metal and camouflaged P–51Bs and Cs photographed at a 14th AF base in China on 16 August 1944. The Merlin-powered Mustang was a distinct improvement over the types it replaced. (USAF/69118)

speed was 441 mph, over 50 mph faster than the Allison variants, and just this factor would have made the P–51B a winner, but performance also increased in every other category. The wing had been strengthened to bear two pylons that could each carry 1,000 lb – a bomb or a drop tank. Testing of the XP–51Bs proceeded rapidly and the production line was soon in motion, production units having minor changes for the airframe and a major change in the cowling which streamlined the carburetor air scoop even further. The different airframe of the P–51B supplanted the early Mustangs on the line and production went fairly smoothly but the flow of Packard engines to NAA moved slowly at first, some airframes having to wait up to six weeks before receiving Packard-built Merlins. Packard went on to eliminate the flow problem and engines were soon reaching the production lines in time to be mated with the airframes.

First production P–51Bs were tested against other Army fighters to find out if the new Mustang was as good as everybody had hoped. Testing found out that the laminar flow airfoil was greatly affected by the marring of the leading edge finish of the wing. Any gaps in the wing's construction were filled on the production line with a special sealer and then sanded flush to achieve the desired airflow but GIs in size 12 combat boots quickly scuffed and chipped the surface as they serviced the Mustang and reloaded the guns.

The conclusions of Army Air Forces Board Project No. (M–1) 50 are set out below:

The P–51B, from sea level to 11,000 ft, is some seven to ten miles per hour slower than the P–51A which is the fastest fighter at this altitude. Between 14,000 and 22,000 ft, the P–51B is about fifteen to twenty mph faster. From 22,000 ft the P–51B, in high blower, widens this speed advantage up to seventy-five mph at 30,000 ft. From sea level, the P–51B gradually gains on the P–38J and the P–47D until, at 16,000 ft, it has a speed of about 420 mph which is about ten mph faster than the P–38J and about twenty mph faster than the P–47D. Above 27,000 ft, the P–51B can no longer get war emergency power, but its speed of about 430 mph at 30,000 ft is equal to that of the P–47D and about twenty mph faster than the P–38J, both using war emergency power. The P–51B is capable of 400 mph at 40,000 ft.

The P–51B is by far the best climbing aircraft of all current American fighters. It takes about 4.5 minutes to get to 15,000 ft as against five minutes for the P–38J and about seven minutes for the P–47D. The P–51B maintains a lead of about .5 minute over the P–38J to 30,000 ft and reaches that altitude in about eleven minutes which is about 6.5 minutes faster than the P–47D.

In zooming the P–51B with the P–47D from level flight at cruising and high speeds, and from high speeds out of dives, the P–51B gains speed rapidly and leaves the P–47D far behind. In zooming, the P–51B with the P–38J, from level flight at crusing speed, the fighters climb evenly at the start. How-

change of mind and both prototypes were redesignated again as XP–51Bs, causing some minor confusion. In order to accommodate the increased orders, because of NAA's rapid expansion with the Mustang, Mitchell bomber and Texan trainer, an increase in size of the Inglewood facility, the building of a new Dallas plant, which produced virtually identical aircraft known as P–51Cs, and yet another newly built plant in Tulsa, Oklahoma resulted.

The actual performance of the XP–51B came out better than the engineers had predicted, an unusual aeronautical event. Top

ever, the P–51B falls off while the P–38J keeps climbing. In zooms from high speeds (425 indicated air speed), the P–51B pulls away from the P–38J and its zoom ends considerably higher.

The diving characteristics of the P–51B are superior to those of any other fighter plane. It is exceptionally easy to handle and requires very little trimming. The P–51B dives away from all other fighters except the P–47D, against which the P–51B loses several hundred feet ahead in the initial pushover and then holds that position, apparently neither gaining nor losing distance.

The new seal-balanced ailerons of the P–51B give the fighter a faster rate of roll at all speeds than any other fighter except the P–47D with which it is equal at cruising speeds.

The search view of the P–51B is better than in the P–51A but is still obstructed above, to both sides, and to the rear, by the canopy construction. The view forward over the nose is considerably improved over the P–51A by the relocation of the carburetor air intake scoop, the elimination of the clear view panel on the left side of the windshield, and lowering of the nose of the engine one and one-half degrees.

The fighting qualities of the P–51B were compared with those of the P–47D–10 and the P–38J–5 and, briefly, with the P–39N–0 and the P–40N. The only maneuver the P–39 and P–40 have that is superior to the P–51B, is a slight advantage in a turning circle. In all other maneuvers, as well as performance, they are both far inferior. The P–51B has good performance at all altitudes, but above

20,000 ft the performance improves rapidly, and its best fighting altitude is between 25 and 35,000 ft. The rate of climb is outstanding, with an average of about 3,000 ft per minute from sea level to 25,000 ft. Above 20,000 ft, the overall fighting qualities of this aircraft are superior to those of all the other types used in the trials.

Now that the much-improved P–51B/C was in production, the main problem was to get as many aircraft to the battlefronts as soon as possible in order to counter the threats posed by new variants of German fighters. Another assembly line was set up at Inglewood – actually 'disassembly' would be a more accurate term – for the breaking down, packing and crating of Mustangs destined for combat. In Britain the USAAF's 354th Fighter Group was chosen to be the first unit to operate the P–51B. After having trained on Bell Airacobras, the Fighter Group embarked in a ship for Britain, minus Airacobras, and arrived on 20 October 1943 as part of the new 9th Air Force. Initial base for the 354th was Greenham Common and it was here that the Mustangs arrived on 11 November.

After the briefest of introductions, aircraft

and crews were sent to the base at Boxted in Essex to prepare for combat missions into occupied Europe. American day bombers had been taking a savage, almost unacceptable, beating at the hands of the *Luftwaffe*. Unescorted raids by 8th Air Force Boeing B–17 Flying Fortresses were being attacked by everything the Germans could get into the air and the Forts, as well-armed as they were, simply could not stand up to the terrific punishment. Ten percent was a common loss factor during the heavy bomber missions and it quite often went higher over targets that were particularly strategic to the German war effort.

The P–51B had an excellent internal fuel capacity but to stretch the fighter's 'legs' even further, a variety of drop tanks was developed

P–51D–20–NAs of the 45th Fighter Squadron, 15th Fighter Group, are seen here escorting Boeing B–29 Superfortresses on the way to Japan. The Mustang's exceptional range combined with the Packard Merlin's reliability meant the Superfortresses could be escorted to and from their epic raids on the Japanese Home Islands. (USAF/57587)

This photograph was taken at a 14th Air Force base in South China just before the field was evacuated and buildings and damaged aircraft blown up to prevent capture by rapidly advancing Japanese on 19 November 1944. The Japanese advances in Central and South China took Americans by surprise. This P-51B carries fearsome tiger's teeth applied over the Olive Drab and Neutral Grey camouflage. Spinner is bare metal. (USAF/56349)

– these being mounted on the pylons under the wing. With fuel consumption running around 65 US gallons an hour (giving a four hour and 45 minute endurance on internal fuel), the Mustang would fall 110–115 US gallons short of the required six-hour mission with the 30 minute reserve that the Army desired for long-range escort fighters. The Mustang did, however, have the lowest fuel consumption rate of any of the Army fighters including the P–47D (140 gph) and P–38J (144 gph).

Development of the drop tank soon became a fine science with aerodynamic tests to ensure that an empty tank would drop cleanly away from the wing and not rise back up in the airflow to strike the airframe. Motion picture cameras were used to record the dropping of a variety of different tanks to make sure that this would not happen since a fighter could easily be knocked down by its own stray drop tank. Subcontractors began to produce tanks in different capacities and out of different materials. A compressed paper unit, pioneered by the British, was particularly useful but the more standard unit was a 75 gallon tank made out of aluminum. Production of the tanks reached a high of 48,000 units during the month of June 1944.

Another method of extending the Mustang's range was to mount an 85 US gallon tank in the fuselage behind the pilot and the last 550 Bs built had the tank as standard, most other aircraft being field modified. This tank increased the internal fuel capacity to 269 US gallons but it also brought some undesirable side effects such as reducing climb, changing the center of gravity and making the controls sluggish above 25,000 ft. However, as the tank was emptied, the Mustang's characteristics once again became normal. The internal tankage, combined with wing fuel tanks, gave the Mustang an amazing radius of action – one that was far beyond the pilot's bladder.

Tactics for the deployment and operation of the P-51B also had developmental problems. Some of the commanders saw the Mustang as an integral part of the bomber formation. Fighters would fly directly with the bombers, their speed severely limited, spark plugs packing up with lead deposits from the low rpm and pilots completely restricted to defensive rather than offensive tactics. German fighters would have the advantage of speed when attacking the bombers and they would also know that

Mustang pilots would not pursue them, merely trying to turn away the attacks.

As pilots of the 354th became more experienced with their new mounts, the first operational mission took place on 1 December as Lt Colonel Don Blakeslee, a proponent of the P–51, led a sweep of the 'Pioneer Mustang Group', as the unit had become known, on a mission over occupied Belgium to familiarize the men with the combat characteristics of the 'B. The Mustang's main role, that of bomber escort, started on 5 December when the Mustangs joined with the Fortresses for a mission into Germany. Operational control of the 354th had been handed over to the 8th Air Force for the bomber escort missions. The first victory over an enemy aircraft did not occur until 16 December when a Bf 110 twin-engine fighter fell to the guns of a 355th FS Mustang. Long-range missions soon became standard and the many problems of operating for hours at high altitude had to be faced – everything from oxygen starvation to the freezing of certain oils and greases. All these problems

were eventually overcome, usually by Yankee ingenuity, but they did cause problems and either delayed or scrubbed some missions.

Pilots and crew chiefs discovered that the problem of fouled plugs could usually be eliminated by the application of power every 15 minutes. These bursts of power would cleanse the plugs and the engine would resume normal running. The windshield had a tendency to collect ice at high altitude and thus hamper vision. Coolant losses were also experienced at high altitude, meaning that the engine would begin to heat up and that the fighter would have to return to a friendly field as quickly as possible before the engine seized. Ammunition belts had a tendency to jam the machine guns during high G maneuvers but, as irritating as they were, most malfunctions were fixed in the field by crew chiefs and engineers, and NAA field representatives passed the information back to the factory where modifications were incorporated into the production line.

The direct linking of the fighters to the

bombers ceased on 6 January 1944 when Lt General James Doolittle took over command of the 8th Air Force. Doolittle, hero of the B–25 attack on Tokyo, immediately saw the problem inherent with not letting fighters roam to pursue and destroy the enemy. He quickly changed the standing orders and the Mustang pilots were now free to attack and destroy the *Luftwaffe* before and after the German fighters attacked the Fortresses and Liberators.

The freeing of the Mustangs to attack the attackers meant that scores rapidly began to rise. Many pilots quickly became aces in the Mustangs during the early months of 1944 as heavy air combat raged across the skies of Europe. As more Mustangs arrived from the factories (P–51Cs had been coming off the Dallas line since August 1943), new groups were rapidly formed and other groups discarded the heavy Thunderbolt for the nimble Mustang. The 357th Fighter Group became the second Mustang unit, flying out of Leiston in February 1944. The third P–51B/C group was the 363rd FG, flying out of Rivenhall, which also became operational in late February. The famous 4th FG traded in their Jugs and were also operational in February, flying

out of Debden. Thus the power and influence of the Mustang quickly began to spread. General Adolph Galland stated that 'the Mustang was the best Allied fighter – perhaps the best of any fighters – of the Second World War. It was a respected and dangerous adversary.' While awaiting trial as a war criminal, Herman Göring claimed that he knew the war was lost when he saw 'American fighters over Berlin.' The mission to Berlin, perhaps the most feared of all the missions flown by Allied airmen, was achieved by Mustangs on 3 March 1944 as they escorted bombers to the target – a trip of over 1,000 miles – through heavy flak barrages, rockets and swarms of enemy fighters. The Mustangs completed the mission and, from that moment on, the long-range fighter had become a reality for the USAAF.

The Royal Air Force was also interested in the P–51B. Very pleased with their earlier Mustangs when operated within their limitations, the RAF pilots were anxious to see what this combination of American airframe with British engine was all about. The P–51B/C in British service was to be known, logically, as the Mustang Mk III. Virtually identical to their USAAF counterparts, except for some special

British equipment, the first Mark IIIs were assigned to No 122 Wing at RAF Gravesend in December 1943. The wing was composed of Nos 19, 65 and 122 Sqns – all of which had previously been flying Spitfires. The British had some of the same problems as did the USAAF as they pressed their Mustangs into service but, at this point, they were not overly concerned about long-range escort missions since their Lancaster and Halifax 'bomber streams' headed to Germany at night and trusted in the cloak of darkness for a modicum of protection. The USAAF demand for the Mustang was such that some RAF Mustang Mark IIIs were 'borrowed' and pressed into American service while the direct aid of the RAF Mustang squadrons was

The classic lines of the North American P–51D in flight. USAAF s/n 44–13926, a P–1D–5–NA built at Inglewood, wears the code E2*S indicating the Mustang was assigned to the 375th Fighter Squadron, 361st Fighter Group. The Insignia Yellow spinner and cowl band were carried by the unit's Mustangs starting in May 1944. The 361st was activated on 10 February 1943 in Richmond, Virginia, and arrived at Bottisham, England, on 30 November 1943 with P–47 Thunderbolts. Mustangs arrived during May 1944 and the 361st racked up 226 German aircraft destroyed in the air with 105 more victories over aircraft on the ground, losing 81 P–47s and P–51s in the process. The 361st had a dozen aces. (USAAF)

often requested during the early long-range missions.

Since the RAF Mustang MK IIIs were usually not needed for any very long-range duties, tactics soon switched to missions that included hit and run raids on Occupied Europe. Mustang Mk III combat missions started during mid-February 1944, as No 122 Wing aircraft raided French ports. One of the main complaints from the British pilots was that the Mustang III suffered from poor vision. Hampered by its 1930's canopy design, the Mustang's combat vision was indeed poor but British engineers at Boscombe Down, the UK

equivalent to Wright Field, designed a one-piece Perspex canopy unit that greatly improved visibility. Called the Malcolm Hood, after its designer, the new unit replaced the built-up, side-hinging canopy structure and was moved back and forth on rails installed on the sides of the fuselage for entry. The one-piece plexiglass canopy was considerably bulged on all sides and was a distinct improvement. Most RAF Mustang Mk IIIs were retrofitted with the Malcolm Hood and many units found their way to the USAAF squadrons. Visibility during high-speed aerial combat was a prime requisite for victory and the search for improved vision was not yet over.

Mustangs were not reserved for operations exclusively out of Britain. Early in 1944, 15th Air Force units in Italy began to receive P–51B/Cs as did Royal Air Force units there. Combat over Italy was by no means less deadly than combat over France and Germany but units in Italy had been a bit neglected, not always receiving the most modern of aircraft

and the Mustang went a long way in helping to rectify this slight.

The skies over China soon became home to Merlin Mustangs as the fighters started equipping units of the 14th Air Force during April 1944. The 14th, separated by 'the Hump' from more normal supply routes, waged a tough battle against a foe that would not give ground while alive. The threatening terrain over which they flew also meant that if a pilot had to bail out his chances at surviving were not good. The Mustang pilots of the 14th were usually hardened individuals, many veterans of the early days with the Flying Tigers, and their Mustangs reflected this glorious past, their cowlings elaborately painted with fierce mouths and glaring eyes.

Back at the main factory in Inglewood, work continued on producing improvements that would make the Mustang a better warplane. A wide variety of underwing armaments, from rockets to bombs to smoke producing canisters, were tested. Updates were con-

Fabulous line-up photograph of the aircraft flown by the 8th AF group commanders. Gentle Annie, MC*R, is from the 79th FS, 20th FG. Receiving Mustangs in July 1944, the 20th destroyed 212 Luftwaffe aircraft in the air, another 237 on the ground, and losing 132 aircraft in combat. (USAF)

stantly added to the production line and a new variation in the form of the F–6C was created by modifying P–51B/Cs into tactical reconnaissance aircraft. The F–6C carried the regular armament but it had the interior of the fuselage modified to house a variety of aerial cameras that were able to photograph targets from ports built into the side of the fuselage. This turned out to be a very popular modification with the photo recon pilots since they could defend themselves against hostile aircraft, unlike the unarmed Lockheed F–5 Lightning that had to rely on height and speed to outrun the enemy.

Throughout the early and middle stages of the war, much consideration had been given on how to camouflage aircraft effectively. Each warring nation had its own ideas; the *Luftwaffe* had complex patterns for their fighters, the Royal Air Force stayed with traditional two-tone upper camouflage, the French had an attractive blending of a wide variety of colors and the American Army settled on the unat-

tractive Olive Drab and Neutral Grey. Each slight increment in top speed usually meant that a better advantage over the enemy could be achieved. Much study was given to the composition of the camouflage colors and their surfaces. Early RAF tests showed that a Mustang Mk I painted with gloss, rather than matte, paint did not really show much of a speed advantage plus it took a considerable number of man hours to keep the finish glossy while the fighter flew from an operational base. Back in the States, testing revealed that a P–51 with its finish sanded and then highly polished would go 21 mph faster than before. This figure caused quite a stir in the USAAF and a small testing program was undertaken whereby a variety of Army aircraft were sanded and highly polished to see how much extra speed could be obtained. The results were very disappointing, an average of a few mph higher was achieved but nothing like the tests with the Mustang. On investigation, it was discovered that the test Mustang had an

extremely poor finish to begin with and was actually flying slower than it should have been before being polished. During a war the Army had considerable manpower at its disposal but it certainly could not waste thousands of hours of airmen's time by constantly polishing combat planes, especially the large bombers.

The next step that the Army considered was stripping all paint off its combat aircraft. By late 1943, enemy attacks on Allied airfields were fairly rare and the value of the camouflage was becoming questionable. There would be a small weight saving with the deletion of the paint but this would not really matter since the vast horsepower reserves of a Mustang would not notice the minor weight savings. However, natural metal aircraft would be easier to maintain since the matte camouflage colors constantly faded, chipped and stained. The natural metal finish also picked up a few mph since it was cleaner. Thus, in late 1943, the Army decided to eliminate the standard Olive Drab and Neutral Grey in favor of natural metal and, by early 1944, fighters were leaving the production lines in gleaming natural aluminum finish.

For the Mustang this new order presented a bit of a problem. To get the desired effects from the laminar flow airfoil, the leading edge of the Mustang's wing had to be filled with a special putty and then carefully sanded to achieve as smooth a finish as possible. The putty would be protected to a degree by the layer of camouflage paint but would be exposed to the elements with its deletion. It was decided to continue the filling and sanding process on the wing and then to spray paint the leading edge (about the first forty percent of the wing) with an aluminum varnish or lacquer, leaving the remaining sixty percent unpainted. In practice it was quite often easier to paint the entire wing and photographs will show combat Mustangs with natural metal fuselages and aluminum painted wings.

As the bare metal Mustangs began arriving at combat units, they looked rather out of place among the darkly-painted combat-stained veterans. Mixed flights of camouflaged and natural metal aircraft were quite common up until the end of the fighting in Europe. The Pacific was another matter since most of the Mustangs being delivered to this theater were of the later, uncamouflaged aircraft. The Army feared that Pacific salt corrosion would play

Red tail stripes signify the 308th FS, 31st FG. American Beauty has a red spinner and stripe around the cowl. Flown by Captain Voll, it carries a tally of 21 victories. (USAF)

*In-flight study of VF*L, a P–51D–5–NA, s/n 44–13961, operated by the 336th FS, 4th FG. The 4th was the only American unit activated in a combat theatre. This event took place on 12 September 1942, when the RAF's three Eagle Squadrons were taken over by the USAAF. The 4th began flying Mustangs in February 1944. The 4th had been the first FG to penetrate German airspace, on 28 July 1943 when the 4th flew a deep penetration mission with its Thunderbolts. By the end of the war, the 4th had destroyed 583.5 German aircraft in the air and a further 469 on the ground. The 4th lost 241 Mustangs and Thunderbolts during 2½ years of aerial combat. (USAF)*

havoc with the unprotected aluminum but very little corrosion was encountered with aircraft in service although this may well have changed if the Pacific War had gone on longer.

In a quest for improved combat vision, P–51B–1–NA 43–12102 was pulled from the Inglewood line and considerably modified to carry a bubble or 'teardrop' canopy. Test pilot Bob Chilton did most of the test flying on this aircraft during September 1943 and found the vision to be greatly improved but, oddly, because the modification looked so streamlined, the top speed and rate of climb were both a bit down. It was found, through wind tunnel

testing, that the built-up turtle deck rear fuselage of the P–51B/C actually offered improved streamlining but the mph loss was greatly offset by the wonderful visibility.

The bubble canopy was incorporated on a new version of the Mustang, the P–51D, and this variant was built in the largest numbers of any Mustang. Inglewood built 6,502 P–51Ds while Dallas cranked out 1,454 Ds and Ks (the K being virtually identical to the D). The new version of the Mustang would have many modifications that came about from experience in the field. The cowling was slightly changed and simplified, the landing gear modified, a V–1650–7 of 1,695 hp (war emergency rating) was installed, wing armament was standardized on six .50 caliber Brownings, the 85 US gallon fuselage tank was also standard and some airframe strengthening was also incorporated.

The D production line was also updated and a dorsal fin was added to the vertical fin to make up for lost keel area through the deletion of the turtleback. The early Ds had experienced some longitudinal stability problems so the new fin was necessary and was retrofitted in the field to the early Ds. The two underwing pylons remained standard but later production Ds were also fitted with five rocket rails under each wing so that a total of ten of the very effective 5 in High Velocity Aircraft Rockets (HVAR) could be carried. A strengthened wing handled the extra load.

The first P–51Ds were sent to Britain and dispersed to squadron and wing commanders who needed the better visibility for guiding their flights. There was a bit of sparring since the earlier aircraft could outclimb and outspeed the commander's new aircraft but the difference was fractional – about five mph difference between the two models. After the initial arrivals, the P–51Ds quickly began to flow from the Army's depots in Ireland and Northern England to the combat units. The depots received the aircraft from the factory, assembled them, stripped off all the protective coatings, tested the engines and test flew the aircraft to make sure they were airworthy after the ocean voyage. Latest modifications were usually added at these depots and the Mustangs were brought up to combat standard and then flown, sometimes by female ferry pilots, to the operational bases. This system worked quite well as it made sure that the aircraft delivered to an operational squadron was as combat-fit as possible although there certainly was no guarantee that a mechanical failure would not ground the aircraft shortly after arrival. If an engine went unserviceable, the squadron mechanics could usually have the Merlin removed overnight and a new one installed and running by the morning. This

assembly-line method of getting the aircraft to front-line bases and keeping them running was a major contributing factor to the Allies' victory.

Now that Mustang escort flights were common practice, many pilots turned their attention to the *Luftwaffe*'s airfields. Why not attack the airfields and destroy the enemy on the ground or at least render their airfields and hangars unserviceable? The idea appealed to Jimmy Doolittle and other commanders, so some P–51 squadrons were released to rampage over Europe, attacking enemy airfields and other targets of opportunity. The P–51D enjoyed a bit of an advantage with its six guns but it was still behind the P–47D Thunderbolt's massive eight-gun armament. The Mustangs did a great deal of damage in these raids but they also began to pay a heavy price, losing more aircraft in ground attack than in aerial combat. The *Luftwaffe* took the defense of their airfields very seriously and the fields were usually heavily ringed with anti-aircraft weapons manned by experienced *Luftwaffe* crews. The Germans had developed anti-aircraft fire into a fine art and many Mustangs were literally shot to pieces or blown out of the air by direct hits from the deadly and effective

88 mm cannon. During these low-level attacks, the vulnerability of the Mustang's cooling system became readily apparent and flak or shrapnel hits in the radiator or maze of cooling tubes often meant that a Mustang pilot would be trading his low-altitude speed for height as he zoomed for altitude, his stricken fighter trailing a sickly white stream of glycol as he struggled for the canopy release and a trip by 'silk elevator' right into the hands of the Germans. Other pilots were not so lucky and flew into the ground at over 400 mph when part of their aircraft's controls were damaged or shot off. The weakness of the cooling system did not make the Mustang an ineffective ground attack machine but its losses did go up considerably, as they did for every type of fighter employed in this hazardous pastime. Other machines such as the Thunderbolt were really better suited for the mission and could absorb more damage. Still, Mustang pilots often returned to Britain with chunks of telephone poles embedded in their wings or wires trailing from their tail surfaces – testimony of just how low they had pressed their attacks.

Mustang pilots would find themselves on seven to eight-hour bomber escort missions one day and then on sea-level attacks on

George Preddy had a slow start on what was to become one of the most distinguished combat careers in the USAAF. Originally assigned to the 49th FG in the Southwest Pacific, Preddy was sent back to the States after a mid-air collision in July 1942. In July 1943, Preddy was sent to England with the 352nd Fighter Group where he flew Thunderbolts. While flying P–47s, Preddy destroyed two enemy aircraft but was forced to jump into the Channel after his flak damaged P–47 could not make it all the way back to England. When the 352nd began to receive Mustangs in the spring of 1944, Preddy really started to come into his own as a top fighter pilot. While flying blue-nosed Mustangs, all named Cripes A' Mighty, Preddy racked up 26.83 aerial victories. His rising score was to be stopped not by the Germans but by his own allies. Preddy was chasing an Fw 190 near Coblenz on Christmas Day 1944, when American ground forces in the area opened up on the low-flying German but their shells smashed into Preddy's Mustang which crashed and exploded. Preddy is seen in the photograph after returning from his 6 August 1944 mission when he shot down six Bf 109s. (USAF/54992)

U.S. ARMY P-51B-10-NA
SERIAL NO. AAF42-106435
CREW WEIGHT 200 LBS

SERVICE THIS AIRPLANE WITH
GRADE 100/130 FUEL. IF NOT
AVAILABLE T.O. DG-3-1 WILL BE
CONSULTED FOR EMERGENCY ACTION
SUITABLE FOR AROMATIC FUEL

***B**ob Chilton, dean of the Mustang test pilots, prepares to take a P-51B up on a short test flight. Chilton became head of the flight test division at NAA and built up over 3,000 hours flying Mustangs. Some days would see Chilton taking as many as ten fighters into the air for checkouts. Bob flew every version of the P-51 but liked the experimental lightweight Mustangs the best because of their high speed and superb handling qualities. (NAA)*

airfields the next. The *Luftwaffe* was being mauled at this point even though German industry was producing increasing numbers of fighters. New German fighter pilots were poorly trained and easy prey for the Mustangs but the experienced German pilots were another matter and many of these aces had *dozens* of Mustangs to their credit.

The Germans were rapidly developing new technology weapons and the Me 262 jet fighter and Me 163 rocket attack aircraft were two machines that gave the Mustang trouble. Allied intelligence had reported that the Germans were developing a jet fighter and it

seemed that the Mustang, with its high top speed, would be the best Allied fighter to tackle the new threat. Me 262s, never available in considerable strength and mistakenly assigned to the ground attack role by Hitler, were often met and defeated by Mustangs, although the Mustang's performance would often be stretched beyond the breaking point and P-51s would return home with popped rivets and deformed airframes. Mustangs would also wait near the jet fighters' home bases and pounce on them as they landed or took off. Still, the jet was superior to the Mustang and, if it had been developed earlier and its technical problems overcome, the outcome of the air war certainly could have been different.

The Me 163 was produced in even smaller numbers than the 262 and the rocket-powered aircraft was plagued with problems but it could blast bomber formations and its very high speed and small size made it an almost impossible target for Mustang pilots.

The P-51D rapidly became the supreme

fighter over Europe. As deliveries from the factories increased, the USAAF eventually re-equipped all but 15 of its Fighter Groups with the bubble-top Mustang. This gave a total of 42 squadrons operating the P-51D!

P-51D squadrons really began to stretch the Mustang's already long range with missions to European targets which terminated in Russia, escorting American bombers. The Russians, never the best of hosts – even to Allied pilots who were directly aiding the Russian fight for survival – eyed the Mustang and bomber pilots with suspect looks and kept them virtually prisoners until it was time for the crews to head back on the long return flights. The Russians demanded large numbers of Mustangs but, perhaps fortunately, only small numbers were supplied to the Soviets.

The P-51D soon showed its outstanding escort capabilities in the Pacific – an area where the Mustang units would have to operate over thousands of miles of uncharted and hostile waters and where engine failure meant almost certain death. The new Boeing B-29 Superfortress bomber held considerable promise for devastating the Japanese home islands but the USAAF knew that the air battles over the islands would be ferocious and that the Mustang's excellent combat qualities would be sorely needed. The American policy of island-hopping had meant that new airfields were frantically being built by Naval Construction Battalions even before the islands were totally secure. The SeaBees built giant runways that could accommodate the Superfortresses and attacks against the home islands were soon underway. The level of damage caused to the enemy even exceeded the USAAF's most optimistic reports. Japanese housing and factories were of a decidedly flimsy nature and the fire storms caused by the Superfortresses' incendiary bombs literally burned away the hearts of many Japanese cities.

With the large drop tanks, Mustangs regularly flew escort missions of over 2,000 miles and provided valuable escort for the big bombers. Early Superfortresses were plagued with engine problems and Mustangs were often called on to escort B-29s with engines out and fend off attacks by Japanese fighters who were hoping to pick off the stragglers.

The result of the deadly battle for control of a miserable little island named Iwo Jima eventually meant that the USAAF would be able to establish a major airfield that would be able to recover damaged B-29s on the way back from Japan and launch more Mustangs for missions over the home islands. By the end of the war in Japan, Mustangs were regularly patrolling over Japan and meeting and defeating the best the enemy had to offer.

LIGHTWEIGHT MUSTANGS

The lightweight Mustang air superiority fighters offered very high performance but were design exercises that led to the last Mustang – the P–51H.

As with earlier Mustangs, the P–51D was subject to changes and improvements on the production line and several new variants were built, including the TP–51D, a two-seat dual control trainer with an enlarged cockpit canopy that was produced in very small numbers, and the F–6D, the tactical recon version of the P–51D/K.

Even though the P–51D was an excellent aircraft, new versions of the Mustang were being planned. One scheme involved navalizing the Mustang for operation from carriers in the Pacific. Testing was carried out with a Mustang equipped with a tail hook and, although the trials were satisfactory, it was

decided that the Navy would stay with the Corsair and Hellcat.

'In order to test optimum performance with the Mustang design,' recalls test pilot Bob Chilton, 'it was decided to proceed with the development of a series of lightweight Mustangs.' The Mustang series was one of the lightest fighter aircraft in quantity production in America during the war. When compared to the monstrous Thunderbolt at a loaded weight of 21,200 lb (N model) or the twin-engined Lockheed Lightning at 20,300 lb (H model), the P–51D was absolutely slim with a loaded weight of 11,600 lb. However, the North American designers realized the benefits of increased weight savings, in terms of longer range, higher altitude, higher speed and increased flight performance and, to gain such desired increases, began studying various ways of reducing the overall weight of the Mustang's basic design.

Aeronautical design had greatly matured in

the few years since the prototype's birth. It has been said that there is nothing like a war to add a quantum jump to the sciences, be they medicine or aeronautics. There was a basic truth in this rather dreadful statement since the NAA design team now knew much more about the deadly art of aerial combat and its effects upon the construction of an airframe.

The first experiment into the lightweight field resulted in the XP–51F which first flew from Mines Field on 14 February 1944. Couched in today's aerospace jargon, the XP–51F would be considered an 'air superiority' fighter, meaning that it was dedicated to only one role; that of a high-altitude, high-

Equipped with a five-blade Rotol propeller, the XP–51G was powered by a Rolls-Royce 14 S.M. engine capable of producing 1675 hp and enabling the XP–51G to climb to 20,000 ft in 3.4 minutes. (NAA)

Photographed at Mines Field on 26 April 1945, XP–51J s/n 44–76027. Powered by an Allison, it had the J's extended bubble canopy and streamlined radiator air scoop. (NAA/105B–0–33C)

S/n 44–64164 was the fifth production P–51H–1–NA out of a group of 20 aircraft. Bob Chilton flew the first P–51H on 3 February 1945. Basically derived from the XP–51F, the H had its cockpit specifically designed for long over-water Pacific missions. The fastest of all production Mustangs, the H would never see combat. (NAA)

performance fighter. When the USAAF contract for the XP–51F was issued during April 1943, there was absolutely no mention of ground attack, dive bombing, reconnaissance or any other role that would detract from the aircraft's primary mission.

The XP–51F was designed to British load factors which were somewhat less critical than those enforced by the USAAF. North American had quickly noted that a maximum weight Spitfire Mk IX weighed in at a full ton less than the P–51D.

The design of the XP–51F dispensed with as much structural weight as possible; everything that was not absolutely necessary was discarded. Two of the .50 caliber machine guns were disposed of with the justification that a burst from four .50s would destroy a target just as effectively. Inspection panels were reduced in number but, at the same time, they were redistributed and made more efficient. The standard landing gear was eliminated and a much slimmer leg and oleo was incorporated along with a smaller wheel, tire and brake. With the reduced size gear unit, the Mustang's famous 'cranked' leading edge was eliminated, thereby saving additional pounds.

Some plastic was even incorporated into the airframe while further weight reductions were gained by simplifying the motor mount and by reducing the number of engine cowling sections.

Absolute attention was also applied to reducing drag and the XP–51F was to have a long, elegant bubble canopy that, while improving pilot vision, would also improve streamlining by its length. The finish of the XP–51F was also a matter of considerable attention and it was completely flush rivetted, with the entire surface, excepting the cowling and inspection panels, being filled with a special putty that had been developed by North American. After drying, the putty was sanded down, reapplied where necessary, and then sanded again before being primed and painted with special lacquer.

Power would be supplied by the standard Rolls-Royce/Packard V–1650–7 and the propeller was to be a special three-blade Aeroproducts Unimatic hydraulic constant speed unit with hollow core blades to save weight. The USAAF contract called for three XP–51Fs. This was changed in June 1943 to include two more machines but these final two would be finished as XP–51Gs. Right from the first, Bob Chilton knew that he had a winner: 'When we were doing the initial ground testing of the engine, we could not run the throttle up unless the aircraft was firmly chained down. On the early test flights I found that I had so much power on my hands that I had to advance the throttle by increments to prevent the plane from taking off prematurely. By the time that I had reached only 30 in of manifold pressure, the F model was off and flying!'

Flight testing of the XP–51Fs was sandwiched in between the many other flight tests that were being conducted by NAA, as Bob Chilton recalled.

We were dealing with such a huge volume of new aircraft that time for testing new projects, unless they were of the highest priority, was strictly limited. On an overall total, the XP–51Fs probably accumulated no more than 100 flying hours.

The USAAF did not like the idea that the XP–51F was built to British loading specifications. They had gotten used to the incredibly rugged strength designed into almost all American fighters. They felt that the Japanese had gone way too far in sacrificing structural strength for additional performance. The USAAF was also none too pleased with the European and British practice of dropping some structural strength in favor of boosted performance. This was not to say that the XP–51F, or any of the lightweight Mustangs, was not a strong aircraft. They were not as strong as the basic D model, however.

Reducing weight and streamlining made the XP–51F into what Bob Chilton fondly remembers 'as my favorite Mustang'. He recalled:

It was not uncommon to climb out of Mines Field at 7,500 fpm. The F handled like a finely-tuned race car and it was hard to find an angle of attack that would keep the aircraft slow enough to achieve its 250 mph climb-out speed. It was not uncommon on test flights to climb to 45,000 ft and that led to some interesting problems. Firstly, the F was, of course, not pressurized and, secondly, flying at altitudes of extreme height was still a bit novel and the personal equipment for high-altitude flying had not kept pace with the aircraft. You would dress with as many layers of clothing as possible, to which was added a heavy flying jacket.

I had been doing some experimental work with the University of Southern California in their new centrifuge, testing the effects of various aeronautical situations on the human body. For the high-altitude flights in the XP–51F, we had obtained a Canadian experimental vest that wrapped completely around the upper torso of the body. Oxygen from the fuselage tanks passed through the vest which made it very tight and uncomfortable with the pressure. However, this pressure was a great help at altitude. I had a British-built manually controlled regulator that hung on a strap around my neck and this device was calibrated so that I could dial the pressure required to keep the oxygen blood level at its correct percentage. In effect, I was having about 18 lb of pressure shoved down my throat which made speaking over the radio extremely difficult. The heavy pressure from the vest helped somewhat but I could only transmit one word at a time and that was only possible when I was exhaling, making it very difficult for the ground personnel to understand my messages.

The heater, at 45,000 ft, was just putting out more frozen air but there were certain benefits. Passing through 30,000 ft it seemed that the air was very clear. But when I broke 35,000 it seemed clear that I had passed into an entirely new strata of really clear air. I could look back and see an almost razor-sharp demarcation line and it made for a very awe-inspiring sight. One day I was flying at 45,000 ft between Los Angeles and San Diego and the air was so clear that I could pick out a specific mountain peak almost 600 miles away in Arizona. The beauty of those high-altitude flights is something I will never forget.

NAA failed to get the benefit of 500-mph publicity from the XP–51F, not due to any lack of work on the part of George Mountain Bear who, as with the NA–73X, spent day after day polishing the surface of the fighter. However, George's hard work could not get the aircraft past the magic mark. The USAAF was content to let the XP–51Fs slip away in obscurity without issuing further contracts for development. It is presumed that the XP–51Fs ended their days on the NAA scrap heap, that is except for one example, FR409, which was transferred to the RAF for further testing.

The two remaining Mustangs on the XP–51F contract were completed as XP–51Gs and the airframe of the G was essentially the same as the F but the powerplant was a Rolls-Royce RM14SM Merlin 145 of 1,500 hp. These engines were supplied directly from Britain and would have been produced in the States by Packard if the G had gone into production.

The first XP–51G, 43–43335, was test flown by Bob Chilton who later commented that this particular machine was flown only a few hours. During this short testing period, the engineers decided to test a different propeller. Normally flown with a four-blade prop, Bob remembers the flight after a five-blade Rotol unit, imported from Britain, was briefly fitted. 'A British technician was sent out with the propeller but it was a full five months before we could get around to testing the unit. The Brit certainly enjoyed his lengthy vacation with trips to Hollywood and other tourist spots. Once we got a breather in our testing program, we had the Rotol unit fitted. The aircraft made just one flight with this propeller and, unfortunately, I was at the controls. The propeller made the XP–51G directionally unstable, especially over 250 mph, when any touch of the rudder would cause the aircraft to start wandering in a most erratic manner.' The normal four-blade unit was re-installed after this first flight and the aircraft was sent off to the USAAF.

The second XP–51G, 43–43336, was assigned to the RAF. Given the serial FR410, this aircraft was also briefly test flown, the vertical fin and rudder increased slightly in height, and fitted with a four-blade Aeroproducts propeller.

The final version of the experimental lightweight Mustangs was the XP–51J. Two J models were built and they were very similar, from firewall back, to the F and G. The main reason for the construction of the J was to test the installation of the Allison V–1710–119 powerplant and the Allison-developed infinitely variable supercharger. With the standard two-stage supercharger unit that was fitted to the Merlin, there was a definite gap between the point when the first stage of the supercharger would become inefficient and the point when the second stage blower would cut in. However, Bob Chilton felt that the Allison left something to be desired and 'the cylinder head design of the Allison had never changed since day one. This caused improper fuel distribution between cylinders, causing popping and detonation when high power settings were applied. We put British plugs on the Allison and this helped but did not cure the problem. However, the supercharger appeared to work just fine and was an improvement on the two-stage system.'

The USAAF was apparently afraid that the British would cancel the license for the Packard-built Rolls Royce Merlin once the war was over, leaving the USAAF with just the Allison as its basic high-performance inline powerplant. The J was specifically built as a countermeasure test program to the non-availability of the Merlin. Once again, it appears that the two XP–51Js did only a minimal amount of flying and were soon relegated to scrap.

A final look at the lightweight Mustangs leaves one with the impression that they were more an exercise in design management than a direct assault on a new generation of propeller-driven fighters. Chief designer Schmued once said that 'can't do' wasn't in his vocabulary and he certainly did prove that the lightweight Mustangs could be built and offer very high performance figures. Army thinking had changed during the developmental time period and the lightweights never achieved the production line but the design goals were usually reached and, in many cases, passed. The lessons from the lightweights would be applied to the ultimate Mustang, the P–51H.

The P–51H embodied much of the design experience of the lightweights. It was the fastest of all Mustangs, at 487 mph, courtesy of a water-injected V–1650–7 that could develop 2,218 hp and the P–51H looked quite a bit like the lightweights but with a more purposeful sit that came of being constructed for combat missions rather than just testing. The bubble canopy had been shortened but the engine installation was kept as simple as on the experimentals with the engine mount being an integral part of the cowling. The lighter undercarriage and simplified wing structure were also retained and the wing could either be

***B**eautiful attention to detail is seen in this close-up view of the XP–51F. The lightweight F had a long bubble canopy to improve streamlining. A simplified cowl allowed easy access to the engine. Note the four-gun wing. (NAA/105–0–11)*

fitted with four or six machine guns with a total of either 1,600 or 1,800 rounds being carried. Two underwing pylons were fitted and these could carry either drop tanks or 1,000 lb bombs. Bob Chilton was in the cockpit of the first P–51H when it flew on 3 February 1945. The systems of the P–51H had been designed with long-range Pacific missions in mind and the cockpit had been made as comfortable as possible for the pilot. Besides a few early models, the P–51H was equipped with a taller fin and rudder to handle the increased torque from the engine.

The fact that the war was rapidly coming to a conclusion meant that the P–51H would be too late to participate in combat missions but the aircraft was equipping squadrons at the end of the war. All further orders for the P–51H were cancelled with the conclusion of hostilities but 555 had been built and these aircraft later served with Air National Guard units, as did many of the earlier D models.

The Mustang had destroyed nearly 5,000 enemy aircraft during aerial combat in the ETO alone and had defeated the best that the Germans and Japanese could offer. However, the Mustang's operational career was far from closed. Korea was just a few years away as were the various Arab/Israeli conflicts as well as the countless 'minor nation' wars in which the Mustang would be employed. The Mustang finally retired from operational roles in 1984, making the North American design the world's longest serving combat aircraft.

THE BAD ANGEL

How a P–51D scored one of World War Two's most unusual victories.

Lieutenant Louis E Curdes yanked the control column of his P–51D Mustang violently to the right and rolled his fighter level, skimming just a few feet above the tropical 'paradise' of Bataan Island. This Japanese-held bastion was located about 150 miles to the north of Luzon in the Philippines and harbored an air strip called Basco which was receiving the devastating attention of the Mustangs of the Third Commando Group. Mustang after Mustang made strafing runs at the Japanese targets, exploding aircraft and collapsing the thatch buildings with a rain of .50 caliber slugs. The time was mid-February 1945 and the Japanese were being blasted all the way back to the Home Islands. What Japanese aircraft that did get into the air were immediately jumped by hordes of P–47s, P–38s, P–51s and naval fighters whose pilots were all eager to add coveted 'setting sun' victory marks to the side of the fuselage. Curdes, however, was to participate in an aerial victory that would add an American flag to his victory score!

Louis Curdes began his combat career with Lockheed P–38 Lightnings in the Mediterranean Theater. Curdes found the big P–38 and its heavy firepower to his liking and accounted for seven German and one Italian aircraft during his combat tour. Curdes also knew how devastating it could be to be knocked from the sky having had to take to his parachute after his P–38 had been chewed up by a *Luftwaffe* fighter. The young pilot from Fort Wayne, Indiana, found himself transferred to the Pacific with the Third Air Commandos in January 1945. The transition from the big Lightning to the more responsive Mustang must have caused some problems but Curdes apparently overcame them quickly and was soon flying combat missions against the Japanese.

The Third Air Commandos were flying their Mustangs out of Mangaldan on the Philippine island of Luzon, just east of Lingayen. Flying over harsh territory and vast stretches of water, the Mustang pilots had to place extreme faith in their crew chiefs and the big Packard-Rolls engines in front of them. Since enemy air activity was constantly decreasing along with the Japanese fortunes of war, the Mustang pilots had to range far and wide in search of targets of opportunity. Anything that moved was fair game for the 51 pilots and they attacked enemy supply depots, shipping and air fields.

The February raid against Basco Strip was to knock out any enemy equipment that looked

halfway serviceable, whether it be aircraft, trucks or gun emplacements. However, the Japanese had other ideas about letting the Americans maraud over the field. Several anti-aircraft emplacements had been carefully concealed around the air strip and these began blazing away when the Mustangs were sighted. The Mustang was not the world's best ground attack aircraft since all the vital plumbing for the cooling system was situated in the lower fuselage, armored only with a thin sheet of aluminum.

One of the strafing Mustangs was caught in a burst of fire from the Japanese defenses and quickly began streaming a whitish trail of glycol, the life blood of any liquid-cooled engine. The pilot wisely traded his speed for altitude and took to his parachute, plopping down a few minutes later in the warm Pacific. While inflating his small life raft, another Mustang climbed for altitude to radio back to base that one of the flock had been knocked down and to send the Dumbo – the rescue PBY Catalina that was maintained for the sole purpose of recovering downed American airmen.

Photographer James P. Gallagher had the good fortune to record the unusual scoreboard on Louis Curdes's Mustang during April 1945 at Lingayen, Luzon, Philippine Islands. Gallagher had met Curdes during March when he made several visits to the Officers' Club of the 49th Fighter Group at Lingayen. Curdes's career as a Mustang pilot was not to continue for long as he was assigned to the 8th Fighter Squadron of the 49th Fighter Group where he once again was able to fly the Lockheed Lightning. (J. P. Gallagher)

In the meantime, Curdes took up a defensive position over his downed comrade in case the Japanese made some effort to capture the flyer. American pilots in the Pacific lived with a very reasonable fear of imprisonment by the Japanese. At least the Germans had signed the Geneva Convention and treated downed aircrews with a fair amount of respect. Not so the Japanese who were brutal in every sense of the word and would often execute pilots for no particular reason. The Japanese themselves considered being taken prisoner an ultimate disgrace of their manhood and samurai tradition.

As Curdes established a lazy racetrack course over the downed pilot, he was a bit startled to notice a lone, twin-engine aircraft heading down toward the Basco Strip. A bit puzzled, Curdes broke off his patrol and headed to the aircraft. Its shape was certainly familiar, the lines of the faithful Douglas C-47 Skytrain were impossible to miss but what was this aircraft doing going into an enemy strip? Closer inspection proved that the transport was carrying full United States Army Air Force markings. Curdes knew that the Japanese had built their own version of the C-47 – codenamed *Tabby* by the Allies – and there was always the possibility that the enemy had captured an American aircraft and was flying the machine on some clandestine mission.

Whatever the situation, it called for immediate action. Curdes targeted the C-47 and pressed the fire control button on the Mustang's control column. A burst of lead from the six .50s smashed into the right wing and engine of the transport which immediately began trailing smoke. The right engine's propeller was feathered but the C-47 continued for the island. Since the nearest American base was hundreds of miles away, Curdes pressed in once again – this time his marksmanship took out the remaining engine and the crew of the C-47 had nowhere to go but down. The transport made a classic belly landing in the still Pacific and doors rapidly popped open as the crew and passengers beat a hasty exit from the sinking aircraft.

A large rubber raft was inflated and the thirteen passengers made themselves as comfortable as possible. Curdes circled overhead and was startled to see that some of the passengers appeared to be women. Running low on fuel he headed back to base to report the encounter and find just what was happening. Upon arrival at Mangaldan, the Mustang pilot discovered that the Douglas was indeed American. Considerably off course and carrying passengers that included Army nurses, the transport's pilot was heading for the enemy strip when Curdes attacked.

Before dawn the next morning, Curdes and a wingman were airborne in their Mustangs. Finding the raft, they set up a defensive patrol until the Dumbo appeared on the scene and rescued all thirteen passengers and crew and the P-51 pilot. It certainly had been a harrowing experience for the C-47 crew but considerably better than the reception they would have received after landing on Bataan.

Curdes must have had mixed thoughts about his escapade and what results the strange aerial victory would have. However, the situation worked out extremely well – the US government was able to pump a lot of propaganda from the incident – and a freshly promoted Captain Louis E Curdes was awarded the Distinguished Flying Cross for shooting down one of his own aircraft!

NORTH AMERICAN P-51 MUSTANG VARIANTS, SERIAL NUMBERS AND SPECIFICATIONS

Variants

NA-73X Handbuilt prototype with civil registration NX19998 (c/n 73-3097) for British requirement. Unarmed with highly polished natural metal finish. the aircraft was powered by a 1,150 hp Allison V-1710-39. Heavily damaged on an early test flight, the prototype was rebuilt and continued a limited flight test program before being scrapped.

XP-51-NA The USAAF acquired two early production Mustang Mk Is (c/n 73-3101 and 73-3107) for testing to see if the aircraft had a combat potential for the Army. These aircraft had carried RAF serials AG348 and AG354 and were assigned Army serials 41-38 and 41-39 for testing. Initially flown in natural metal finish, the aircraft went through a number of paint schemes. Powered by 1,150 hp Allison V-1710-39. One aircraft survives in flyable condition with the Experimental Aircraft Association Museum.

P-51-NA Similar to RAF Mustang Mk I, 150 aircraft were constructed with four 20 mm cannon in the wing, and with American style instruments, radios and controls replacing British items. Carrying construction numbers 91-11981 through 91-12130, these aircraft were given RAF serials FD418 through FD567. 57 were converted to P-51-1-NA standards (later F-6A-NA) and carried two K24 fuselage cameras (serials 41-37320 through 41-37339; 41-37352 through 41-37366; 41-37368 through 41-37371; 41-37412 through 41-37429. One aircraft (41-37426, FD524) was transferred to the US Navy as BuNo 57987. Most aircraft were delivered in RAF style camouflage or in USAAF Olive Drab and Neutral Gray. NAA designation NA-91.

P-51A-NA Similar to P-51-NA but the wing cannon were replaced by four .50 caliber Browning machine guns. 1,200 hp Allison V-1710-81. Two underwing racks for bombs or drop tanks. 50 P-51As were transferred to the RAF to replace aircraft kept by Army for P-51-1-NA conversion, and 35 were later converted to F-6B-NA. Production stopped at P-51A-10 in order to change the line over to Merlin-powered machines. The NAA designation was NA-99.

A-36A-NA P-51A optimised for ground attack with NAA designation NA-97, the aircraft retained machine gun armament but had dive brakes mounted above and below the wing. Powered by 1,325 hp Allison V-1710-87. The underwing racks could each carry a 500 lb bomb. 500 were built (42-83663 through 42-84162; c/n 97-15881 through 97-16380) with 42-83685 being supplied to the RAF as EW998. Delivered in Olive Drab and Neutral Gray finish.

XP-51B-NA Two P-51-NAs (41-37352, 41-37421) were rebuilt with 1,380 hp V-1650-3 Merlin engines, with many other detail modifications made to areas such as the radiator, cowling and ailerons. Originally redesignated as XP-78-NA before switching to P-51B. Delivered in Olive Drab and Neutral

Gray camouflage. The NAA design number was NA-101.

P-51B-NA A total of 1,988 B models were constructed, of which 71 B-10-NA were converted to F-6C-NAs. Early versions were powered with the 1,380 hp V-1650-3 and armed with four .50 caliber Browning machine guns in the wing; later versions had the V-1650-7 and six .50 caliber wing guns. 550 B-5s became P-51B-7s with the addition of a fuselage fuel tank. Two underwing racks held drop tanks or bombs. The fuselage fuel tank (75 US gallons) was also retrofitted to earlier aircraft. Aircraft were delivered in Olive Drab and Neutral Gray camouflage until USAAF changed to all natural metal combat aircraft. NAA design number NA-102 through B-1, and NA-102 for remaining aircraft.

P-51C-NT The C was basically identical to the B except for the fact that it was built at NAA's new Dallas, Texas, plant. A total of 1,750 Cs was completed including 20 converted to F-6C-NTs. The C-1 was powered with the V-1650-3 but the remaining 1,400 aircraft carried the more powerful V-1650-7. The four .50 caliber guns were supplied with 1,260 rounds of ammunition. NAA designation NA-103 for 1943 aircraft, and NA-111 for 1944 machines.

XP-51D-NA This designation covered the conversion of two P-51B-10 aircraft (42-106539, 42-106540) with cut-down rear fuselage and bubble-canopy to improve vision. The wing was modified to hold six .50 caliber Browning air-cooled machine guns with 1,880 rounds of ammunition. There were many other refinement modifications. They were finished in Olive Drab and Neutral Gray. NAA designation NA-106.

P-51D-NA Production version of the Mustang with bubble canopy. Four P-51D-1-NAs were completed with the original-style canopy before the introduction of the bubble canopy with the D-5. A total of 6,502 bubble canopy Ds built at NAA's Inglewood plant. A dorsal fin was introduced soon after production commenced to compensate for a loss of keel surface after the removal of the top rear fuselage. Production was also undertaken at Dallas with the designation P-51D-NT, a total of 1454 being built from D-5-NT through D-20-NT. Many small refinement modifications were introduced throughout production. The D-25-NA had two sets of rocket stub launchers under each wing panel to carry 5 in rockets. Six .50 caliber wing guns. Dallas delivered 136 F-6D-20-NT/-25-NT tactical recon aircraft. Most aircraft were delivered in natural metal finish. NAA design number NA-109 through NA-124.

TP-51D Ten P-51Ds modified for dual control training with extensive work carried out in the cockpit area for the provision of a second seat and full instrument panel. Part of the rear fuselage was cut away to make more room for the second seat (the first conversion used standard cockpit space and regular canopy) and a larger, longer canopy was installed. After the war, further TPs (designated TF by this time) were built from random airframes by Temco in Dallas.

P-51E-NT Original designation for Dallas-built D but dropped in favor of D-NT.

XP–51F–NA Three Fs were built (c/n 105–26883 through 105–26885) to test the concept of a low-weight, high-performance redesigned Mustang. The laminar flow wing differed from those on earlier Mustangs. They were built to lower strength British specifications so that the airframe would be as light as possible. The third F was supplied to the RAF for testing. They had a reduced armament of four .50 caliber guns, V–1650–7 engines and three-blade propellers. The NAA design number was NA–105.

XP–51G–NA Also designated NA–105. The last two of the project batch of Fs were built as Gs with 1,675 hp Rolls-Royce Merlin (c/n 105–25931, 105–25932) and five blade Rotol propellers, which proved to make flight characteristics unstable. One machine was sent to the RAF as FR410. All NA–105 Mustangs were delivered in sprayed silver finish, except for RAF examples which were camouflaged in standard RAF European day fighter finish.

XP–51J–NA Also designated NA–105. The last two of the lightweight experimental Mustangs (c/n 105–47446, 105–47447) were similar to the F and G but were powered by 1,500 hp Allison V–1710–119 engines. Tests were inconclusive as the engine did not perform up to full power specifications.

P–51H–NA The production lightweight Mustang, with NAA designation of NA–126, incorporating some of the lightweight lessons learned from the F, the H was a stronger, more 'Americanized' fighter than the NA–105. Streamlining was quite advanced. The armament consisted of six .50 caliber Brownings and provision for two 1,000 lb bombs and six 5 in HVAR rockets under the wings. They had a V–1650–9 engine that was capable of producing 2,218 hp in the war emergency rating with water injection. The vertical tail was changed several times with the first few machines, finally settling on a taller unit. One F–51H was supplied to the RAF. A total of 555 Hs was built. The NAA design number was NA–126.

P–51K–NT The same as the P–51D–NT but built with an Aeroproducts propeller instead of the Hamilton Standard unit. A total of 1,500 Ks was built, including 163 as F–6K–NTs; 594 were transferred to the RAF as Mustang IV. With the K–10–NT, underwing rocket stubs for four 5 in rockets were added. NAA design number NA–111.

P–51L–NT A P–51H–NA variant with V–1650–11 engine. An order for 1,700 was cancelled, including 44–91004 through 44–92003. NAA design number NA–129.

P–51M–NT Dallas-built version of the P–51H–NA with V–1650–9A engine. One was completed (45–11743, c/n 124–48496 but the remaining order for 1,628 was cancelled with the end of the war.

Royal Air Force Variants

Mustang Mk I 620 built, ten transferred to Soviets while two went to the USAAF. Allison V–1710–39 of 1,150 hp. Four .50 caliber guns in wing, two .30 caliber weapons in lower nose. Provision for one F24 camera behind the pilot's seat.

Mustang Mk IA Same as Mk I but with four 20 mm cannon in the wing. Part of order kept by USAAF.

Mustang Mk II Fifty aircraft similar to P–51A.

Mustang Mk III 852 aircraft, some transferred to RAAF and USAAF. Similar to P–51B/C.

Mustang Mk IV/IVA 281 aircraft similar to USAAF P–51D/K. Many Ks were designated as Mk IVA.

Mustang Mk V One XP–51F–NA. The RAF also received single examples of the XP–51G, A–36 and P–51H.

Mustang Mk X Four Mustang Mk Is (AL963, AL975, AM203, AM208) converted with Rolls-Royce Merlin 61 or 65 engines with four-blade propellers and different radiators, for trials.

Serial Numbers

XP–51–NA	41–38, 41–39
P–51–NA	41–37320 through 41–37469
P–51A–1–NA	43–6003 through 43–6102
P–51A–5–NA	43–6103 through 43–6157
P–51A–10–NA	43–6158 through 43–6312
XP–51B–NA	41–37352, 41–37421 (both converted P–51–NAs)
P–51B–1–NA	43–12093 through 43–12492
P–51B–5–NA	43–6313 through 43–6352; 43–6353 through 43–6752; 43–6753 through 43–7112
P–51B–10–NA	43–7113 through 43–7202; 42–106429 through 42–106538; 42–106541 through 42–106738
P–51B–15–NA	42–106739 through 42–106908; 42–106909 through 42–106978; 43–24752 through 43–24901
P–51C–1–NT	42–102979 through 42–103328
P–51C–5–NT	42–103329 through 42–103378; 42–103379 through 42–103778
P–51C–10–NT	42–103779 through 42–103978; 43–24902 through 43–25251; 44–10753 through 44–10782
P–51C–11–NT	44–10783 through 44–10817
P–51C–10–NT	44–10818 through 44–10852
P–51C–11–NT	44–10853 through 44–10858
P–51C–10–NT	44–10859 through 44–11036
P–51C–11–NT	44–11037 through 44–11122
P–51C–10–NT	44–11123 through 44–11152
XP–51D–NA	42–106539, 42–106540 (converted P–51B–1s)
P–51D–5–NA	44–13253 through 44–14052
P–51D–10–NA	44–14053 through 44–14852
P–51D–15–NA	44–14853 through 44–15252; 44–15253 through 44–15752

P–51D–20–NA	44–63160 through 44–64159; 44–72027 through 44–72126; 44–72127 through 44–72626
P–51D–25–NA	44–72627 through 44–73626; 44–73627 through 44–74226
P–51D–30–NA	44–74227 through 44–75026
P–51D–5–NT	44–11153 through 44–11352
P–51D–20–NT	44–12853 through 44–13252
P–51D–25–NT	44–84390 through 44–84989; 45–11343 through 45–11542
TP–51D	45–11443, 45–11450; 44–84610 through 44–84611
XP–51F–NA	43–43332 through 43–43334
XP–51G–NA	43–43335, 43–43336
P–51H–1–NA	44–64160 through 44–64179
P–51H–5–NA	44–64180 through 44–64459
P–51H–10–NA	44–64460 through 44–64714
P–51H–NA	44–64715 through 44–65159 (cancelled)
XP–51J–NA	44–76027, 44–76028
P–51K–1–NT	44–11353 through 44–11552
P–51K–5–NT	44–11553 through 44–11952
P–51K–10–NT	44–11953 through 44–12752; 44–12753 through 44–12852
P–51L–NT	44–91004 through 44–92003 (cancelled)
P—51M–NT	45–11743

Royal Air Force Serial Numbers

Mustang Mk I	AG345 through AG663; AG664; AL958 through AM257; AP164 through AP263
Mustang Mk IA	FD418 through FD567
Mustang Mk II	FR890 through FR939
Mustang Mk III	FB110 through FB399; FR411; FX848 through FX999; FZ100 through FZ197; HB821 through HB961; HK944 through HK947; HK955 through HK956; KH421 through KH640; SR406 through SR440
Mustang Mk IV	KH641 through KH670
Mustang Mk IVA	KH671 through KH870; KM100 through KM492; TK586; TK589; KM744 through KM799 (cancelled)
XP–51G	FR410 (designated as Mk IV)
Mustang Mk V	FR409 (XP–51F)
P–51H–NA	KN987
A–36A	EW998

Specifications

XP-51

Span	37 ft
Length	32 ft 3 in
Height	12 ft 2 in
Wing area	233 sq ft
Empty weight	6,280 lb
Loaded weight	8,400 lb
Max. speed	382 mph
Cruise speed	300 mph
Ceiling	30,800 ft
Rate of climb	2,500 fpm
Range	625 to 1,040 miles
Powerplant	Allison V-1710-39 of 1,150 hp

P-51

Overall dimensions	as XP-51
Empty weight	6,550 lb
Loaded weight	8,800 lb
Max. speed	387 mph
Cruise speed	307 mph
Ceiling	31,300 ft
Rate of climb	2,200 fpm
Range	350 to 1,175 miles
Powerplant	Allison V-1710-39 of 1,150 hp

P-51A

Overall dimensions	as XP-51
Empty weight	6,430 lb
Loaded weight	9,000 lb
Max. speed	390 mph
Cruise speed	305 mph
Ceiling	31,400 ft
Rate of climb	2,300 fpm
Range	350 to 2,550 miles
Powerplant	Allison V-1710-81 of 1,200 hp

XP-51B

Span	37 ft
Length	32 ft 3 in
Height	13 ft 8 in
Wing area	233 sq ft
Empty weight	7,050 lb
Loaded weight	8,880 lb
Max. speed	441 mph
Cruise speed	n/a
Ceiling	42,000 ft
Rate of climb	3,600 fpm
Range	n/a
Powerplant	Packard V-1650-3 of 1,380 hp

P-51B

Overall dimensions	as XP-51B
Empty weight	6,980 lb
Loaded weight	11,800 lb
Max. Speed	439 mph
Cruise speed	362 mph
Ceiling	41,500 ft
Rate of climb	30,000 ft in 12.1 minutes
Range	400 to 2,700 miles
Powerplant	Packard V-1650-7 of 1,490 hp

P-51D

Overall dimensions	as XP-51B
Empty weight	7,100 lb
Loaded weight	11,600 lb
Max. speed	437 mph
Cruise speed	362 mph
Ceiling	41,900 ft
Rate of climb	30,000 ft in 13 minutes
Range	up to 2,800 miles
Powerplant	Packard V-1650-7 of 1,490 hp

P-51H

Span	37 ft
Length	33 ft 4 in
Height	13 ft 8 in
Wing area	233 sq ft
Empty weight	6,590 lb
Loaded weight	11,100 lb
Max. speed	487 mph
Cruise speed	380 mph
Ceiling	41,500 ft
Rate of climb	30,000 ft in 12.5 minutes
Range	850 to 2,400 miles
Powerplant	Packard V-1650-9 of 2,218 hp

XP-51F

Span	37 ft $\frac{1}{4}$ in
Length	32 ft 2$\frac{3}{4}$ in
Height	8 ft 8 in
Wing area	233 sq ft
Empty Weight	5,635 lb
Loaded weight	9,060 lb
Max. speed	466 mph
Cruise speed	379 mph
Ceiling	42,000 ft
Rate of climb	19,500 ft in 4.8 minutes
Range	2,100 miles
Powerplant	Packard V-1650-7 of 1,695 hp

XP-51G

Overall dimensions	as XP-51F
Empty weight	5,750 lb
Loaded weight	8,885 lb
Max. speed	472 mph
Cruise speed	315 mph
Ceiling	45,700 ft
Rate of climb	20,000 ft in 3.4 minutes
Range	1,865 miles
Powerplant	Rolls-Royce Merlin 145M of 1,910 hp

XP-51J

Span	37 ft
Length	32 ft 11 in
Height	13 ft 8 in
Wing area	233 sq ft
Empty weight	6,030 lb
Loaded weight	9,140 lb
Max. speed	491 mph (not verified)
Cruise speed	n/a
Ceiling	43,700 ft
Rate of climb	20,000 ft in 5 minutes
Range	n/a
Powerplant	Allison V-1710-119 of 1,500 hp

Vultee XP-54
Swoose Goose — The Winner That Lost

Built to compete in an innovative specification contest, Vultee's fighter was a victim of too much cleverness.

The American aircraft industry had been sluggish at best when responding to new concepts for pursuit aircraft designs during the 1930s. Most manufacturers liked the idea of sticking to the tried and true formula of two wings, two machine guns and a steel tube fuselage and wood wings covered with cotton fabric. This formula was not conducive to high performance and it is small wonder that new American bombing aircraft during the 1930s were outstripping the pursuits in speed and firepower. The situation was remedied by a few far-thinking individuals in the Army Air Corps who insisted that a specification be drawn up that would allow for a massive creative effort on the part of the aeronautical industry to create new fighting aircraft.

Major Ed Powers, Chief of the Engineering

The prototype XP–54 in flight on its one-way trip from Vultee Field to Norton AAFB where the complicated Lycoming XH–2470 powerplant, developing 2,300 hp, turned into garbage. Serial number 41–1211 was scrapped almost immediately. The only surviving part was the complex nose gun armament section which was shipped off to Eglin AFB for static firing tests. The second Swoose Goose was left in natural metal finish. Instead of a predicted top speed of 510 mph, the XP–54 was able to obtain only a lowly 380 mph. (Vultee)

Section in the Office of the Chief of Staff, gathered a group of individuals concerned about the direction in which the country's airpower was headed and came up with a lengthy document that was to have an interesting effect on American fighter aircraft. The specification was called Request for Data R–40C and was issued to all interested manufacturers during 1940. The document, drawing from hard lessons observed in Spain, France, and Britain, was sent out in the early part of 1940 and, in effect, freed manufacturers from all previous restraints and opened the fighter design field to any and all comers.

R–40C let the designers have complete creative control – their aircraft could have any

One of the most distinctive looking fighter prototypes produced during World War Two, too many untried systems and concepts doomed the Swoose Goose to failure. Vultee employees seemed to find a bit of humor with the aircraft and affixed an insignia under the canopy that employed a Vultee V along with a half goose/half buzzard in somewhat questionable flight. Guns were never installed in either prototype although the complex swivel system was installed. The XP–54 featured one of the first forms of ejection seat since, in case of bail out, the pilot would have an extremely difficult time clearing the pusher propeller so the seat was designed to slide directly down its entry rails and drop off with the pilot still attached. The pilot would then have to release himself from the falling seat and activate the parachute. (USAAF)

engine or engines desired, they could be of any shape or size, they could carry as many guns as desired and – in an interesting decision – they could be monoplanes or biplanes. Anything and everything was open for study and speculation while the Army sat back to see what would happen. The aeronautical companies, scenting fat contracts in the wind, devoted considerable effort in creating paper aircraft to submit to the Army review board.

The Army Air Corps set up a grading panel to review the fighters and established a system called Figure of Merit (FOM) which would grade the fighters on a possible top score of 1,000 points. Factors such as top speed, maneuverability, armament, and overall performance were to be figured into the FOM. The FOM was then to be divided by the estimated price provided by the manufacturer and the resulting figure, the Dollar FOM, was to influence the Air Corps on what fighter should be ordered.

As designs began to flood into the Army office set aside for the evaluation it soon became evident that some form of classification was needed to clarify the different types of aircraft into some form of similar catagory. Accordingly three classes were established and comprised highly radical, unorthodox, and

conventional. Designs were then sifted into these categories where they could be compared against each other. It is significant to note that not one biplane was submitted and virtually all the fighter designs were constructed out of the new all-metal stressed skin form of manufacture.

Designs from Bell, Curtiss, Vultee, and almost every other company that had any hope of producing a fighter aircraft were carefully studied by the Army board and the final winner in the FOM was a Vultee design that grabbed 817.9 out of a possible 1,000 points. The Vultee aircraft certainly fell into the highly radical category as few beasts such as this had ever been envisioned. The aircraft was given the designation Model 84 by Vultee and it was planned from the start as a large pusher with twin booms that tapered back to the tail surfaces. Power was to be supplied by a Pratt & Whitney X–1800 but when P&W cancelled all liquid-cooled powerplants, Vultee had to substitute the Lycoming XH–2470, a liquid-cooled monster with four banks of six cylinders. Since the engine was larger and heavier, Vultee designers had immediately to revise specifications for the aircraft – the first in a constant upward weight spiral which had a very detrimental effect on the Model 84.

The Army placed an order for the Model 84 on 8 January 1941 and assigned XP–54 to the design. Originally planned to gross in at around 8,500 lb, the Vultee quickly shot up to 18,000 lb and did not stop there. The fuselage pod was a long rather elegant affair that contained all armament, pilot, fuel and engine with a long-stroke nose landing gear leg. Originally designed to take a contra-rotating propeller, the change of engine also brought along a four blade Hamilton Standard unit that had a diameter of 11 ft 6 in. The armament of the XP–54 – which for some reason had now been dubbed 'Swoose Goose' by the employees at Vultee – was one of the strangest features of an already unusual aircraft. Originally planned to carry an armament of six .50 caliber air cooled Browning machine guns, the armament section was capable of pivoting three degrees upward and six degrees downward. It was reasoned that this installation would aid in deflection shots and come in particularly useful when the aircraft was strafing ground targets and could fly straight and level while the nose was depressed for firing. Needless to say, this little device weighed a lot and added to the increasing complexity of what was to have been a basic pursuit aircraft.

Cooling the massive powerplant that had been tightly cowled at the rear of the fuselage pod caused a number of problems. The entire center section of the wing, which had been given an inverted gull form much like Vought's Corsair, was to house all radiators and intercoolers in what was hoped to be an efficient unit that could supply the engine's cooling needs while not interfering with overall streamlining. Redesigning was still going on when, on 11 March 1942, a second prototype of the XP–54 was ordered by the Army. At this time the designers decided to throw out the six .50 calibers in the nose and go with something with a bit more punch. Accordingly two Oldsmobile T–9 37 mm cannon, which were extremely popular with the folks over at Bell, were installed in the nose along with two .50 calibers. Since the cannon had a rather slow muzzle velocity, another weight increasing plan was added to the concept. All four guns would still be capable of

swiveling downwards for strafing but the two cannon could be tilted upwards a bit for air-to-air firing so they would have the same trajectory as the .50s. This system was controlled by a complex gun sight that computed range and angle.

In the meantime it was becoming a bit obvious that the XP–54's increasing weight problem was going to detract significantly from overall performance. Vultee had originally given the Army a proposed top speed of 510 mph which was wildly optimistic and, even with weight reduced to the original specification, could never have been achieved. To give the XP–54 better high altitude performance it was decided to fit a turbosupercharger to the Lycoming XH–2470 and the unit was installed on the bottom of the rear section of the fuselage pod. The supercharger meant that the cockpit of Swoose Goose would have to be pressurized and this was not a bad idea as there was a fear of carbon monoxide fumes leaking into the pilot's compartment from the engine section. Accordingly the canopy and pilot's section were sealed off as a separate compartment and entrance was provided by a rather novel means. The pilot would press a button on the bottom of the fuselage which would activate an electric motor that would lower the pilot's seat on rails and the pilot would get in the seat, strap in, press another button and the whole contraption would slowly rise back into the fuselage.

Addition of extra armor and self-sealing fuel tanks were also doing their part to decrease range and performance. The engineers were extremely worried about range since fuel tanks could not be fitted in the wing panels because of all the cooling devices.

The aircraft was not completed until January 1943 and, since Vultee Field was getting a bit small for test work with advanced aircraft, the Swoose Goose was disassembled, loaded on trucks and driven out to the sun-drenched Mojave Desert where it was put back together and flown for the first time on 15 January for a half hour hop. As with the XP–85, the XP–54 was was a great idea at the time it was conceived but it just did not work out and the fighters already on production

lines (none of which stemmed from R–40C) were better aircraft than the Goose. The prototype continued a limited testing program, plagued by problems from all the added complexities, but it did manage to log over 60 hours before being transferred to Wright Field on 28 October where the Lycoming almost immediately turned into garbage, suspending further flying. Another blow soon came when the entire Lycoming XH–2470 program was cancelled by the Army. The second prototype was ready to fly by this time and it made a short hop from Vultee Field (apparently felt long enough if the aircraft was making a one-way flight!) to nearby Norton AAFB on 24 March 1944 where the second Lycoming also gave up the ghost. It had been decided that the first prototype would supply parts for the second aircraft but since the engines of both were dead orders were given to scrap both aircraft. Thus both XP–54s were gone almost before anyone realized and the massive amounts of money spent on a questionable program receded into history for there was still a war to be fought and won.

VULTEE XP–54 SWOOSE GOOSE SERIAL NUMBERS AND SPECIFICATIONS

Serial Numbers

XP–54	41–1210 and 41–1211

Specifications

XP–54 Swoose Goose

Span	53 ft 10 in
Length	54 ft 9 in
Height	13 ft
Wing area	456 ft sq
Empty weight	15,262 lb
Loaded weight	19,335 lb
Max. speed	380 mph
Cruise speed	315 mph
Ceiling	37,000 ft
Rate of climb	2,000 fpm
Range	500 miles
Powerplant	Lycoming XH–2470–1 of 2,300 hp

Curtiss XP-55
Ascender — Curtiss' Try For The Future

The XP–55 was beset with design problems but at least it had a funny name.

The second place honors in the Army's R–40C design contest for new and different fighting aircraft went to the Curtiss-Wright Corporation's Airplane Division. Curtiss and chief designer Don Berlin had submitted a paper airplane to the Army in 1939 that had the company designation of Model 24. Berlin had interpreted R–40C in a manner completely departing from the conventional lines

of the P–40 series of fighters. The Model 24 was to look like nothing else that had ever rolled out of the Curtiss factory for it was to have a sweptback wing, a pusher engine and a unique nose mounted elevator.

Power was to come from the Pratt & Whitney X–1800 inline liquid-cooled sleeve valve engine that was promising high power ratings with low frontal area. During 1939, Curtiss was on top of the America fighter aircraft market and the future looked nothing but rosey. Little did company management realize

Curtiss engineers and flight crew pose by the third and last XP–55 built, 42–78847. All Ascenders were finished in the standard Olive Drab and Neutral Gray camouflage scheme. The third aircraft incorporated a number of modifications over the first machine including lengthened wing tips and increased area to the forward elevator. Number three was also later fitted with four .50 caliber machine guns for armament testing. This aircraft was lost during a test flight at Wright Field. Note how the cooling gills were in the fully opened position (located immediately before the engine spinner) while the aircraft was on the ground. Modified several times, the XP–55 was never able to overcome heating problems with the rear mounted Allison V–1710. (Curtiss)

that, after the P–40, Curtiss would produce one failure after another, eventually resulting in the demise of the company as an airframe manufacturing concern. Mis-management and poor aircraft designs resulted in this unlikely departure from the American aeronautical scene and, unfortunately, the radical new fighter was to be listed as one of the failures.

Berlin hoped that his new aircraft would have a top speed of just over 500 mph and the Army was duly impressed and, on 22 June 1940, awarded a contract to Curtiss rating the Model 24 as outstanding and second only in the contract dollar figure of merit (FOM) to the XP–54. Berlin decided that such a radical aircraft should be flown in some form of low-powered mock-up form before metal was actually cut for the real fighting machine. The simplest way to test the theories behind the XP–55 was to quickly build a simple full-scale flying prototype that could be put into the air for a flight test program in the shortest possible time. The Model 24B was built out of wood, steel tube and fabric and had fixed landing gear

and extremely simple flight instruments and systems but it was faithful to the overall layout of the Model 24. Power came from an inline Menasco C68–5 rated at 275 hp. The attractive prototype was put on a railroad car and shipped to Muroc Dry Lake where it was assembled and flown for the first time on 9 November 1941. Trouble for the full-size machine was in the offing from the very first flight of the lightweight prototype when test pilot Harvey Gray reported that the Model 24B was extremely lacking in stability. Curtiss engineers spent several weeks trying to correct the deficiency. The aircraft had odd wingtip rudders that were like the ones featured on the plans for the full-size fighter and it was thought that enlarging these would help a bit while the fixed fin area above and below the engine was also enlarged. The Model 24B had started out life on strictly Curtiss money but the Army was impressed by the company's dedication to the project and eventually provided funds that would transfer the aircraft to their ownership. The top speed of the Model 24B was well under 200 mph but, once it got back into the air, it

The Curtiss Model 24B was a full scale lightweight flying mockup for the XP–55. Powered by a Menasco inline engine and capable of about 180 mph, the 24B was used to prove the feasibility of the XP–55's layout. Originally built as a private company project, the 24B was purchased by the Army and eventually transferred to NACA for further testing. Built of wood and steel tube and covered with fabric, the 24B featured a second cockpit for an observer directly over the wing. (USAF/167812)

was flown regularly in proving flights. However, doubts still persisted about the possible handling problems with the XP–55 when the contract for three prototypes was signed on 10 July 1942.

The contract was immediately in trouble with the cancellation of the Pratt & Whitney X–1800 engine program and Curtiss was left with little but the dated and underpowered Allison to install in the new fighter. The Allison V–1710 started life in the early 1930s and was reaching the end of its developmental potential when it was chosen for the XP–55. Producing only 1,275 hp in its V–1710–95 version compared to the hoped for 2,200 hp from the X–1800, it was obvious that performance was going to suffer drastically.

Scott Field in Illinois was chosen as the site for the first flight of the prototype XP–55 which was disassembled at the factory and sent by railroad car. The first flight was made on 13 July 1943 after a couple of days of taxi trials and was anything but anticlimatic. Test pilot Harvey Gray found that the XP–55 did not want to become airborne and that the nose mounted elevator seemed to be almost totally useless. Barely in the air by the end of the runway, Gray gently turned the XP–55 around and got it safely back on the field. Curtiss engineers immediately enlarged the surface of the elevator which seemed to alleviate the problem.

Testing continued and more problems with the stability of the aircraft came to light, the XP–55 tending to yaw without warning during maneuvers. Stalls were also a problem and the XP–55 was prone to what has become known as the 'deep stall', which is a stall from which chances of recovery are slim.

The luckless Gray was flying the first prototype of the XP–55 during November when he entered a series of stall tests that were going to spell doom for the first aircraft. With gear and flaps down, Gray pulled up the nose of the XP–55, reduced power and waited for the stall. However, when it came it was violent and with little warning, flipping the aircraft upside down. The Allison was not capable of running in the inverted position so it stopped and the XP–55 fell in a straight line towards earth. Gray, after moving the controls through an unsuccessful series of stall recovery techniques, quickly thought about his situation, unstrapped his safety harness, jettisoned the canopy and, with some difficulty, exited the plummeting aircraft. The XP–55 continued its upside-down plunge and impacted with an Illinois farm field, exploded and burned.

This accident left Curtiss in a panic and several modifications were tried by which the stall problem, it was hoped, could be reduced or eliminated. The limits of the elevator travel were increased and wing tips of greater area were added on the third XP–55 which was under construction. The second XP–55 had flown on 9 January 1944, and was not modified but, instead, was placed under a strict set of flight rules that governed the attitudes in which the aircraft could be placed. Testing of the third aircraft presented problems when it was discovered that the larger elevator could stall itself during rotation. The third aircraft, which first flew on 25 April 1944, was fitted with four .50 caliber Browning machine guns in the nose for armament testing. At this point it was obvious, as with the other aircraft that had originated from R–40C, that the XP–55 would not achieve production. The powerplant was not developing enough horsepower to propel the XP–55 at its original design estimate of over 500 mph but tests had shown that, even with the lowly Allison, the XP–55 was capable of just under 400 mph which is a tribute to the attention paid by Berlin to low frontal area and reduced drag.

Limited testing with the XP–55 continued during the war but the destruction of the third prototype during a demonstration flight at Wright Field towards the end of the war finished off the series. The second aircraft was pushed out to pasture and the engineering team for the XP–55 at Curtiss went on to other projects. Even though an early form of stall warning had been fitted to the XP–55 most test pilots considered the aircraft to be very dangerous with extremely poor handling characteristics. Many problems were encountered with the cooling of the rear mounted powerplant and the problem of engine temperatures almost always being in the red was never resolved.

At least the Curtiss personnel had a sense of humor when they picked the official name of Ascender for the XP–55 for, even if a bit school-boyish, it was the only double meaning name to get past the government bureaucrats during the war for, as the engineers had stated, the XP–55 flew 'ass-end first'.

Ascender 42–78846 is currently held in storage by the National Air and Space Museum for eventual restoration.

CURTISS XP–55 ASCENDER SERIAL NUMBERS AND SPECIFICATIONS

Serial Numbers

CW–24B	42–39347
XP–55	42–78845 through 42–788847

Specifications

XP–55 Ascender

Span	40 ft 7 in
Length	29 ft 7 in
Height	11 ft 7 in
Wing area	209 sq ft
Empty weight	5,325 lb
Loaded weight	7,710 lb
Max. speed	390 mph
Cruise speed	300 mph
Ceiling	36,500 ft
Rate of climb	3,500 fpm
Range	635 miles
Powerplant	Allison V–1710–95 of 1,275 hp

Northrop XP—56
Black Bullet — The Tailless Fighter

Last of the contracted aircraft from the R–40C design circular, Northrop's fighter exhibited extremely unpleasant flying characteristics.

The Army's R–40C design circular eventually produced three aircraft that were built, all being unorthodox and all, in varying degrees, being failures. The last aircraft to be ordered from R–40C was the Northrop N–2B. Jack Northrop had formed his new company, Northrop Aircraft Incorporated, at Hawthorne, California, during August 1939 after he had split from the Douglas plant at El Segundo. Northrop's designs were, of course, always in the forefront of aviation development with such record setting machines as the Lockheed Vega and Northrop Gamma. However, with his new company Northrop wished to set his corporate sights on the lucrative military aircraft market. Entering the R–40C contest, which encouraged outrageous aircraft design, Northrop hoped that his N–2B would prove to be the military market for his long-championed flying wing configuration.

Entering the N–2B to the Army in late 1939,

Northrop and his small group of engineers waited with crossed fingers as the military pored over the paper aircraft. Two prototypes were ordered by the Army on 26 September 1940 at a price of $411,000 and the new aircraft were given the designation of XP–56. Northrop had envisioned an aircraft that would be radical in structure as well as appearance. Much of the airframe of the XP–56 would be made out of heavy thickness magnesium that would be bonded together in Northrop's own patented Heliarc system that would weld the magnesium together with a welding flame surrounded by a mantle of helium gas. Magnesium would combine the advantages of lightweight with its very tough tensile strength while the unique shape of the XP–56 showed off Northrop's creativity to its full extent. Virtually a flying wing with the fuselage being a mere pod for the carriage of the guns, pilot and engine, the XP–56 sported a pusher engine, a small dorsal fin, and a large ventral fin under the rear fuselage. Wingtips had a pronounced down-turn while the stubby creation sat on large tricycle landing gear.

Power for the new fighter was to be supplied by the Pratt & Whitney X–1800, which really should have been designated H–2240 (the H for its configuration and the 2240 for the number of cubic inches) but, because of military secrecy, the new engine had its horsepower rating applied as a designation. The P&W X–1800 borrowed the sleeve-valve design from the powerplants being produced by Bristol in England but the engine was doomed to die an early death when a change in management at P&W and Army opinion opted that the famous company stick to developing

Number two Northrop XP–56 Black Bullet, 42–38353, parked on the dry lake bed at Muroc. The second aircraft had a number of different features when compared to the first XP–56 and these included the large fin on top of the fuselage pod in an attempt to gain more stability, bellows rudders (the openings of which can be seen at the extreme wingtips), and various other small detail changes. However, flying qualities of both aircraft were extremely poor and the second prototype made only ten short test hops before being judged unsafe. Proposed armament was to include two 20 mm cannon and four .50 caliber machine guns but these were never installed. Camouflage was Olive Drab and Neutral Gray with the national insignia being added to the ventral fin. (Northrop)

Head-on view emphasises the clean lines of the Northrop XP-56. Test pilot Harry Crosby found the Black Bullet, as the type had been nicknamed at the factory, to be a difficult beast in the air. Flown for the first time on 23 March 1944, Crosby quickly learned that the second aircraft needed immense amounts of runway before it staggered into the air and, once airborne, the XP-56 lacked stability. (Northrop/74-03418)

Flight time on both XP-56s amounted to just a few hours as the machines were extremely unpleasant in the air. The second prototype was eventually transferred to the NACA wind tunnel at Moffett Field for additional testing but the Army was soon convinced that they had a failure on their hands and the project was dropped. (Northrop/9119-034)

radial engines instead of liquid-cooled inline powerplants. The X–1800 was felt to have a considerable development life before attaining maturity but the dropping of the engine left Northrop a bit in the lurch.

The decision to replace the inline X–1800 with the radial R–2800 was quickly reached but a great deal of redesign had to be undertaken on the rear portion of the XP–56 in order to shoehorn the radial into the space that should have been occupied by the slimmer inline. Pratt & Whitney also had some redesigning to do in order to convert the R–2800 into a pusher by the addition of concentric drive shafts and an explosive cord that wrapped around the gear box which would blow off the Curtiss Electric contra-rotating six blade propeller unit in case the pilot had to make a hasty exit without wanting to become so much instantly sliced meat. The cooling ducts that had been installed in the wing roots to supply air in the inline were retained and the hot air was exhausted out of a ring directly in front of the spinner.

The prototype XP–56 emerged from its Hawthorne hangar during March of 1943 resplendent in a coat of silver paint that was added to protect the sensitive magnesium surface; this was to be eventually replaced by standard camouflage. Engine runs revealed heating problems with the buried R–2800 and a number of adjustments were undertaken to make the engine run at a cooler temperature. Eventually the XP–56 was taken apart and trucked out to the desolate Muroc Dry Lake where it was put back together for taxi tests. During these high speed runs it was found that the XP–56 was extremely unstable on the ground, tending to violently yaw from the left to right with no warning. A new brake system was fitted but, although helping the problem, did not completely eliminate the disconcerting situation.

Northrop test pilot John Myers finally got the XP–56, which had been named the Black Bullet by factory workers for reasons unknown, into the air for a very brief and very low hop on 30 September. Myers held the beast just a few feet off the ground as he roared along the rock-hard prehistoric dry lake bed. Myers had an extremely unpleasant time with the fighter and found the aircraft almost uncontrollable. Quickly back on the ground, Myers recommended that the small hump on the top of the fuselage that passed as a fin be drastically enlarged in hopes of improving directional stability. The aircraft was modified but was soon destroyed when it flipped upside down following a problem on takeoff with the nose landing gear. Myers was severely injured with a broken back but his head was saved from being smashed by the polo helmet that he had started wearing when flying the XP–56!

Harry Crosby flew the second Black Bullet directly out of Hawthorne on 23 March 1944. This aircraft featured a number of modifications over the first prototype including the larger fin, bellows rudders mounted in the wing tips, and an Olive Drab and Neutral Gray camouflage scheme. The bellows rudders took air in through an opening in the anahedral wing tip and, when the pilot operated the rudder pedals, opened a valve that actuated the bellows, causing the airflow to change the direction of the aircraft. Crosby found that the number two Black Bullet was equally as unpredictable as the first, a ground speed of 160 mph being needed before the XP–56 would sluggishly lift into the air – a circumstance which must have proved exceptionally thrilling considering the not overly generous length of the runway at Northrop Field.

Crosby found that, although improved, the flight characteristics of the second XP–56 left a great deal to be desired and that the P&W R–2800–29 was not developing full power. The aircraft was eventually to be transferred to the NACA wind tunnel at Moffett Field for checking but a few more flights convinced Northrop and the Army that they had a failure that no amount of modification could improve. After only ten flights the XP–56 was parked and left, Northrop going on to bigger and better projects.

The XP–56 proved little except that magnesium could be welded for an aircraft structure. Designed to carry two 20 mm cannon and four .50 caliber machine guns in the nose, neither prototype was ever fitted with armament. Somehow, the second XP–56 survived the mass scrappings of aircraft following the end of the war and today can be seen at Hawthorne Airport, Southern California (home of today's Northrop) where it is being restored to taxiing condition by retired Northrop employees.

NORTHROP XP–56 BLACK BULLET SERIAL NUMBERS AND SPECIFICATIONS

Serial Numbers

XP–56	41–786 and 42–38353

Specifications

XP–56 Black Bullet

Neither XP–56 completed manufacturer's flight trials so performance estimates should be regarded as overly optimistic.

Span	42 ft 6 in
Length	27 ft 6 in
Height	11 ft
Wing area	306 sq ft
Empty weight	8,700 lb
Loaded weight	12,145 lb
Max. speed	465 mph
Cruise speed	396 mph
Ceiling	33,000 ft
Rate of climb	3,125 fpm
Range	445 miles
Powerplant	Pratt & Whitney R–2800–29 of 2,000 hp

Lockheed XP-58 Chain Lightning — The Fighter That Could Not Fight

The massive Lockheed XP–58 was built for a requirement that really did not exist.

World War Two stirred a frenzy of aircraft building by United States manufacturers. Many of these aircraft were the epitome of function while others were virtually useless and left their creators wondering why they were built in the first place. Unfortunately, the Lockheed XP-58 falls into the latter classification. It had the misfortune to go through more redesign, re-engining, and reclassification than almost any other fighter.

In 1940 when the British Aircraft Purchasing Commission was searching America for combat aircraft that could aid the situation back home, they found that the Lockheed P-38 Lightning might be the ideal answer for a long-range fighter that could escort Royal Air Force bombers on raids into Germany – something that the short-range Spitfires were incapable of doing. The Army, at the same time, was also extremely interested in the P–38 and considered the aircraft to be one of the hottest weapons available to the Air Corps. A conflict could arise if production of American aircraft

First and last Lockheed XP–58, 41–2670, on a test flight near the company's Burbank, California, plant during July 1944. Originally conceived as a marginally larger P–38, the XP–58 grew to a monstrous 40,000 lb and was plagued by design and mission changes. The huge aircraft certainly could not have succeeded as a day fighter for it was far too large to actively engage enemy fighters but it did have possibilities as a night fighter but that role was to be occupied by the Northrop P–61 Black Widow. The massive booms housed the radiators and cooling systems for the ungainly Allison V–3420s that powered the aircraft. Note the turret mockups and the gunner's rear facing position at the extreme end of the fuselage pod. (Lockheed)

was disrupted while an order for British aircraft was negotiated. Never an organization to let an opportunity slip by, the Army came to an interesting agreement with Lockheed officials whereby Lockheed would build, in exchange for the Army granting 'permission' to build Lightnings for the British, a prototype 'improved' Lightning at no cost to the Army. The agreement seemed to leave everyone happy except (eventually) the RAF who found out that their Model 322–61 Lightning was vastly inferior (due, we might add, to modifications wanted by the British against the protests of Lockheed) to the Air Corps version and the two RAF prototypes were returned to America and the order cancelled.

However, work was progressing on the design of the Army's 'free' aircraft. The concept for the improved Lightning was an interesting one for, once again, it harkened back to some rather dismal 1930s aeronautical thinking. One of the big fears for the more excitable members of the public during the 1930s had been expressed by lurid stories and illustrations carried in some of the more 'yellow journal' Sunday tabloids which depicted vast fleets of bombers in the 'next war' droning over major cities and flattening them as they beat off attacks by ineffective interceptors. Reasoning at the time figured that a massive, ultra-heavily armed fighter could blast its way

into the envisioned solid wall of bombers and break apart the formations by sheer fire-power. It seems that little realistic thought was given to these future super bombers along with the fact that Japan, Germany and any other possible hostile nation had nothing even approaching this high-altitude multi-engine fleet. Nevertheless, the concept of a super fighter remained as an idea that intrigued the Army, RAF, and *Luftwaffe* and each group would try to eventually build their own version.

Back at Lockheed the super Lightning program was beginning to take form as an enlarged P–38 capable of wading into formations of enemy bombers or escorting the Army's own strategic bombers and warding off attacks by hostile fighters. A heavy armament was proposed for the aircraft, which had taken the designation XP–58, and would include a 20 mm cannon (soon increased to two cannons) and two Browning air cooled .50 caliber machine guns in the nose along with a .50 caliber mounted in each tail boom to ward off attacks from the rear. A gunner would be seated behind the pilot with a remote control sight to fire the tail guns. At this time, the XP–58 was seen as being a bit larger than the P–38 and powered by two Continental IV–1430 engines which had originally been designed in the late 1930s.

The Army wanted some commonality between the P–38 and XP–58 and requested that Lockheed use as many interchangeable parts as possible. The Continental engine was, of course, an untried factor but the company had a good reputation of building reliable powerplants for a wide variety of civilian and smaller military aircraft. The only other American high-performance inline engine available in quantity was the Allison and the shortcomings of this powerplant have already been discussed in other chapters so the prospect of a new military liquid-cooled engine was very welcome. Continental had sent the specifications for their IV–1430 to the Army back in the late part of 1939 but the Army had wanted more horsepower than the engine could produce (1,600 hp) and the project was shelved. A proposal for a mated version of the engine (designated H–2860 and capable of 3,200 hp) was also dropped because the Army felt that

The XP–58 after arrival at Wright Field where it underwent limited testing before being scrapped, having flown for a bit over 20 test flights before leaving the Lockheed factory. The XP–58 was completely outclassed by other fighter aircraft already in service and its large size handicapped any possible fighting performance. The propellers on the Allison V–3420s rotated in opposite directions ('handed'), as on the P–38 Lightning. (USAF)

the other more established engine companies would come up with similar engines in a shorter space of time. Both decisions were to prove to be incorrect and, with a historical hindsight, it appears that both engines could have been successfully developed especially with the lead times available if they had been ordered in 1939. With the emergence of the XP–58, the IV–1430 was dusted off and given a full development contract.

As Lockheed studied the Army requirement it quickly became apparent that the aircraft was beginning to grow at an alarming rate and that greater power would be needed. The first change in consideration of the XP–58's power-plants came during the middle of 1940 when the IV–1430s were dropped in favor of yet another new engine. This time the choice fell upon the Pratt & Whitney H–2600 which was a ponderous sleeve-valve (a type of engine favored by the Bristol Company in England) capable of 2,200 hp. This liquid-cooled giant fell by the wayside when Hap Arnold decided that Pratt & Whitney should spend its time and resources developing the incredibly successful R–2800 series of radials. Pratt & Whitney proposed that Lockheed install the R–2800 in the XP–58 but Lockheed felt that a different powerplant was needed.

There must have been a great deal of frustration in the Lockheed design department at the company's Burbank factory when the Wright R–2160 Tornado was selected for the XP–58. Each engine change also meant extensive interior changes to the aircraft's motor mounts, cowlings, interior plumbing and radiator set-up. The Tornado was an interesting engine as it used six rows of seven cylinders, was liquid-cooled, and was capable of pumping out at least 2,500 hp. The Army appeared to be interested in the engine when, during November 1940, it issued a contract for engines to be supplied to the XP–58.

The concept of extra power may have been a curse for the XP–58 as both the Army and Lockheed immediately began considering other items that they could tack onto the fighter to take advantage of the power and the proposed top speed of at least 450 mph. One of the first considerations was in the field of armament. The original armament was not all that heavy so Lockheed decided to install two turrets in the fuselage pod, one on top and one below, each with two .50 caliber machine guns while the nose section would take the very heavy armament of four 37 mm cannon, a burst from which would demolish any aircraft, be it bomber or fighter. To adequately equip the cabin area for high altitude fighting, the Army and Lockheed agreed that the aircraft should be pressurized. The weight of the extra guns, ammunition, turrets, sighting

mechanism, and pressurization system was making the weight of the XP–58 soar.

As metal cutting started on the first XP–58, the second prototype was delayed so additional fuel tanks could be designed that would increase the aircraft's range on internal fuel to just over 3,000 miles. During the middle of 1941, Wright completed its first entire R–2160 and every bit of extra power that the elegant engine could produce would be needed for the gross weight of the XP–58 had almost doubled and now was approaching 36,000 lb!

By 1942 it should have been clear to the Army that the massive formations of enemy bombers were just not going to appear. In fact it seems that the Axis had virtually neglected the development of an efficient four engine bombing aircraft that could penetrate vast distances and defend itself against enemy fighter attacks – certainly one of the real failings of the German and Japanese aircraft industries. The need for a porcine behemoth to wade into imagined bomber formations – without first being blown out of the sky itself – was just non-existent. However, both concerns in the XP–58 program seemed to ignore this fact but the Army Air Force pulled a surprise late in 1942 when it suddenly, and radically, changed the XP–58's role – it would now be dedicated to ground attack!

Admittedly the four 37 mm cannon in the nose would be a powerful weapon in the ground attack mission but the aircraft was extremely large (hence making a good target for all those enraged infantry men being strafed) and the plumbing system for the liquid-cooled engines was a nightmare that would have easily been destroyed or damaged by even the lightest flak. The size of the XP–58 meant that it could carry even larger weapons than the 37 mm cannons so the Army began investigating the possibilities of installing a massive 75 mm cannon in the nose in place of the other guns. In the low level role the pressurization and turrets could be deleted but, because of extra armor and ammunition, the gross weight of the aircraft actually edged up a few more pounds.

The decision on the ground attack mission did not mean that the program was going to enjoy a voyage through smooth waters. On the contrary, the requirements and problems were going to become more complex. Once again, the Army changed missions and the XP–58 went back to attacking bombers and any fighter that would sit still and let the lumbering twin-boom monster shoot it down. To make matters more difficult, Wright was having a great deal of trouble with the Tornado and could not guarantee a delivery date to even match the very slow development schedule of the XP–58 so the Army called for yet another

engine change. This time it was the ugly and not particularly promising Allison V–3420 which was an H–engine made by joining two of the company's V–1710s together.

It was back to the drawing board at Lockheed, where much cursing was probably being done by the accountants who had been tallying the rising cost of the Army's 'free' fighter. New cowlings, tail booms, radiators, and interior plumbing were once again designed and, finally, a fix was put on the project and construction began to rapidly proceed although by mid 1943 it must have been evident to all concerned that the XP–58 did not fit in to a war that was being fought and won by aircraft such as the Mustang, Thunderbolt, and Lightning.

Dubbed Chain Lightning by Lockheed employees, the XP–58, in a note of perhaps final irony, lifted into the air over Burbank, California, on 6 June 1944 – the day of the Allied invasion of Fortress Europe. By this time the second XP–58 had been cancelled but the first prototype continued limited flight testing and completed over 20 flights before being transferred to Wright Field where it is thought that the aircraft flew only a very few times before eventually being scrapped. Apparently the XP–58 had nice handling qualities once in the air but the complex engines and all the associated plumbing and systems made the Chain Lightning a maintenance nightmare and fires within the turbosuperchargers were a frequent problem and the flames kept scorching the tail surfaces and booms. The aircraft never had the turrets, armament, or pressurization system installed and the XP–58 served as a monument to an expensive idea that had gone wrong – very wrong.

LOCKHEED XP–58 CHAIN LIGHTNING SERIAL NUMBERS AND SPECIFICATIONS

Serial Number

XP–58	41–2670

XP–58 Chain Lightning

Span	70 ft
Length	49 ft 4 in
Height	13 ft 7 in
Wing area	600 sq ft
Empty weight	31,625 lb
Loaded weight	39,190 lb
Max. speed	435 mph
Cruise speed	275 mph
Ceiling	40,000 ft
Rate of climb	2,660 fpm
Range	1,400 miles
Powerplant	Two Allison V–3420s of 3,000 hp each

PART THREE

Bell P-59A
Airacomet — America's First Jet Fighter

The Airacomet was America's first entry into the jet age, yet it was an aircraft that was destined for little more than a training role.

If there was one statement that could be made of Larry Bell, president of Bell Aircraft Corporation, it was that he was not afraid of new ideas. His Airacuda and Airacobra had deeply impressed Army Air Force officials with their advanced, if flawed, concepts and the name of Bell would not be left out of future discussions involving new or advanced technology for combat aircraft.

During the time that Bell was setting up shop to build aircraft in New York, an equally creative and far-thinking fellow was struggling to get his new and revolutionary ideas accepted in England. Frank Whittle, a young Royal Air Force officer, was developing workable ideas for a new form of aircraft powerplant. Whittle, as a cadet at the RAF College in 1928, had written a term paper advocating the development of gas turbine engines for aircraft power. This, of course, was during the period when the RAF was operating nothing but biwinged aircraft that dated back to World

A rather dramatic portrait shows an XP–59 on the hardstand at Muroc with the pilot in full cold weather flying gear getting ready to mount up. The flat Dark Olive Drab and Neutral Gray finish is shown to good advantage in this view. The two 37 mm cannon were mounted on either side of the landing light and were equipped with 40 rounds of ammunition apiece. Cannon armament was never all that much favored by World War Two American aircraft designers but cannons were a mainstay of the Bell fighter designs. (Bell Aircraft Corporation)

The first Bell XP–59A in flight over the Mojave Desert, an ideal testing location for the super-secret aircraft as the site was far removed from regular population. The family lines from the Airacobra and Kingcobra are evident in this view, particularly in the wing area. The XP–59A was kept as simple as possible making the craft look a bit like a child's model glider. After a few short hops in ground effect, the Airacomet made its first flight on 1 October 1942 with test pilot Bob Stanley at the controls. The Airacomet exhibited few vices but it was underpowered and above 300 mph it exhibited a lack of directional stability which made for a poor gun platform. (Bell Aircraft Corporation)

War One and had a difficult time struggling past the 100 mph mark. Reaction to the paper was one of academic interest but, much like stating that it would be nice for a man to travel to the moon, the idea was not favored by the RAF and, although it was termed a *nice* concept, no action was undertaken in official circles to study the feasibility of a new technology powerplant. The Air Ministry was still locked in the biplane era!

Whittle, of course, did not forget the idea and continued the development and pursuit of his dream, filing for a British patent during January 1930. With patent application in hand, Whittle next approached the Air Ministry to try to gain some development funds for the project. Whittle, however, was turned down by the Air Ministry (a British institution that, at that time, was not known for its far thinking) so he tried the privately owned British aircraft factories but was again met by rejection on the grounds that the transfer of the concept from paper to an actual working engine was beyond the bounds of current technology.

Depressed and set back by running into what seemed insurmountable brick walls, Whittle even let the patent for his revolutionary idea lapse. However, the situation brightened considerably in 1935 when two ex-RAF friends of Whittle's came forward and offered

to invest some very needed money and a firm called Power Jets Limited was incorporated legally during March 1936. Whittle and his partners worked on the design of the gas turbine at a frantic pace and, a few months later, a contract was issued to the British Thomson-Houston Company for the construction of the first Whittle turbine engine.

Of course, any revolutionary idea is not usually the exclusive product of any one mind, no matter how great that mind is and, across the North Sea in the heart of Germany, other scientists were at work on new propulsion systems for aircraft and rockets. Their eventual aim, or rather the aim of their masters, was perhaps not as altruistic as Whittle's, for the newly developing and highly secret *Luftwaffe* had need for aircraft of advanced technology and high performance.

In the United States the idea of gas turbine power for aircraft was really not even dis-

cussed among the major aircraft manufacturers as, once again, the reality of the concept seemed to be far in the future. Certainly the moving pictures starring those interchangeable heroes, Buck Rogers and Flash Gordon, caught the public's imagination with their fast-moving rocket ships. During the 1930s the term 'jet' was usually applied to craft powered by rockets or other forms of non-airbreathing engines.

Back in England, Whittle had gotten his first experimental engine running and, although the power output was very low, results were extremely encouraging. Testing was carried out during 1937 and the struggling company's efforts were finally rewarded with government notice and a contract for an airworthy engine. Gloster Aircraft Company was contracted to build a test airframe, known as the E.28/39, to test the concept. Engine and airframe were mated and flown for the first

time on 15 May 1941 but the honor for the first gas turbine powered aircraft flight had already been taken by the Germans on 27 August 1939 when the Heinkel He 178 first took to the air, powered by an engine developed by Hans von Ohain.

The military in the United States was not unaware of the new advances being made in gas turbine and rocket propulsion and several high-level discussions took place culminating in a visit by General Hap Arnold to England during April 1941, when he observed several test hops by the E.28/39. Arnold, impressed by the concepts being developed by the English designers, contacted the State Department in Washington with a view towards carrying out discussions on an agreement for a transfer of gas turbine technology between Britain and the United States. The agreement was drawn up during September and called for the production of three aircraft and 15 gas turbine, or jet,

Clearly showing tall tail surfaces of the XP–59A, Bob Stanley pilots the aircraft above the Mojave Desert. Note that this is a later photograph and the newer style insignia has been applied. The General Electric I–A engines that powered the XP–59A were capable of producing 1,250 lb of thrust each. Early photographs of the XP–59A prototypes show that they did not carry the serial number in the standard position on the fin and rudder, probably for security reasons. The serials were added at a later date. (General Electric)

engines. The Whittle engines were to be constructed by General Electric as Arnold held the view that the main engine manufacturers such as Allison, Pratt & Whitney, and Wright were too busy on current reciprocating engine projects along with the fact that these 'traditional' engine builders might not take kindly to the idea of a totally new powerplant.

The decision as to the airframe manufacturer came about during a series of discussions involving a number of diverse factors and Bell

This YP-59A, 42-108783, was modified to a two-seat configuration with the second cockpit located in the nose with just a small windshield to protect the occupant. The Airacomets were rather unique for having these open cockpit second positions, the only jet aircraft to be so modified. Mystic Mistress was used as a mother aircraft during the development of radio controlled equipment for drone aircraft in the latter part of 1944 and the early part of 1945. The first 'robot' aircraft was another YP-59 but it was destroyed during a radio-controlled take off. A P-59B replaced the wrecked Airacomet for the remainder of the trials. Before its conversion to a two seater, the Mistress had been used for Airacomet weapons trials and it was with this aircraft that test pilots determined that the Airacomet series of aircraft would make poor gun platforms. (E. Deigan)

Aircraft Corporation in Buffalo, New York, was awarded the contract to build the three twin-engine airframes. Several reasons were advanced for the order in favour of Bell and included the fact that Bell was close to the General Electric facilities, that Bell was not overly burdened with the rapidly growing new combat aircraft construction programs as were other manufacturers, that the Bell design staff was small but highly innovative, and that Bell had a number of test sites which were far from the public eye.

General Arnold immediately called a meeting with Bell and his chief designer, Harland Poyer, to discuss the feasibility of Bell Aircraft handling the project. Both men were highly enthusiastic and felt confident that the new fighter could be constructed. When Bell and Poyer returned to their factory they selected a

small group of aeronautical engineers who were sworn to secrecy as Arnold had impressed on the two the need for an absolute blackout on what was going on at the New York factory. The small group of men, with only a very rough generalized sketch of the powerplant to go on, developed a $\frac{1}{20}$th scale model of their proposed fighter within the amazingly short period of two weeks.

As the design of the aircraft progressed, the problem of designation cropped up. Wanting to maintain their silence on the project, Bell and the USAAF decided to designate the aircraft as the XP-59A. The XP-59 was a projected fighter design that had been drawn up in the past by Bell engineers. The aircraft was a propeller-driven pusher fighter with twin booms, somewhat like the Lockheed P-38. It was thought that the dusting off of this old designation, with the addition of an A, would make any spies think that Bell was merely doing some additional developing of a previously thought out design. The company assigned the jet aircraft the Bell model number of 27.

The problem of security was a very real one for aeronautical companies in those dark days immediately before America's entry into World War Two. It was known that the Germans had a fairly effective spy network operating in the country, misguidedly assisted by many citizens of German heritage. Bell engineers were moved into an old car factory

where they could prepare their drawings and concepts away from prying eyes while another old building on the main street of Buffalo was rented as the site for the actual construction of the three prototypes. In the meantime, negotiations were proceeding smoothly with the British in regards to the transfer of license rights for the building of the new jet engine.

It was decided that the American program could be considerably aided by shipping an entire Whittle unit to the Buffalo factory. Accordingly, one of the early Whittle units that had been used in the taxiing tests of the Gloster fighter was carefully packaged and inserted into a special carrier in the bomb bay of a Consolidated B-24 Liberator bomber. The flight went well but the secret nature of the mission was nearly ruined by overly anxious customs officials who demanded to see what the aircraft was carrying in its bomb bay. High-ranking government sources quickly stamped out any further interest in the crate and the engine was transferred to General Electric who had built a special test cell for the Whittle engine at their Lynn, Massachusetts, facility.

General Electric was a bit dismayed about the quality of the engineering drawings that had accompanied the powerplant as they felt that the drawings were a bit overly basic and that certain parts of the engine were not covered at all. General Electric quickly requested that their engineers be allowed to make design changes on areas that they felt were inadequate and to proceed on constructing the parts for the engine that were not detailed in the drawings. This was approved and, by a massive effort of all those concerned, the first General Electric Type I–A was run on 18 March 1942, the first of thirty such powerplants to be constructed for the XP–59. The 'I' designation was another security ploy, hoping to disguise the engine as a turbosupercharger, a main stable of the General Electric building program. The engine produced 1,250 lb of thrust but had a number of developmental problems, including exceedingly high exhaust gas temperature. Frank Whittle made a special visit to General Electric to deliver new, more detailed drawings and he stayed around long enough to help iron out the problems with the I–A.

Meanwhile, Bell's design team was proceeding at a fast pace but had encountered a number of problems due to the security of the project. A wind tunnel model had been tested in the tunnel at Wright Field but the engineers wanted to test a larger model in the huge NACA wind tunnel to help develop the design of the air intakes. The request was not granted as it was felt that the use of the NACA wind tunnel would not be a security controlled operation.

With the very limited time at hand, Bell engineers could not be overly creative in the design of the XP–59A so they stuck to principles that had been tried and proven with their Airacuda and Airacobra projects and the XP–59A's lines owed a great deal to these two aircraft. Construction of the XP–59A was absolutely conventional for the time period, with no new manufacturing techniques being employed. The design was basically the simplest carrier for the two General Electric jets that could be built. The design drawings were carefully monitored so as not to let any of the employees in the manufacturing section know exactly what the newly built parts were going to be incorporated with. The airframe of the XP–59A was all metal except for the use of fabric covered control surfaces and flaps, a feature that seems outdated but, at the time, was adequate for other high-performance aircraft. However, testing revealed that the fabric did distort under high speeds and the fabric on the tail surfaces was always in danger of catching fire in the event of an engine 'hot start'. The fabric was replaced with metal after the first Airacomets had been built. Bell's

tricycle landing gear was also employed on the XP–59A as the nose wheel offered much improved ground handling, as had been discovered with the modified Airacuda and the Airacobra.

As construction of the Airacomets progressed the problem of how to get the aircraft out of the rather small building cropped up. A large hole was knocked in the wall of the second floor of the old building where the fighters were being built and a simple crane was installed to carefully lower the crated components of the fighters on to flat cars on the railway spur line that passed next to the building.

It was obvious from the beginning that the new aircraft could not be tested from the Buffalo airport where Bell did its flight test work on the more conventional aircraft. The question of where to find a spot where the

The second production P–59A built, 44–22610. After a careful USAAF analysis of the Airacomet it was concluded that the Airacomet was 'not operationally or tactically suited for combat nor is it believed that any modifications to this aircraft, short of a completely new design, would improve its combat suitability.' The 50 production Airacomets that were built were used for training purposes. (Bell Aircraft Corporation)

physical testing could be undertaken with complete secrecy was a vexing one. Two USAAF officers associated with the Bell project were given the task of scouting the country to find a suitable site. After some consideration they finally settled on the USAAF's Muroc Bombing and Gunnery Range in the middle of Southern California's Mojave Desert. Since few people in their right mind would set up residence in such an unlikely hell hole, it would be easy for USAAF security personnel to keep watch on the very few residents. Accordingly, plans were undertaken to move the disassembled aircraft to Muroc for the intensive testing program. The USAAF did not even have to worry about runways for the rock-hard smooth surface of the Muroc Dry Lake offered virtually miles of unobstructed runway, ideal for the testing of a new aircraft that might want to quit flying at any moment and leave the hapless pilot frantically searching for a landing spot. The selection of Muroc was to have far-reaching importance for the USAAF

for the area eventually became the site of Edwards AFB, home for America's most famous aircraft and spacecraft testing programs.

In the early morning hours of 19 September 1942, the first XP-59 with its three I-A engines, associated mechanics and security guards arrived at the wind-swept desolation of Muroc; the crew were a bit dismayed to see that construction work on their hangars and barracks was not *quite* finished. However, inflamed with the enthusiasm for their new project, the men dug into their spartan surroundings and prepared their charge for testing.

Veteran Bell test pilot Bob Stanley had been picked to handle the test flights and he had been in close contact with the engineers at Bell and General Electric in order to pick up any hints concerning the unusual beast that he was to take into the air for the first time. Along with learning the systems of his new charge, Stanley and his fellow troops from Bell and the

USAAF had to lend a hand in finishing the hangar and barracks since all the civilian contract workmen had to be dismissed with the arrival of the jet!

With a first flight date set for 2 October, much hard work was called for from all involved with the project. The assembly of the aircraft and the mating of the engines went smoothly and no damage had been incurred in the long train trip from the East Coast. Initial engine runs took place on 26 September and Stanley began to make taxi tests with the aircraft to get a feel of the controls. During several of the high speed taxi tests actual lift off occurred for a few moments. On 1 October Bob Stanley made history when he lugged the XP-59A into the air after a lengthy take off run across the surface of the dry lake. Four flights were made during the day, all of short duration and all with the landing gear firmly in the fixed down position. A number of important people gathered for the 'first' test flight of the XP-59A on 2 October and they watched as Bob Stanley

made two flights in the Olive Drab and Neutral Gray camouflaged jet, one flight climbing to an altitude of 10,000 ft. Looking back on the program, it is amazing how smoothly everything went, especially considering the nature of the highly experimental jet engines with their unknown operational life times. In fact, since the jets were an unknown quantity Bell and General Electric decided that it would be wise to change the powerplants after a few flights rather than risk engine failure.

By the start of the new year, the other two XP–59As were at Muroc, being assembled and readied to join the testing program. In order to obtain more test data, the first XP–59A had a second cockpit cut into the forward nose

This side view of 44–22610 shows the installation of the three .50 caliber Browning machine guns and the 37 mm cannon in the nose. Production models of the Airacomet were left in their bare metal finish. The production Airacomets had a slightly bulged hood to help improve pilot headroom and visibility. (Bell Aircraft Corporation)

position with a small windshield installed on top of the fuselage. An observer's seat was placed in the cockpit and the unfortunate individual that had to man this rather exposed position would record data while the pilot concentrated on flying the fighter. Several Airacomets were modified this way, certainly the first and last open cockpit installation on a jet fighter.

Back at the factory work was progressing on the second batch of Airacomets, 13 YP–59As. However, problems at General Electric were cutting into the delivery schedule of the completed aircraft, General Electric had to face many new problems in producing the jet engines so it was perhaps to be expected that the schedule would slip.

The YP–59A was basically similar to the first three aircraft but some design detail refinements had been added. The throw over canopy of the XP–59A had been replaced by a more conventional hood that slid back and forth on rails. The aircraft was built to hold the more powerful I–16 engines but, since these were not available on time, smaller jet pipes were added to the first few YP–59As so that they could fly with the less powerful I–A or I–14B engines. The first two YP–59s flew during August and September of 1943. The Airacomet, as the jet fighter became known after a Bell employee contest to pick a suitable name, was no speed demon, attaining a maximum speed of about 390 mph at 35,000 ft. The initial armament of the XP–59A had been a proposed load of two 37 mm cannon mounted in the nose. These heavy cannon would have destroyed anything in the air but it was decided to settle on an armament of one 37 mm cannon and three .50 caliber machine guns in the YP–59A. Armament testing with the YP–59As brought forth a rather surprising fact: the Airacomet was a poor gun platform above 290 mph as it became directionally unstable above that speed, especially when the guns were fired.

Heavy rains in the early part of 1943 over the Muroc area stopped all test flying when the Muroc Dry Lake suddenly stopped being dry and the entire area flooded. Accordingly all test flying was moved to nearby Victorville Army Air Force Base during March 1943 and, since the area was more populated, the Airacomets were fitted with canvas covers over their nose sections and curious little propellers were tacked on to the nose to hide the real propulsive means. However, once in the air the deception proved to be a bit fruitless as the local citizenry soon became used to the strange howling 'jet' noise emitted by the Airacomets as they carved trails in the bright blue California sky.

By April the prehistoric sea bed surface of

the dry lake had once again hardened to its smooth rock like finish and the Airacomets moved back for continued testing, building up the knowledge of operating the sensitive jet engines. The I–16 engines, being more powerful, were also not as reliable and very few of the engines made it to their recommended service life of 50 hours before being pulled out and overhauled.

The YP–59As at Muroc were tested against the Republic Thunderbolt and Lockheed Lightning with discouraging results; the Airacomet could not hold its own with the propeller-driven fighters. The only plus in the Airacomet's favor was that it could out turn the large Lightning. General Hap Arnold reviewed the test results and concluded that the Airacomet would not be the first mass-produced operational jet fighter for the USAAF. However, Arnold did praise the test program and the dedication of the Bell and General Electric employees in developing an experimental aircraft that would put America in the front of all jet fighter development.

Accordingly, activity at Muroc was cut back and Bell employees began to pack up their tools and belongings for the trip back to New York. The Bell test facility had assembled and flown three XP–59As and six YP–59As for a total of 242.5 hours with a mishap. It was certainly a proud record that would establish Muroc as the world's top aircraft testing base. As the Bell program closed down at Muroc, Lockheed entered the facility with its new XP–80, the first prototype of the aircraft that became the USAAF's first operational jet fighter.

Even though the Muroc program was closed down, testing of the Airacomet still continued. The XP–59As were modified to YP–59A standard by the modification of the tail and wing tips and the replacement of the fabric on the control surfaces with metal. It was decided that Bell should produce 300 production-version Airacomets. However, this order would have absorbed the entire General Electric run of I–16 jets while deleting 600 Kingcobras from the Bell production line. The Kingcobra was needed to supply the Russian Lend-Lease order for aircraft so the production run on the P–59A was cut to 100 Airacomets. A formal order was issued on 11 March 1944 for the production of 100 aircraft at $123,477 per example. Bell engineers had been working on ways of improving the performance of the Airacomet and had decided to install added fuel tanks in the outer wing panels to extend the range beginning with the 21st airframe; the new designation of P–59B–1 would be applied. A distinct surprise to the Bell organization came on 10 October when Larry Bell was notified that the Airacomet production line would be stopped with the 39th aircraft. Bell negotiated with the USAAF and came to an agreement that, for economic reasons, it would be best to cancel the Airacomet at the 50th airframe. Thus the total production of the Airacomet would consist of 20 P–59A–1s and 30 P–59B–1s with acceptance of the type being completed by 27 August 1945.

Production versions of the Airacomet were scattered around the country. A number were dispatched to various Air Force facilities for familiarity training while some aircraft were stored by Bell for lack of engines. The majority of the Bell order went to the 412th Fighter Group at Santa Maria, California. Here the Airacomets were used to train new pilots in the art of jet flying. In January 1946, Santa Maria was closed down and the Airacomets were scattered to the four winds. A number went to the Aberdeen Proving Ground in Maryland where they were used as targets, others were scrapped or sent to schools where they could be used as mechanical training aids. A few survived to eventually be displayed in museums as examples of American aeronautical creativity. By 1950, not one example of

the Airacomet remained airworthy and that included the three examples that had been transferred to the US Navy as that service's first jet fighter.

Although achieving little in the form of operational history, the Bell Airacomet did forge an important link in the development of the American jet fighter as stated by Larry Bell on 7 January 1944:

'We believe that the hundreds of successful flights made by Bell jet-propelled ships opens a new chapter in American aviation history.

'Bell Aircraft has built the first American fighter planes powered by jet propulsion engines constructed by the General Electric Company from British designs.

'They prove a new scientific principle – that planes can fly without propellers. Once a principle is proved, count on the engineering genius of the Allied Powers to develop it into greater performance records, not only to help speed the day of victory but to pave the way towards new achievements in a postwar aviation world.'

BELL P–59A AIRACOMET SERIAL NUMBERS AND SPECIFICATIONS

Serial Numbers

XP–59A	42–108784/8786
YP–59A	42–108771/8783
P–59A–1	44–22609/2628
P–59B–1	44–22629/2658

Specifications

XP–59A Airacomet

Span	49 ft
Length	38 ft 10 in
Height	12 ft 3¾ in
Wing area	200 sq ft
Empty weight	7,950 lb
Loaded weight	11,700 lb
Max. speed	389 mph
Cruise speed	280 mph
Ceiling	40,000 ft
Rate of climb	1,200 fpm
Range	520 miles
Powerplant	Two General Electric I–A turbojets of 1,250 lb thrust each

Curtiss P-60
The Search For Success

Each subsequent version of the ill-starred Curtiss P–60 seemed to be farther and farther away from the success that the company needed.

As mentioned previously in this volume, mismanagement and poor designs at Curtiss led the company from being America's largest producer of pursuit aircraft at the start of World War Two to being a fourth rate company by 1945 whose designs were looked upon with a mixture of contempt and humor by the more successful aircraft manufacturers. Perhaps no other aircraft outlines the Curtiss downfall in fortunes than the P–60, a series of unattractive fighters whose history is as complex as their performance was poor.

During 1940 Curtiss was quite pleased with the large numbers of P–40s that were beginning to pour from the Buffalo, New York, factory but, realizing that times were rapidly changing, work was instigated on the production of a superior fighter aircraft that could eventually take over where the P–40 left off. In order to speed the production of a new fighter it was planned to use a wing based on the laminar flow airfoil (as used on the new P–51) with a fuselage that was basically that of an updated P–40D. Power was to be supplied by a Rolls-Royce Merlin V–1650–1 built by Packard in the United States. An eight gun .50 caliber armament was to be fitted and the new aircraft was designated the XP–60. The XP–60 owed much of its design to the early uncompleted XP–53 which was to be a follow-on to the unsuccessful XP–46. The XP–53 was to have had a laminar wing and was to have been powered by the Continental XIV–1430–3 but problems with the engine led to the project being dropped. However, the partially completed XP–53 airframe was used for static and equipment tests for the XP–60.

Even though Curtiss had spent considerable time attempting to produce a clean airframe, getting rid of the primitive gear retracting layout of the P–40 in favor of a flush retracting gear, the resulting aircraft was quite unattractive – looking a bit like a stretched P–40. The XP–60 made its first flight on 18 September 1941 and performance with the V–1650–1 was not all that spectacular – top speed being estimated at 380 mph. Curtiss also proposed another version of the P–60 that would be powered by an Allison with a turbo-supercharger. The Army looked upon this aircraft with a bit more favor as they felt that Packard would be hard pressed to produce the numbers of Merlin engines needed.

The ungraceful XP–60D in the air. When the basic XP–60 was modified to include a larger vertical tail and an uprated Rolls-Royce engine the designation was switched from XP–60 to XP–60D. The XP–60 featured a laminar flow wing, to which Curtiss had pinned unreasonable expectations, and a fuselage that was basically similar to that of a P–40D. Curtiss found that, during testing, it was extremely difficult to keep the fine finish, needed for perfect laminar flow, on the wing surface. Although designed to carry eight .50 caliber machine guns in the wing, the XP–60 never had the armament installed. First flown on 18 September 1941, the aircraft never completed a full flight test program. (Curtiss)

The new aircraft carried the Curtiss designation of Model 95A and the Army designation of XP–60A. This aircraft was to utilize the same wing as the XP–60 but an entirely new fuselage was to be built. The final result was a squat looking machine with little elegance. The Allison was installed under an extremely bulky cowling along with a General Electric turbosupercharger that was to be the aircraft's undoing. The Army seemed to like the XP–60A and ordered 1,950 aircraft in a contract dated 31st October 1941 with deliveries to begin in September of the next year. However, a further look at the XP–60A convinced the Army that the aircraft was not what they wanted and, less than a month later, the contract was cancelled which was a big blow to Curtiss. The Army suggested that Curtiss proceed with a new version of the P–60 design that would have considerably more performance or set up a production line to build the

Most powerful looking of the P–60 series was the XP–60C which featured a contra-rotating Aeroproducts propeller and a Pratt & Whitney R–2800–53 of 2,000 hp. The XP–60C was basically an XP–60A airframe fitted with the new propeller and engine combination. Originally designed to take the new Chrysler XIV–2220 engine of 2,300 hp, the aircraft was equipped with the Pratt & Whitney unit when it became apparent that the Chrysler unit was not a feasible project. To save weight armament had been reduced to only four .50 caliber guns. The XP–60C ran into problems when the Army felt that Pratt & Whitney would have a hard time producing the R–2800 modified for contra-rotating props in sufficient numbers for production. (Curtiss)

Republic P–47 Thunderbolt under contract. Curtiss was not overly thrilled with building another manufacturer's aircraft and work went ahead on producing an improved version of the P–60A.

Pearl Harbor meant a rapid change in the Army's plans for acquiring aircraft and contracts were worked out with Curtiss whereby the company would construct a series of prototypes based on the P–60 – along with setting up production for at least 2,400 P–47G Thunderbolts, so Curtiss did not escape the fate of producing someone else's aircraft.

Problems in getting the XP–60A into the air continued and the aircraft was damaged when the turbosupercharger caught fire during ground runs. The unit kept giving considerable trouble so it was finally removed and the engine's exhaust system revised before the first flight was made on 1 November 1942. Minus the General Electric unit, the XP–60A's performance was less than sparkling. Since the contract had been cancelled, testing on the XP–60A was extremely sporadic and only a few flights were undertaken.

The next step in the P–60 saga was the XP–60C which was to have an experimental Chrysler XIV–2220 but problems with the powerplant forced abandonment of the proposal and it was decided that the XP–60C design would be modified to take the Pratt & Whitney R–2800–53 radial. The XP–60C had a rather formidable look, with the big radial

and the contra-rotating Aeroproducts propeller with a diameter of 12 ft 2 in. In order to make an attempt to reduce the rapidly increasing overall weight, the XP–60C was to be equipped with only four .50 caliber guns so the requirement of the aircraft having an eight gun armament was not met. Curtiss predicted a top speed of over 400 mph for the new fighter and the Army, once again, was interested in the P–60 series. A contract for 500 Pratt & Whitney-engined fighters with the designation P–60A–1–CU was drawn up in November 1942 but problems soon arose. It was felt by the Army that Pratt & Whitney would have trouble producing the special version of the R–2800 needed for the contra-rotating propeller. It was decided that the R–2800–10 with a four blade propeller would be substituted for the contra-rotating unit and the XP–60B, which was basically identical to the XP–60A, except for the General Electric turbosupercharger being replaced with a Wright unit, was modified to take the R–2800–10 and a new designation, XP–60E, was applied.

By this time the XP–60C was ready to fly and it took to the air for the first time on 27th January 1943 and displayed fairly pleasant flying characteristics. The XP–60E soon followed the XP–60C into the air, flying for the first time on 26 May but, during an early test flight, the engine quit and the aircraft was damaged in the ensuing crash landing. This accident led to a further problem in keeping the

P–60 series in a clear progression of order for the XP–60C had its engine and contra-rotating prop removed and the Pratt & Whitney R–2800–10 installed so that flight testing could continue at a fast pace. The damaged XP–60E was repaired at Curtiss using the wings of the XP–60A (which had been withdrawn from flying and broken down for parts after a couple of test flights) and the engine and contra-rotating propellers from the XP–60C. So, in effect, the aircraft had reversed identities.

Limited flight testing resumed after the repair work and the single propeller variant was not as fast but the reduction in weight from the dropping of the heavier unit did aid overall performance a bit. Once again the Army took a hard look at the whole project and, once again, cancelled the whole mess – feeling that their P–47 and P–51 could do everything better than the P–60s. When the contract was cancelled on 3 June 1943 it was decided to finish off the first two YP–60A–1–CUs, which were on the production line and partially completed, as YP–60Es.

The YP–60E looked considerably different from the previous P–60 aircraft since it dispensed with the built-up turtledeck behind the cockpit and added a bubble canopy atop the fuselage. The YP–60E also featured a redesigned and cleaned up cowling, a six gun wing and increased internal fuel. Curtiss did not like the idea of proceeding with the aircraft, which they had finally realized was a failure, but the Army insisted that the prototypes be completed and the first was eventually flown on 15th July 1944, while the other prototype was never completed and was junked. Unfortunately, the YP–60E enjoyed as little success as the previous aircraft for it was only flown twice before testing was dropped in order to 'save funds' which was a curious statement since the entire P–60 project had expended over $8,875,000 and countless man-hours – an expenditure that was made in the face of the fact that the P–60 series was never going to be a success.

The YP–60E was pushed out in the weeds during the later part of 1944 but, somehow, it survived the massive scrappings at the end of the war to appear at the 1947 Cleveland National Air Races with the civil registration NX21979. Flown by Jimmy DeSanto, the YP–60E's string of bad luck continued when DeSanto bailed out during a qualifying race and the YP–60E slammed into the earth and exploded.

The P–60 series spelled an inglorious end to the Curtiss domination of the American propeller-driven fighter market.

CURTISS P–60 SERIAL NUMBERS AND SPECIFICATIONS

Serial numbers

XP–60	41–19508
XP–60A	42–79423
XP–60C	42–79424
XP–60E	42–79425
YP–60E	43–32763

Specifications

All performance figures for the P–60 series should be regarded as manufacturer's estimates since the aircraft did not complete rigorous flight testing.

XP–60

Span	41 ft 5 in
Length	33 ft 4 in
Height	14 ft 4 in
Wing area	275 sq ft
Empty weight	7,008 lb
Loaded weight	9,961 lb
Max. speed	380 mph
Cruise speed	n/a
Ceiling	29,000 ft
Rate of climb	3,500 fpm
Range	n/a
Powerplant	Rolls-Royce Packard V–1650–1 of 1,120 hp

XP–60A

Span	41 ft 4 in
Length	33 ft 8 in
Height	12 ft 4 in
Wing Area	275 sq ft
Empty weight	7,806 lb
Loaded weight	10,160 lb
Max. speed	420 mph
Cruise speed	n/a
Ceiling	35,200 ft
Rate of climb	2,560 fpm
Range	n/a
Powerplant	Allison V–1710–75 of 1,425 hp

XP–60C

Span	41 ft 4 in
Length	34 ft 1 in
Height	15 ft
Wing area	275 sq ft
Empty weight	8,698 lb
Loaded weight	10,785 lb
Max. speed	414 mph
Cruise speed	n/a
Ceiling	37,900 ft
Rate of climb	3,890 fpm
Range	n/a
Powerplant	Pratt & Whitney R–2800–53 of 2,000 hp

XP–60E

Span	41 ft 4 in
Length	33 ft 11 in
Height	15 ft
Wing area	275 sq ft
Empty weight	8,574 lb
Loaded weight	10,667 lb
Max. speed	410 mph
Cruise speed	n/a
Ceiling	38,000 ft
Rate of climb	4,200 fpm
Range	n/a
Powerplant	Pratt & Whitney R–2800–10 of 2,000 hp

YP–60E

Span	41 ft 4 in
Length	33 ft 7 in
Height	13 ft 11 in
Wing area	275.15 sq ft
Empty weight	8,285 lb
Loaded weight	11,520 lb
Max. speed	405 mph
Cruise speed	n/a
Ceiling	34,000 ft
Rate of climb	4,200 fpm
Range	n/a
Powerplant	Pratt & Whitney R–2800–18 of 2,100 hp

Northrop P-61
Black Widow — Nocturnal Warrior

This Northrop design had the distinction of being the only specifically-built USAAF night fighter.

Today, Northrop Aircraft Corporation is known as a company that lavishly premiers its new aircraft to the news media and the public. Warplanes such as the F–18 Hornet and F–20 are presented with a certain amount of flash and pageantry, yet Northrop's first production fighter was uniquely presented to the public

during World War Two in a manner that would gladden any publicist's heart.

A very cool night had fallen over the Los Angeles Coliseum on 8 January 1944 but the chilly evening did not discourage the more than 100,000 spectators who packed the seats. Even though the war was going full bore, America was not that affected by blackouts or shortages compared to Britain which was reeling under a heavy series of restrictions on the civil populace along with a distinct lack of

edible foodstuffs. The war workers in the Coliseum were watching a gala Army-Navy entertainment show while stuffing in hot dogs, popcorn, and Coke. These massive shows seemed to be very popular with fun-starved war workers and soldiers who thought that anything Bob Hope or Betty Grable did was just great. Suddenly the Coliseum's lights dimmed and nearby searchlights began stabbing the night sky. An announcer – who would have done Walter Winchell proud – came on over

the public address system and launched into a perfect 1940's piece of rabid propaganda; 'Look! In the night skies, something fast and dark flashing through the searchlights. ... What you saw – if you looked fast enough – was America's newest fighting plane, the Northrop P–61 Black Widow.'

All this excitement produced considerable backslapping among the blue collar workers along with statements on how the new 'secret' fighter was going 'to get the Japs and Nazis'. Unfortunately, the new fighter was not all that secret – it had been the mount of a cartoon strip character for many months, but it is doubtful if enemy agents had been reading the funny papers. (When questioned on how he got information on the new fighter, the artist – who lived near Hawthorne – stated that he had seen the new fighter flying almost every day and simply liked the way it looked!)

Posing for a camera plane while on a test flight over the Southern California coast, this P–61B 42–39728 gives a good idea of the size of what was to be the USAAF's largest fighter aircraft. With all three crew members firmly strapped in and all three wearing the baseball caps that were popular with American World War Two airmen, the Black Widow displays its factory-fresh camouflage scheme. Camouflage for night fighters was a subject for great debate during the early years of World War Two and it finally fell to the Office of Scientific Research's Camouflage Section at the Massachusetts Institute of Technology to develop a paint that would render the night fighter 'invisible' when trapped in the enemy's searchlights. The best finish was found to be a very glossy black, which was virtually invisible in 80 per cent of the passes made through test searchlight beams. However, when the results of the test became known during the middle of October 1943, orders had already been issued to Northrop to paint the first Black Widows Olive Drab and Neutral Gray and conversion to the new paint scheme (called Jet or Anti-searchlight paint) did not take place until February 1944. (Northrop)

The Northrop P–61 Black Widow was to establish the Hawthorne, California, company as a major airframe builder and was to provide the USAAF with its only specifically-built night fighter of World War Two. Genesis for the aircraft, which was also to become the Army's largest – in the terms of size – production fighter, went back to 1940 when Britain was fighting for its survival and American observers were sent to England for neutral observation of the war situation and to foresee possible future military trends. One of the items that bothered the Americans most was the *Luftwaffe's* ability to roam over London at night, dropping heavy bomb loads and, for the most part, frustrating the attempts of the Royal Air Force fighters to intercept them. When the results were reported back to the USAAF planners, specifications were drawn up for an aircraft that could successfully intercept and destroy enemy aircraft at night. At this point, the art of night fighting was in an early stage of development. During World War One, brave pilots forced their BE2s, Sopwith Camels and other primitive aircraft to great heights to intercept and attack German Gothas and Zeppelins that were marauding over Britain. Such interceptions relied more on personal skill and bravery than any organized system of fighting. After World War One, development of the night fighter was virtually dropped as production was concentrated on more conservative combat aircraft. The Germans took advantage of this lack of night fighters to bring their war of terror to British cities after unacceptable daylight losses brought on by the stubborn RAF fighters made the day raids impossible. Various attempts were made to use Spitfires, Hurricanes and Defiants as night interceptors. Vectored to their approaching targets by pioneering British airborne radar, the pilots were pretty much on their own for the finding of the enemy aircraft and the attack. The night played strange tricks on the airmen's eyes and

aircraft that appeared close were quite often far away or *vice versa*. Other problems began to crop up with night fighters. Exhaust flames blinded the pilots so dampers or shields were fitted over exhaust stacks. The Spitfire, although an excellent day fighter, proved to be tricky to handle at night, its narrow track landing gear making night operations difficult. The more primitive Hurricane became an excellent night interceptor because it was much easier to handle both in the air and on the ground. The Defiant, with its lack of forward firing guns and slow top speed, did not enjoy much success but it was pressed into service with vigor since it was available in some numbers. Airborne radar-equipped Blenheims and Beaufighters soon followed and proved more successful – especially the powerful Beaufighter.

Visions of long-range enemy bombers attacking the coasts of America haunted military men for little was available to stop advanced aircraft from roaming at will over the night-time coastal towns. Anti-aircraft protection was inadequate – much of the equipment dated back to World War One – and searchlights were available only in limited numbers while shelters for the public were lacking.

The only production military aircraft that Northrop had built up until this time was the N–3PB, a sleek single-engine, twin-float patrol bomber that was manufactured for Norway – who purchased 24 of the machines. John Northrop and his design staff began work on the Army proposal during October 1940 but the project was beset with a variety of problems and it was a long time before the first aircraft flew from the Hawthorne plant. After putting in considerable overtime in the engineering department, Northrop presented the Army with the initial concept for the new night fighter during the first part of December but the Army wanted some minor changes and Northrop Specification NS–8A was submitted once again on 17 December and approved by the Army.

The new design was given the designation of XP–61 and the Army allocated $1,167,000 for the production of two prototypes, associated support items and a wooden wind tunnel model that could be used in the tunnels at Wright and Langley Fields. The original aircraft specification underwent many changes during the engineering stage, resulting in a lengthy time period before production of an actual flying prototype. For a start, the XP–61 would become the largest fighter that the Army had procured; its size easily matched that of any medium bomber, and the complexity of the new systems and techniques that were to be incorporated into the fighter also posed many delays. The initial design called for

USAAF s/n 41–19509 was the first XP–61 prototype. Seen at the Hawthorne factory, the prototype was finished in natural metal with yellow cowlings and spinners. The turret aerodynamic shape had been fitted but the canopies did not feature the armor glass windscreens of later variants. The engine set-up for the XP–61 was different in the original proposal. The aircraft (Northrop Specification NS–8A) was to have been powered by two Pratt & Whitney R–2800–A5G engines with a complex ducted spinner cooling system but the system was shelved and the engines that the prototype first flew with on 26 May 1942 were R–2800–25S Double Wasps and these were soon changed in favor of R–2800–10s. (Northrop)

a unique twin boom configuration with the crew of three housed in a large pod mounted to a sturdy center section. This fuselage nacelle would also house the radar and part of the armament. The wing was built up on two spars with stressed skin and cantilever structure and was assembled from six panels. The twin booms would house the two Pratt & Whitney R–2800–A5G engines with cooling air being supplied via ducted spinners, an idea that seemed to be left over from several unsuccessful Cleveland air racers. Each boom would carry a large fuel tank and construction of the

unit would be out of welded magnesium alloy. However, working with this new material posed insurmountable problems as the metal was extremely difficult to weld and work with. Armament was to be heavy and would consist of four 20 mm cannons mounted in the wing structure along with two .50 caliber Browning machine guns mounted in a remote controlled belly turret and four similar weapons mounted in another turret on top of the fuselage nacelle. This would give a considerable punch that was certain to knock down any enemy night intruder, an important consideration learned in the night skies over Britain when the initial surprise attack had to achieve victory for, once warned, the enemy aircraft could easily shake off the pursuer in the inky blackness.

Changes soon took place as the Army requested that the new aircraft should carry a heavier fuel load, a wise consideration when viewing the vast distances of the Pacific. Northrop was able to increase the fuel load but was faced with another problem when, during March 1941, the military decided to standardize on a different model of the P&W R–2800

which would have meant an entire firewall-forward redesign. The Army-Navy Standardization Committee was formed to help smooth out the problems of supply by reducing the number of different items that were required to keep the military machine moving. Standardization was an excellent idea and was certainly responsible for the eventual American victory in the war that was rapidly drawing near. However, at the moment, it was giving John Northrop nothing but headaches. As so often is the case, after a few days, the Standardization Committee reversed its decision and Northrop was able to continue with the project without having to take time out for the troublesome redesign.

A full scale mock-up of the new fighter was constructed in a walled-off area in one of the Northrop hangars and Army observers were eagerly inspecting the creation as it began to grow in size. The Army put forth a recommendation that again resulted in construction delays when a panel of officers suggested that the 20 mm cannon be removed from the wings and mounted in the fuselage nacelle, thereby centering the firepower into a very lethal punch. The recommendation resulted in a number of structural modifications that were time consuming. The cannon were mounted in a large tray that was attached to the belly in place of the ventral turret and its two machine guns which were disposed of.

As October turned into November, Northrop was trying to cure the problems caused by the use of magnesium in the tail booms while coping with another serious situation: the inability of General Electric to supply the complex remote controlled top turret for the first prototype on time. Further delays resulted from a rather unusual Royal Air Force contract for Vultee Vengeance attack bombers and, in order to produce the aircraft in the least amount of time, Northrop was subcontracted to produce 400 of the machines and this resulted in the rapidly growing Corporation having to set up new facilities to build the RAF aircraft, resulting in some slowdown on the XP–61 project. The Vultee/Northrop Vengeances were delivered to the RAF starting in January 1942 and concluding during April 1943.

The Army was rapidly becoming more and more concerned with the night fighting situation in the European war and towards the end of 1941 – before the first XP–61 had even been completed – a contract was issued for 150 production aircraft, followed during February 1942 by another contract for 410 machines.

For the first flight of the XP–61, Northrop contracted with veteran test pilot and aviation showman Vance Breeze to make the initial hop. At this time the dapper Breeze was at the height of his glory – flying around the country to test new military and civil aircraft and making quite a name for himself in the press. It is not known how much money Breeze got for the XP–61 flight but it was probably considerable since he seemed to have a gift for talking aeronautical firms out of large amounts for his testing efforts, a situation that usually offended the much lower paid company test pilots who undertook the risky daily work of testing out production machines and modifications.

On 26 May 1942, the prototype XP–61 stood on the ramp at Hawthorne while mechanics made final checks on the airframe and engines. Breeze, attired in a natty flight suit, poked his head inside the wheel wells and various inspection panels as he made his own check. The aircraft was left in natural metal finish with yellow cowlings and spinners. The spinners were of the more conventional variety rather than the complex ducted affairs which had been dropped during the design formulation. Some minor problems had risen during the weeks before the first flight, one of them being the sudden lack of availability of Curtiss Electric propellers. Hamilton Standard units were substituted but, during ground running, the propellers created a heavy vibration that was unsuitable. Northrop began checking for a way to cure the vibration but, in one of the many changes of face that occurred with the XP–61 program, Curtiss suddenly decided that they could supply the originally specified propellers. The problem with late deliveries of the General Electric turrets still remained and an aerodynamic shape complete with gun barrels was fitted to the top of the fuselage nacelle for flight testing.

The Hawthorne runway runs east–west and takeoffs are usually made into the prevailing westerly sea breezes coming off the nearby Pacific. Breeze started the R–2800s, signalled to the mechanics to pull the auxiliary power carts from the engines, and began to taxi. At the runup area, Breeze spent some time running up the engines until he was satisfied with their performance. Centering the XP–61's nose wheel on the runway's dividing stripe, Breeze advanced the throttles and after a fairly short takeoff run, lifted the XP–61 gracefully into the air. Breeze stayed near the airfield as he climbed for some altitude. After testing the controls and a few different power settings for about 15 minutes, Breeze headed back to Hawthorne for a smooth landing. Breeze reported that he felt the general flying characteristics of the aircraft were good but noted that the engines were not developing full power. Of course, much flying had to be done before the

The third YP–61, 41–18878, is seen on the ramp at Wright Field during 1946. By this time, 878 had seen service with several experimental and training units and was showing the effects of hard use. The 13 service test YP–61s were built between August and September 1943 and were fully equipped with top turrets and other military items. Flight testing soon revealed problems with the turret when the guns were swung, this causing extreme airframe vibration. A complete fuselage nacelle was shipped to Wright Field for wind tunnel testing. The YPs were fitted with reinforced turrets which had only two guns and all except 37 of the production run of 200 P–61As were built without the turret while aerodynamic problems were sorted out.

The streamlined turret atop a P–61A–I–NO. When the turret was eliminated from the majority of A models due to the aerodynamic buffeting problem, engineers were a bit surprised to find that top speed was increased by only three miles per hour. Note how rapidly the Olive Drab paint weathered and scuffed. (Northrop)

Opposite top
The fourth P–61A, 42–5488, is seen in its Olive Drab and Neutral Gray camouflage scheme. The aircraft was retained by the factory for testing and had its rudders, cowlings and spinners painted yellow. The R–2800 engines were oil-throwers as can be seen by the stained condition of the tail booms. The numbers carried on the nose were part of a factory coding system. The first 45 Black Widows were built with R–2800–10 engines and designated P–61A–I–NOs. (Northrop)

Very detailed view of the pilot's cockpit of P–61A–I–NO 42–5488. The dual throttle arrangement is seen on the pilot's left. Interphone button was on the left of the control wheel while the 20 mm cannon firing button was on the right with the trigger for the .50 caliber machine guns located on the right side of the wheel. Note the thick section of armor glass mounted in the front windshield. (Northrop)

flight envelope was completely explored but Northrop was very pleased that the huge new fighter handled so well.

As with most prototype aircraft of this period, certain necessary changes in design were made evident by the early test flights. The XP–61 had a horizontal stabilizer of new design installed to help improve control characteristics. Although the P–61 program had been given a high priority, problems plagued the prototypes and delayed production. Engine failure on the XP–61 called for the redesign of several powerplant elements by Pratt & Whitney engineers, while Northrop had determined that the rear spar area was slightly under specified strength and had limited the maneuvers the XP–61 could perform. Test flights of the XP–61 – while in company hands – were carried out minus the SCR–720 radar which the military considered highly secret and would install in the XP–61 only when it reached the guarded safety of Muroc Dry Lake or Wright Field.

The SCR–720 was, of course, the heart of the P–61 project. The closing days of the 1930s had seen much developmental work in the field of radar, both in Britain and in America. Once again, American techniques of mass production helped spur the development of radar and the first functioning microwave radar unit in the US was operating in Boston during January 1941. The unit had parts from Westinghouse, Bell, Sperry, General Electric along with a British magnetron. A second prototype radar unit was built to be installed in an aircraft and, on 10 March, a Douglas

B–18A took off with the unit installed in the aircraft's nose. At first the radar was extremely limited in range; perhaps a field of only five miles could be 'painted' on the radar operator's scope. Once again the American engineers tackled the problem of range with skill and enthusiasm and the unit was soon reaching out eight miles, and more range was in the offing. The Army was impressed by the prototype radar set and, during February 1941, 15 production sets were ordered for the upcoming XP–61 and Douglas A–20. The set was designated A1–10 and one unit was even installed in a Royal Canadian Air Force Boeing 247 transport for testing. This aircraft eventually headed for England for demonstrations. The British were impressed and ordered ten units for installation in the Bristol Beaufighter but this project was later dropped when the designers felt that the radar would not fit into the Beaufighter's nose and the radar units were assigned for other purposes. After the 108th unit of American radar had been built, a number of updates, modifications and some British components were installed to produce a new unit, the SCR–720. The Army and Northrop had carefully studied the primitive British night fighters and the new XP–61 had been built with its large nose entirely free to house nothing but radar. The radar operator was given the best position in the XP–61, installed above and behind the pilot in his own cockpit with an excellent forward view. The SCR–720 unit was delivered by Western Electric during November 1942 and some of the first sets were installed in the last of the Douglas P–70

Mechanics of the 547th Night Fighter Squadron work on their P–61As based at the Lingayen air strip, Luzon, Philippines. The 547th was a very interesting outfit, its pilots being a diverse mixture of USAAF, RAF, and RCAF officers who had had previous night fighting experience in Europe and were gathered together to aid the newly formed Black Widow squadrons in the Pacific. The squadron was activated on 1 March 1944 at Hammer Field, California, and trained at nearby Visalia Army Air Force Field from 31 May through 5 August before being transferred to the Pacific. Along with the P–61, the squadron operated P–70s and P–38M night fighters. The unit was inactivated on 20 February 1946. (USAF/63392)

conversions. The SCR–720 was an advanced piece of equipment, even having anti-jamming features that would help seek an enemy aircraft out even if it was dispersing 'chaff' – small bits of aluminum foil – to confuse the radar by forming a 'cloud' around the radar target or by giving off multiple images. Additional improvements gave the radar a longer range and better reliability and, thus, the P–61 was equipped with long searching night eyes that could easily hunt the enemy in the dark battlegrounds of the air.

The prototype P–61 had been equipped with the curiously named Zap flaps, but these units had to be built to very close production tolerances so a decision was made to install conventional flaps and spoiler-type ailerons that were somewhat similar to the units fitted in advanced sailplanes. The sheer complexity of the P–61 was the aircraft's greatest downfall since the many problems encountered with the first machines meant that deliveries to the combat areas were seriously compromised. Handling qualities were fine but the new systems let Northrop down.

The second XP–61 entered the flight test program during November of 1942 and more problems quickly appeared during the gun firing tests. The blast from the four 20 mm cannon jarred the fuselage pod structure and the canopies and various hatches and panels had to be strengthened to prevent them from being blown off during firing. Problems with airframe buffeting were also encountered and fixes had to be made to stop flap shaking which took place when the XP–61 started to build up speed. The Army test pilots liked the way the XP–61 flew and were impressed by the handling qualities of such a large aircraft. After further testing and problem solving repairs, the Army recommended that the aircraft should be accepted into the inventory.

The news of the XP–61's acceptance was greeted with jubilation at the Northrop factory during July 1943 and the small airfield was alive with activity as new buildings and hangars were being erected to house P–61 production along with Northrop's many war-effort projects. John Northrop did not get his favorite flying wing concept with the XP–61 but he had put the company on the map with America's first specifically built night fighter. At this time, work was already well progressed on the 13 service test YP–61s which featured most of the changes worked out on the prototypes, including the replacement of the magnesium in the booms as mentioned earlier. These aircraft began to come off the line during August with deliveries being completed by the end of the next month. However, a curious problem regarding the P–61's armament system had come to light at this time. Testing of a scale model in a wind tunnel had revealed that airframe buffeting was incurred when the guns were rotated and elevated. Further testing in the Wright Field wind tunnel with an entire P–61 nacelle highlighted the problem and the YP–61s were fitted with a structurally reinforced turret minus two of the .50 caliber weapons.

Since the P–61As were on the production line during the turret problem, the first batch of aircraft was fitted with turrets but the remaining P–61As were without the unit and its four machine guns. Comparing photographs indicates that the first 37 P–61As were either built in an out of serial number order or that later turretless P–61As were retrofitted with the turret and machine guns. By this time the P–61 had picked up the name Black Widow but the impression that most of these early aircraft were painted in all-black night fighter schemes is incorrect and needs explaining.

During the 1930s the Army had experimented with various camouflage paint schemes for aircraft operating under the cover of darkness. The Army wanted a black finish that would absorb the beams of the enemy's searchlights. However, the flat black finish that was first tested lit up with a silver glow every time the test aircraft was caught in the searchlight beams. Testing revealed that the rough, matte surface color actually picked up and intensified the searchlight's beam. Other experiments revealed that a smooth flat black surface paint was apparently more effective in dispersing the searchlight beam. The Camouflage Section of of the Office of Scientific Research at the famous Massachusetts Institute of Technology advanced the theory that a very glossy black paint would be the most suitable finish for a night fighter as the paint would reflect the light away from the aircraft. The new color was called Jet Black but, when tested, the Army did not agree with the theory and, in the Army's tests, the colors of Neutral Gray, Dull Black, and Jet Black were all found to be visible in the beam of anti-aircraft searchlights. The Army felt that Neutral Gray had the additional advantage of blending in with the sky on a brightly moonlit night. The Army then recommended that all night fighters be finished in the standard Olive Drab/Neutral Gray color scheme.

Back at MIT the researchers were a bit puzzled that the new Jet Black had failed the test. Upon further investigation they found that the Jet Black had been applied over an existing rough camouflage scheme which resulted in a glossy but rough finish. The test aircraft should have been stripped of all former paint and then resprayed with the Jet Black for a smooth and glossy finish. The paint scheme was correctly applied to another test aircraft and this time the results were most impressive. The aircraft was found to be virtually invisible in 80 per cent of the passes through the searchlight cones. These tests were undertaken during October 1943 and, by the time the Army was informed through the chain of command, the new results were too late to affect the first P–61s.

During October the Army had also issued camouflage orders to Northrop to paint the Black Widows in the Olive Drab/Neutral Gray paint scheme that had proven superior during the June 1943 tests. One of the Army commanders not knowing what the other was doing was to make the introduction of the Jet Black scheme a definite late arrival, the first Jet Black Widows not coming off the production line until late February 1944. A number of the early camouflaged Widows were repainted in the field but, once again, the paint was usually incorrectly applied over the old camouflage or, worse yet, a flat black color somewhat like the shade and texture that the Royal Air Force favored was applied, this usually being quickly eaten off the tail booms by the vast quantity of oil spewed out by the R–2800s. Jet Black was also occasionally applied to special mission aircraft.

With the service test YP–61s busily undergoing evaluation by various Army fields and with the first production aircraft coming off the line at Hawthorne it looked like the Black Widow would finally get into the war for which it was designed. The first production P–61As went to the 348th Night Fighter Squadron for training. The 348th was activated as a night fighter squadron on 1 October 1942 and was initially allocated A–20s and P–70s at its Orlando Air Base in Florida. The 348th also received some of the YP–61s and the pilots were most impressed by the new mount which could outfly the P–70 in all respects. When the squadron began to receive

The setting sun outlines a Black Widow that has been prepared for a night mission. The P–61 was to claim the title of the largest and heaviest fighter to see operational service with the USAAF.

Spray-on plastic preservative had not been completely perfected when Black Widows were being shipped overseas for service in the Pacific, so the airframes were carefully wrapped with protective canvas covers and all openings were sealed and the tires were smeared with a preservative goo. These P-61s are seen at Hickam Field, Oahu, Hawaii, on 19 April 1944. (USAF/63405)

P-61As, it was attached to the 481st Night Fighter Operational Training Group and the instructors and pilots quickly set out to establish night fighter procedures and operational tactics for the new fighters. In an effort to get the fighters to Europe as quickly as possible, the 422nd Night Fighter Squadron was shipped to England during March 1944. This squadron was activated on 1 August 1943 and trained at Orlando before heading to Charmy Down, England, on 7 March and then to Scorton on 6 May. Detached units of the 422nd NFS also operated from a number of other British bases including Hurn. The 425th NFS soon followed but slow delivery of the Black Widows meant that the units were understrength for a period of time. By this

time, the *Luftwaffe* was licking wounds that were to prove mortal and the great numbers of enemy aircraft that had characterized the first years of the war over Europe were now past history and the pickings for the Widows were slim. Four other Black Widow units joined the first two, these being the 414th, 415th, 416th and 417th but these NFS were also initially hampered by the lack of aircraft.

The available Black Widows did a considerable amount of flying and supported the post D-Day Invasion activities as well as actions in Northern France, the Rhineland, Ardennes-Alsace, and Central Europe. Pickings were slim but when the P-61 found a target, the target was usually destroyed or heavily damaged. The following Encounter Report was made by Capt Bob Elmore and Lt Leonard Mapes on the night of 17 December 1944:

'After several unsuccessful chases, a vector was given for a target at four miles and below our aircraft. After letting down in an orbit to keep from overshooting, AI contact was

secured at 4.5 miles. The range was closed to 1,000 ft when a visual was secured but it was necessary to close to 500 ft before the target could be identified, from 12 o'clock 15 degrees, as a Ju 88 flying on a heading of 270 degrees at 4,000 ft. We pulled to 100 ft dead astern before opening fire. First burst caused a white explosion in the fuselage and another longer one set both engines on fire. For a moment or two, the enemy aircraft went into a gradual climb, then it fell away to port, went straight down flaming fiercely and exploded when it struck the ground.'

The Black Widows usually operated individually at night and therefore did not receive the publicity of the day fighter units operating over Europe. Yet the P-61s in Europe fought a dark and dangerous war with a *Luftwaffe* who, although weakened, could still strike deadly blows. The Black Widow squadrons never received their full complement of aircraft and, at one time, were even threatened with receiving another machine

instead of the Black Widow. When the 422nd and 425th NFS of the Eighth Air Force arrived in Britain, there was considerable controversy going on as to whether the de Havilland Mosquito would make a better night fighter for the USAAF instead of the P-61; the use of the Mosquito would also help balance the scale of the Lend-Lease Program. Test flights between the P-61A and the Mosquito NF Mk XVII proved inconclusive, with each aircraft having good and bad points, so the USAAF went ahead with the plans to bring the P-61A squadrons up to strength.

The 425th NFS was the first unit to get up to strength with Widows, having 16 aircraft by the end of July 1944. Some of the first action seen by the 425th NFS was the interception of the Fiesler V-1 'Buzz Bombs' that were being sent against London by Hitler who was intent upon the destruction of Britain's capital city. The V-1, even though it was unmanned and flew on a pre-programmed course, was a deadly customer and had to be treated with considerable respect. The V-1 was fast, pro-

pelled by its Argus pulse-jet engine that let out a weird wail as it passed overhead, but it could be caught by the latest Allied fighters flying with their throttles wide open. The Buzz Bombs were dangerous to approach and shoot at from the rear since their warhead was armed and ready to go off. Some of the braver RAF pilots would catch up with a V-1 and gingerly slide their wing under the V-1's stubby mainplane and then slowly raise their wing until the air pressure would cause the V-1's wing to rise and send the deadly bomb off course, toppling its gyro control system in the process. Other methods of destruction included making beam attacks but, once again, the attacking aircraft was always in danger of being hit by exploding debris.

Members of the 425th began encountering the bombs in considerable numbers as they roared along at about 350 mph, usually at the fairly low altitude of 3,500 to 4,000 ft, dragging a tail of flame. One pilot made the mistake of pursuing a V-1 until he was 100 ft behind the aircraft. Carefully lining up the victim in

Sometimes the Black Widows did not stay so black. This P-61 of the 418th NFS is seen at Atsugi, Japan, shortly after the end of the war. Some of the P-61s had been repainted in the field and the black camouflage did not hold up in the humid South Pacific weather as this example illustrates. It seems that the oil from the R-2800s which usually covered the tail booms also aided in stripping the poorly applied paint off the aircraft. Note the drop tanks placed on the ground and the crescent moon insignia applied to the rudder. Unfortunately the serial number on the tail boom has also been obliterated. The 418th Night Fighter Squadron was activated on 1 April 1943 at Orlando, Florida, and was eventually disbanded on 20 February 1947 after flying a mix of P-70s, P-38Ms, B-25s and Widows. The squadron's aircraft carried a large insignia on the nose of their P-61s that can be seen on the aircraft in the photograph but it is in as poor condition as the rest of the paint so the description of the insignia from official records is in order: 'Over and through a blue-green disc, a king bee black and golden orange, wearing a red crown, holding aloft a lighted lantern proper with the right foreleg, and grasping a gray machine gun in the left foreleg, tip-toeing across a white cloud formation in base, and peering over the edge with a look of ferocity on his face; a crescent moon and two stars of yellow in background.' (J. P. Gallagher)

his gun sight, the pilot pressed the cannon button and the V–1 blew up directly in front of the Widow. The explosion temporarily blinded the pilot who soon found himself struggling with the controls of the damaged P–61A. The fighter made it back to base but the fabric on some of the control surfaces had burned off and the aircraft was coated with charred fuel and debris from the V–1. This dangerous sideline gained nine official victories for the 422nd and 425th NFS.

As the 422nd and 425th pilots began to gain more time in their aircraft it soon became obvious that there were not enough German aerial targets left to employ the attentions of the night fighters full time. Since the Black Widow was known as a superb handling

machine and had, along with the reliability of two engines, the powerful punch of four 20 mm cannon, then, the Army reasoned, why should the P–61 not be employed as a night intruder? Attacking enemy rolling stock and positions was a dangerous proposition in daylight since the pilots would be facing *Luftwaffe* anti-aircraft batteries which were just about the most accurate in the world. Under the cover of darkness much of the risk from flak would be eliminated but the danger of flying into the ground or other obstructions grew in alarming proportion.

Lack of spares for the Widows meant that the two night fighter squadrons were only able to field about ten aircraft each. The terrible winter of 1944–45 and the vigorous attack of the last ditch German Ardennes offensive put every flying Widow into the air to attack any German target of opportunity. The P–61As went after tanks, trains, and troop concentrations with great effectiveness, for few targets could stand up to the concentrated fire of the four cannon. Trains were favorite targets and the Widows were able to chew up quite a

number before the incredibly harsh December weather stopped most flying. A German officer who was captured near the end of the war stated that the best part of the offensive was during December when the rolling stock could move freely without the threat of attack from the P–61s.

The 414th, 415th, 416th and 417th NFS were assigned to the Twelfth Air Force but, once again, the lack of aircraft and parts kept their participation at a minimum. The 414th NFS was the first to become operational, switching from the Bristol Beaufighters they had been flying, in January 1945. This squadron managed to send a detachment of aircraft to strengthen the 422nd NFS to aid in attacking German positions. Pilots of the 414th managed to rack up five kills while flying Widows.

Thus the participation in the European War by P–61s was limited but when they did get into action they gave a good account and the 422nd NFS managed to produce three aces who flew the Widow. The Pacific, however, produced more action for the P–61.

Twenty-second P–61B, a –1–NO serial number 42–39419, is seen at the Hawthorne factory in its jet night camouflage scheme and yellow cowlings and spinner and number 938 which indicates that the machine was held by Northrop for testing purposes. The aircraft is carrying the top turret, a feature that was not very common on the very early B model Widows. More Bs were built than any other P–61 variant. (Northrop)

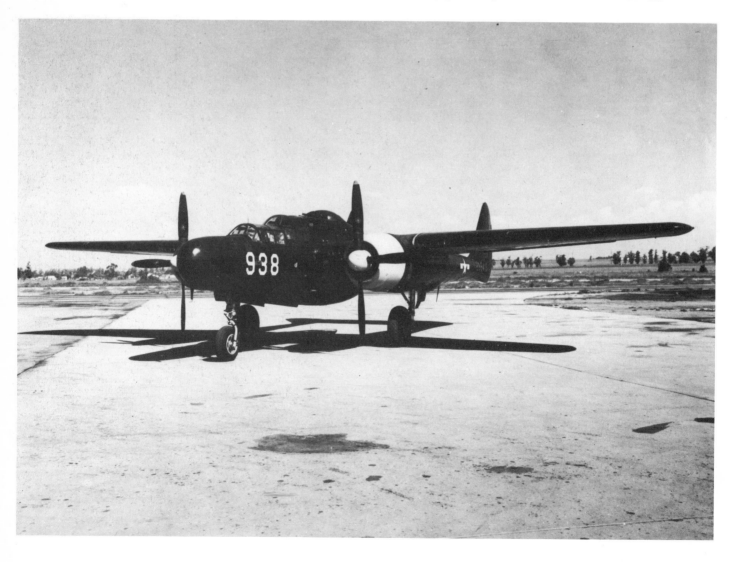

While deliveries of the first Black Widows to training and combat squadrons were taking place, design work was continuing at the factory to improve the P–61's combat performance. As can be seen in the characteristics chart that accompanies this chapter, Northrop and Pratt & Whitney were constantly attempting to improve the power output from the basic R–2800 engine. The first 45 P–61A–1s were equipped with the –10 variant that produced 2,000 hp but the P–61A–5 had upgraded –65 powerplants that could pump out 2,250 hp each at war emergency power ratings. Water injection, which gave a brief but rapid boost in engine performance, was added to the A–10 series. Many small design detail changes distinguished the various sub-variants of Black Widows and some of these features were retrofitted to earlier models. The P–61A–11 was the first Widow to be equipped with two under-wing racks that could carry extra fuel tanks or two 1,600 lb bombs. The provision of additional fuel tanks significantly stretched the Widow's range which was to prove particularly useful for its combat role in the Pacific.

The ability to carry bombs also meant that the Widow had changed from a pure night fighter to a night intruder, a mission by which the P–61 could be employed to destroy not only enemy aircraft at night but also hit fortifications or troop concentrations under the cover of darkness.

The first major change on the Black Widow production line which would result in a new model number was the P–61B which, although basically similar to the P–61A, had a number of significant improvements. To give more room for equipment in the nose, that area was increased in length by eight inches. Problems had been reported with early P–61s of skin wrinkling. The vast area of the wing was prone to wrinkle after high speed flights or after high g combat maneuvers had taken place. The internal structure was not failing but the unsightly skin wrinkles were disconcerting for the aircrew and reduced performance. To remedy the problem, light weight stiffeners were incorporated into the wing. During combat maneuvers, the Widow sometimes had a tendency to shed the large

plexiglass fairing that covered the rear of the fuselage nacelle behind the gunner's position. When this huge piece let go the noise sounded like the aircraft was breaking up, causing panic in the crew – especially to the gunner who occupied the rear position. Strengthening the mounting of the unit to the nacelle alleviated the problem but did not solve the tendency of the unit to break away during high g maneuvers. A warning notice was applied to the interior of the rear nacelle stating that no member of the crew should sit on the plexiglass bubble while the P–61 was in flight. Along with a number of small detail changes, the P–61B was powered by the R–2800–65 and wing racks were standard. The B–10, in another attempt to increase range and war-

Interior view of the radar operator's compartment in a P–61B. The early radar fitted in these aircraft provided constant headaches for maintenance crews as the units were prone to breaking down, especially during rigorous flight maneuvers. The radar operator had an excellent view from his position above and behind the pilot. Note how the radar scope is lined with fur to protect the operator's face. (Northrop)

load, was fitted with four underwing racks and, on the B-15, the turret with four .50 calibre Browning machine guns was reinstalled as standard (earlier models were also retrofitted). General Electric was able to supply an improved turret and fire control system and these were installed on the P-61B-20. a total of 450 B models were constructed before production was handed over to the variant of the P-61 which incorporated improvements learned from reports coming in from the combat zones where the Widow was beginning to see action.

All versions of the P-61 had a particularly 'deadly' look; an indication of an aircraft that was designed for just one purpose: war. The size of the Black Widow and its unusual configuration (particularly when painted in the Jet camouflage) gave a menacing impression. Yet the P-61 was an extremely docile aircraft with well-harmonized controls that pleased pilots and gave them the confidence to dogfight with smaller, supposedly more nimble, fighter aircraft. The P-61 had a surprisingly short turning radius for an aircraft so

large and the Widow's turning ability was put to good use by pilots who were able to cut off enemy aircraft attempting to turn inside of the Black Widow. If there were complaints coming from the combat pilots, then they usually centered on two points: climb performance and top speed. The pilots wanted more of each and felt that with the improved performance parameters the Widow would be almost impossible to defeat, even when engaging the enemy's latest fighters.

The P-61C was the answer to the combat reports and – if the earlier P-61s had a deadly appearance – then the P-61C looked downright evil. While retaining the basic configuration of the B, the P-61C was powered by Pratt & Whitney R-2800-73 powerplants that were equipped with General Electric CH-5 turbosuperchargers which were fed via large air intakes beneath the engine nacelles. This combination of engine and turbosupercharger was able to pump out 2,800 hp per engine. Performance was also aided by the addition of new propellers – two huge Curtiss Electric four blade propellers which were of the latest

Seen on 2 May 1945, P-61B-15-NO 42-39724A, waits at the large aircraft depot in Newark, New Jersey, where aircraft were readied for shipment to Europe. The aircraft is carrying four fuel tanks, two inboard of the engines and two outboard. This photograph also shows the entry hatch ladder behind the landing gear. Note the rows of P-51D Mustangs in the background that are being prepared for shipment by sea.

Seen before delivery at Northrop is P-61B-20-NO 43-8237. The -20 had a new General Electric upper turret and fire system with improved reliability. The massive spread of the P-61's wing and tail is clearly evident in this view. (Northrop)

Another turretless P–61B is seen during the freezing winter of 1945 in Europe. This Black Widow carries a respectable mission tally under the pilot's cockpit and is unusual in the fact that it still retains D-Day stripes on the tail booms while the stripes that were under the wings have been removed or repainted. (A. Meryman)

Black Widows on the prowl. A formation of three P–61Bs is seen on a mission over the Pacific, the grey exhaust stains of the R–2800 engines are readily apparent as they streak the top of the wing and extend the length of the tail booms. Pilots found the large P–61 to be easy to fly with a good speed range but a bit lacking in top speed.

paddle-blade style; the immense width of each blade would be able to offer more power in the rarified upper atmosphere. These various additions increased the weight of the C model to 32,200 lb but Northrop figured that the greater weight would be taken care of by the increased power. The acceleration offered by the new engines meant that attacking targets at night from the rear would be more hazardous because of the chance of overshooting and suddenly becoming the hunted rather than the hunter. Since perspective changes greatly at night and judging the distance to the target is much more difficult, the chance of ramming also had to be considered. To help alleviate this problem, an effective system of airbrakes was installed above and below the wing of the P–61C. The brakes could be instantly deployed by the pilot while pursuing a target and they would quickly decrease the speed of the Widow. However, many pilots preferred the earlier versions of the P–61, finding them lighter on the controls and more responsive to fighter-type maneuvers. The

P-61C, even with its extra power, was
thought to be a bit sluggish and, when heavily
loaded, was an earth lover of the first magni-
tude – often requiring a runway of at least
15,000 ft in order to safely stagger airborne.
The conclusion of World War Two stopped
P-61C production after 476 aircraft had been
constructed.

The Army felt that the P-61 could be
effectively employed in the Pacific Theater of
operations where the aircraft's radar and long
range capabilities could be fully realized while
hunting and destroying Japanese marauders.
General George C. Kenney remembers that,
'Early in June 1943, the 421st Night Fighter
Squadron flew in five new P-61 night fighters
to replace the obsolescent P-70s in New
Guinea.' The 421st was activated on 1 May
1944 and, like many other Widow units, took
initial training at Orlando, Florida, where the
unit was attached to the 481st Night Fighter
Operational Training Group until heading for
the New Guinea area and the Fifth Air Force
after becoming operational. Gen Kenney further recalls, 'As soon as Mokmer drome was
secured, V Fighter Command's new airborne
control center was flown in to relieve the
assault fighter control center at Bosnek. This
improved control and warning system, aided
by the arrival of the detachment of 421st Night
Fighter Squadron P-61s (one of them trailed
and shot down a Mitsubishi Dinah bomber
over Japen Island on the night of 7 July to score
the first P-61 victory in the Southwest Pacific),
made Japanese raids against Biak-Owi increasingly hazardous...'

The arrival (along with the 418th and
547th NFS at later dates) of the 421st NFS

solved a number of problems. On 25 October
1944, the unit moved to Tacloban, Leyte,
where operations were rapidly undertaken
against a variety of Japanese targets. On the
night of 29 November, the 421st was ordered
to intercept a Japanese convoy that was steaming to Ormoc in the Leyte Gulf. Gen Kenney
recalls the interception: 'I ordered the squadron of P-61 night fighters that we had just
gotten into Tacloban, to heckle the convoy all
night and see if we could keep them from
unloading.

'The heckling worked. Both merchant vessels were still off-shore with the decks piled
high with boxes and crowded with troops
when our attack hit them just after daybreak.
Both vessels were sunk and seven out of 15 Jap
airplanes flying as cover were added to the
score of our 49th Fighter Group.'

The aircraft of the 421st NFS carried an
insignia that rather typified the colorful American combat aircraft insignia during World
War Two and is worth recounting from the
official description: 'Over and through a
medium blue disc, border yellow orange, edged
black, BUGS BUNNY proper, wearing brown
aviator's helmet and grey and white goggles,
seated in cockpit of a caricatured tan aircraft,
and holding aloft a carrot proper in the right
forepaw, focusing a grey spotlight with white
beam with left forepaw; two grey machine
guns emitting fire from muzzle proper in nose
of aircraft.'

One of the more unusual kills of the Pacific
Theater occurred when a 548th NFS Black
Widow of the Seventh Air Force intercepted a
Boeing B-29 bomber that was heading back to
Iwo Jima after a raid on Osaka. The P-61 drew

*After the war, the P-61 equipped the
Stateside night fighter squadrons for several
years. This P-61B-20-NO is seen at Hamilton Field
near San Francisco. It carries four bare metal tanks
under the wings and the staggered arrangement of
the four .50 caliber machine guns in the upper
turret can be seen. The jet camouflage scheme was
prone to weathering and was usually in need of
repainting or touching up. The PK codes were
assigned to the Black Widow as postwar 'buzz
numbers'.*

alongside of the bomber and could see crewmen frantically gesturing from different positions in the aircraft. Thinking that the bomber
boys were just waving a friendly greeting, the
P-61 banked away to look for more lucrative
targets. However, the P-61 pilot noticed that
the B-29 was still transmitting an emergency
IFF (Identification Friend or Foe) signal and
came back for a closer look. This time the Black
Widow crew was able to spot considerable
damage in the nose area of the bomber,
apparently from a direct hit of anti-aircraft fire.
The B-29 had taken the hit over target and the
pilot had been killed instantly while the copilot
was seriously wounded but able to control the
bomber. Many of the aircraft's systems were
damaged or completely knocked-out. The
bomb bay doors were shut and the lethal load
of bombs still rode in their shackles. The P-61
managed to guide the mortally wounded bomber back to Iwo Jima where the crew abandoned ship during two runs over the island.
However, the damaged bomber continued to
fly and showed no sign of faltering – thus it was
an extremely dangerous item as it droned
through Allied airspace. The P-61 crew was
ordered to down the aircraft once it was over
open sea. Closing to firing distance, the pilot
pumped in several bursts from the cannon and

machine guns but the B–29 did not even shudder – it just kept on flying!

The Superfortress was a tough bird – as the Japanese fighters had found out as the B–29s reduced the Home Islands to ashes. The perplexed Widow pilot pressed home several more attacks and the cannon fire tore huge holes in the B–29 but the aircraft continued on a straight-line course. Finally one wing dropped slightly and the P–61 was able to shoot out two engines and the bomber spun into the ocean.

Such exotic kills were not commonplace and most P–61 crews found themselves flying hour after hour of boring night patrols occasionally punctuated by moments of terror and elation as enemy aircraft were encountered, tracked and destroyed. The Japanese were masters at single plane or small formation raids on Allied bases at night – causing more confusion and loss of sleep than any real damage. These raids were counterproductive to the war effort and occasionally did cause real damage when a stray bomb hit a fuel or ammunition dump. The increasing number of Black Widows in the Pacific began to stem these raids and more and more Japanese bombers would fail to return to their bases in the early morning hours.

The Seventh Air Force (formerly the Hawaiian Air Force) operated three Black Widow Squadrons – the 6th, the previously

mentioned 548th and 549th NFS in its Central Pacific area of operations. The Seventh was equipped with a fairly wide variety of aircraft types and was fated to fight in some of the lesser-known areas of war where combats over the vast stretches of Pacific Ocean often went unheralded. The 6th NFS had a long and distinguished history, dating back to World War One when it had been organized as the 6th Aero Squadron on 13 March 1917. The 6th became a night fighter squadron on 9 January 1943 and began to receive and train with Black Widows as soon as they were available from the factory. Training out of the Hawaiian Islands, the 6th worked up to operational status with the P–61s before departing to the Central Pacific. A detachment of the seven Widows from the 6th moved to Aslito Airfield on Saipan during June 1944 to begin operations against very active Japanese night intruders. The Widows first made contact during the night of 27 June with a prowling Kate but contact was difficult and, although shots were fired, a probable kill could not be registered against the obsolete enemy aircraft. The luck of the 6th NFS picked up on the night of 6 July when two P–61s intercepted marauding Betty bombers and flamed two of the fast bombers, one taking 134 rounds of 20 mm shells before blowing up.

The 6th NFS racked up victories against the

enemy, making the proposition of attacks against newly-won American installations more and more costly. However, Japanese attacks against Saipan became more and more concerted, especially after B–29 raids out of Saipan began hitting the Home Islands with savage attacks. The enemy sometimes would come in at high altitude, sometimes at low level – whatever tactic the Japanese pilots would feel to be the best procedure to counter American radar and night fighters. On the night of 25 December, two Betty bombers fell victim to the P–61A flown by Lt Dale Haberman (pilot) and Lt Raymond Mooney (radar

observer). The following is the official combat reported filed by the crew of *Moonhappy*:

'Scrambled from Condor Base then to Coral Base and vectored to the north of the Island at altitude of 15,000 ft. Coral Base ordered figure 8 orbits since they had no Bogies in the vicinity. Controller notified pilot that there were no Bogies in the vicinity but much Snow [fuzzy radar image] was in the area. Contact made with airborne radar at five miles. Control notified ... reported Bogies in vicinity but could give no information. Went into starboard orbit but airborne radar kept picking up Bogie which seemed to be in orbit. Bogie straightened out and headed north. Chased Bogie to the north and let down to 9,000 feet when visual contact was made, opened fire at 1,500 feet and closed to 700 feet. Bogie made violent turns and hits observed to go into

wings and fuselage. Bogie was in a slight dive indicating 300 mph, Bogie last seen to roll to port in semblance of split-S and nose straight down with fires observed coming from the right wing and engine. Visual lost as Bogie was at 6,000 feet still going straight down, apparently out of control.

'At the same time the Radar Observer called for a starboard turn as a second Bogie was out about two miles. Closed fast on second Bogie letting down to 4,500 feet where visual was made at about 2,500 feet. Closed in to 700 feet and opened fire with hits observed to spray the entire ship. Bogie exploded with its debris hitting P–61 with damage to left cowling. Bogie went down in flames and [was] seen to hit the water. At the time ... location was estimated as 100 miles north of the Island. Returned to vicinity of Island and brought in to land as fuel was low.'

The 548th and 549th Night Fighter Squadrons joined the Seventh Air Force on the bitterly contested island of Iwo Jima on 7 and 24 March 1945. The 549th was to remain on Iwo for the rest of the war (with detachments at Saipan and Guam) while the 548th moved to Ie Shima to provide night defense. During May, the 548th NFS operated intruder missions over the Home Island of Kyushu during which time five victories were recorded.

The Tenth Air Force – another unit that was small in numbers but big in achievements – operated in the Indo-China area during the war, which was another forgotten outpost but this did not mean that the war there was any less savage or deadly. The 427th Night Fighter Squadron was assigned to the Tenth (and later transferred to the Fourteenth AF during November 1944) as the only Black Widow squadron operated by that Air Force. The 427th was activated on 1 February 1944 at Hammer Field, Fresno, California, which was to become a center on the West Coast for Black Widow training. The squadron moved to Pomigliano, Italy, on 12 August and was stationed there until 20 September (flying only four missions) when they were sent to Pandaveswar, India, on 31 October and then on to Myitkyina, Burma (with a detachment to Kunming, China), during December. For the next few

months the 427th was occupied with flying 73 defensive patrols without encountering any enemy aircraft. On the night of 22 February 1945, the P–61As of the 427th began night intruder patrols. Some of the Black Widows were modified in the field with bazooka-like rocket tubes while others were equipped to carry a variety of explosive devices including napalm. During the first four night intruder actions, the Widows delivered an impressive array of ordnance that included one ton of bombs, two napalm bombs, and 26 4.5 rockets. Just over 1,800 rounds of 20 mm ammunition were also expended. The Widows went after troop concentrations and supply dumps with a considerable amount of success. However, as targets became fewer and fewer in Burma, most of the missions were being flown by the detachment in China. Enemy aircraft were rarely encountered and the P–61s were mainly employed in attacking ground targets.

The Fourteenth Air Force in China also had one P–61 squadron (besides the 427th NFS which was assigned at a later date) – the 426th NFS. The 426th was activated on 1 January 1944 at Hammer Field where training was undertaken. During August the unit headed for India and then arrived at Chengtu, China, on 5 November 1944 from which detachments were sent to Kunming and Hsian. The

426th moved to a number of bases within China as the fortunes of war rapidly changed against the Japanese. As with the 427th, the 426th operated mainly against ground targets as aerial activity by the enemy was almost non-existent.

Black Widows also equipped the 418th and 550th Night Fighter Squadrons of the Thirteenth Air Force in the South Pacific. The 418th NFS was activated on 1 April 1943 at Orlando, Florida, and, during November, moved to the New Guinea area where the squadron operated from a wide number of airfields as the fortunes of war dictated rapid changes. The 418th saw considerable action against enemy intruders as the squadron moved from New Guinea to the Schouten Islands to Leyte to Mindoro to Okinawa and, finally, to Japan as part of the occupation

After the war, the Black Widow was chosen to participate in weather research and at least 16 P–61Bs were modified into P–61Gs, which meant that all war material such as guns and armor were eliminated. Some aircraft were apparently completely stripped of the jet camouflage. The aircraft were flown into thunderstorms, a decidedly hazardous task. This P–61G, formerly a P–61B–20–NO, 43–8298, is seen during 1946 when it was assigned to the All Weather Flying Center at Wright Field, Ohio. Aircraft is wearing the unit's special red and yellow paint trim. Note the various new aerials and instruments protruding from the nacelle.

forces, making the 418th one of the most widely deployed Black Widow squadrons. The 418th suffered some bad luck during the landings on Mindoro when, on 15 December 1944, Japanese *Kamikaze* aircraft broke through the screen of protecting Army fighters and crashed into two LSTs, sinking both. One of the LSTs carried the majority of equipment for the 418th! However, the unit was able to recoup its losses and get back into operation. On 27 January 1945, Black Widows from the 418th were active, operating from their base on Mindoro, when Lt Bertram C. Tompkins encountered a Japanese aircraft. The following is from the pilot's combat report:

'Approximately 1½ hours after becoming airborne the GCI controller vectored me onto a Bogey approaching from the northwest. F/O Wertin made radar contact with Bogey at 0010 at a distance of six miles and altitude of 10,000 ft on heading of 280 degrees. He directed me to 2,000 ft directly behind and below Bogey and I obtained a visual and identified it as a Tony. I closed to 150 ft and fired one short burst. The Tony exploded and fell burning into the water approximately twenty miles west of base. No evasive action was used by enemy aircraft.

'Immediately GCI vectored me onto second Bogey, which was twenty miles southeast of me. F/O Wertin made radar contact at six miles and directed me to 3,000 ft. directly behind and slightly below the Bogey, where I got a visual. I closed to 300 ft and fired one burst, and enemy aircraft exploded and fell to the water burning. Kill was made approximately five miles west of Mindoro coast. E/A was identified as a Tony. Violent evasive action was used.'

As the war ground on to a conclusion, Northrop attempted a number of different versions of the P-61, only one of which reached production. The XP-61D was intended to be a version of the Black Widow optimized for high altitude operation. A P-61A-5 (USAAF s/n 42-5559) was pulled for modification to XP-61D standards during February 1944. The regular engines were taken off and R-2800-17 powerplants with CH-5 turbosuperchargers were installed in their place. Since the Northrop plant was near bursting with work on the P-61 and various other war-related projects, series production was to be assigned to the Goodyear Aircraft Corporation. Initial design and mock-up work was to be undertaken by Northrop while Goodyear would complete final design and production work. A second P-61A, this time a -10, was brought into the program for conversion as the second XP-61D (USAAF s/n 42-5587). Work on the conversion proceeded smoothly and the first XP-61D flew during November 1944 and tests indicated that high-altitude performance was considerably improved but constant engine failures put the program behind time and, after the first P-61C

had been completed, the XP-61D program was abandoned.

With the introduction of the B-29 bomber program, the Army felt that a high-performance long-range fighter was needed to escort the big bomber. Northrop proposed the XP-61E as the needed aircraft. Two P-61B-10 aircraft (USAAF serials 42-39549 and 42-39557) were obtained for the conversion work which involved a new fuselage nacelle that eliminated the upper structure and turret. Since the aircraft was to be a day fighter, the radar was dropped and four .50 caliber Browning machine guns were installed in the nose. The crew of two was seated in tandem under a huge bubble canopy (reportedly the largest blown plexiglass structure). Additional internal fuel cells were installed to secure the range needed for the aircraft's escort role. The aircraft offered reasonable performance but, due to changing fortunes of war, was not proceeded with. The XP-61F was to be a similar conversion of the P-61C to long-range day-fighter configuration but work was never started on the project.

One XP-61E was converted into the XF-15

*W*earing the title **Thunderstorm** *on its nose gear door, the P-61C-1-NO, 43-8354, flew in the weather tests along with the P-61Gs. The Black Widows quite often encountered violent weather during their flying, as evidenced by the amount of paint worn off the nose radome.*

reconnaissance aircraft. The highly modified nose section was able to house a wide variety of cameras and performance was superior to the other photo-reconnaissance aircraft of the time. The Army was impressed with the XF–15 and a pre-production XF–15A was ordered and this aircraft was converted from a P–61C. The Army established a requirement for 320 F–15 Reporters, as the type was named, and an initial order for 175 aircraft was awarded to Northrop during June 1945. However, only 36 F–15As were built up from partially completed P–61C airframes when the contract was suddenly cancelled during 1947. The F–15A carried its crew of two under a large bubble canopy similar to the XP–61E. Both crew positions had full flight controls and featured reclining seats so that one crewman could sleep while the other flew during long reconnaissance missions. In addition to the normal fuel tanks, the F–15A carried a huge 500 gallon tank just behind the rear crewman and drop tanks could also be installed. The F–15A could mount up to six cameras which could be arranged in 24 positions and was capable of carrying 17 different types of aerial cameras. Some postwar use was made of the F–15As including assignment of one aircraft to NACA but most soon found their way to the smelter. One F–15A survived to become a

survey aircraft in Mexico and then a fire bomber in California but it was destroyed in a takeoff accident during the late 1960s.

The last modification to the basic P–61 design was the modification of some P–61B and C aircraft to P–61G configuration. At least 16 aircraft were converted during 1945 to the G configuration for weather reconnaissance missions. All war related items were stripped, including guns and armor, and special weather and radio equipment was installed. Some of these aircraft participated in 'Operation Thunderstorm', during which the Black Widows were flown directly into huge thunderstorms to gather scientific data. As a reflection on the strength of the Black Widow, it can be noted that none of the P–61s were torn apart by the violent forces of nature present inside the thunderheads.

A few units soldiered on with the P–61 after the end of the war and these included the 51st Fighter Group's 16th, 25th and 26th squadrons and the 347th Fighter Group's 4th, 68th and 339th squadrons – all based in the Pacific. The P–61 formed the basis of America's first all-weather fighter squadrons and served with 52nd All-Weather Fighter Group which included the 2nd and 5th squadrons and the 325th All-Weather Fighter Group with the 317th, 318th and 319th squadrons. By 1950

Another P–61C–1–NO, 43–8327, assigned to 'Project Thunderstorm' at Wright Field during 1947. The Black Widow did not remain in active service for very long after the end of World War Two and by 1950 the Widow was just a memory as the USAF was rapidly converting to a jet fighter force.

the Black Widow had virtually disappeared from the new USAF's inventory which was now directed to the purchase of jet aircraft. So efficient was the scrapping of the Black Widow force that the USAF was forced to search the world during the 1960s when an example was sought for the USAF Museum. One example was found in France where it had been used as a training aid by Air France mechanics. Air France generously donated the aircraft to the USAF Museum where it can be seen today. The National Air and Space Museum in Washington DC also has a P–61 in storage for eventual restoration and display.

Aside from occupying the historically significant slot as the Army's first specifically-built night fighter, the P–61's career can be summed up by stating the fact that it was too late to see significant combat in Europe and the Pacific. The many production delays of the advanced fighter denied the aircraft its rightful place as the finest night fighter built by any nation during World War Two.

NORTHROP P–61 BLACK WIDOW VARIANTS, SERIAL NUMBERS AND SPECIFICATIONS

Variants

XP–61 Two built, originally fitted with P&W R–2800–25S engines but these were replaced with R–2800–10s when they would not develop full power. They were not fitted with the upper turret (aerodynamic form fitted instead). SCR–720 radar was fitted when delivered to USAAF. Hamilton Standard propellers were replaced with Curtiss Electric units because of vibration problems. Natural metal finish.

YP–61 R–2800–10 engines. Thirteen service testing aircraft equipped with dorsal barbettes and military equipment built and delivered between August and September 1943. They suffered buffeting problems because of the upper turret, and the turret was reinforced and two guns were removed. Booms were made of welded magnesium alloy but building proved a problem and the units were redesigned for production in aluminum.

P–61A R–2800–10/–65 engines. Production version: 45 were built as A–1s with R–2800–10 engines; 35 as A–5s with 2,250 hp R–2800–65 engines were constructed; 100 as P–61A–10s were built with a water injection system for the engines; and 20 as A–11s had provision for carrying two 165 US gallon drop tanks under the wing. The first models were delivered in Olive Drab and Neutral Gray finish but later variants were delivered with overall glossy black finish. The first 37 P–61As were delivered with the top turret but because of the buffeting problem the remainder were built without the turret but some were later fitted with the turret.

P–61B R–2800–65 engines. The most numerous Black Widow variant with 450 built, it was basically the same as the A but with important military updates. The nose was lengthened by 8 inches to accommodate more radar gear, cartridge ejection doors for the cannon were eliminated, and it had automatic cowl flaps and night binoculars. 62 B–1s were built, similar to the A–11 but without the fuel tank/bomb rack provision. Racks were reintroduced on the B–2, –5, –11 and –16 (a total of 99 built) variants which also had minor updates. Strengthened wings on the B–10 (45 constructed), –15, –16, –20 and –25 (250 of all variants built) meant that the Widow could carry four 165 US gallon drop tanks or four 1,600 lb bombs. The first 200 B models did not have the top turret which was added to production aircraft with the B–15 (153 constructed), –16 (six built), –20 (84) and –25 (seven). Various minor changes were carried through the entire series and most models had the more important changes fitted in the field.

P–61C R–2800–73 engines with General Electric CH–5 turbochargers with large intakes under cowlings. 41 were built, with 476 cancelled after VJ-Day. Paddle-blade Curtiss Electric propellers, airbrakes fitted above and below the wings. The dorsal turret was installed on all aircraft and four .50 caliber machine guns with 560 rpg in the top turret, plus four

20 mm cannon in the underfuselage with 200 rpg. P–61Cs were finished in glossy black (Night).

XP–61D R–2800–14 engines with GE CH–5 turbosuperchargers, with paddle-blade Curtiss Electric propellers. An attempt to improve the high-altitude performance of Black Widow, design work and the conversion of aircraft was carried out by Goodyear Aircraft Corporation on two P–61A airframes. Aircraft were left in natural metal finish, and plane 791 (USAAF s/n 42–5559) had yellow cowlings and spinners. Development of the project abandoned with advent of P–61C.

XP–61E R–2800–65 engines. Two were built from converted P–61B airframes (first one being USAAF s/n 42–39549) as long-range escort fighter prototypes. The fuselage nacelle was modified by the elimination of the turret and turtledeck, a large bubble canopy was added, the nose radar was deleted and four .50 caliber machine guns added. The design of the canopy (at that time the largest blown plexiglass unit built) differed on the two aircraft; one rolled back, the other was hinged to swing open to the left. Extra fuel tanks were added to the center and rear nacelle. The second XP–61E was lost during testing on 11 April 1945, and development was discontinued due to the rapidly changing fortunes of war. The remaining XP–61E was converted into the XF–15 prototype.

P–61G R–2800–65 engines. Sixteen aircraft were converted postwar from P–61B airframes, stripped of armament and armor, and used by the USAF for weather research. Records on these aircraft are incomplete but it should be noted that P–61Cs were also used in the weather research program.

XF–15 R–2800–65 engines. Photographic recon. conversion of the surviving XP–61E. The configuration was basically same as for the XP–61E except that all armament was deleted and the nose was modified to carry a variety of cameras. It had a natural metal finish.

XF–15A R–2800–73 engines. One built, a conversion of a P–61C (USAAF s/n 43–8335) airframe to the general configuration of the XF–15, with natural metal finish with yellow cowlings and spinners.

F–15A R–2800–73 engines. The production version of the XF–15/A prototypes. The requirement for 320 Reporters (as the type was named) and an initial order for 175 aircraft was awarded during June 1945. Only 36 Reporters were completed (many surplus new P–61C parts were used in construction) before the contract was cancelled during 1947. The canopy slid fore and aft on tracks over the crew of two.

F2T–1 R–2800–10 engines. Twelve (according to company records, other sources state five aircraft) P–61As were transferred from USAAF stocks for use by the USMC as night fighter trainers. The aircraft were flown without armament from Miramar MCAS, California, and were left in overall black camouflage.

Serial Numbers

XP–61	41–19509, 41–19510
YP–61	41–18876 through 41–18888
P–61A	42–5485 through 42–5634; 42–393487 through 42–39397
P–61B	42–39398 through 42–39757; 43–8231 through 43–8320
P–61C	43–8321 through 43–8361
F–15A	45–59300 through 45–59335
F2T–1N	52750 through 52761

Specifications

XP–61

Span	66 ft
Length	48 ft 11 in
Height	14 ft 8 in
Wing area	663 sq ft
Empty weight	19,245 lb
Loaded weight	28,870 lb
Max. speed	370 mph
Cruise speed	200 mph
Ceiling	33,100 ft
Rate of climb	2,900 fpm
Range	1,200 miles
Powerplant	Two Pratt & Whitney R–2800–10 of 2,000 hp each

YP–61

Span	66 ft
Length	48 ft 11 in
Height	14 ft 8 in
Wing area	663 sq ft
Empty weight	21,910 lb
Loaded weight	28,830 lb
Max. speed	370 mph
Cruise speed	200 mph
Ceiling	33,000 ft
Rate of climb	2,900 fpm
Range	1,200 miles
Powerplant	Two Pratt & Whitney R–2800–10 of 2,000 hp each

P–61A–5

Span	66 ft
Length	48 ft 11 in
Height	14 ft 8 in
Wing area	663 sq ft
Empty weight	20,965 lb
Loaded weight	32,400 lb
Max. speed	369 mph
Cruise speed	222 mph
Ceiling	33,100 ft
Rate of climb	2,700 fpm
Range	n/a
Powerplant	Two Pratt & Whitney R–2800–65 of 2,000 hp each, 2,250 hp at war emergency power

P–61B

Span	66 ft
Length	49 ft 7 in
Height	14 ft 8 in
Wing area	662.36 sq ft
Empty weight	23,450 lb
Loaded weight	36,200 lb
Max. speed	330 mph
Cruise speed	225 mph
Ceiling	33,100 ft
Rate of Climb	2,550 fpm
Range	610 miles
Powerplant	Two Pratt & Whitney R–2800–65 of 2,000 hp each, 2,250 hp at war emergency power

P–61C

Span	66 ft
Length	49 ft 7 in
Height	14 ft 8 in
Wing area	662.36 sq ft
Empty weight	24,000 lb
Loaded weight	40,300 lb
Max. speed	430 mph
Cruise speed	307 mph
Ceiling	41,000 ft
Rate of climb	2,600 fpm
Range	1,725 miles max
Powerplant	Two Pratt & Whitney R–2800–73 of 2,100 hp each, 2,800 hp at war emergency power

XP–61D

Span	66 ft
Length	48 ft 11 in
Height	14 ft 8 in
Wing area	663 sq ft
Empty weight	23,205 lb
Loaded Weight	39,715 lb
Max. speed	430 mph
Cruise speed	315 mph
Ceiling	43,000 ft
Rate of climb	2,500 fpm
Range	1,050 miles
Powerplant	Two Pratt & Whitney R–2800–77 of 2,100 hp each, 2,800 hp at war emergency power

XP–61E

Span	66 ft
Length	49 ft 7 in
Height	13 ft 5 in
Wing area	664 sq ft
Empty weight	21,350 lb
Loaded Weight	40,181 lb
Max. speed	376 mph
Cruise speed	n/a
Ceiling	30,000 ft
Rate of climb	2,500 fpm
Range	2,250 miles
Powerplant	Two Pratt & Whitney R–2800–65 of 2,000 hp each

F–15A

Span	66 ft
Length	50 ft 4 in
Height	13 ft 5 in
Wing area	662 sq ft
Empty weight	n/a
Loaded weight	32,190 lb
Max. Speed	440 mph
Cruise speed	315 mph
Ceiling	41,000 ft
Rate of climb	n/a
Range	4,000 miles
Powerplant	Two Pratt & Whitney R–2800–73 of 2,800 hp each

Curtiss XP-62
Ungainly Heavyweight

This prototype was an attempt to fill an order for a high-altitude, heavily-armed fighter.

During January 1941 the Army Air Corps approached the Curtiss-Wright Corporation with the request to undertake a study concerning a large heavyweight fighter that would be capable of flying at high altitude with a formidable battery of weapons. The fighter would be wanted for protecting the new high-altitude bombers then on the drawing boards and would need to be pressurized like the bombers. The Army wanted the aircraft to carry either eight 20 mm cannons or twelve .50 caliber Browning machine guns and fly at speeds over 450 mph, truly amazing requirements for the time.

Curtiss decided to utilize the new Wright R–3350–17 which was being developed for the B–29 along with a turbosupercharger to be installed in the bottom rear of the fuselage structure. A number of proposals were submitted to the Army and extensive changes were undertaken on each 'paper' airplane.

The Curtiss XP–62 was certainly not a thing of beauty. The bulky fuselage accommodated the huge Wright R–3350 and its contra-rotating propeller, the cockpit pressurization system which was fed from an engine-driven blower via an armored duct, and the turbosupercharger which was fitted under the rear fuselage in the manner of the Republic P–47. The XP–62 only made a few flights and there is some doubt if the pressurization system was ever installed. Originally to carry an armament of either eight 20 mm cannons or 12 .50 caliber machine guns, the awesome aerial arsenal was reduced to four 20 mm cannon, but these were never installed in the prototype. The aircraft was scrapped in 1944 and full flight test results were never obtained. It was finished in the standard Dark Olive Drab upper surfaces with Neutral Gray undersurfaces. (USAF)

Weights and speeds went up and down as both the Army and Curtiss tried to make up their minds on exactly what would fill the specifications. Finally, on 1 January 1942, the Army recommended that the cannon armament be reduced to four and the airframe be lightened. Curtiss in turn submitted production plans for 100 P–62s with delivery to begin during May 1943. The Army approved these plans on 27 May 1942 and work immediately began on the prototype XP–62.

The all-metal stressed skin fighter was ugly from the start. The canopy, with its 14 separate panels, looked a bit like a fly's eye while the fat fuselage dropped all attempts at grace in order to hold the massive R–3350, pressurized cockpit and turbosupercharger. The pressurization system was to run off an engine-driven blower and travel to the cockpit via a heavily armored duct. Curtiss designer Don R. Berlin and his team put a considerable amount of effort into this creation but with little reward for, on 27 July – just two months after the contract was signed – the Army changed its mind and cancelled the project completely, feeling that the aircraft would disrupt vital deliveries of Curtiss-built P–47G Thunderbolts. Another reason for the cancellation was that the XP–62 would offer very little more when compared to the Republic heavyweight and that the XP–62's complexity would lead to lengthy developmental problems.

Since the prototype was well on its way to completion, the Army decided to finish the aircraft and use it for a flying test bed. The XP–62 made its first flight on 21 July 1943, from the company's Buffalo plant but the pressurization system had not been installed. Soon after the first flight the second prototype, the XP–62A, was cancelled by the Army. The aircraft was never fitted with any armament and it is doubtful that the pressurization system was ever installed. It is thought that very few flights were made with the XP–62 before it was scrapped in 1944.

The XP–62 did not really have a chance to prove its intended concept. By the time it had flown the Army had firmed up its fighter program to concentrate on the P–38, P–47 and P–51, all of which offered good performance at high altitudes even if they did not have the XP–62's power and pressurization system.

CURTISS XP–62 SERIAL NUMBER AND SPECIFICATIONS

Curtiss Serial Number

XP–62   41–35873

Specifications

XP–62

Flight testing of the XP–62 was never completed and all performance figures should be regarded as estimates.

Span	53 ft 8 in
Length	39 ft 6 in
Height	16 ft 3 in
Wing area	420 sq ft
Empty weight	11,773 lb
Loaded weight	16,651 lb
Max. speed	448 mph
Cruise speed	340 mph
Ceiling	35,700 ft
Rate of climb	2,300 fpm
Range	1,500 miles
Powerplant	Wright R–3350–17 of 2,300 hp

Bell P-63 Kingcobra — The Lend-Lease Fighter

The P–63 gained all of its combat successes with foreign air forces.

The pilot of the North American P–51C had been carefully stalking his prey for the past few miles, ducking in and out of the valleys and canyons of the huge billowing white clouds that covered the arid plains below. The well-weathered Olive Drab Mustang stood out against the stark white backdrop but then so did its prey which was painted a gaudy shade of orange. The Mustang pilot switched on his guns and sight and closed on his target. Pressing the firing button on his control stick he cursed as the first burst went wide, alerting the target and causing its pilot to tuck the aircraft into a tight left turn behind the pillar of

a cloud. Racked over in an even tighter turn, the Mustang pilot advanced the throttle and roared in for a deflection shot. This time his well-aimed bursts were right on target and hits scored all over the other plane. Instead of bursting into flames, the target's landing lights began winking in a frantic manner while the 'enemy' pilot rocked his wings to signal that the attack had been successful. The 'enemy' was a highly modified Bell P–63 Kingcobra that had been built as a flying target, while the P–51 pilot was an advanced fighter student from one of the many fields scattered over the vast Texas plain. This was about as close to combat as the Kingcobra would come while serving in the USAAF. Fellow Kingcobras saw considerable action with the Soviets and some

fighting with the French *Armée de l'Air* but as an American-operated fighter the P–63 would remain in the unique role of being shot at but never shooting back!

The genesis of the Kingcobra is directly traceable to the XP–39E. As noted in an earlier chapter, the XP–39E Airacobra was an attempt to update the inadequate P–39 series of aircraft through some fairly drastic modifica-

*R*ather elegant in line, the Bell P–63 Kingcobra still suffered from the less than adequate performance offered by the Allison V–12 engine. This first production P–63A, 42–68871, is seen on a test flight near the Bell factory. The underwing gun pods and pylons are shown to good advantage. Camouflage scheme is overall Dark Olive Drab with Neutral Gray undersurfaces. (Bell)

The prototype P–63, 42–78015, sits on the Bell ramp amid earlier Airacobras. The Kingcobra was an attempt to redefine the P–39 and rectify the mistakes and poor handling qualities of the Airacobra. (Bell)

tions. The basic P–39 fuselage was left intact but the three XP–39Es were fitted with a new laminar-flow wing with square tips and each aircraft was flown with a different form of modified tail surface. It had been proposed to equip the XP–39Es with the Continental V–1430–1 engine but this powerplant proved to be troublesome and not ready in time for flight trials so the XP–39Es were fitted with the Allison V–1710–47 of 1,325 hp. The aircraft were extensively tested and, while performance was better than the standard Airacobra, it was not judged worth putting the aircraft into production since new types already under production would be able to outperform the XP–39E.

The knowledge gained in the testing of the XP–39E with its new technology laminar-flow wing was not lost because of the cancellation of a production contract. Design of a new fighter to replace the Airacobra had begun at

the Bell plant during 1941. Although bearing a great deal of resemblance to the earlier Airacobra, it was, in fact, a completely new aircraft with very few interchangeable parts. The new fighter was larger in all aspects than the Airacobra and Bell hoped that many of the flaws that had been discovered in the operational use of the P–39 would be eliminated. However, while meeting its design goals, the P–63 Kingcobra was already dated by the rapid advancement of wartime aeronautical technology.

The original order for the XP–63 was issued by the Army on 27 June 1941 and consisted of specifications for two aircraft. Work proceeded at a rapid pace and the first prototype was ready for flight on 7 December 1942, exactly one year after the disaster at Pearl Harbor. Originally some thought had been given to installing the Continental engine in the new fighter but the Allison V–1710–47 (the same

series of powerplant that had equipped the XP–39Es) was installed. The Kingcobra was a sleek looking aircraft, its beautifully finished laminar-flow wing helping improve performance considerably. The Kingcobra followed the same construction techniques as the P–39 and armament remained basically the same: one 37 mm cannon and two .50 caliber machine guns in the nose section and one podded .50 caliber weapon mounted under each outer wing panel, somewhat similar to the P–39Q. Testing of the prototype quickly ran into problems when the first aircraft was destroyed in a crash. The second prototype, first flown on 5 February, barely lasted three months before it was also written off in an accident. The loss

Bell Airacobras were used in the P–63 program to test various engineering theories. XP–39E, 41–19502, was the second example used in the tests and had a different wing, modified air scoop, and redone tail surfaces.

Many P–63s were utilized at Stateside training bases and this flight of 4th Air Force P–63A–6 aircraft was on a training mission out of Chico Army Air Field, California. (USAF)

of both prototypes did not seem to stem the Army's eagerness to procure the new fighter and flight testing continued with the XP–63A which had been ordered during June 1942 and first flown on 26 April 1943.

Bell and Army test pilots reported that the new fighter handled extremely well, that its performance was considerably better than the P–39's, and that it had no dangerous flying characteristics. The Kingcobra was a large aircraft and certainly did not follow the European trend of smaller, more compact fighting machines. All characteristics in the combat maneuverability regime were considered good but, unfortunately, good was not good enough in 1943 when production Kingcobras would be running into fighters such as the Focke-Wulf Fw 190 which was causing near panic in RAF and USAAF units that were having to meet Kurt Tank's 'Butcher Bird' in the deadly skies over Europe. Once again, Bell seemed to be behind the eight-ball with their new fighter design but a market was to be found for the P–63.

America's new ally, the Soviet Union, although fondly looked upon by the period's politicians, was viewed with considerable alarm by high-ranking American and British military officials. The fact that the Soviets were clamoring for every available piece of military hardware and industrial equipment was viewed in some circles as filling a need that went beyond the grave military crisis. The Soviets, for their part, never seemed to be satisfied with the Allied supply effort – always demanding more and better aircraft. Fortunately, the danger of giving the best and newest fighters and bombers to the Soviets was

*T*he P–63, like the P–39, had a cockpit that was not dissimilar with family sedans of the period so it is interesting to note that the entire Kingcobra cabin was subcontracted to the Hudson Motor Car Company. A complete cabin is seen being installed on a Kingcobra fuselage in this 14 October 1944 photograph. (Bell)

Opposite

*T*he international flavor of the Kingcobra is apparent in this view. A USAAF aircraft is to the rear, with a Russian Kingcobra in the middle and a French machine in the foreground. (Bell)

*B*ell P–36A–6, 42–69012, is seen undergoing static testing at Bell. The purpose of this particular experiment was to see if the cabin doors would release while the fuselage was being subjected to unusual stress. (Bell)

recognized as folly. The Russians demanded Mustangs and Thunderbolts and Lightnings but the Americans suddenly realized that they had an excellent market for Airacobras and Kingcobras.

The Lend-Lease policy supplied American factories with valuable production contracts that would keep the supply lines going until newer and better combat aircraft could be built. The first Lend-Lease aircraft sent to the Russians was a small batch of Curtiss Tomahawks diverted from a Royal Air Force order. Other aircraft such as Curtiss O–52 observation planes – a type that had been totally rejected by the Army – and North American B–25Bs were shipped by sea to bolster the Soviet defenses. More aircraft followed, including larger orders for P–40s, but aircraft being shipped disassembled on convoys were quite often sent to the bottom during the effective attacks by roving packs of German U-Boats. The first Bell Airacobras were warmly received by the Russians who liked the cannon and thought the aircraft much better than the P–40. During 1944 the Russians began taking deliveries of the Republic P–47 which came via

Iran, and the Kingcobra which came via the Alaska ferry route. The Soviets only got 195 Thunderbolts but they did get 4,719 Airacobras and 2,400 Kingcobras. Out of a total 14,798 aircraft supplied by America, the Soviets received 14,018 – the difference being lost during convoy shipment or crashing during ferry flights. However, this large number of aircraft was considered to be totally insufficient by the Russians – when compared to the almost 300,000 aircraft built in America during World War Two, the Soviets felt that they were being short-changed by the capitalists. However, the Soviets apparently got their own back when they did not pay for most of the Lend-Lease equipment nor destroy or return it according to the terms of the contract. American military fear of giving the Soviets advanced equipment was well-taken when a Boeing B–29 Superfortress had to make an emergency landing in Russian territory after a bombing mission to Japan late in the war. The Russians eventually returned the American crew but they kept the bomber, disassembled the craft, made blueprints of each part and, eventually, produced a nearly identical copy of

During World War Two, the Airacobra and Kingcobra turned Bell from a small aircraft manufacturer into one of the world's largest. This Kingcobra was the 10,000th fighter manufactured by the company. (Bell)

Opposite above
Two P–63As were sent to the Royal Air Force to test the laminar flow wing. Both received standard day fighter camouflage and one machine was modified with a bubble canopy. The X on the forward fuselage was to denote the experimental role. (MoD)

Finding the fighter ideal for their purposes, the biggest user, of course, of the Kingcobra was the Soviet Union. These Kingcobras are seen ready for the ferry flight to Alaska where they would be picked up by Soviet pilots. The aircraft were painted in standard USAAF camouflage. The drop tanks on these machines are natural metal. (Bell)

A virtual field full of Soviet Kingcobras is seen at the Bell plant prior to a mass delivery flight. (Bell)

the big four-engined plane. The USSR had always wanted American heavy bombers but their requests had been politely turned down. By careful copying they now had their own version of the Superfortress which equipped Soviet heavy bomber units well into the 1950s.

Little is known about the Soviet operation of the Kingcobras that they received via the Alaskan pipeline. Soviet pilots would pick up the fighters and ferry them to a dispersal base outside of Moscow where they would be

assigned to active squadrons. It is not known if there were any Soviet aces who flew the Kingcobra but it is probably a safe assumption to presume that the Kingcobra did rack up victories over the *Luftwaffe* since there were quite a few Russian aces who flew the Airacobra. Undoubtedly the Russians appreciated the fine flying qualities of the Kingcobra which did not have any of the vices attributed to the earlier Bell product. There is no record of a Kingcobra ever going through the strange maneuver described as tumbling. The faster

speed and the punch from the updated 37 mm cannon certainly wreaked havoc on German armor and soft-skinned vehicles. During the severe Russian winters, the German rolling stock would quite often be stuck and would present excellent targets for bands of marauding Soviet Kingcobras and Airacobras. German anti-aircraft guns had achieved a high state of art and the Bell fighters, like all liquid-cooled aircraft, proved to be vulnerable to damage. Shells could destroy or damage the radiators or cooling lines and the fighter pilot

would have only a few minutes to decide whether to try a crash landing or bail out before his engine quit. Losses among the Soviet fighter forces were extremely high, many German pilots remembering that they could not shoot down the red-starred fighters fast enough. As Soviet factories, located well behind the line of action, began tooling up for mass-production and the flow of new aircraft to front-line squadrons picked up, the hard-pressed Germans felt as if they were facing a tidal wave of aircraft. German production could not keep up with the massive numbers of Soviet aircraft aided by Lend-Lease equipment and, even though the average German pilot was considerably superior to his Soviet counterpart, it was only a matter of time before the lack of availability of aircraft and supplies began to take their toll on the *Luftwaffe*.

Back in the United States, as the flow of Kingcobras continued smoothly on the Alaskan pipeline, Bell engineers busied themselves with modifications and improvements to the basic design. The next variant, following the P–63A, was the P–63C which featured an improved Allison V–1710–117, more armor

Interesting photo of USAAF Kingcobras in their training role. At low altitude, a mix of natural metal and camouflaged P–63s are seen escorting a flight of Boeing B–29s on a practice raid. (USAAF)

against the possibility of damage during ground attack, extra fuel capacity and a distinguishing long ventral fin (from the P–63C–5–BE on) that extended from the rear portion of the rudder to almost the trailing edge of the wing. Armament remained unchanged but, in many instances, the podded .50 caliber wing guns were removed by the Soviets in the field. The P–63C was a fine looking aircraft and the extra military power available for longer periods from the Allison along with the additional stability from the ventral fin made the Kingcobra a popular aircraft with the pilots. Bell cranked out 1,227 P–63Cs, many going to the Soviets. Most of the P–63As had been delivered in the standard Olive Drab and Neutral Gray camouflage but the P–63Cs assigned to the USAAF were left in natural metal finish except for the wing which had all seams carefully filled and sanded then painted with a smooth coat of silver paint. This

P–63D, s/n 43–11718, was possibly the most attractive Kingcobra built. Powered by an Allison V–1710–109, the fighter featured a longer wing, a full bubble canopy and no ventral fin. The armor plate behind the pilot was fashioned out of armor glass in order not to restrict visibility. (Bell)

P–63 airframes were used for a large variety of aerodynamic experiments including this testing of a 'butterfly' tail. (Bell)

Heavy and sluggish on the controls, the RP–63s were not particularly well liked by the pilots. Nor were the student gunners who had a habit of firing at the RPs after they would break away from their 'attack'. During the break, the unarmored underbelly of the Kingcobra was exposed and the fragmenting bullets could do plenty of damage and several Kingcobras were knocked down in this manner. Painted in a bright orange, Frangible Sal is 42–69647, a number that does not fall into known RP serial blocks. (USAF)

The P–63 finally got to see a 'combat' role with the USAAF in a most unusual manner. Given a layer of a newly developed aluminum armor, modified P–63s were sent against fledgling gunners for actual practice in shooting at a live target. Fortunately, the bullets were made of a material that would shatter on impact with the armor. (USAF)

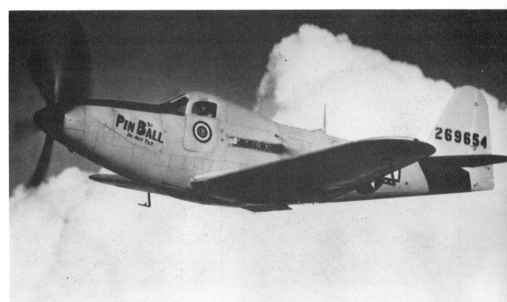

R P–63, Pin Ball – Do Not Tilt, is seen in flight. The heavily armored cockpit restricted the pilot's vision. (USAF)

*T*he Bell P–36F, powered by an Allison V–1710–135, featured a totally redesigned tail unit that incorporated a larger, swept-back vertical tail. Otherwise similar to the P–63E, only one example of the F was constructed but this aircraft is still airworthy and flies with the Confederate Air Force. (Bell)

Opposite above

*N*ext to the Russians, the French were the second largest foreign user of the Kingcobra. After World War Two, the French deployed P–63 units to Indo-China where they attacked the Viet Minh. The Kingcobra was not suited to the tropical climate and rigors of Indo-China and the aircraft was less than successful. (Bell)

*B*ell's Kingcobra production line illustrates just how important women were to America's war effort. Known as Rosie the Riveters, the women aircraft workers freed men for combat jobs while keeping up the immense aircraft output from the nation's factories. (Bell)

smooth surface was necessary to preserve the benefits of the laminar-flow airfoil. However, P–63Cs that were to be delivered to the Russians were camouflaged in the Olive Drab and Neutral Gray scheme with red stars surrounded by a thin white trim line.

Limited production or experimental variants of the Kingcobra included the P–63D, P–63E and P–63F. The P–63D was basically a P–63C without the ventral fin that had a large bubble canopy installed along with an uprated Allison V–1710–109 of 1,425 hp. The bubble canopy slid back along the fuselage when opening and this made the relocation of the air scoop mandatory. The scoop was moved far enough back so that the canopy could clear the unit when in the fully opened position. The large bubble gave the Kingcobra pilot excellent visibility since he was located on the forward edge of the wing. The unit could be jettisoned in face of an emergency but the quaint car doors were gone. Plans were instigated for the production of the P–63D but these never came to fruition. The P–63E was basically similar to the D with its ten inch increased wing span but it did not have the bubble canopy and retained

the familiar car doors. Plans to produce almost 3,000 P–63Es were also shelved when it became apparent that the fighter would be just too outdated. Thirteen P–63Es were produced and these were used for a variety of miscellaneous tasks. The final Kingcobra was the P–63F, two of which were constructed, and it was the most easily recognizable variant since it had a greatly increased vertical fin that gave the machine a distinctive look. The P–63F was powered by an Allison V–1710–135 of 1,425 hp that gave a top speed of over 430 mph. Once again, plans for production were shelved because, no matter how it was modified, the Kingcobra was just too dated to warrant further production. The prototype P–63F, 43–11719, survived the post-war scrappings and still flies regularly (now painted in *ersatz* Russian markings) from its home base in Texas.

The United States Army Air Force retained a considerable number of Kingcobras and these machines were used for a variety of missions. Some were sent to advanced training units, some were used as base hacks, but the majority were put to one of the strangest uses of any

military aircraft. Concerned by the poor gunnery scores of its student fighter pilots, the USAAF and Bell put together plans for a highly modified version of the Kingcobra that would provide 'live' practice. Five RP–63A–11–BE Kingcobras (based on the P–63A–9) were manufactured that were gutted of all armament and armor. An extra-thick tough skin weighing almost 1,500 pounds was placed over vital areas of the airframe while the rear portion of the canopy was also sheeted over. Sensors were installed in the skin and ran to a control board in the cockpit which in turn was hooked to the landing lights and to extra lights added to the airframe. The dorsal engine air intake was replaced with a clam shell unit and the aircraft were painted in a variety of bright colors. These machines were to serve just one purpose: flying targets. Student fighter pilots had their machine guns supplied with frangible bullets that would splinter and disintegrate upon impact with the skin of the Kingcobra. The RP–63s were sent to gunnery bases around the country where they became victims over and over again for the young fighter pilot trainees. The students would

End of the line. Virtually all USAAF
Kingcobras ended up in scrapyards
immediately after World War Two. (W. T. Larkins)

attack the Kingcobras and if their bursts hit home, the panel in the pilot's cockpit would register the hits and set the landing lights and other additional lights blinking madly. Due to the bright colors with which the aircraft were painted and the blinking lights, the Kingcobras were dubbed 'Pin Ball machines.' The idea worked and the practice gave students a taste of real combat. Other RPs were produced in greater quantity and these included 95 RP–63A–12s which had additional fuel and 200 RP–63Cs with the Allison V–1710–117, finishing the run with 32 RP–63Gs powered with the Allison V–1710–135. Other modifications included a V-tail testing arrangement on one P–63, but it is not known if the aircraft flew in this configuration, and two P–63s that were given to the Navy to test swept-back wings.

Two P–63As were sent to the Royal Air Force where they were evaluated to test the effectiveness of the laminar flow wing – a feature that would later appear on the Supermarine Spitfire. Both these aircraft received standard day fighter camouflage and were marked with a large X on the nose to denote the experimental role. One aircraft was also fitted with a bubble canopy but it is not known if this feature was also tested for future British combat aircraft. Both Kingcobras were scrapped after their testing programs ended.

The only other operators of the Kingcobra were the *Armée de l'Air* and the *Fuerza Aerea Hondurena*. France received around 300 aircraft from American stocks towards the end of World War Two. The famous *Normandie-Niemen* operated P–63s from Saigon in Vietnam during September 1949. The P–63s were used against the rapidly spreading Viet Minh with uncertain results. The Kingcobras were getting old and were unsuited to operating in the extreme Indo-China jungle climate where engines would regularly overheat. The cooling system for the Allison was also prone to damage from Viet Minh groundfire. The Kingcobras were replaced by the French with Grumman Hellcats and Bearcats as soon as those aircraft were made available from America. Honduras received a small number of P–63s, the only South American country to get them, after signing the Rio Pact of 1947. Operated with a few P–38s, these aircraft formed an operational squadron but it is thought that the aircraft were rarely flown. The survivors of both types were returned to the USA in the early 1960s and soon became collector's items. The Kingcobra thus gained the distinction of fighting with two air forces and operating marginally with another while never seeing real action with the USAAF. Yet the Army's Kingcobras were constantly being 'shot down' over and over again! Today about three P–63s remain flyable and are very popular with airshow audiences.

BELL P–63 KINGCOBRA VARIANTS, SERIAL NUMBERS AND SPECIFICATIONS

Variants

XP–63 V–1710–47 engine. Two built, both crashed. No armament.

XP–63A V–1710–93 engine. One built, production prototype. 37 mm cannon and two .50 caliber nose guns and two .50 caliber guns in pods under wing.

P–63A V–1710–93 engine. 37 mm cannon and two .50 caliber nose guns and two .50 caliber guns in pods under wing. Most were transferred to Russia. The P–63A–6 carried outboard underwing shackles for drop tanks or two 500 lb bombs. Another drop tank or 500 lb bomb could be carried under the fuselage. The P–63A–7 had a four-blade Aeroproducts propeller of smaller dimensions. The P–63A–9 introduced an improved Oldsmobile M10 37 mm cannon with 58 shells. The P–63A–10 had increased armor protection. A total of 1,725 was built.

P–63B Proposed Merlin-powered Kingcobra. Not built.

P–63C V–1710–117 engine. Similar to the P–63A–10 except for the engine. 37 mm cannon and four .50 caliber guns in nose and wing. The P–63C–5 had a ventral fin for increased stability. Most were transferred to USSR or France. A total of 1,227 was built.

P–63D V–1710–109 engine. Longer wing, bubble canopy and no ventral fin. One was built.

P–63E V–1710–109 engine. Similar to the P–63D, except it did not have the bubble canopy but it did have the ventral fin. 37 mm cannon, two .50 caliber nose guns and two .50 caliber podded wing guns. Thirteen were built.

P–63F V–1710–135 engine. Similar to P–63E but with much larger vertical tail. One was built.

RP–63A–11 The first target Kingcobra, based on the P–63A–9, they had no armament or standard armor, but had a special thick skin weighing 1,488 lb on vital portions. The rear of the canopy was covered over. Sensors were fitted to record hits, and a red light on the spinner flashed when aircraft was hit. A clam-shell intake replaced the air intake behind canopy. Five were built.

RP–63A–12 As P–63A–11 but with increased internal tankage of 126 gallons. A total of 89 was built.

RP–63C V–1710–117. Total of 200 was built.

RP–63G V–1710–135. Targets had designations changed after the war in 1948 to QF–63A, QF–63C, and QF–63G. A total of 32 was built.

Serial Numbers

XP–63	41–19511 and 41–19512
XP–63A	42–78015
P–63A	42–68861 through 42–69879; 42–69975 through 42–70685
P–63C	42–70686 through 42–70860; 43–10818 through 43–10892; 43–11133 through 43–11717; 44–4001 through 44–4427
P–63D	43–11718
P–63E	43–11720 through 43–11721; 43–11725 through 43–11735
P–63F	43–11719, 43–11722
Kingcobra Mk I	FR408 (P–63A, 42–68937), FZ440 (P–63A–9–BE, 42–69423)

Kingcobras built as targets:

RP–63A	42–69880 through 42–69974
RP–63C	43–10933 through 43–11132
RP–63G	43–11723 through 43–11724; 45–57283 through 45–57312

A total of 2,421 Kingcobras were transferred to the Soviet Union.

Specifications

XP–63

Span	38 ft 4 in
Length	32 ft 8 in
Height	12 ft
Wing area	248 sq ft
Empty weight	6,185 lb
Loaded weight	8,400 lb
Max. speed	421 mph
Cruise speed	341 mph
Ceiling	45,500 ft
Rate of climb	3,670 fpm
Range	587 miles
Powerplant	Allison V–1710–47 of 1,325 hp

P–63A

Span	38 ft 4 in
Length	32 ft 8 in
Height	12 ft 7 in
Wing area	248 sq ft
Empty weight	6,375 lb
Loaded weight	10,500 lb
Max. speed	408 mph
Cruise speed	378 mph
Ceiling	43,000 ft
Rate of climb	3,100 fpm
Range	490 miles
Powerplant	Allison V–1710–95 of 1,325 hp

P–63C

Span	38 ft 4 in
Length	32 ft 8 in
Height	12 ft 7 in
Wing area	248 sq ft
Empty weight	6,800 lb
Loaded weight	10,700 lb
Max. speed	410 mph
Cruise speed	356 mph
Ceiling	38,600 ft
Rate of climb	3,150 fpm
Range	320 miles
Powerplant	Allison V–1710–117 of 1,510 hp

P–63D

Span	39 ft 2 in
Length	32 ft 8 in
Height	11 ft 2 in
Wing area	255 sq ft
Empty weight	7,076 lb
Loaded weight	11,000 lb
Max. speed	437 mph
Cruise speed	n/a
Ceiling	39,000 ft
Rate of climb	2,650 fpm
Range	700 miles
Powerplant	Allison V–1710–109 of 1,425 hp

P–63E

Span	39 ft 2 in
Length	32 ft 8 in
Height	12 ft 9 in
Wing area	255 sq ft
Empty weight	7,300 lb
Loaded weight	11,200 lb
Max. speed	410 mph
Cruise speed	n/a
Ceiling	n/a
Rate of climb	3,400 fpm
Range	725 miles
Powerplant	Allison V–1710–109 of 1,425 hp

North American P-64 Fighter From A Trainer

North American Aviation was enjoying great success with its diverse line of training aircraft so, the company reasoned, why not make a silk purse out of a sow's ear?

The management of North American Aviation certainly seemed to be correct when congratulating themselves on the Company's move to sunny Southern California during 1935. North American had been formed out of a complex conglomeration of aeronautical and manufacturing companies but the company's first aircraft, the porcine three-seat O–47 observation platform, was not setting the world on fire. The prototype of the observation aircraft had been built by General Aircraft (to be renamed the Manufacturing Division of North American) in Dundalk, Maryland, before the move west. The management of the

new aircraft company had found very reasonable manufacturing space situated at Mines Field (location of today's sprawling Los Angeles International Airport) and the good weather, combined with close proximity to the rapidly developing aircraft industry that seemed to be making the Los Angeles area home, made the new North American location ideal. Now all the company needed was aircraft to build!

North American immediately set to work constructing several hundred O–47s to satisfy the Army Air Corps contract. The portly aircraft was efficient at its job but times were rapidly changing and the day of the slow, lightly armed observation aircraft had come and gone. North American designers set their sights on a number of other projects that were to include trainers, bombers, and fighters –

including the famous P–51, but that was yet to come.

The last prototype aircraft to be constructed at the Dundalk facility was a rather crude looking little trainer that had received the designation NA–16. What was not known at

With horizontal elevator in the full up position, an Air Corps instructor runs up the Wright R–1820–77 of the base's P–64 prior to a flight. The six P–64s were assigned to various training bases in the United States where they were to act as advanced fighter trainers. However, the delightful handling qualities of the aircraft made them pets of the instructors who used them to blow-off steam after a hard day's work of instructing in low performance aircraft such as the Vultee BT–13s in the background. The P–64 was a fine aerobatic performer and, with armament removed, was capable of a championship display in the hands of a skilled pilot. Note that this aircraft has apparently been sprayed in darker colours than were originally applied to the Thai machines although the general camouflage pattern has been basically followed. (P. M. Bowers)

S even NA–50s were produced for Peru in 1939, the first fighter variant to come from the NA–16 trainer family. The rudder was off the Navy's SNJ–2 series while the basic design of the aircraft came from the NA–26, a two-seat trainer that was the first version of the NA–16 series to have retractable landing gear. The NA–50 featured all-metal construction except for the control surfaces which were fabric covered. A primitive sight system was mounted in front of the windshield. (NAA)

A fully operational NA–50 for Peru is seen at Mines Field prior to delivery. Both machine guns with extended blast tubes have been installed in the aft cowling while four 100 lb bombs have been mounted under the wing. All stencilling on the aircraft is in Spanish. (NAA)

Its Texan ancestry is clearly evident in this view of the first NA–50 for Peru. Finished in overall natural metal, the Peruvian national insignia was painted in red, white and red on the rudder and above and below each outer wing panel. Two or three NA–50s were lost in combat when Peru and Ecuador clashed in 1941 but the NA–50s provided valuable ground support, dive bombing and strafing enemy positions. At least one NA–50 remained active until the late 1950s with the Cuerpo de Aeronautica del Peru, giving aerobatic demonstrations. The three-blade propeller fitted to the R–1820–77 was built by Hamilton Standard. (NAA)

the time was that variants of the NA–16 were to put North American on the aeronautical map and, when production of the final variant concluded, over 17,000 of the rugged trainers had been produced. More than 4,500 other examples were to be manufactured under license by foreign companies, a success story that has rarely been equalled in the aeronautical field.

The NA–16 was first flown in April of 1935 and then traveled to Wright Field, Ohio, for extensive testing by Army Air Corps pilots. Powered by a Wright R–975 Whirlwind of 400 hp, the little aircraft had tandem seating with open cockpits and non-retractable landing gear. The Wright Field pilots liked the aircraft and recommended that it be chosen as the new Army Air Corps basic training aircraft. Several changes in the design were also suggested by Wright Field including the in-

Opposite above
The first NA–68 for Thailand seen parked on the dirt ramp at Mines Field. While similar to the NA–50, the NA–68 differed in a number of small design details. The tail group was from an AT–6 while the landing gear had been reinforced. The positions for the fuselage mounted .30 caliber Browning air cooled machine guns had been moved to the front cowling while large fairings covered the breeches for the 20 mm cannons. External wing racks could also carry a load of small bombs. The NA–68 was camouflaged in light earth tones on the upper surfaces while the lower surfaces were left in their shiny natural metal finish. (NAA)

The prototype NA–68 carried the civil registration NX25607 on the rudder and under the left wing and on top of the right wing. Fuselage appears to be painted in the base coat of the camouflage color while a painted position for the Thai roundel can be clearly made out under the wing. Mottling on the rear fuselage is from the sun's reflection off the highly polished aluminum skin of the wing. (NAA)

A poor quality print but the only view known of an NA–68 in flight. The photograph is of the prototype NX25607 just as the landing gear is retracting into the wells. At this stage in testing the twin cannon armament had been added. Note the primered positions for the roundels which had not yet been painted. (NAA)

A P–64 parked at an Air Corps base. This particular example, one of six taken into service by the Army after the invasion of Thailand still retains the breech covers for the 20 mm cannon. None of the P–64s were fitted with armament while in American service. On the original print 'U.S. Army' is visible under the wings.

stallation of a Pratt & Whitney R–1340 of 600 hp, streamlined fairings enclosing the gear struts, and a sliding enclosure for the cockpits. North American quickly instituted these changes on the prototype which then acquired the company designation of NA–18, the first in 63 different North American assignment numbers given to its trainer series as it underwent constant changes to conform to the wants of customers or to accommodate new features such as different engines and retractable landing gear. Eventually named Texan in American use and Harvard in Commonwealth operation, North American's trainer was to fly on into aviation history. The vast number of changes that the trainer underwent are outside the scope of this volume but one of the most interesting modifications of the basic airframe is the subject of this chapter.

North American reasoned that, as the 1930s progressed towards the 1940s and world unrest grew, many small and third world nations would need some form of pursuit aircraft to guard their interests. The main factor in such an aircraft would, of course, be cost. In order to keep cost at an absolute minimum the engineers dragged out their rather shopworn NA–16 blueprints, set up their slide rules and developed the NA–50.

The NA–50 drew its lines from the NA–26, the first version of the NA–16 with retractable landing gear. The NA–50 was of all metal construction except for the fabric covered control surfaces. A Wright R–1820–77 of 870 hp was added and, for armament, the NA–50 was equipped with two .30 caliber Browning air-cooled machine guns firing through the propeller arc from their location on the upper decking. Internal provisions were installed in the wings for the mounting of four racks, capable of carrying up to a total of 550 lbs of bombs. Thus armed, the small aircraft could be considered 'sort of a fighter' but it certainly would not want to come up against aircraft like the Spitfire or Bf 109. First flying from Mines Field during February 1939, the NA–50 caught the attention of a delegation from the South American country of Peru who were impressed by the modern features such as the retractable landing gear, enclosed cockpit, and all-metal construction. Peru went on to order seven NA–50s which were quickly completed and ready for delivery by May 1939.

Peru had a number of long-standing feuds with its neighbor Ecuador and, when border fighting between the two countries' armies broke out in 1941, the NA–50s were ordered into action. The fighters flew patrols over the combat zone and aided the ground troops by dive bombing and strafing the enemy forces. During the action several NA–50s were lost in fighting, including at least one downed by anti-aircraft fire. After this brief combat indoctrination, the NA–50s operated by Peru faded into obscurity.

Back at Mines Field, the sales department was looking for more customers for the NA–50 as the seven-plane order from Peru did not cover the development costs. The Kingdom of Thailand was extremely nervous of its Japanese neighbor who had occupied vast chunks of Indochina and, in an attempt to bolster its antiquated forces, signed a contract with North American for six fighting aircraft that were very similar to the Peruvian NA–50s. The Thai aircraft had improved tail surfaces of the same type featured on the AT–6 and an improved armament of one 20 mm cannon under each outer wing panel. The cannon breeches were enclosed in fairings while the long barrels protruded to the front of the engine cowling. These various changes added yet another model number to the already burgeoning NA–16 family: NA–68. The aircraft for Thailand were camouflaged in light earth colors and crated for ocean shipment. However, once on the high seas between California and Hawaii, the cargo ship was recalled when news of the Japanese invasion of Thailand reached the American government.

North American uncrated their charges, assembled the aircraft and delivered them to the Army. There was no way that six underpowered aircraft could be pressed into any sort of fighting role so it was decided to utilize the aircraft in an advanced training role, flying beside its stablemate the Texan. In an ironic note, the Army realized that the aircraft would need a designation to fit into the American system and, since it was built as a fighting aircraft, was assigned the number P–64 for its training role!

The P–64s were dispersed to various training bases in America where they were usually flown by overworked instructors who enjoyed the aircraft's superior performance and nice handling qualities. With all armament removed the P–64 became known as quite an aerobatic ship and many World War Two student pilots recall sparkling performances etched in the air by the P–64.

With the end of the War the P–64s found their way to the vast aeronautical scrapyards in Arizona. At one such field, North American employee Jack Canary came across a staked-down P–64, its paint peeling in the intense desert sun. Canary remembered the delightful handling qualities of the aircraft and, hating to see the machine melted down into pots and pans, paid a small sum and flew the bedraggled machine back to Southern California. Canary flew the machine for several years then sold it. The P–64 went through a number of owners including a rainmaker in Mexico, returning to the United States in the early 1960s before being purchased by Paul Poberezny, president of the Experimental Aircraft Association. The last surving P–64 is now preserved in that organization's famous museum and it is flown occasionally, a monument to the trainer that became, however briefly, a fighter.

NORTH AMERICAN P–64 SERIAL NUMBERS AND SPECIFICATIONS

Serial Numbers

P–64	41–19082 through 41–19087

Specifications

P–64

Span	37 ft 3 in
Length	27 ft
Height	19 ft
Wing area	227 sq ft
Empty weight	4,660 lb
Loaded weight	6,800 lb
Max. speed	270 mph
Cruise speed	235 mph
Ceiling	27,500 ft
Rate of climb	n/a
Range	635 miles
Powerplant	Wright R–1820–77 of 870 hp

Vultee P-66 Vanguard — The Multi-Purpose Design

Vultee thought that a number of diverse military aircraft stemming from one basic design would be a fine idea, but the theory did not quite work in practice.

The concept of a multi-purpose military aircraft design has intrigued aeronautical engineers since the beginning of military aviation. The idea of coming up with a basic design that could be added to or subtracted from in order to create everything from a trainer to a fighter certainly had plenty of appeal, for such an aircraft would be cost-efficient and could be manufactured in its different versions with a minimum of trouble and retooling. Different engines could be added to the basic design to create low-powered trainers or high-horsepower fighters. A variety of outer wing panels could be equipped with machine guns or cannon while shackles could be attached for dive bombing or ground support roles. The center section could also be adapted for single-seat fighter, dual control trainer, or tandem ground attack configurations. Landing gear could be fitted in the fixed position for training aircraft while retractable heavy duty units could easily be mated to the center section for combat roles.

The investigation into this 'all-in-one' aircraft really picked up during the 1930s, perhaps spurred on by the Bill Barnes pulp novels featured in the popular *Air Trails* magazine. The fictional Barnes created a wide variety of bizarre aircraft, many of which featured common components, in which he was constantly doing battle with the various forces of evil around the world. Bill Barnes, apparently, had never heard of the idea of wind tunnel testing and, while that exacting science was still at an admittedly early stage of development, it also appears that the real aeronautical engineers

Vultee Model 48C Vanguard in flight. Given the civil license NX28300 because the prototypes were developed as company projects rather than under government contracts, the Model 48C was the definitive version of the prototype Vanguards. This aircraft flew for the first time on 6 September 1940; 144 examples had been ordered by the Swedish government on 6 February 1940. The Model 48C was basically similar to the earlier Model 48X except for an uprated engine and the provision for four wing and two nose mounted machine guns. Close examination of this photograph reveals that the ports for the wing machine guns have been retouched out while no attempt has been made to cover over the distinctive nose gun positions. (Vultee)

Although NX21755 was the first P–48, this designation should not be confused with the Army pursuit numbering system as it was merely the Vultee model assignment. This view of the P–48 shows the aircraft after it had been rebuilt following an accident during landing when test pilot Vance Breese hit another aircraft and tore a landing gear leg off the fighter. Breese made a skillful crash landing and Vultee decided to rebuild and modify the Vanguard to remove the streamlined cowling and extended drive shaft which they had hoped would contribute to a significant increase in top speed. Actually the Vanguard performed better without the streamlined modifications since their removal also shed a considerable amount of weight. No provision was made for armament in this aircraft. (Vultee)

Another of the planes evolved from the multi-purpose specification created by Vultee was the BC–3. The BC–3, stemming from the BC–51, was a basic combat trainer that had a limited attack potential. The BC–3 never went beyond the prototype stage but its lines clearly reflect the common ancestry. This aircraft survived the war and appeared on the US Civil Register in the late 1940s as NX21753, the number that it carried during its testing life with Vultee. (Vultee)

involved in the process of creating a multi-purpose aircraft were not paying all that much attention to the hard lessons that had been learned in the field of military aviation.

Vultee Aircraft in Downey, California, was attracted by the idea of an all-in-one military aircraft during the late 1930s as orders for military aircraft were on a rocketing upward spiral all over the world. After much consideration, Vultee evolved a plan that would see a basic airframe form at least four distinct military planes. These would range from a basic trainer to a single-seat combat aircraft. Vultee chose to employ a common tail group, rear fuselage, and wing while switching around these elements to specifically designed components for specific roles. The four aircraft that Vultee envisioned would include a single-seat fighting aircraft that would carry the company designation of P–48 (this designation had nothing to do with the Army's numbering of pursuit designs). The next step would be a basic combat trainer that could be employed in light combat duties designated BC–51. A step down from the BC–51 would be the B–54 which would be employed as an advanced trainer. Bringing up the rear position was the B–54D which would be constructed as a simple basic trainer. Oddly, it was the low man on the totem pole that would achieve the most success, but more of that later.

The shining star of the multi-role concept was undoubtedly the P–48 which was being bred as a sleek fighter that would have done Bill Barnes proud. Vultee wanted to come up with a nose configuration that would slim the radial engine installation into a sleek unit that would resemble the most closely cowled liquid-cooled powerplant. To achieve the long lines needed for streamlining, the engineers added an extra-long drive shaft to the Pratt & Whitney R–1830–S4C4–G of 1,200 hp that had been chosen for the fighter. The extended drive shaft placed the propeller, a three-blade Hamilton Standard unit, far in front of the engine and Vultee carefully wrapped a sleek cowling around the engine. Cooling was to be provided by an adjustable air intake that was installed directly behind and under the back plate for the gracefully formed spinner. Much was made of this installation and Vultee claimed that they had created a unit that offered the simplicity of a radial powerplant coupled with the elegant streamlining of a sleek inline engine.

The P–48 was wheeled out of the Vultee main hangar at Vultee Field and, after a number of ground tests, was flown for the first time during September 1939 by none other than Vance Breese, who has already been mentioned in this volume. Breese was, at this time, riding the crest of his popularity – conforming well to the public's (and apparently corporation's) idea of a dashing test pilot. Breese, however, was not all that pleased with his new mount and he found the engine cooling to be dreadfully inadequate while

When the order for 144 Vanguards for export to Sweden was blocked because of US government policy, Vultee and the government tried to interest Britain in purchasing the aircraft. Accordingly, two examples were painted in full Royal Air Force camouflage and assigned serial numbers. BW208, the first of the two aircraft, is seen at Vultee Field in Downey, California, during inspection. The fellow in uniform is the great Royal Flying Corps World War One ace, William Bishop. Bishop was once again in uniform for World War Two and he participated in a number of decision making roles. Bishop was viewing the aircraft to see if it would make a good combat trainer for the huge RAF training bases located in Canada. (Vultee)

handling was not what it should have been. The engineers responsible for the sleek, but non-functional, cowling must have cringed when the adjustable air scoop was fixed in the wide open position and, with indignity heaped upon indignity, another air scoop was cut in the top of the cowling. Even these modifications did not help all that much and the engine temperature needle kept climbing over the red line as the Pratt & Whitney heated up under its tight wrappings. So when Breese, while coming in to land on 9 May, rammed a Lockheed Sirius and tore off a landing gear leg, necessitating a skillful crash landing, Vultee decided it was time to modify NX21755, as the P–48 had been registered.

The damaged airframe of the prototype was hauled back to the hangar and work began immediately to convert the aircraft to the configuration of the second prototype – known as the Model 48X which had flown on 11 February 1940. Actually, at this point, it

*A*n extremely interesting view of what appears to be the Model 48X making a mock firing pass on a Vultee V–II dive bomber. The aircraft has been finished in a complex water-based camouflage scheme similar to those worn by Curtiss P–36s illustrated elsewhere in this volume. It is not known if the Vanguard prototype participated in any of the pre-World War Two war games in which many aircraft wore unusual and temporary camouflage schemes. (Vultee)

*E*xcellent view of a P–66 at the Vultee factory finished in Army markings and camouflage. Upper surfaces were sprayed Dark Olive Drab while the lower surfaces were finished in Neutral Gray. This particular P–66, 42–6955 can be distinguished as one of the later aircraft built because of the smaller amount of plexiglass covering the area behind the pilot's seat. The wide track of the landing gear is also apparent from this high angle. (Vultee)

This photograph of a late production P–66 poses something of a mystery as the coding on the tail does not conform to any of the Army serials. The aircraft could have been one of the Chinese machines being readied for shipment without national markings applied, a fairly common practice. (Vultee)

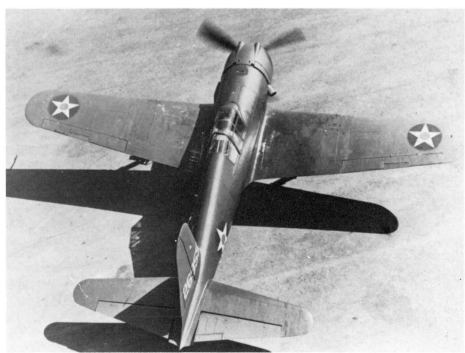

With the Pratt & Whitney R–1830–S3C4–G running, the P–66 heads out for the Vultee runway. Little is known of the 15 P–66s that were impressed into Army service although most of the aircraft were apparently assigned to various training fields in the American southwest. (Vultee)

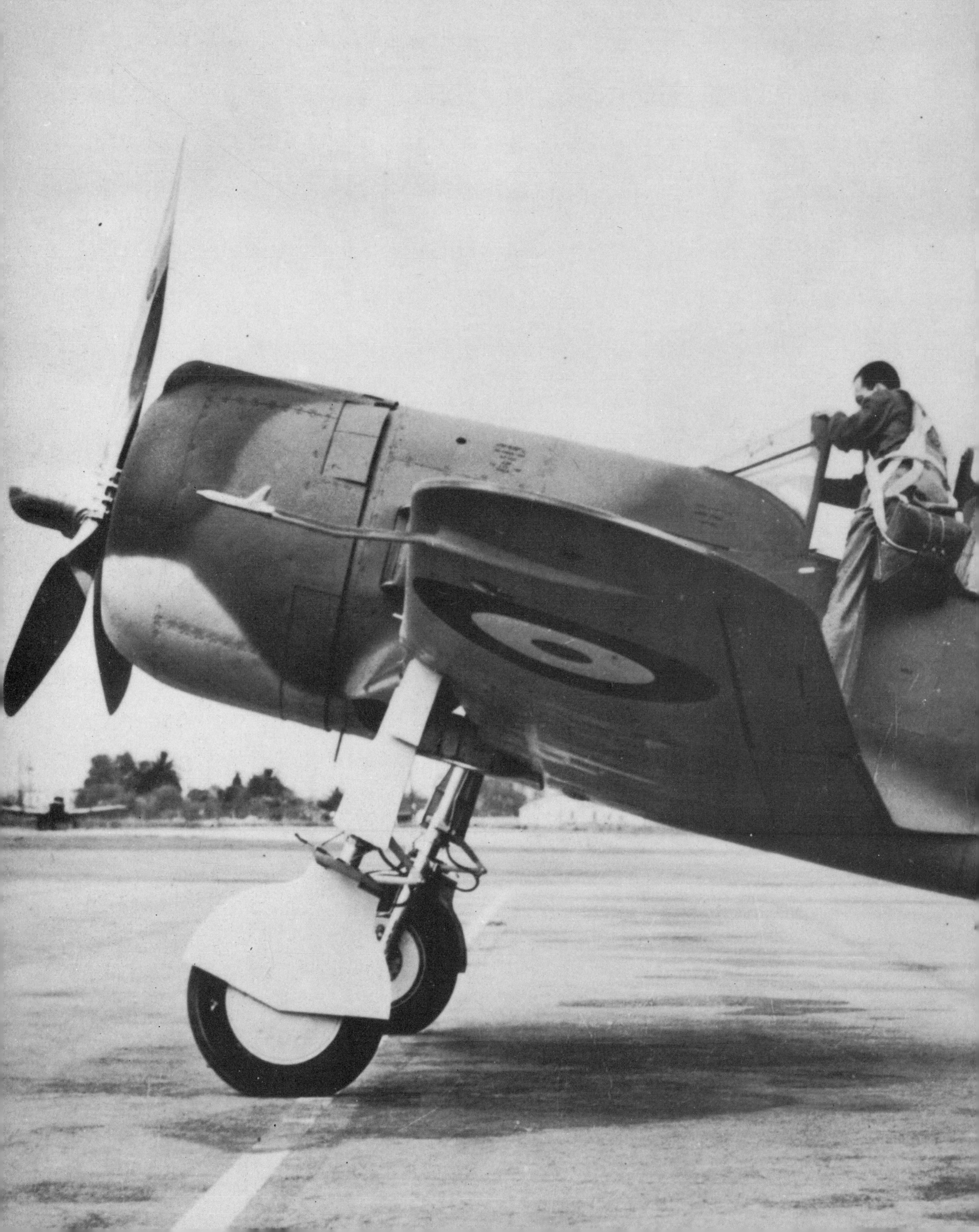

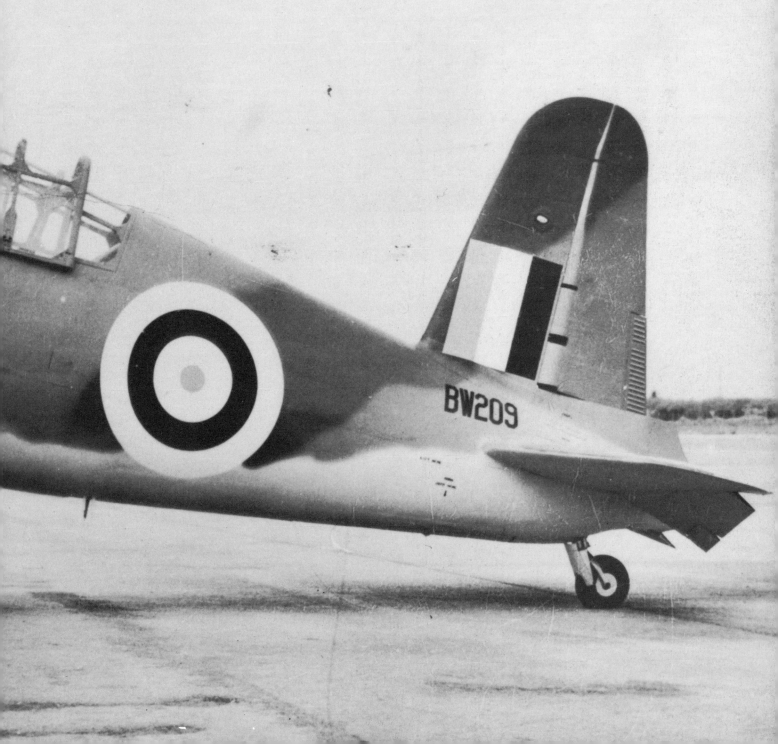

The second RAF Vanguard, BW209, is seen shortly before a test flight. BW209 was camouflaged in semi-matte Dark Earth and Dark Green upper surfaces while the under surfaces were sprayed in Sky Type S. The fuselage roundel is a standard RAF Type A with an overall diameter of 49 inches with a seven inch Yellow band, Blue band, and White band, and a seven inch Red center. The under wing roundel is 56 inches in diameter while the upper wing roundel was a standard upper wing Type B roundel with a Blue band of 16.8 inches in width and a Red center 22.4 inches in diameter. (Vultee)

should have seemed obvious to Vultee that their fighter entry was way too late to enter the rapidly developing combat aircraft market and its top projected speed of less than 350 mph was woefully inadequate for a new fighter.

However, Vultee apparently did not let reality stand in its way and proceeded at full speed with its multi-purpose project. The BC–51 combat trainer had emerged as the BC–3 and was undergoing testing while the lowly B–54D had turned into the highly successful BT–13 Valiant trainer. Back on the fighter end of the project, things were not going at all well. The first two aircraft were flying – both with standard open cowlings around their engines – and actually benefited from the dropping of the streamlined cowling, as the extra weight of the cowling and long drive shaft had completely detracted from the limited advantages of the streamlining. The two aircraft were not identical as the second machine was fitted with a wing that featured dihedral in the center section and also in the outer wing panels in an attempt to overcome some of the Vanguard's, as the design had been named by Vultee, stability problems. The Model 48X (registered NX19999, since these were private development aircraft and not funded under government contract) also had a

strengthened landing gear and carried provision for an armament of two machine guns in the nose, firing through the propeller arc, and one machine gun mounted in each wing but this armament was never fitted. In order to help cure stability problems, both prototypes were eventually fitted with tail groups that offered more control and keel surface. The Model 48X was the fastest of the series and achieved almost 360 mph at 15,000 ft.

While work on the prototypes was proceeding, the Vultee sales department began searching for potential customers for their fighter. Europe was looked on as a likely market as England seemed to be snapping up everything that could be made in America that had the capability to get into the air. Like North American and their NA–50 design, Vultee also cast an eye at the third world countries, many of which were being threatened by the worldwide advance of the Axis.

One country that was casting wary eyes at the Axis *and* at one of the free world's 'allies' was Sweden. Sweden had the rather unfortunate position to be so located as to be desired by both Germany and Russia while wanting to maintain a policy of individual freedom. Sweden's military was equipped with outmoded aircraft and weapons and when, during November 1939, Soviet forces spilled into Finland, with whom Sweden had a mutual defense pact, the Swedes were hard-pressed to assemble a force of Gloster Gladiator fighters

and Hawker Hart light bombers, both biplanes, to send to Finland.

Swedish representatives visited the American aircraft factories in search of combat aircraft that could be quickly built and delivered. Vultee, perhaps somewhat to their surprise, became the recipient of a contract for 144 Model 48C Vanguards. The first Model 48C, which also had a civil registration – NX28300 – was basically similar to the Model 48X and differed only in powerplant and various detail changes. A different version of the Pratt & Whitney engine, the R–1830–S3C4–G, which offered a better horsepower output at high altitudes, was installed and the armament layout called for the installation of four .30 Browning air cooled machine guns in the wings while two .50 caliber Browning guns were installed in the upper decking of the cowling to fire through the propeller arc. The first of the Swedish fighters was ready for delivery in September but a curious change in political climate prevented the Swedes from ever receiving their Vanguards.

The Swedish expeditionary force sent to aid Finland against the Russian invasion of that country was frowned upon by the Roosevelt administration who viewed such a move contrary to the huge American propaganda effort attempting to build up the image of Soviet Russia as a bunch of peace-loving workers who only wanted to stop an incursion of the Axis so they could get back to farm and factory.

Very well-worn Vanguard seen in Army camouflage. Aircraft has had its landing gear doors rather crudely cut off while a large ADF 'bullet' has been added under the center section.

Roosevelt apparently was not taking the fact that the Soviets had signed a non-aggression pact with Hitler. The government reasoned that any move against the Russians was a move against the Allies and quickly put a ban on the export of the fighters to Sweden. Sweden was not going to get its Vanguards, nor its Seversky P–35s which had been ordered at about the same time. What to do with the Vanguards became a bit of a problem.

The immediate market for the fighters would seem to be Britain who was buying just about any combat aircraft that it could get its hands on. Accordingly two Vanguards were painted up in full Royal Air Force markings, with serials BW208 and BW209, but, after some preliminary testing, the offer was dropped although a study of RAF records indicates that the serial block of BW208 through BW307 was assigned for 100 Vanguards that the RAF apparently was going to procure as an advanced contract trainer.

The next export market that seemed to be the most likely place to dispose of the Vanguards was China who was having considerable difficulty finding aircraft that could match the performance of the invading Japanese fighters. Records indicate that 129 Vultee Vanguards were shipped off to China for service but little is known of their combat record. The remaining 15 Vanguards were retained in the United States where they were dispersed from the Downey factory to the various southwest Army training bases for use as advanced trainers. As with the P–64, the problem with designation arose and the Vanguards were assigned the P–66 slot. Once again it was a case of a training aircraft receiving a fighter designation. Little is known of the P–66's history and it does not appear that any examples survived past 1945.

It is interesting to note that the multi-purpose aircraft program was not quite the success that was intended. The Vanguard never really got anywhere, the BC–3 only achieved prototype stage, but the BT–13, as previously mentioned, became one of the Army's most important and successful basic training aircraft and was produced in thousands. Vultee was merged with Consolidated and eventually took up the name Convair which in turn was swallowed up by the giant General Dynamics. The multi-purpose aircraft was not really forgotten and the TFX program developed by Secretary of Defense Robert S. McNamara under the administration of John F. Kennedy was eventually awarded to the Convair division of General Dynamics. The main thrust of the program was to produce a joint service jet warplane capable of performing many tasks. The TFX became the F–111 and whether the ultra-expensive program really lived up to expectations depends on a number of rather partisan views – both pro and con. At least the little P–66 must have felt somewhat vindicated.

VULTEE P–66 VANGUARD SERIAL NUMBERS AND SPECIFICATIONS

Serial Numbers

P–66	42–6832 through 42–6975

Note: all P–66s were assigned Army serials even though the majority were supplied to China and only 15 were taken on strength by the Army as advanced trainers.

Specification

P–66 Vanguard

Span	36 ft
Length	28 ft 5 in
Height	9 ft 5 in
Wing area	197 sq ft
Empty weight	5,230 lb
Loaded weight	7,050 lb
Max. speed	342 mph
Cruise speed	330 mph
Ceiling	25,000 ft
Rate of climb	2,100 fpm
Range	900 miles
Powerplant	Pratt & Whitney R–1830–S3C4–G (–33) of 1,200 hp

McDonnell XP-67
Elegant First Try

McDonnell's first attempt to build a fighter resulted in an extremely unusual aircraft.

The world-famous company that is currently responsible for the majority of the free world's fighter aircraft had a very humble beginning at Lambert Field in St Louis, Missouri, during 1939. James S. McDonnell, who would go on to build the F–4 Phantom II, F–15 Eagle and F–18 Hornet, was the son of a cotton farmer. At an early age, he began to show considerable interest in the new science of aeronautics. Gaining a degree from Princeton in 1921, McDonnell went on to become a pilot in the Army Air Service. For a number of years McDonnell went from one aircraft manufacturer to another on a variety of jobs, always picking up vital knowledge that was essential for his future plans. McDonnell's first aeronautical creation was a two place monoplane built in 1928 to compete in the Daniel Guggenheim contest for a 'safe' aircraft. The little Doodlebug was quite revolutionary and proved that a number of advanced theories could be applied to light aircraft but the Great Depression of 1929 killed off any chance of mass production.

After the Doodlebug McDonnell went back to working for different aircraft corporations, again picking up vital facts in running corporations that would serve him in the future. In 1938 McDonnell resigned from his last job and began seeking financial support for devel-

*T*he XP–67 is rolled out from the McDonnell plant at Lambert Field. Note the air intakes which were revised after the aircraft caught fire. The large tires fitted to the aircraft would have permitted operation off grass airfields. Also note the early propellers. Pilot had relatively good visibility from the pressurized cockpit. (McDonnell)

*S*een on 13 March 1944, the XP–67 in flight northwest of St Louis, Missouri. The 'blended' contours of the fuselage made for an extremely low profile. Aircraft was finished in standard Army camouflage of Olive Drab upper surfaces with Neutral Gray under surfaces. Dark Green dappling had been added around the leading and trailing edges of the flying surfaces. Cooling and turbocharger problems plagued the XP–67 during its brief flying career. By the time the aircraft had made its appearance, the bomber formations that it was to seek out and destroy had, of course, disappeared as the Axis was pushed closer and closer to defeat. (McDonnell)

oping his own company. The search for funds was accomplished and the McDonnell Aircraft Corporation came into business.

The first order of business for the new corporation was to find business – and in a hurry! McDonnell had carefully studied the Army Air Corps Circular Proposal R–40C (previously mentioned in other chapters) and decided that the company should create its own advanced fighter design to enter into the contest so that the company could have an actual aircraft of its own rather than having to rely on subcontracted work from other manufacturers.

The design for the new fighter was daring in the extreme. To be powered by the experimental Allison V–3420 or Pratt & Whitney H–3130, the aircraft would be propelled by two pusher propellers mounted behind the wings and driven by the means of a complex arrangement of angled drive shafts and gears

from the engine which would be mounted in the mid-fuselage position. McDonnell reasoned that this means of propulsion would leave the nose area free for a very heavy battery of cannon. The Air Corps reviewed the design submission but felt that the project was too ambitious and overly complicated. However, they were impressed by the amount of creative thinking that went into the proposal and told McDonnell that they would be pleased to consider future proposals from the new company. This developing contact between the company and the Army paid off when the Army issued a contract to McDonnell for two experimental fighter aircraft on 26 September 1941.

The new fighter, in many ways, was just as radical as McDonnell's first paper airplane that the Army had rejected. Aimed from the start as a fighter that would engage and destroy bomber formations, the new aircraft was given the designation XP–67. McDonnell and his designers felt that the overall efficiency of a fighting aircraft could be improved if the fuselage contours were 'blended' into an airfoil shape that would complement the wing's lifting abilities. The fuselage of the XP–67 took on a flattened shape that gave the appearance of having been pressed in a hydraulic vice. This new shape blended the wing, nacelles, and fuselage into what appeared, at first glance, to be one unit. The result was an attractive and functional looking fighter.

Power for the XP–67 was to be supplied by two Continental IV–1430–17/19 engines that were to produce 1,300 hp for takeoff but, via the use of turbosuperchargers, the horsepower rating would increase to 1,600 per engine at 25,000 ft. The engines were cowled in some of

the most attractive nacelles ever to grace a fighting aircraft, although some problems with cooling were encountered and the air inlets were changed several times. The engines drove two four-bladed propellers that were changed several times during testing. Eventually it seems that the final choice consisted of two Curtiss Electric propellers with large root cuffs. The engines rotated in opposite directions and utilized thrust augmentors to gain some extra speed advantage from the engine's gasses after they had passed through the turbosuperchargers.

One of the most startling features of the XP–67 was its incredibly heavy armament. Originally planned to carry six .50 caliber machine guns and four 20 mm cannon, the armament package was changed to six 37 mm

At a later date, the XP–67 with modified air intakes and 10 ft 6 in diameter Curtiss propellers. Designed to carry the incredibly heavy armament of six Oldsmobile M–4 37 mm cannon, the gun package was never fitted to the prototype but the armament would have guaranteed knocking any bomber out of the sky. Problems with the experimental Continental IV–1430 powerplants meant that the full horsepower rating of 1,300 hp at take-off and 1,600 hp at altitude were never achieved. (USAF)

*F*ront view of the *XP–67* shows off the aircraft's unusual lines to advantage. The idea of blending the fuselage into part of the lifting surface contributed to increased performance by helping to eliminate drag. The dihedral in the horizontal stabilizer is readily apparent. (McDonnell)

*E*xhaust gases from the Continental powerplants and turbochargers were gathered and ejected through exhausts in the extreme rear portion of the nacelles. This form of thrust augmentation added a bit of propulsive thrust. (McDonnell)

*P*lan view of the McDonnell XP–67 illustrates how the whole airframe was 'blended' to give an airfoil shape. From this angle it appears the fuselage is little more than a pod, giving an idea of the effectiveness of the streamlined shape. The leading edges of the flying surfaces were painted Dark Green for a dappled effect. (McDonnell/D4E–3238)

*T*he white crosses on the fuselage were for photographic recording purposes during the XP–67's early test flights. The immense size of the nacelles for the Continental IV–1430 engines also illustrate the high degree of streamlining applied to the units. The exhaust came directly out of the back of each nacelle, adding a small amount of jet thrust. (McDonnell/D4E–2507)

cannon with some consideration being given to later arming the XP–67 with a single 75 mm cannon. The punch from the six Oldsmobile M–4 cannon of 37 mm would have blown any bomber ever made out of the air and it was decided that this would be the final armament package with 45 rounds per cannon. The installation of this armament package would have been extremely heavy but it certainly would have made the XP–67 the king of the bomber destroyers. The armament, however, was never fitted during the test flights.

With a projected top speed of 472 mph at high altitude, the XP–67 was fitted with a pressurized cockpit for the single pilot. The pressurization presented some problems, especially with the aircraft's aft sliding canopy but the McDonnell design team overcame these obstacles and soon had a perfectly functioning unit.

The first XP–67 was rolled out of the factory during December 1943 and was finished in the standard Olive Drab and Neutral Gray finish with some green dappling around the leading and trailing edges of the flying surfaces. During high-speed taxi tests the new fighter received damage when one of the turbosupercharger units cracked and caught on fire, burning the interior structure of the nacelle. The turbos were to be a sore point on the XP–67 since they were prone to catching fire and, being buried inside the nacelle, the fire would not be noticed until the exterior paint began to smoke and blister!

First flight of the aircraft was made on 6 January 1944 and was extremely short due to cooling and turbo problems. The turbo compartments were encased with stainless steel firewalls to help prevent the spread of any possible fire while the air ducts were completely revised. The test flights started up once again but were of short duration. Number four flight was marred when the engine rpm ran away and damaged both powerplants. Continental had to prepare replacements for the experimental engines and this caused further delay. Testing of the aircraft was taken up during March by the Army and it was soon apparent that the engines were not giving their advertised power ratings but general handling characteristics of the fighter were thought to be satisfactory. Various other changes were made to the XP–67 during its testing period and these included adding some more dihedral to the horizontal stabilizer and the inclusion of a dorsal fin.

On a test flight on 6 September, the right engine of the XP–67 began burning after takeoff and the Army pilot managed to make a successful emergency landing but a brake stuck and the aircraft slewed around into the wind where the fire was able to grow and do considerable damage to the airframe. Since the need for a bomber destroyer was, by 1944, virtually non-existent, the XP–67 program was cancelled. The second prototype – to which some thought was being given of installing turbosupercharged Rolls-Royce Packard Merlins, and a jet in the rear of each nacelle – was nearing completion, but it was decided to scrap the aircraft rather than prepare it for flight.

The XP–67 was an extremely original first try at a combat aircraft and, if bomber formations had existed for the production version of the fighter, it certainly would have made an impressive showing with its six 37 mm cannon. However, McDonnell learned many lessons from this aircraft and the creative spirit did not depart the company for, even as the XP–67 was being cancelled, work was progressing on manufacturing the Navy's first jet fighter – the FD–1 Phantom – the first of a long line of famous warplanes to issue from the St Louis company.

McDONNELL XP–67 SERIAL NUMBERS AND SPECIFICATIONS

Serial Numbers

XP–67	42–11677 and 42–11678 (scrapped before completion)

Specifications

XP–67

Span	55 ft
Length	44 ft 9 in
Height	15 ft 9 in
Wing area	414 sq ft
Empty weight	17,750 lb
Loaded weight	25,400 lb
Max. speed	405 mph
Cruise speed	270 mph
Ceiling	38,000 ft
Rate of climb	2,600 fpm
Range	2,384 miles
Powerplant	Two Continental XIV–1430–17/19 at 1,350 hp each at takeoff and 1,600 hp each at altitude.

Douglas P-70
Havoc — The Make-Shift Night Fighter

This A–20 Havoc conversion was a stop-gap measure until specifically designed night fighters could be built.

Quite often aircraft designers find themselves completely surprised to find that the military is employing 'their' creation in an entirely different role from which it was designed. The history of military aviation is studded with examples of aircraft that became famous (or infamous) when they were used in roles for which they were not designed. One can think of the little de Havilland Tiger Moth primary trainers with light bombs strapped under their wings searching for German U-boats and land-

ing craft in the dark days of World War Two when the invasion of Britain appeared to be imminent or, in more modern reference, the Republic F–105 and McDonnell Douglas F–4 Phantom, both multi-Mach fighters that found themselves dropping iron bombs on primitive Vietnamese 'hootches' during the 1960s and 1970s, a far cry from their original high altitude interception role.

During the Battle of Britain, the *Luftwaffe* found that daylight bombing raids in their underpowered and lightly armed Heinkel He 111s and Dornier Do 17s were distinctly dangerous as Spitfires and Hurricanes slashed into the bomber formations with little regard

to Göring's notion that the Royal Air Force had been destroyed as a fighting unit. Wrecked German bombers littered the pastoral British countryside and the German high command realized that something had to be done im-

Army Air Force 42–53794 started out life as an A–20G–5 before it was converted to a P–70A–2. These aircraft retained the standard nose armament of four or six .50 caliber Browning machine guns rather than the ventral armament pack carried by other Nighthawks. These aircraft were apparently used just for the training role and were painted in the standard Olive Drab upper surfaces and Neutral Gray lower surfaces rather than the overall Matt Black that had been specified for the night fighting role. This aircraft carries the name of that popular wartime cartoon GI, Sad Sack. (H. W. Kulick)

Close-up view of another P–70A–2, this one named Eight-Ball, shows off the forward armament of four .50 caliber machine guns under a very beat-up nose cone. Entry to the P–70A–2 was via a rear hatch and through the canopy hatch. The P–70 was a single-pilot aircraft. Slow speed and poor rate of climb kept the Nighthawk from achieving any combat glory although it was a comfortable and smooth aircraft to fly. (H. W. Kulick)

Opposite above

Army Air Force 39–736 was the first production P–70. Modified from the first production run of A–20s, the P–70 was fitted with two 1,600 hp Wright R–2600–11 radials, British AI Mk IV radar and a ventral gun pack with four 20 mm cannon in place of the bomb bay. The P–70 was painted overall Matt Black. The nose antenna has been very cleverly retouched out of the photograph by a military censor. The aircraft is seen during evaluation at Wright Field. (USAF/26218)

Opposite below

The RAF, stuck with a number of French DB–7s after the fall of that country, decided that the aircraft could profitably be employed as night fighters and intruders. Extra armor plate, noses with various combinations of .303 caliber machine guns, matt-black paint schemes, and flame dampening exhausts converted the aircraft for the night role. Some of the aircraft were modified to have a dual night fighter/light bomber role. (Air Ministry/10695D)

An interim P–70A–2 night fighter is seen soon after take off from the Douglas factory. The nose-mounted armament of four .50 caliber machine guns is evident in this view. (Douglas/49–17–4)

mediately to stop the heavy losses in aircraft and trained aircrews, many of whom had fought with the Condor Legion in Spain. The German change in tactics was really quite simple and the results were much more profitable than the daylight raids. The change in tactics simply meant that the Germans would be 'touring' Britain by night. The RAF was sorely pressed to meet and destroy the enemy at night for it had no proven night fighter and the Germans were able to do a great deal of

damage and disrupt the sleeping pattern of millions of people with their nocturnal raids. Spitfires and Hurricanes were sent up into the black skies, aided by searchlights, in an attempt to seek out and destroy the enemy. However excellent these two aircraft were as daylight interceptors, as night fighters they fell far short of the impressive victories that they had racked up during the Battle.

The Spitfire was basically unstable and tricky to handle at night, especially when pilots were trying to return to poorly lighted airfields after a mission and were having to cope with the Spitfire's difficult ground handling characteristics; few Spitfire night sorties were flown. The slower Hurricane had more success since it was a more docile and stable

aircraft when compared to the Spitfire, and had better pilot visibility from the cockpit. A number of modifications had to be made to the Hurricanes that were being adapted to the night fighting role. These included glare shields over the exhaust ports so that the pilot would not be blinded by the flames from his own engine's exhaust, and all black (Night) paint jobs that would help cut down on the enemy's chances of seeing the fighter in the moonlight. There was special training for the pilots, who were also subjected to wandering around during daylight hours with virtually black 'sun' glasses in order to improve their night vision. The entire subject of attacking enemy aircraft at night had to be completely rethought as the Germans began appearing in

*A*waiting scrapping after the war at Chino,
California, this Douglas P–70B–2, 42–54053, was
originally an A–20G–10 built at Santa Monica
before conversion to night fighter status. This
aircraft was used in the training role and never had
the ventral gun pack fitted. Note the open bomb
bay doors. Finished in Olive Drab and Neutral
Gray with a black radome, silver-doped
replacement rudder, and a red-bordered national
insignia that should have been done away with in
1943. (W. T. Larkins)

*T*his Nighthawk carried the unusual
designation of TP–70B–2–SM to denote its
strictly training role. Finished in overall Matt
Black, the P–70 is seen in the vast scrapyard at
Chino after the end of the war. Note the open
bomb bay doors, indicating that the aircraft was
never fitted with the ventral gun pack while
performing its job as a trainer for the P–61. The
serial number is repeated under the left wing. The
P–70B–2 was fitted with either the SCR720 or
SCR729 radar array. (W. T. Larkins)

ever increasing numbers, and it soon became apparent that the single-engine fighter was not really going to be the answer. Pilots were overworked at night, trying to fly the aircraft and catch the raiders at the same time was an exhausting task, and the fact that the fighters had only one engine did not give the greatest safety margin, especially flying over a Britain that was almost totally blacked out.

The Royal Air Force was desperately searching for aircraft that could be converted to the night fighting role when they realized that the Havocs that had been taken on strength from the French order plus the Havocs that they had on order from the Douglas factory had plenty of internal room, fairly good performance, and were available in some number. Accordingly

plans were quickly sketched out for the conversion of the Havocs (or Bostons as they were called by the RAF at that time before later standardization with the American name) into night fighters. Around one hundred ex *Armée de l'Air* aircraft were modified as Havoc Mk III (also known as Havoc Mk I Pandora) night fighters and had an overall matt black camouflage paint scheme, flame dampening exhausts and a modified nose with eight .303 machine guns. These aircraft were to have varying degrees of success in intercepting the enemy but the installation of AI Mk IV or V radar in the nose helped the pilot zero in on the nearly invisible enemy. The British development in the building and operation of radar was, at the time, far in advance of anything that the Germans or Americans had and was a primary reason for the RAF's defeat of the German bomber forces, whether they came over in daylight or night raids. One of the strangest modifications to the Havoc in RAF service was the installation of a 2,700 million candlepower searchlight in the nose of about 30 of the twin-engine machines. These aircraft, termed Turbinlite Havocs, were unarmed and were supposed to hunt out enemy aircraft with their radar, illuminate them, and then have their Hurricane escort attack and destroy the German bomber. Needless to say, the idea was over-ambitious and did not work. However, the RAF had started the development of very sophisticated night fighter tactics with the Havoc and these tactics were applied to the deadly Beaufighter and Mosquito which soon entered hostile night skies in search of the enemy.

Back in the United States, the British use of the Havoc was not lost on the Army. Northrop had sent a proposal for an advanced night fighter to the Army but it would not be ready for several years and the fact that some sort of stop-gap night fighter was needed immediately led the Army to the Douglas factory in Santa Monica. Douglas was gearing up for massive Army orders for the Havoc but they were also having serious problems with the turbosupercharged Wright R–2600–7 powerplants. Cooling difficulties and defects with the turbo-superchargers led the Army to revise its initial order for the A–20, as the aircraft was designated, to include modifications on 60 of the planes which would convert them to the P–70 night fighter. The –7 engines were substituted with 1,600 –11s that were not turbosupercharged while the British AI Mk IV radar was placed in the nose with antenna being mounted on the nose and from the wings. A ventral pack with armament was installed in place of the bomb bay and included four 20 mm cannon with 60 rounds per gun. Deliveries of the fighters began in April of 1942 and were completed during September of that year.

The next batch of P–70s, which had been dubbed the Nighthawk by Douglas but not by the Army, consisted of 39 P–70A–1s, which were stock A–20Cs that were converted to night fighters by the Army during 1943. These aircraft had the 1,600 hp R–2600–23 engines and carried up to eight .50 caliber machine guns in the ventral pack along with uprated radar and other small improvements. The P–70A–2 came about from modifying 65 A–20Gs to the same basic standard as the P–70A–1.

The P–70B–1 was a one-off conversion from an A–20G that featured the new SCR720 radar set in the nose. Since this radar filled the nose section of the aircraft, all armament, six .50 caliber machine guns, had to be fitted in separate gun packs, three on each side of the fuselage. The P–70B–2 was built in the most numbers, 105 aircraft, of any of the Nighthawk series and they were converted from A–20Gs and Js and featured the improved SCR720 or SCR729 radar while up to eight .50 caliber machine guns were fitted in the ventral pack.

The P–70 series of fighters was not a success due to the fact that the Nighthawk really did not have enough power to handle the hot new Axis fighters that were appearing in the night skies over Europe and the Pacific. The P–70 was a pleasant enough aircraft to fly, as was the Havoc bomber version, and did not have any vices. The tricycle landing gear was particularly welcome, with its ease of ground handling, during night operations.

Most of the P–70s were shipped off to the 481st Night Fighter Operational Training Group in Orlando, Florida, where future night fighter crews were able to practice and hone their skills on the Nighthawk. This Group was responsible for developing the effective American night fighter tactics of interception that came in very useful later during the war. The Nighthawks equipped over a dozen understrength squadrons and were flown quite regularly. Since the Northrop P–61 was taking longer than planned to develop, the Army decided to send the Nighthawks to combat zones where their crews could begin plying their deadly trade. Five squadrons were sent overseas with P–70s but at least one, the 427th Night Fighter Squadron, was equipped with early P–61s in Italy before they even had the chance to become operational with the Nighthawk. One night fighter squadron of P–70s was sent to the 475th Fighter Group in the Pacific during May of 1943 but the pilots were not pleased with the aircraft. As the official USAAF history states: 'The service command had to work over the P–70 to increase its speed, ceiling and maneuverability before it would be equal to the demands made upon it.' During the Bougainville campaign the Japanese pilots flying at night were able to rack up a number of successes. As long as General Twining 'continued to rely upon the P–70 ... he was unable to counter the Japanese ... who were piling up a fairly respectable list of successes, particularly against shipping.'

Admiral Halsey was extremely concerned by the attacks on his ships and requested that a new fighter, perhaps the British Mosquito, be rushed to the area to help counter the Japanese night air raids but this was denied and night defense fell to P–38s operating in conjunction with searchlights at higher altitudes, while Navy F4U–2Ns patrolled the medium altitudes with radar equipped Venturas, and the limited number of available P–70s covered the beaches at low altitude. This combination eventually beat back the Japanese night attacks on the important island.

The 6th Night Fighter Squadron was the first P–70 unit to reach the Pacific, arriving in September 1942 in Hawaii, but it was transferred to Guadalcanal in March (except for one small detachment of aircraft left in Hawaii to guard against the decreasing possibility of future Japanese attacks). The 421st Night Fighter Squadron operated a small number of P–70s out of New Guinea but, once again, the aircraft were quite often unable to catch Japanese raiders and in June 1943, five new P–61s arrived to replace the Nighthawks.

The combat career of the P–70 is largely lost to time but it was, at best, limited to whatever enemy aircraft could be surprised before they could take advantage of their superior speed and escape the clutches of the Nighthawks. The best statement that could be made about the P–70 series is that it did give valuable training that enabled the new night fighting P–61 to have experienced air crews that were familiar with the entirely new world of aerial combat at night.

DOUGLAS P–70 NIGHTHAWK SERIAL NUMBERS AND SPECIFICATIONS

Serial Numbers

XP–70	39–735
P–70	39–736 to 39–740, 39–742 to 39–744, 39–746 to 39–747, 39–749 to 39–797

The remaining P–70 variants were modified from production aircraft and their serial numbers fell in a random pattern that is difficult to compile since the P–70 was not a commonly photographed aircraft.

Specifications
P–70 Nighthawk

Span	61 ft 4 in
Length	47 ft 7 in
Height	17 ft 7 in
Wing area	464 sq ft
Empty weight	16,031 lb
Loaded weight	21,264 lb
Max. speed	329 mph
Cruise speed	270 mph
Ceiling	28,250 ft
Rate of climb	1,500 fpm
Range	1,000 miles
Powerplant	Two Wright R–2600–11 engines of 1,600 hp each

Republic XP-72
Wasp Major Thunderbolt

This variant of the Thunderbolt was cancelled because of changing requirements.

Perhaps the most aggressive appearing of all American propeller-driven fighters built during World War Two was Republic's XP–72. The aircraft, having all the powerful determination of its P–47 heritage, was powered by the massive Pratt & Whitney R–4360 Wasp Major which, in its early versions, could produce 3,500 horsepower. The combination of the battle-proven Thunderbolt airframe and the huge P&W powerplant gave the XP–72 the look of awesome performance and power.

Immediately after the flight of the prototype Thunderbolt, the Republic design team began drawing up plans for a fighter that could outperform the P–47. Alex Kartveli led his team to plan for two aircraft, one built around the Wright R–2160 and the other around the P&W R–4360. The Army approved of both projects and assigned the designation XP–69

An impression of power is given by the XP–72 in this view of the second prototype, 43–6599. Differing in a number of small design details from the first aircraft, 6599 was equipped with the Aeroproducts contra-rotating propeller which was not installed on the first aircraft because of problems with the unit. Armament on the XP–72 had been cut down to six .50 caliber machine guns from the eight guns carried by the P–47 in order to save weight. The second aircraft was also fitted with underwing pylons which could have carried extra fuel tanks or bombs. (Republic)

to the Wright-powered machine while XP–72 went to the P&W airframe. The Wright engine was capable of producing 2,500 hp and would have been mounted behind the pilot's compartment with a drive shaft to the propeller, similar to the Bell Airacobra. The experimental Wright powerplant featured 42 cylinders and a turbosupercharger. Intended for high-altitude work, the XP–69 was to have a pressurized cockpit and carry a heavy cannon armament. However, the much more powerful XP–72 seemed more promising and work was stopped on the XP–69, after a mockup had been built, when a contract for two prototype XP–72s was issued by the Army to Republic on 18 June 1943.

At the time of the contract, the Pratt & Whitney engine was still very much in the experimental stage but company engineers were placing great faith in the new powerplant and felt that, with development, the engine could produce well over 4,000 horsepower. The cowling around the 28 cylinder R–4360 was a work of art and beautifully streamlined, making the bulk of the radial engine appear to be almost slim. A turbosupercharger was fitted to the rear fuselage mated (as in the Thunderbolt) with the R–4360–13 but plans were to eventually install the –19 powerplant with a fluid coupling drive for a fan-driven centrifugal compressor that would supercharge the en-

gine (this never came about). To get the amount of air needed for the unit, a large scoop was built into the belly of the XP–72, giving the aircraft the appearance of having an inline powerplant with a belly radiator scoop, not unlike the P–51. However, cooling for the P&W was provided via a narrow opening behind the large spinner that fitted over the propeller hub. Exhaust was vented via NACA ejector stacks that added a bit of extra thrust.

The airframe of the XP–72 was very similar to the Thunderbolt's and the same wing section, the Republic S3 airfoil, was fitted. The S3 went back to 1932 when it was designed by Alexander de Seversky himself, certainly a tribute to fine design since the wing was being used on aircraft with top speeds that were only being vaguely dreamed of in 1932. An ample bubble canopy was mounted atop the fuselage. Six .50 caliber machine guns were to be placed in the wing instead of the Thunderbolt's normal battery of eight in order to help keep weight down.

First flown on 2 February 1944, the prototype XP–72 gracefully lifted into the air from Republic's Farmingdale factory – the powerful rumbling of its R–4360 unlike anything else in the air. Originally it had been intended to fly the prototype with an Aeroproducts contra-rotating propeller but that company was hav-

The beautifully cowled R–4360–13 on the XP–72 was a masterpiece of aeronautical craftsmanship. The small air opening directly behind the large spinner rammed cooling air over the 24 cylinders of the Pratt & Whitney 'corn cob' radial. The large opening for the turbosupercharger can be seen directly below the wing leading edge. The prototype never flew with the contra-rotating propeller but was equipped instead with this four blade unit when teething problems slowed delivery of the six blade propeller. (Republic)

Nearly identical views of the two XP–72s provide an interesting look at some of the design differences between the two aircraft. The most apparent, of course, is the change in propeller units. Other small differences include a larger stainless steel plate behind the ejector stacks and some minor paneling details. Note how the aircraft's designation was carried on the vertical fin with the serial number. (Republic)

ing teething problems with the unit so the XP-72 flew with a large four-blade propeller with small root cuffs. Test pilot Lowery Brabham had to lift off and land the XP-72 in a three-point attitude because of the large size of the propeller. The XP-72 displayed excellent handling qualities and had very few developmental problems. The potential power from the P&W engine was well illustrated when, without the turbosupercharger installed, one low-level run with the R-4360-13 netted a speed of 480 mph. The idea had been to use the XP-72 as an interceptor, much like the RAF's Spitfire. The power reserves from the huge radial would have meant that the aircraft could have become airborne and climbed to battle height in very short order. Unfortunately, times had changed and attacks from German and Japanese bombers or fighters on Allied factories and bases were doubtful at this late date in the war. The emphasis had shifted to long-range deep penetration fighters.

By the time that the second prototype had flown in the middle of 1944 (this time with the Aeroproducts' contra-rotating propeller) the order for 100 P-27As powered by R-4360-19 engines had been cancelled and work had switched to the new jet fighters under development. The production P-72A would have been fitted with the new infinitely variable supercharger that would have given peak performance at 25,000 ft with an estimated top speed of almost 550 mph.

It is thought that the XP-72s were used for a limited amount of testing, especially trying out the operation of the R-4360. However, the war was rapidly changing and the XP-72s were soon forgotten. For a new aircraft the XP-72 performed in a manner that was little short of amazing – very few snags were encountered with engine or airframe and the performance was excellent. One wonders what a few squadrons of strategically placed P-72As could have done to Hitler's V-1 assault on the United Kingdom.

The two prototypes are presumed to have been scrapped soon after the end of the war.

REPUBLIC XP-72 SERIAL NUMBERS AND SPECIFICATIONS

Serial Numbers

XP-72	43-6598 and 43-6599

Specifications

XP-72

Span	40 ft 11 in
Length	36 ft 7 in
Height	16 ft
Wing area	300 sq ft
Empty weight	11,475 lb
Loaded weight	17,492 lb
Max. speed	490 mph
Cruise speed	300 mph
Ceiling	42,000 ft
Rate of climb	5,000 fpm
Range	1,200 miles
Powerplant	Pratt & Whitney R-4360-13 of 3,450 hp

Fisher XP-75 Eagle — The Spare Parts Fighter

Like the Republic XP–72, the Eagle was originally built for a requirement that no longer existed when the fighter was completed.

America's greatest asset during World War Two was the ability to convert its factories into producing quality war material on a mass production line basis. The American mastery of the production line, especially in the automotive field, has been the envy of the rest of the industrial world. The ability to churn out huge amounts of material on a production line was a fact not lost on the Army in the years before America entered World War Two. Up until that time aircraft manufacture had been a rather haphazard affair but the large contracts that were starting to flow in from countries anxious to obtain new combat aircraft and the orders coming from the Army which was frantically trying to re-equip with more modern aircraft caused manufacturers to adopt Detroit-style techniques for the building, assembling, and test flying of military aircraft.

After America entered World War Two, and new automobiles were no longer being manufactured, the military turned its eye on the factories in Detroit and, in fairly short order, the same companies that had been building new cars were now bashing out tanks, guns, military components and aircraft. The speed with which the conversion from civilian to military manufacture was effected, and the quality of most of the items, spoke well of American industrial prowess.

That giant of the automotive world, General Motors, was tied directly to aviation since it

One of the production P–75A Eagles seen undergoing an engine run-up with its tail section firmly strapped down. The production aircraft used a modified Curtiss P–40 wing with an extended and squared-off wing tip. Ailerons were also longer than on the standard P–40 wing. Landing gear unit was modified from the Vought F4U Corsair's main gear. The Eagle did feature excellent pilot visibility from the bubble canopy mounted well forward on the fuselage. However poor performance and bad handling qualities spelled doom for the design. (Fisher)

Although the armament was never in fact installed, the camouflaged prototype Eagle was to carry ten .50 caliber machine guns. Six fuel tanks – two ahead of the engine and four in the center section – had a capacity of 534 US gallons and drop tanks could be installed under the wings for additional range. As can be seen in this view, the exhaust was routed through the the fuselage and expelled via streamlined ports on the side and top of the fuselage. (Fisher)

Opposite above
The prototype XP–75 Eagle, 43–46950, is seen after roll-out from the factory still in its primer finish. Curtiss P–40 wing and Douglas SBD Dauntless tail assembly are easily identified. The canopy – the windshield and sliding portion – were from a P–40, tapered back to a knife edge, giving the unit a curious gothic appearance. (Fisher)

A close-up view of the front end of the prototype Eagle illustrates the hefty Aeroproducts contra-rotating propeller assembly. The engine for the P–75 was a curious affair, General Motors Allison Division mated the heads and cylinder banks of two V–1710s to a common crankcase to produce the V–3420. The engine was installed mid-fuselage behind the pilot and a long drive shaft drove the propeller. (Fisher)

owned Allison, chief supplier, at that time, of liquid-cooled aero engines to the Army. Allison wanted to sell its new V–3420 (basically a joined together pair of V–1710 engines) and, during 1942, General Motors decided to convert its Fisher Body plant in Cleveland, Ohio, to an aviation plant that would construct a new fighter built around the V–3420.

The Army, during 1942, was in need of high-performance interceptors that had a very high rate of climb and sufficient firepower to do fatal damage to enemy bomber and fighter formations. Drawing upon this need, General Motors came up with a fighter that was submitted to, and accepted by, the Army. A contract was issued to Fisher during October of that year for the construction of two prototype fighters.

The aircraft proposed by General Motors was a bit different from the average run of the mill interceptor for, besides having the powerful but experimental V–3420, the new XP–75 (as the aircraft had been designated) was to be built from a conglomeration of parts acquired from aircraft already in production!

This unique direction in design was supposed to produce a fighter that would blast the Axis from the air. In fact, one aero historian has stated that the P–75 designation was picked as a symbol of victory, just as the French 75 gun of World War One had been a symbol of defeating the Kaiser's best. True or not, much press was given to this new 'wonder' plane even before it was ready to fly.

Allison was having its own problems with the V–3420 which was not living up to the power requirements published in their brochures. General Motors on the other hand was busy gathering bits and pieces of other warplanes for their new fighter which, in another burst of patriotic fervor, had been dubbed 'Eagle'. Originally the outer wing panels were to come from the North American P–51 and were to be mated to a center section that would give an inverted gull shape much like the Corsair's. However, this was modified and the outer wing panels were taken from the Curtiss P–40, not a particularly wise choice since the airfoil was outdated, and the inverted gull was dropped in favor of a straight-through center section. The tail section was pulled from the Douglas Dauntless while the main landing gear came from the Vought F4U. General Motors began stirring these bits and pieces around, adding newly designed sections where necessary, and the resulting aircraft was a curious looking beast.

It had been decided that the best place to mount the V–3420 was amidship, like the P–39 Airacobra, with a long drive shaft that would be connected to a contra-rotating propeller. Armament was to be six .50 caliber machine guns in the P–40 wing and four more in the nose but armament was never fitted to any of the Eagles.

The new sections of the Eagle were of conventional all-metal stressed skin construction and the first aircraft flew on 17 November

Opposite above
Six escort fighter Eagle prototypes were
ordered on 6 July 1943, and these were followed
by six production P–75A–1–GCs – the only aircraft
of the 2,500 unit order to be completed before the
contract was cancelled. Army Air Force
s/n 44–44550 was the second of the production
Eagles. The double-scoop radiator intakes are
shown to advantage in this view along with the
deeper fuselage for extra fuel tanks. (Fisher)

The six production Eagles had a much more
refined look than the previous prototypes. A
totally new and enlarged tail unit was added in the
hope of correcting stability problems while a
bubble canopy from a P–47D–25–RE got rid of the
built-up affair. A long ventral fin was also added to
the rear fuselage for stability. The production
Eagles were left in a natural metal finish and were
not camouflaged. (Fisher)

1943. The flight tests were anything from
encouraging as the engine was acting up,
stability was poor, there were problems with
the center of gravity and performance was well
below what had originally been specified.

However, by the time the prototype Eagle
had flown the Army had changed its mind on
the original requirement. Like the XP–72, the
Eagle was no longer needed as a fast climbing
interceptor; the Army's main need now was
for a long-range penetration fighter.

Fisher, going along with the Army's wishes,
decided to contract for a further six prototypes
that would meet the long-range requirement.
At the same time the Army placed orders for
2,500 Eagles, a curious move in the light of the
obvious fact that the Eagle was probably not
going to be a world-beater. The second prototype was in the air soon after the first and
continued testing revealed that the engine was
still not giving full power and that control
forces were heavy and the aircraft unrespons-
ive. In the air the XP–75 was a strange looking
affair, its 'borrowed' parts being immediately

As mission requirements rapidly changed, the
Army, in 1943, ordered Fisher to modify the
Eagle into a long-range escort fighter rather than
the interceptor that had originally been planned. A
second batch of prototypes was constructed and
these incorporated a number of modifications
including a reworked Dauntless tail section that
had more fin, but less rudder, area for improved
stability. The canopy was also modified to get rid of
the ungainly 'sharp' trailing edge. The main landing
gear had streamlined fairings installed on the oleo
legs but the tail wheel remained fixed.

identifiable. The pilot was seated well forward of the wing under a cockpit canopy that bordered on hideous but the view was quite exceptional although some complaints were registered by the test pilots about the clanking and whirring drive shaft that ran between their legs. Air for the radiators was provided by an unusual twin-section scoop positioned under the rear fuselage, somewhat like the one on the Mustang.

Work was continuing on the six long-range Eagles and the Fisher plant was having time to make some changes. Extra fuel tanks were installed while a new rear fuselage with a large, attractive vertical fin and rudder was added, dropping the Dauntless look for that portion of the Eagle. A new bubble canopy that opened to the rear was also installed which helped improve the aircraft's looks. The uprated V-3420-23 was installed in the engine bay on these aircraft.

Testing of the six long-range Eagles was equally frustrating as problems with the engine continued while performance was well below estimates. The Eagle was big and awkward in the air and had none of the grace or fine handling characteristics of a fighter. The Army, with the successful P-38, P-47 and P-51 now in the inventory in large numbers,

decided to drop the P-75 contract and it was terminated on 6 October 1944. Several production aircraft were either complete or nearing completion at this time and the Army agreed to have work continue on this small batch so that the aircraft could be used as test beds for the Allison engine.

The first five production Eagles were completed and several were transferred to Eglin Air Base in Florida for further testing, but the first prototype was destroyed in a crash soon after arrival. The other aircraft were flown only occasionally before being completely withdrawn from testing. One Eagle managed to survive being scrapped and this curious aircraft is now on display at the United States Air Force Museum in Dayton, Ohio.

Born out of desperation, the P-75 was never really capable of being the aircraft that the military wanted. A totally new wing would have been required to aid performance while the untried powerplant was not a wise choice for an aircraft needed in a short period of time. An interesting experiment perhaps, but the P-75 can certainly be classified as a failure. The name Eagle lives on in the USAF inventory with the magnificent McDonnell Douglas F-15 Eagle high-performance fighter, a far cry from the 'spare parts fighter' of 1943.

FISHER P-75 EAGLE SERIAL NUMBERS AND SPECIFICATIONS

XP-75	43-46950 and 43-46951
	44-32161 through
	44-32166
P-75A-1-GC	44-44549 through
	44-44554

Specifications

P-75A Eagle

Even though a number of Eagles were completed, final performance testing was never achieved and these figures should be regarded as overly high since they were the original manufacturer's specifications.

Span	49 ft 4 in
Length	41 ft 4 in
Height	15 ft 6 in
Wing area	347 sq ft
Empty weight	11,255 lb
Loaded weight	19,420 lb
Max. speed	404 mph
Cruise speed	250 mph
Ceiling	40,000 ft
Rate of climb	4,200 fpm
Range	1,150 miles
Powerplant	Allison V-3420-23 of 2,600 hp

Bell XP-77
The Wooden Midget

Bell learned that lightweight and small size did not necessarily equate to high performance.

The year immediately preceding America's entry into World War Two was a time of indecision for the country's aeronautical community. Japanese expansion in the Far East had dispelled the stereotyped image of Japanese airmen as buck-tooth, near-sighted bumblers. The air forces of the Empire had ruthlessly rolled over all opposition and disquieting reports had been received by Amer-

ican intelligence sources that spoke of deadly new aircraft capable of outperforming anything in the air.

The news from Europe was equally appalling. The Continent had fallen to Hitler's *blitzkreig* in an astoundingly short period of time. France's *Armée de l'Air* had been touted as the most modern air force in free Europe yet it had been blasted out of the sky by the *Luftwaffe's* Messerschmitt Bf 109s, a fighter that drove fear into the hearts of military planners, for it appeared unstoppable. A defeated British Ex-

Bell XP–77 43–34916 during a test flight. Originally planning to mount a supercharged Ranger V–770–9 of 500 hp, Bell engineers had to settle for the V–770–6 which had the same horsepower but was not supercharged and whose performance rapidly fell off at altitudes above 12,000 ft. The XP–77 had been designed to mount a 20 mm cannon firing through the prop shaft, a Bell trademark, but this weapon was dropped during an early weight cutting redesign and only the two .50 caliber Browning air cooled machine guns in the nose with 200 rpg were left as armament. The weight-cutting program was not entirely successful and the proposed operational weight of 3,000 lb was never achieved and performance consequently suffered. Restricted from aerobatic maneuvers, this aircraft was destroyed when the pilot attempted an Immelmann but the aircraft fell into an inverted spin and crashed. (Bell)

Seen at the Bell factory in New York is the first XP–77, 43–34915. Featuring all-wood construction for the basic airframe, the XP–77 was covered with stressed plywood that had been impregnated with plastic/resin bonding. The skin was then attached to the framework with nails and glue. The fuselage and wing were integral units and the cockpit was sealed off by fume-proof bulkheads that separated the pilot from the engine and fuel tank. Doped overall silver, the XP–77 carries the name of Bell test pilot Jack Woolams under the windscreen. Woolams went on to race a modified Bell P–39, Cobra I, in the Cleveland Air Races after the War but was killed in the crash of the aircraft during qualification trials. (Bell)

peditionary Force was pulled off the beaches at Dunkirk in one of the most amazing rescue operations known to man. The Royal Air Force was battered but not destroyed and, in the months of quiet given by Hitler's curious stopping at the beaches of France, was able to regroup and rearm with the Spitfires and Hurricanes that were being produced by factories whose employees were working a 24-hour shift. While the RAF had been given much needed time, the situation on the high seas was not as optimistic. The *Unterseeboots* were prowling the seas and sinking just about

anything that crossed the sights of their periscopes.

The fact that Britain was an island nation that depended upon its ocean lanes for vital and strategic building materials was not lost upon Hitler and his generals. The Germans felt that if the shipping lanes to Britain could be closed then the nation would eventually have to surrender or sign a peace agreement as the nation's factories ground to a halt from lack of raw supplies. The sleek German submarines traversed the Atlantic, blasting anything bound for Britain and, in feats of extreme military daring, even ventured into American harbors and river mouths to sink supply shipping. The sight of blazing ships just off America's resort beaches in the year before that country's entry into the War, caused a quiet wave of panic to grip many citizens and politicians. Admittedly, America was extremely rich in natural resources but what if those resources were committed fully during a war, and what if the Germans decided to throw a U-Boat blockade around the nation's harbors? During 1940 the submarine was a

menace for which there was no cure, as the fine art of anti-submarine warfare did not come until later in the war, and the idea of Hitler's blood-thirsty U-Boats isolating the nation seemed very real.

Preparing or engaging for a war utilizes vast quantities of resources classified as strategic materials. These range from aluminum for aircraft, iron and steel for weapons, tanks and shipping, and oil for fuel. Military planners were giving a great deal of thought to weapons that could be constructed from non-strategic materials that were in good supply with little threat of being rationed.

The innovative design team at Bell Aircraft Company began to draw up plans for possible aircraft that could be constructed of non-strategic materials and still deliver the high performance needed for modern combat aircraft. Bell had been paying attention to the brief bits of news coming from Asia that told of new Japanese aircraft that were rolling over the opposition like a scythe through wheat. Bell designer Bob Woods undertook the project of constructing a high performance fighter

aircraft out of non-strategic materials to prove that such a concept could be carried out with less man hours than building a conventional aluminum fighter.

Bell envisioned an aircraft with a slim high-aspect ratio wing with a single spruce spar. The ribs of the wing and the formers of the fuselage would be wood while the stressed skin would be plastic/resin-bonded wood that would be attached with nails and glue to the structure and then given a protective covering of doped-on cotton fabric. The design, originally given the title of Tri-4, would feature the tricycle landing gear that had become a Bell trademark while armament would be kept to a 20 mm cannon firing through the prop shaft and two .50 caliber air cooled Browning machine guns with just 200 rounds per gun.

The Mitsubishi A6M Zeke, possibly the best dogfighting aircraft in the history of aerial warfare, was making itself felt over China when, on 30 October 1941, Bell submitted their completed proposal to the Army. Bell felt that the small size of the Tri-4 would be of considerable advantage in the twisting, turn-

ing world of aerial combat. One problem that had given the engineers nightmares was the selection of a powerplant for the fighter. Small size, plenty of power and a sleek frontal area were required, as streamlining was extremely important for the miniature fighter. The only American-built engine that could have been considered was the Ranger V-770, a 12 cylinder, air cooled, supercharged powerplant that was probably the *worst* engine made by an American aeronautical company during World War Two. Of course, Bell could not know of the problems that were going to develop with the V-770 when they specified the engine for the Tri-4 as Ranger was building its fairly reliable inline six cylinder engine for the Fairchild series of primary trainers. However, the V-12 was to prove a bit more than Ranger could handle.

General Hap Arnold seemed to be impressed by Bell's paperwork and, on 16 May 1942, he issued orders that the Army procure 25 fighters. On paper the concept looked good with a top speed of over 400 mph on its 500 hp engine. Arnold specified that the Tri-4 be

The prototype XP-77 after the end of the War at the Wright Field Victory Air Display in a revised paint scheme. The original concept of an agile, lightweight fighter built of non-strategic materials just did not live up to army expectations. Test pilots did not give the Bell aircraft favorable marks because of poor handling qualities, excessive vibration and a small and extremely noisy cockpit. (W. T. Larkins)

equipped with a shackle for carrying a small bomb or depth charge so that the aircraft could participate in a ground attack role.

It soon became apparent that Ranger could not deliver the supercharged V-770-9 on schedule so the company offered to supply Bell with the V-770-6 that they were building for the Navy and that could develop 500 hp but only below 12,000 ft, with performance rapidly falling off above that altitude. Only six of these non-supercharged powerplants could be offered in time for testing trials so the Army cut the number of aircraft ordered to six. At this time the aircraft, which had been re-designated as the D-6 Project by the Bell design department, was assigned the Army pursuit number of XP-77.

As work progressed on the XP-77, it soon

became clear that the weight of the aircraft was going to take a sharp rise and, since weight in a fighter of this size was the most important design factor, Bell realized that they were in trouble. It appears that the 20 mm cannon was dropped at this point in an effort to save weight. The original design weight of 3,700 lb loaded had risen well over 4,000 lb and a concerted effort to lighten the prototype to 3,000 lb, the recalculated weight needed to achieve performance, was undertaken. The program dragged on and costs rose so the Army reduced its prototype XP–77 order down to two aircraft. At this time both Bell and the Army must have realized that the XP–77 was not going anywhere and an order dropping any further consideration of the supercharged V–770–9 was issued.

The first completed prototype did not fly until 1 April 1944, which was an amazingly long development span for such a simple aircraft but it should be noted that Bell was swamped with work on the P–39, B–63, and P–59. After a few flights the Army realized that they were holding a tiger by the tail as the XP–77 was prone to instability and extreme airframe vibration, possibly due to the fact that the V–770 was mounted on a rigid engine bearer along with apparent aileron flutter at higher speeds.

The prototype XP–77 was taken to Wright Field for more testing but, at such a late date in the war, it appears that the aircraft was only occasionally flown during this period. The second aircraft was retained by Bell for further testing and it was transferred to the Army's testing ground at Eglin Field in Florida, along with the first prototype which had been pulled from Wright Field. At Eglin the aircraft were flown fairly extensively and test pilots' reports were less than satisfactory. During a hard landing, the pilot flying the first XP–77 was

considerably surprised to find himself skidding along the runway as the nose gear collapsed. Restrictions on the aircraft did not permit any violent maneuvers such as power dives, spins, and snap rolls. The pilots who flew the aircraft disliked the amount of cockpit noise from the V–770 while mechanics were not pleased with the engine's reliability. In fact, the Navy had equipped the Curtiss Seamew floatplane with the V–770 and had intended the aircraft to replace the earlier SOC but the new aircraft was totally unreliable and extremely unpopular with pilots and most Seamews, which could be equipped with landing gear for shore operations, were left sitting in aircraft depots. One unlucky Navy ferry pilot recounted a flight in the underpowered Seamew in which he had to deliver the aircraft from a ferry depot to a base in central California, a distance of about 300 miles. During this short flight he experienced three forced landings with engine problems and the ferry flight finally culminated when the engine exploded and burst into flames. The pilot made a hasty exit over the side and, while descending in his parachute, watched the Seamew punch a hole in a farmer's field.

After a bit over two months of testing the second aircraft was returned to Wright Field. During a test flight, a pilot attempted an Immelman but the XP–77 fell into an inverted spin from which he could not recover. Jettisoning the canopy, the pilot fell free while he watched from his parachute as the XP–77 converted itself to first class kindling when it impacted with the Ohio countryside.

The crash put an end to a program that could and would not go anywhere. The war was so advanced by this time that victory was in sight and an underpowered fighter like the XP–77 had no place alongside machines such as the P–51, P–38, and P–47 which were fully

operational. Perhaps the XP–77 could be classified as an interesting experiment for it did prove that small underpowered and lightly armed fighters could only engage an enemy if and when the enemy chose to do battle. The program also showed that a non-strategic fighter was not easier to build. Certainly these were not qualifications for a fighter and the XP–77 concept was quickly dropped from any future Army requirements. The surviving XP–77 ended up its days as a base 'gate guardian' before it finally deteriorated and was hauled to the base dump and unceremoniously burned.

BELL XP–77 SERIAL NUMBERS AND SPECIFICATIONS

Serial Numbers

XP–77	43–34915 and 43–34916

Specifications

XP–77

Span	27 ft 6 in
Length	22 ft 11 in
Height	10 ft 11 in
Wing area	100 sq ft
Empty weight	2,760 lb
Loaded weight	3,583 lb
Max. speed	335 mph
Cruise speed	270 mph
Ceiling	30,000 ft
Rate of climb	3,650 fpm
Range	650 miles
Powerplant	Ranger V–770–7 (Army designation for Navy V–770–6) of 500 hp

Northrop XP-79
The Flying Ram

Northrop's flying wing fighter was built to one of the strangest specifications of World War Two.

John K. Northrop was always fascinated with the idea of the flying wing. Such a concept seemed, during the 1920s, to be straight out of one of the 'new fangled' science fiction pulp magazines that were available down at the corner drug store for a dime apiece. Northrop envisioned a flying wing that would cut down on building costs (because of the lack of fuselage and tail group), have excellent lifting capabilities (because all the surface of the aircraft would be devoted to an airfoil shape), and have high performance (the flying wing would have much less drag and better streamlining than the average aircraft).

Northrop was employed by several aviation firms where his creative genius was diverted into designing conventional aircraft that were record breakers but the idea of a flying wing

The XP–79B was an advanced aircraft with a primitive purpose: a jet-powered flying wing to ram enemy bombers. Made of high strength magnesium reinforced with armor plating, the XP–79B had provisions for cockpit pressurization and four .50 caliber machine guns but neither were installed. The landing gear for the XP–79B was a curious arrangement consisting of two forward gear legs and two rear gear legs with large tires; all four units retracted up into the wing. Army interest in the XP–79B terminated when the aircraft crashed on its first flight. (Northrop)

took some time before being put into physical shape. In 1928, after working for Lockheed and designing the world-famous, record setting Vega, Northrop made his first attempt to branch out on his own. He formed the very small Avion Corporation at Burbank, California, and busily set to work on his flying wing concept. The new aircraft did not have a number designation but was simply known as 'The Flying Wing' which was fairly safe since it was the only aircraft of its type. The Flying Wing got off the ground from Burbank Airport in 1929 and made a few successful turns over the field before coming back for a landing. The aircraft was then taken out to Muroc Dry Lake in the Mojave Desert for more extensive testing. Originally a tractor with a conventional tail mounted on twin booms, The Flying Wing was modified to a pusher engine and made many test flights. During this year Avion was turned into the Northrop Aircraft Corporation as part of the huge United Aircraft and Transport Corporation, an early day aviation conglomerate that also included Boeing. In 1939 Northrop once again struck out on his own and formed Northrop Aircraft Inc at Hawthorne, California (still its home today).

Going back to The Flying Wing, Northrop found himself in the middle of the Great Depression, a period of time when most aviation companies were doing everything to keep

their heads above water – many failing in the process. Northrop reverted to conventional aircraft, feeling that the economic times were just not right for the continued development of such a radical aircraft. Northrop's so-called 'conventional' aircraft were world beaters. The Alphas, Betas, Deltas and Gammas roared across the world, breaking records wherever they went. The beautiful all-metal, low-wing Northrops became known for their high-performance and efficiency. As the 1930s began to turn middle-aged, Northrop turned his talents to aircraft with a more military bent, such as the 3–A, BT–1 and A–17. However, the flying wing idea was never all that far in the back of his mind.

When Northrop started the new company in Hawthorne, attention was immediately turned to gaining contracts that would ensure the firm's survival. Subcontracts were obtained from some of the larger aviation manufacturers before a contract for 24 seaplane patrol bombers called N–3PBs was received from Norway. As early as 1940 Northrop was ready to give the flying wing concept another try. Designated N–1M, the new aircraft was a true flying wing with no conventional tail surfaces. Quickly built from wood and steel tubing so that the new ideas could be tested in the air, the N–1M made its first test flight on 3 July 1940, with that dapper test pilot Vance Breese

at the controls. Breese felt that the N–1M handled unusually well and seemed to require less horsepower for the same performance that could be expected from a conventional aircraft. The N–1M had two Lycoming 65 hp powerplants driving twin pusher propellers. The configuration of the N–1M, given the experimental civil registration NX28311, changed several times as different wing tips, engines and propellers were experimented with. Over 200 flights were flown with the N–1M and Jack Northrop felt that his ideas had been proven and the time had come for bigger and better wings with military and commercial potential. The N–1M was retired from flying but, unlike so many other aircraft of the period, it survived and is on display at the National Air and Space Museum.

Other flying wing projects soon followed and included the XP–56 (covered in another chapter of this volume), the N–9M, MX–324/334, JB–1, and XP–79. The XP–79 was a totally revolutionary concept, both in airframe and mission role. Northrop had begun construction of America's first 'rocket plane', the MX–334, during 1943 under the terms of a highly secret USAAF contract. Known at Northrop as 'Project 12' details of the aircraft were not even released until 1947. The new plane was small, its wing spanned only 32 ft, and the pilot was positioned in a prone cockpit

An interesting view of the MX–324 after the war when the vertical fin had been removed; whether the aircraft flew in this configuration is not known. Possibly the most embarassing method of entry on any aircraft ever built, the pilot of the Wing had to clamber up from the trailing edge and slither on his stomach into the small triangular opening – Freud would have loved it! Note that the aircraft has 'Prototype – Northrop Flying Wing' stenciled on the wing leading edge. Development work on the MX–324/334 was applied directly to the XP–79B.

Development of the XP–79B really started with the MX–324/334 series of gliders and rocket-powered wings. These aircraft were of extremely basic construction – steel tube and wood – and would help prove Northrop's theories regarding the flying wings. The pilot, as in the XP–79B, reclined on a specially built seat that would aid in tolerating high G forces. The landing gear was fixed and the vertical fin, which was wire braced, looked like it had been tacked on as an after-thought. An MX–324 is seen on display at the Victory Air Show held at Wright Field at the end of World War Two. (W. T. Larkins)

on the theory that he would be less subject to crushing G forces while on his stomach. The MX–324 was a glider that would test the feasibility of the idea while the MX–334 would be the actual powered article. The MX–324 testing proceeded during 1943, a P–38 being used as a tow plane after attempts to get the aircraft into the air while being towed behind a car had failed.

The gliders had some problems and Harry Crosby, a Northrop test pilot and famed pre-war racing pilot, had a close brush with disaster that was to prove prophetic. During a tow flight, Crosby got into the prop turbulence of the P–38 and the glider flipped upside down and entered into a spin from which he could not recover. Crosby frantically worked the controls but the glider seemed to have a mind of its own, and it suddenly stopped spinning but remained inverted. Crosby jettisoned the two part canopy and hatch and climbed out onto the wing from where he managed to kick himself free from the wing which was now descending in ever-tightening circles. Crosby was in for an unpleasant surprise as he floated down in his parachute and noticed that the glider was closing in on him as he dangled in the harness of his chute. However, luck, this time, was on Crosby's side for he managed to avoid being hit by the glider, and they came down in the desert, a short distance apart.

The MX–334 was in the air on 2 October 1943 for unpowered testing while Aerojet Corporation completed its XCAL–200 rocket engine. The engine was powered by monoethylaniline fuel that was oxidized with red fuming nitric acid and, on 23 June 1944, the MX–334 made its first powered flight and flew into history as America's first rocket propelled aircraft. Capable of 3.5 minutes of power, the MX–334 accumulated much useful research data but was never considered militarily feasible and besides, Northrop was on to a much more exciting project.

Development of the XP–79 had actually started just after work had begun on the MX–334. The Army felt that the XP–79 would actually be capable of military operations and was most anxious to test fly the new aircraft. The XP–79 was to be unique in a number of different areas. Firstly, the aircraft was to be manufactured of magnesium; secondly, it was to be rocket powered, and, thirdly, it was designed to knock enemy aircraft out of the air by ramming them! Now, unfortunately, there are no records to see who was responsible for this idiotic and totally unworkable idea but it should be noted that other countries, including Russia and Germany, were actually considering flying rams and had built a number of aircraft to undertake the role, usually with fatal results to everyone involved. It is quite logical to presume that an aircraft hitting another one at high speed will cause at least one of the machines to crash. The amazing part is that the Army and Northrop considered the idea feasible for, no matter how strongly the flying ram was built, it would probably suffer at least some damage which would most probably render it non-airworthy.

Construction of the XP–79 proceeded at a fast pace after the contract was awarded for the construction of three machines in January of 1943. Performance with a 2,000 lb thrust Aerojet rocket would be over 500 mph at 40,000 ft but flight time would probably be less than half an hour due to the limited fuel burn of the rocket. Aerojet had so many problems with the rocket that the XP–79 and engine contract for two aircraft was dumped by the Army. At the same time a new contract was awarded to develop the third XP–79 to be powered by two Westinghouse jets and the new designation of XP–79B was assigned.

The pilot would also be in a prone position in the XP–79B, flanked by the two jets. The aircraft would blast off from its base with the aid of JATO packs as the enemy bomber formations approached. Climbing rapidly to 40,000 ft, the XP–79B would then dive into the formation and try to cut off the wing or tail of a bomber. The idea is ridiculous today and certainly could not have been less so in 1943. Instead of ramming the enemy why not take advantage of the XP–79B's tremendous speed to make several passes into the bomber formation and try to blast as many of the bombers with cannon or machine gun fire? Apparently some of the Army brass were having second thoughts about the project for it was ordered that the XP–79B be equipped with four .50 caliber Browning machine guns.

The pilot lay on his stomach with his head projecting into an acrylic plastic windshield that had a section of armor glass mounted in front of the pilot's face. The pilot controlled the pitch and roll of the XP–79 with a cross-bar control rod while the maneuvering brakes were operated with foot pedals. The XP–79B was fitted with elevons and the bellows-rudder as described in the section on the XP–56. The pressurized cockpit was entered from an overhead hatch and the hatch could be released for escape.

The airframe was built entirely of heavy gauge magnesium that was reinforced with steel armor plate and had been heliarc-welded. The leading edge skin was $\frac{3}{4}$ in thick while armor plate of a $\frac{1}{4}$ in thickness was installed at a 45 degree angle just inside the leading edge.

Painted overall white and given the serial 43–52437, the prototype was mounted on a truck at the Northrop factory and covered in canvas. Taken to the Muroc Dry Lake testing facility, the XP–79B flew for the first time on 12 September 1945 with Harry Crosby at the controls. As the aircraft accelerated down the rock-hard surface of the dry lake, an Army fire truck pulled out in front of the flying ram's path, Crosby chopped the throttle but then applied power as the truck got out of the way. The aircraft climbed to 10,000 ft and appeared to be travelling at over 400 mph when a turn was attempted. Something went drastically wrong and the turn developed into a nose-down spin. Crosby tried to gain control of the aircraft but, when this appeared impossible, he jettisoned the escape hatch and attempted to exit the rapidly falling aircraft. As he fell from the airplane, he was struck by the rotating wing and never opened his parachute. The XP–79B slammed into the floor of the desert

and exploded, the magnesium making for an exceptionally hot fire and there was soon nothing left of the XP–79B.

By 1943 it should have been clear to all concerned that vast formations of enemy bombers were simply not going to materialize and that the method of destroying the enemy by ramming was preposterous. However, a great amount of energy and money was expended on the project which, in the end, did nothing to advance the science of aviation and killed one of America's better known pilots.

NORTHROP XP–79B SERIAL NUMBERS AND SPECIFICATIONS

Serial Numbers

XP–79B   43–52437

Specifications

XP–79B

Since the XP–79B did not complete its first flight, performance figures should be regarded as estimates.

Span	38 ft
Length	14 ft
Height	7 ft
Wing area	278 sq ft
Empty weight	5,840 lb
Loaded weight	8,670 lb
Max. speed	525 mph
Cruise speed	n/a
Ceiling	40,000 ft
Rate of climb	6,000 fpm
Range	n/a
Powerplant	Two Westinghouse 19–B axial-flow jets of 1,345 lb thrust each

Lockheed P-80A
Shooting Star — USAAF Combat Jet

Taking up where the Bell Airacomet failed, this Lockheed product went on to set records.

In a war that had already produced countless unpleasantries, 25 July 1944 was a day that was to hold a nasty new surprise for the Allies. The crew of a photo-reconnaissance Mosquito was heading at 30,000 ft towards Munich to record the results of a bombing raid. The pilot was probably a bit lulled into complacence by the fact that the Mosquito was a very fast aircraft and, at the height he was flying, the chances of interception were remote. Suddenly the reverie or boredom that is caused by lengthy flight, even over enemy territory, was torn apart when a stream of tracers shot past the Mosquito's canopy at an extremely close distance. The Royal Air Force pilot probably mentally jumped out of his uncomfortable bucket seat but reactions, instilled by vigorous training and actual combat flights, immediately set in and the pilot racked the Mosquito over in a hard bank, feeling the blood flow from his brain as the crushing force of G pushed him

This high angle aerial view makes evident the clean angles of the Shooting Star. YP–80A 44–83031 exhibits the fine finish applied to the early jet fighters. Note that the pilot still retains the World War Two style leather helmet and has not yet opted for the rather crude early 'hard hats' that became essential pieces of equipment in the jet age. Tony LeVier found that even though he was tightly strapped into his seat, the P–80 could gyrate with considerably more force than most propeller-driven aircraft and he was stunned almost to the point of unconsciousness when his head was slammed into the side of the canopy when the Gray Ghost lost its tail on a test flight. (Lockheed/F7931)

The aircraft that started Lockheed's venture into the jet age, XP–80 44–83020, at Muroc Dry Lake. Nicknamed Lulu-Belle, the prototype jet was finely finished with a lusterless medium green (FS 595A 34092) on the upper surfaces while lusterless gray was applied to the under surfaces (FS 595A 36440). Note the original blunt tips on the flying surfaces, which were eventually changed to the rounded configuration that became standard on production machines. Being a prototype, it was quite unusual for the XP–80 to have the six .50 caliber machine guns installed in the nose. (Lockheed/LF8479)

down into his parachute. The aircraft that had made the unexpected firing pass shot past the turning Mosquito, giving the crew a shock because they had never seen anything like it. Shock, however, quickly gave way to a fight for survival as the strange aircraft hauled around for another firing pass. Throttles to the firewall with the Merlins screaming like banshees on Halloween, the Mosquito could have shown a clean pair of heels to most German combat aircraft but this damn thing was turning on them and coming back with a vengeance. More tracers blasted past the Mosquito as the aerial struggle continued but luck held with the Britons as the shells kept missing while the Mosquito roared back to Blighty and the *Luftwaffe* antagonist eventually turned away. With the enemy gone, the shaking crew suddenly realized that their ultra-fast pursuer did not have propellers! Well, the usually bored intelligence officer was going to perk up

his ears after this mission and to hell with the photographs of Munich.

The aircraft that the Mosquito crew tangled with was the first recorded combat with the *Luftwaffe*'s newest fighter – the jet-powered Messerschmitt Me 262, an aircraft which, if it had been deployed correctly instead of being wasted by the direct orders of Adolf Hitler could have lengthened the war by a considerable period and have taken the lives of many more Allied aircrew.

As explained in the chapter on the Bell Airacomet, both the Americans and British had functioning jet aircraft but they were not operational nor would they have been suitable for combat missions in the deadly aerial arena over a devastated Europe. However, a new aircraft had already taken shape and flown in America that was to become the United States Army Air Force's first practical jet fighter.

With the failure of the Bell Airacomet in

mock battles with the Republic P–47 and Lockheed P–38, the Army knew that a new aircraft would have to be designed, and designed in a minimum of time to give the USAAF the type of combat aircraft that would be needed if the war were to drag on for several more years. Lockheed Aircraft Corporation had expressed an interest in the exciting new concept of jet-powered flight as early as 1939 but the military did not want the company to divert time and resources from producing the vitally important P–38 Lightning and Hudson bomber. After the failure of the experimental Airacomet, the Army turned its attention back to the Burbank, California, factory and issued an invitation to Lockheed to produce a fighter designed around the rather primitive British de Havilland Halford H–1 Goblin jet powerplant. Fortunately Lockheed had in its possession one of the greatest aircraft designers of all time, Clarence L. 'Kelly' Johnson, who held the title

of Chief Research Engineer. Johnson, who has always seemed to be ages ahead of his contemporaries, was extremely excited with the prospect of designing and building a jet fighter and the extreme time restrictions that the Army demanded did not seem to deter him.

The original invitation to Lockheed had been extended during May 1943 and on 15 June, Kelly and his hard working staff were briefing Army officials on a new fighter which they felt would considerably advance the state of combat aeronautics and deliver to the war zones an aircraft that would help the Allies hold the acendency of the air that they were beginning to gain. Johnson has always been known for his philosophy of 'make it simple and then make it even simpler' and he impressed the Army Air Force with the fact that Lockheed could build a jet combat aircraft for them in a time period that seemed almost absurdly short.

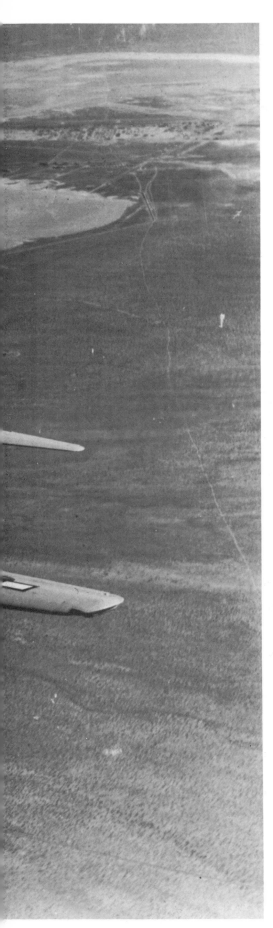

Lockheed had given the jet plans the designation of Project MX–409 and the Army was so impressed with Johnson's enthusiasm and plans that they gave Lockheed the go-ahead to proceed with the new project on 17 June with the designation XP–80 and a budget of almost half a million dollars. The one catch was that the aircraft had to be delivered within an incredibly short 180 days from contract approval!

However short that period of time may have seemed, Johnson and his crew of engineers were able to have the completed XP–80 ready for ground testing in just 141 days – a record probably only emulated by the North American NA–73X. The shape of the XP–80 was as simple as possible, keeping with Johnson's design philosophies. Armament would be centered in the nose section like the P–38, a tricycle landing gear would provide good ground handling characteristics, a bubble canopy would afford excellent visibility, the fuselage would easily separate into two sections behind the wing to afford easy access to the engine while the wing would be a new thin airfoil design to take advantage of the possibilities of high-speed flight offered by the new powerplant. In one month's time, Lockheed had a design mock-up of the XP–80 ready for

the Army to approve and then it was on to cutting metal for the actual aircraft. The company had built up a great deal of experience with wind tunnel testing and they realized that small sections of such a high-performance aircraft as the XP–80 could affect performance to an abnormal degree so special attention was paid to keeping smooth, flowing contours on the design. It should be stressed that the XP–80 was strictly an experimental aircraft with a goal of getting into the air and compiling as much performance data as possible – and not a fighter that could readily be pressed into combat. Combat considerations would come later as data from the XP–80 could be assimilated and refined.

Heavy amounts of overtime meant that the airframe was rapidly taking shape but Johnson was worried about the British having the engine delivered to Burbank in time to mate with the completed airframe. After considerable time had been spent on transAtlantic messages, the Halford unit arrived on 2 November and installation was begun as soon as the unit was uncrated. On 9 November, the XP–80 had been painted, checked out, weighed and was complete in almost every detail. It would not have been advisable to test fly the prototype from the Burbank runway

Left
Here Tony LeVier flies the first XP–80A 44–83021 over Muroc Dry Lake on an early test flight. Finished in grey lacquer, the prototype was dubbed the Gray Ghost. The baked-on finish was difficult to apply and maintain and the second XP–80A was left unpainted to test differences in performance. It was soon found that the painted aircraft was marginally faster but that as soon as the paint became chipped or scuffed in the field the margin of speed disappeared and it was ruled that Shooting Stars should be delivered in a natural metal finish, but this did not happen until the 470th aircraft. (Lockheed/S6893)

An early production P–80A–1–LO, 44–85121, on the line at Wright Field in Ohio, finished in the grey paint scheme and proudly carrying the maker's decal and name on the nose section. The six .50 caliber Browning air cooled machine guns were mounted together in the nose and were easily accessible via the large hinged panel that covered most of the nose section. The bubble canopy, mounted forward of the wing, offered the pilot exceptional visibility. This aircraft had earlier been the mount for Capt John S. Babel's historic one-stop speed dash across the USA on 26 January 1946 with two other P–80As.

Assigned to the Wright Field Flight Test Division, P–80A–1–LO 44–85247 was photographed during 1946. This aircraft was one of three that participated in the 1946 National Air Races at Cleveland, Ohio, where the specially painted Shooting Stars thrilled the huge crowd with a dazzling display of jet performance. The aircraft were raced around the pylon course set aside for the unlimited propeller-driven racers but the combination of high speed and high G forces had a detrimental effect on the Shooting Star's airframe as can be seen by the skin wrinkling under the fuselage codes.

because of its easy access to the public so, instead, it was decided that the XP–80 would be carefully disassembled, wrapped in canvas and shipped by truck to the Mojave Desert where it could be tested at Muroc Army Air Field.

Trouble was soon to arise at Muroc when, during engine test runs, the suction created by the jet caused the side mounted air intakes to collapse almost sucking the nearby Kelly Johnson into the intake! Since jet engines were extremely limited items at the time, the Lockheed team was very concerned over possible damage to the unit from ingestion of pieces of metal from the intake. The engine was pulled

from the airframe and carefully studied. Instead of finding damage from metal ingestion, the team was dismayed to find that the engine, while only being slightly damaged from material ingestion, appeared to suffer a fatigue defect from the manufacturing process. The British violently disagreed with this conclusion and felt that the entire fault lay with the intake duct which, de Havilland had claimed before actual testing had begun, would collapse on starting. In retrospect, it seems most likely that the duct was at fault, for the design of the all-important air intake was an entirely new science and, after the initial failure, Johnson designed a new duct although it still gave some trouble with the production run of aircraft. Desperately needing a new engine, Lockheed was relieved when de Havilland pulled the jet from the second Vampire prototype and shipped the unit to Burbank.

Since the basic contract had been fulfilled before the specified date and because of the new nature of the project, the Army was understanding of the fact that Lockheed needed a bit more time to redesign the intakes

and receive the next powerplant. By the morning of 8 January 1944, the XP–80, nicknamed *Lulu-Belle* by the workers, was ready to try its wings. The new engine had been installed and the reworked intakes did not fail during trial engine runs. The prehistoric lake bed at Muroc was wet from the winter rains which harden the surface to a smooth, rock-like finish during the spring and this was the cause of some concern. However, a close check of the surface by test pilot Milo Burcham indicated that the desert floor would bear the weight of *Lulu-Belle* for the first flight. A crowd of military and industrial observers had gathered on the blustery morning to watch pre-war race pilot Burcham climb into the XP–80, strap in and start the Halford, which roared with the strange Goblin-like wail that gave the engine its eventual name. Burcham advanced the throttle and felt the XP–80 slowly accelerate down the natural runway. Speed gradually built up and Burcham gently eased the aircraft into the air, accompanied by cheers and applause from the gathered crowd. In a few minutes Burcham and *Lulu-Belle* were back on

P–80A–I–LO 44–85106 in the famous 'Hat in the Ring' markings of the 94th Fighter Squadron, a unit that can trace its history back to World War One. Note the duct splitter plate which had been devised to help prevent the 'duct rumble' that occured when low-energy air gathered between the duct and fuselage skin and was trapped, producing a disconcerting racket – especially during descents. Note the taping over fuselage seams below the canopy.

the ground after the landing gear would not retract. A quick check indicated that the gear handle had not gone through an override position, thus failing to retract. Burcham also voiced some complaints about the lateral stability of the aircraft, which he considered to be overly sensitive. This sensitivity was apparently due to the fact that the hydraulic boost combined with the very slick airframe of the XP–80 made the aircraft's controls ultra-responsive. Johnson figured that there was nothing wrong with this responsiveness and advised Milo that the aircraft would have to be flown with a very gently hand until the pilot could get used to the sensitive feel. Burcham agreed to this method and climbed aboard the XP–80 for a second flight that morning and, this time, the seasoned test pilot treated the spectators to a spectacular show of high speed flight at just a few feet above the lake bed followed by an impressive series of rolls during a steep climb. Burcham was pleased with the solid feel of the aircraft as it easily neared 500 mph and the Lockheed team was visibly pleased with the more protracted second flight.

Testing began to swing into a frantic pace at Muroc as the XP–80 started logging flight hours. A camera was placed in the cockpit to record instrument readings while the pilot could concentrate on flying, rather than attempting to jot down test notes on a knee-pad while controlling the aircraft. Burcham began to get used to the XP–80's sensitive controls and was very pleased with the extremely high rate of roll of the aircraft, which was much higher than that of any piston-engine fighter with the added plus of not having to fight the torque generated by a large piston powerplant. Takeoff acceleration was nothing to brag about and the contemporary fighters could easily outdistance the XP–80, but once the jet began to gain some airspeed it was a completely different story and the day of the propeller-driven fighter was soon to be just history.

Burcham found out that *Lulu-Belle*, while generally a pleasant handling machine, had a few nasty surprises in store. The stall characteristics were virtually non-existent and the aircraft would snap quickly to the right. Johnson thought the problem over and, after some

more wind tunnel testing, added a wing fillet to help the stall problems. Burcham still found the aircraft difficult in the stall and had a hard time getting used to the lateral stability which required constant hands-on flying to keep the aircraft at a level attitude.

As the initial flight testing progressed, Lockheed and the Army reached agreement on the Model L–141; two aircraft were to be built in equally record time as the XP–80, with the first to be delivered 150 days after the letter of intent was issued, and the second example to follow in 180 days time. The Model L–141 was to be a bit different from the XP–80 and was to be bigger, heavier and faster. These two machines would be designated XP–80A by the Army and would incorporate combat systems that had been left out of the XP–80 to expedite getting the aircraft into the air. At this point it was decided to equip the XP–80As with the General Electric I–40 jet of 4,000 lb thrust which would increase the performance of the fighter dramatically.

Lockheed and the Army entered into the XP–80A contract on 10 February 1944, but the dramatic events in Europe escalated the contracts at a feverish pace. Four days later another contract for 13 YP–80A service test aircraft was issued and, just a few more days later, a production order for 500 P–80As powered by the I–40 was drawn up.

Initially, engines built under license from de Havilland by Allis-Chalmers were to power the P–80 series but delays in getting a production line set up at Allis-Chalmers and problems in dialog with the British maker led the Army to abandon the Halford series in favor of the more technically advanced I–40 which would give the added thrust that the fighter needed. The General Electric unit – later to be redesignated J33 – had evolved from the British Whittle jet.

While contract negotiations were proceeding at a rapid rate in the Burbank offices, the XP–80 was slowly building up flying hours at Muroc. Armament (six .50 caliber Browning machine guns) had been added along with improved fillets, rounded wing tips, changes in the horizontal stabilizer and modifications to internal systems in an effort to improve performance and handling characteristics and gain data for the new XP–80A. The Halford H–1B jet could not, because of the position of the engine, develop full power and the optimum 10,500 rpm could not be achieved – 9,500 rpm being about tops. This meant that thrust decreased from the projected 3,000 lb to 2,240 lb but, even so, the XP–80 was the first aircraft in the United States to pass the 500 mph mark. Constant Army monitoring of the XP–80's airframe and flight results provided a large amount of data, most exceedingly favorable, and the changes requested by the Army were considered rather few in view of the radical nature of the jet aircraft, along with the fact that the XP–80 had been designed and built in such a short time.

The *Lulu-Belle* was progressing in its test program most satisfactorily when another Lockheed test pilot who had also been a well-known pre-war racer returned to Burbank from a tour teaching USAAF pilots the finer points of flying the twin-engine P–38 Lightning. Tony LeVier was a skilled pilot who had gained respect from his contemporaries during the Cleveland Air Races where pilots pitted their lives for prize money and the pursuit of speed. LeVier, in his memoirs, recalls meeting up with *Lulu-Belle* for the first time:

'When I returned to Burbank, Milo and Jim White had both flown *Lulu-Belle* several times. Milo was now Lockheed's chief pilot, succeeding the late Marshall Headle, and his successor as chief engineering pilot had not yet been appointed. Joe Towle, who had been Milo's assistant in engineering, was now the senior pilot in our department, and one of the first things he did when I reported back to work was to have me checked out in jets. Early in June 1944, Jim and I flew up to Muroc in our twin-engine Cessna and I walked over to *Lulu-Belle* and climbed in.

'I had always dreamed about the perfect airplane and how it would fly, but little did I realize I would ever see it. This was probably the closest thing to it in the entire world. I will never forget my first flight in this little airplane, any more than I would forget my solo flight back in 1930.

'This was the most effortless flight I had ever known. Without propeller noise or vibration, the XP–80 accelerated smoothly down the runway, and as it reached flying speed it went into the air with no more than a slight pull

Very colorfully marked F–80A–10–LO 44–85275A in natural metal finish. The rear fuselage stripes probably denoted that this aircraft was flown by a squadron or group commander. Note how the Shooting Star's codes changed from PN to FN when, on 11 June 1948, the USAF revised the designation applied to fighter aircraft from 'P' for pursuit to 'F' for fighter. Bombs could be carried in place of the wing tip fuel tanks.

back on the control stick. After the gear and flaps were up it seemed almost like something you would dream about – hoping some day you would have an opportunity to fly such an airplane, and then wake up and wonder why it couldn't be possible. Here I was actually in it.

'After I had flown jets quite a while I often said that a pilot wasn't very good who couldn't have gotten used to *Lulu-Belle* in a very few minutes. It was the most simple airplane to fly that you could imagine, considering what we had been flying previously. You had a few engine instruments, the usual flight instruments, and that was it. To go faster all you had to do was move the throttle forward, or pull it back to slow down – no regulation of the propeller, no fuss about mixture control or cowl flaps, no worry about head temperatures or whether the oil would run too hot – there wasn't such a thing. It was all very simple. This airplane even had an automatic starting system. All you did was get in, buckle yourself into the seat and hit the switch. Its only disadvantage was the engine, which was low on thrust. To make the XP–80 really good we needed at least 4,000 lb thrust, and we got it on the next version of this airplane.'

The larger and heavier XP–80As with their rounded tips on the flying surfaces were completed and delivered in June and July of 1944. Both aircraft, after initial ground testing at Burbank, were transferred to Muroc for flight testing. Flight testing did not go as smoothly as with *Lulu-Belle* because it seemed that some of the flight problems originally encountered had been magnified with the two aircraft. LeVier recalled: '*Lulu-Belle* was a great airplane because there was practically nothing wrong with it. But as is so often the case, the changes we made to stretch it out created problems. We had lengthened the fuselage, moved the cockpit forward, moved the engine to the rear and put a larger gas tank in the fuselage. These changes and others added up to a practically new airplane, and we had to test it to prove it would work.'

LeVier was chosen to take the XP–80A into the air for the first time and he, Kelly Johnson and engineers from General Electric carefully went over the untried I–40. The jet was to develop at least 4,000 lb thrust but it was decided to put limitations on the unit since it was so new. Full power was achieved at 11,500 rpm but LeVier was instructed by GE to hold power to 10,500 rpm and reduce to 10,000 rpm immediately after takeoff. Engine time, even ground runs, were counted in

minutes as nobody really knew how long the I–40 would hold together. As LeVier wrote: 'We were faced with a brand-new airplane and a brand-new engine, and it is a tough combination when you have to develop both at the same time.'

Lulu-Belle had been painted a non-standard shade of green with gray under surfaces but the first XP–80A, in an attempt to gain every bit of speed possible, had its metal surface filled and sanded and then painted with a high gloss light grey lacquer that was then highly polished. Because of the grey finish the first XP–80A picked up the nick-name of *Grey Ghost*. The second XP–80A, in a comparison test, was left in its natural finish to see if there would be a large speed difference between the aircraft with a view towards establishing a policy of military jets carrying the customized finish, and if it justified the amount of work needed to finely paint the jets.

The *Grey Ghost* took to the air for the first time on 10 June but problems developed very quickly for LeVier. After about half an hour in the air, LeVier came back to Muroc with the right flap down and the left flap firmly in the up position, a very dangerous set-up that made the XP–80A difficult to control. LeVier had checked out the lake bed before takeoff and thought that the surface was too rough for use so he elected to use the base's normal 6,000 ft runway for the flight. During the first flight, it seemed to LeVier that, even though the engine power was reduced, the XP–80A was handling poorly with performance being particularly sluggish. A tremendous blast of heat was pouring into the cockpit from near the throttle position, making the throttle so hot that LeVier had trouble holding on to the control.

'I had my test card fastened to my knee on my left leg, which is normal procedure on a test flight, and was planning to check each point during my climb and note the various characteristics of stability and control. Then I would proceed to 10,000 ft to conduct landing gear and flap tests, stall the airplane, make a few maneuvers and speed runs, and finally pick up Jim White in *Lulu-Belle*.

'However, I dismissed the test card from my mind almost immediately after leaving the ground, as I knew I had a real problem on my hands. As I reduced power to 10,000 rpm my speed dropped to 160 mph and I was just barely able to keep the plane airborne. It skimmed the ground for a considerable distance, and only after several minutes of circling around over the desert was I finally able to get up enough speed to start climbing to test altitude, which was around 260 mph.'

Once this height was achieved LeVier began going through the landing gear tests and stalls. The XP–80A showed the same problem of dropping rapidly to the right when the stall occurred. LeVier carried out a few more tests but the heat, problems with performance, and extremely turbulent air were beginning to take a toll on the test pilot. LeVier decided to call it a day and headed back to Muroc, lowering the flaps and finding the jamming malfunction. Riding the controls with considerable force to keep the jet level, LeVier knew that further reduction in airspeed could cause the fighter to flip over on its back with a safe recovery doubtful. 'Although it required full stick to the right to fly the airplane, I figured that as long as I held 180 mph I would be able to control it down close to the ground, where I could cut my power. If the wing did tend to drop at that point I would be almost on the ground and it wouldn't be too dangerous. This I did and it worked out fine.'

The faults of this first flight were quickly set upon. Lack of stability was traced to a center of gravity problem and lead weights were added to the nose to correct the problem. The torrent of hot air entering the cockpit was traced to a faulty pressurization valve but it was evident that this was only a temporary fix and that a combination cooling/pressurization system would have to be devised. The problem of flap retraction was traced to a simple mechanical defect but other problems arose in the next few flights that had Kelly Johnson back at the drawing board and puzzling over the new world of jet flight.

During the first few test flights with the XP–80A two problems came up that were most perplexing. The first, which occurred during descent, was a strange combination of noises that issued forth from the engine ducts while the second mystery was an aileron vibration that occurred at Mach 0.8 and, if let to continue, could possibly tear the aileron from the wing. Wind tunnel testing showed that the noises in the intake came from a layer of low energy air that gathered inside the duct near the fuselage skin. This was eliminated by a design change within the air duct. The aileron vibration was eventually eliminated – after a number of fixes that did not work – by increasing the tension on the aileron cable rigging.

LeVier took the second XP–80A, the *Silver Ghost*, aloft for its first flight on 1 August and this aircraft had a small second seat crammed behind the pilot's position so an observer could ride, in extreme discomfort, and check flight characteristics while the pilot concentrated on putting the aircraft through its paces. There was some doubt if a pilot could escape from the XP–80A in the case of an emergency, especially at high speed, for these early jets were not equipped with ejection seats, which had not yet been fully developed. The chances for the observer getting out of his cramped position were not even thought about, except perhaps by the observer. The *Silver Ghost* was also equipped to carry extra fuel tanks that would hang from the wing tips where Johnson figured that they would considerably cut down on the drag caused by normal positioning midway under the wing. The idea worked and soon became a standard feature on fighter aircraft the world over.

The heavily instrumented *Silver Ghost* began to gather reams of valuable data as the Army breathed down Lockheed's collective neck for faster development as the Me 262s began to attack the massive bomber formations over Europe. The Me 262 and the rocket-powered Me 163 *Komet* were effective weapons that could have delayed the conclusion of the war but Hitler, obsessed with the idea of the enemy invading the sacred territory of the *Reich*, threw the effectiveness of the Me 262 away by ordering most of the production run to be equipped for ground attack and thereby eliminating one of the *Luftwaffe*'s few chances of stopping the bombers and their escorting fighters that were pounding Germany to rubble. In Britain, work was rapidly progressing on the Gloster Meteor and de Havilland Vampire, jet fighters that were needed to attack and destroy the dreaded V–1 that was hitting that country in considerable numbers. The V–1 could be attacked, under ideal conditions, by propeller-driven fighters but the advantage of the speed offered by the jet would make the attacks on the pulse-jet powered robot bombs less dangerous and more effective. There was also considerable concern that a faster, more advanced version of the V–1 would be sent against Britain that only a jet fighter could catch.

The 13 pre-production YP–80As began deliveries on 13 September 1944 and the aircraft were quickly dispersed to testing and training units. The second YP–80A had its nose section modified at the Lockheed factory to carry a camera pack and was designated XF–14 to indicate its photo reconnaissance role. Losses of photo reconnaissance aircraft to the German jets was mounting at an alarming rate over Europe, and the USAAF, needing the vital photographs of enemy installations, wanted to rush modifications of the basic P–80A design into an aircraft that could carry a battery of cameras at high speed. Kelly Johnson designed a nose section that could easily be installed in place of a regular fighter gun-nose and required no major modification of the airframe.

Trouble for the P–80A program, which had been given the official name of Shooting Star, began in earnest when the third YP–80A crashed on takeoff on 20 October killing veteran test pilot Milo Burcham. The YP–80A's engine quit shortly after liftoff and Burcham attempted a straight in crash landing but the fighter slammed into the side of one of the many gravel pits that surrounded the airfield and was completely destroyed. The accident came as a severe blow to the Lockheed team but an investigation was immediately launched and the cause of the crash was traced to a broken drive shaft in the fuel pump that caused a total loss of fuel pressure to the engine at a vital point during the takeoff. A new fuel pump was designed and installed in production aircraft that would serve as a backup unit in case of main pump failure. Exploring the new jet age was just beginning to get costly.

Tony LeVier took over the position as Chief Engineering Test Pilot after Burcham's death and the Shooting Star program continued at a rapid pace. LeVier flew Lulu-Belle and the Grey Ghost against a variety of current Army fighters including the P–38, P–47 and P–51 and a number of bomber types. The contest was never in doubt as the P–80s were able to best the propeller-driven aircraft virtually every time. At Muroc, where the tests against the current aircraft were being conducted, test pilot Ernie Claypool was killed during a night test when the YP–80A he was flying collided with the B–25 bomber that had been sent along to determine the effects of the jet exhaust at night. LeVier forged ahead in his new role and, as one of his first duties, picked a new staff of pilots. 'I preferred younger pilots,' LeVier wrote, 'feeling that any lack of experience they might have would be offset by their aptitude and interest in test work. I felt that first of all a pilot has to be eager to do experimental flying, and secondly he must be qualified; without these two things you do not have the right man.'

LeVier went on to pick Herman 'Fish' Salmon, Stanley Beltz, Roy Wimmer, and the famous stunt pilot Harold Johnson who was older than the others but useful for his wisdom and experience. Salmon became one of Lockheed's most famous pilots and also established quite a name for himself, as did LeVier, in the air races that followed the war. After retiring from Lockheed in 1968, Salmon tested a number of other diverse aircraft and he specialized in ferrying old transports and unusual aircraft. During the summer of 1980, news that Herman Salmon died at the controls of an ageing Lockheed Constellation that he was ferrying to Alaska saddened the aviation community.

To continue tests involving the duct noise problems, LeVier took the Grey Ghost up for a test flight at Muroc on 20 March 1945. The jet climbed to 15,000 ft and LeVier began to descend to check the noise at high speed at about 10,000 ft. At 11,000 ft the aircraft began to shake wildly and then the nose pitched down and the jet swung to the left in a violent tumble. The tail of the Grey Ghost had separated from the fuselage and LeVier was pinned in the cockpit as the jet plunged towards the ground. The violence of the plunge was such that LeVier could not gather his wits to jettison the canopy because, even though he was strapped in, he was being slammed into the cockpit sides with such force that he was momentarily stunned. The tumbling seemed to lessen for a moment and LeVier was able to blow the canopy off the aircraft. Frantically releasing his safety belts, he was thrown out of the aircraft by another violent maneuver. Letting himself fall for some distance to slow down his rate of descent, LeVier opened his parachute but was horrified to see that the Grey Ghost was now falling along with him, only 100 ft away! Fortunately the tumbling aircraft did not hit his parachute but LeVier was injured when he violently slammed into the desert floor because of a high wind. A construction worker saw him fall and helped the best he could until a jeep could be found to drive LeVier to the hospital. Two crushed vertebrae were the result of the rough landing and Tony had to spend five weeks in the hospital while his spine healed. It was six months before he flew again.

The cause of the loss of the Grey Ghost was traced to failure of the engine's turbine wheel which damaged the fuselage structure causing the tail to come off during the descent. The design of the turbine wheel was reconsidered and, after finding that the original process of manufacturing the wheel left impurities in the metal, the method of manufacture was changed to eliminate any possibility of this happening.

One of the most interesting aspects of the YP–80A's career was a project called 'Extravision' in which four YP–80As were to be sent to Europe. The aircraft involved were serialed 44–83026 through 83029 and two were crated and sent to England while the remaining two travelled to Italy along with ground crews and spare parts. The two YP–80As were assembled and flown in England on 27 January 1945 after being assigned to the Eighth Air Force but, the next day, 44–83026 crashed after exploding in the air and killing the USAAF pilot. The aircraft, unfortunately, were never committed to engaging the enemy. For some reason both the USAAF and RAF declined to engage their early jet prototypes in combat against enemy aircraft for fear of having the machines fall into enemy hands, which is a rather curious attitude since the Luftwaffe's operational fighters were just as, if not more, advanced. The remaining YP–80A was left with the British and transferred to Rolls-Royce where it was used for engine testing but it was written off on 14 November 1945 when the engine flamed out and the aircraft had to make a forced landing.

The war in Europe was rapidly drawing to a conclusion but it was anyone's guess on just how long the fight to defeat the Japanese in the Pacific would last. Military commanders of all the Allied nations knew that the enemy would fight to the death to hold onto the home islands and they also knew that their own armies would need the best and most modern equipment available. The USAAF felt that Lockheed alone would not be able to provide the large number of P–80s that would be needed for the fight in the Pacific so plans were drawn up with North American Aviation to produce the Shooting Star under license. The USAAF wanted at least 1,000 P–80As from Lockheed during 1945 and an order for 1,000 P–80Ns was placed with North American on 19 January 1945. The N was identical to the A and the military assigned the same priority to the P–80A that they had to the B–29 but the P–80N was cancelled on 26 May, probably due to the development of the atomic bomb.

The first production P–80A was handed over to the USAAF during February 1945 on schedule and aircraft began to flow into the USAAF's training pipeline. Since the P–80A was an entirely new aircraft on the production lines and was capable of such outstandingly high performance, the aircraft had to be built to much closer tolerances than previous propeller-driven aircraft. Parts suppliers were also having trouble getting their equipment to the Burbank factory for installation while engine deliveries were running behind time. The concern for engine deliveries on time caused the USAAF to open a second production line at the Allison division of General Motors and, during 1946, all responsibility for production of the I–40 for the P–80A was transferred to Allison.

As the production aircraft were delivered accidents began to happen at an alarming rate. Within a short time three production P–80As and a YP–80A were involved in fatal accidents and, on 6 August 1945, America's greatest combat ace, Major Richard I. Bong, was killed during an acceptance flight at Burbank. The death of Bong brought a major investigation into the Shooting Star program. Col. Charles J. Langmack recalls Bong's brief period of service at Lockheed:

'When Major Bong came to Lockheed he was assigned to my office, the Army Air Force Plant Representative's Office. I assigned him to flight operations flying acceptance flights on P–38 and P–80A aircraft. I was in charge of all flying of Army Air Force aircraft built by Lockheed and I was in charge of the investigation board which detailed Bong's accident. Bong and I were in flight operations at the same time on the day of the accident. He was clearing for his P–80A acceptance flight and I was filing a flight plan to one of Lockheed's sub-assembly plants with my Douglas C–47 staff ship.

'My C–47 was parked near the intersection off the East-West/North-South runways. I was still looking over or checking a few things on my airplane as Richard Bong went by on his takeoff run. I watched as he cleared the boundary and then, just a second or two later, the engine flamed out just as Bong had started a very shallow right turn with about fifty to sixty feet of altitude. The P–80A had nowhere near efficient climbing speed.

'Within a split second after the engine quit, the P–80A stalled and went in at a very steep angle, striking the ground with a terrific impact and huge fuel explosion. Richard Bong did not bail out of the aircraft as there just was not enough time.

'The USAAF investigation did not find conclusive information that Bong had failed to turn on the boost pump for backup on takeoff. Richard's body was well within the radius of scattered parts of the Shooting Star which covered approximately a block and a half in diameter.'

The day after Bong's crash the USAAF grounded all YP– and P–80A aircraft until the investigation could be carried out in detail. There had been 15 accidents since the first Shooting Star crash and six of these had been fatal. On 1 September, P–80s involved in testing were allowed back into the air but, the next day, Japan surrendered and the war was over. The investigation concluded that some crashes were due to pilot error, some (like Le Vier's) were due to structural failure, and some such as Major Bong's were due to engine failure. The end of the war threw the P–80 program into confusion.

After the excitement and celebration of the war's end, the Lockheed plant went back to

Many F–80As were modified as radio-controlled drones for a variety of tasks. Some served as targets for new missiles and guns while others were flown through the residue from atomic bomb blasts to test fallout patterns. This QF–80A–1–LO 44–85462A sprouts a number of aerials for its specialized mission. The aircraft was painted overall bright red to warn other planes that might venture too close that this was a non-piloted aircraft. Note the hook mounted under the fuselage to catch cables stretched across the runway to bring the drone to a quick halt so that the engine and all systems could be shut down.

work with the grim news that the USAAF had cancelled 2,631 P–80As that were on order. The P–80A was to completely take the place of the P–38 Lightning after the war and a new version of the Shooting Star, called the P–80Z was planned. The P–80Z was to be a heavier, longer range, more combat-ready aircraft and 240 of the remaining 917 aircraft on contract were to be delivered as P–80Zs. However, after much consideration and revision of the original concept, the P–80Z emerged as the P–80B (other versions of the P–80 besides the prototypes and the A model are outside the scope of this volume).

The demoralizing crashes plus the slow-down in orders after the war made Johnson and Lockheed realize that they had to get some favorable publicity for the Shooting Star so they decided to go after a transcontinental speed record with a later all-out assault on the absolute speed record, but first they had to get the USAAF's final restrictions lifted. Five P–80As were assigned to undergo 100 hours of testing each and to perform regular flight maneuvers, landings and takeoffs, but no violent combat maneuvers. After the testing was completed with few problems, the P–80A · was put back into full flight status but troubles soon developed with the Allison J33–9 equipped aircraft and they had to be grounded for inspection. Shooting Stars with J33–11 jets could continue flying.

To go all out for the transcontinental record, three P–80As were especially prepared with all armament removed and extra fuel added. One aircraft would attempt to go the whole distance without refuelling while the other two would land once for fuel. The race began at Long Beach Municipal Airport on 26 January 1946 and LaGuardia Field in New York was the target with Topeka Army Air Force Base in Kansas designated as the refuelling point. The aircraft took off with about 15 minutes between each launch and the flight was virtually text book perfect with the single P–80A arriving at LaGuardia after four hours, 13 minutes, 26 seconds with an average speed of 580.93 mph. The two Shooting Stars which had stopped to refuel also set records. The record run generated considerable publicity for the P–80A which was badly needed and other Shooting Stars were soon setting records and captivating the public with the concept of jet flight. One P–80A zipped between New York and Washington, DC, in 29 minutes, 15

The Shooting Star became the first jet aircraft for a number of Air National Guard units who were eager to turn in their old World War Two propeller fighters for the jets even though the jets were not exactly in pristine condition by the time the USAF passed them on to the ANG. This RF–80A–25–LO 44–85160 was assigned to the Alabama ANG.

seconds at an average speed of 438.9 mph. The Shooting Stars were also entered into the popular Cleveland Air Races but high speeds at low altitudes while pulling Gs going around pylons had detrimental effects on the airframes and officials eventually ruled the jets out from the pylon races.

Considerable effort went into the assault on the world speed record and Kelly Johnson and Lockheed had a number of modifications to the basic P–80A before the aircraft was ready to assault the speed record. At the time, the British were holding the speed record of 606 mph with their twin-jet Gloster Meteor, and Lockheed felt that a standard P–80A with a few additional modifications would be able to fly at at least 635 mph, a figure that the British would have a hard time bettering. P–80A 44–85213 was taken to Muroc Dry Lake and had its armament removed and an extra fuel tank installed in its place. The aircraft's surface was carefully filled, painted and polished and the Fédération Aéronautique International approved the speed trials course of just under two miles that Lockheed and the USAAF had set up. However, the aircraft did not live up to expectations and achieved only 596 mph. Some of the runs were made when the air was rough and the pilot commented that flights should only be made in the calm early morning air when turbulence was at an absolute minimum. The rough air bounced the P–80A so

drastically that the paint chipped and flaked off the airframe and to make matters worse, the British had raised the record to 616 mph. About this time the engineers began to understand the meaning of critical Mach number which meant that, if even more powerful engines were added, the rise in speed would be very small because the airframe was reaching the speed at which it could not go any faster. Lockheed then modified P–80A 44–85200 into the P–80R racing configuration. The airframe was lightened, a new model of the J33 engine was installed, a very small canopy and windshield helped cut down on drag, a sharp leading edge to the wing was added, and every possible seam and joint was filled and sanded smooth.

The GE J33–23 could develop 4,600 lb of thrust and on 19 June 1947, Col Al Boyd and the P–80R made their runs over Muroc and were able to attain an average speed of 623.8 mph, bettering the British record by a healthy margin. Kelly Johnson had proven that an American jet aircraft could capture the world's speed record and that American technology could be supreme in the jet field, which it has remained until this day. The P–80R is preserved in the USAF Museum as a monument to the brave test pilots who risked their lives during the early days of the jet over the lake bed at Muroc.

The P–80B and P–80C went on to set other

records in performance and in combat during the Korean War. When that conflict started the P–80 was the most numerous jet aircraft in the Far East Air Force and helped blunt the North Korean advance as they carried out countless ground attack missions. A P–80 also participated in the first jet-to-jet aerial combat when it met and defeated a North Korean MiG–15 fighter. However, the USAAF's first combat jet, the P–80A, did not see combat in Korea. The newly formed United States Air Force was in dire need of new jet qualified pilots and the P–80As were retained stateside to train the pilots that were to win the air war over Korea. The Shooting Star proved one of the most useful of all military aircraft designs for, in short order, it spawned first, the two-seat dual control TF–80C trainer which became the T–33, the world's most widely used jet trainer, and then the F–94 Starfire all-weather interceptor.

The original XP–80 *Lulu-Belle* was retired from flying in 1946 and held in storage for the National Air and Space Museum where it has recently been restored back to its original configuration, even down to the non-standard green paint used on the upper surfaces.

Although eventually eclipsed in Korea by the F–84 and F–86, the Shooting Star was there when needed and America's first combat jet did much to help win that country's fight for freedom.

LOCKHEED P–80 SHOOTING STAR SERIAL NUMBERS AND SPECIFICATIONS

Serial Numbers

XP–80	44–83020
XP–80A	44–83021 through 44–83022
YP–80A	44–83023 through 44–83035
P–80A	44–84992 through 44–85491; 45–8301–through 45–8363
FP–80A	45–8364 through 45–8477

Specifications

XP–80

Span	37 ft
Length	32 ft 10 in
Height	10 ft 3 in
Wing area	240 sq ft
Empty weight	6,287 lb
Loaded weight	8,620 lb
Max. speed	502 mph
Cruise speed	n/a
Ceiling	41,800 ft
Rate of climb	3,000 fpm
Range	n/a
Powerplant	De Havilland H–1B of 2,460 lb thrust

YP–80A

Span	39 ft
Length	34 ft 6 in
Height	11 ft 4 in
Wing area	238 sq ft
Empty weight	7,225 lb
Loaded weight	9,600 lb
Max. speed	553 mph
Cruise speed	410 mph
Ceiling	48,500 ft
Rate of climb	5,000 fpm
Range	560 miles
Powerplant	General Electric J33 of 4,000 lb thrust

P–80A

Span	39 ft 11 in
Length	34 ft 6 in
Height	11 ft 4 in
Wing area	238 sq ft
Empty weight	7,920 lb
Loaded weight	14,500 lb
Max. speed	558 mph
Cruise speed	410 mph
Ceiling	45,000 ft
Rate of climb	4,580 fpm
Range	540 miles
Powerplant	Allison J33–A–11 of 4,000 lb thrust

Vultee XP-81
The Combination Fighter

This daring design was an attempt to mix new sources of propulsion with a long combat range.

If there was one category in which American fighter designs excelled during World War Two then that category was range. British and European fighters during the early days of the War were almost point-defense machines, that is, they were meant to do one basic function – rise from their bases, climb quickly to intercept the enemy, do battle, and return quickly to

their nearby base to refuel and rearm. The fighters were not meant to travel long distances escorting bombers or searching out prey. The weak point of both the Spitfire and the Messerschmitt Bf 109 was their lack of range. In the Battle of Britain the Bf 109s that were escorting the German bombing aircraft had extremely limited time over England, meaning that the bombers were often left to the mercy of the Royal Air Force fighters – this limited range was even more of a critical factor when considering that the German bases were

The pilot's cockpit was placed well forward of the wing, giving outstanding visibility. The tricycle landing gear worked extremely well and test pilots reported that the XP–81, in its limited flying program, handled well on the ground. Production aircraft were to have been fitted with wing pylons for the carriage of a variety of stores. A large intake on either side of the upper fuselage supplied the jet in the rear section with air. (Consolidated Vultee)

The XP–81's large size is apparent in this view of the prototype. The laminar flow wing's clean finish was essential to get the maximum performance from the airfoil. Both XP–81 prototypes are still in existence, although in poor condition, and it is hoped that one of the combination fighters will eventually be put on display in the USAF Museum as a tribute to the many experimental aircraft built for the USAAF during World War Two. (Convair/A1028)

just on the other side of the Channel in defeated France. On the other hand, the Spit-fires often had to break combat and let a damaged enemy escape because they were running out of fuel.

As the war progressed and the American B–17 Flying Fortresses of the 8th Air Force arrived in England to carry out a steady bombing of German and occupied Europe, the matter of range became very critical. The B–17s could fight all the way to Berlin and back but, for a good portion of the mission, they were subjected to intense attacks by everything that the *Luftwaffe* could get into the air. Allied fighters had such limited range that they could only escort the bombers part of the way to the target before turning back. The *Luftwaffe* was smart enough to avoid engaging with the Allied fighters and would wait until they turned back before pouncing on the bombers. The bombers began to take fearful losses and the entire Allied strategic bombing campaign was threatened.

America did not seem to have the curious blinders that blocked out the advantage of long range as did the British whose fighters, even

A view of the prototype, 44–91000, over Muroc Dry Lake shows the very attractive lines of the Consolidated Vultee XP–81 to advantage. The NACA-developed laminar flow wing aided the aircraft's proposed high speed and long range. An armament of six .50 caliber air cooled Browning machine guns was proposed but never fitted. The YP–81 was to have had the more powerful TG–110 in the nose and six 20 mm cannons fitted in the wing. (Consolidated Vultee)

today, have traditional 'short legs'. Perhaps the vast distances across the country and the fact that potential adversaries were thousands of miles away contributed to aircraft such as the Mustang, Thunderbolt, and Lightning which were fast, powerful, and long ranging. With these aircraft the bomber streams were assured of excellent protection to and from the target and the *Luftwaffe* was destroyed while trying to break through the bombers' protective cover.

During the middle of the War it became obvious to many military planners that the fighting in the Pacific was, in many ways, going to be more difficult than aerial combat over Europe. First, there were incredibly vast distances of ocean to fly over and, secondly, it seemed that just about every available island was in the hands of the Japanese. The American policy of 'island hopping' is beyond the scope of this book but, briefly, it was hoped to stage massive amphibious invasions of strategic Japanese-held islands, secure them, and build airfields which would point a path of destruction directly at the Empire. It was a plan with many question marks, for mass landings on this scale had never been tried and the enemy was known to be ferocious and reluctant to give ground even in the face of certain defeat. If the island campaign failed or was delayed then a new breed of combat aircraft would be needed, aircraft that could cover the distances of the Pacific, bomb Japan, and return. Fighters would also be needed to protect the bombers.

Consolidated Vultee, Vultee having merged with Consolidated and moved from its small field at Downey to the larger Lindbergh Field in San Diego, was asked to consider the possibility of a high-performance fighter with very long range. The engineers at Consolidated Vultee decided to approach the problem in a unique manner. Instead of taking the tried and true powerplants such as the Rolls-Royce Packard Merlin or P&W R–2800 and then design around them, they opted for the new world of jet power. The company roughed out a design that would take advantage of the new turboprop engine being developed by General Electric and would have the equally new General Electric I–40 jet in the tail for additional bursts of power.

To accommodate these new powerplants and the needed fuel an airframe of considerable size was required. After initial work had been undertaken, the Army issued a contract for two prototypes on 11 February 1944. The turboprop was to be the TG–100 (later redesignated as the XT–31–GE–1) which was to develop over 2,300 hp. A turboprop is basically a jet engine to which a conventional propeller has been added. This arrangement, while incapable of pure jet speeds, has certain advantages such as improved fuel consumption. The jet in the tail was eventually changed to the J33–GE–5 which was capable of producing 3,750 lb of thrust. The aircraft, which had been designated XP–81, began to take shape as a large but very clean fighter. A NACA-developed laminar flow wing offered long range and high speed with its fairly high aspect ratio which would also give good high altitude performance.

General Electric was having its share of trouble with both engines, the turboprop being the first to be built for an American aircraft. The first XP–81 was quickly finished and ready for flight testing in January of 1945 but the turboprop was still a long way from being ready. To get the aircraft into the air so that some testing could be carried out, Consolidated Vultee obtained a QEC (quick engine change) unit from a P–51D. The motor mount for the V–1650–7 Merlin was adapted to the firewall of the XP–81 and the fighter was disassembled and trucked out to Muroc Dry Lake where the first flight was made on 11 February 1945, exactly one year after the aircraft had been ordered. The Merlin installation, with its large air intake and radiator in place of the turboprop's large exhaust pipe, was no beauty but it did get the airplane in the air where test pilots found that the handling qualities of the big jet were quite good.

The war in the Pacific had changed since the XP–81 concept was first considered and the island hopping campaign was proving to be a success, although an extremely bloody one for the Marine and Army troops involved. SeaBees had created miracles by hacking airstrips out of jungle and coral in a matter of days and, as the last bits of work were being completed, the B–29s, Mustangs, and Thunderbolts would arrive – pushing the war right to the heart of the Empire. The need for an aircraft such as the XP–81 quickly diminished and a contract for 13 YP–81s was cancelled. In the meantime, the first prototype was taken back to San Diego where the belated turboprop had finally arrived but the aircraft languished at the airfield until after the end of the War and the first flight with both means of propulsion installed was not made until 21 December 1945. The turboprop gave considerable trouble and was over 1,000 hp lower in output than had been promised by GE! Only a few flights were made before the aircraft was dumped and available records are not clear if the second prototype ever took to the air. The XP–81 was strictly a test bed and its proposed armament of six .50

caliber guns was never installed. The design of the aircraft was sound but the new powerplants gave too much trouble – as was to be expected – and the turboprop never powered an operational American fighter, although that type of engine did see considerable use and success on a wide variety of military and civil transports. It was thought that the XP–81s were scrapped until just a few years ago both planes were found sitting on a forgotten section of Edwards AFB where they had been used as targets for high altitude photo testing. The aircraft, minus engines and many other parts, are now being held by the USAF as possible candidates for preservation, which would be a fitting tribute for their first turboprop powered fighter.

CONSOLIDATED VULTEE XP–81 SERIAL NUMBERS AND SPECIFICATIONS

Serial Numbers

XP–81	44–91000 and 44–91001

Specifications

XP81

Since the XP–81 completed very few test flights these figures should be regarded as estimates.

Span	50 ft 6 in
Length	44 ft 10 in
Height	14 ft
Wing area	425 sq ft
Empty weight	12,800 lb
Loaded weight	19,500 lb
Max. speed	507 mph (estimated)
Cruise speed	n/a
Ceiling	35,500 ft
Rate of climb	4,500 fpm
Range	2,500 miles
Powerplant	One General Electric XT–31–GE–1 of 2,300 hp and one J33–GE–5 of 3,750 lb thrust

North American P-82 Twin Mustang — A Successful Mating

To cope with the vast distances of the Pacific Ocean, North American attempted to exploit the best assets of the P–51 in a twin-engine fighter.

When America entered World War Two it was realized that the powerful German war machine would have to be stopped before Britain and Russia fell to the Nazi onslaught. On the West Coast of America, especially California, the near-hysterical attitude over a possible Japanese invasion (a physical impossibility since the Japanese did not have the logistics or manpower to attempt such a feat during 1942) brought about the imprisonment of virtually all Japanese-American citizens who

were quickly gathered – their property immediately confiscated – and herded into bleak and depressing concentration camps that were usually located in desert areas. Anything oriental was immediately suspect and, during the dark days of 1942, it was not uncommon for the anti-aircraft guns that were defending Los Angeles to begin blazing away at suspected Japanese aerial intruders. Of course the near panic was not helped by reports of continuing defeats in the Pacific along with occasional Japanese military ventures such as when a submarine surfaced off Santa Barbara, California, and randomly shelled an oil refinery. The panic generated by the event was considerable but it was not until after the war that the

actual reason for the shelling was found to be more personal than military. The submarine commander had visited the refinery before the war on an exchange visit and had tripped and torn his uniform on some cactus. This had rankled the officer enough that he had held a very strong memory of regaining his 'honor'. However, to the beach-side citizens it seemed as if the invasion had started.

A banking view of 44–83887, the second XP–82, shows the clean and graceful lines of the Twin Mustang. The unique twin fuselage concept of the XP–82 meant extended range over the single-engine fighters already in operation while two pilot operation would cut down on the fatigue factor for long flights. Lineage from the P–51 fighter endowed the P–82 with excellent performance. (USAF/A–32650)

Much of America's vast military-industrial power was directed towards supplying the battlelines on the European front while the war in the Pacific was regarded, for the first year or so, as almost more of a back-burner operation. Once a definite foothold had been gained in the European conflict then more and more attention was focused on defeating the Japanese. One of the stumbling blocks in the Pacific war was the problem of distance. The distance between American held bases and the Japanese homeland was vast and planners realized that the homeland must be heavily punished if the war was to be fought to a victorious conclusion. Thus began the deadly 'island hopping' battles to wrest islands away from the enemy so that airfields could be constructed which would bring the bombers closer and closer to the home islands. New aircraft were also needed for the long flights over the water and the Boeing B–29 Superfortress bomber was given top priority in design and construction. USAAF planners realized that, if certain island bases could not be gained, a long-range escort fighter would be needed to protect the bomber formations that would be striking the home islands.

During 1943, North American Aviation Inc began initial design work on a unique appearing fighter. NAA reasoned that the excellent long-range abilities of their single-engine Mustang could be considerably enhanced by mating two Mustang fuselages to a common center section and rectangular tailplane. This set-up would enable a second pilot to be carried in the extra fuselage who could also aid in navigation and other chores which would considerably ease the strain of single-pilot operations over water. The twin engines would also add a large margin of safety. North American gave the project the designation of NA–120. The Army liked the proposal and issued contract AC–2029 on 7 January 1944 for two prototypes.

Designated XP–82, the new aircraft was to be powered by Packard-built Rolls-Royce Merlin V–1650–23/25 engines that were fitted with opposite rotating (handed) propellers that would virtually eliminate the problems of torque. The fuselages resembled those for the

Several different pod installations were tried on the two experimental Twin Mustang night fighters. Note the openings for the six .50 caliber machine guns immediately above the radar pod. (NAA)

When the USAAF decided it needed a night fighter to replace the Northrop Black Widow, two of the meager run of 20 P–82Bs were pulled aside for conversion to night fighters. Serial number 44–65170 was given the designation of P–82D and was equipped with APS–4 radar while the scope and operator's equipment were installed in the cockpit of the right fuselage. The radar was mounted in a huge pod attached to the underside of the wing center section.

light-weight experimental Mustang prototypes but, in fact, were new designs that had little to do with the previous aircraft.

Armament for the XP–82 was to be carried in the new center section and not in the outer wing panels as in the previous Mustang fighters. The landing gear arrangement for the new fighter was rather different; each fuselage had its own tail wheel while the main landing gear legs were attached at the root of the outer wing panel and retracted into the wing center section. Ground handling of the XP–82 was a bit stiff but not all that much different from the original Mustang. Wing pylons were provided on the outer panels for the carriage of fuel tanks or bombs and rockets.

The first XP–82 flew from the North American plant in Los Angeles on 15 April 1945 with NAA test pilot Bob Chilton at the controls. The first flight went well and the Army appeared to be impressed with the machine

which offered long-range and high-performance. The third aircraft to be built was designated XP–82A and was equipped with Allison V–1710–119 engines with propellers that rotated in the same direction. This aircraft was built as a hedge against the possibility that the British might cancel the license for Packard building the Rolls-Royce Merlin when the war in Europe came to an end. This was later to prove a wise move.

The new fighter was given the name Twin Mustang, which seemed singularly fitting. On 8 March 1944 the Army had issued a contract for 500 Twin Mustangs that would be designated P–82Bs (NA–123) which would be powered by V–1650–23/25 Merlins and incorporate a number of detail differences from the prototypes. The P–82B was to have four underwing pylons for four 1,000 lb bombs, fuel tanks, or rockets. In addition to the six .50 caliber Browning machine guns in the center

*P*rowling the coast of Southern California, the P–82C (44–65169) was fitted with SCR720 radar in the huge pod, one of several different pod styles that the P–82C carried during its testing career. Note that the high gloss Black camouflage paint has already begun to weather. Codes and serials were painted in matte 619 Red. (NAA)

*U*ndoubtedly the most famous P–82B was 44–65168, Betty Jo, which went on to set a record for non-stop flight between Hawaii and New York with an overall time of 14 hours, 33 minutes and an average speed of 334 mph over the 5,051 mile distance. Seen here on a test flight from the North American factory, Betty Jo was named for the pilot's wife but by mistake the factory had added an extra 'e' to the name which was later removed. (NAA)

section, a large pod could be attached under the center section that could carry eight .50 caliber weapons and their ammunition, giving the very heavy forward firing armament of 14 large caliber machine guns.

North American rapidly constructed the tooling and jigs for production of the new fighter but, just as work was getting started on the aircraft, the atomic bombs were dropped on Japan and the war was over. The Army had little need for a new fighter, especially a propeller-driven one, and the order for 500 P–82Bs was slashed to just 20 aircraft.

The Army still needed a decent performing night fighter to replace the Northrop P–61 Black Widow and the P–82B, on second examination, seemed that it might provide an ideal platform for airborne radar. The tenth and eleventh P–82Bs were pulled aside for conversion to P–82C and P–82D night fighters. The aircraft were identical in airframe but

had different radar systems installed. The P–82C (44–65169) was fitted with the SCR720 in a large central pod while the P–82D (44–65170) was equipped with APS–4 radar. Both aircraft were given gloss black paint schemes to fit in with new roles. The scopes and controls for the radar sets were installed in the right fuselage cockpit while aerials for the radar bristled from the outer wing panels.

The P–82Bs, with one exception, led a relatively quiet existence during their service life. That exception was P–82B 44–65168 which was fitted with extra fuel tanks in the fuselage space behind the pilots' seats and four huge 310 gallon drop tanks were suspended from the outer panel wing pylons. Nicknamed *Betty Jo* for Lt Col Robert E. Thacker's wife, the P–82B flew, with Thacker as pilot and Lt John Ard as copilot, on 27 February 1947 from Hickam Field, Hawaii, to New York. A new

record was set when *Betty Jo* landed 14 hours, 33 minutes later in New York after a non-stop flight of 5,051 miles with an average speed of 334 mph even though three fuel tanks would not jettison and had to be carried the entire distance, increasing drag and making the aircraft unstable for the pilot to fly.

The P–82C and P–82D proved that the Twin Mustang would make a very good night fighter and orders were eventually issued for other variants that are outside the scope of this volume since they were built after the war, but the following brief run-down covers the types and their differences. The NA–144 was the P–82E powered by Allisons and 100 were built as day fighters; 100 Allison-equipped P–82F (NA–149) night fighters were manufactured with APS–4 radar; and the last Twin Mustang variant was the P–82G (NA–150) of which 50 were built. The P–82G carried the SCR720 radar set. The first P–82E was begun in early

Lt Col Robert Thacker, pilot and Lt John Ard, copilot, are seen taxiing the P–82B at LaGuardia Field after their record-setting flight. Note the three fuel tanks that would not jettison. Thacker fought in both theaters during the War and had 3,000 hours of military flying time to his credit. While a member of the 7th Bomb Group, Colonel Thacker participated in the memorable flight of 13 Flying Fortresses that departed from Hamilton Field, California, and landed at Hickam Field, Hawaii, on 7 December 1941 during the height of the Japanese attack on the field. (NAA)

Betty Jo was fitted for its non-stop Honolulu to New York flight with these four huge 310 gallon gasoline tanks to carry part of the extra fuel needed for the trip. The tanks were the largest ever carried by a fighter aircraft and the pilots ran into a bit of trouble when three of the tanks would not jettison after they ran dry, causing extra drag and making the Twin Mustang more difficult to fly. (NAA)

1946 and the Twin Mustang line at Inglewood eventually closed down in March 1949, when the last P–82G was built.

The Twin Mustang would probably have served a very average military life if it had not been for the outbreak of the Korean War when America's Air Force had run down to meager levels of aircraft and manpower. The Twin Mustangs that were stationed with the Far East Air Force were thrown immediately into the fighting and the first kill of the Korean War was scored by a P–82 crew. The Twin Mustangs did a considerable amount of damage to the advancing North Koreans, strafing troop concentrations, destroying bridges and rolling stock, and engaging the enemy aircraft whenever they appeared. Parts were in limited supply for the Twin Mustangs and they were phased out as newer and more numerous aircraft became available. After the end of the Korean War a number of surviving P–82Gs were transferred to the Alaskan Air Command where, after winterization, they were designated as F–82Hs. A couple of Twin Mustangs are in museums today while the Confederate Air Force maintains the only airworthy example, a P–82B.

NORTH AMERICAN P–82 TWIN MUSTANG SERIAL NUMBERS AND SPECIFICATIONS

Serial Numbers

XP–82	44–83886 and 44–83887
XP–82A	44–83888
P–82B	44–65160 through 44–65179
P–82C	44–65169
P–82D	44–65170
P–82E	46–255 through 46–354
P–82F	46–405 through 46–504
P–82G	46–355 through 46–388

Specifications

P–82B

Span	51 ft 3 in
Length	38 ft 1 in
Height	13 ft
Wing area	408 sq ft
Empty weight	13,405 lb
Loaded weight	22,000 lb
Max. speed	482 mph
Cruise speed	227 mph
Ceiling	41,600 ft
Rate of climb	3,500 fpm
Range	1,400 miles
Powerplant	Two Packard V–1650–23/25 of 1,860 hp each

Bell XP-83
The Jet Escort

Bell's second jet-powered design was aimed at providing the range and performance for the long over-water distances that were being flown in the Pacific while on the way to targets in Japan.

Bell's historic development of the P–59A Airacomet did not lead to the performance nor the contracts that the company hoped would be forthcoming from the USAAF. The rather straightforward angular design of the Airacomet combined with the very early jet engines hindered performance but, as with all early jet aircraft, one of the most perplexing problems was the ability of the turbojets to gobble fuel at alarming rates. The huge fuel consumption ruled out using the new jet fighters on long-range escort missions such as the lengthy over-water flights being undertaken by the P–51s escorting B–29 bombers to Japan.

Designers at Bell reasoned that if the airframe of a fighter was considerably expanded then extra fuel tanks could be added that would extend range. Provisions could be made in the wing for the carriage of auxiliary droppable fuel tanks. Bell initiated design work on the aircraft during March 1944, and the preliminary drawings looked very much like a scaled-up Airacomet. Bell chose to retain the Airacomet's simple layout for ease of production but the airframe on the new aircraft was cleaned up. The new fighter could carry almost 1,000 gallons of fuel internally while drop tanks would boost the total to 1,750 gallons, giving a range at economy power settings of just over 2,000 miles.

The USAAF tendered a contract to Bell for the development and production of two XP–83 prototypes on 31 July 1944, and work was rapidly undertaken to complete the machines with the first XP–83 flying on 27 February 1945, under the control of Bell test pilot Jack Woolams.

The large XP–83 was not an unattractive aircraft. Left in natural bare metal finish, the XP–83's cockpit (which was pressurized) was

In the air the Bell XP–83 was a well-proportioned aircraft but lack of performance prevented the USAAF from ordering the fighter. The XP–83 helped pioneer the difficult road of jet experimentation that would eventually lead to a workable long-range jet fighter. (Bell)

After the end of World War Two, the prototype Bell XP–83, 44–84990, is seen at Wright Field, Ohio. The tinted bubble canopy and armament of six nose-mounted .50 caliber machine guns are clearly visible. Looking like a scaled-up Airacomet, the XP–83 was not able to achieve the performance that the USAAF was looking for. (W. T. Larkins)

situated far ahead of the wing's leading edge, giving the pilot excellent visibility. The sliding portion of the bubble canopy was darkly tinted to cut down on glare at high altitude. Looking like an enlarged Airacomet, the XP–83 had its engines – two General Electric J33–GE–5 turbojets of 4,000 lb st each – mounted beneath the wing roots. This set-up would give the XP–83 pilot minimum trouble with asymmetric control if one of the engines failed. The engine installation also left the fuselage free for the carriage of as much fuel as possible.

The prototype XP–83, 44–84990, was designed for an armament of six .50 caliber air-cooled Browning machine guns mounted in the nose but future plans called for possible installation of either 20 mm or 37 mm cannon – Bell apparently being unable to free themselves from their fascination with the slow firing 37 mm cannon. Early testing, however, quickly revealed that the XP–83 was not a high performance aircraft, although its flight qualities were pleasant. Aircraft that were being built or under design offered much more performance and, during 1945, development of the project was abandoned.

The Bell XP–83 paved the road for development of the long-range jet fighters that were built during the 1950s but, at this time, early jets such as the XP–83 could still be outperformed – if not in top speed – by many of the last generation of propeller-driven fighters such as the North American P–82 Twin Mustang. The XP–83 was the last fighter design to come from Bell although the company would go on to set new aeronautical records with their experimental research aircraft and helicopters.

BELL XP–83 SERIAL NUMBERS AND SPECIFICATIONS

Serial Numbers

XP–83	44–84990 and 44–84991

Specifications

XP–83

Span	53 ft
Length	45 ft
Height	14 ft
Wing area	431 sq ft
Empty weight	14,105 lb
Loaded weight	27,500 lb
Max. speed	522 mph
Cruise speed	n/a
Ceiling	45,000 ft
Rate of climb	3,000 fpm
Range	1,730 miles
Powerplant	Two General Electric J33–GE–5 turbojets of 4,000 lb static thrust each

POSTWAR –
THE LAST OF THE GREATS

America's aircraft production output was enormous during World War Two, with sub-types proliferating, but hundreds of war-weary and surplus aircraft were struck off at the war's end. The lastest, however, continued to serve with Air National Guard units or to undergo development, while the P–80 served with distinction during the Korean War.

*A*fter the war, many P–51Ds and P–51Hs equipped America's new Air National Guard squadrons. This P–51H of the New York ANG is seen after the collapse of the right gear leg during landing. (NY ANG)

*T*he American production output the Germans and Japanese could not even touch. Seen in early 1945, these rows of P–51D–20–NAs literally disappear into the dawn mist at Mines Field. (NAA)

*C*olorful P–47N–20–RA 44–89238A assigned
to the post-war All Weather Flying Center.
Carrying the Center's standard colors, the N was
painted in red and yellow trim.

*I*nteresting view of a post-war P–47N–1–RE
taken with a K–20 aerial camera. This angle
illustrates to advantage the different wing shape of
the N. The N–1 carried 556 gallons of fuel
internally. The new long-range wing had four
interconnected self-sealing fuel cells for a total of
200 gallons.

A formation of P–47N–5–RE Thunderbolts on a test flight from the Farmingdale factory. Easiest identification feature of the N was the squared-off wing tips. The small antennas for the AN/APS–13 tail warning radar can be seen on the vertical fin. This model of the N had provisions installed for catapult launching. (Republic)

N ote the application of the large buzz numbers on the side of the fuselage of P–47N–5–RE, seen after the war. This colorful aircraft carried pre-war style red, white and blue tail stripes.

Northrop's heavy-hitting P–61 Black Widow – the first specifically designed and built night fighter for the Army Air Force – had good performance and long range, ideal attributes for a photo reconnaissance aircraft. Production P–61A night fighters began entering service during October 1943 and more advanced versions quickly followed, including the P–61B and C. There was consideration given to making a day fighter out of the Black Widow and two XP–61Es were built using P–61B airframes. These aircraft had radar and the large top turret deleted, with the center pod fuselage being much smaller and more streamlined. A large bubble canopy was added for the two-man crew and power came from two 2000 hp P&W R–2800–65 radials, giving a top speed over 400 mph and a range of 2,250 miles. However, Army policy deleted the new day fighter and diverted funds from the project into the development of the very similar F–15A Reporter which had all armament removed and mountings and ports for a variety of aerial cameras installed. Engines were uprated to R–2800–C powerplants that pushed the top speed of the design near 440 mph. Larger turbosuperchargers – the scoops can be seen under the engine nacelles – gave excellent high altitude performance. The post-war military economy did not offer the Northrop F–15A Reporter a large role and only 36 were built and delivered during 1946. (Northrop)

38335

Even though built in such small numbers, it was an excellent performing aircraft and handled much like the fighter from which it was derived – its top speed being higher than the P–61. Cameras were mounted in positions located in the extreme nose and offered a wide field of view. The aircraft spanned 66 ft and was 49 ft 7 in long. The large paddle blade Curtiss-Electric propellers offered excellent high-altitude 'bite' in the thin air. (Northrop)

Although the P–80 was the USAAF's first combat-worthy jet aircraft, it saw no combat during World War Two but it had a long service life in America and other countries – the basic design changing into equally classic all-weather fighters and advanced trainers. One derivation of the basic P–80 airframe was the XF–14–LO, s/n 44–83024. This machine, a YP–80A–LO, was converted to have a modified nose that would carry cameras instead of six .50 caliber machine guns. The concept's success led to orders for the F–14–10 (designated RF–80A in June 1948), basically a stock P–80 airframe with a new nose that hinged upward to reveal mounts and installations for camera gear that could include K–17 and K–22 cameras. The aircraft in the photograph, s/n 44–84998, was a P–80A–1–LO that was modified as an F–14A development aircraft. Thirty-eight P–80A–5–LOs were converted to F–14As while 114 were built new. The F–14As were originally powered by 3850 lb thrust General Electric J33–GE–11s but, in 1953, 98 were overhauled and refitted with new 5,400 lb thrust Allison J33–A–35 turbojets. As can be seen, the camera bay could be worked on without a platform or ladder. Photo ports were installed in the side of the nose and on the undersurface. Contrasted with the photographer's Rolleiflex, this massive 40-inch aerial camera could be carried in the camera bay, shooting down. Adjustable racks provided secure clamps for different sizes of cameras. (Lockheed/AD7229)

FP-80A-LO (an interim designation between F-14A and RF-80A) s/n 44-85483 seen on a test flight from the Burbank factory, with large buzz numbers on the rather ungainly blunt photo nose that replaced the more streamlined unit which held six .50 caliber machine guns. By this point in production the baked-on gray finish had been replaced by bare metal. The dive brake has been deployed to slow the FP-80A down so that the pilot could formate with the photo plane. Early P-80s were finished in a very precise manner to allow as high a speed as possible – the entire airframe was covered with a special body putty that was then sanded down to a very smooth finish, and a special gray enamel paint was then sprayed over the airframe and baked in a special oven. In active service it was impossible to maintain and soon gave way to a natural aluminum finish on the P-80 series. (Lockheed/H661)

The harsh and deadly environment of the Korean War proved the value of the RF-80. Countless missions were flown to record the movements of an aggressive North Korea as the enemy poured south. The photographs let the hard-pressed American defenders study enemy movements and encampments and then hit the targets with deadly results, slaughtering North Koreans and blunting the force of the invasion so that additional Allied reinforcements could be brought into the fight. The RF-80 was not capable of tangling with MiG-15 fighters and standing orders stated that photo-pilots were to turn back and head for home at the first sight of MiGs. Missions would only be continued if the target was of vital importance and if heavy air cover was being provided by F-86 Sabres. Illustrated are the various camera options that could be carried by an RF-80C of the 67th Tactical Reconnaissance Wings based at Taegu Air Base (K-2) during 1951. (USAF)

Bibliography

Balchen, Col. Bernt; Ford, Maj. Corey; LaFarge, Maj. Oliver. *War Below Zero.* Houghton Mifflin, NY, 1944

Bell, Dana. *Air Force Colors.* Vols 1 and 2. Squadron/Signal Publications, Texas, 1979 & 1980

Bledsoe, Marvin. *Thunderbolt: Memoirs Of A World War Two Fighter Pilot.* Van Nostrand Reinhold, NY, 1982

Bowers, Peter M. *Curtiss Aircraft 1907–1947.* Putnam, London, 1981

Carter, Kit. *The Army Air Forces In World War II Combat Chronology.* GPO, Washington, DC, 1975

Chennault, Claire Lee. *Way Of A Fighter.* G. P. Putnam's Sons, NY, 1949

Craven, W. F. and Cate J. L. *The Army Air Forces In World War II.* Vols 1–5. University of Chicago Press, Illinois, 1948

Cross, Roy and Scarborough, Gerald. *P–51 Mustang.* Patrick Stephens, London, 1973

David, Burke. *Get Yamamoto.* Random House, NY, 1969

Francillon, R. J. *McDonnell Douglas Aircraft Since 1920.* Putnam, London, 1982

Freeman, Roger. *Thunderbolt.* Macdonald and Jane's, London, 1978
   Mustang At War. Doubleday, NY, 1974
   The Mighty Eighth. Doubleday, NY, 1970
   Mighty Eighth War Diary. Jane's, London, 1981
   Camouflage and Markings USAAF 1937–1945. Ducimus, London, 1974

Godfrey, John T. *The Look Of Eagles.* Random House, NY, 1958

Green, William. *Famous Fighters Of The Second World War.* Doubleday, NY, 1962

Hall Jr, Grover C. *1000 Destroyed.* Morgan, Dallas, TX, 1961

Hansell Jr, Maj. Gen. Haywood S. *The Air Plan That Defeated Hitler.* self-published, Atlanta, GA, 1972

Hardy, M. J. *The North American Mustang.* Arco, NY, 1979

Hess, William N. *P–47 Thunderbolt At War.* Ian Allan, London, 1976
   A–20 Havoc At War. Scribner's, NY, 1979

Johnson, Robert S. *Thunderbolt!* Rinehart & Co., NY, 1958

Kenney, George C. *General Kenney Reports.* Duell, Sloan and Pearce, NY, 1949

Lord, Walter. *Incredible Victory.* Harper & Row, NY, 1967

MacCloskey, Brig. Gen. Monro. *Torch And The Twelfth Air Force.* Richards Rosen Press, NY, 1971

McDowell, Ernest and Hess, William. *Checkertail Clan.* Aero, Fallbrook, CA, 1978

McEwen Jr, Charles. *422nd Night Fighter Squadron.* 422nd NFS Association 1983

Mahurin, Col. Walker. *Honest John.* G.P. Putnam's Sons, NY, 1962

Morris, Danny. *Aces and Wingmen.* Neville Spearman, London, 1972

Mosley, Leonard. *The Reich Marshal.* Doubleday, NY, 1974

Noah, Joseph W. *Wings God Gave My Soul.* Charles Baptie Studios, Annandale, VA, 1974

Pentland, Geoff. *RAAF Camouflage and Markings 1939–45.* Vol. 1. Kookaburra, Australia

Prange, Gordon W. *Miracle At Midway.* McGraw-Hill, NY, 1982

Sims, Edward H. *American Aces Of World War II.* Macdonald, London, 1958
   Greatest Fighter Missions. Harper & Row, NY, 1962

Smith, Herschel. *Aircraft Piston Engines.* McGraw-Hill, NY, 1981

Stafford, Gene and Hess, William. *Aces Of The Eighth.* Squadron/Signal, TX, 1973

Stiles, Bert. *Serenade To The Big Bird.* W. W. Norton, NY, 1947

Sweeting, C. G. *Combat Flying Clothing.* Smithsonian Press, Washington DC, 1984

Thruelsen, Maj. Richard and Arnold, Lt Elliot. *Mediterranean Sweep.* Duell, Sloan and Pearce, NY, 1944

Toliver, Raymond and Constable, Trevor. *Fighter Aces Of The USA.* Aero, Fallbrook, CA, 1979

Turner, Richard E. *Big Friend, Little Friend.* Doubleday, NY, 1976

Van Haute, Andre. *Pictorial History Of The French Air Force.* Ian Allan, Surrey, UK, 1974

Wagner, Ray. *American Combat Planes.* Doubleday, NY, 1982

Weal, John. *Combat Aircraft Of World War Two.* MacMillan, NY, 1977

Weatherill, David. *Aces, Pilots and Aircraft Of The 9th, 12th and 15th USAAF.* Kookaburra, Melbourne, Australia, 1979

Wooldridge Jr, E. T. *The P–80 Shooting Star.* Smithsonian Press, Washington DC, 1979

Y'Blood, William T. *Red Sun Setting.* Naval Institute Press, Annapolis, MD, 1981

Index

S

T

U

V

W

Y

Z